THE **ORGB** SOLUTION

 W9-BXT-881

Print + Online

ORGB⁵ delivers all the key terms and core concepts for the **Organizational Behavior** course.

ORGB Online provides the complete narrative from the printed text with additional interactive media and the unique functionality of **StudyBits**—all available on nearly any device!

What is a StudyBit™? Created through a deep investigation of students' challenges and workflows, the StudyBit™ functionality of **ORGB Online** enables students of different generations and learning styles to study more effectively by allowing them to learn their way. Here's how they work:

COLLECT WHAT'S IMPORTANT
Create StudyBits as you highlight text, images or take notes!

WEAK
FAIR
STRONG
UNASSIGNED

RATE AND ORGANIZE STUDYBITS
Rate your understanding and use the color-coding to quickly organize your study time and personalize your flashcards and quizzes.

 StudyBit™

TRACK/MONITOR PROGRESS
Use Concept Tracker to decide how you'll spend study time and study YOUR way!

85%

PERSONALIZE QUIZZES
Filter by your StudyBits to personalize quizzes or just take chapter quizzes off-the-shelf.

○ CORRECT
○ INCORRECT
○ INCORRECT
○ INCORRECT

ORGB5

Debra L. Nelson, Oklahoma State University
James Campbell Quick, University of Texas, Arlington

Vice President, General Manager, 4LTR Press: Neil Marquardt

Product Director, 4LTR Press: Steven Joos

Product Manager: Laura Redden

Content/Media Developer: Daniel Celenza

Product Assistant: Lauren Dame

Marketing Manager: Emily Horowitz

Sr. Content Project Manager: Martha Conway

Manufacturing Planner: Ron Montgomery

Production Service: MPS Limited

Sr. Art Director: Bethany Casey

Internal Designer: KeDesign/Ted & Trish Knapke

Cover Design: Curio Press, LLC/Lisa Kuhn

Cover Image: Arthimedes/Shutterstock.com

Special Page Images: Computer and tablet illustration: © iStockphoto.com/furtaev; Smart Phone illustration: © iStockphoto.com/dashadima; Feedback image: Rawpixel.com/Shutterstock.com

Intellectual Property Analyst: Diane Garrity

Intellectual Property Product Manager: Betsy Hathaway

Design images: Teamwork concept: Danielala/Shutterstock.com; Fast Fact: A_KUDR/Shutterstock.com; Hot Trend: Blablo101/Shutterstock.com; By the Numbers: pio3/Shutterstock.com

© 2017, 2015 Cengage Learning®

ALL RIGHTS RESERVED. No part of this work covered by the copyright herein may be reproduced or distributed in any form or by any means, except as permitted by U.S. copyright law, without the prior written permission of the copyright owner.

Unless otherwise noted, all items © Cengage Learning.

For product information and technology assistance, contact us at **Cengage Learning Customer & Sales Support, 1-800-354-9706**

For permission to use material from this text or product, submit all requests online at **www.cengage.com/permissions**
Further permissions questions can be emailed to **permissionrequest@cengage.com**

Library of Congress Control Number: 2015960055

Student Edition ISBN: 978-1-305-66390-9

Student Edition with Online: 978-1-305-66391-6

Cengage Learning
20 Channel Center Street
Boston, MA 02210
USA

Cengage Learning is a leading provider of customized learning solutions with employees residing in nearly 40 different countries and sales in more than 125 countries around the world. Find your local representative at **www.cengage.com**

Cengage Learning products are represented in Canada by Nelson Education, Ltd.

To learn more about Cengage Learning Solutions, visit **www.cengage.com**

Purchase any of our products at your local college store or at our preferred online store **www.cengagebrain.com**

Printed in the United States of America
Print Number: 01   Print Year 2016

Arthimedes/Shutterstock.com

CONTENTS

Part 1
INTRODUCTION

Dusit/Shutterstock.com

Part 2
INDIVIDUAL PROCESSES AND BEHAVIOR

Rawpixel/Shutterstock.com

6 Learning and Performance Management 84

7 Stress and Well-Being at Work 100

Part 3 INTERPERSONAL PROCESSES AND BEHAVIOR

BrAt82/Shutterstock.com

8 Communication 118

9 Work Teams and Groups 136

10 Decision Making by Individuals and Groups 152

11 Power and Political Behavior 170

12 Leadership and Followership 186

13 Conflict and Negotiation 204

Part 4 ORGANIZATIONAL PROCESSES AND STRUCTURE

Iurii/Shutterstock.com

14 Jobs and the Design of Work 222

15 Organizational Design and Structure 238

16 Organizational Culture 258

17 Career Management 274

18 Managing Change 292

1 | Organizational Behavior and Opportunity

LEARNING OUTCOMES

1-1 Define organizational behavior.

1-2 Identify four action steps for responding positively in times of change.

1-3 Identify the important system components of an organization.

1-4 Describe the formal and informal elements of an organization.

1-5 Identify factors that contribute to the diversity of organizations in the economy.

1-6 Describe the opportunities that change creates for organizational behavior.

1-7 Demonstrate the value of objective knowledge and skill development in the study of organizational behavior.

After finishing this chapter go to **PAGE 15** for **STUDY TOOLS.**

HUMAN BEHAVIOR IN ORGANIZATIONS

Human behavior in organizations is complex and often difficult to understand. Organizations have been described as clockworks in which human behavior is logical and rational, but they often seem like snake pits to those who work in them.[1] The clockwork metaphor reflects an orderly, idealized view of organizational behavior devoid of conflict or dilemma because all the working parts (the people) mesh smoothly. The snake pit metaphor, on the other hand, conveys the daily conflict, distress, and struggle in organizations. Each metaphor reflects reality from a different perspective—the organization's versus the individual's. The snake pit metaphor expresses the dark side of human behavior, which is seen at its extreme in cases of road rage and workplace violence. Workplace incivility has become commonplace in many organizations, with an estimated 50% of workers saying that they experience uncivil behavior weekly. Incivility has negative affective, cognitive, and behavioral consequences for instigators, targets, and witnesses of such negative behaviors.[2] In contrast, the clockwork metaphor expresses the view of organizations as healthy and productive systems in which individuals have a clear sense of the shared vision and values, are personally invested in outcomes, feel that their contributions are significant, and receive support and respect from the organization's leadership.[3]

This chapter serves as an introduction to the complex subject of organizational behavior. The first section provides an overview of human behavior in organizations, its interdisciplinary origins, and its responses to change. The second section presents an organizational context within which behavior occurs. The third section highlights the **opportunities** that exist in times of **change** and **challenge** for people at work.[4] The fourth section addresses the ways people learn about organizational behavior and explains how the text's pedagogical features relate to the various learning styles. The final section presents the plan for the book.

We can define **organizational behavior** as the study of individual behavior and group dynamics in organizations. The study of organizational behavior is primarily concerned with the psychosocial, interpersonal, and behavioral dynamics in organizations. However, organizational variables that affect human behavior at work are also relevant to the study of organizational behavior. These organizational variables include jobs, the design of work, communication, performance appraisal, organizational design, and organizational structure.

1-1a Understanding Human Behavior

The vast majority of theories and models of human behavior fall into two basic categories: that of an internal perspective and that of an external perspective. The internal perspective looks at workers' minds to understand their behavior. It is psychodynamically oriented, and its proponents understand human behavior in terms of the thoughts, feelings, past experiences, and needs of the individual. The internal perspective explains people's actions and behavior in terms of their histories and personal value systems. The idea of this perspective is that internal processes of thinking, feeling, perceiving, and judging lead people to act in specific ways; therefore, people are best understood from the inside, and their behavior is best interpreted alongside their thoughts and feelings. The internal perspective has given rise to a wide range of motivational and leadership theories.

The external perspective, on the other hand, focuses on factors outside the person to understand behavior, that is, external events, consequences, and environmental forces. This perspective excludes consideration of a person's history, feelings, thoughts, and personal value system in interpreting actions and behavior. Thus, it has given rise to an alternative set of motivational and leadership theories, which are covered in Chapters 5 and 12. The internal and external perspectives offer alternative explanations for human behavior. For example, the internal perspective might say Mary is an outstanding employee because she has a high need

Organizations have been described as clockworks, but they often seem like snake pits.

Danielala/Shutterstock.com

opportunities Favorable times or chances for progress and advancement.

change The transformation or modification of an organization and/or its stakeholders.

challenge The call to competition, contest, or battle.

organizational behavior The study of individual behavior and group dynamics in organizations.

for achievement, whereas the external perspective might say it is because she is extremely well paid for her work. Kurt Lewin combined both perspectives with his claim that behavior is a function of both the person and the environment.[5]

1-1b Interdisciplinary Influences

Organizational behavior is a blended discipline that has grown out of contributions from numerous earlier fields of study. The sciences of psychology, sociology, engineering, anthropology, management, and medicine have all contributed to our understanding of human behavior in organizations.

Psychology, the science of human behavior, was developed during the closing decades of the nineteenth century. Psychology traces its origins to philosophy and the science of physiology. One of the most prominent early psychologists, William James, held a degree in medicine (MD). Since its beginnings, psychology has branched into a number of specialized fields, including clinical, experimental, military, organizational, and social psychology. Organizational psychology frequently overlaps with organizational behavior; for instance, both investigate work motivation.[6] Johnson & Johnson, Valero Energy, and Chaparral Steel all used psychological research on American military personnel from the World War I era to develop their sophisticated personnel selection methods.[7]

Sociology, the science of society, has contributed greatly to our knowledge of group and intergroup dynamics. Because sociology takes society rather than the individual as its point of departure, sociologists focus on the variety of roles within a society or culture, the norms and standards of behavior in groups, and the consequences of compliant and deviant behavior. Individuals have a role set that is determined by their social position, and roles affect how people interact within organizations. The Professional Role Behaviors Survey, for example, studied how the roles of various

Lightspring/Shutterstock.com

medical practitioners changed during hospital restructuring and these changes influenced organizational behavior and culture.[8]

Engineering is the applied science of energy and matter. It enhances our understanding of the design of work. Frederick Taylor took basic engineering ideas and applied them to human behavior at work, influencing the early study of organizational behavior.[9] With his engineering background, Taylor placed special emphasis on human productivity and efficiency in work behavior. Job preparation and performance shifted from a long apprenticeship and a creative, problem-solving approach to work to training in and automated performance of simplified tasks. A study published in 1990 showed that Taylor's notions of performance standards and differential piece-rate systems were still shaping organizational goal-setting programs at Black & Decker, IBM, and Weyerhaeuser at that time.[10]

Anthropology, the science of human learned behavior, is especially important to our understanding of *organizational culture*. In fact, anthropological research has been used to examine the effects of efficient organizational cultures on organizational performance[11] and the ways pathological personalities may lead to dysfunctional organizational cultures.[12] In one case study, Schwartz used a psychodynamic, anthropological mode of inquiry to explore corporate decay at General Motors and NASA.[13]

Management, originally called *administrative science*, is the study of overseeing activities and supervising people in organizations. It includes the design, implementation, and management of various administrative and organizational systems. March and Simon take the human organization as their point of departure to investigate administrative practices that enhance the effectiveness of the system.[14] Management is the first discipline to take the modern corporation as the unit of analysis, a viewpoint that distinguishes its contribution to the study of organizational behavior.

Medicine, the applied science of treating diseases to enhance an individual's health and well-being, focuses on both physical and psychological health as well as industrial mental health.[15] As modern care defeats acute diseases, medical attention is shifting to more chronic diseases such as hypertension and to issues involved in occupational

psychology The science of human behavior.

sociology The science of society.

engineering The applied science of energy and matter.

anthropology The science of human learned behavior.

management The study of overseeing activities and supervising people in organizations.

medicine The applied science of healing or treating diseases to enhance an individual's health and well-being.

health and well-being.[16] These trends have contributed to the growth of corporate *wellness programs* such as Johnson & Johnson's "Live for Life Program." Moreover, *ergonomics* has gained increasing attention as a way to prevent medical problems resulting from poor design of workstations, resulting in the loss of billions of dollars from higher healthcare costs and lower worker productivity.[17] Such costs can be cut nearly in half by implementing the results of medical research into better workplace design.[18]

1-2 BEHAVIOR IN TIMES OF CHANGE

Early research of individuals and organizations in the midst of environmental change found that people often experience change as a threat and respond by relying on well-learned and dominant forms of behavior.[19] That is, people often become rigid and reactive in the midst of change, rather than open and responsive. This behavior works well in the face of gradual, incremental change. However, rigid and well-learned behavior may be a counterproductive response to significant change, such as outsourcing. Prompted by dramatic advances in Internet and networking technology, outsourcing has been unavoidable in much of American industry.[20] Yet factors such as employee attrition and the potential for data loss have caused many companies to modify their outsourcing strategies to keep both talent and information within the organization.[21] Big changes disrupt people's habitual behavior and force them to learn new skills, often creating discomfort and discontent. To such employees, Eric Brown, CEO of Johnson Products Company, Inc., recommends looking for the positive opportunities in change and viewing challenge as a good rather than bad experience. His action steps for adapting to change are to (1) have a positive attitude, (2) ask questions, (3) listen to the answers, and (4) be committed to success.[22]

Success is never guaranteed, however, and change sometimes results in failure. Some of the world's greatest leaders, such as Winston Churchill, experienced dramatic failures before they achieved lasting success. It was their capacity to learn from the failure and to respond positively to new opportunities that helped them overcome early setbacks. Knowing this, one venture capitalist with whom the authors have worked likes to ask an executive who is seeking to build a business to tell him about his or her greatest failure. He wants to hear how the executive responded to the failure and what he or she learned from the experience.

So change carries both the risk of failure and the opportunity for success; our behavior often determines the outcome. Moreover, success can come through the accumulation of small wins and through the use of microprocesses, as has been found with middle managers engaged in institutional change.[23]

1-3 THE ORGANIZATIONAL CONTEXT

A complete understanding of organizational behavior requires an understanding of both human behavior and of the organizational context—that is, the specific setting—within which behavior is acted out.

1-3a Organizations as Open Systems

Just as two different perspectives offer complementary explanations for human behavior, two views shape complementary explanations of organizations. Organizations are open systems of interacting components, including people, tasks, technology, and structure. These internal components also interact with components in the organization's task environment.

Today, the corporation is the dominant organizational form for much of the Western world, but other organizational forms have dominated other societies. Religious organizations, such as the temple corporations of ancient Mesopotamia and the churches in colonial America, can often dominate society.[24] So can military organizations, such as the clans of the Scottish Highlands and the regional armies of the People's Republic of China.[25] All of these societies are woven together by family organizations, which themselves may vary from nuclear and extended families to small, collective communities.[26] The purpose and structure of religious, military, and family organizational forms varies, but people within different organizations often behave alike. In fact, early discoveries about power and leadership in work organizations were remarkably similar to findings about power and leadership within families.[27]

Because organizations are so varied in function, manufacturing products such as aircraft components or delivering services such as money management, for example, we must first understand the open system components of an organization and its task environment in order to see how the organization performs.

Accordingly, Katz and Kahn in one study, and Leavitt in another, established open system frameworks for understanding organizations.[28] The four major internal components are task, people, technology, and structure. These four components, along with the organization's inputs, outputs, and key elements in the task environment, are depicted in Figure 1.1. The **task** of the organization is its mission, purpose, or goal

task An organization's mission, purpose, or goal for existing.

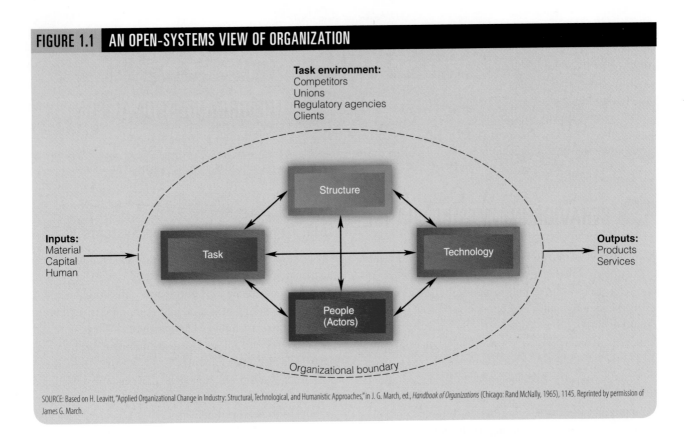

FIGURE 1.1 AN OPEN-SYSTEMS VIEW OF ORGANIZATION

Task environment:
Competitors
Unions
Regulatory agencies
Clients

Inputs:
Material
Capital
Human

Structure

Task

Technology

People
(Actors)

Outputs:
Products
Services

Organizational boundary

SOURCE: Based on H. Leavitt, "Applied Organizational Change in Industry: Structural, Technological, and Humanistic Approaches," in J. G. March, ed., *Handbook of Organizations* (Chicago: Rand McNally, 1965), 1145. Reprinted by permission of James G. March.

for existing. The **people** are the human resources of the organization. The **technology** is the wide range of tools, knowledge, and/or techniques used to transform inputs into outputs. The **structure** involves the systems of communication, authority and roles, and workflow.

In addition to these major internal components, the organization as a system also has an external task environment composed of different constituents such as suppliers, customers, and federal regulators. Thompson describes the task environment as that element of the environment related to the organization's degree of goal attainment, or its basic task.[29] A number of organizations are using or considering the use of Twitter as a way of networking into elements of their task environments.[30] For example, NASA uses Twitter to update followers on the status of upcoming shuttle flights.

The organization system works by taking inputs, converting them into throughputs, and delivering outputs to its task environment. *Inputs* are the human, informational, material, and financial resources used by the organization. *Throughputs* are the materials and resources as they are transformed by the organization's technology component. Once the transformation is complete, they become *outputs* for customers, consumers, and clients. The actions of suppliers, customers, regulators, and other elements of the task environment affect the organization and the behavior of people at work. The role of modern corporations has expanded to include corporate social responsibility. Customers expect these organizations to be good corporate citizens, creating social value as well as financial wealth for their shareholders.[31]

1-4 THE FORMAL AND INFORMAL ORGANIZATION

The open systems view of organizations suggests that they are designed like clockwork (recall the clockwork metaphor described at the beginning of this chapter), with a neat, precise, interrelated functioning. The **formal organization** is the official, legitimate, and most visible part of the organization, and it enables people to think of organizations in logical and rational ways. The snake pit metaphor mentioned earlier originates from the study of the **informal organization**, which is unofficial and

people The human resources of an organization.

technology The tools, knowledge, and/or techniques used to transform inputs into outputs.

structure The systems of communication, authority and roles, and workflow.

formal organization The official, legitimate, and most visible part of the system.

informal organization The unofficial and less visible part of the system.

Formal Organizational Elements Help Make Marriott a Great Place to Work

Marriott is no Google, and it doesn't strive to be. Marriott employees **love** working at Marriott, and a large part of their affinity for the hotel chain can be attributed to its formal employee policies, from its hiring, flexible scheduling, and career development programs to its wide-ranging perks and benefits. These formal organizational elements have had a positive impact on worker attitudes and desire to remain with the company. Marriott employees consider each other as family rather than colleagues. By far, it is the company's recruitment and hiring practices that have the most positive effect on organizational outcomes.

Source: Marriott International, Inc.

Marriott's EVP of HR believes that due to the company's practice of "hiring friendly and training technically," it has experienced lower turnover and increased numbers of employees who not only believe in serving their customers, but delight in doing so.

SOURCE: L. Gallagher, "Why Employees Love Marriott," *Fortune*, 171 (March 15, 2015), 112–118.

---

less visible. The **Hawthorne studies**, conducted during the 1920s and 1930s, first suggested the importance of the informal elements. During the so-called interview study, the third of the four Hawthorne studies, the researchers began to fully appreciate the informal elements of the Hawthorne Works as an organization.[32] The formal and informal elements of the organization are depicted in Figure 1.2.

FIGURE 1.2 FORMAL AND INFORMAL ORGANIZATION

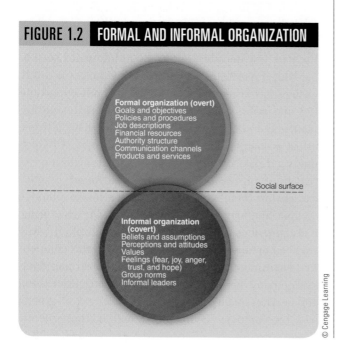

Formal organization (overt)
Goals and objectives
Policies and procedures
Job descriptions
Financial resources
Authority structure
Communication channels
Products and services

Social surface

Informal organization (covert)
Beliefs and assumptions
Perceptions and attitudes
Values
Feelings (fear, joy, anger, trust, and hope)
Group norms
Informal leaders

© Cengage Learning

Because the formal and informal elements of an organization can sometimes conflict, we must understand both. Such conflicts erupted in many organizations during the early years of the twentieth century and were embodied in the union–management strife of that era. Sometimes these formal–informal conflicts escalated into violence. For example, supervisors at the Homestead Works of U.S. Steel during the 1920s were issued pistols "just in case" they felt it necessary to shoot unruly, dangerous steelworkers. However, during that same era, the progressive Eastman Kodak company provided financial backing for employees' neighborhood communities, such as Meadowbrook in Rochester, New York. Kodak's concern for employees and attention to informal issues made unions unnecessary at the company.

The informal elements of the organization are often points of diagnostic and intervention activities in organizational development, though the formal elements must always be considered because they provide the context for the informal.[33] It is the informal elements involving people's feelings, thoughts, and attitudes about their work that most affect their behavior and performance, but individual behavior plays out in the context of both the formal and informal elements of the

Hawthorne studies Studies conducted during the 1920s and 1930s that suggested the importance of the informal organization.

The open systems view of an organization suggests that it is designed and run like clockwork.

system, becoming, in the process, organizational behavior. Employees' moods, emotions, and dispositions all influence critical organizational outcomes such as job performance, decision making, creativity, turnover, teamwork, negotiation, and leadership.[34]

1-5 DIVERSITY OF ORGANIZATIONS

Most attempts to explain or predict organizational behavior rely heavily on factors within the organization and give less weight to external environmental considerations.[35] Yet organizational behavior always occurs in the

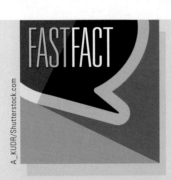

FASTFACT

The United States Economy

The U.S. economy is the largest in the world, with a gross domestic product of more than $17.7 trillion in 2014. The largest sectors are service (46%), product manufacture of nondurable goods (15%), and durable goods (8%). Taken together, the production of products and the delivery of services account for 69% of the U.S. economy. Government and fixed investments account for the remaining 31%.

SOURCE: U.S. Bureau of Economic Analysis, "Table 1.1.5 Gross Domestic Product," http://www.bea.gov/iTable/iTable.cfm?ReqID=9&step=1#reqid=9&step=3&isuri=1&903=5, accessed March 24, 2015.

context of a specific organizational setting, so students can benefit from being sensitive to that industrial context and from developing an appreciation for the diversity of various organizations.[36]

Large and small organizations operate in each sector of the economy: the private, manufacturing, service, government, and nonprofit sectors. In the private sector are a great variety of organizations that play an important role in the economy. The manufacturing sector includes the production of basic materials, such as steel, and the production of finished products, such as automobiles and electronic equipment. The service sector includes transportation, financial services, insurance, and retail sales. The government sectors, which provide essential infrastructure, and nonprofit organizations are important to our collective well-being because they meet needs that other sectors do not address. For example, in France, the not-for-profit Action Tank has discovered a solution for poor consumers who find access to even low-cost products and services out of their reach.[37]

Hundreds of small, medium-sized, and large organizations contribute to the economic health and human welfare of the United States. Throughout this book, we provide examples from a variety of organizations to help you develop a greater appreciation for your own organization and for others in the diverse world of private business enterprises and nonprofit organizations.

1-6 CHANGE CREATES OPPORTUNITIES

Global competition, which is a leading force driving change at work, has increased significantly during the past few decades, especially in industries such as banking, finance, and air transportation. As a result, change has accelerated and, with it, both opportunities and risks. Corporate competition creates performance and cost pressures, changes that have a ripple effect on people and their behavior at work. Although one such risk for employees is the marginalization of part-time professionals, good management practice can ensure their integration.[38] Furthermore, although competition may lead to downsizing and restructuring, it also provides the opportunity for revitalization.[39] And small companies don't necessarily lose in this competitive environment. Scientech, a small power and energy company, needed to enhance its managerial talent and service quality to meet the challenges of growth and big-company competitors, and it consequently

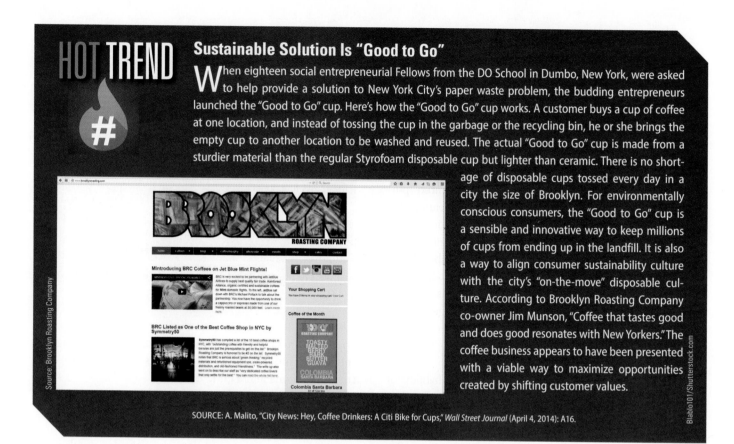

Source: Brooklyn Roasting Company

Blablo101/Shutterstock.com

HOT TREND

Sustainable Solution Is "Good to Go"

When eighteen social entrepreneurial Fellows from the DO School in Dumbo, New York, were asked to help provide a solution to New York City's paper waste problem, the budding entrepreneurs launched the "Good to Go" cup. Here's how the "Good to Go" cup works. A customer buys a cup of coffee at one location, and instead of tossing the cup in the garbage or the recycling bin, he or she brings the empty cup to another location to be washed and reused. The actual "Good to Go" cup is made from a sturdier material than the regular Styrofoam disposable cup but lighter than ceramic. There is no shortage of disposable cups tossed every day in a city the size of Brooklyn. For environmentally conscious consumers, the "Good to Go" cup is a sensible and innovative way to keep millions of cups from ending up in the landfill. It is also a way to align consumer sustainability culture with the city's "on-the-move" disposable culture. According to Brooklyn Roasting Company co-owner Jim Munson, "Coffee that tastes good and does good resonates with New Yorkers." The coffee business appears to have been presented with a viable way to maximize opportunities created by shifting customer values.

SOURCE: A. Malito, "City News: Hey, Coffee Drinkers: A Citi Bike for Cups," *Wall Street Journal* (April 4, 2014): A16.

improved its performance. Thus, competition spurred its increased success.

Product and service quality are the major ways that companies can win in a competitive environment. IBM, Control Data Services, Inc., Northwest Airlines (now Delta), and Southwest Airlines all used problem-solving skills to achieve high-quality products and services in their attempts to deal with competitive forces. Change in the coffee industry has been a key stimulus for both Caribou Coffee and Starbucks as they innovate and improve.

Too much change, however, leads to chaos, and too little change leads to stagnation. Also, winning in a competitive industry can be a transient victory; staying ahead of the competition requires constant change.

1-6a Global Competition in Business

Managers and executives in the United States face radical change in response to increased global competition. According to noted economist Lester Thurow, this competition is characterized by intense rivalry between the United States, Japan, and Europe in core industries.[40] As a result, all categories of employees face increased pressure to be productive and to add value to the firm.

Moreover, corporate warfare and competition make employment uncertain for people in companies or industries that pursue cost-cutting strategies to achieve economic success. Five months after taking over as CEO of Microsoft, Satya Nadella notified employees of impending organizational changes, not limited to job cuts, required for the technology giant to return to its core business.[41] The global competition in the automotive industry among Japanese, U.S., and European car companies exemplifies the intensity that other industries can expect in the future.

Some people feel that the future must be the focus in coming to grips with this international competition, whereas others believe we can deal with the future only by studying the past.[42] Global, economic, and organizational changes have dramatic effects on the study and management of organizational behavior.

1-6b Customer Focused for High Quality

Global competition has challenged organizations to become more customer focused, to meet changing product and service demands, and to exceed customers' expectations of high quality. Quality has the potential to give organizations in viable industries a competitive edge against international competition. By aiming to be number one in experience, for example, Caribou Coffee competes with a customer-focused, high-quality approach.

Quality has become a rubric for products and services of high status. *Total quality* is defined in many ways.[43] *Total quality management (TQM)* is the total dedication to continuous improvement and to customers so that the customers' needs are met and their expectations exceeded. This customer-oriented philosophy of management has important implications for virtually all aspects of organizational behavior. Quality cannot be optimized because customer needs and expectations are always changing, but it is embedded in highly successful organizations. Part of what has catapulted Toyota to the top of the auto industry is its attention to quality and detail throughout the organization. Even though TQM consulting has experienced a boom-to-bust cycle, the main concepts underlying its initial rise in popularity are here to stay.

Quality improvement enhances the probability of organizational success in increasingly competitive industries. One study of 193 general medical hospitals examined seven TQM practices and found them positively related to the financial performance of the hospital.[44] Indeed, quality improvement is an enduring feature of an organization's culture and of the economic competition we face today. It leads to competitive advantage through customer responsiveness, results acceleration, and resource effectiveness.[45] In evaluating quality improvement ideas for people at work, three key questions should be asked: (1) Does the idea improve customer response? (2) Does the idea accelerate results? (3) Does the idea increase the effectiveness of resources? A "yes" answer means the idea should be implemented to improve quality.

Six Sigma is a philosophy for company-wide quality improvement developed by Motorola and popularized by General Electric. Characterized by its customer-driven approach, through its emphasis on using quantitative data to make decisions and its priority of saving money,[46] it has evolved into a high-performance system for executing business strategy. Part of its quality program is a twelve-step problem-solving method specifically designed to lead a Six Sigma "Black Belt" to significant improvement within a defined process. It tackles problems in four phases: (1) measure, (2) analyze, (3) improve, and (4) control. In addition, it forces executives to align the right objective and targets, and it forces quality improvement teams to mobilize for action in order to accelerate and monitor sustained improvement. Six Sigma is set up so that that it can be

TABLE 1.1	CONTRASTING SIX SIGMA AND TOTAL QUALITY MANAGEMENT
Six Sigma	**Total Quality Management**
Executive ownership	Self-directed work teams
Business strategy execution system	Quality initiative
Truly cross-functional	Largely within a single function
Focused training with verifiable return on investment	No mass training in statistics and quality Return on investment
Business results oriented	Quality oriented

SOURCE: M. Barney, "Motorola's Second Generation," *Six Sigma Forum Magazine* (May 2002): 13.

applied to a range of situations, from manufacturing settings to service work environments. Table 1.1 contrasts Six Sigma and TQM.

Any quality control method has some success and some failure, and some methods may work better in a given organization than others due to differences in organizational culture. One study, with a strong emphasis on exploring statistical modeling techniques, compared Six Sigma to two other methods for quality improvement (specifically, Taguchi's methods and the Shainin system) and found it to be the most complete strategy of the three.[47] On the other hand, statistical data on the actual economic effect of Six Sigma is lacking, and the method has come under some critique.[48] It is important for managers to consider which of a variety of options is best for their organization.

1-6c Behavior and Quality at Work

Whereas total quality may draw on reliability engineering or just-in-time management, total quality improvement can succeed only when employees have the skills and authority to respond to customer needs.[49] Total quality has important direct effects on the behavior of employees at all levels in the organization, not just on employees working directly with customers. Thus, chief executives can advance total quality by engaging in participative management, being willing to change things, focusing quality efforts on customer service (not cost cutting), including quality as a criterion in reward systems, improving the flow of information regarding quality-improvement successes or failures, and being actively and personally involved in quality efforts. While serving as chair of Motorola, George Fisher emphasized

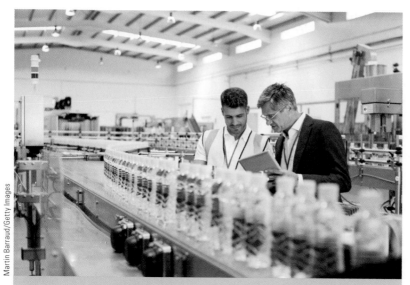

Quality is customer-oriented philosophy of management with important implications for virtually all aspects of organizational behavior

have excelled by integrating innovation into every aspect of healthcare delivery, from leadership and goal-setting to patient care.[50]

According to George H. W. Bush, "Quality management is not just a strategy. It must be a new style of working, even a new style of thinking. A dedication to quality and excellence is more than good business. It is a way of life, giving something back to society, offering your best to others."[51]

Quality is one watchword for competitive success. Organizations that do not respond to customer needs find their customers choosing alternative product and service suppliers who are willing to exceed customer expectations. Keep in mind, however, that total quality isn't a panacea for all organizations, and it doesn't guarantee unqualified success.

the behavioral attributes of leadership, cooperation, communication, and participation as important elements in the company's Six Sigma program.

Quality improvement is crucial to competitive success. The U.S. Department of Commerce sponsors an annual award in the name of Malcolm Baldrige, former secretary of commerce in the Reagan administration, to recognize companies excelling in quality improvement and management. The Malcolm Baldrige National Quality Award examination evaluates an organization in seven categories: leadership, information and analysis, strategic quality planning, human resource utilization, quality assurance of products and services, quality results, and customer satisfaction. Hospitals and health systems that have won the Malcolm Baldrige Award

1-6d Managing Organizational Behavior in Changing Times

Over and above the challenge of quality improvement to meet international competition, managing organizational behavior during changing times is challenging for at least three other reasons: (1) the increasing globalization of organizations' operating territory, (2) the increasing diversity of organizational workforces, and (3) the continuing demand for higher levels of moral and ethical behavior at work.

Each of these three issues is explored in detail in Chapter 2 and highlighted throughout the text as they appear intertwined with contemporary organizational practices. For example, the issue of women in the

HOT TREND

Four Things That Worry Business

Dominic Barton is global managing director of McKinsey Consulting. Ninety percent of his clients are Fortune 100 CEOs and other world leaders, including governments and nonprofit organizations. This provides him with good insight into what is consuming leaders' energies in a global and uncertain business climate. The following are four concerns that are consistent for many global business leaders:

- Anticipating the effects of geopolitics
- Keeping up with fast-moving technologies
- Protecting systems from threats of cyberattacks
- Responding to shifts in economic market power

SOURCE: G. Colvin, "Four Things That Worry Business," *Fortune* (October 27, 2014): 32.

How Do You Learn?

To gain a better understanding of yourself as a learner so that you can maximize your potential and develop strategies for specific learning environments, you need to evaluate the way you prefer to learn and process information. "What about You?" on the Chapter Review Card offers a short learning-style assessment.

workplace concerns workforce diversity and at the same time overlaps with the globalization issue. Gender roles are often defined differently in various cultures, and sexual harassment often plagues organizations in the United States, Europe, Israel, and South Africa.

1-7 LEARNING ABOUT ORGANIZATIONAL BEHAVIOR

The study of organizational behavior is based on scientific knowledge and applied practice. It involves abstract ideas, such as valence and expectancy in motivation, as well as concrete matters, such as observable behaviors and medical symptoms of distress at work. Therefore, learning about organizational behavior includes at least three activities, as shown in Figure 1.3. First, the science of organizational behavior requires the mastery of a certain body of **objective knowledge**. Objective knowledge results from research, experimentation, and scientific observation. Second, the practice of organizational behavior requires **skill development** based on knowledge and an understanding of oneself in order to master the abilities essential to success. Third, both objective knowledge and skill development must be applied in real-world settings.

Learning can be challenging and fun if student diversity is addressed in the learning process, when students have more options and can take greater responsibility as coproducers.[52] Teaching and learning styles should be aligned carefully, and educators should be aware that teaching is no

objective knowledge Knowledge that results from research and scientific activities.

skill development The mastery of abilities essential to successful functioning in organizations.

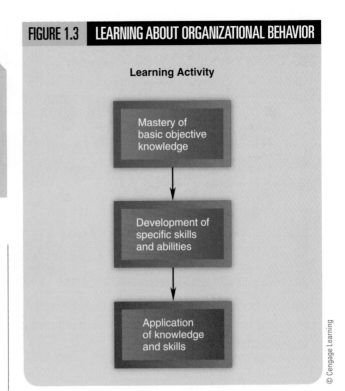

FIGURE 1.3 **LEARNING ABOUT ORGANIZATIONAL BEHAVIOR**

Learning Activity

Mastery of basic objective knowledge

Development of specific skills and abilities

Application of knowledge and skills

© Cengage Learning

longer merely verbal and visual but has now become virtual.[53] If you are a visual learner, use charts, maps, PowerPoint slides, videos, the Internet, notes, or flash cards and write things out for visual review. If you are an auditory learner, then listen, take notes during lectures, consider taping them so that you can fill in gaps later, review your notes frequently, and recite key concepts aloud. If you are a tactile learner, trace words as you are saying them, write down facts several times, and make study sheets.

1-7a Objective Knowledge

In any field of study, objective knowledge is developed through basic and applied research. Since the early research on scientific management, research on organizational behavior has continued to provide objective knowledge involving theories, conceptual models, and various research findings. In this book, the objective knowledge in each chapter is reflected in the supporting notes. Mastering the concepts and ideas that come from these notes enables you to discuss intelligently topics such as motivation, performance, leadership,[54] and executive stress.[55]

We encourage instructors and students of organizational behavior to think critically about the objective knowledge that has been gained in the study of organizational behavior. Only by engaging in critical thinking can one question or challenge the results of specific research or consider how such research should be applied in a particular work setting. Rote memorization does not prepare students to appreciate the complexity of specific theories or the intricacies of interrelated concepts, ideas, and topics. Critical thinking, by contrast, enables students to identify inconsistencies and limitations in the current body of objective knowledge.

Critical thinking, based on knowledge and understanding of basic ideas, leads to inquisitive exploration and is a key to accepting the responsibility of coproducer in the learning process. A questioning, probing attitude is at the core of critical thinking. The student of organizational behavior should evolve into a critical consumer of knowledge related to organizational behavior—one who is able to intelligently question the latest research results and distinguish plausible, sound, new approaches from fads that lack substance or adequate foundation. Ideally, the student of organizational behavior develops into a scientific, professional manager who is knowledgeable in the art and science of organizational behavior.

1-7b Skill Development

Learning about organizational behavior requires doing as well as knowing. Furthermore, the development of skills and abilities requires that students be challenged by the instructor and by themselves. The "What about You?" features on the Chapter Review Cards give you a chance to learn about yourself, challenge yourself, and apply what you are learning.

The U.S. Department of Labor tries to ensure that people acquire the necessary skills to be successful in the workplace.[56] The essential skills identified by the department are (1) resource management skills, such as time management; (2) information management skills, such as data interpretation; (3) personal interaction skills, such as teamwork; (4) systems behavior and performance skills, such as cause–effect relationships;

and (5) technology utilization skills, such as troubleshooting. Many of these skills, such as decision making and information management, are directly related to the study of organizational behavior.[57] Employers increasingly demand that workers possess effective teamwork and collaboration skills. Eighty percent of employers surveyed cited the ability to work in groups as a highly desirable attribute of recruits.[58]

Developing skills is different from acquiring objective knowledge because it requires structured practice and feedback. A key function of experiential learning is engaging the student in individual or group activities that are systematically reviewed, leading to new skills and understandings. However, objective knowledge acquisition and skill development are interrelated, as shown in Figure 1.4. The student engages in an individual- or group-structured activity and then systematically reviews that activity, gaining new or modified knowledge and skills.

If skill development and structured learning occur in this way, there should be an inherently self-correcting element to learning because of the modification of the student's knowledge and skills over time.[59] To ensure that skill development does occur and that the learning is self-correcting as it occurs, three basic guidelines must be followed.

First, students must accept responsibility for their own behavior, actions, and learning. This is key to the

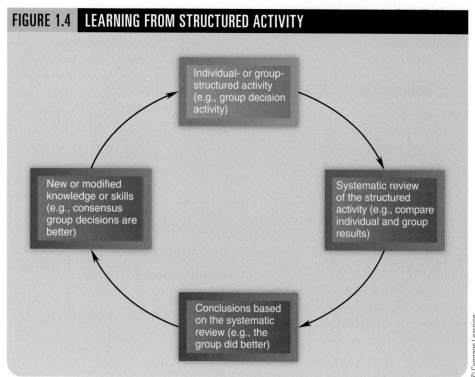

FIGURE 1.4 LEARNING FROM STRUCTURED ACTIVITY

Individual- or group-structured activity (e.g., group decision activity)

Systematic review of the structured activity (e.g., compare individual and group results)

Conclusions based on the systematic review (e.g., the group did better)

New or modified knowledge or skills (e.g., consensus group decisions are better)

© Cengage Learning

pio3/Shutterstock.com

BY THE NUMBERS

1920s
supervisors at U.S. Steel issued pistols

$17.7 trillion
U.S. gross domestic product in 2014

3
activities involved in learning organizational behavior

12
steps in the GE Six Sigma problem-solving method

46%
of the U.S. GDP comes from the service sector

coproducer role in the learning process. A group cannot learn for its members. Members must accept responsibility for what they each individually do and learn. Denial of responsibility helps no one, least of all the learner.

Second, each student must actively participate in the individual- or group-structured learning activity. Structured learning is not passive; it is active. In group activities, everyone suffers if just one person adopts a passive attitude. All must actively participate.

Third, each student must be open to new information, new skills, new ideas, and experimentation. This does not mean that students should be indiscriminately open. It does mean that students should have nondefensive, open attitudes so that they can learn and adjust to new ideas.

1-7c Application of Knowledge and Skills

Understanding organizational behavior includes an appreciation and understanding of working realities as well as of science and of oneself. One of the advantages of structured, experiential learning is that a person can explore new behaviors and skills in a comparatively safe environment. Fortunately, losing your temper in a classroom activity and learning about the potentially adverse impact on other people will have dramatically different consequences from losing your temper with an important customer in a tense work situation. Thus, learning spaces

> **Learning about organizational behavior requires doing as well as knowing.**

that offer the interface of student learning styles with institutional learning environments give learners safe spaces to engage their brains to form abstract hypotheses, to actively test these hypotheses through concrete experiences, and to reflectively observe the outcomes in behavior and experience.[60] The ultimate objective of skill application and experiential learning is that one transfers the process employed in learning from structured activities in the classroom and learning spaces to learning from unstructured opportunities in the workplace.

Although organizational behavior is an applied discipline, students are not "trained" in organizational behavior. Rather, they are "educated" in organizational behavior and are coproducers in learning. The distinction between these two modes of learning is found in the degree of direct and immediate applicability of either knowledge or skills. As an activity, training ties objective knowledge or skill development more directly to specific applications. By contrast, education enhances a person's residual pool of objective knowledge and skills that may then be selectively applied later—sometimes significantly later—when the opportunity presents itself. Hence, education is consistent with the concept of lifelong learning. Especially in a growing area of knowledge such as organizational behavior, the student can think of the first course as the outset of lifelong learning about the subject.

STUDY TOOLS 1

LOCATED AT BACK OF THE TEXTBOOK

☐ Rip out chapter review card

LOCATED AT WWW.CENGAGE.COM/LOGIN

☐ Track your knowledge and understanding of key concepts in business using 4LTR Press Online

☐ Review key term flashcards and create your own using StudyBits

☐ Create and complete practice quizzes based off of your notes and StudyBits

☐ Complete Online activities such as Matching and Fill-in-the-Blank exercises

☐ View chapter highlight box content, including the chapter videos, key exhibits and executive profiles.

2 | Challenges for Managers

Ollyy/Shutterstock.com

LEARNING OUTCOMES

2-1 Describe the factors that affect organizations competing in the global economy.

2-2 Explain how cultural differences form the basis of work-related attitudes.

2-3 Describe the challenges and positive influences diversity brings to today's business environment.

2-4 Discuss the role of ethics, character, and personal integrity in the organization.

2-5 Explain five issues that pose ethical dilemmas for managers.

2-6 Describe the effects of technological advances on today's workforce.

After finishing this chapter go to **PAGE 33** for **STUDY TOOLS.**

Key challenges that managers face today stem from the fact that business is increasingly global in scope.[1] Globalization is driven by the spread of economic logics centered on freeing, opening, deregulating, and privatizing economies to attract investment as well as technological innovations that are revolutionizing communication.[2] The resulting challenges for managers can be viewed as both opportunities and threats.

Chief executive officers of U.S. corporations have cited three challenges managers must overcome to remain competitive: (1) globalizing the firm's operations to compete in the global village; (2) leading a diverse workforce; and (3) encouraging positive ethics, character, and personal integrity.[3]

Companies like Coca-Cola, are transnational and are recognized around the world (sign is from Berlin, Germany)

2-1 COMPETING IN THE GLOBAL ECONOMY

Only a few years ago, business conducted across national borders was referred to as *international* activity, a term implying that the individual's or the organization's nationality is held strongly in consciousness.[4] *Globalization*, by contrast, suggests that the world is free from national boundaries and is borderless.[5] U.S. workers now compete with workers in other countries. Organizations from other countries, such as the auto manufacturers Honda, Toyota, Nissan, and Daimler Benz, are establishing subsidiaries in the United States.

Similarly, what were once called *multinational organizations* (organizations that did business in several countries) are now referred to as **transnational organizations**, indicating that the global viewpoint supersedes national issues.[6] Transnational organizations such as 3M, Dow Chemical, and Coca-Cola operate worldwide across long distances and employ a multicultural mix of workers.

2-1a Social and Political Changes

Social and political upheavals have led organizations to change the way they conduct business as a result of thinking globally. Toyota, for example, is one Japanese company thinking big, thinking globally, and thinking

What major challenges must managers overcome to remain competitive?

differently by learning to speak to the 60-million-strong Generation Y, or so-called millennials.[7]

Business ventures in China have become increasingly attractive to U.S. companies. One challenge U.S. managers have tackled is understanding the Chinese way of doing business, ways that have been shaped by the Communist Party, socialism, feudalistic values, and **guanxi** (building networks for social exchange). Once *guanxi* is established, individuals can ask favors of each other with the expectation that the favor will be returned. Thus, many Chinese use *guanxi*, or personal connections, to conduct business or obtain jobs.

The concept of *guanxi* is not unique to China. There are similar concepts in many other countries, including Russia and Haiti. It is a broad term that can mean anything from strongly loyal relationships to ceremonial gift giving, sometimes seen as bribery. *Guanxi* is more common in societies with underdeveloped legal support for private businesses.[8]

Americans can learn to build their own *guanxi* in order to interact effectively with Chinese managers. This would involve understanding the Chinese chain of command and negotiating slow, general agreements. Using the foreign

transnational organization An organization in which the global viewpoint supersedes national issues.

guanxi The Chinese practice of building networks for social exchange.

government as a local franchisee may be effective in China. For example, KFC's operation in China is a joint venture between KFC (60%) and two Chinese government bodies (40%).[9]

The opening of trade barriers is a third issue that affects organizations competing in a global economy. In 1993, the European Union integrated fifteen nations into a single market by removing trade barriers. At that time, the member nations of the European Union were Austria, Belgium, Denmark, Finland, France, Germany, Greece, Ireland, Italy, Luxembourg, the Netherlands, Portugal, Spain, Sweden, and the United Kingdom. By 2007 Bulgaria, Cyprus, the Czech Republic, Estonia, Hungary, Latvia, Lithuania, Malta, Poland, Romania, Slovakia, and Slovenia had also joined. Europe's integration provides many opportunities for U.S. organizations to engage 494 million potential customers. Companies such as Ford Motor Company and IBM, which entered the market early with wholly-owned subsidiaries, were able to capitalize on their much anticipated head start.[10] Competition within the European Union will intensify, however, as will competition from Japan and the former Soviet nations.

The United States, Canada, and Mexico dramatically reduced trade barriers with the North American Free Trade Agreement (NAFTA), which took effect in 1994. Organizations found promising new markets for their products, and many companies located plants in Mexico to take advantage of low labor costs. Prior to NAFTA, Mexico placed heavy tariffs on U.S. exports. The agreement immediately eliminated many of these tariffs and provided that the remaining tariffs be phased out over time.

Given these changes, managers must think globally and adopt a long-term view. Entering global markets requires long-term strategies.

2-1b Cultural Differences

One key for any company competing in the global marketplace is to understand diverse cultures. Whether managing culturally diverse individuals within a single location or managing individuals at remote locations around the globe, organizations must appreciate the

expatriate manager A manager who works in a country other than her or his home country.

differences among cultures. Edgar Schein suggests that to understand an organization's culture or, more broadly, any culture, one should dig below the surface of visible artifacts and uncover the basic underlying assumptions at the core of the culture.[11]

Microcultural differences (i.e., differences within cultures) are key to our understanding of the global work environment.[12] One such difference is the gap between generations, which Toyota, as previously mentioned, is addressing by learning to speak to the 60-million-strong millennial Generation Y.[13]

When considering differences among cultures, symbols are extremely important because they can generate misunderstanding or inhibit communication if they are interpreted incorrectly. Consider the thumbs-up sign, which means approval in the United States but is an obscene gesture in Australia. Consider also the Windows icon representing a manila file folder, which is meaningless to Europeans who have never used such folders.[14]

Do cultural differences translate into differences in work-related attitudes? To answer this question, the pioneering Dutch researcher Geert Hofstede, with his colleagues, surveyed 160,000 managers and employees of IBM working in sixty different countries. Thus, the researchers were able to study individuals from the same company in the same jobs but living in different countries. They found that national culture explains more differences in work-related attitudes than does age, gender, profession, or position in the organization. Five dimensions of cultural differences that formed the basis for work-related attitudes were identified (Figure 2.1).[15]

Management careers have taken on a global dimension in that working in transnational organizations may give managers the opportunity to work in other countries. **Expatriate managers**, those who work in a

---

FIGURE 2.1 HOFSTEDE'S DIMENSIONS OF CULTURAL DIFFERENCES

Individualism	Collectivism
High power distance	Low power distance
High uncertainty avoidance	Low uncertainty avoidance
Masculinity	Femininity
Long-term orientation	Short-term orientation

SOURCE: Based on Academy of Management, P.O. Box 3020, Briarcliff Manor, NY 10510-8020. Cultural Constraints in Management Theories. G. Hofstede, Academy of Management Executive 7 (1993).

country other than their home country, benefit greatly from knowledge of cultural differences.

International executives are executives whose jobs have international scope, whether they have an expatriate assignment or deal with international issues. What kind of competencies should an individual develop to prepare for an international career? Some key competencies are integrity, insightfulness, risk taking, courage to take a stand, and ability to bring out the best in people. Learning-oriented attributes of international executives include cultural adventurousness, flexibility, openness to criticism, desire to seek learning opportunities, and sensitivity to cultural differences.[16] Further, strong human capital generally has a positive effect on internationalization.[17] Notice that all these qualities are based on core competencies and the ability to learn from experience.

Because workplace customs vary widely, understanding cultural differences becomes especially important for companies that are considering opening foreign offices. It is wise to do the research in advance. Consulate offices and companies operating within the foreign country provide excellent information about national customs and legal requirements. Table 2.1 presents a business guide to cultural differences in three countries: Japan, Mexico, and Saudi Arabia.

Another reality affecting global business practices is the cost of layoffs in other countries. As the economy has become more global, downsizing has presented challenges worldwide. For example, dismissing a forty-five-year-old middle manager with twenty years of service and a $50,000 annual salary varied in cost from a low of $13,000 in Ireland to a high of $130,000 in Italy.[18] Laying off this manager in the United States would have cost approximately $19,000. The wide variability in costs stems from the various legal protections that certain countries give workers. In Italy, laid-off employees must receive a so-called notice period payment (one year's pay if they have nine years or more of service) plus a severance payment (based on pay and years of service). U.S. companies operating overseas often adopt the European tradition of training and retraining workers to avoid overstaffing and potential layoffs. Appreciating the customs and rules for doing business in another country is essential to global success.

2-2 CULTURAL DIFFERENCES AND WORK-RELATED ATTITUDES

Hofstede's work has implications for work-related attitudes. We'll now take a closer look at how his five dimensions of cultural differences are manifest in a variety of countries.

2-2a Individualism versus Collectivism

In cultures where **individualism** predominates, the social framework is loose and employees put loyalty to themselves and their families ahead of loyalty to their company and work group. Cultures characterized by **collectivism**, on the other hand, are tightly knit social frameworks in which individual members depend strongly on others and group decisions are valued and accepted.

North American and European cultures are individualistic in orientation. Managers in Great Britain and the Netherlands, for example, emphasize and encourage individual achievement. In contrast, in collectivist cultures, such as Israeli *kibbutzim* and Japan, people view group loyalty and unity as paramount. Collectivistic managers seek to fit harmoniously within the group and encourage their employees to do the same. The world's regions are patterned with varying degrees of this cultural difference.

2-2b Power Distance

Power distance relates to the acceptance of the unequal distribution of power. In countries with a high power distance, bosses are afforded more authority, which is seldom bypassed, titles are used, and formality is the rule. Managers and employees in such countries see one another as fundamentally different kinds of people. India, Venezuela, and Mexico all demonstrate high power distance.

In societies with low power distance, people believe in minimizing inequality. People at various power levels in these countries are less threatened by and more willing to trust one another. Managers and employees judge each other on a basis of equality. Managers are given authority only if they have expertise. Employees frequently bypass the boss in order to get work done in countries with a low power distance, such as Denmark and Australia.

2-2c Uncertainty Avoidance

Cultures with high **uncertainty avoidance** are concerned with security and tend to avoid conflict. People in such

individualism A cultural orientation in which people belong to loose social frameworks and their primary concern is for themselves and their families.

collectivism A cultural orientation in which individuals belong to tightly knit social frameworks and depend strongly on extended families or clans.

power distance The degree to which a culture accepts unequal distribution of power.

uncertainty avoidance The degree to which a culture tolerates ambiguity and uncertainty.

TABLE 2.1 BUSINESS GUIDE TO CULTURAL DIFFERENCES

Country	Appointments	Dress	Gifts	Negotiations
Japan	Punctuality is a necessity. It is considered rude to be late.	Conservative dress is the norm for men and women in large to medium-sized companies, though pastel shirts are common. One may be expected to remove shoes in temples and homes, as well as in some ryokan (inn) style restaurants. In that case, slip-on shoes should be worn.	Important part of Japanese business protocol. Gifts are typically exchanged among colleagues on July 15 and January 1 to commemorate midyear and the year's end, respectively.	Business cards (*mishit*) are an important part of doing business and key for establishing credentials. One side of your card should be in English and the other in Japanese. It is an asset to include information such as membership in professional associations.
Mexico	Punctuality is not always as much of a priority. Nonetheless, Mexicans are accustomed to North Americans arriving on time, and most Mexicans in business, if not government, will try to return the favor.	Dark, conservative suits and ties are the norm for most men. Standard office attire for women includes dresses, skirted suits, or skirts and blouses. Femininity is strongly encouraged in women's dress.	Not usually a requirement in business dealings, though presenting a small gift is generally appreciated as a gesture of goodwill. If giving a gift, be aware that inquiring about what the receiver would like to receive may offend.	Mexicans avoid directly saying "no." A "no" is often disguised in responses such as "maybe" or "we'll see." You should also use this indirect approach in your dealings. Otherwise, your Mexican counterparts may perceive you as being rude and pushy.
Saudi Arabia	It is customary to make appointments for times of day rather than precise hours. The importance Saudis attach to courtesy and hospitality can cause delays that prevent keeping to a strict schedule.	The only absolute requirement of dress code is modesty. For men, this means covering everything from navel to knee. In public, women are required to cover everything except the face, hands, and feet by wearing an *abaya* (standard black cloak) and headscarf.	Should only be given to the most intimate of friends. For a Saudi to receive a present from a lesser acquaintance is so embarrassing that it is considered offensive.	Business cards are common but not essential. If used, the common practice is to have both English and Arabic printed on the same side so that neither language is perceived as less important by being on the reverse of the same card.

SOURCE: Adapted from information obtained from business culture guides accessed online at http://www.executiveplanet.com.

cultures tend to seek consensus in an effort to moderate the threat of life's inherent uncertainty. Cultures with low uncertainty avoidance tolerate ambiguity better. People are more willing to take risks and are more comfortable with individual differences. Conflict is seen as constructive, and people accept dissenting viewpoints. Accordingly, Norwegians and Australians value job mobility because they have low uncertainty avoidance; Japan and Italy are characterized by high uncertainty avoidance, and so, not surprisingly, their cultures emphasize career stability.

2-2d Masculinity versus Femininity

In cultures characterized by traditional **masculinity**, assertiveness and materialism are valued. Men, the idea goes, should be assertive, tough, and decisive, whereas women should be nurturing, modest, and tender.[19] Money and possessions are very important in this viewpoint, and performance is what counts. Achievement is

> In cultures with low power distance, managers are more likely to consult employees and work with them to achieve harmonious results.

admired. Cultures characterized by traditional **femininity** emphasize relationships and concern for others. Men and women are expected to assume both assertive and nurturing roles. Quality of life is very important, and people and the environment are emphasized.

2-2e Time Orientation

Cultures also differ in **time orientation**. A culture's values may be oriented toward the future (long-term orientation) or toward the past and present (short-term orientation).[20] In China, which has a long-term orientation, values such as thrift and persistence, which look toward the future, are emphasized. Russians generally have a short-term orientation and particularly value respect for tradition (past) and meeting social obligations (present).

Hofstede found the United States to be the most individualistic country of any he studied. It ranked among the countries with weak power distance, and its level of uncertainty avoidance indicated a tolerance of uncertainty. The United States also ranked as a masculine culture with a short-term orientation. These values have shaped U.S. management theory, so Hofstede's work casts doubt on the universal applicability of U.S. management theories. Because these dimensions vary widely, management practices should be adjusted to account for cultural differences. Managers in transnational organizations must learn as much as they can about other cultures in order to lead their culturally diverse organizations effectively.

2-2f Developing Cross-Cultural Sensitivity

In today's multicultural environment, it is imperative that organizations help their employees recognize and appreciate cultural differences. One way companies do this is through cultural sensitivity training. IBM's cultural sensitivity program, Global Citizens Portfolio, consists of flexible spending accounts that employees can use to enhance their training and in turn benefit the company.[21] Another way to develop sensitivity is by using cross-cultural task forces or teams. The Milwaukee-based GE Medical Systems Group (GEMS),

In masculine cultures, assertiveness and materialism are valued over relationships.

Peppersmint/Shutterstock.com

masculinity A cultural orientation in which assertiveness and materialism are valued.

femininity A cultural orientation in which relationships and concern for others are valued.

time orientation Whether a culture's values are oriented toward the future (long-term orientation) or toward the past and present (short-term orientation).

with 19,000 employees working worldwide, has developed a vehicle for bringing together managers from each of its three regions (the Americas, Europe, and Asia) to work on a variety of business projects. Their Global Leadership Program forms several work groups made up of managers from various regions and has them work together on important projects, such as worldwide employee integration, to increase employees' sense of belonging throughout the GEMS international organization.[22] Because cultural differences are constantly in flux, it is important for managers to foster up-to-date knowledge of relevant cultural trends.

The globalization of business affects all parts of the organization, but particularly human resource management. Human resource managers must adopt a global view of human resource planning, recruitment and selection, compensation, and training and development. This means that they must possess a working knowledge of the legal systems in various countries as well as of global economics, culture, and customs. Not only do HR managers prepare U.S. workers to live outside their native country, but they also help foreign employees interact with U.S. culture. Global human resource management is a complex field, one that is critical to organizations' success in the global marketplace.

 ## 2-3 THE DIVERSE WORKFORCE

Cultural differences contribute a great deal to the diversity of the workforce, but other forms of diversity are important as well. **Diversity** encompasses all forms of difference among individuals, including surface-level differences such as gender, national origin, age, and race and deep-level differences such as personality, religion, social status, and sexual orientation. Largely because of demographic changes in the working population, diversity has garnered increasing attention in recent years. Managers feel that dealing with diversity is a paramount concern for two reasons: first, they need to motivate diverse work groups, and, second, they must communicate with employees who have different values and language skills.

Several demographic trends are affecting organizations. By the year 2020, the workforce will be more culturally diverse, more female, and older than ever. Thus, workforce demographic change and diversity are critical challenges for the study and management of organizational behavior.[23] The theories of motivation, leadership, and group behavior based on research in a

diversity All forms of difference among individuals, including culture, gender, age, ability, religion, personality, social status, and sexual orientation.

workforce of one composition may not be applicable in a workforce of a very different composition.[24] This may be especially problematic if ethnic, gender, and/or religious differences lead to conflict between leaders and followers in organizations. Still another factor in diversity involves individuals with disabilities because recent legislation and new technologies have helped more such people enter the workforce. Hence, learning to work together with an open mind is an increasingly important skill. Alcon Laboratories, the Swiss-owned and Fort Worth-based international company whose mission is to improve and preserve eyesight, is an example of the kind of organization that offers diversity training to help employees learn to work together.

2-3a Ethnic Diversity

The globalization of business is not the only force promoting cultural and ethnic diversity in the workplace. Changing domestic demographics also affect organizations' cultural diversity. By 2020, minorities will constitute more than one-half of the new entrants to the U.S. workforce. Yet African Americans and Hispanic Americans are overrepresented in declining occupations, thus limiting their opportunities. Further, African Americans and Hispanic Americans tend to live in a few large cities that are facing severe economic difficulties and high crime rates. Minority workers are less likely to be prepared because they are less likely to have had satisfactory schooling and on-the-job training, which will likely put them at a disadvantage within organizations. It need not be this way. For example, Coca-Cola has made substantial progress on diversity by monitoring its human resource systems, and companies such as Motorola already recognize and meet these needs by focusing on basic skills training.[25]

In sum, the globalization of business and changing demographic trends present organizations with a culturally diverse workforce, creating both challenge and risk. The challenge is to harness the wealth of differences provided by cultural diversity. The risk is that prejudices and stereotypes may prevent managers and employees from developing synergies to benefit the organization. Diversity of the workforce was a major factor in the innovation that drove the dot-com boom in Silicon Valley, illustrating that the benefits of a diverse workforce make good management of these challenges and risks important.[26]

2-3b Gender Diversity

The number of women in the U.S. labor force reached its peak in 1999 with a rate of 60%. Since then, the participation rate for women (as for men) declined to 57.2% in 2013.[27]

HOT TREND

Working Women Work to Preserve their Identities During Pregnancy

Pregnant working women use numerous strategies to protect and maintain their professional images during pregnancy. Some strategies are used to maintain their image as a viable resource. Such practices include keeping up the same pace of work as they did before they became pregnant and failing to ask colleagues or supervisors for special accommodations. Other strategies are used to avoid stigmatization and negative outcomes such as pregnancy discrimination. These "decategorization" strategies include concealing their pregnancies with clothing, denying pregnancy-related health problems such as nausea, or downplaying their pregnancies by minimizing attention to their conditions. Practicing these strategies will help working women retain their legitimacy and protect against adverse actions that have the potential to halt their post-pregnancy careers.

SOURCE: L. M. Little, V. S. Major, A. S. Hinojosa, and D. L. Nelson, "Professional Image Maintenance: How Women Navigate Pregnancy in the Workplace," *Academy of Management Journal*, 58 (2015), 8–37.

Women are better prepared to contribute in organizations than ever before because they earn 51% of all doctorates, 60% of master's degrees, and 57% of all bachelor's degrees.[28] But their share of authority and compensation is not increasing commensurately with their education and participation in the workforce. Not only has there been little recent increase in the number of women CEOs, but the number of women positioned to move into top jobs has also dropped. Half of the males in the workforce occupy line positions, compared to only one-quarter of women in business.[29] American Express is an exception to the rule. Rated as one of the top 50 companies for executive women in 2015 by the National Association for Female Executives (NAFE), American Express not only places women in top positions, it also provides them training and experiences that expand their skills.[30] Nonetheless, median weekly earnings for women persist at a level of 81% of their male counterparts' earnings.[31] Because benefits are tied to compensation, women also receive fewer benefits.

The **glass ceiling** is a transparent barrier that keeps women from rising above a certain level in organizations. In the United States, it has been rare to find women in positions above middle management.[32] Although growth in opportunities for women to attain executive positions has recently stagnated, the situation is improving for women in the boardroom. Women currently hold 19% of board seats in S&P 500 companies, up from 15% in 2010.[33] Research has shown that companies that have gender-diverse board leadership performed better across dimensions of corporate social performance (CSP).[34] The ultimate glass ceiling may well be the professional partnership. Although women account for 34% of legal professionals, they account for only 21% of the partners.[35]

Globally, the leadership picture for women is improving. For example, the number of female political leaders has grown dramatically worldwide in recent decades. In the 1970s, there were only five such leaders. In the 1990s, twenty-one female leaders came into power, and today women around the world are leading major global companies. Note, however, that these global female business leaders do not come predominantly from the West. In addition, a large number of women have founded entrepreneurial businesses.

Removing obstacles to women's success presents a major challenge for organizations. If they do not help the increasing numbers of female employees achieve their potential, they risk underutilizing the talents of half the U.S. workforce.

Women are better prepared to contribute in organizations than ever before.

glass ceiling A transparent barrier that keeps women from rising above a certain level in organizations.

Therefore, it is wise for organizations to develop policies that promote equity in pay and benefits, to encourage benefit programs of special interest to women, and to provide equal starting salaries for jobs of equal value. Corporations that shatter the glass ceiling share several practices:

1. Upper managers demonstrate support for the advancement of women.

2. Leaders incorporate practices into their diversity management programs to ensure that women perceive the organization as attractive.[36]

3. Women are represented on standing committees addressing key strategic business issues and are targeted for participation in executive education programs.

4. Systems are put in place to identify women with high potential for advancement.[37]

Companies such as IBM and Ernst & Young work for diversity not only by offering excellent programs for advancing and developing women executives, but also by judging supervisors based on their active support for such endeavors.[38]

2-3c Age Diversity

The graying of the U.S. workforce is another source of workplace diversity. Older Americans, aged 65 or older, number 41 million, or 13% of the U.S. population. That equates to more than one in every eight individuals. The number of middle-aged Americans (aged 45 to 64 years) increased by 33% during the same period. The 65 and over population is projected to increase to 80 million by 2040.[39]

This change in worker profile has profound implications for organizations. The job crunch among middle-aged workers will intensify as companies seek flatter organizational structures and eliminate middle-management jobs. Older workers are often higher paid, and companies that employ large numbers of aging baby boomers may find these pay scales a handicap to competitiveness.[40] Paid volunteerism, however, can be a draw to younger generations.[41] Conversely, a more experienced, stable, reliable, and healthier workforce can pay dividends to companies. A recent study showed that age diversity among employees in Western companies had a positive impact on profitability.[42] The baby boomers are well trained and educated, and their knowledge is a definite asset to organizations.

The aging workforce is increasing intergenerational contact at work.[43] As organizations flatten, workers traditionally segregated by old corporate hierarchies find

The "graying" of the U.S. workforce is another source of workplace diversity.

themselves working together. Four generations are cooperating: the *silent generation* (people born from 1930 through 1945), a small group that includes most organizations' top managers; the *baby boomers* (people born from 1946 through 1964), whose substantial numbers give them a strong influence; the *baby bust generation*, popularly

Men: The Secret Weapon for Increasing Gender Diversity at the Top

The numbers of women CEOs at Fortune 500 firms have virtually been unchanged since 2010. Women held 14.6% of the top jobs at these firms in 2013. How can U.S. corporations help women advance? Recruit men. That's exactly what Cardinal Health Inc. did. Mike Kaufmann is a powerful senior executive at Cardinal Health. Kaufmann advanced through the management ranks at Cardinal while balancing work and family. He is also the head of the women's networking group, intent on pushing gender equity and diversity at the top. Kaufmann, along with about sixty male bosses from Cardinal, spent six months learning to improve women's career prospects by building alliances with them. According to Kaufmann, "men must be highly involved to change the balance of power in senior management." The strategy has had a positive effect. Now, half of Cardinal's six operating presidents are women, compared with just a third five years ago.

SOURCE: J. S. Lublin, "Men Pitch In to Boost Women at Work: Why Men Are Joining the Networks of Corporate Women," *Wall Street Journal (Online)*, March 10, 2015.

known as *Generation X* (those born from 1965 through 1976); and the subsequent generation, tentatively called *Generation Y, millennial,* or the *baby boomlet* (those born after 1976).[44] The millennial often bring new challenges to the workplace because of their early access to technology and their continuing connection to parents.[45]

The differences in attitudes and values among these four generations can be substantial, and managers struggle to integrate their workers into a cohesive group. Most leadership positions are currently held by members of the silent generation. Baby boomers tend to (1) regard the silent generation as complacent, (2) strive for moral rights in the workplace, and (3) take a more activist position regarding employee rights. The baby busters, newer to the workplace, are often impatient, want short-term gratification, and value a greater balance between family and work. They scorn the achievement orientation and materialism of the baby boomers. Members of Generation Y, on the other hand, place high importance on independence and creativity, and they are less inclined to settle for work that is not in line with their values.

Younger workers may have false impressions of older workers, viewing them as resistant to change, unable to learn new work methods, less physically capable, and less creative than younger employees. Research indicates, however, that older employees are more satisfied with their jobs, more committed to the organization, and more internally motivated than their younger cohorts.[46] Research also indicates that direct experience with older workers reduces younger workers' negative beliefs.[47] Motivating aging workers and helping them maintain high levels of contribution to the organization is a key task for managers.

Source: McDonald's

McJOBS is a plan by McDonald's to recruit, train and retain individuals with disabilities.

2-3d Ability Diversity

Employees with different abilities present yet another form of diversity. Individuals with disabilities are an underutilized human resource. An estimated 50 million individuals with disabilities live in the United States, and their unemployment rate is estimated to exceed 50%.[48] Nevertheless, they have entered the workforce in greater numbers since the Americans with Disabilities Act went into effect in the summer of 1992. The act defines a person with a disability as "anyone possessing a physical or mental impairment that substantially limits one or more major life activities."[49] Under this law, employers are required to make reasonable accommodations to permit workers with disabilities to perform jobs. The act's protection encompasses a broad range of illnesses that produce disabilities, including acquired immune deficiency syndrome

Can Knowledge of Stereotypes Increase Stereotypical Behavior?

Researchers tested the assertion that individuals who are aware of the prevalence of stereotypes would work harder to prevent stereotypical judgments and subsequent biased behavior. In three separate studies, researchers investigated the effect of differing levels of stereotype messaging on expressions of bias, social judgments, and behaviors against three commonly stereotyped groups (i.e., older adults, women, and overweight individuals). The findings suggest that, contrary to popular belief, individuals will be *more* prone to practice stereotypical behaviors when they are presented with information about the prevalence of stereotypes than people who are presented with information about the rarity or nonexistence of stereotyping. When individuals are explicitly presented with information about the prevalence of stereotyping, they will be less likely to be intentional about reducing unwanted behavior.

SOURCE: M. M. Duguid and M. C. Thomas-Hunt, "Condoning Stereotyping? How Awareness of Stereotyping Prevalence Impacts Expression of Stereotypes," *Journal of Applied Psychology,* 100 (2015), 343–359.

(AIDS), cancer, hypertension, anxiety disorders, dyslexia, blindness, and cerebral palsy, to name only a few.

Some companies recognized the value of employing workers with disabilities long before the legislation. In 1981, McDonald's created McJOBS, a corporate plan to recruit, train, and retain individuals with disabilities, which has hired more than 9,000 mentally and physically challenged individuals.[50] Its participants include workers with visual, hearing, or orthopedic impairments; learning disabilities; and developmental disabilities. McJOBS holds sensitivity training sessions with managers and crew members before workers go onsite to help workers without disabilities understand what it means to be a worker with a disabling condition. Most McJOBS workers start part-time and advance according to their abilities and the opportunities available.

2-3e Sexual Orientation and Gender Identity

Another type of workplace diversity is sexual orientation and gender identity. Increasing numbers of employees identify as gay, lesbian, bisexual, or transgender (LGBT). Because many in the LGBT community are not "out," the exact population cannot be determined. Nearly 49% of bisexual employees reported that they had not come out to anyone at their workplace. A recent Gallup poll, however, found that nearly 4% of Americans identify as LGBT. Another study found that an estimated 9 million individuals or 4% of the U.S. population is lesbian, gay, or bisexual.

LGBT workers present organizations with opportunities and challenges. Sixty-two percent of Fortune 500 companies offer domestic partner health benefits, and 87% have nondiscrimination policies that include sexual orientation. While gay and transgender employees have become more commonplace in organizations, they still experience unfair treatment including discrimination, harassment, or violence in the workplace.[51] Organizations that treat all employees fairly and respectfully despite their sexual identity will have an advantage in attracting and recruiting potential employees, customers, and clients. Research has found a positive connection between companies' adoption of LGBT-friendly policies and their stock price. The decision to offer LGBT-friendly HR policies often depends on external factors such as state and local policies and pressure to match competitor offerings. The demographic composition of the board can also affect whether companies offer HR benefits to same-sex employees. Companies that have more women board members are more likely to adopt LGBT-friendly HR policies.[52] Dallas-based AT&T was listed as number one of the top ten companies for LGBT employees for its employee development practices especially designed to promote inclusion of LGBT employees as well as women, veterans, and people with disabilities.[53]

2-3f Valuing Diversity

Diversity involves more than culture, gender, age, ability, and personality. It also encompasses religion, social status, and sexual orientation. These diversity types lend heterogeneity to the workforce.

Managers must combat prejudice and discrimination to manage diversity. *Prejudice* is an attitude, whereas *discrimination* describes behavior. Both diminish organizational productivity in that they present obstacles to promoting and compensating good workers fairly. Discrimination poses challenges to an organization's ability to attract and recruit prospective workers, retain good human talent, and maintain positive work environments that employees perceive as fair and inclusive.[54] The potential for unfair treatment increases as the workforce becomes increasingly diverse. Combating stereotypes is essential. For example, a recent study revealed that male bosses sometimes hold certain stereotypes that negatively influence their interaction with female employees of color.[55] Open communication can help clarify misperceptions and clear the way for advancement.

Diversity helps organizations in many ways. Some organizations recognize the potential benefits of aggressively working to increase the diversity of their workforces. Yum! Brands' Kentucky Fried Chicken (KFC) tries to attract and retain female and minority-group executives. A president of KFC's U.S. operations said, "We want to bring in the best people. If there are two equally qualified people, we'd clearly like to have diversity."[56]

In an effort to understand and appreciate diversity, Alcon Laboratories developed a diversity training class called Working Together. The course takes advantage of two key ideas. First, people work best when they are valued and when diversity is taken into account. Second, when people feel valued, they build relationships and work together as a team.[57] Even majority-group managers may be more supportive of diversity training if they appreciate their own ethnic identity. One evaluation of diversity training found that participants preferred training with a traditional title and a broad focus.[58] Further, women were found to react more positively to diversity training than were men.

A conclusion from the evaluation was that companies should measure the effects of training so that they can monitor its positive payoffs.

Managing diversity helps companies become more competitive, but effective diversity management involves more than simply being a good corporate citizen or complying with affirmative action.[59] Managing diversity requires a painful examination of employees' hidden assumptions. Having empathy, being able to see and understand the viewpoints of others, is an essential component of Emotional Intelligence (EI) and important for developing and maintaining relationships with others, whether minority or majority. Biases and prejudices about people's differences must be uncovered and dealt with so that differences can be celebrated and used to their full advantage.

2-3g Diversity's Benefits and Problems

Although diversity has the potential to enhance organizational performance, it may pose some problems as well. Table 2.2 summarizes the main benefits and problems with diversity at work. The first main benefit of diversity management is that it helps firms attract and retain the best available human talent. The companies topping the lists of the best places to work are usually excellent at managing diversity. A second benefit is that diversity aids marketing efforts. Just as workforces are diversifying, so are markets. A diverse workforce, therefore, can improve a company's marketing plans by drawing on insights from various employees' cultural backgrounds. Third, diversity promotes creativity and innovation. The most innovative companies, such as Hewlett-Packard, deliberately build diverse teams to foster creativity. Fourth, diversity improves problem solving. Diverse groups bring more expertise and experience to bear on problems and decisions, and they encourage higher levels of critical thinking. Fifth, diversity enhances organizational flexibility

because it makes an organization challenge old assumptions and become more adaptable. These five benefits add up to competitive advantage for companies with well-managed diversity.

We must also recognize diversity's potential problems. Five problems are particularly notable: resistance to change, lack of cohesiveness, communication problems, interpersonal conflicts, and slower decision making. People are attracted to and are more comfortable with others like themselves. Thus, it stands to reason that workers may resist diversity efforts when they are forced to interact with others unlike themselves. Managers should be prepared for this resistance rather than naively assuming that everybody supports diversity. Another difficulty with diversity is the issue of cohesiveness, that invisible glue that holds a group together. Cohesive groups have higher morale and better communication, but diverse groups take longer to achieve cohesiveness, so they may also take longer to develop high morale.

Another obstacle to performance in diverse groups is communication. Culturally diverse groups may encounter special communication barriers. Misunderstandings can lower work group effectiveness by creating conflict and hampering decision making.[60]

2-4 ETHICS, CHARACTER, AND PERSONAL INTEGRITY

Managers frequently face ethical dilemmas and tradeoffs. Merck & Company is an example of a company that manages ethical issues well, and its emphasis on ethical behavior has consistently earned it a place on *Business Ethics'* list of top 100 corporate citizens.[61] For many organizations, however, unethical conduct sometimes occurs despite their best attempts to prevent such problems. The toughest problems for managers to resolve include employee theft, environmental issues, comparable worth of employees, conflicts of interest, and sexual harassment.[62]

Ethical theories help us understand, evaluate, and classify moral arguments; make decisions; and then defend conclusions about what is right and wrong. Ethical theories can be classified as consequential, rule-based, or character theories.

TABLE 2.2 THE BENEFITS AND PROBLEMS OF DIVERSITY	
Benefits	**Problems**
> Attracts and retains the best talent	> Resistance to change
> Improves marketing efforts	> Lack of cohesiveness
> Promotes creativity and innovation	> Communication problems
> Results in better problem solving	> Interpersonal conflicts
> Enhances organizational flexibility	> Slower decision making

© Cengage Learning

2-4a Consequential Theories of Ethics

Consequential theories of ethics emphasize the consequences or results of behavior. John Stuart Mill's *utilitarianism*, a well-known consequential theory, suggests that the consequences of an action determine whether it is right or wrong.[63] Good is the ultimate moral value, and we should maximize good effects for the greatest number of people. But do good ethics make for good business? Right actions do not always produce good consequences, and good consequences do not always follow right actions. And how do we determine the greatest good? The protection of what is good for minorities is critically important in a free, good society.

Corporations and business enterprises tend to subscribe to consequential ethics, partly due to the persuasive arguments of the Scottish moral philosopher Adam Smith.[64] He believed that the self-interest of human beings is God's providence, not the government's. Smith set forth a doctrine of *natural liberty*, presenting the classical argument for open-market competition and free trade. Within this framework, people should be allowed to pursue what is in their economic self-interest, and the natural efficiency of the marketplace will then serve the well-being of society. However, Smith was mindful of the interests of others and argued for three key virtues: prudence, which is good self-care; justice, which is doing no harm to others, and beneficence, which is doing good for others.[65]

Heartland Arts/Shutterstock.com

2-4b Rule-Based Theories of Ethics

Rule-based theories of ethics emphasize the character of the act itself, not its effects, in arriving at universal moral rights and wrongs.[66] Moral rights, the basis for legal rights, are associated with such theories. In a theological context, the Bible, the Talmud, and the Koran are rule-based guides to ethical behavior. Immanuel Kant worked toward the ultimate moral principle in formulating his *categorical imperative*, a universal standard of behavior.[67] Kant argued that individuals should be treated with respect and dignity and that they should not be used as a means to an end. He argued that we should put ourselves in the other person's position and ask whether we would make the same decision if we were in that person's situation.

2-4c Character Theories of Ethics

Virtue ethics, of which **character theories** of ethics are a type, offer an alternative to understanding behavior in terms of self-interest or rules. Character theories of ethics emphasize the character of the individual and the intent of the actor instead of the character of the act itself or its consequences. These virtue-ethics theories are based on Aristotle's view of ethics, which focused on an individual's inner character and virtuousness rather than on outward behavior. Thus, the good person who acted out of virtuous and right intentions was one with integrity and ultimately good ethical standards. Robert Solomon is the best known advocate of this Aristotelian approach to business ethics.[68] He advocates a business ethics theory centered on the individual within the corporation, emphasizing personal virtues as well as corporate roles. Solomon's six dimensions of virtue ethics are community, excellence, role identity, integrity, judgment (*phronesis* in Greek), and holism. We previously noted Smith's three key virtues. At the heart of character and virtue ethics is emotional intelligence, a central component in leader and follower development. The Goolsby Leadership Academy at the University of Texas at Arlington emphasizes the development of emotional competencies, such as empathy, compassion, and self-control. For the emotionally competent person of good character, integrity comes first.[69] Organizational factors may negatively affect an otherwise virtuous individual. Workers who experience

> **People need ethical theories to guide them through complex, difficult, and often confusing moral choices and ethical decisions.**

consequential theory An ethical theory that emphasizes the consequences or results of behavior.

rule-based theory An ethical theory that emphasizes the character of the act itself rather than its effects.

character theory An ethical theory that emphasizes the character, personal virtues, and intent of the individual.

A_KUDR/Shutterstock.com

FASTFACT

A Slippery Slope Toward Unethical Behavior

Researchers have found evidence of a "slippery slope" effect whereby minor indiscretions lead to major infractions over time when left unchecked. This evolution of unethical behavior is explained by individuals' capacity to morally disengage from self-sanctions and guilt normally associated with unethical behavior. Instead, each incremental unethical act is accompanied by an increased scope of what is deemed permissible. It is recommended that managers address each instance of unethical behavior, whether considered minor or major, as it occurs to prevent unethical behavior from snowballing in the future.

SOURCE: D. T. Welsh, L. D. Ordonez, D. G. Snyder, and M. S. Christian, "The Slippery Slope: How Small Ethical Transgressions Pave the Way for Larger Future Transgressions," *Journal of Applied Psychology*, 100 (2015), 114–127.

increased anxiety and feel threatened at work may engage in unethical behavior despite having good intentions.[70]

2-4d Cultural Relativism

Cultural relativism contends that there are no universal ethical principles and that people should not impose their own ethical standards on others. Local standards guide ethical behavior. Cultural relativism encourages individuals to operate under the old adage of "When in Rome, do as the Romans do." Unfortunately, people who adhere strictly to cultural relativism may avoid difficult ethical dilemmas by denying their own accountability.

2-5 ETHICAL DILEMMAS FACING THE MODERN ORGANIZATION

People need ethical theories to guide them through complex, difficult, and often confusing moral choices and ethical decisions. Contemporary organizations experience a wide variety of ethical and moral dilemmas. In this section, we address employee rights, sexual harassment, organizational justice, and whistle-blowing. We conclude with a discussion of social responsibility and codes of ethics.

2-5a Employee Rights

Managing the rights of employees at work creates many ethical dilemmas in organizations. Drug testing, free speech, downsizing and layoffs, and due process are but a few of the employee rights issues that managers face.

These dilemmas include privacy issues related to technology. Many feel that computerized monitoring constitutes an invasion of privacy. Using employee data from computerized information systems presents many ethical concerns. New software allows employers to tap into their employees' address books and e-mail contacts to obtain new potential clients and discern who in the company might be best suited to approach them.[71] Safeguarding the employee's right to privacy while preserving access to the data for those who need it forces managers to balance competing interests.

The reality of AIDS in the workplace also illustrates the difficulties managers face in balancing various interests. Managers may encounter a conflict between the rights of HIV-infected workers and the rights of their coworkers who feel threatened. But laws protect HIV-infected workers. The Americans with Disabilities Act (ADA) requires employees to treat HIV-infected workers as disabled individuals and to make reasonable accommodations for them. But ADA cannot encompass all of the ethical dilemmas involved.

Confidentiality may also present challenges. Employers are not required to make concessions to coworkers, but they are obligated to educate, reassure, and provide emotional support to them. Some employees with HIV or AIDS fear stigmatization or reprisals and do not want their condition known by their coworkers. Management should discuss the ramifications of trying to maintain confidentiality and should assure affected employees that every effort will be made to prevent negative consequences for them in the workplace.[72]

How does a manager protect the dignity of the HIV-infected employee and preserve the morale and productivity of the work group when so much prejudice and ignorance surround this disease? Many organizations, such as Wells Fargo, believe the answer is education.[73] Wells Fargo has written an AIDS policy to address confidentiality, employee socialization, coworker education, and counseling.

2-5b Sexual Harassment

According to the Equal Employment Opportunity Commission, sexual harassment is unwelcome verbal or physical sexual attention that affects an employee's

Sexual harassment costs the typical *Fortune* 500 company $6.7 million per year in absenteeism, turnover and lost productivity.

job conditions or creates a hostile working environment.[74] Supreme Court rulings tend to blame companies when managers create a sexually hostile working environment. Sexual harassment is more likely to occur in some organizations than in others—for example, in male-dominated workplaces.[75] In some organizations, employees risk their jobs by complaining of sexual harassment or are not taken seriously, and perpetrators are rarely punished. Managers can defend themselves by demonstrating that they took action to eliminate workplace harassment and that the complaining employee did not take advantage of company procedures to deal with harassment. Even the best sexual harassment policy, however, will not absolve a company when harassment leads to firing, demotions, or undesirable working assignments.[76]

There are three types of sexual harassment. *Gender harassment* includes crude comments or behaviors that convey hostility toward a particular gender. *Unwanted sexual attention* involves unwanted touching or repeated pressures for dates. *Sexual coercion* consists of implicit or explicit demands for sexual favors by threatening negative job-related consequences or promising job-related rewards.[77] Recent theory has focused attention on the aggressive behavior of sexual harassers.[78]

Sexual harassment costs the typical *Fortune* 500 company $6.7 million per year in absenteeism,

distributive justice The fairness of outcomes that individuals receive in an organization.

turnover, and lost productivity. Valeant Pharmaceuticals International paid out millions to settle four sexual harassment complaints against former CEO Milan Panic. Plaintiffs may now sue for compensatory and punitive damages in addition to back pay. And these costs do not take into account the negative publicity that sexual harassment cases may attract. Moreover, victims of sexual harassment who do not report the problem are less satisfied with their work, supervisors, and coworkers, and they may psychologically withdraw at work. They may suffer poorer mental health and even exhibit symptoms of post-traumatic stress disorder in conjunction with the harassment experience. Some victims report alcohol abuse, depression, headaches, and nausea.[79]

Several companies have created comprehensive sexual harassment programs. Atlantic Richfield (ARCO), owned by British Petroleum and a player in the male-dominated energy industry, has a handbook on preventing sexual harassment that includes phone numbers of state agencies where employees can file complaints. The openness seems to work. Lawsuits rarely happen at ARCO. When employees make sexual harassment complaints, the company investigates thoroughly. ARCO fired the captain of an oil tanker for sexually harassing coworkers. Not all sexual behavior among employees is harmful or harassing in nature. Workplace interactions between organizational members that have sexual connotations but not perceived by any of the parties as being threatening or harassing are considered social sexual behavior. Examples of social sexual behavior include flirting, sharing sexual stories or jokes, complimenting physical appearance, or gentle touching. Social sexual behavior in the workplace can have numerous psychological, emotional, and relational benefits for those involved. Among the benefits are increased self-esteem, energy, vigor, and creativity. There is also evidence that social sexual behavior can enhance group cohesion and camaraderie.[80]

2-5c Organizational Justice

Organizational justice also generates moral and ethical dilemmas at work. **Distributive justice** concerns the fairness of outcomes individuals receive. For example, during former President George H. W. Bush's 1992 visit, Japanese CEOs questioned the distributive justice of keeping American CEOs' salaries so high while many companies were struggling and laying off workers.

Procedural justice concerns the fairness of the process by which outcomes are allocated. The ethical questions in procedural justice examine the process by which an organization distributes its resources. Has the organization used the correct procedures in allocating resources? Have the right considerations, such as competence and skill, been brought to bear in the decision process? And have the wrong considerations, such as race and gender, been excluded from the decision process? One study of work scheduling found that advance notice and consistency, two dimensions of procedural justice, reduced voluntary turnover.[81] Some research suggests cultural differences in the effects of distributive and procedural justice.[82]

2-5d Whistle-Blowing

Whistle-blowers are employees who inform authorities of wrongdoings by their companies or coworkers. Depending on their situations, whistle-blowers may be perceived as either public heroes or vile wretches. Those seen as heroes generally report serious and high-magnitude ethical breaches widely perceived as abhorrent.[83] Others may see the whistle-blower as a wretch if they feel the act of whistle-blowing is more offensive than the situation reported. One of the most well-known whistleblowers, Edward Snowden is hailed as a hero by some for revealing the extent of the U.S. government domestic surveillance program. However, others consider Snowden a disgruntled NSA contractor who participated in industrial espionage.[84]

Whistle-blowing is a powerful influence on corporate America because committed organizational members sometimes engage in unethical behavior in an intense desire to succeed. Organizations can manage whistle-blowing by explaining the conditions that are appropriate for disclosing wrongdoing. Clearly delineating wrongful behavior and the appropriate ways to respond are important organizational actions.

2-5e Corporate Social Responsibility

Corporate **social responsibility** is an organization's obligation to behave ethically in its social environment. Ethical conduct at the individual level can translate into social responsibility at the organizational level. Multiple stakeholders in society expect organizations to engage in socially responsible actions. Servant leaders play an important role in creating, implementing, and sustaining socially responsible behaviors.[85]

Current concerns include protecting the environment, promoting worker safety, supporting social issues,

FIGURE 2.2 THE FOUR-WAY TEST

The Four-Way Test
of What We Think, Say, or Do

1. Is it the TRUTH?

2. Is it FAIR to all concerned?

3. Will it build GOODWILL and better friendships?

4. Will it be BENEFICIAL to all concerned?

© Cengage Learning

and investing in the community, among others. Some organizations, such as IBM, loan executives to inner-city schools to teach science and math. Some companies have even tried to build a brand around social responsibility, such as the Just Coffee Cooperative, which sponsors trips to coffee-producing regions in order to build customer loyalty to the cause and their brand.[86] Firms that are seen as socially responsible have a competitive advantage in attracting applicants.[87] American Apparel, however, tried to build a brand around the fact that they produce garments locally rather than in foreign sweatshops but found that, as attractive as its ethics might have been to customers, sex appeal was more effective in actually selling its product.[88]

2-5f Codes of Ethics

Most mature professions guide their practitioners' actions and behavior with codes of ethics. For example, the Hippocratic oath guides doctors. A profession's code of ethics becomes a standard against which members can measure themselves in the absence of internalized standards.

A similar professional code of ethics does not exist for business. However, Rotarian Herbert J. Taylor developed the four-way test, shown in Figure 2.2, in a major business turnaround during the 1930s as a way to create strategic advantage through good character and moral behavior. Now used in more than 166 nations by 1.2 million Rotarians, this test focuses the questioner on key ethical and moral questions.

procedural justice The fairness of the process by which outcomes are allocated in an organization.

whistle-blower An employee who informs authorities of the wrongdoings of her or his company or coworkers.

social responsibility The obligation of an organization to behave ethically in its social environment.

Beyond the individual and professional level, corporate culture is another excellent starting point for addressing ethics and morality. Sometimes regulations articulate a corporation's ethics. For example, the Joint Ethics Regulation (DOD 5500.7-R, August 1993) specifies the ethical standards that all U.S. military personnel must follow. In other cases, corporate ethics appear as a credo. Johnson & Johnson's credo, shown in Figure 2.3, helped hundreds of employees ethically address criminal tampering with Tylenol products.

Individual codes of ethics, professional oaths, and organizational credos must all be anchored in a moral, ethical framework because ethical theories are the only way to question and improve our current standards. However, even though a universal right and wrong may exist, it would be hard to agree on a single code of ethics to which all individuals, professions, and organizations can subscribe.

Dcwcreations/Shutterstock.com

FIGURE 2.3 THE JOHNSON & JOHNSON CREDO

We believe our first responsibility is to the doctors, nurses, and patients, to mothers and all others who use our products and services. In meeting their needs everything we do must be of high quality. We must constantly strive to reduce our costs in order to maintain reasonable prices. Customers' orders must be serviced promptly and accurately. Our suppliers and distributors must have an opportunity to make a fair profit.

We are responsible to our employees, the men and women who work with us throughout the world. Everyone must be considered as an individual. We must respect their dignity and recognize their merit. They must have a sense of security in their jobs. Compensation must be fair and adequate, and working conditions clean, orderly, and safe. Employees must feel free to make suggestions and complaints. There must be equal opportunity for employment, development, and advancement for those qualified. We must provide competent management, and their actions must be just and ethical.

We are responsible to the communities in which we live and work and to the world community as well. We must be good citizens—support good works and charities and bear our fair share of taxes. We must encourage civic improvements and better health and education. We must maintain in good order the property we are privileged to use, protecting the environment and natural resources.

Our final responsibility is to our stockholders. Business must make a sound profit. We must experiment with new ideas. Research must be carried on, innovative programs developed and mistakes paid for. New equipment must be purchased, new facilities provided, and new products launched. Reserves must be created to provide for adverse times. When we operate according to these principles, the stockholders should realize a fair return.

SOURCE: "Our Credo," http://www.jnj.com/wps/wcm/connect/c7933f004f5563df9e22be1bb31559c7/jnj_ourcredo_english_us_8.5x11_cmyk.pdf?MOD=AJPERES.

STUDY TOOLS 2

LOCATED AT BACK OF THE TEXTBOOK

☐ Rip out chapter review card

LOCATED AT WWW.CENGAGE.COM/LOGIN

☐ Track your knowledge and understanding of key concepts in business using 4LTR Press Online

☐ Review key term flashcards and create your own using StudyBits

☐ Create and complete practice quizzes based off of your notes and StudyBits

☐ Complete Online activities such as Matching and Fill-in-the-Blank exercises

☐ View chapter highlight box content, including the chapter videos, key exhibits and executive profiles.

3 | Personality, Perception, and Attribution

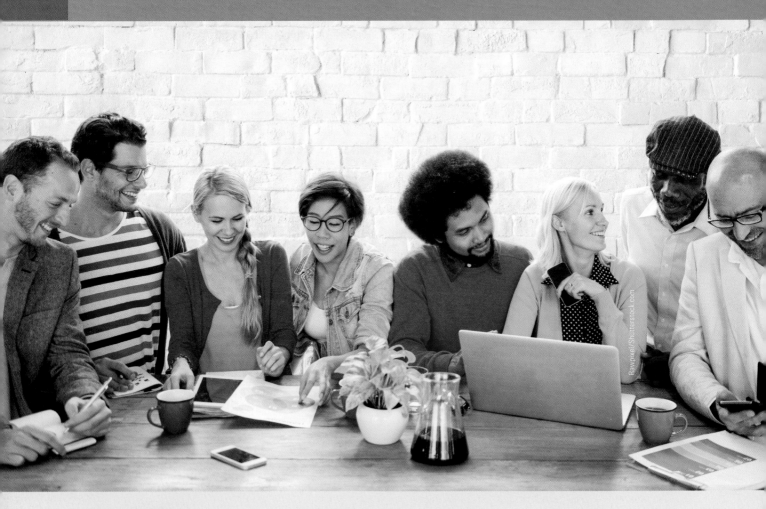

Rawpixel/Shutterstock.com

LEARNING OUTCOMES

3-1 Describe individual differences and explain why they are important in understanding organizational behavior.

3-2 Articulate key personality traits and explain how they influence behavior in organizations.

3-3 Discuss how personality theories may be applied in organizations.

3-4 Define social perception and explain the factors that affect it.

3-5 Identify five common barriers to social perception and explain the difficulties they cause.

3-6 Explain the attribution process and how attributions affect managerial behavior.

After finishing this chapter go to **PAGE 51** for **STUDY TOOLS.**

3-1 INDIVIDUAL DIFFERENCES AND ORGANIZATIONAL BEHAVIOR

Over the next two chapters, we'll explore the concept of **individual differences**. Individuals are unique in terms of their skills, abilities, personalities, perceptions, attitudes, emotions, and ethics. Hence, individual differences represent the essence of the challenge of management. Managers must often work with people who possess a multitude of varying characteristics, so the more managers understand individual differences, the better they can work with others.

The basis for understanding individual differences stems from Kurt Lewin's early contention that behavior is a function of the person and the environment.[1] He expressed this idea in an equation: $B = f(P, E)$, where B = behavior, P = person, and E = environment. Lewin's idea has been developed further by the **interactional psychology** approach.[2] Basically, this approach says that we must know something about the person and something about the situation in order to understand human behavior. There are four basic propositions of interactional psychology:

1. Behavior is a function of continuous, multidirectional interaction between the person and the situation.

2. The person is active in this process, both changing his or her situations and being changed by them.

3. People vary in many characteristics, including cognitive, affective, motivational, and ability factors.

4. Two aspects of a situation are important: the objective situation and the person's subjective view of the situation.[3]

The interactional psychology approach points out the need to study both persons and situations. The *person*

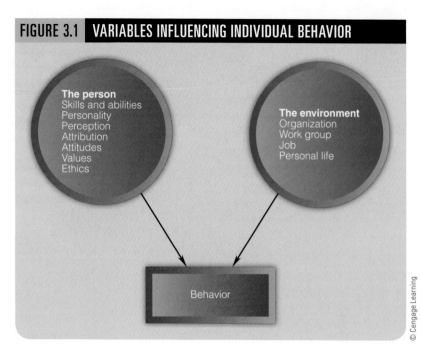

FIGURE 3.1 VARIABLES INFLUENCING INDIVIDUAL BEHAVIOR

The person
Skills and abilities
Personality
Perception
Attribution
Attitudes
Values
Ethics

The environment
Organization
Work group
Job
Personal life

Behavior

© Cengage Learning

> Individuals are unique in terms of their skills, abilities, personalities, perceptions, attitudes, emotions, and ethics.

Danielala/Shutterstock.com

consists of individual elements such as personality, perception, attribution, attitudes, emotions, and ethics. The *situation* consists of the environment the person operates in, including the organization, work group, personal life situation, job characteristics, and other environmental influences. The effect of personal and environmental differences on organizational behavior is shown visually in Figure 3.1. In this chapter, we'll address skills and abilities, personality, perception, and attribution. Chapter 4 will deal with attitudes, emotions, and ethics.

3-1a Skills and Abilities

Many skills and abilities influence work outcomes. Nearly 100 years ago, Charles Spearman introduced the concept of *general mental ability (GMA)* as a measure of an individual's innate cognitive intelligence.[4] GMA, which includes a person's skills and abilities, is the single best predictor of work performance across many occupations and across different cultures.[5]

individual differences
The way in which factors such as skills, abilities, personalities, perceptions, attitudes, values, and ethics differ from one individual to another.

interactional psychology
The psychological approach to understanding human behavior that involves knowing something about the person and about the situation.

PERSONALITY AND ORGANIZATIONS

What makes an individual behave consistently in a variety of situations? **Personality** is the relatively stable set of characteristics that influences an individual's behavior and lends it consistency. Although researchers debate what determines personality, we conclude that it has several origins. One determinant is heredity. Researchers have found that identical twins who were separated at birth and raised in very different situations nevertheless shared personality traits and job preferences. In fact, about half of the variations in traits such as extraversion, impulsiveness, and flexibility were shared by identical twins who grew up separately.[6] Thus, genes appear to influence personality.

Environment also determines personality, shaping it through family influences, cultural influences, educational influences, and other environmental factors. Two major theories of personality are the trait theory and the integrative approach. Each theory has influenced the study of personality in organizations.

3-2a Trait Theory

Some early personality researchers believed that we must break down behavior patterns into a series of observable traits in order to understand individuals. According to **trait theory**, the combination of these traits forms an individual's personality. Gordon Allport, a leading theorist, saw traits as broad, general guides that lend consistency to behavior.[7] Thousands of traits have been identified over the years. Raymond Cattell, another prominent theorist, identified sixteen traits that formed the basis for differences in individual behavior. He described traits in binary pairs such as self-assured/apprehensive, reserved/outgoing, and submissive/dominant.[8]

One popular personality classification involves the so-called Big Five. These traits (described in Table 3.1) include extraversion, agreeableness, conscientiousness, emotional stability, and openness to experience.[9] The Big Five

personality A relatively stable set of characteristics that influence an individual's behavior.

trait theory A personality theory that advocates breaking down behavior patterns into a series of observable traits in order to understand human behavior.

TABLE 3.1	THE BIG FIVE PERSONALITY TRAITS
Extraversion	The person is gregarious, assertive, and sociable (as opposed to reserved, timid, and quiet).
Agreeableness	The person is cooperative, warm, and agreeable (rather than cold, disagreeable, and antagonistic).
Conscientiousness	The person is hardworking, organized, and dependable (as opposed to lazy, disorganized, and unreliable).
Emotional stability	The person is calm, self-confident, and cool (as opposed to insecure, anxious, and depressed).
Openness to experience	The person is creative, curious, and cultured (rather than practical with narrow interests).

SOURCES: P. T. Costa and R. R. McCrae, *The NEO-PI Personality Inventory* (Odessa, Fla.: Psychological Assessment Resources, 1992); J. F. Salgado, "The Five Factor Model of Personality and Job Performance in the European Community," *Journal of Applied Psychology* 82 (1997): 30–43.

are broad, global traits associated with behaviors at work. For example, from preliminary research, we know that introverted and conscientious employees are less likely to be absent from work.[10] Individuals with high agreeableness tend to rate others more leniently on peer evaluations, while those with high conscientiousness tend to be tougher raters.[11] People who are less agreeable and less conscientious are more likely to engage in workplace deviance, behavior that is counterproductive.[12] Across many occupations, conscientious people are more motivated and perform better than others.[13]

But different patterns of the Big Five traits are related to high performance in different occupations and work situations. For customer service jobs, individuals high in emotional stability, agreeableness, and openness to experience perform best. Managers with emotional stability and extraversion are top performers.[14] People who are emotionally stable (as opposed to neurotic) hold up better in decision making under time and social pressure, and people who are more agreeable have a tougher time making decisions under pressure.[15] Studies have also shown that an extreme amount of any trait harms organizations. Interestingly, highly conscientious and emotionally stable individuals perform worse on the job than those with more moderate levels of both traits.[16] The reasons could be that very conscientious individuals may be overly rigid, inflexible, and compulsive, paying too much attention to small details at the expense of larger goals. Similarly, very high levels of emotional stability may result in extreme overcontrol of emotions, making a person less socially competent than those who have more moderate levels of this personality trait.

The Big Five framework is helpful for understanding cultural differences and has held up well when applied to Western cultures, particularly among Spanish and Mexican populations.[17] But it remains to be seen whether the Big Five traits will emerge in studies of non-Western cultures.[18] Personality traits are also relevant to *cultural intelligence*, which, in the workplace, means how we adapt to cultural differences.[19]

But the trait approach has many critics. Some theorists argue that simply identifying traits is not enough because personality is dynamic and never completely stable. Further, early trait theorists tended to ignore the influence of situations.[20] The trait theory also tends to ignore process, that is, how we get from a trait to a particular outcome.

3-2b Integrative Approach

In response to the criticisms of trait theory, researchers have taken a broader, more **integrative approach** to the study of personality.[21] This integrative approach focuses on both personal dispositions and situational variables as combined predictors of behavior. *Dispositions* are the tendencies of an individual to respond to situations in consistent ways. They include emotions, cognitions, attitudes, expectations, and fantasies.[22] Influenced by both genes and experiences, dispositions can be modified.

A recent study of how personality affects status offers a good example of how an integrative approach can be applied to better understand organizations. The study looked at a variety of personality variables that affected not only the actual status held by an individual, but how that individual perceived his or her status as well as how the person's status was viewed by others. The most important variable was leadership identity, though the leader's self-perception was determined largely by emotional stability and agreeableness. Meanwhile, extraversion and conscientiousness most affected how the leader was perceived by others.[23]

3-2c Personality Characteristics in Organizations

Managers should learn as much as possible about personality in order to understand and better relate to their employees, which is why we devote much attention to the subject of personality in this text. Although researchers have identified hundreds of personality characteristics, we have selected a few with particularly strong influences on individual behavior in organizations. *Core self-evaluation (CSE)* involves a broad set of personality traits that articulates an individual's concept of himself or herself.[24] CSE is concerned with people's locus of control, self-esteem, generalized self-efficacy, and emotional stability. It predicts both goal-directed behavior and performance, even in non-U.S. cultures (e.g., Japan).[25] All these aspects of CSE will be examined shortly. In addition to the traits associated with CSE, we will consider the personality traits of self-monitoring and positive/negative affect.

Can managers predict the behavior of their employees from their personalities? Not completely. Recall that the interactional psychology model (Figure 3.1) requires both dispositional and situational variables to predict behavior. As we consider the following personality variables, then, keep in mind that they are only one piece of the personality puzzle.

When weighing the role of situation, it is important to understand that situations vary in strength. **Strong situations** overwhelm the effects of individual personalities. These situations are interpreted in the same way by different individuals, evoke agreement on the appropriate behavior in the situation, and provide cues to appropriate behavior. For example, at performance appraisal sessions, employees know to listen to their bosses and to contribute when asked to do, so this is a strong situation.

Weak situations are open to many interpretations. They provide few cues to appropriate behavior and no obvious rewards for any particular behavior. Individual personalities thus have a greater influence in weak situations than in strong situations. An informal meeting without an agenda might be a weak situation. Because organizations present combinations of strong and weak situations, personality affects behavior more in some situations than in others.[26]

Following are explanations of the various aspects of personality involved in CSE plus the traits of self-monitoring and positive/negative affect. Locus of control, self-efficacy, self-esteem, and the effects of emotional stability together constitute the core self-evaluations. CSE is a strong predictor of both job satisfaction and job performance, next only to GMA.[27]

LOCUS OF CONTROL An individual's generalized belief about internal (self) versus external (situation or others) control is called **locus of control**. People who believe they control what happens to them

integrative approach The broad theory that describes personality as a composite of an individual's psychological processes.

strong situation A situation that overwhelms the effects of individual personalities by providing strong cues for appropriate behavior.

locus of control An individual's generalized belief about internal control (self-control) versus external control (control by the situation or by others).

have an internal locus of control, whereas people who believe that circumstances or other people control their fate have an external locus of control.[28] In an organization, people with an internal locus of control (called *internals*) often report higher job satisfaction, exhibit superior job performance, are more likely to assume managerial positions, and tend to prefer participative management styles more than those with an external locus of control (*externals*).[29]

Internals and externals have similar positive reactions to being promoted, including high job satisfaction, job involvement, and organizational commitment. However, internals remain happy long after the promotion, whereas externals' joy over the promotion is short-lived. This might occur because externals do not believe their own performance led to the promotion.[30]

Knowing about locus of control can prove valuable to managers. Because internals believe they control what happens to them, they will want to exercise control in their work environments. Internals don't react well to close supervision, so managers should give them considerable voice in how work is performed. Externals, by contrast, may appreciate more structured work settings and prefer not to participate in decision making.

SELF-EFFICACY People's **general self-efficacy** is their overall view of themselves as being able to perform effectively in a wide variety of situations.[31] Employees with high general self-efficacy have more confidence in their job-related abilities and other personal resources (e.g., energy, influence over others) that help them function effectively on the job. People with low general self-efficacy often feel ineffective at work and may express doubts about performing new tasks well. Previous success or performance is one of the most important determinants of self-efficacy. People who trust their own efficacy tend to attempt difficult tasks, persist in overcoming obstacles, and experience less anxiety when faced with adversity.[32] Because they are confident in their capability to provide meaningful input, they value the opportunity to participate in decision making.[33] High self-efficacy has also been related to higher job satisfaction and performance.[34]

Another form of self-efficacy, called *task-specific self-efficacy*, describes a person's belief that she or he can perform a specific task. ("I believe I can do this sales presentation today.") In contrast, general self-efficacy is broader. ("I believe I can perform well in just about any part of the job.")

SELF-ESTEEM Self-esteem is an individual's general feeling of self-worth. Individuals with high self-esteem have positive feelings about themselves, perceive themselves to have strengths as well as weaknesses, and believe their strengths are more important than their weaknesses.[35] Individuals with low self-esteem view themselves negatively. They are more strongly affected by what other people think of them, and they compliment individuals who give them positive feedback while cutting down people who give them negative feedback.[36]

Evaluations from others affect our self-esteem. You might be liked for who you are, or you might be liked for your achievements. Being liked for who you are is more stable, and people with self-esteem stemming from this type of reaction from other people are usually able to be less defensive and more honest with themselves. Being liked for your achievements is more unstable; self-esteem resulting from this type of reaction waxes and wanes depending on the magnitude of achievements.[37]

Self-esteem affects attitudes and behavior in organizations. People with high self-esteem perform better and are more satisfied with their jobs.[38] They tend to seek out higher-status jobs.[39] A work team made up of individuals with high self-esteem is more likely to succeed than a team with low or average self-esteem.[40]

High self-esteem, however, can be too much of a good thing. People with inflated self-esteem may brag inappropriately when they find themselves in stressful situations.[41] Very high self-esteem may also lead to overconfidence and relationship conflicts.[42] Such individuals may shift their social identities to protect themselves when they do not live up to some standard. For example, if Denise outperforms Teresa on a statistics exam, Teresa may convince herself that Denise is not really a

Yellowj/Shutterstock.com

general self-efficacy An individual's general belief that he or she is capable of meeting job demands in a wide variety of situations.

self-esteem An individual's general feeling of self-worth.

Blablo101/Shutterstock.com

HOT TREND

High Self-Monitors Are Good Networkers

High self-monitors resemble good actors who are able to play different roles for different audiences. They have strong motives to succeed in social interactions, use humor in conversations, and speak first to break awkward silences. In addition, a recent study showed that high self-monitors are also likely to be social network brokers, connecting previously unacquainted people with each other. High self-monitors, when viewed by others as empathetic, can be effective at connecting people and building networks.

SOURCE: A. M. Kleinbaum, A. H. Jordan, and P. G. Audia, "An Altercentric Perspective on the Origins of Brokerage in Social Networks: How Perceived Empathy Moderates the Self-Monitoring Effect," *Organization Science*, published online February 13, 2015.

good person to compare herself with because Denise is an engineering major and Teresa is a physical education major. Teresa's high self-esteem protects her from this unfavorable though, in truth, valid comparison,[43] which might otherwise prompt her to improve her knowledge of statistics.

Self-esteem may be strongly affected by situations. Success tends to raise self-esteem, whereas failure lowers it. Managers should thus encourage employees to raise their self-esteem by giving them appropriate challenges and opportunities for success.

SELF-MONITORING Self-monitoring—the extent to which people base their behavior on cues from other people and situations—has a huge impact on behavior in organizations.[44] High self-monitors pay attention to what is appropriate in particular situations and to the behavior of other people, and they behave accordingly. Low self-monitors, by contrast, pay less attention to situational cues and act from internal states instead. As a result, low self-monitors behave consistently across situations. High self-monitors, because their behavior varies with the situation, appear more unpredictable and less consistent but in practice are actually more effective at work because they respond appropriately to changes in the organizational situation. For example, one study of managers at a recruitment firm found that high self-monitors were more likely to offer emotional help people dealing with work-related anxiety. Low self-monitors, on the other hand, were unlikely to offer such emotional support.[45]

According to our research, high self-monitors get promoted because they accomplish tasks by meeting the expectations of others and because they seek out central positions in social networks.[46] They are also more likely to use self-promotion to make others aware of their skills and accomplishments.[47] However, the high self-monitors' flexibility may not be suited for every job, and the tendency to move may not fit every organization.[48]

Because high self-monitors base their behavior on cues from others and from the situation, they demonstrate higher levels of managerial self-awareness. This means that, as managers, they assess their own workplace behavior accurately.[49] Managers who are high self-monitors are also good at reading their employees' needs and changing the way they interact with employees.[50]

We can further speculate that high self-monitors respond more readily to work group norms, organizational culture, and supervisory feedback than do low self-monitors, who adhere more to internal guidelines for behavior ("I am who I am"). In addition, high self-monitors may support the trend toward work teams because they can easily assume flexible roles.

POSITIVE/NEGATIVE AFFECT Individuals who focus on the positive aspects of themselves, other people, and the world in general are said to have **positive affect**.[51] In contrast, those who accentuate the negative in themselves, others, and the world are said to possess **negative affect** (also called *negative affectivity*).[52] Individuals with positive affect are more satisfied with their jobs.[53] They are also more likely to help others at work and engage in more organizational citizenship behaviors.[54] Employees with positive affect have fewer absentee days.[55] Positive affect has also been linked to more life satisfaction and better performance across a variety of life and work domains.[56] Individual affect influences the work group as well. Positive individual affect produces positive team affect, which promotes cooperation and reduces conflict.[57] In particular, leader affectivity influences the affectivity of his or her subordinates. Thus, positive affect is a definite asset in work settings. Managers can encourage it by allowing people to participate in decision making and by providing pleasant working conditions.

self-monitoring The extent to which people base their behavior on cues from other people and situations.

positive affect An individual's tendency to accentuate the positive aspects of herself or himself, other people, and the world in general.

negative affect An individual's tendency to accentuate the negative aspects of himself or herself, other people, and the world in general.

3-2d Proactive Personality

Proactive personalities identify opportunities and act on them; they show initiative, take action, and persevere until they effect change. People who are not proactive fail to identify, let alone seize, opportunities to effect change.[58] Proactivity has been positively related to job performance, career success, and job search success.[59] Additionally, leaders who identify themselves as proactive are viewed as more charismatic by their subordinates.[60]

3-3 APPLICATION OF PERSONALITY THEORY IN ORGANIZATIONS

To apply personality theories in their organizations, managers first must measure the personalities of their organizations' members. Projective tests, behavioral measures, and self-report questionnaires can all be used to measure personality.

3-3a Common Personality Measurement Tools

During **projective tests**, individuals are shown a picture, abstract image, or photo and are asked to describe what they see or to tell a story about it. The rationale behind projective tests is that each individual responds to the stimulus in a way that reflects his or her unique personality. The Rorschach ink blot test is commonly used to assess personality.[61] Like other projective tests, however, it has low reliability. The individual being assessed may look at the same picture and see different things at different times. In addition, the assessor might apply her or his own biases in interpreting the information about the individual's personality.

Behavioral measures of personality examine an individual's behavior in a controlled situation. We might assess a person's sociability, for example, by counting the number of times he or she approaches strangers at a party. The behavior is scored to produce an index of personality. Some potential problems with behavioral measures include the observer's ability to stay focused and the way the observer interprets the behavior. Additionally, some people behave differently when they know they are being observed.

The most common method of assessing personality is the **self-report questionnaire**. An individual responds to a series of questions, usually in an agree/disagree or true/false format. One of the more widely recognized questionnaires is the *Minnesota Multiphasic Personality Inventory (MMPI)*, a comprehensive test assessing a variety of traits that can help diagnose several neurotic or psychotic disorders. Another self-report questionnaire, the *NEO Personality Inventory*, measures the Big Five traits. Self-report questionnaires also suffer from potential biases. It is difficult to view your own personality objectively. People often answer the questionnaires in terms of how they want to be seen rather than as they really are.

3-3b Carl Jung and the Myers-Briggs Type Indicator® Instrument

Another approach to applying personality theory in organizations is the Jungian approach and its measurement tool, the *Myers-Briggs Type Indicator® (MBTI)*. This instrument was developed to measure ideas about individual differences advocated by the Swiss psychologist Carl Jung. Many organizations use the MBTI instrument, and we will focus on it as an example of how some organizations use personality concepts to help employees appreciate diversity.

Jung built his work on the notion that people are fundamentally different but also fundamentally alike.

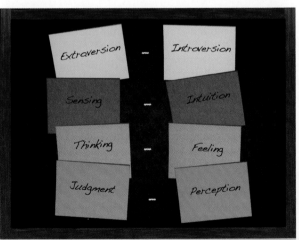

The Myers-Briggs Type Indicator is a common way to measure differences in individuals

---

projective test A personality test that elicits an individual's response to abstract stimuli.

behavioral measures Personality assessments that involve observing an individual's behavior in a controlled situation.

self-report questionnaire A common personality assessment that involves an individual's responses to a series of questions.

TABLE 3.2 — TYPE THEORY PREFERENCES AND DESCRIPTIONS

Extraversion	Introversion
Outgoing	Quiet
Publicly expressive	Reserved
Interacting	Concentrating
Speaks, then thinks	Thinks, then speaks
Gregarious	Reflective

Sensing	Intuition
Practical	General
Specific	Abstract
Feet on the ground	Head in the clouds
Details	Possibilities
Concrete	Theoretical

Thinking	Feeling
Analytical	Subjective
Clarity	Harmony
Head	Heart
Justice	Mercy
Rules	Circumstance

Judging	Perceiving
Structured	Flexible
Time oriented	Open ended
Decisive	Exploring
Makes lists/uses them	Makes lists/loses them
Organized	Spontaneous

SOURCE: Adapted from *Introduction to Type*®, Sixth Edition by Isabel Briggs Myers. Copyright 1998, 2011 by CPP, Inc. All rights reserved.

His classic treatise *Psychological Types* proposed that the population was made up of two basic types: Extraverted types and Introverted types.[62] He went on to identify two types of Perceiving (Sensing and Intuition) and two types of Judgment (Thinking and Feeling). Perceiving (how we gather information) and Judging (how we make decisions) represent the two universal basic mental functions.

Jung suggested that human similarities and differences could be understood by combining preferences. We prefer and choose one way of doing things over another. We are not exclusively one way or another; rather, we have a preference for Extraversion or Introversion, just as we have a preference for right-handedness or left-handedness. Jung's type theory argues that no preferences are better than others. Differences are to be understood, celebrated, and appreciated.

During the 1940s, the mother-daughter team of Katherine Briggs and Isabel Briggs Myers became fascinated with individual differences among people and with Jung's work. They developed the **Myers-Briggs Type Indicator® (MBTI) instrument** to put Jung's type theory into practical use. The MBTI instrument is used extensively in organizations as a basis for understanding individual differences. More than 2 million people complete the instrument per year in the United States, and it is frequently used by *Fortune* 500 companies.[63] The MBTI instrument has been used in career counseling, team building, conflict management, and understanding management styles.[64]

THE PREFERENCES There are four scale dichotomies in type theory: extraversion/introversion, sensing/intuition, thinking/feeling, and judging/perceiving. Table 3.2 shows these preferences. The combination of these preferences makes up an individual's psychological type.

EXTRAVERSION/INTROVERSION The **Extraversion/Introversion** preference represents where you find energy. Jung's theory holds that the Extraversion/Introversion preference reflects the most important distinction among individuals. The Extraverted type (E) is energized by interaction with other people. The Introverted type (I) is energized by time alone. Extraverted types typically have a wide social network, whereas Introverted types have a more narrow range of relationships. As articulated by Jung, this preference has nothing to do with social skills. Many introverts have excellent social skills but prefer the internal world of ideas, thoughts, and concepts. Extraverts represent approximately 49 percent of the U.S. population, and introverts represent about 51 percent, indicating a fairly even split.[65] Our U.S. culture rewards and nurtures extraverts. In work settings, extraverts prefer

Myers-Briggs Type Indicator® (MBTI) instrument An instrument developed to measure Carl Jung's theory of individual differences.

Extraversion Being energized by interaction with other people.

Introversion Being energized by spending time alone.

Who Says Introverts Can't Be Leaders?

Do you have to be an extravert to be a leader? Some of the most influential leaders in business and politics would disagree—they're introverts!

- Larry Page, CEO and cofounder of Google
- President Barack Obama
- Marissa Mayer, CEO of Yahoo
- Warren Buffett, famous investor and philanthropist, CEO of Berkshire Hathaway
- Hillary Clinton, former Secretary of State
- Mark Zuckerberg, cofounder of Facebook

Introverted leaders may succeed because of their natural capacity for introspection and thoughtful communication. They spend a lot of time listening and are more open to others' ideas, collaborating with others before making important decisions. Rather than interacting with a great number of people, introverts form genuine, deep ties to a smaller network of people they can rely on.

It's important to remember that introversion means getting energy from time alone. It has nothing to do with social skills; in fact, many of the leaders mentioned above have great social skills.

SOURCE: S. Cole, "7 Famous Leaders Who Prove Introverts Can Be Wildly Successful," *Fast Company*, http://www.fastcompany.com/3032028/the-future-of-work/7-famous-leaders-who-prove-introverts-can-be-wildly-successful, accessed June 18, 2014.

variety and do not mind being interrupted by phone calls or visits. They communicate freely but, on the negative side, may say things that they regret later.

Introverts prefer to concentrate quietly and think things through privately. They are detail oriented and do not mind working on a project for a long time; but they dislike telephone interruptions and may have trouble recalling names and faces.

Sensing Gathering information through the five senses and focusing on what actually exists.

Intuition Gathering information through a "sixth sense" and focusing on what could be.

SENSING/INTUITION The **Sensing/Intuition** preference represents perception or information gathering. The Sensing type (S) pays attention to information gathered through the five senses and to what actually exists. The Intuitive type (N) pays attention to a "sixth sense" and to what could be rather than to what actually exists.[66] Approximately 70 percent of people in the United States are Sensing types.[67]

At work, Sensing types prefer specific answers to questions and can be frustrated by vague instructions. They like jobs yielding tangible results and would rather use established skills than learn new ones. Intuitive types like solving new problems and are impatient with routine details. They enjoy learning new skills more than actually using them. They tend to think about several things at once and may appear absentminded. They like figuring out how things work just for the fun of it.

THINKING/FEELING The **Thinking/Feeling** preference describes the way we prefer to make decisions. The Thinking preference (T) makes decisions in a logical, objective fashion, whereas the Feeling preference (F) makes decisions in a personal, value-oriented way. The general U.S. population is divided 40/60 on the Thinking/Feeling type preference, respectively. But, interestingly, the majority of males are Thinking types, whereas the majority of females are Feeling types. It is the one preference in type theory that has a strong gender difference. Thinking types tend to analyze decisions, while Feeling types sympathize. Thinking types try to be impersonal, whereas Feeling types base their decisions on how the outcome will affect the people involved.

In work settings, Thinking types tend to show less emotion. They also tend to be less comfortable with others' emotional expressions and respond more readily to other people's thoughts. They tend to be firm minded and like putting things into a logical framework. Feeling types, by contrast, are comfortable with emotion in the workplace. They enjoy pleasing people and receiving frequent praise and encouragement.

JUDGING/PERCEIVING The **Judging/Perceiving** dichotomy reflects one's orientation to the outer world. The Judging preference (J) loves closure. They prefer to lead planned, organized lives and like making decisions. On the other hand, Perceivers (P) prefer flexible and spontaneous lives and like to keep options open. Imagine two people, one with a preference for Judging and the other for Perceiving, going out for dinner. J asks P to choose a restaurant, and P suggests ten alternatives. J just wants to decide and get on with it, whereas P wants to explore all the options.

Judging types love getting things accomplished and delight in checking off completed tasks on their calendars. Perceiving types generally adopt a wait-and-see attitude, collecting new information instead of drawing conclusions. Perceiving types are curious and welcome new information. They may start many projects without finishing them.

THE SIXTEEN TYPES The preferences combine to form sixteen distinct types, as shown in Table 3.3. For example, the ESTJ type has Extraversion, Sensing, Thinking, and Judging preferences. ESTJs see the world as it is (S); make decisions objectively (T); and like structure, schedules, and order (J). Combining these qualities with their preference for interacting with others makes them ideal managers. ESTJs are dependable, practical, and able to get any job done. They are conscious of the chain of command and see work as a series of goals to be reached by following rules and regulations. They may have little tolerance for disorganization and have a high need for control. Research results from the *MBTI Atlas* show that most of the 7,463 managers studied were ESTJs.[68]

The MBTI instrument has been found to have good reliability and validity as a measurement instrument for identifying type.[69] There are no good or bad types; each has its own strengths and weaknesses. Type influences learning style, teaching style, and choice of occupation. A study of the MBTI types of engineering students at Georgia Tech determined that STs and NTs were more attracted to engineering. Es and Fs were more likely to withdraw from engineering courses.[70] Type can also determine an individual's decision-making and management styles.

HOW COMPANIES USE MBTI Recent studies have focused on the relationship between type and specific managerial behaviors. The Introverted type (I) and the Feeling type (F), for example, appear to be more effective at participative management than their counterparts, the Extraverted type and the Thinking type.[71] Companies such as AT&T, ExxonMobil, and Honeywell use the MBTI instrument in their management development programs to help employees understand the different viewpoints of others in the organization. The MBTI instrument can also be used for team building, and resources are available to help managers learn how to do so effectively.[72] Hewlett-Packard and Armstrong World Industries use the MBTI instrument to show teams that diversity and differences lead to successful performance.

Managers value type theory for its simplicity and accuracy. But information from the MBTI instrument can be misused in organizational settings.[73] Some inappropriate uses include labeling one's coworkers, claiming results as a convenient excuse that one simply can't work with a particular coworker, and avoiding responsibility for learning to work flexibly with others. Although personality type is not an excuse for inappropriate behavior, if used well, type theory helps managers develop interpersonal skills. It also helps in building teams that capitalize on individuals' strengths and foster appreciation of individual team members' differences.

> **Thinking** Making decisions in a logical, objective fashion.
>
> **Feeling** Making decisions in a personal, value-oriented way.
>
> **Judging** Preferring closure and completion in making decisions.
>
> **Perceiving** Preferring to explore many alternatives with flexibility and spontaneity.

TABLE 3.3 CHARACTERISTICS FREQUENTLY ASSOCIATED WITH EACH TYPE

SENSING TYPES		INTUITIVE TYPES	
ISTJ	**ISFJ**	**INFJ**	**INTJ**
Quiet, serious, earn success by thoroughness and dependability. Practical, matter-of-fact, realistic, and responsible. Decides logically what should be done and works toward it steadily, regardless of distractions. Takes pleasure in making everything orderly and organized—work, home, and life. Values traditions and loyalty.	Quiet, friendly, responsible, and conscientious. Committed and steady in meeting obligations. Thorough, painstaking, and accurate. Loyal, considerate, notices and remembers specifics about people who are important, concerned with how others feel. Strives to create an orderly and harmonious environment at work and at home.	Seeks meaning and connection in ideas, relationships, and material possessions. Wants to understand what motivates people and is insightful about others. Conscientious and committed to firm values. Develops a clear vision about how best to serve the common good. Organized and decisive in implementing his or her vision.	Has an original mind and great drive for implementing ideas and achieving goals. Quickly sees patterns in external events and develops long-range explanatory perspectives. When committed, organizes a job and carries it through. Skeptical and independent, has high standards of competence and performance for self and others.
ISTP	**ISFP**	**INFP**	**INTP**
Tolerant and flexible, quiet observer until a problem appears, then acts quickly to find workable solutions. Analyzes what makes things work and readily gets through large amounts of data to isolate the core of practical problems. Interested in cause and effect, organizes facts using logical principles, values efficiency.	Quiet, friendly, sensitive, and kind. Enjoys the present moment, and the immediate environment. Likes to have his or her own space and to work within a selected time frame. Loyal and committed to personal values and to people who are important to him or her. Dislikes disagreements and conflicts, does not force opinions or values on others.	Idealistic, loyal to values and to people who are important to him or her. Wants an external life that is congruent with values. Curious, quick to see possibilities, can be a catalyst for implementing ideas. Seeks to understand people and to help them fulfill their potential. Adaptable, flexible, and accepting unless a value is threatened.	Seeks to develop logical explanations for everything that interests him or her. Theoretical and abstract, interested more in ideas than in social interaction. Quiet, contained, flexible, and adaptable. Has unusual ability to focus in depth to solve problems in area of interest. Skeptical, sometimes critical, always analytical.
ESTP	**ESFP**	**ENFP**	**ENTP**
Flexible and tolerant, takes a pragmatic approach focused on immediate results. Finds theories and conceptual explanations boring. Wants to act energetically to solve the problem. Focuses on the here and now, spontaneous, enjoys each moment that he or she can be active with others. Enjoys material comforts and style. Learns best through doing.	Outgoing, friendly, and accepting. Exuberant lover of life, people, and material comforts. Enjoys working with others to make things happen. Brings common sense and a realistic approach to his or her work and makes work fun. Flexible and spontaneous, adapts readily to new people and environments. Learns best by trying a new skill with other people.	Warmly enthusiastic and imaginative. Sees life as full of possibilities. Makes connections between events and information very quickly, and confidently proceeds based on the patterns he or she sees. Wants a lot of affirmation from others, and readily gives appreciation and support. Spontaneous and flexible, often relies on his or her ability to improvise and verbal fluency.	Quick, ingenious, stimulating, alert, and outspoken. Resourceful in solving new and challenging problems. Adept at generating conceptual possibilities and then analyzing them strategically. Good at reading other people. Bored by routine, will seldom do the same thing the same way, apt to turn to one new interest after another.
ESTJ	**ESFJ**	**ENFJ**	**ENTJ**
Practical, realistic, matter-of-fact. Decisive, quickly moves to implement decisions. Organizes projects and people to get things done, focuses on getting results in the most efficient way possible. Takes care of routine details. Has a clear set of logical standards, systematically follows them and wants others to do so also. Forceful in implementing plans.	Warmhearted, conscientious, and cooperative. Wants harmony in the environment, works with determination to establish it. Likes to work with others to complete tasks accurately and on time. Loyal, follows through even in small matters. Notices what others need in their day-to-day lives and tries to provide it. Wants to be appreciated for who he or she is and for his or her contribution.	Warm, empathetic, responsive, and responsible. Highly attuned to the emotions, needs, and motivations of others. Finds potential in everyone, wants to help others fulfill their potential. May act as a catalyst for individual and group growth. Loyal, responsive to praise and criticism. Sociable, facilitates others in a group, and provides inspiring leadership.	Frank, decisive, assumes leadership readily. Quickly sees logical and inefficient procedures and policies, develops and implements comprehensive systems to solve organizational problems. Enjoys long-term planning and goal setting. Usually well informed, well read, enjoys expanding knowledge and passing it on to others. Forceful in presenting ideas.

NOTE: I = Introversion; E = Extraversion; S = Sensing; N = Intuition; T = Thinking; F = Feeling; J = Judging; and P = Perceiving.

SOURCE: Adapted from *Introduction to Type*, Sixth Edition by Isabel Briggs Myers. Copyright 1998 by Peter B. Myers and Katharine D. Myers. All rights reserved.

3-4 SOCIAL PERCEPTION

Perception is another psychological process that creates individual differences. As the primary vehicle through which we come to understand ourselves and our world, perception adds meaning to information gathered via the five senses of touch, smell, hearing, vision, and taste. Virtually all management activities rely on perception. Here, we focus specifically on **social perception**, or the process of interpreting information about another person.

The *selection interview* highlights the importance of perception. The consequences of a bad match between an individual and the organization are devastating for both parties, so accurate data must be gathered. First interviews are typically brief, and the candidate is usually one of many seen by an interviewer during a day. The interviewer often makes an accept or reject decision in the first four to five minutes based on her or his perception of the candidate.[74]

Another aspect of the importance of perception was shown by a study that found increased conflict related to perceptions of dissimilarity in values between CEOs and top management teams. Even if, in reality, there was no difference in values, the mere perception of differences increased conflict. This study highlights the importance of managers paying attention to how their employees perceive organizational decisions because their perceptions influence their behavior.[75]

Perception is often culturally determined. Based on our cultural backgrounds, we tend to perceive things in certain ways. Read the following sentence: *Finished files are the result of years of scientific study combined with the experience of years.* Now quickly count the number of *Fs* in the sentence. Individuals who speak English as a second language see all six *Fs*. Most native English speakers report that there are three *Fs* because they are culturally conditioned to ignore unimportant words like *of*.[76] Culture can affect our interpretation of the data we gather as well as the meaning we add to it. In other words, our culture can affect our social perception. Valuing diversity, including cultural diversity, has been recognized as a key to international competitiveness, so managers need good social perception skills.[77]

Three major categories of factors influence our perception of others: characteristics of ourselves as perceivers, characteristics of the target person we are perceiving, and characteristics of the situation in which the interaction takes place. Figure 3.2 models social perception.

3-4a Characteristics of the Perceiver

Several characteristics of the perceiver can affect social perception. The perceiver uses *perceptual lenses* to shape his or her view of the target, especially if it is a new encounter. Perceptual lenses are filters used by the perceiver to

social perception The process of interpreting information about another person.

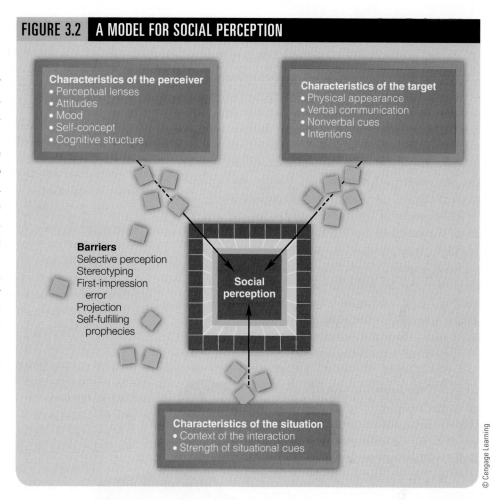

FIGURE 3.2   A MODEL FOR SOCIAL PERCEPTION

Characteristics of the perceiver
- Perceptual lenses
- Attitudes
- Mood
- Self-concept
- Cognitive structure

Characteristics of the target
- Physical appearance
- Verbal communication
- Nonverbal cues
- Intentions

Barriers
Selective perception
Stereotyping
First-impression error
Projection
Self-fulfilling prophecies

Social perception

Characteristics of the situation
- Context of the interaction
- Strength of situational cues

© Cengage Learning

make a quick initial assessment. The most often used lenses include the trust lens (are you friend or foe?), the power lens (are you useful to me?), and the ego lens (which of us is superior?). You can use knowledge of perceptual lenses to ensure that you're perceived accurately. For the trust lens, project warmth and competence through appropriate eye contact, smiling, and good posture. For the power lens, make yourself instrumental through assurances that you can help the perceiver reach mutual goals. For the ego lens, be modest and inclusive, and create a sense of "us."[78]

The perceiver's *attitudes* also affect social perception. Suppose you are interviewing candidates for a very important position in your organization—a position that requires negotiating contracts with suppliers, most of whom are male. You may feel that women are not capable of holding their own in tough negotiations. This attitude will doubtlessly affect your perceptions of the female candidates you interview.

Mood can have a strong influence on the way we perceive someone.[79] We think differently when we are happy than we do when we are depressed. We also remember information that matches our mood state better than information that is inconsistent with it. When in a positive mood, we form more positive impressions of others. When in a negative mood, we tend to evaluate others unfavorably.

Another factor that can affect social perception is the perceiver's *self-concept*. An individual with a positive self-concept tends to notice positive attributes in another person. In contrast, a negative self-concept can lead a perceiver to pick out negative traits in another person. The better we understand ourselves, the more accurate our perceptions of others.

Cognitive structure, an individual's pattern of thinking, also affects social perception. Some people tend to perceive physical traits such as height, weight, and appearance more readily. Others focus on central traits, or personality dispositions. Cognitive complexity allows a person to perceive multiple characteristics of another person rather than attending to just a few traits.

The way you dress influences how people perceive you.

3-4b Characteristics of the Target

Characteristics of the target (the person being perceived) influence social perception in various ways. *Physical appearance* plays a big role in our perception of others. The perceiver will notice physical features such as height, weight, estimated age, race, and gender. Clothing says a great deal about a person. Blue pinstriped suits, for example, suggest banking or Wall Street. Perceivers tend to notice physical appearance characteristics that contrast with the norm, that are intense, or that are new or unusual.[80] A loud person, one who dresses outlandishly, a very tall person, or a hyperactive child will be noticed because he or she contrasts with what is commonly encountered. Novel individuals such as newcomers or minorities also attract attention.

Physical attractiveness often colors our entire impression of another person. Interviewers rate attractive candidates more favorably and award them higher starting salaries.[81] But people who are perceived as physically attractive face some nonbeneficial stereotypes as well.

Verbal communication from a target affects our perception of him or her. We listen to the topics discussed and his or her tone of voice and accent, and we make judgments based on this input.

Nonverbal communication conveys a great deal of information about the target. Eye contact, facial expressions, body movements, and posture all are deciphered by the perceiver in an attempt to form an impression of the target. Awareness of cultural differences is particularly important when it comes to nonverbal communication because some nonverbal signals mean very different things in different cultures. The "okay" sign in the United States (forming a circle with the thumb and forefinger) is an insult in South America. Facial expressions, however, seem to have universal meanings. Individuals from different cultures can recognize and decipher expressions the same way.[82]

The *intentions* of the target are inferred by the perceiver who observes the target's behavior. We may see our boss appear in our office doorway and think, "Oh no! She's going to give me more work to do." Or we may perceive that her intention is to congratulate us on a recent success. In any case, the perceiver's interpretation of the target's intentions affects the way the perceiver views the target.

Stefan Randholm/Flickr/Getty Images

3-4c Characteristics of the Situation

The situation in which the interaction between the perceiver and the target takes place, the *social context*, also influences perception. Meeting your professor in his or her office affects your impression differently than meeting your professor in a local restaurant would. Social context is very important in Japan. Business conversations after working hours or at lunch are taboo. If you try to talk business during these times, you may be perceived as rude.[83]

The *strength of situational cues* also affects social perception. As discussed earlier in the chapter, some situations provide strong cues about appropriate behavior. In these situations, we assume that the individual's behavior can be accounted for by the situation and may not reflect the individual's disposition. This is the **discounting principle** in social perception.[84] For example, you may encounter an automobile salesperson who has a warm and personable manner, asks about your work and hobbies, and seems genuinely interested in your taste in cars. Yet you probably cannot assume that this behavior reflects the salesperson's personality because of the influence of the situation. This person is trying to sell you a car and probably treats all customers in this manner.

3-5 BARRIERS TO SOCIAL PERCEPTION

It would be wonderful if all of us had accurate social perception skills. Unfortunately, barriers often prevent us from perceiving others accurately. Five barriers to social perception are selective perception, stereotyping, first-impression error, projection, and self-fulfilling prophecies.

Selective perception is our tendency to prefer information that supports our viewpoints. Individuals often ignore information that threatens their viewpoints. Suppose, for example, that a sales manager is evaluating the performance of his employees. One employee does not get along well with colleagues and rarely completes sales reports on time. This employee, however, generates the most new sales contracts in the office. The sales manager may ignore the negative information, choosing to evaluate the salesperson only on contracts generated. The manager is exercising selective perception.

A **stereotype** is a generalization about a group of people. Stereotypes reduce information about other people to a workable level so that it can be compiled efficiently. Stereotypes become even stronger when they are shared with and validated by others.[85] Some stereotypes

are accurate and serve as useful perceptual guidelines, but, of course, many are inaccurate and do much harm, generating false impressions that may never be tested or changed.

In multicultural work teams, members often form impressions of foreign coworkers based on stereotypes before getting to know them as individuals. Asians, for example, are sometimes pushed toward career choices that fit with a stereotype that Asians excel at math and science, setting aside what a particular individual's strengths and talents may actually be. Stereotypes such as these can compromise the productivity of the work team,

---

Is "Bossy" a Negative Stereotype for Women?

Strong, powerful women often get stereotyped as bossy, and it's seldom a compliment. Strong, assertive men, in contrast, are referred to as powerful or decisive. Sheryl Sandberg, COO of Facebook, teamed with former Secretary of State Condoleezza Rice and Girl Scouts' CEO Anna Maria Chavez to launch "Ban Bossy" (banbossy.com) to combat the stereotype by banning the word. The idea is that girls often don't want to lead because they don't want to be disliked and called bossy—meaning too aggressive, ambitious, and political and overstepping bounds. Many women joined the campaign, including Beyoncé, who said in her TV ad for the campaign, "I'm not bossy. I'm the boss."

The campaign has generated controversy, with some women arguing that rather than banning the "bossy" word, women should reclaim it by not worrying about being labeled as such, and by being confidently assertive.

All parties would probably agree that the stereotype exists. The key for both sexes lies in being assertive and strong while still being respectful. Neither sex fares well as leaders when seen as abrasive.

SOURCES: A. Fisher, "How Women Can Respond to That Other B-Word: Bossy," *Fortune*, http://fortune.com/2014/04/24/how-women-can-respond-to-that-other-b-word-bossy/, accessed April 20, 2014; J. Humphrey, "The End of Bitchy: Addressing Stereotypes of Women at Work," *Fast Company*, http://www.fastcompany.com/3041942/strong-female-lead/the-end-of-bitchy-addressing-stereotypes-of-women-at-work, accessed February 5, 2015.

---

discounting principle The assumption that an individual's behavior is accounted for by the situation.

selective perception The tendency to select information that supports our individual viewpoints while discounting information that threatens our viewpoints.

stereotype A generalization about a group of people.

lower morale, and result in limited opportunities for individuals. The more accurate information employees have about their coworkers and their backgrounds, however, the less likely stereotypes are to play a role in how individuals are perceived both in terms of group dynamics and individual advancement.[86]

Attractiveness is a powerful stereotype. We assume that attractive individuals are also warm, kind, sensitive, poised, sociable, outgoing, independent, and strong. However, a study of romantic relationships showed that most attractive individuals do not fit the stereotype apart from possessing good social skills and being popular.[87] Some individuals may seem to us to fit the stereotype of attractiveness because our behavior elicits from them behavior that confirms the stereotype. Consider, for example, a situation in which you meet an attractive fellow student. Chances are that you respond positively to this person because you assume she or he is warm, sociable, and so on. Even though the person may not possess these traits, your positive response may bring out these behaviors in the person. Thus, your interaction may be channeled to confirm the stereotype.[88]

Stereotyping pervades work life. When an individual's behavior contrasts with a stereotype of his or her group, he or she is treated more positively (given more favorable comments or pats on the back). For example, a female softball player might receive more applause for a home run hit than a male teammate because some people may stereotype women as less athletic than men and hold female players to a lower standard. Either way, the contrast is still part of stereotyping.[89]

First impressions are lasting impressions, so the saying goes. We tend to remember what we perceive first about a person, and sometimes we are quite reluctant to change our initial impressions.[90] **First-impression** occurs when we observe a very brief bit of a person's behavior in our first encounter and infer that this behavior reflects what the person is really like. Such primacy effects can be particularly dangerous in interviews, given that we form first impressions quickly and that these impressions may be the basis for long-term employment relationships.

What factors do interviewers rely on when forming first impressions? Perceptions of the candidate, such as whether they like the person, whether they trust the person, and whether or not the person seems credible, all influence the interviewer's decision. Something as seemingly unimportant as the pitch of your voice can leave a lasting impression.

Speakers with lower vocal pitch are believed to be more competent, more dominant, and more assertive than those with higher voices. Men whose voices are high enough that they sound feminine are judged the least favorably of all by interviewers. This finding is ironic, given that research has found that students with higher vocal pitch tend to earn better grades.[91]

Projection, also known as the *false-consensus effect*, causes inaccurate perceptions of others. When we project, we assume that our own beliefs and values are commonly held and normative, and we overestimate the number of others who share them. People who are different are viewed as unusual and even deviant. Projection occurs most often when you surround yourself with others similar to you. You may overlook important information about others when you assume we are all alike and in agreement.[92]

Self-fulfilling prophecies, also called the *Pygmalion effect*, interfere with social perception in that our expectations affect the way we interact with others such that we provoke the very response we expect. Early studies of self-fulfilling prophecy were conducted in elementary school classrooms. Teachers were given bogus information that some of their pupils had high intellectual potential. These pupils were chosen randomly; there were really no differences among the students. Eight months later, the "gifted" pupils scored significantly higher on an IQ test. The teachers' expectations elicited growth from these students because they had given them tougher assignments and more feedback on their performance.[93]

A manager's expectations of an individual affect both the manager's behavior toward the individual and the individual's response. For example, suppose your initial impression is that an employee has the potential to move up in the organization. Chances are you will spend a great deal of time coaching and counseling the employee, providing challenging assignments, and grooming the individual for success. Managers can harness the power of the Pygmalion effect to improve productivity in the organization simply by expecting positive results from a group of employees.[94]

3-5a Impression Management

Most people want to make favorable impressions on others. This is particularly true in organizations where individuals compete for jobs, favorable performance

first-impression Forming lasting opinions about an individual based on initial perceptions.

projection Overestimating the number of people who share our own beliefs, values, and behaviors.

self-fulfilling prophecy Allowing expectations about people to affect our interaction with them in such a way that those expectations are fulfilled.

FASTFACT

A_KUDR/Shutterstock.com

"Faking Good" Is Our Default Mode of Impression Management

Scientists have examined the brains of people engaged in either "faking good" (giving the best impression) or "faking bad" (giving an undesirable impression) using fMRI, sophisticated brain imaging technology. Faking bad activates distinct regions of the brain and takes longer, whereas faking good happens more quickly and doesn't show as much patterned brain activity. This indicates that faking good may be so well-practiced that it's the default form of impression management.

SOURCE: T. F. D. Farrow, J. Burgess, I. D. Wilkinson, and M. D. Hunter, "Neural Correlates of Self-Deception and Impression Management," *Neuropsychologia* 67 (2015): 159–174.

evaluations, and salary increases. The process by which individuals try to control the impressions others have of them is called **impression management**. Individuals use several techniques to control others' impressions of them.[95]

Some impression management techniques are *self-enhancing*. Name-dropping, or mentioning an association with important people in the hope of improving one's image, is often used. Controlling one's appearance is another self-enhancing technique for impression management. Individuals dress carefully for interviews because they want to "look the part" in order to get the job. Self-descriptions, or statements about one's characteristics, are used to manage impressions as well.

Another group of impression management techniques are *other-enhancing*. They focus on the individual on whom one is trying to make an impression rather than on oneself. People often use flattery and favors to win approval. Agreeing with someone's opinion can create a positive impression. People with disabilities, for example, often use other-enhancing techniques. They may feel that they must take it upon themselves to make others comfortable interacting with them. Impression management techniques help them prevent potential avoidance by others.[96]

Leaders, as the face of organizations, engage in impression management. If the company is in a highly publicized decline and their own compensation depends on company performance, leaders increase their

impression management behaviors.[97] And firms often tailor their impression management techniques to different stakeholders such as local press, international press, and financial analysts, to manipulate each group's view of the company's performance.[98]

So impression management does seem to influence others' impressions. As long as the impressions conveyed are accurate, this process benefits organizations. If the impressions are found to be false, however, the result is a strongly negative overall impression. Furthermore, excessive impression management can lead to the perception that the user is manipulative or insincere.[99]

3-6 ATTRIBUTION IN ORGANIZATIONS

Human beings are innately curious. We want to know *why* people behave the way they do. We also seek to understand and explain our own behavior. **Attribution theory** explains how we pinpoint the causes of our own behavior (and therefore our performance) and that of other people.[100]

3-6a Internal and External Attributions

We can attribute events to an internal source of responsibility (something within the individual's control) or an external source (something outside the individual's control). Suppose you perform well on an exam. You might say you aced the test because you are smart or because you studied hard; this internal attribution credits your ability or effort. Alternatively, you might make an external attribution for your performance by saying it was an easy test or that you had good luck.

Attribution patterns differ among individuals.[101] Achievement-oriented individuals attribute their success to ability and their failures to lack of effort—both internal causes. Failure-oriented individuals attribute their failures to lack of ability and may develop feelings of incompetence (or even depression) as a result.[102] Women managers are less likely to attribute their success to their own ability. This may be because they are adhering to social norms that compel women to be modest or because they believe that success has more do to with hard work than ability.[103]

impression management The process by which individuals try to control the impressions others have of them.

attribution theory A theory that explains how individuals pinpoint the causes of their own and others' behavior.

John Lund/Heather Hryciw/Blend Images/Getty Images

3-6b Attributional Biases

The attribution process may be affected by two very common problems: The first is the tendency to make attributions to internal causes when focusing on someone else's behavior, known as the **fundamental attribution error**.[105] The other error, **self-serving bias**, occurs when focusing on one's own behavior. Individuals tend to make internal attributions for their own successes and external attributions for their own failures.[106] In other words, when we succeed, we take credit for it; when we fail, we blame the situation on other people.

Both biases were illustrated in a study of healthcare managers asked to cite the causes of their employees' poor performance.[107] The managers claimed that internal causes (their employees' lack of effort or lack of ability) explained their employees' poor performance. When the employees were asked to pinpoint the cause of their own performance problems, they blamed a lack of support from the managers (an external cause), which illustrates self-serving bias.

There are cultural differences in these two attribution errors. In fatalistic cultures, such as India, people tend to believe that fate is responsible for much that happens. People in such cultures tend to emphasize external causes of behavior.[108] In China, people are taught that hard work is the route to accomplishment. When faced with either a success or a failure, Chinese individuals first reflect on whether they tried hard enough or whether their attitude was correct. Thus, in analyzing a cause, they first look to their own effort.[109]

The way individuals interpret the events around them has a strong influence on their behavior. People in general try to understand the causes of behavior so that they can predict and control future behavior, and managers certainly do this. Hence, they use attributions in all aspects of their jobs. Especially in evaluating performance and rewarding employees, managers must

Attribution theory has many applications in the workplace. The way you explain your own behavior affects your motivation. If you believe careful preparation and rehearsal led to your successful presentation, you're likely to take credit for the performance and to have a sense of self-efficacy about future presentations. If, however, you believe that you were just lucky, you may not be motivated to repeat the performance because you believe you had little influence on the outcome.

Luck or Skill?

Lots of attributions are made during employment interviews when candidates are asked to explain the causes of previous performance. Candidates want to give interviewers reasons to hire them ("I work well with people, so I'm looking for a managerial job"). Research shows that successful candidates make different attributions for negative outcome than unsuccessful ones. Successful candidates are willing to make internal attributions for negative events. Unsuccessful candidates blame negative outcomes on things beyond their control, giving interviewers the impression that they failed to learn from the event and that they will likely blame others when something goes wrong in the workplace.[104]

fundamental attribution error The tendency to make attributions to internal causes when focusing on someone else's behavior.

self-serving bias The tendency to attribute one's successes to internal causes and one's failures to external causes.

determine the causes of behavior and a perceived source of responsibility.

Attribution theory explains how performance evaluation judgments can lead to differential rewards. A supervisor attributing an employee's good performance to internal causes such as effort or ability may give a larger raise than a supervisor attributing the good performance to external causes like help from others or good training. Managers are often called on to explain their own actions as well, and in doing so they make attributions about the causes of their own behavior. We continue our discussion of attributions in Chapter 6.

STUDY TOOLS 3

LOCATED AT BACK OF THE TEXTBOOK

☐ Rip out chapter review card

LOCATED AT WWW.CENGAGE.COM/LOGIN

☐ Track your knowledge and understanding of key concepts in business using 4LTR Press Online

☐ Review key term flashcards and create your own using StudyBits

☐ Create and complete practice quizzes based off of your notes and StudyBits

☐ Complete Online activities such as Matching and Fill-in-the-Blank exercises

☐ View chapter highlight box content, including the chapter videos, key exhibits and executive profiles.

4 | Attitudes, Emotions, and Ethics

Kaleidoscopic/Shutterstock.com

LEARNING OUTCOMES

4-1 Explain the ABC model of an attitude.

4-2 Describe how attitudes are formed.

4-3 Identify sources of job satisfaction and commitment.

4-4 Distinguish between organizational citizenship and workplace deviance behaviors.

4-5 Identify the characteristics of the source, target, and message that affect persuasion.

4-6 Discuss the definition and importance of emotions at work.

4-7 Contrast the effects of individual and organizational influences on ethical behavior.

4-8 Identify the factors that affect ethical behavior.

After finishing this chapter go to **PAGE 69** for **STUDY TOOLS.**

4-1 ATTITUDES

An **attitude** is a psychological tendency expressed when we evaluate a particular entity with some degree of favor or disfavor.[1] Since we respond favorably or unfavorably toward many things such as coworkers, our own appearance, or politics, we have attitudes toward many things. Attitudes are closely linked to behavior in general, so they are an important factor in organizational behavior. Managers complain about workers with "bad attitudes" and conduct "attitude adjustment" talks. Poor performance attributed to bad attitude can often stem from lack of motivation, minimal feedback, lack of trust in management, or other problems. On the positive side, recognition and praise from colleagues and supervisors can positively impact an individual's attitudes and job performance.[2]

Thus, managers should understand the antecedents to attitudes as well as their consequences. They also need to understand the different components of attitudes, how attitudes are formed, the major attitudes that affect work behavior, and how to use persuasion to change attitudes.

4-1a The ABC Model

An individual does not have an attitude until he or she responds to an entity (person, object, situation, or issue) on an affective, behavioral, or cognitive basis. We can break attitudes down into three components, as depicted in Table 4.1. These three components compose what we call the *ABC model* of an attitude.[3]

Affect is the emotional component of an attitude. It refers to an individual's feeling about something or someone. Statements such as "I like this" or "I prefer that" reflect the affective component of an attitude. Affect can be measured by self-report questionnaires as well as physiological indicators such as blood pressure, which show emotional changes by measuring physiological arousal.

TABLE 4.1   THE ABC MODEL OF AN ATTITUDE

	Component	Measured By	Example
A	Affect	Physiological indicators Verbal statements about feelings	I don't like my boss.
B	Behavioral intent	Observed behavior Verbal statements about intentions	I want to transfer to another department.
C	Cognition	Attitude scales Verbal statements about beliefs	I believe my boss plays favorites at work.

SOURCE: Adapted from M. J. Rosenberg and C. I. Hovland, "Cognitive, Affective, and Behavioral Components of Attitude," in M. J. Rosenberg, C. I. Hovland, W. J. McGuire, R. P. Abelson, and J. H. Brehm, eds., *Attitude Organization and Change* (New Haven, Conn.: Yale University Press, 1960).

We may be supportive, passive, or hostile, depending on our attitude.

Danielala/Shutterstock.com

The second component is *behavioral intent* toward an object or person. Here, it is important to note that a behavioral intent may not actually lead to a particular behavior. But often it does. Our attitudes toward women in management, for example, may be inferred from observing the way we treat a female supervisor. We may be supportive, passive, or hostile, depending on our attitude. The behavioral component of an attitude is measured by observing behavior or by asking a person about behavior or intentions.

The third component of an attitude, *cognition* (thought), reflects a person's perceptions or beliefs. Cognitive elements are evaluative beliefs measured by attitude scales or by asking about thoughts. The statement "I believe Japanese workers are industrious" reflects the cognitive component of an attitude.

The ABC model shows that we must assess all three components to understand an attitude. Suppose, for example, you want to evaluate your employees' attitudes toward *flextime* (flexible work scheduling). You would want to determine how they feel about the policy (affect), whether they would participate in it (behavioral intention), and what they think about it (cognition). The most common method of attitude measurement, however, is the attitude scale, which measures only the cognitive component.

attitude A psychological tendency expressed by evaluating something with a degree of favor or disfavor.

affect The emotional component of an attitude.

4-1b Cognitive Dissonance

As rational beings, people prefer consistency (consonance) between their attitudes and behavior. Anything that disrupts this consistency causes tension (dissonance), which motivates individuals to change either their attitudes or their behavior to maintain consistency. The tension produced by a conflict between attitudes and behavior is **cognitive dissonance**.[4]

Suppose, for example, a salesperson is required to sell damaged televisions for the full retail price without revealing the damage to customers. She believes, however, that this is unethical, which creates a conflict between her attitude (concealing information from customers is unethical) and her behavior (selling defective TVs to uninformed customers). Uncomfortable with the dissonance, she will try to resolve the conflict. She might change her behavior by refusing to sell the defective TV sets. Alternatively, she might rationalize that the defects are minor and that the customers won't be harmed by not knowing about them. These are attempts by the salesperson to restore equilibrium between her attitude and behavior, thereby eliminating the tension from cognitive dissonance.

Managers need to understand cognitive dissonance because employees often find themselves in situations in which their attitudes conflict with their behavior. Employees who display sudden shifts in behavior may be attempting to reduce dissonance. Some employees find the conflicts between strongly held attitudes and required work behavior so uncomfortable that they leave the organization to escape the dissonance.

A salesperson who tries to sell a damaged product for full price may experience cognitive dissonance.

iStockphoto.com/Chris Rose

Direct experience with something strongly influences attitudes toward it. How do you know that you like biology or dislike math? You have probably formed these attitudes from experience studying the subjects. Research has shown that attitudes derived from direct experience are stronger, held more confidently, and more resistant to change than attitudes formed through indirect experience.[5] These attitudes are powerful because of their availability; they are easily accessed and active in our cognitive processes.[6] When attitudes are available, we can call them quickly into consciousness.

In **social learning**, the family, peer groups, religious organizations, and culture shape an individual's attitudes indirectly.[7] Children adopt certain attitudes when their parents reinforce attitudes they approve. This is evident from the fact that very young children express political preferences similar to those held by their parents. Later, peer pressure molds attitudes through group acceptance of individuals who express

4-2 ATTITUDE FORMATION

Attitudes are learned. Our responses to people and issues evolve over time. Two major influences on attitudes are direct experience and social learning.

cognitive dissonance A state of tension produced when an individual experiences conflict between attitudes and behavior.

social learning The process of deriving attitudes from family, peer groups, religious organizations, and culture.

Learning from Observing A Model

For an individual to learn from observing a model, four processes must take place:
1. The learner must focus attention on the model.
2. The learner must retain what was observed from the model. Retention is accomplished in two basic ways:
   • The learner "stamps in" what was observed by forming a verbal code for it.
   • The learner forms a mental image of himself or herself behaving like the model—what is known as *symbolic rehearsal*.
3. The learner must reproduce the behavior through practice.
4. The learner must be motivated to learn from the model.

© Cengage Learning

popular attitudes and through sanctions, such as exclusion from the group, placed on individuals who espouse unpopular attitudes. Substantial social learning occurs through *modeling*, in which individuals acquire attitudes by observing others. After overhearing other individuals expressing opinions or watching them engage in behaviors that reflect an attitude, the observer adopts the attitude.

Culture also plays a definitive role in attitude development. Consider, for example, the contrast in the North American and European attitudes toward vacation and leisure. The typical vacation in the United States is two weeks. In Europe, longer vacations are the norm. In some countries, *holiday* means everyone taking a month off. The European attitude is that an investment in longer vacations is important to health and performance.

4-2a Attitudes and Behavior

The correspondence between attitude and behavior has concerned organizational behaviorists and social psychologists for quite some time. Can attitudes predict behaviors such as being absent from work or quitting your job? Some studies suggested that they can, because attitudes and behavior are closely linked, while others found no relationship at all. Researchers also focused on when attitudes predict behavior and when they do not. Attitude–behavior correspondence depends on five things: attitude specificity, attitude relevance, timing of measurement, personality factors, and social constraints.

Individuals possess both general and specific attitudes. You may favor a woman's right to reproductive freedom (a general attitude) and prefer pro-choice political candidates (a specific attitude) without attending pro-choice rallies or donating to Planned Parenthood. That you don't perform these behaviors appears to weaken the link between your attitude and behaviors. However, given a choice between a pro-choice and an anti-abortion political candidate, you will probably vote for the pro-choice candidate. In this case, your attitude seems quite predictive of your behavior. The more specific the attitude, the stronger is its link to behavior.[8]

Another factor that affects the attitude–behavior link is relevance.[9] Attitudes that address an issue in which we have some self-interest are more relevant for us, and our subsequent behavior is consistent with our expressed attitude. Consider a proposal to raise income taxes for those earning $150,000 or more. If you are a student, you may not find the issue of great personal relevance. Individuals in that income bracket, however, might find it highly relevant. Their attitude toward the issue would be strongly predictive of whether they would vote for the tax increase.

The timing of the measurement is still another factor affecting attitude–behavior correspondence. The shorter the time is between the attitude measurement and the observed behavior, the stronger the relationship. For example, voter preference polls taken close to an election are more accurate than earlier polls.

Personality factors also influence the attitude–behavior link. One personality disposition that affects the consistency between attitudes and behavior is *self-monitoring*. Recall from the discussion of personality characteristics in Chapter 3 that low self-monitors rely on their internal states when making decisions about behavior, while high self-monitors are more responsive to situational cues. Low self-monitors therefore display greater correspondence between their attitudes and behaviors.[10] High self-monitors may display little correspondence between their attitudes and behavior because they behave according to signals from others and from the environment.

Finally, *social constraints* affect the relationship between attitudes and behavior.[11] The social context provides information about acceptable attitudes and behaviors.[12] New employees in an organization are exposed to the attitudes of their work group.[13] A newcomer from Saudi Arabia may hold a negative attitude toward women in management because this attitude prevails in his home culture. He sees, however, that his work group members respond positively to their female supervisor. His own behavior may therefore be compliant because of social constraints even though it is inconsistent with his attitude and cultural belief system.

4-2b Work Attitudes

Attitudes at work are important because, directly or indirectly, they affect work behavior. Chief among the things that negatively affect employees' work attitudes are demanding jobs over which employees have little control.[14] A study concerned with how to prevent turnover in nursing found that commitment to the profession was one factor, but nurses' attitudes were significantly affected by whether or not they had flexibility in their schedules, could get enough time off, and had opportunities to learn new skills and advance. A major factor was the tension between patient care and hospital profits. The nurses in this study said that they felt called to make a difference in their patients' lives, but sometimes worried they could not offer patients adequate care and attention due to competing interests.[15] In contrast to the nursing situation in that study, another study found that a positive psychological climate was enough to generate positive attitudes and good performance in various jobs.[16]

4-3 JOB SATISFACTION

Job satisfaction is a pleasurable or positive emotional state resulting from the appraisal of one's job or job experiences.[17] It has been treated both as a general attitude and as satisfaction with five specific dimensions of the job: pay, the work itself, promotion opportunities, supervision, and coworkers.[18]

An individual may hold different attitudes toward various aspects of a job. For example, an employee may like her job responsibilities but be dissatisfied with the opportunities for promotion. Characteristics of individuals also affect job satisfaction.[19] Those with high negative affectivity are more likely to be dissatisfied with their jobs. Challenging work, valued rewards, opportunities for advancement, competent supervision, and supportive coworkers are dimensions of the job that can lead to satisfaction. What may surprise you is that pay is only marginally related to job satisfaction. Well-paid individuals are only slightly more satisfied than relatively poorly paid individuals.[20]

There are several measures of job satisfaction. One of the most widely used measures comes from the *Job Descriptive Index (JDI)*. This index measures the specific facets of satisfaction by asking employees to respond "yes," "no," or "cannot decide" to a series of statements describing their jobs. Another popular measure is the *Minnesota Satisfaction Questionnaire (MSQ)*.[21] This survey also asks employees to respond to statements about their jobs using a five-point scale that ranges from very dissatisfied to very satisfied. Figure 4.1 presents some sample items from each questionnaire.

Managers and employees believe that happy or satisfied employees are more productive at work. Most of us feel more satisfied than usual when we believe that we are performing better than usual.[22] But research on the relationship between job satisfaction and performance has shown it to be more complex than that. If job satisfaction always improved performance, then the manager's job would simply be to keep workers happy. Although this may be the case for certain individuals, research has shown that job satisfaction for most people is only one of several causes of good performance. Another view holds that good performance causes satisfaction, yet some high performers are not satisfied with their jobs. It is important to consider all of the potential variables when considering job satisfaction.[23]

The lack of a clear relationship between satisfaction and performance can be explained by the intervening role of rewards. Employees who receive valuable rewards are more satisfied. In addition, employees who receive rewards that are contingent on performance (the higher the performance, the larger the reward) tend to perform better. Rewards thus influence both satisfaction and performance. The key to influencing both satisfaction and performance through rewards is that the rewards are valued by employees and are tied directly to performance.

Andresr/Shutterstock.com

job satisfaction A pleasurable or positive emotional state resulting from the appraisal of one's job or job experiences.

FIGURE 4.1 **SAMPLE ITEMS FROM SATISFACTION QUESTIONNAIRES**

Job Descriptive Index

Think of the work you do at present. How well does each of the following words or phrases describe your work? In the blank beside each word given below, write

Y	for "Yes" if it describes your work
N	for "No" if it does NOT describe it
?	if you cannot decide

WORK ON YOUR PRESENT JOB:

_____ Routine
_____ Satisfying
_____ Good

Think of the majority of the people who you work with now or the people you meet in connection with your work. How well does each of the following words or phrases describe these people? In the blank beside each word, write

Y	for "Yes" if it describes the people you work with
N	for "No" if it does NOT describe them
?	if you cannot decide

COWORKERS (PEOPLE):

_____ Boring
_____ Responsible
_____ Intelligent

Minnesota Satisfaction Questionnaire

1 = Very dissatisfied
2 = Dissatisfied
3 = I can't decide whether I am satisfied or not
4 = Satisfied
5 = Very satisfied

On my present job, this is how I feel about:

_____ The chance to work alone on the job (independence)
_____ My chances for advancement on this job (advancement)
_____ The chance to tell people what to do (authority)
_____ The praise I get for a good job (recognition)
_____ My pay and the amount of work I do (compensation)

SOURCE: The Job Descriptive Index is copyrighted by Bowling Green State University. The complete forms, scoring key, instructions, and norms can be obtained from the JDI Office, Department of Psychology, Bowling Green State University, Bowling Green, OH 43403. Minnesota Satisfaction Questionnaire from D. J. Weiss, R. V. Davis, G. W. England, and L. H. Lofquist, *Manual for the Minnesota Satisfaction Questionnaire* (University of Minnesota Vocational Psychology Research, 1967).

4-4 ORGANIZATIONAL CITIZENSHIP VERSUS WORKPLACE DEVIANCE

Job satisfaction encourages **organizational citizenship behavior (OCB)**—behavior that is above and beyond the call of duty. Satisfied employees are more likely to help their coworkers, make positive comments about the company, and refrain from complaining when things at work go poorly.[24] Going beyond the call of duty is especially important to organizations using teams, as employees in teams depend on extra help from each other to get things accomplished.

Satisfied workers are more likely to want to give something back to the organization—that is, to engage in OCBs because they want to reciprocate their positive experiences.[25] Often, employees may feel that their OCBs are not recognized because they occur outside the confines of normal job responsibilities, but they do indeed influence performance evaluations. Employees who help others, suggest innovations, and develop their skills receive higher performance ratings.[26]

OCBs can be directed at different facets of an organization, determined according to individual attitudes. For example, affect tends to direct OCBs toward other people, while cognition directs OCBs toward the organization.

Culture plays a role in where OCBs are directed. In collectivist teams, people who perform OCBs directed toward individuals are rated highly. In individualistic cultures, people who direct their OCBs toward the organization are rated more highly.[27]

When OCBs are the norm within a team, members are more likely to engage in OCBs. The impact of one person's OCB can spread throughout an entire team and spill over into the organization.[28] It should be recognized, though, that employees who over-engage in OCBs can become exhausted because of the toll it takes on their personal energy resources.[29] Organizations can help individuals avoid fatigue and exhaustion from OCBs by providing a supportive environment, encouraging strong teamwork, and by not pressuring employees for OCBs.[30] The impact of one worker's OCBs can thus spread throughout an entire department.

Researchers have found a strong link between job satisfaction and organizational performance, although, as

> **organizational citizenship behavior (OCB)** Behavior that is above and beyond the call of duty.

mentioned earlier, the relationship between the two factors is more complex than one might think. Nevertheless, overall, companies with satisfied workers have better performance than companies with dissatisfied workers.[31] This may be due to the more intangible elements of performance, such as OCB, that contribute to organizational effectiveness but aren't necessarily captured by measuring individual job performance.

Job satisfaction connects to other important outcomes. Dissatisfied workers are more likely to skip work and quit their jobs, driving up the cost of turnover. Furthermore, dissatisfied workers report more psychological and medical problems than do satisfied employees.[32]

One factor that leads to dissatisfaction at work is a misfit between an individual's values and the organization's values, or a lack of *person–organization fit*. People who feel that their values don't mesh with the organization's values experience job dissatisfaction and eventually leave the organization.[33]

Like all attitudes, job satisfaction is influenced by culture. A recent study of job satisfaction rates in forty-nine countries found a close link between job characteristics and job satisfaction in countries with higher incomes, higher individualism, and lower power distance than in countries with lower incomes, lower individualism (higher collectivism), and higher power distance.[34] As employees from different cultures may have differing job expectations, there may be no single prescription for increasing the job satisfaction of a multicultural workforce. Researchers found in China's hotel and restaurant industry that high-performance human resource practices such as promotions from within, flexible job assignments, long-term results-oriented appraisals, and job security fostered service-oriented OCBs. Such OCBs were in turn linked to lower turnover and higher productivity at the organizational level.[35]

When employees are dissatisfied with their jobs, they are more likely to engage in **workplace deviance behavior (WDB)**, which is defined as any voluntary, attitude-driven, counterproductive behavior that violates organizational norms and causes some degree of harm to organizational functioning. Examples of such behavior include gossiping about coworkers, sabotaging others' projects, and theft from the company or colleagues.[36] Negative events in the business world, such as downsizing and technological insecurities, are generally considered responsible for spikes in workplace deviance. Layoffs, for example, may inspire employees to develop negative attitudes, to feel anger and hostility toward the organization, and to retaliate. Even when an employee keeps her job but believes the procedure used to determine the layoff is unfair, she may still take revenge against the manager.[37] Perceived unfairness at work is a major cause of deviance, sabotage, and retaliation. Managers must prevent and manage WDB to keep it from harming performance, and one way to do that is to encourage positive attitudes among employees.

4-4a Organizational Commitment and Job Satisfaction

The strength of an individual's identification with an organization is known as **organizational commitment**. There are three kinds of organizational commitment: affective, continuance, and normative. **Affective commitment** is an employee's intention to remain in an organization because of a strong desire to do so. Affective commitment encompasses loyalty and a deep concern for the organization's welfare based on three factors: a belief in the goals and values of the organization, a willingness to put forth effort on behalf of the organization, and a desire to remain a member of the organization.[38]

Continuance commitment is an employee's tendency to remain in an organization because he cannot afford to leave.[39] Sometimes employees believe that they will lose a great deal of their investments in time, effort, and benefits if they leave. **Normative commitment** is a perceived obligation to remain with the organization. Individuals who experience normative commitment stay with the organization because they feel they should.[40]

Certain organizational conditions, such as participation in decision making and job security, encourage commitment. And so do job characteristics such as autonomy, responsibility, role clarity, and interesting work.[41] Affective and normative commitments are related to lower rates of absenteeism, higher quality of work, increased productivity, and overall performance.[42] Managers should encourage affective commitment in particular because committed individuals expend more task-related effort and are less likely to leave the organization.[43]

---

workplace deviance behavior (WDB) Any voluntary counterproductive behavior that violates organizational norms and causes some degree of harm to organizational functioning.

organizational commitment The strength of an individual's identification with an organization.

affective commitment Organizational commitment based on an individual's desire to remain in an organization.

continuance commitment Organizational commitment based on the fact that an individual cannot afford to leave.

normative commitment Organizational commitment based on an individual's perceived obligation to remain with an organization.

Managers can increase affective commitment by communicating their appreciation of employees' contributions and concern for employees' well-being.[44] Affective commitment also increases when the organization and employees share the same values and when the organization emphasizes values like moral integrity, fairness, creativity, and openness.[45] Negative experiences at work, such as perceived age discrimination, diminish affective commitment.[46]

Affective and normative commitments are related to lower rates of absenteeism, higher quality of work, increased productivity, and overall performance.

4-5 PERSUASION AND ATTITUDE CHANGE

The days of command-and-control management, in which executives simply told employees what to do, are over. Modern managers must instead aim to change employee attitudes and thus need to be skilled in the art of persuasion.[47] Through persuasion, one individual (the source) tries to change the attitude of another person (the target) in regard to a certain issue (the message). Certain characteristics of the source, target, and message affect the persuasion process.

4-5a Source Characteristics

Three major characteristics of the source affect persuasion: expertise, trustworthiness, and attractiveness.[48] A source who is perceived as an expert is particularly persuasive. Testimonials, for example, are the third most effective technique in advertising, after corporate responsibility and emotional appeal. Endorsers of a product are effective when they are perceived as trustworthy, attractive, or similar to the consumer, or when they represent an image the consumer would like to adopt.[49]

4-5b Target Characteristics

Individuals with low self-esteem are more likely to change their attitudes in response to persuasion than are individuals with high self-esteem. Individuals who hold very extreme attitudes are more resistant to persuasion, and people who are in a good mood are easier to persuade.[50] Undoubtedly, individuals differ widely in their responsiveness to persuasion. Managers must recognize these differences and realize that their attempts to change attitudes may not be universally accepted.

4-5c Message Characteristics

Suppose you want to persuade your employees that an unpopular policy is a positive change. Should you present one side of the issue or both sides? Given that your employees are already negatively inclined toward the policy, you will have more success in changing their attitudes if you present both sides. This shows support for one side of the issue while acknowledging that another side does exist. Moreover, refuting the other side rather than ignoring it makes it harder for the targets to hang on to their negative attitudes.

Persuasion is a delicate skill. Undisguised deliberate attempts at changing attitudes may drive employees' attitudes in the opposite direction. This is most likely to occur when the target of the persuasive communication feels her or his freedom is threatened.[51] Less threatening approaches are less likely to elicit negative reactions. The emotional tone of the message is also important. Messages framed with the same emotion as that felt by the receiver are more persuasive.[52]

4-5d Cognitive Routes to Persuasion

The source, target, and message characteristics are weighed differently in the two cognitive routes to persuasion, the central route and the peripheral route, as shown in the *elaboration likelihood model* of persuasion in Figure 4.2.[53] The routes are differentiated by the amount of elaboration, or scrutiny, that the target is motivated to give to the message.

The *central route* to persuasion involves direct cognitive processing of the message's content. In this route, individuals think carefully about issues that are personally relevant. The listener may nod his head at strong arguments and shake his head at weak ones.[54] Logical and convincing arguments are needed to change attitudes by this route.

In the *peripheral route* to persuasion, the individual is not motivated to pay much attention to the message's content because she is distracted or perceives the message as personally irrelevant. Instead, she is persuaded by characteristics of the persuader such as expertise, trustworthiness, and attractiveness. The individual may also be persuaded by statistics, the number of arguments presented, or the method of presentation—none of which relate to the actual content of the message.

FIGURE 4.2 | THE ELABORATION LIKELIHOOD MODEL OF PERSUASION

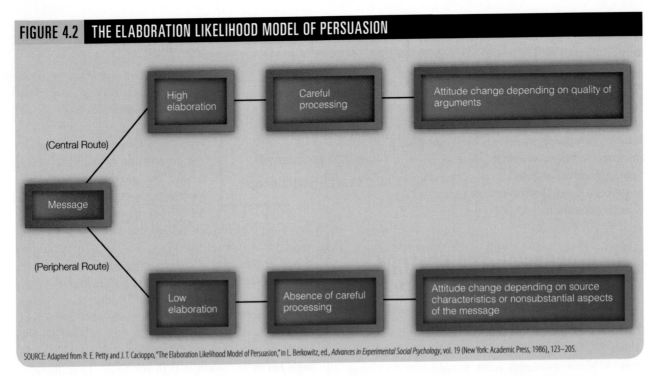

SOURCE: Adapted from R. E. Petty and J. T. Cacioppo, "The Elaboration Likelihood Model of Persuasion," in L. Berkowitz, ed., *Advances in Experimental Social Psychology*, vol. 19 (New York: Academic Press, 1986), 123–205.

The elaboration likelihood model shows that the target's level of involvement with the issue is important. That involvement also determines which route to persuasion will be more effective. In some cases, attitude change comes about through both the central and the peripheral routes. To cover all of the bases, managers should structure the content of their messages carefully, develop their own effective persuasive attributes, and choose a method of presentation that will appeal to the audience.[55]

4-6 EMOTIONS AND MOODS AT WORK

Emotions are discrete and fairly short-lived feelings that have a specific, known cause. An emotion like anger, for example, may arise because a colleague was rude to you. Or you may feel happy because you got a promotion. *Moods*, on the other hand, are typically classified as positive or negative and are made up of various emotions. Moods typically last longer than emotions and don't have a specific cause. Traditional management theories did not place a premium on studying the effects of employees' moods and emotions because they were thought to be bad for rational decision making at work. Ideas about management centered around the stereotypical ideal employee who kept his emotions in

emotions Mental states that include feelings, physiological changes, and the inclination to act.

check and behaved in a totally rational, nonemotional manner. Research has proven that emotions and cognitions are intertwined and that both are normal parts of human functioning and decision making.[56]

4-6a Emotions

Emotions (e.g., anger, joy, pride, hostility) are short-lived, intense reactions to an event. Employees have to cope with both positive and negative events at work on a daily basis, and these events, in turn, lead to emotions. When events at work are positive and goals are being met, employees experience positive emotions. But when events at work are perceived as negative, the opposite can be true.[57] Emotions, in turn, impact both work attitudes and work behaviors.

Different emotions relate to specific facets of job satisfaction. Gratitude, for example, may be related to satisfaction with coworkers or satisfaction with supervisors. Interest, a feeling of curiosity or fascination, may relate to satisfaction with the work itself.[58] Positive emotions produce better cognitive functioning, physical and psychological health, and coping mechanisms.[59] Individuals differ in their capacity to experience both positive emotions (e.g., happiness, pride) and negative emotions (e.g., anger, fear, guilt).[60] People who experience positive emotions tend to do so repeatedly.[61] Overall, people who experience positive emotions are more successful across a variety of life domains and report higher life satisfaction. Negative emotions, on the other hand, lead to unhealthy

Intuit's Emotional Connection with Customers

Intuit, the makers of personal finance software such as QuickBooks, Quicken, and TurboTax, started out with an emphasis on design. Over the years, the company strayed from that focus, but CEO Brad Smith wanted to "design for delight" by thinking about emotions—how customers feel about Intuit products, and whether they take pleasure from using them. To make this happen, the number of designers at Intuit increased 600 percent. They began paying attention to user ratings to see whether the emotion they were creating was the emotion they wanted customers to experience. TurboTax, for example, is the market-leading tax software, and consumers spend six billion hours each year using it. Doing taxes is drudgery, but in the end most taxpayers (70 percent) get refunds, and for some it's the biggest check they will get all year. TurboTax was designed to minimize the hassle and speed the path to a big windfall, a positive emotional event, for customers.

Intuit also incorporated emoticons into its customer interfaces. Smiley faces can be used to show elements that customers like, and sad faces are posted by customers when they hit a snag. Creating emotional connections with customers through product design has paid off. TurboTax revenue increased 7 percent in one year from the redesign. Intuit holds 60 percent of the market share in the do-it-yourself tax software category, while their closest competitor holds 18 percent.

Source: Intuit

SOURCE: B. Smith, "Intuit's CEO on Building a Design-Driven Company," *Harvard Business Review*, January–February (2015): 35–38.

---

coping behaviors and lowered cardiovascular function and physical health.[62]

4-6b Moods

Moods are feeling states that are more enduring than emotions and have no clear cause. Moods are one level above emotions since they are made up of a variety of emotions. Individuals experiencing a strongly positive mood at work feel excited, enthusiastic, and peppy, while individuals experiencing a less positive mood feel dull and sluggish. Individuals experiencing a negative mood at work feel distressed, hostile, or jittery, while those experiencing a less negative mood are calm and relaxed.[63]

Moods may be particularly important in the workplace because they last longer than emotions. Positive moods at work lead to better work performance and OCBs and decrease deviance.[64] Negative moods lead to more turnover intentions and absenteeism.[65] Interestingly, negative moods also increase altruistic behavior and subsequently improve the mood of the altruistic individuals.

4-6c Emotional Contagion at Work

Emotions have far-reaching influence on workplace behavior. They drive employee decision making and are even used as a manipulative tool to ensure desired outcomes from conflicts or negotiations.[66] The influence of emotion at work is extended by **emotional contagion**, which is the dynamic process through which emotions are transferred from one person to another, either consciously or unconsciously, through nonverbal channels.

Emotions need to be managed at work because they spread easily. Emotional contagion occurs primarily through nonverbal cues and the basic human tendency to mimic each other's facial expressions, body language, speech patterns, vocal tones, and even emotions. Contagion affects any job involving interpersonal interaction. Positive emotions that travel through a work group due to emotional contagion produce cooperation and

emotional contagion A dynamic process through which the emotions of one person are transferred to another, either consciously or unconsciously, through nonverbal channels.

task performance.[67] The opposite occurs when negative emotions destroy morale and performance.

When organizations and their employees experience change and/or huge losses, they may struggle to recover. Good leaders can help by using compassion to heal and rebuild employee morale.[68] Organizations need to give employees a comfortable place to share their mutual grief and trauma. These issues can be resolved by caring leaders who are willing to share their emotions with employees.

Edyta Pawlowska/Shutterstock.com

4-6d Emotional Intelligence

Emotional intelligence (EI) is the ability to recognize and manage emotion in oneself and in others. EI is made up of several types of abilities: perceiving, understanding, facilitating, and regulating emotion.[69] This type of intelligence is thought to be an important ability for many types of jobs and to be a fundamental aspect of leadership (see Chapter 12 for more information). EI seems to facilitate job performance in a sequential fashion. Having the ability to perceive emotions allows one to better understand emotions, which then increases emotion regulation. Being able to regulate your emotion, in turn, helps as you display appropriate emotions in the workplace, which allows you to perform better at work. Emotional intelligence helps

you avoid amygdala hijacks, in which the emotional brain runs away with the rational brain. Jet Blue flight attendant Steven Slater's famous rant and exit from the airplane is a well-documented example of an amygdala highjack. Such losses of self-control, if frequent or extreme enough, can cost you your career!

Although self-report measures are often used to measure EI, they are not always accurate, since individuals do not always have a good perspective as to their own abilities. Studies indicate that colleagues are quite accurate in rating an individual's emotional intelligence. Whereas others tend to rate us on our behavior, we tend to rate ourselves on our intentions.[70] Because emotional intelligence shows in our work behavior, the perceptions of coworkers and bosses are essential in understanding our own emotional intelligence.

4-6e Emotional Labor

It is clear that moods and emotions impact employees and organizations a great deal. Positive moods and emotions bring about positive outcomes. This can be particularly true for highly interpersonal jobs like customer service representatives, flight attendants, and, oftentimes, professors,

Google's SIYLI Develops Emotional Intelligence and Mindfulness

Google uses its Search Inside Yourself Leadership Institute (SIYLI) to train leaders in mindfulness practices and emotional intelligence skills. Based on studies of neuroscience, the program is focused on helping leaders become more resilient, more creative, and happier. SIYLI's cofounder and chair, Chade-Meng Tan, is a Google engineer who believes work should be fun and enjoyable, and that it should create the conditions for world peace. Meng, also known as Google's Jolly Good Fellow, connected with emotional intelligence guru Daniel Goleman and mindfulness pioneer Jon Kabat Zinn to create the program, which was tested and refined at Google over a four-year period.

SIYLI is an intense two-day experience in which participants learn to train their attention, develop self-knowledge and self-mastery, and create useful mental habits. More than a thousand Google employees have been through SIYLI training, and there's a lengthy waitlist to get in. Now, SIYLI is offered worldwide. Maybe Meng's vision of creating world peace is not so far-fetched.

SOURCE: silyi.org

Blablo101/Shutterstock.com

HOT TREND

Mindful Facebooking and Less Burnout

The use of social media at work is controversial. Some believe it's a healthy break from demanding work, but others feel it is inappropriate and not a good break because it can be emotionally taxing and detract from getting work done. Some companies even have policies prohibiting the use of social media at work.

Research shows that *mindfulness*, which is bringing a quality of attention to moment-by-moment experience in a nonjudgmental way, can make Facebooking a more effective way of taking a break. People who are mindful can regulate their social media use and not be carried away by the pleasant or unpleasant emotions they experience while Facebooking. Individuals who use Facebook mindfully report lower levels of burnout.

SOURCE: P. Charoensukmongkol, "Mindful Facebooking: The Moderating Role of Mindfulness on the Relationship Between Social Media Use Intensity at Work and Burnout," *Journal of Health Psychology*, published online February 15, 2015.

who are expected to express positive emotions and suppress any anger or hostility they may be feeling. *Emotional labor* is the work that employees do to control their feelings and expression of emotions in the workplace and is a type of emotion regulation.[71]

Often organizations have specific rules regarding emotional expression called *display rules*. There are two primary types of emotional labor used to meet these display rules: deep acting and surface acting. *Deep acting* involves attempting to feel the emotion one is displaying. Picturing a beautiful mountain vista or thinking about a pleasant memory are examples of deep acting. *Surface acting* is faking an emotion to meet the display rules. Surface acting causes *emotional dissonance*, or a discrepancy between one's felt emotion and one's expressed emotion. Surface acting can result in negative outcomes such as burnout, negative mood, and work withdrawal. Deep acting, in general, seems to have positive consequences and has been related to positive mood at work as well as high-quality customer service performance and reduced burnout.[72]

4-7 ETHICAL BEHAVIOR

Ethics is the study of moral values and moral behavior. **Ethical behavior** involves acting in ways consistent with one's personal values and the commonly held values of the organization and society.[73] Paying attention to ethical issues pays off for companies. In the early 1990s, James Burke, then CEO of Johnson & Johnson, put together a list of companies committed to ethics. The group included Johnson & Johnson, Coca-Cola, Gerber, Kodak, 3M, and Pitney Bowes. A recent study showed that over a forty-year period, the market value of these organizations grew at an annual rate of 11.3 percent, as compared to 6.2 percent for the Dow Jones industrials as a whole.[74] Doing the right thing can have a positive effect on an organization's performance.[75]

Ethical behavior in firms can also lead to practical benefits, particularly by attracting new talent. Firms with better reputations attract more applicants, creating a larger hiring pool, and evidence suggests that respected firms can choose higher-quality applicants.[76] For example, Timberland's strong value system helps the company attract and recruit the best talent and maintain a solid reputation with investors.

Failure to handle situations ethically can hurt companies. Employees who are laid off or terminated are very concerned about the quality of treatment they receive. Honestly explaining the reasons for the dismissal and preserving the dignity of the employee will reduce the likelihood of employees initiating a claim against the company. One study showed that less than 1 percent of employees who felt the company was being honest filed a claim. More than 17 percent of those who felt the company was being less than honest filed claims.[77] Conversely, ethical actions can be a boon to organizations. Australia's former prime minister, Kevin Rudd, apologized publicly for the ill treatment of Aborigines on the part of the national government. Even before the issue of financial compensation was addressed, this action built trust and hope among Australians of all races.[78]

Unethical behavior by employees can affect individuals, work teams, and even the organization. Organizations thus depend on individuals to act ethically. For this reason, more and more firms are starting to monitor their employees' Internet usage. Although some employees complain that this monitoring violates their privacy, the courts tend to disagree, arguing that companies have the right to monitor employees' use of company-owned hardware and software.

ethical behavior Acting in ways consistent with one's personal values and the commonly held values of the organization and society.

A_KUDR/Shutterstock.com

FASTFACT

What Is a B Corp?

B Corps (Certified Benefit Corporations) are companies that use the power of business as a force for good. To be designated a B Corp, a company must meet tough standards in environmental performance, social responsibility, accountability, and transparency. Today, there are more than one thousand certified B Corps in more than thirty countries representing sixty different industries. B Corps aim not only to be the best in the world but also to be the best for the world. For example, when compared to other sustainable businesses, B Corps are more likely to donate at least 10 percent of their profits to charity, use on-site renewable energy, and use suppliers from low-income communities. B Corps you may recognize include Ben & Jerry's, Patagonia, Warby Parker, and Klean Kanteen, among others.

SOURCE: bcorporation.net

Michael Smyth was fired from his job with Pillsbury Company after employees read inflammatory comments he made in several e-mails to his supervisor. Smyth sued for wrongful termination, claiming that the firm had violated his right to privacy after telling employees their e-mail would remain confidential. Despite these promises, the court ruled that Smyth had no reasonable expectation of privacy while using the firm's equipment. Further, it said, Smyth's right to privacy was outweighed by the firm's need to conduct business in a professional manner. Only future court cases will clarify where a firm's effort to monitor potentially unethical behavior actually violates its own ethical code.[79] Nonetheless, today's high-intensity business environment only increases the need for strong ethics programs.

Managers often struggle to align the ideal of ethical behavior with the reality of everyday business practices. Violations of the public's trust are costly. When Mattel recalled 20.5 million toys that were manufactured in China because they contained lead, its public image suffered greatly. The company attempted to undo the damages through a national advertising campaign.[80] Firms can experience lower accounting returns and slow sales growth for as long as five years after having been convicted of illegal corporate behavior.[81]

Individuals face complex ethical issues at work. A one-week review of *The Wall Street Journal* revealed more than sixty articles dealing with ethical issues in business.[82] As Table 4.2 suggests, few of these issues are clear-cut. They depend on the specifics of the situation,

TABLE 4.2	ETHICAL ISSUES FROM ONE WEEK IN THE LIFE OF *THE WALL STREET JOURNAL*
1. Stealing	Taking things that don't belong to you
2. Lying	Saying things you know aren't true
3. Fraud and deceit	Creating or perpetuating false impressions
4. Conflict of interest and influence buying	Bribes, payoffs, and kickbacks
5. Hiding or divulging information	Concealing information that another party has a right to know or failing to protect personal or proprietary information
6. Cheating	Taking unfair advantage of a situation
7. Personal decadence	Aiming below excellence in terms of work performance (e.g., careless or sloppy work)
8. Interpersonal abuse	Behaviors that are abusive of others (e.g., sexism, racism, emotional abuse)
9. Organizational abuse	Organizational practices that abuse members (e.g., inequitable compensation, misuses of power)
10. Rule violations	Breaking organizational rules
11. Accessory to unethical acts	Knowing about unethical behavior and failing to report it
12. Ethical dilemmas	Choosing between two equally desirable or undesirable options

SOURCE: Kluwer Academic Publishers and Journal of Business Ethics, 11, 1992, 255–265, A Menu of Moral Issues: One Week in the Life of The Wall Street Journal, J. O. Cherrington and D. J. Cherrington, with kind permission from Springer Science+Business Media B.V.

and their interpretation depends on the characteristics of the individuals examining them. Consider lying, for instance. Many business people tell white lies. Is this acceptable? The perception of what constitutes ethical versus unethical behavior in organizations varies among individuals.

© Cengage Learning

FIGURE 4.3 INDIVIDUAL/ORGANIZATIONAL MODEL OF ETHICAL BEHAVIOR

Individual influences
Value systems
Locus of control
Machiavellianism
Cognitive moral development

Ethical behavior

Organizational influences
Codes of conduct
Ethics committees or officers
Training programs
Ethics communication systems
Norms
Modeling
Rewards and punishments

4-8 FACTORS THAT AFFECT ETHICAL BEHAVIOR

Two sets of factors—individual characteristics and organizational factors—influence ethical behavior.[83] In this section, we'll look at the individual influences on ethical behavior. Ethical decision making requires three qualities of individuals[84]:

1. The competence to identify ethical issues and evaluate the consequences of alternative courses of action.

2. The self-confidence to seek out different opinions about the issue and decide what is right in terms of a particular situation.

3. Tough-mindedness—the willingness to make decisions when all that needs to be known cannot be known and when the ethical issue has no established, unambiguous solution.

Which individual characteristics lead to these qualities? According to our model, they are value systems, locus of control, Machiavellianism, and cognitive moral development. Figure 4.3 illustrates these, as well as the organizational influences, which we will examine throughout the remainder of the book.

4-8a Values

Different values generate different ethical behaviors. **Values** are enduring beliefs that a specific mode of conduct or end state of existence is personally or socially preferable to an opposite or converse mode of conduct or end state of existence.[85] This definition was proposed by Rokeach, an early scholar of human values. As individuals grow and mature, they learn values, although these may change as an individual develops a sense of self. Cultures, societies, and organizations shape values. Parents and other respected role models influence value development by providing guidance about what is right and wrong. Like general beliefs about right and wrong, values form the basis for ethical behavior. Though values vary widely among individuals, we use them to evaluate our own behavior and that of others.

INSTRUMENTAL AND TERMINAL VALUES Rokeach distinguished between two types of values: instrumental and terminal. **Instrumental values** shape the acceptable behaviors that can be used to achieve some goal or end state. Instrumental values identified by Rokeach include ambition, honesty, self-sufficiency, and courage. **Terminal values** influence the goals to be achieved or the end states of existence. Rokeach identified happiness, love, pleasure, self-respect, and freedom among the terminal values.

values Enduring beliefs that a specific mode of conduct or end state of existence is personally or socially preferable to an opposite or converse mode of conduct or end state of existence.

instrumental values Values that shape the acceptable behaviors that can be used to achieve some goal or end state.

terminal values Values that influence the goals to be achieved or the end states of existence.

TABLE 4.3 INSTRUMENTAL AND TERMINAL VALUES

INSTRUMENTAL VALUES		
Honesty	Ambition	Responsibility
Forgiveness	Open-mindedness	Courage
Helpfulness	Cleanliness	Competence
Self-control	Affection/love	Cheerfulness
Independence	Politeness	Intelligence
Obedience	Rationality	Imagination
TERMINAL VALUES		
World peace	Family security	Freedom
Happiness	Self-respect	Wisdom
Equality	Salvation	Prosperity
Achievement	Friendship	National security
Inner peace	Mature love	Social respect
Beauty in art and nature	Pleasure	Exciting, active life

SOURCE: Based on *The Nature of Human Values* by Milton Rokeach.

Table 4.3 gives a complete list of instrumental and terminal values. Terminal and instrumental values work in concert by providing individuals with goals to strive for and acceptable ways to achieve those goals.

Americans' rankings of instrumental and terminal values have been remarkably stable over time.[86] The highest ranked instrumental values were honesty, ambition, responsibility, forgiveness, open-mindedness, and courage. The highest ranked terminal values were world peace, family security, freedom, happiness, self-respect, and wisdom.

Age also affects values. Baby boomers' values contrast with those of the baby busters, who are beginning to enter the workforce. The baby busters value family life and time off from work and want to balance work and home life. This contrasts with the more driven, work-oriented value system of the boomers. The baby boomers place a huge emphasis on achievement values at work. Their successors in Generations X and Y are markedly different. Generation X values self-reliance, individualism, and balance between family and work life. Generation Y values freedom in scheduling and embraces a work-to-live mind-set rather than the live-to-work approach of the baby boomers.[87]

WORK VALUES Work values influence individuals' perceptions of right and wrong on the job.[88] Four work values are achievement, concern for others, honesty, and fairness.[89] *Achievement* is a concern for the advancement of one's career; it drives people to work hard and seek opportunities to develop new skills. *Concern for others* is shown in caring, compassionate behaviors such as encouraging others or helping them with difficult tasks. These behaviors also constitute organizational citizenship. *Honesty* is providing accurate information and refusing to mislead others for personal gain. *Fairness* means remaining impartial while recognizing different points of view.

Individuals rank these values in terms of their relative importance in their work lives.[90] Employees who share their supervisor's values are more satisfied with their jobs and more committed to the organization.[91] Values also have profound effects on job choice. Although traditionally pay and advancement potential have had the strongest influences on job choice decisions, one study found that three other work values—achievement, concern for others, and fairness—had greater influence.[92] This means that organizations recruiting job candidates should pay careful attention to individuals' values and to the messages their organizations send about company values.

CULTURAL DIFFERENCES IN VALUES Organizations facing the challenges of an increasingly diverse workforce and a global marketplace must understand culture's influence on values. Doing business in a global marketplace often means encountering a clash of values among different cultures. Consider loyalty, for example. In Japan, loyalty means "compassionate overtime." Even when you have no work yourself, you should stay late to provide moral support for your peers who are working late.[93] In contrast, Koreans value loyalty to the person for whom one works.[94] In the United States, family and other personal loyalties are held above loyalty to the company or one's supervisor.

Cultures differ in the individual contributions they value at work. Collectivist cultures like China and Mexico value a person's contributions to relationships in the work team. By contrast, individualist cultures (the United States, the Netherlands) value a person's contribution to task accomplishment. Both collectivist and individualist cultures, however, value rewards based on individual performance.[95] Iran's collectivist managers demonstrate little tolerance for ambiguity, high need for structure, and willingness to sacrifice for the good of society—all values they derive from Islam, which promotes belonging, harmony, humility, and simplicity.[96]

Values also affect individuals' views of what constitutes authority. French managers value authority as a right of office and rank. Their behavior reflects this value, as they tend to exercise power based on their position in the organization. By contrast, managers from the Netherlands value group inputs to decisions and expect employees to challenge and discuss their decisions.[97]

We may be prone to judging the value systems of others, but we should resist this tendency. Tolerating diverse values can help us understand other cultures. The value systems of other nations are not necessarily right or wrong; they are merely different.

4-8b Locus of Control

Another individual influence on ethical behavior is locus of control. Recall from Chapter 3 that individuals with an internal locus of control believe that they control events in their lives and that they are responsible for their own experiences. Those with an external locus of control believe that outside forces such as fate, chance, or other people control what happens to them.[98]

Internals are more likely than externals to take personal responsibility for the consequences of their ethical or unethical behavior. Externals are more apt to believe that external forces caused their ethical or unethical behavior. Research has shown that internals make more ethical decisions than do externals.[99] Internals also are more resistant to social pressure and are less willing to hurt another person even if ordered to do so by an authority figure.[100]

4-8c Machiavellianism

Machiavellianism also influences ethical behavior. Niccolò Machiavelli was a sixteenth-century Italian statesman famous for writing *The Prince*, a guide for acquiring and using power.[101] He suggested that manipulating others was the best way to achieve power. **Machiavellianism**, then, is a personality characteristic involving one's willingness to do whatever it takes to get one's own way.

A high-Mach individual operates from the notion that it is better to be feared than loved. High-Machs tend to be deceitful, have a cynical view of human nature, and care little for conventional notions of right and wrong.[102] They are skilled manipulators, relying on their persuasive abilities. Low-Machs, in contrast, value loyalty and relationships. They are less willing to manipulate others for personal gain and are concerned with others' opinions.

High-Machs believe that the desired ends justify any means, so they feel it's fine to manipulate others in order to achieve a goal.[103] They are emotionally detached from other people and focus on the objective aspects of situations. High-Machs are also more likely to engage in ethically questionable behavior.[104] Employees can counter Machiavellian individuals by focusing on teamwork instead of one-on-one relationships where high-Machs have the upper hand. Making interpersonal agreements public reduces their susceptibility to Machiavellian manipulation.

4-8d Cognitive Moral Development

An individual's level of **cognitive moral development** also affects ethical behavior. Psychologist Lawrence Kohlberg proposed that as individuals mature, they move through a series of six stages of moral development (Table 4.4).[105] With each successive stage, they become less dependent on other people's opinions of right and wrong and less self-centered (focusing less on their own interests). At higher levels of moral development, individuals are concerned with broad principles of justice and with their self-chosen ethical principles. Kohlberg's model focuses on the decision-making process and on how individuals justify ethical decisions. His cognitive developmental theory explains how people decide what is right and wrong and how the decision-making process changes through interaction with peers and the environment.

Cognitive moral development occurs at three levels, each consisting of two stages. At Level I, called the *premoral level*, a person's ethical decisions are based on rewards, punishments, and self-interest. In Stage 1, people obey rules to avoid punishment. In Stage 2, people obey rules only if it is in their immediate interest to do so.

> **Machiavellianism** A personality characteristic involving one's willingness to do whatever it takes to get one's own way.
>
> **cognitive moral development** The process of moving through stages of maturity with regard to making ethical decisions.

TABLE 4.4   KOHLBERG'S STAGES OF COGNITIVE MORAL DEVELOPMENT

Level I	Premoral	Reward, punishment, self-interest
Level II	Conventional	Expectations of other people and society
Level III	Principled	Universal values and personal ethical principles

© Cengage Learning

At Level II, the *conventional level*, people focus on the expectations of others. In Stage 3, individuals try to live up to the expectations of people close to them. In Stage 4, they broaden their perspective to include the laws and norms of the larger society. They fulfill duties and obligations to contribute to society.

At Level III, the *principled level*, universal values determine what is right. The individual sees beyond laws, rules, and the expectations of other people. In Stage 5, individuals are aware that people have diverse value systems. They uphold their own values even if others disagree. Individuals in Stage 5 make decisions based on principles of justice and rights. For example, someone who decides to picket an abortion clinic just because his religion bans abortion is not a Stage 5 individual. A person who arrives at the same decision through a complex decision process based on justice and rights may be a Stage 5 individual. The key is the process rather than the decision itself. In Stage 6, the individual follows self-selected ethical principles. Stage 6 individuals act according to their own self-selected

ethical principles, even when these principles conflict with a law.

As individuals mature, their moral development passes through these stages in an irreversible sequence. Research suggests that most adults are in Stage 3 or 4. Most adults thus never reach the principled level of development (Stages 5 and 6).

Kohlberg's model of cognitive moral development has been supported by a great deal of research since it was proposed more than thirty years ago. Individuals at higher stages of development are less likely to cheat, more likely to engage in whistle-blowing, and more likely to make ethical business decisions.[106]

But Kohlberg's model has also been criticized. Carol Gilligan, for example, argues that the model does not take gender differences into account. Kohlberg's model was developed from a twenty-year study of eighty-four boys.[107] Gilligan contends that women's moral development follows a different pattern, one based not on individual rights and rules but on responsibility and relationships. Women and men face the same moral dilemmas but approach them from different perspectives—men from the perspective of equal respect and women from the perspective of compassion and care. But researchers who reviewed the research on these gender differences concluded that the differences may not be as strong as Gilligan originally suggested.[108]

In general, though, evidence supports the idea that men and women view ethics differently. A large-scale review of sixty-six studies found that women were more likely than men to perceive certain business practices as unethical. Young women were more likely than young men to see breaking the rules and acting on insider information as unethical. Both sexes agreed that collusion, conflicts of interest, and stealing are unethical. It takes about twenty-one years for this gender gap to disappear. Men seem to become more ethical with more work experience; the longer they are in the workforce, the more their attitudes resemble those held by women. That said, age and experience are related for both sexes. Experienced workers of either sex are more likely to think that lying, bribing, stealing, and colluding are unethical.[109]

Individual differences in values, locus of control, Machiavellianism, and cognitive moral development all influence ethical behavior in organizations. Organizations might use this knowledge to promote ethical behavior by hiring individuals who share the organization's

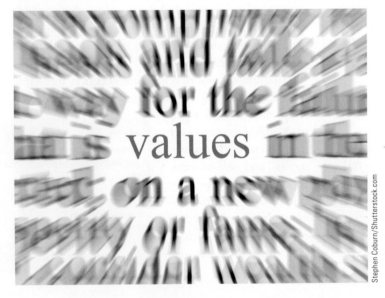

Stephen Coburn/Shutterstock.com

values or hiring only internals, low-Machs, and individuals at higher stages of cognitive moral development. Such strategies, however, obviously present both practical and legal problems.

Training may be a safer way to use this knowledge. Evidence suggests that training can increase cognitive moral development. Organizations could help individuals move to higher stages of moral development by providing educational seminars. That said, values, locus of control, Machiavellianism, and cognitive moral development are fairly stable in adults.

The best way to use the knowledge of individual differences may be to recognize that they help explain why ethical behavior differs among individuals and to focus managerial efforts on creating a work situation supporting ethical behavior.

Most workers are responsive to external influences. They do not act as independent ethical agents but look to their organization for guidance. Managers can offer such guidance by exercising the organizational influences listed in Figure 4.3. They can encourage ethical behavior through codes of conduct, ethics committees, ethics communication systems, training, norms, modeling, and rewards and punishments, as shown in Figure 4.3. We discuss these areas further in Chapter 16.

STUDY TOOLS 4

LOCATED AT BACK OF THE TEXTBOOK

☐ Rip out chapter review card

LOCATED AT WWW.CENGAGE.COM/LOGIN

☐ Track your knowledge and understanding of key concepts in business using 4LTR Press Online

☐ Review key term flashcards and create your own using StudyBits

☐ Create and complete practice quizzes based off of your notes and StudyBits

☐ Complete Online activities such as Matching and Fill-in-the-Blank exercises

☐ View chapter highlight box content, including the chapter videos, key exhibits and executive profiles.

5 | Motivation at Work

Monkey Business Images/Shutterstock.com

LEARNING OUTCOMES

5-1 Define motivation and articulate different views of how individuals are motivated at work.

5-2 Explain Maslow's hierarchy of needs and its two main modifications.

5-3 Discuss how the needs for achievement, power, and affiliation influence an individual's behavior in the workplace.

5-4 Describe the two-factor theory of motivation.

5-5 Explain two new ideas in human motivation.

5-6 Describe the role of inequity in motivation.

5-7 Describe the expectancy theory of motivation.

5-8 Describe the cultural differences in motivation.

After finishing this chapter go to **PAGE 83** for **STUDY TOOLS.**

5-1 MOTIVATION AND WORK BEHAVIOR

Motivation is the process of arousing and sustaining goal-directed behavior. Motivation theories attempt to explain and predict observable behavior. They may be broadly classified into internal, process, and external theories. *Internal theories* of motivation give primary consideration to variables within the individual that lead to motivation and behavior. Maslow's hierarchy of needs is a good example of an internal theory. *Process theories* of motivation, such as expectancy theory, emphasize the nature of the interaction between the individual and the environment. *External theories* of motivation focus on the elements in the environment, including the consequences of behavior, as the basis for understanding and explaining people's behavior at work. Any single motivation theory explains only a small portion of the variance in human behavior, so researchers have developed many alternative theories to account for unexplained behavior. A comprehensive approach to understanding motivation, behavior, and performance must consider three elements of the work situation—the individual, the job, and the work environment—and how these elements interact.[1]

5-1a Internal Needs

Philosophers and scholars have theorized for centuries about human needs and motives. During the past century, researchers have focused on motivation in a business context.[2] Max Weber, an early German sociologist, argued that the meaning of work lies not in the work itself but in its deeper potential for contributing to a person's ultimate salvation.[3] Weber, and later Milton Blood, understood this *Protestant ethic*, with its foundations in Calvinist thought, as the fuel for human industriousness. The Protestant ethic encouraged hard work on the grounds that prosperous workers were more likely to find a place in heaven.

Sigmund Freud proposed a more complex motivational theory, suggesting that a person's organizational life was founded on the compulsion to work and the power of love.[4] He emphasized the unconscious mind's influence on human motivation. **Psychoanalysis** is Freud's method for delving into the unconscious mind to better understand a person's motives and needs. Thus, the psychoanalytic approach can help explain irrational and self-destructive behaviors such as suicide or workplace violence.[5] Analyzing a person's unconscious needs and motives can help us understand such traumatic work events. The psychoanalytic approach also helps explain deviant behavior in the workplace.

Freud's thought served as the basis for subsequent *need theories* of motivation. Research suggests that people's deeper feelings transcend culture, with most people caring deeply about the same few things. Factors that make employees motivated and loyal to the organization include fair compensation and the trust and respect of their supervisors. Intrinsic motivation varies by the individual and has a positive effect on individual personality traits. For example, an employee who performs a work task for the pure satisfaction of doing so tends to be more conscientious, open to experience, and agreeable the following day.[6] Managers who are more supportive and less controlling appear to elicit more intrinsic motivation from their employees.

5-1b External Incentives

Most economic assumptions about human motivation emphasize financial incentives. The Scottish political economist and moral philosopher Adam Smith argued that a person's **self-interest** was determined by God, not the government.[7] Smith laid the cornerstone for the free enterprise system of economics when he formulated the so-called invisible hand and the free market to explain the motivation for individual behavior. The "invisible hand" refers to the unseen forces of a free market system that shape the most efficient use of people, money, and resources for productive ends. Smith assumed that people are motivated by self-interest for economic gain to provide

> A comprehensive approach to understanding motivation, behavior, and performance must consider all three elements of the work situation and how they interact.

Danielala/Shutterstock.com

motivation The process of arousing and sustaining goal-directed behavior.

psychoanalysis Sigmund Freud's method for delving into the unconscious mind to better understand a person's motives and needs.

self-interest What is in the best interest of and benefit to an individual.

Intrinsic Factors and External Incentives Work Together to Improve Employee Performance

Which affects employee performance more, intrinsic rewards or external incentives? According to a recent study, it depends. Researchers reviewed four decades of research and nine previous meta-analyses to answer that question along with other questions about the relative impact of intrinsic versus extrinsic motivation on performance outcomes. They found that both are instrumental. However, the most *important* method depended on the performance context. Intrinsic motivation was a better predictor of performance when quality was desired. For those tasks that require a great deal of personal investment, require judgment, or are complex, intrinsic motivation mattered most. On the other hand, external incentives were a better predictor of performance for quantity, when tasks were straightforward, noncomplex, and repetitive. Motivation tactics do not work in isolation. Managers should consider the desired performance to determine whether to rely on intrinsic rewards or external incentives to motivate employee behavior.

SOURCE: C. P. Cerasoli, J. M. Nicklin, and M. T. Ford, "Intrinsic Motivation and Extrinsic Incentives Jointly Predict Performance: A 40-Year Meta-Analysis," *Psychological Bulletin* 140 (2014): 980–1008.

the necessities and conveniences of life. Thus, employees are most productive when motivated by self-interest.

The more collective wealth an economy can produce, the better individuals can fulfill their self-interest. Technology and labor efficiency are two ways of promoting greater collective wealth. Technology is crucial to Smith's view because he believed that the productivity of a nation's labor force determines its wealth. Therefore, a more efficient and effective labor force yields greater abundance for the nation. Technology acts as a force multiplier for the productivity of labor.[8]

Frederick Taylor, the founder of *scientific management*, also examined labor efficiency and effectiveness.[9] His goal was to change the relationship between management and labor from one of conflict to one of cooperation.[10] Taylor believed the basis of the conflict was the division of the profits. Instead of continuing this conflict, labor and management should work together to enlarge total profits.

Early organizational scholars assumed that people were motivated by self-interest and economic gain. Consequently, they developed differential piece-rate systems of pay emphasizing external incentives. Modern management practices, such as employee recognition programs, flexible benefit packages, and stock ownership plans, stem from Smith's and Taylor's original theories. They emphasize external incentives, which may take either strictly economic form or more material form, such as outstanding employee plaques. Whataburger has developed the WhataGames in which the best employees compete for bragging rights and medals.[11] This training-and-loyalty exercise reduces turnover and builds commitment.

Some approaches, however, suggest that economic motives alone are not sufficient and need to be combined with other external motives. The Hawthorne studies, mentioned in Chapter 1 as the first to recognize informal aspects of an organization, also studied what motivates people to be productive. They confirmed the positive effects of pay incentives on productivity but also demonstrated the importance of social and interpersonal motives.[12] Other people constitute yet another external motive. Executives have recently championed so-called enlightened self-interest. Self-interest is concern for one's own needs; enlightened self-interest recognizes others' interests as well.

In still other approaches, external and internal motivations are combined. Psychological ownership considers both psychological needs and external incentives to motivate workers. One study of 800 managers and employees in three different organizations found that "feelings of ownership" of an organization increased organizational citizenship behavior.[13]

 ## 5-2 MASLOW'S NEED HIERARCHY

Abraham Maslow, a psychologist, proposed a theory of motivation that went beyond just physical and economic needs to emphasize psychological and interpersonal needs as well. The core of Maslow's theory is a hierarchy of five categories of need.[14] Although he recognized that factors other than one's needs (e.g., culture) determine behavior, his theory focused on specifying people's internal needs. As shown in Figure 5.1, Maslow labeled the five levels of his *need hierarchy* as physiological needs, safety and security needs, love (social) needs, esteem needs, and the need for self-actualization. He conceptually derived the five need categories from the early thoughts of William James and John Dewey, coupled with the psychodynamic thinking of Sigmund Freud and Alfred Adler.[15]

One distinguishing feature of Maslow's need hierarchy is the *progression hypothesis,* which suggests that as one level of need is met, a person progresses to the next higher level of need as a source of motivation. Hence, people progress up the hierarchy as they successively gratify each level of need. Maslow understood the lowest level of ungratified needs to motivate behavior, although some research has challenged this view.[16]

Managers can make the most of Maslow's need hierarchy for success in their teams by recognizing that each individual has a unique set of needs and therefore gearing incentives to meet various needs. An ergonomic work space, for example, can fill physiological needs by making an employee comfortable in the work space. The need for security might be filled by a good retirement plan. Some employees have a high need for social interaction, and opportunities for after-work tennis or racquetball may fill those needs. Needs for status and self-actualization can be filled by opportunities to

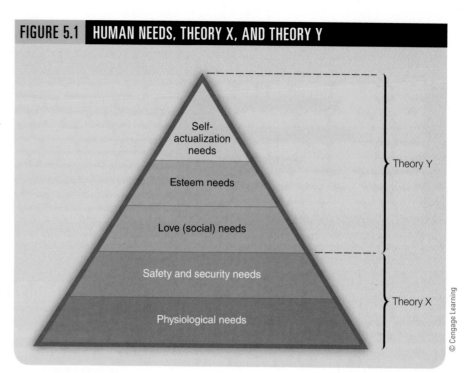

FIGURE 5.1 HUMAN NEEDS, THEORY X, AND THEORY Y

© Cengage Learning

Sergey Nivens/Shutterstock.com

Self-interest is concern for one's own needs; enlightened self-interest recognizes others' interests as well.

work with higher-ups or to work on projects that particularly suit the individual's skills and interests.[17]

5-2a Theory X and Theory Y

Maslow's need hierarchy has been applied to organizational behavior in two key ways. Douglas McGregor strove to explain motivation by grouping the physiological and safety needs as lower-order needs and the social, esteem, and self-actualization needs as upper-order needs. According to McGregor's theory, managers can make one of two sets of assumptions about an individual depending on the factors that motivate his or her behavior. McGregor's **Theory X** assumptions are appropriate for employees motivated by lower-order needs, while **Theory Y** assumptions apply to employees motivated by higher-order needs. These assumptions are listed in Table 5.1 and have been mapped onto Maslow's hierarchy, from which they derive, in Figure 5.1.[18] McGregor understood the responsibility of management to be the same under both sets of assumptions. Specifically, "Management is responsible for organizing the elements of productive enterprise—money, materials, equipment, people—in the interest of economic ends."[19] Theory Y assumptions have inspired employee participation programs, and

Theory X A set of assumptions managers might apply to individuals who are motivated by lower-order needs.

Theory Y A set of assumptions managers might apply to individuals who are motivated by higher-order needs.

TABLE 5.1 | MCGREGOR'S ASSUMPTIONS ABOUT PEOPLE

Theory X	Theory Y
> People are by nature indolent. That is, they work as little as possible.	> People are not by nature passive or resistant to organizational needs. They have become so as a result of experience in organizations.
> People lack ambition, dislike responsibility, and prefer to be led.	> The motivation, the potential for development, the capacity for assuming responsibility, and the readiness to direct behavior toward organizational goals are all present in people. Management does not put them there. It is a responsibility of management to make it possible for people to recognize and develop these human characteristics for themselves.
> People are inherently self-centered and indifferent to organizational needs.	
> People are by nature resistant to change.	
> People are gullible and not very bright, the ready dupes of the charlatan and the demagogue.	> The essential task of management is to arrange conditions and methods of operation so that people can achieve their own goals best by directing their own efforts toward organizational objectives.

SOURCE: Excerpted by permission of the publisher, from the "MacGregor's Assumptions about People" from Management Review, November 1957, American Management Association, New York, NY. All rights reserved. www.amanet.org

Fortune 1000 corporations use employee involvement to encourage high-performance achievements.[20] Employees are more likely to identify with and motivated to achieve organizational outcomes when leaders formulate messages appropriately.[21] Whole Foods founder and CEO John Mackey relies on Maslow's hierarchy of needs in motivating employees.[22]

5-2b ERG Theory

Clayton Alderfer recognized Maslow's contribution to understanding motivation yet believed that the original need hierarchy didn't accurately identify and categorize human needs.[23] He proposed the **ERG theory** of motivation, which grouped human needs into only three basic categories: existence, relatedness, and growth.[24] Alderfer classified Maslow's physiological and physical safety needs in an *existence need* category. The interpersonal safety, love, and interpersonal esteem needs were reclassified in a *relatedness need* category. Finally, a *growth need* category encompassed Maslow's self-actualization and self-esteem needs.

ERG theory also supplemented Maslow's original progression hypothesis with a *regression hypothesis*. Alderfer's regression hypothesis suggests that when people are frustrated by their inability to meet needs at the next higher level in the hierarchy, they regress to the next lower category of needs and intensify their desire to gratify those needs. Hence, ERG theory explains both progressive need gratification and regression when people face frustration.

ERG theory A theory that organizes human needs into the categories of existence, relatedness, and growth.

manifest needs Learned or acquired needs that are easily perceived.

need for achievement A manifest need that concerns excellence, competition, challenging goals, persistence, and overcoming difficulties.

5-3 McCLELLAND'S NEED THEORY

A second major need theory of motivation focuses on personality and learned needs. Henry Murray developed a long list of motives and manifest needs in his early studies of personality.[25] Inspired by Murray's work, David McClelland identified three learned, or acquired, needs, called **manifest needs** because they are easily perceived.[26] These are the needs for *achievement*, *power*, and *affiliation*. Some individuals have a high need for achievement, while others have a moderate or low need for achievement. The same is true for the other two needs. A manager may have a strong need for power, a moderate need for achievement, and a weak need for affiliation. Different needs are dominant in different people, and each need has different implications for people's behavior. Companies such as American Express recognize the importance of such diverse employee needs by creating and maintaining family-friendly policies.

5-3a Need for Achievement

The **need for achievement** encompasses excellence, competition, challenging goals, persistence, and overcoming difficulties.[27] People with a high need for achievement thus seek performance excellence, enjoy difficult and challenging goals, persevere, and are competitive. The *Murray Thematic Apperception Test (TAT)*, a projective test such as those discussed in Chapter 3, was used as an early measure of the achievement motive. It was further developed by McClelland and his associates, although it has been criticized, and alternative instruments have been developed.[28]

McClelland found that people with a high need for achievement perform better than those lacking such a need. Such individuals share these three characteristics: First, they set goals that are moderately difficult yet achievable. Second, they like to receive feedback on their progress toward these goals. Third, they do not like having external events or other people interfere with their progress toward the goals.

In addition, high achievers (1) often hope and plan for success; (2) may be quite content to work alone or with other people, whichever is more appropriate to their task; and (3) like being very good at what they do so and, accordingly, tend to develop expertise and competence in their chosen endeavors. Groups consisting of high-achieving members may experience conflict over how to get work tasks accomplished as members attempt to demonstrate their individual task-related contributions.[29] The need for achievement is consistent across countries for adults who are employed full-time, but researchers have found international differences in the tendency for achievement.[30] Achievement tendencies are highest in the United States, an individualistic culture, and lowest in collectivist societies such as Japan and Hungary.[31]

5-3b Need for Power

The **need for power** includes the desire to influence others, the urge to change people or events, and the wish to make a difference in life. The need for power is interpersonal because it involves influence over other people. McClelland distinguishes between *socialized power*, which is used for the benefit of many, and *personalized power*, which is used for individual gain. The former is a constructive force, while the latter may be a very disruptive or even destructive force.

According to McClelland's research, the best managers have a very high need for socialized power as opposed to personalized power.[32] They are concerned for others; have an interest in organizational goals; and want to be useful to the larger group, organization, and society. For example, the CEO of Management Sciences for Health, Jonathan D. Quick, MD, displayed a high need for interactive, or socialized, power on the McClelland need profile while showing a very low need for imperial power, both of which are strong positive traits.

5-3c Need for Affiliation

The **need for affiliation** is an urge to establish and maintain warm, close, intimate relationships with others.[33] People with a high need for affiliation are motivated to express their emotions to others and expect them to do the same in return. They find conflicts disturbing and are strongly motivated to work through any such barriers to closeness. The need for relationships is important not only in McClelland's theory but also in each of the theories we have discussed so far.

Over and above these three needs for achievement, power, and affiliation, Murray's manifest needs theory also included the need for autonomy. This is the desire for independence and freedom from constraints. People with a high need for autonomy prefer to work alone and to control the pace of their work. They dislike bureaucratic rules, regulations, and procedures.

Figure 5.2 shows the parallel structures of Maslow's, McGregor's, Alderfer's, and McClelland's theories of motivation.

> **need for power** A manifest need that concerns the desire to influence others, change people or events, and make a difference in life.
>
> **need for affiliation** A manifest need to establish and maintain warm, close, intimate relationships with other people.

FIGURE 5.2 — NEED THEORIES OF MOTIVATION

	Maslow	McGregor	Alderfer	McClelland
Higher order needs	Self-actualization Esteem — Self / Interpersonal Belongingness (social and love)	Theory Y	Growth Relatedness	Need for achievement Need for power Need for affiliation
Lower order needs	Safety and security — Interpersonal / Physical Physiological	Theory X	Existence	

© Cengage Learning

HOT TREND

The Best Way to *Really* Motivate Your Team

Managers have spent inordinate amounts of time grappling with how to compensate their sales forces in ways that allowed their teams to easily measure their own output while balancing risks with rewards. For most companies, the result was a commissioned-based compensation plan, often based on research conducted using lab experiments. Recent studies of sales-force compensation use research with company pay and sales data and field experiments with actual sales representatives. These studies suggest that managers use a mix of bonuses and commissions to engage a broad range of salespeople with different motivations and needs.

SOURCE: D. J. Chung, "How to Really Motivate Salespeople," *Harvard Business Review* (April 2015): 54–61.

5-4 HERZBERG'S TWO-FACTOR THEORY

In developing his *two-factor theory of motivation*, Frederick Herzberg departed from need-based theories and examined the critical incident experiences of people at work.[34] Herzberg's original study included 200 engineers and accountants in western Pennsylvania during the 1950s. He asked them to describe two important incidents at their jobs: one that was very satisfying and made them feel exceptionally good at work and another that was very dissatisfying and made them feel exceptionally bad.

Herzberg and his colleagues believed that people had two sets of needs:

motivation factor A work condition that satisfies the need for psychological growth.

hygiene factor A work condition that generates dissatisfaction due to discomfort or pain.

one based on avoiding pain and one stemming from the desire for psychological growth. Conditions in the work environment would affect one or the other of these two needs. Work conditions related to satisfaction of the need for psychological growth were labeled **motivation factors**. Work conditions related to dissatisfaction caused by discomfort or pain were labeled **hygiene factors**. Motivation factors relate to job satisfaction, and hygiene factors relate to job dissatisfaction.[35] Table 5.2 lists the motivation factors and hygiene factors included in the following discussion.

5-4a Motivation Factors

Job enrichment involves building motivation factors into a job and, according to Herzberg, creates job satisfaction. In his original research, Herzberg identified motivation factors as responsibility, achievement, recognition, advancement, and the work itself. When these factors are present, they improve a worker's effort and performance. Table 5.2 lists salary as a motivational factor based on some studies. Acceptance of this idea has led many organizational reward systems to include financial benefits such as stock options as part of an employee's compensation package.

Motivation factors lead to positive mental health. They challenge people to grow, contribute to the work environment, and invest themselves in the organization. The absence of these factors does not lead to dissatisfaction, but rather to feelings of neutrality. Motivation factors are the more important of the two sets of factors because they directly affect a person's drive to do a good job. When they are absent, a person lacks the motivation to perform well and achieve excellence.

TABLE 5.2 THE MOTIVATION-HYGIENE THEORY OF MOTIVATION	
Motivation factors that contribute to job satisfaction when they are present:	Hygiene factors that contribute to job dissatisfaction when they are absent:
> Achievement	> Company policy and administration
> Recognition of achievement	> Supervision
> Work itself	> Interpersonal relations
> Responsibility	> Working conditions
> Advancement	> Salary
> Growth	> Status
> Salary	> Security

© Cengage Learning

iQoncept/Shutterstock.com

5-4b Hygiene Factors

Hygiene factors are completely distinct from the motivation factors and are unrelated to the drive to achieve and do excellent work. While motivation factors create job satisfaction if present or feelings of neutrality if absent, absent or insufficient hygiene factors result in job dissatisfaction. Herzberg's hygiene factors include company policy and administration, technical supervision, interpersonal relations with one's supervisor, working conditions, salary, and status. Good hygiene factors cannot stimulate psychological growth or human development, but they are necessary to prevent job dissatisfaction.

When these hygiene factors are poor or absent, the dissatisfied employee complains about poor supervision, poor medical benefits, or whatever hygiene factor is poor. One method that employees use to determine the quality of supervision they receive is by the level of fairness they perceive the supervisor uses when enacting company policies. However, the supervisor's motives may have a greater impact on employee perceptions of workplace fairness.[36] Many companies have initiated formal flextime policies to reduce dissatisfaction and persuade women leaders to come back to work.[37] Even in the absence of good hygiene factors, employees may still be very motivated to perform their jobs well if the motivation factors are present.

Two conclusions can be drawn. First, hygiene factors are important to a certain level but unimportant beyond that threshold. Second, the presence of motivation factors is essential to enhancing employee motivation to excel at work.

5-4c Critique of the Two-Factor Theory

One critique of the theory surrounded the classification of the two factors. Some data have shown that a factor may not fit exclusively into either the hygiene or motivation categories. For example, employees generally classify pay as both a hygiene factor and a motivation factor. A second critique of the theory does not account for individual differences. Differences in age, sex, social status, education, or occupational level may influence the classification of factors. A third concern is that intrinsic job factors like the workflow process may be more important in determining satisfaction or dissatisfaction on the job. Finally, much of the supporting data for the theory is based on the *critical-incident technique*. Despite the critiques, Herzberg's was the first motivation theory developed specifically to predict motivation in work settings, thus having important implications for the design of work as we will discuss in Chapter 14.[38]

5-5 TWO NEW IDEAS IN MOTIVATION

Two new ideas in motivation have emerged in the past decade. One centers on eustress, strength, and hope. This idea comes from the new discipline of *positive organizational behavior*. A second new idea centers on positive energy and full engagement, translating what was learned from high-performance athletes for the use of *Fortune* 500 executives and managers.

5-5a Eustress, Strength, and Hope

Eustress (for "euphoria + stress") is healthy, normal stress.[39] Stress is the energy we experience when confronted with a challenging or difficult situation. Such situations can produce *distress*, a negative response such as frustration or fear, which leads to unhealthy and unproductive results, or eustress, a positive response to challenges that generates energy and motivates an individual to achieve. Eustress leads us to invest in strengths, find meaning in work, display courage and principled action, and draw on positive emotions at work.[40] This positive perspective on organizational life encourages optimism, hope, and health for people at work. Instead of focusing on the individual's needs or the rewards or punishment meted out in the work environment, the idea of encouraging eustress is to focus on the individual's interpretation of or response to events. An assumption underlying

eustress Healthy, normal stress.

eustress is that although things happen that are out of our control, we can control our response to a situation. Thus, we can control distress by reframing our perspective on a situation. Eustress is a healthy and positive motivational force for individuals who harness its energy for productive work and organizational contributions.

5-5b Positive Energy and Full Engagement

The second new concept in motivation, Jim Loehr's *full engagement* idea, uses lessons learned from professional athletes.[41] The central tenets are that an individual should manage energy rather than time and should strategically disengage from certain activities to balance the power of full engagement.[42] This approach suggests that individuals do not need to be activated by unmet needs but are already activated by their own physical, emotional, mental, and spiritual energy. Managers should therefore help individuals learn to manage their energy so that they can build positive energy and capacity for work.

Loehr's concept stresses the role of energy recovery in overall performance. Some individuals work best by putting forth productive energy for short periods and then taking time to rest and reenergize. This mimics the human body's potential to build or enhance its capacity, enabling the individual to sustain a high level of performance in the face of increasing work demands. Organizations with high levels of employee engagement have strong financial performance, even in volatile economic conditions.[43]

5-6 SOCIAL EXCHANGE AND EQUITY THEORY

Equity theory is a social exchange process approach to motivation that focuses on the interaction between an individual and the environment. In contrast to needs theories based on internal motivation, equity theory is concerned with the social processes that influence motivation and behavior. Power and exchange are important considerations in understanding human behavior.[44] Accounting for such external factors, Amitai Etzioni developed three categories of exchange relationships that people have with organizations: committed, calculated, and alienated involvements.[45] Committed relations have high positive intensity, calculated relationships have low positive or low negative intensity, and alienated relationships have high negative intensity. Committed relationships may characterize a person's involvement with a religious group, and alienated relationships may characterize a person's incarceration in a prison. These three categories will be discussed further in Chapter 11.

5-6a Demands and Contributions

Calculated involvements are based on the notion of social exchange in which each party in the relationship demands certain things of the other and contributes accordingly to the exchange. Business partnerships and commercial deals are both calculated involvements. When both parties to the exchange benefit, the relationship has a positive orientation. When losses occur or conflicts arise, the relationship has a negative orientation. Figure 5.3 offers a model for examining calculated exchange relationships.

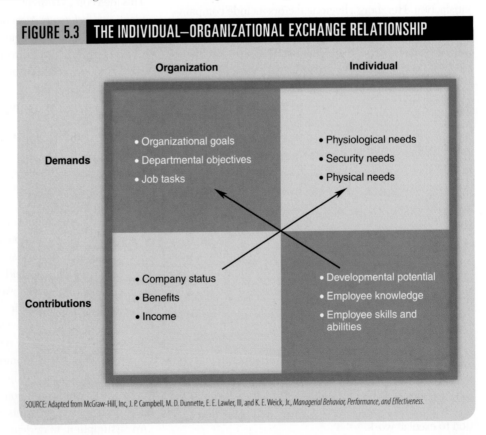

FIGURE 5.3   THE INDIVIDUAL–ORGANIZATIONAL EXCHANGE RELATIONSHIP

Organization | Individual

Demands
- Organizational goals
- Departmental objectives
- Job tasks

- Physiological needs
- Security needs
- Physical needs

Contributions
- Company status
- Benefits
- Income

- Developmental potential
- Employee knowledge
- Employee skills and abilities

SOURCE: Adapted from McGraw-Hill, Inc, J. P. Campbell, M. D. Dunnette, E. E. Lawler, III, and K. E. Weick, Jr., *Managerial Behavior, Performance, and Effectiveness.*

DEMANDS Each party to the exchange makes demands on the other. The organization expresses its demands on the individual in the form of goal or mission statements, job expectations, performance objectives, and performance feedback. The individual expresses demands, or needs, in the form of expectations of the organization. Employee need fulfillment and the feeling of belonging are both important to a healthy exchange and to organizational membership.[46] These needs may be viewed from the perspective of Maslow, Alderfer, Herzberg, or McClelland. When employees are well taken care of by the company, they take care of the business even in very difficult times.

CONTRIBUTIONS Just as each party to the exchange makes demands on the other, each also contributes to the relationship. These contributions are the basis for satisfying the demands expressed by the other party. Employees satisfy organizational demands through a range of contributions, including their skills, abilities, knowledge, energy, professional contacts, and native talents. As people grow and develop over time, they are able to increasingly satisfy the range of demands and expectations placed on them by the organization.

In a similar fashion, organizations contribute to the exchange relationship to meet individual needs. These contributions include salary, benefits, advancement opportunities, security, status, and social affiliation. Some organizations are richer in resources and better able to meet employee needs than other organizations. One of the concerns that both individuals and organizations have is whether the relationship is a fair deal or an equitable arrangement for both members of the relationship. Social exchange relationship perceptions are influenced by executive leadership style, organizational culture, and employment approach, which in turn have an effect on commitment and performance, though not organizational citizenship behavior (OCB), discussed in Chapter 4.[47]

5-6b Adams's Theory of Inequity

Ideas about social process and exchange advocated by Etzioni and others provide a context for understanding fairness, equity, and inequity in work relationships. Stacy Adams developed the idea that **inequity** in the social exchange process is a particularly important motivator. Adams's *theory of inequity* suggests that people are motivated when they find themselves in situations of inequity, or unfairness.[48] Inequity occurs when a person receives more or less than she believes she deserves based on her effort and/or contribution. Inequity creates tension, which in turn motivates a person to take action to resolve the inequity.

A perception of inequity arises when people consider their inputs (their contributions to the relationship) and their outcomes (the organization's contributions to the relationship) according to an input/outcome ratio, which they compare to that of a generalized "other," or *comparison other*. Figure 5.4 shows two inequity scenarios for a single situation, one negative and one positive. The negative inequity in (b) could occur, for example, if the comparison other earned a higher salary, while inequity in (c) could occur if the person had more vacation time, all else being equal in both cases. Although not illustrated in the example, nontangible inputs such as emotional investment and nontangible outcomes such as job satisfaction may enter into a person's equity equation.

Pay inequity has been a thorny issue for women in some companies. Eastman Kodak and other companies have made real progress in addressing the issue of pay equity.[49] Globalization also presents a challenge for pay equity. As organizations grow internationally, they may have trouble determining pay and benefit equity/inequity across national borders.

Adams considers a situation in which there is inequity in only one variable to be a first level of inequity. A more severe, second level of inequity would occur, for example, in a situation where the inputs of a person experiencing negative inequity, as in Figure 5.4(b), are also greater than those of the comparison other. Inequalities in one (inputs or outcomes) coupled with equality in the other (inputs or outcomes) are experienced as a less severe inequity than inequalities in both inputs and outcomes. One drawback of Adams's theory is that it does not provide a way of determining whether some inputs or some outcomes are more important than others.

> **inequity** A situation in which a person perceives that he or she is receiving less than he or she is giving or is giving less than he or she is receiving.

jeafish Ping/Shutterstock.com

FIGURE 5.4 EQUITY AND INEQUITY AT WORK

© Cengage Learning

5-6c The Resolution of Inequity

Once a person establishes the existence of an inequity, she might use a number of strategies to restore equity. Adams's theory provides seven basic strategies for restoring equity: (1) alter the person's outcomes, (2) alter the person's inputs, (3) alter the comparison other's outcomes, (4) alter the comparison other's inputs, (5) change who is used as a comparison other, (6) rationalize the inequity, and (7) leave the organizational situation.

Each of the first four strategies could involve a wide variety of tactics. For example, if an employee has a strategy to increase his income by $11,000 per year to restore equity, the tactic might be a meeting between the employee and his manager concerning the issue of salary equity. Another tactic would be for the person to work with the company's compensation specialists.

The selection of a strategy and a set of tactics is a sensitive issue with possible long-term consequences. In this example, a strategy aimed at reducing the comparison other's outcomes may have the desired short-term effect of restoring equity but reduce morale and productivity in the long term. The equity theory does not include a hierarchy predicting which inequity-reduction strategy a person will or should

equity sensitive An individual who prefers an equity ratio equal to that of his or her comparison other.

benevolent An individual who is comfortable with an equity ratio less than that of his or her comparison other.

entitled An individual who is comfortable with an equity ratio greater than that of his or her comparison other.

choose, but it is nevertheless a reminder of the importance of fairness. Pay dispersion (the amount of allowable differences between employee pay) has the ability to enhance or diminish employee motivation. Employees will generally be motivated when pay dispersion strategies are based on performance.[50]

5-6d New Perspectives on Equity Theory

Equity theory has been revised in light of new theories and research. One important theoretical revision proposes three types of individuals based on preferences for equity.[51] **Equity sensitives** prefer equity based on the originally formed theory. In other words, they want the relationship between their own input and output to be equal to that of their comparison other. Equity sensitivity contributes to the extent to which employees feel obligated to help in the workplace. Equity sensitive employees who monitor resources they receive from their supervisors may feel less obligated to engage in helping behaviors if they perceive they have been provided with fewer resources.[52] **Benevolents** are comfortable with an equity ratio less than that of their comparison other.[53] These people may be thought of as givers. **Entitleds** are comfortable only with an equity ratio greater than that of their comparison other.[54] These people may be thought of as takers.

Equity in pay is an important factor in motivation because pay is often thought to relate to a person's self-imposed performance expectations. But one study suggests that a person's organizational position also influences self-imposed performance expectations and may be a more important factor than pay.[55] Specifically, a two-level move up in an organization with no additional pay creates a higher self-imposed performance expectation than a one-level move up with modest additional pay. Similarly, a two-level move down in an organization with no reduction in pay creates a lower self-imposed performance expectation than a one-level move down with a modest decrease in pay.

Unfortunately, inequity and organizational injustice can also generate dysfunctional behavior.[56] More seriously, workplace injustice can trigger aggressive reactions that harm both individuals and the organization. Fortunately, only a small number of individuals respond to such unfairness through dysfunctional behavior.[57]

Increasing, decreasing, or constant experiences of inequity over time may have very different consequences for people.[58] Equity theory can help companies implement two-tiered wage structures such as the one used by American Airlines in the early 1990s. In a two-tiered system, one group of employees receives different pay and benefits than another group of employees. Such a system can, however, generate perceptions of inequity, especially where the value of equal pay for equal work is strongly held. Research suggests that unions and management may want to consider work location and employment status (part-time versus full-time) prior to implementing a two-tiered system.[59]

Increasing Valence by Connecting Employees with End-Users

SF photo/Shutterstock.com

When farmers purchase a John Deere tractor, they are invited to visit the factory with their families to see where their tractor is made. Before the tractor leaves the factory, assembly line workers greet the farmer with a golden key and watch the farmer start the tractor for the first time. Olive Garden employees read letters from customers describing how they spent special occasions at the restaurant. One Silicon Valley start-up company invites its existing and potential customers to monthly happy hours to interact with its employees. When scholarship program call-center employees heard directly from scholarship recipients about the impact the scholarships had on their lives, call-center employees were motivated to work harder, increasing their weekly revenue by 400%.

For each group of workers, the opportunity to meet with and engage their end-users helped them understand the "why" of their work. One of the most important ways that managers can instill a sense of meaning in their employee's work is to put them in touch with their end-users, a reward that employees will value.

SOURCE: V. Loder, "How Great Leaders Motivate Their Teams," *Forbes* (February 25, 2015), http://www.forbes.com/sites/vanessaloder/2015/02/25/how-great-leaders-motivate/

5-7 EXPECTANCY THEORY OF MOTIVATION

In addition to individual needs and social exchange, motivation can also be explained in terms of an individual's perception of the performance process. Victor Vroom's *expectancy theory* of motivation is a cognitive process theory founded on two basic notions. First, Vroom assumes that people expect certain outcomes of behavior and performance, which may be thought of as rewards, or consequences of behavior. Second, people believe there is a correlation between the effort they put forth, the performance they achieve, and the outcomes they receive. Expectancy theory has been used in a wide variety of contexts, including test-taking motivation among students.[60]

The key constructs in the expectancy theory of motivation are the valence of an outcome, expectancy, and instrumentality.[61] **Valence** is the value, or importance, one places on a particular reward. **Expectancy** is the belief that effort leads to performance (e.g., "If I try harder, I can do better"). **Instrumentality** is the belief that performance is related to rewards (e.g., "If I perform better, I will get more pay"). Figure 5.5 models the expectancy theory notions of effort, performance, and rewards.

Valence, expectancy, and instrumentality all influence a person's motivation. The perceived relationship between effort and performance varies from person to person and from activity to activity. One person might believe that an increase in effort has a direct, positive effect on performance. Another person might have a very different set of beliefs about the link between effort and performance. In a similar fashion, people's beliefs about the link between performance and reward vary. From a motivation perspective, it is the person's belief about the relationships between these constructs that is important, not the actual nature of the relationship.

Managers can use expectancy theory to design *motivation programs*.[62] Sometimes called *performance planning* or *evaluation systems*, these motivation programs are meant to enhance a person's belief that effort will improve performance and therefore lead to better pay. Valence and expectancy are particularly important in establishing priorities for people pursuing multiple goals.[63]

valence The value or importance one places on a particular reward.

expectancy The belief that effort leads to performance.

instrumentality The belief that performance is related to rewards.

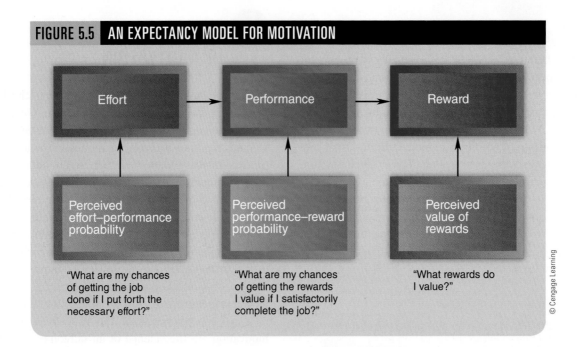

FIGURE 5.5 AN EXPECTANCY MODEL FOR MOTIVATION

Effort → Performance → Reward

Perceived effort–performance probability
"What are my chances of getting the job done if I put forth the necessary effort?"

Perceived performance–reward probability
"What are my chances of getting the rewards I value if I satisfactorily complete the job?"

Perceived value of rewards
"What rewards do I value?"

© Cengage Learning

Valence is the third key idea within the expectancy theory of motivation. Different people value different rewards. One person prefers salary to benefits, whereas another person prefers just the reverse. In fact, employees vary greatly with respect to the link between work and pay, as well as how much they value money.[64]

5-7a Motivational Problems

Expectancy theory attributes motivational problems to three basic causes: disbelief in a relationship between effort and performance, disbelief in a relationship between performance and rewards, and lack of desire for the rewards offered. If the motivational problem stems from the person's belief that effort will not improve performance, the solution lies in altering this belief. The person can be shown how an increase in effort or an alteration in the kind of effort put forth can be converted into improved performance.

If the motivational problem is related to the person's belief that performance will not result in rewards, the solution also lies in altering that belief. The person can be shown how an increase in performance or a somewhat altered form of performance will be converted into rewards. If, however, the motivational problem is related to the value placed on certain rewards, there are two possible solutions: to alter the value placed on the rewards or to alter the rewards themselves.

Research results on expectancy theory have been mixed.[65] The theory predicts job satisfaction accurately, but its complexity makes it difficult to test the full model, and the measures of instrumentality, valence, and expectancy have only weak validity.[66] In addition, measuring expectancy constructs is time-consuming, and the values for each construct change over time for an individual. Finally, the theory assumes that the individual is totally rational and acts as a minicomputer, calculating probabilities and values. In reality, the theory may be more complex than the way people typically function.

5-7b Motivation and Moral Maturity

Expectancy theory predicts that people will work to maximize their personal outcomes. This is consistent with Adam Smith's idea of working for one's own self-interest. Both suggest that people work to benefit themselves alone. Expectancy theory cannot explain altruistic behavior. Therefore, it may be necessary to consider an individual's **moral maturity** in order to understand altruistic, fair, and equitable behavior. Moral maturity is the measure of a person's cognitive moral development, as discussed in Chapter 4. Morally mature people behave based on universal ethical principles, while morally immature people behave based on egocentric motivations.[67]

moral maturity The measure of a person's cognitive moral development.

FASTFACT

A_KUDR/Shutterstock.com

Moral Acts Depend on Language

When faced with ethical dilemmas, individuals who voice their decision using a foreign language rather than their native tongue will likely make decisions that are less ethical. Communicating in a learned language allows individuals to psychologically distance themselves from issues and make less emotional, utilitarian decisions.

SOURCE: A. Lukis, "Moral Decisions May Depend on Language; People Make More Pragmatic Decisions in Languages Other Than Their Native Tongue," *Wall Street Journal* (May 12, 2014).

5-8 CULTURAL DIFFERENCES IN MOTIVATION

Most motivation theories in use today have been developed by and about Americans.[68] When researchers have examined the universality of these theories, they have found cultural differences, at least with regard to Maslow's, McClelland's, and Herzberg's theories. For example, while self-actualization is the pinnacle need for Americans in Maslow's need hierarchy, security may be the most important need for people in cultures with a high need to avoid uncertainty.[69] Although achievement is an important need for Americans, research suggests that other cultures do not value achievement as much as Americans do.

The two-factor theory has been tested in other countries as well. Results in New Zealand did not replicate the results found in the United States; supervision and interpersonal relationships were important motivators in New Zealand, as opposed to the importance of hygienic factors as in America.[70] Researchers examining equity theory in cross-cultural contexts have suggested reexamining equity preferences, selection of referent others, and reactions to inequity.[71] Finally, expectancy theory may hold up well in cultures that value individualism but break down in more collectivist cultures that value cooperative efforts. In collectivist cultures, rewards are more closely tied to group and team efforts, and expectancy theory is ill equipped to deal with such differences.

ChameleonsEye/Shutterstock.com

In places like New Zealand (pictured), supervision and interpersonal relationships are important motivators.

STUDY TOOLS 5

LOCATED AT BACK OF THE TEXTBOOK

☐ Rip out chapter review card

LOCATED AT WWW.CENGAGE.COM/LOGIN

☐ Track your knowledge and understanding of key concepts in business using 4LTR Press Online

☐ Review key term flashcards and create your own using StudyBits

☐ Create and complete practice quizzes based off of your notes and StudyBits

☐ Complete Online activities such as Matching and Fill-in-the-Blank exercises

☐ View chapter highlight box content, including the chapter videos, key exhibits and executive profiles.

6 | Learning and Performance Management

Science Source/Getty Images

LEARNING OUTCOMES

6-1 Describe behavioral theories of learning.

6-2 Describe social and cognitive theories of learning.

6-3 Explain how goal setting can be used to direct learning and performance.

6-4 Define performance and identify the tools used to measure it.

6-5 Explain the importance of performance feedback and how it can be delivered effectively.

6-6 Identify ways managers can reward performance.

6-7 List several strategies for correcting poor performance.

After finishing this chapter go to **PAGE 99** for **STUDY TOOLS.**

6-1 BEHAVIORAL MODELS OF LEARNING IN ORGANIZATIONS

Learning is a change in behavior acquired through experience. It helps guide and direct motivated behavior. Learning may begin with the cognitive activity of developing knowledge about a subject, which then leads to a change in behavior. Alternatively, the behaviorist approach to learning assumes that observable behavior is a function of its consequences. Behaviorists argue that learning stems from classical and operant conditioning.

6-1a Classical Conditioning

Classical conditioning is the process of modifying behavior by pairing a conditioned stimulus with an unconditioned stimulus to elicit an unconditioned response. Its discovery is largely the result of Russian physiologist Ivan Pavlov's experimentation on animals (primarily dogs).[1] During the early 1900s, Pavlov's professional exchanges with Walter B. Cannon and other American researchers brought his ideas to prominence in the United States.[2]

Classical conditioning builds on the natural reaction of an unconditioned response to an unconditioned stimulus. In dogs, this might be the natural production of saliva (unconditioned response) in response to the presentation of meat (unconditioned stimulus). By presenting a conditioned stimulus (e.g., a ringing bell) simultaneously with the unconditioned stimulus (meat), the researcher made the dog develop a conditioned response (salivation). After enough trials, the dog salivated at the sound of a bell, even when no meat was presented.

As demonstrated by B. F. Skinner, classical conditioning may occur similarly in humans.[3] For example, people working at a computer terminal may get lower back tension (unconditioned response) from poor posture (unconditioned stimulus). If they become aware of that tension only when the manager appears (conditioned stimulus), then they may develop a conditioned response (lower back tension) to the appearance of the manager.

But classical conditioning has limited applicability to hu-man behavior in organizations for three reasons. First, humans are more complex than dogs and less amenable to simple cause-and-effect conditioning. Second, the behavioral environments in organizations are complex and not very amenable to single stimulus–response manipulations. Third, the human capacity for decision making can override simple conditioning.

6-1b Operant Conditioning

Operant conditioning is the process of modifying behavior by following specific behaviors with positive or negative consequences.[4] These consequences influence behavior through three strategies: reinforcement, punishment, and extinction. Management pioneer Fred Luthans and his colleagues used *organizational behavior modification (OBM)* to shape behavior in a variety of organizations.[5] OBM employs three types of consequences: financial reinforcement, nonfinancial reinforcement, and social reinforcement. A major review of OBM's influence in organizations found that it had significant and positive influence on task performance in both manufacturing and service organizations but that the effects were most powerful in manufacturing organizations.[6] In a study of pay for performance, more productive employees chose performance-based compensation over fixed compensation when given a choice.[7] However, regardless of which pay scheme employees chose, all produced more under a pay-for-performance scheme. And while attitudes about pay for performance continue to vary according to cultural values, research suggests that its use may be rising cross-culturally.[8]

6-1c Reinforcement Theory

Reinforcement theory holds that reinforcement enhances desirable behavior, whereas punishment and extinction diminish undesirable behavior. This theory is central to the design and administration of organizational reward systems, which are a key factor in attracting and retaining top employees. Strategic rewards help motivate behavior, actions, and accomplishments, all of which advance the organization toward specific business

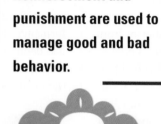

> Reinforcement and punishment are used to manage good and bad behavior.

Danielala/Shutterstock.com

learning A change in behavior acquired through experience.

classical conditioning Modifying behavior by pairing a conditioned stimulus with an unconditioned stimulus to elicit an unconditioned response.

operant conditioning Modifying behavior through the use of positive or negative consequences following specific behaviors.

goals.[9] In addition to cash rewards such as bonuses, strategic rewards include training and educational opportunities, stock options, and recognition awards such as travel.

Reinforcement and punishment represent the positive and negative consequences of behavior. **Positive consequences** are the results that the person finds attractive or pleasurable. They might include a pay increase, bonus, promotion, transfer to a more desirable geographic location, or praise from a supervisor. **Negative consequences** are the results that the person finds unattractive or aversive. They might include disciplinary action, an undesirable transfer, a demotion, or harsh criticism from a supervisor. The recipient of the consequences defines them as positive or negative. Therefore, individual personality differences as well as gender and cultural differences may be important in their classification.

Following a specific behavior with a positive or negative consequence either reinforces or punishes that behavior.[10] Thorndike's *law of effect* states that behaviors followed by positive consequences are more likely to recur and behaviors followed by negative consequences are less likely to recur.[11] Figure 6.1 shows how positive and negative consequences may be applied or withheld in the strategies of reinforcement and punishment.

REINFORCEMENT Reinforcement is a strategy to cultivate desirable behavior by either bestowing positive consequences or withholding negative ones. Positive reinforcement occurs when a positive consequence (like a bonus) follows a desirable behavior (like a successful business year). Marriott International provides positive reinforcement by honoring ten to twenty employees each year with its J. Willard Marriott Award of Excellence. Each recipient receives a medallion engraved with the words that express the basic values of the company: dedication, achievement, character, ideals, effort, and perseverance. A recent field experiment examining the reward practices of an Israeli high-tech manufacturing factory sought to better understand the type of short-term bonus (monetary or nonmonetary)

Positive consequences, such as travel opportunities, have a significant impact on task performance.

with the most positive effect on worker productivity and the circumstances under which short-term bonuses reinforced employee behavior. One group of employees was incentivized with monetary bonuses in the form of cash and family meal vouchers; the other group, with nonmonetary bonuses in the form of a note providing them with positive feedback. Employees who received monetary and nonmonetary bonuses increased their productivity by over 5%. Similarly, productivity decreased for both sets of employees once they were no longer being incentivized for their performance. However, the performance decrease took longer for the employees who had been incentivized with a simple note acknowledging their good performance than those who received cash or the meal voucher.[12]

Bosses Being Asked to Accentuate the Positive

Employers such as VMWare, Inc., Wayfair, Inc., and Boston Consulting Group (BCG) are asking their managers to ease up on the negatives when doling out employee feedback. Instead, managers are being asked to "accentuate the positive" and urged to use praise and emphasize small victories rather than focus on what workers do wrong. For example, it was once normal practice for BCG managers to evaluate employee performance by calling attention to their missteps and areas for improvement. According to Michelle Russell, a BCG partner, "We would bring them in and beat them down a bit." After the feedback session, the company noticed that some employees would not return. Rather than motivate them to improve their performance, the harsh feedback resulted in employees feeling disheartened and shaken, with reduced confidence. Now BCG managers are expected to focus on a particular worker's strength and to mention no more than one or two areas that require improvement. Yahoo Chair Maynard Webb acknowledges that overly positive feedback may lead to managers overlooking serious performance problems, but agrees that people tend to perform better when they're encouraged and inspired.

SOURCE: R. Feintzeig, "You're Awesome! Firms Scrap Negative Feedback—Managers Ease Up on Harsh Reviews; in Past, 'We'd Beat Them Down a Bit,'" *Wall Street Journal* (February 11, 2015): B.1.

positive consequences
Results of a behavior that a person finds attractive or pleasurable.

negative consequences
Results of a behavior that a person finds unattractive or aversive.

reinforcement A strategy to cultivate desirable behavior by either bestowing positive consequences or withholding negative consequences.

FIGURE 6.1 REINFORCEMENT AND PUNISHMENT STRATEGIES

	Reinforcement (desirable behavior)	Punishment (undesirable behavior)
Positive consequences	Apply	Withhold
Negative consequences	Withhold	Apply

SOURCE: Table from Organizational Behavior Modification by Fred Luthans and Robert Kreitner. Copyright © 1985, p. 58 by Scott Foresman and Company and the authors. Reprinted by permission of the authors.

behavior) refrains from doing so when the employee is on time (desirable behavior). The employee avoids the negative consequence (a reduction in pay) by exhibiting the desirable behavior (being on time to work).

When managers design organizational reward systems, they consider not only the type of reinforcement but also how often to provide it, according to continuous or intermittent schedules, as shown in Table 6.1.

Negative reinforcement occurs when managers withhold a negative consequence after an employee demonstrates a desirable behavior. For example, a manager who reduces an employee's pay (negative consequence) if the employee comes to work late (undesirable

6-1d Punishment

Punishment is a strategy to discourage undesirable behavior. One way to punish a person is to follow an

punishment A strategy to discourage undesirable behavior by either bestowing negative consequences or withholding positive consequences.

TABLE 6.1 SCHEDULES OF REINFORCEMENT

Schedule	Description	Effects on Responding
Continuous	Reinforcer follows every response.	Steady, high rate of performance as long as reinforcement follows every response. High frequency of reinforcement may lead to early satiation. Behavior weakens rapidly (undergoes extinction) when reinforcers are withheld. Appropriate for newly emitted, unstable, low-frequency responses.
Intermittent	Reinforcer does not follow every response.	Capable of producing high frequencies of responding. Low frequency of reinforcement precludes early satiation. Appropriate for stable or high-frequency responses.
Fixed ratio	A fixed number of responses must be emitted before reinforcement occurs.	A fixed ratio of 1:1 (reinforcement occurs after every response) is the same as a continuous schedule. Tends to produce a high rate of response that is vigorous and steady.
Variable ratio	A varying or random number of responses must be emitted before reinforcement occurs.	Capable of producing a high rate of response that is vigorous, steady, and resistant to extinction.
Fixed interval	The first response after a specific period of time has elapsed is reinforced.	Produces an uneven response pattern varying from a very slow, unenergetic response immediately following reinforcement to a very fast, vigorous response immediately preceding reinforcement.
Variable interval	The first response after varying or random periods of time have elapsed is reinforced.	Tends to produce a high rate of response that is vigorous, steady, and resistant to extinction.

SOURCE: F. Luthans and R. Kreitner, *Organizational Behavior Modification* (Glenview, Ill.: Scott, Foresman, 1985). Copyright © by Scott Foresman and Company and the authors. Reprinted by permission of the authors.

undesirable behavior with a negative consequence. For example, a professional athlete who is excessively offensive to an official (undesirable behavior) may be ejected from the game (negative consequence). The other way to punish a person is to withhold a positive consequence following an undesirable behavior. For example, a salesperson who puts little effort into his pitch (undesirable behavior) won't likely receive a large commission check (positive consequence).

Punishment sometimes has unintended results. Because punishment is discomforting to the individual being punished, it can bring about negative psychological, emotional, performance, or behavioral consequences (such as workplace deviance), especially when applied too often. Being aware of this potential consequence of a generalized negative response and decreased motivation to work better, some managers use the threat of punishment—rather than actually applying the punishment—to scare workers into greater effort whenever possible.[13]

EXTINCTION An alternative to punishing undesirable behavior is **extinction**—a strategy to weaken a behavior by attaching no consequences (either positive or negative) to it. This strategy may require time and patience, but the absence of consequences eventually weakens a behavior. Extinction may be most effective when used in conjunction with the positive reinforcement of desirable behaviors. For example, complimenting a sarcastic colleague for constructive comments (reinforcing desirable behavior) while ignoring sarcastic comments (extinguishing undesirable behavior) may prove doubly effective. Extinction is not always the best strategy, however. In cases of dangerous or seriously undesirable behavior, punishment might better deliver a swift, clear lesson.

> Managers can empower employees and help them develop self-efficacy by providing job challenges, offering coaching and counseling, and rewarding employees' achievements.

6-2 SOCIAL AND COGNITIVE THEORIES OF LEARNING

In addition to behaviorist theory, social and cognitive theories of learning have been proposed.

extinction A strategy to weaken a behavior by attaching no consequences to it.

task-specific self-efficacy An individual's internal expectancy to perform a specific task effectively.

6-2a Bandura's Social Learning Theory

Albert Bandura's social learning theory offers a complementary alternative to Pavlov's and Skinner's behaviorist approaches.[14] Bandura asserts that learning occurs when we observe other people and model their behavior. Because employees look to their supervisors for acceptable norms of behavior, they are likely to pattern their own actions after the supervisor's. Central to Bandura's social learning theory is the notion of **task-specific self-efficacy**, an individual's internal expectancy to perform a specific task effectively. Individuals with high self-efficacy believe that they have the ability to get things done. Self-efficacy is higher in a learning context than in a performance context, especially for individuals with a high learning orientation.[15] There are four sources of task-specific self-efficacy: prior experiences, behavior models (witnessing the success of others), persuasion from other people, and assessment of current physical and emotional capabilities.[16] Evidence suggests that self-efficacy leads to high performance on a wide variety of physical and mental tasks.[17] Employees with high self-efficacy are more likely to learn new things and seek out variety in conducting their job tasks.[18] Prior success can also enhance one's self-efficacy. For example, women who trained in physical self-defense increased their self-efficacy in self-defense and new tasks.[19]

Alexander Stajkovic and Fred Luthans drew on Bandura's ideas of self-efficacy and social learning to expand their original work in behavioral management and OBM into a comprehensive framework for performance management.[20] Bandura saw the power of social reinforcement, recognizing that financial and material rewards often follow or coincide with the approval of others, whereas punishments often follow social disapproval. Thus, Stajkovic and Luthans saw that self-efficacy and social reinforcement influence behavior and performance at work and have suggested that managers can be confident that employees with high self-efficacy will perform well.

Managers can empower employees and help them develop self-efficacy by providing job challenges, offering coaching and counseling for improved performance, and rewarding employees' achievements. Managers can also remove organizational barriers that stand in the way of employees making progress in meaningful work.[21] Given the increasing diversity of the workforce, managers may want to target their efforts toward women and minorities, who tend to have lower than average self-efficacy.[22]

6-2b Cognitive Theories of Learning

The cognitive approach to learning is based on the *Gestalt* school of thought and draws on Jung's theory of personality

TABLE 6.2 PERSONALITY FUNCTIONS AND LEARNING

PERSONALITY PREFERENCE	IMPLICATIONS FOR LEARNING BY INDIVIDUALS
Information gathering	
Intuitors	Prefer theoretical frameworks. Look for the meaning in material. Attempt to understand the grand scheme. Look for possibilities and interrelations.
Sensors	Prefer specific, empirical data. Look for practical applications. Attempt to master details of a subject. Look for what is realistic and doable.
Decision making	
Thinkers	Prefer analysis of data and information. Work to be fair-minded and evenhanded. Seek logical, just conclusions. Do not like to be too personally involved.
Feelers	Prefer interpersonal involvement. Work to be tender-hearted and harmonious. Seek subjective, merciful results. Do not like objective, factual analysis.

SOURCE: From Type Talk at Work by Otto Kroeger and Janet Theusen, copyright © 1992 by Janet Theusen and Otto Kroeger. Used by permission of Delacorte Press, an imprint of The Random House Publishing Group, a division of Random House, Inc.

differences, discussed in Chapter 3. Recall the distinction between introverts (who need to study, concentrate, and reflect) and extraverts (who need to interact with other people). Introverts learn best alone, whereas extraverts learn best by exchanging ideas with others.

The personality functions of intuition, sensing, thinking, and feeling all have learning implications, which are listed in Table 6.2. Each person has a preferred mode of gathering information and a preferred mode of evaluating and making decisions about that information. For example, an intuitive thinker may want to skim research reports about implementing total quality programs and then, based on hunches, decide how to apply the research findings to the organization. A sensing feeler may prefer viewing videos of interviews with people in companies that implemented total quality programs and then identify people in the organization most likely to be receptive to the approaches presented.

6-3 GOAL SETTING AT WORK

Goal setting is the process of establishing desired results that guide and direct behavior. Goal-setting theory is based on laboratory studies, field research experiments, and comparative investigations by Edwin Locke,

Gary Latham, John M. Ivancevich, and others.[23] Goals crystallize the sense of purpose and mission that drives success.

6-3a Characteristics of Effective Goals

Various organizations define the characteristics of effective goals differently. As one example, Sanger-Harris, a former retail organization, used SMART goals. SMART stands for Specific, Measurable, Attainable, Realistic, and Time-bound. Specific and challenging goals focus attention on exactly what will be accomplished and inspire peak performance. People who set specific, challenging goals consistently outperform those with easy or unspecified goals, as Figure 6.2 shows. Subconscious thought may have a positive effect as well. Two studies of subconscious motivation found that goals that were ingrained but not explicitly expressed significantly enhanced task performance for difficult conscious goals, though not for easy goals.[24]

Measurable, quantitative goals provide opportunities for feedback about goal progress. Qualitative goals are also valuable. The Western Company of North America (now part of BJ Services Company) allows about 15% of a manager's goals to be of a qualitative nature.[25] An example of a qualitative goal is improving customer relations. To assess its progress, this qualitative goal might be quantified using measures like the number of complaints or the frequency of compliments.

Time-bound goals enhance measurability. Many organizations work on standardized cycles of time, such as quarters or years. If there is any uncertainty about the time period of the goal effort, the time limit should be explicitly stated.

The prioritizing of goals allows efficient resource allocation. As time, energy, or other resources become available, a person can work through her list of goals in order of importance.[26] Priority helps direct a person's efforts and behavior.

Goal setting can serve three functions. First, it can increase work motivation and task performance.[27] Second, it can reduce stress caused by conflicting or confusing expectations.[28] Third, it can improve the accuracy and validity of performance evaluation.[29] Let's look at each of these functions in some detail.

goal setting The process of establishing desired results that guide and direct behavior.

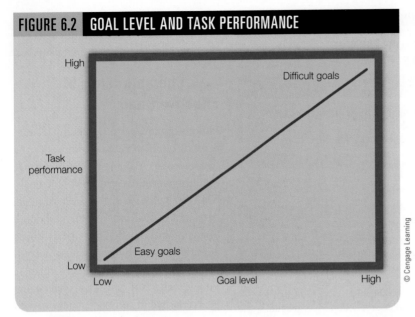

FIGURE 6.2 GOAL LEVEL AND TASK PERFORMANCE

High

Task
performance

Difficult goals

Easy goals

Low

Low   Goal level   High

© Cengage Learning

6-3b Goals Increase Work Motivation and Task Performance

Goals often increase employee effort and motivation, which in turn improve task performance. The higher the goal is, the better the performance. People work harder to reach difficult goals. Figure 6.2 depicts this positive relationship.

Managers who use goal setting should ensure employee participation, supervisory commitment, and useful performance feedback. Participation encourages employees to accept and commit to the goal, two prerequisites to goal accomplishment. Employee participation is especially important in the accomplishment of difficult goals.[30] And when a difficult goal is assigned, acceptance and commitment are considered essential prerequisites to accomplishment.

Supervisory goal commitment reflects an organization's commitment to goal setting. Indeed, organizational commitment is a prerequisite for successful goal-setting programs such as *management by objectives (MBO)*, discussed shortly.[31] The organization commits to the program, and the supervisors and employees commit to its specific work goals.

The supervisor also provides employees with interim performance feedback on their progress toward goals. Such performance feedback is most useful for goals that are specific, and specific goals improve performance most when interim feedback is given.[32] When approached correctly, even negative performance feedback can improve performance.[33] For example, assume an insurance salesperson has a goal of selling $500,000 worth of insurance in six months but has sold only $200,000 after

management by objectives (MBO)
A goal-setting program based on interaction and negotiation between employees and managers.

three months. During an interim performance feedback session, the supervisor helps the salesperson identify his problem—that he is not focusing his calls on the likeliest prospects—and gets him back on track to achieve his goal. Feedback is most helpful when it provides practical advice and is timely.

6-3c Goals Reduce Role Stress, Conflict, and Ambiguity

Goal setting also reduces the *role stress* associated with conflicting and confusing expectations because it clarifies the task–role expectations for employees. Supervisors, coworkers, and employees all provide task-related information. A fourteen-month evaluation found that goal setting reduced conflict, confusion, and absenteeism.[34]

Because goal setting improves role clarity, it generally improves communication between managers and employees.[35] This is why FedEx encourages managers to include communication-related targets in their annual MBO goal-setting process.[36]

6-3d Goals Improve Performance Evaluation

The third major function of goal setting is improving the accuracy and validity of performance evaluation. One of the best methods for this is **management by objectives (MBO)**—a goal-setting program based on interaction and negotiation between employees and managers.

According to Peter Drucker, who developed the concept of MBO over fifty years ago, the objectives-setting process begins with the employee writing a so-called employee's letter to the manager. The letter explains the employee's general understanding of the scope of the manager's job as well as the scope of the employee's own job. The employee lays out a set of specific objectives to be pursued over the next six to twelve months, and after some discussion and negotiation, the manager and the employee finalize these items into a performance plan.

Drucker considers MBO a participative and interactive process. This does not mean that goal setting begins at the bottom of the organization. It means that goal setting is applicable to all employees; both lower-level organizational members and professional staff influence the goal-setting process.[37] Most goal-setting programs are designed to enhance performance, especially when incentives are associated with goal achievement.[38]

The two central ingredients in goal-setting programs are planning and evaluation. The *planning* component consists of organizational and individual goal setting, two essential and interdependent processes.[39] In planning, individuals and departments usually develop operational and tactical plans to support the corporate objectives. The idea is to formulate a clear, consistent, measurable, and ordered set of goals to articulate *what* to do. Operational support planning then determines *how* to do it. The concept of *intention* encompasses both the goal (*what*) and the pathways that lead to goal attainment (*how*).[40]

The *evaluation* component of goal setting consists of interim reviews conducted by managers and employees and formal performance evaluation. The interim reviews are designed to help employees take self-corrective action. The formal performance evaluation occurs at the close of a reporting period, usually once a year. Effective performance reviews must be tailored specifically to the business, be reflective of what goes on internally, and be easily adapted to changes.[41]

Because goal-setting programs are somewhat mechanical by nature, they are most valuable and easily implemented in stable, predictable industrial settings. They are less useful in small, unpredictable organizations. Neither individual personality differences nor gender nor cultural differences appear to threaten the success of goal-setting programs, making them useful tools for a large, diverse workforce.[42]

Goal setting can increase work motivation and task performance, reduce stress, and improve the accuracy of performance evaluation.

6-4 PERFORMANCE: A KEY CONSTRUCT

Performance is most often called *task accomplishment*, the term *task* coming from Frederick W. Taylor's conception of a worker's required activity.[43] Some early management research found that performance standards and differential piece-rate pay inspired high levels of performance, while other early research found that stress improved performance up to an optimum point.[44] Hence, outcomes and effort are both important to good performance.

Predicting job performance has been a concern for over a century. Early World War I–era theories focused on intelligence and *general mental ability (GMA)*. Research has found GMA highly predictive of job knowledge in both civilian and military jobs.[45] Researchers have found mixed EI (emotional intelligence) to be a valid predictor of job performance. Mixed EI consists of personality traits, such as extraversion and conscientiousness, as well as affect and

Deloitte's Performance Management Redesign

Ask any company the HRM process that has the most significant impact on employee performance, and it will likely point to its performance management system. Companies use performance management systems to evaluate the work of its employees, then train, promote, and pay them based on the outcomes. Big 4 consulting firm, Deloitte is no different.

For years, Deloitte has used a performance management process that is similar to the process used by many companies, one characterized by once-a-year rankings of employees, cascading goals and objectives, backward-looking assessments, and 360-degree surveys to capture multiple impressions of employee performance. Recently, Deloitte announced a major overhaul of its performance management system. Why? Three discoveries. First, the once-a-year "batch" process of evaluating employee performance against goals did not reflect the need to evaluate real-time employee performance. The process needed to allow for more agility. Next, Deloitte realized that 62% of an employee's evaluation on certain criteria actually reflected the idiosyncrasies of the rater. For instance, how tough a rater evaluated an employee's strategic thinking skills depended on how much of a strategic thinker the rater was. Finally, a study of their own work teams found that employees who believed they had a chance to use their strengths at work were the highest performers. Deloitte's redesigned performance management is characterized by compensation decisions that are separate from daily performance, regular or per-project "performance snapshots," and weekly check-ins with managers to help keep performance on track.

TonyV3112/Shutterstock.com

SOURCE: M. Buckingham and A. Goodall, "Reinventing Performance Management," *Harvard Business Review* (April 2015): 40–50.

self-perceived abilities.[46] But before job performance can be predicted, it must be defined.

6-4a Performance Management

Performance management is a process of defining, measuring, appraising, providing feedback on, and improving performance.[47] Defining performance in behavioral terms is an essential first step in the process. Done well, the performance management process leads to increased employee engagement, whereby workers know exactly what's expected of them and have the skills and abilities to meet those expectations.[48] Once defined, performance can be measured and assessed so that workers can receive feedback and managers can set goals to improve performance. Positive performance behaviors should be rewarded, and poor performance behaviors should be corrected.

6-4b Defining Performance

Managers must clearly define performance if their employees are to perform well at work. Most work performance is multidimensional. For example, a sales executive's performance will require administrative, financial, and interpersonal skills. Knowing the skills and behaviors needed to succeed in a position is a prerequisite to measuring and evaluating job performance.

Although different jobs require varying skills and behaviors, *organizational citizenship behavior (OCB)* spans many jobs. Recall from Chapter 4 that OCB is behavior above and beyond the call of duty. Employee involvement programs enhance OCB by engaging employees in the work environment.[49] OCB emphasizes collective performance rather than individual performance. It is but one of many dimensions to consider when defining the requirements of a specific job.

Performance appraisal is the evaluation of a person's performance. Accurate appraisals help supervisors fulfill their dual roles as

evaluators and coaches. As the latter, a supervisor encourages growth and development. As the former, a supervisor makes judgments about employees' roles in the organization. Keeping an employee's position within the company in mind lends greater contextual significance to the appraisal process.[50]

Performance appraisals give employees feedback on performance, identify their developmental needs, and influence promotion, demotion, termination, selection and placement decisions.

6-4c Measuring Performance

Ideally, actual performance matches measured performance, but this is actually seldom the case. Since operational performance generates more quantifiable data, it is easier to measure than managerial performance. Recent research measuring motivation for task performance has found that wording and context may influence the validity of direct self-reports.[51] Accuracy of self-performance evaluations is also important. The more accurately individuals evaluate their performance on a task, the better their performance will be on a subsequent task.[52]

Performance appraisal systems should improve the accuracy of measured performance and increase its parity with actual performance. The extent of their agreement is called the *true assessment*, as Figure 6.3 shows. Performance measurement problems such as

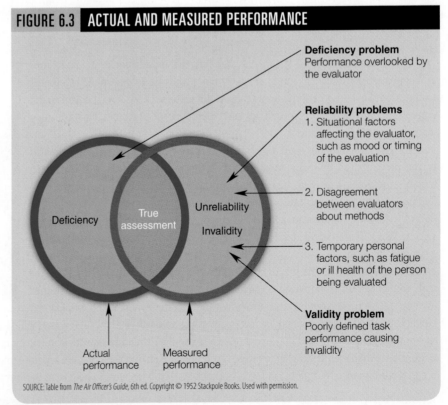

FIGURE 6.3 ACTUAL AND MEASURED PERFORMANCE

Deficiency problem
Performance overlooked by the evaluator

Reliability problems
1. Situational factors affecting the evaluator, such as mood or timing of the evaluation
2. Disagreement between evaluators about methods
3. Temporary personal factors, such as fatigue or ill health of the person being evaluated

Validity problem
Poorly defined task performance causing invalidity

Deficiency / True assessment / Unreliability / Invalidity

Actual performance — Measured performance

SOURCE: Table from *The Air Officer's Guide*, 6th ed. Copyright © 1952 Stackpole Books. Used with permission.

performance management
A process of defining, measuring, appraising, providing feedback on, and improving performance.

performance appraisal The evaluation of a person's performance.

TABLE 6.3	OFFICER EFFECTIVENESS REPORTS, CIRCA 1813

Alexander Brown, Lt. Col., Comdg.—A good-natured man.

Clark Crowell, 1st Major—A good man, but no officer.

Jess B. Wordsworth, 2nd Major—An excellent officer.

Captain Shaw—A man of whom all unite in speaking ill. A knave despised by all.

Captain Thomas Lord—Indifferent, but promises well.

Captain Rockwell—An officer of capacity, but imprudent and a man of violent passions.

1st Lt. Jas. Kearns—Merely good, nothing promising.

1st Lt. Robert Cross—Willing enough, has much to learn, with small capacity.

2nd Lt. Stewart Berry—An ignorant unoffending fellow.

Ensign North—A good young man who does well.

SOURCE: J. C. Benton, *The Air Officer's Guide*, 6th ed. (Mechanicsburg, Penn.: Stackpole Books 1952). Copyright © 1952 Stackpole Books. Used with permission.

deficiency, unreliability, and invalidity contribute to inaccuracy. *Deficiency* occurs when important aspects of a person's actual performance are overlooked. Unreliability results from poor-quality performance measures. *Invalidity* stems from inaccurate definition of the expected job performance.

Table 6.3, a sample of officer effectiveness reports from a nineteenth-century infantry company, demonstrates the bias of early performance appraisals. Even contemporary executive appraisals have a dark side, arousing the defenses of managers and executives. Addressing emotions and defenses is important to the effectiveness of appraisal sessions.[53] Some performance review systems lead to forced rankings of employees, which may be controversial or counterproductive. Although a recent study found that supervisors were reluctant to give negative feedback overall, they were more likely to emphasize social factors when describing the performance of ethnic minorities.[54]

Many performance-monitoring systems use modern electronic technology to measure the performance of vehicle operators, computer technicians, and customer service representatives. For example, such systems might record the rate or the total number of keystrokes for a computer technician.

Sometimes employees are unaware that their performance is being measured. What constitutes inappropriate electronic monitoring of an employee? The ethics of monitoring performance differ by culture. For example, firms in the United States and Sweden generally respect individual privacy more than those in Japan or China.

Goal setting and MBO are results-oriented performance appraisal methods that do not necessarily rely on modern technology. Like performance-monitoring systems, they focus on observable, verifiable results, instead of subjective, judgmental performance dimensions. Goals established during planning serve as the standard for measuring subsequent performance. However, managers who adhere rigidly to a results-oriented approach risk overlooking performance opportunities.

6-5 PERFORMANCE FEEDBACK

Feedback sessions create stress for both supervisors and employees. Early research at General Electric found, not surprisingly, that employees responded constructively to positive feedback but often responded defensively to critical or negative feedback. In response to negative feedback, they shifted responsibility for the problem, denied it outright, or provided a wide range of excuses.[55] In a study of 499 Chinese supervisor–subordinate pairs, supervisors responded positively to employees who sought performance feedback if their motive was performance enhancement or improvement but not so positively if the employee's motive was to influence how their supervisor perceived them.[56]

Both supervisor and employee should try to make performance feedback a constructive learning experience, since feedback has long-term implications for the employee's performance and for the supervisor-employee working relationship. American Airlines follows three guidelines for providing evaluative feedback.[57] First, supervisors refer to specific, verbatim statements and specific, observable behaviors displayed by the employee. This specificity enhances the acceptance of the feedback while discouraging denial. Second, the feedback focuses on changeable behaviors, not intrinsic or personality-based attributes. Third, the session is planned ahead of time and the person who will receive the feedback is notified so that both parties can be ready.

Supervisors should start coaching and counseling sessions with something positive. Once the session is under way and rapport is established, the evaluator can introduce more difficult and negative material. No one is perfect, so everyone can learn and grow through performance feedback and review sessions. Critical feedback is the basis for improvement. Managers should be aware, however, that although specific feedback can improve initial performance, it may also undermine the learning needed for later, more independent performance.[58]

6-5a 360-Degree Feedback

Many organizations use **360-degree feedback**, which is based on multiple sources of information, to improve the accuracy of performance appraisals. Evidence suggests that including self-evaluations in this process makes evaluation interviews more satisfying, more constructive, and less defensive.[59] Some dislike the fact that self-evaluations often conflict with supervisory evaluations.[60] However, these disagreements are part of the full picture of the person's performance. The 360-degree feedback method provides a well-rounded view of performance from superiors, peers, followers, and customers.[61]

As an illustration of the benefits of a 360-degree feedback evaluation, consider a mid-level civilian executive working in a large military organization. The executive is positive, compliant, and deferential toward superiors but largely indifferent toward peers. With followers, he is tough and demanding, bordering on abusive. Without each of these perspectives, the executive's performance cannot be accurately assessed.

Adding a systematic coaching component can improve 360-degree feedback.[62] By focusing on enhanced self-awareness and behavioral management, feedback coaching improves performance, satisfaction, and commitment, and reduces turnover. Separating the performance feedback component from the management development component also improves the 360-degree method.[63] The feedback component contains quantitative feedback and performance measures, while the management development component emphasizes qualitative feedback and competencies for development.

6-5b Developing People and Enhancing Careers

Good performance appraisal systems develop people and enhance careers. They should explore individual growth needs and future performance. However, in order to coach and develop employees successfully, the supervisor must establish mutual trust. This means she must be vulnerable and open to challenge from the subordinate while maintaining responsibility for the subordinate's best interests.[64] Good supervisors are skilled, empathetic listeners who encourage employees to discuss their aspirations.[65]

Employees must also take active responsibility for future development and growth. This might mean challenging the supervisor's ideas about future development and expressing their own goals. Passive, compliant employees cannot accept responsibility for themselves or achieve full emotional development. Individual responsibility is a key characteristic of the culture of the steel manufacturer Gerdau Ameristeel. The company joke is that the company manages by "adultry" (pun intended). Gerdau Ameristeel treats people like adults and expects adult behavior from them.

Peshkova/Shutterstock.com

6-5c Key Characteristics of an Effective Appraisal System

Effective performance appraisal systems have five key characteristics: validity, reliability, responsiveness, flexibility, and equitability. *Validity* means capturing multiple dimensions of a person's job performance. *Reliability* means collecting evaluations from multiple sources and at different times throughout the evaluation period. *Responsiveness* means allowing the person being evaluated to have some input. *Flexibility* means staying open to modification based on new information such as federal requirements. *Equitability* means evaluating fairly against established criteria, regardless of individual differences. High-quality performance appraisals with these characteristics have a positive effect on employee participation in voluntary informal learning activities.[66]

FedEx has incorporated a novel and challenging approach to evaluation in its blueprint for service quality. All managers at FedEx are evaluated by their employees through a survey-feedback-action system. Employees, in turn, evaluate their managers using a five-point scale on twenty-nine standard statements and ten local option ones. Low ratings suggest problem areas requiring management attention. One year the survey revealed that

360-degree feedback A process of self-evaluation and evaluations by a manager, peers, direct reports, and possibly customers.

HOT TREND

Treat Your Career Like a Startup

Career development is a joint responsibility for supervisors and employees. In today's work environment, it takes creativity and an entrepreneurial spirit to navigate careers. Experts suggest thinking like you're launching a business from the ground up. How?

- Rather than focus on short-term gains, think about long-term goals and what skills and experiences you will need to get there.
- Choose the company you want to work for by determining the type of people with whom you want to work. Consider whether these are people who will train you or lead you to other opportunities.
- Know your strengths and market yourself appropriately so that employers see that there is a "product-market" fit.
- Realize that uncertainty is the name of the game. When things don't go as planned, seek feedback and adapt.

The bottom line. Answer to your "inner venture capitalist" by understanding your competitive advantage. Only then will employers be willing to *invest* in you.

SOURCE: E. Fry, "How to Approach Your Own Career Like an Entrepreneur," *Fortune* 171 (January 1, 2015): 84–89.

employees thought upper management was not paying attention to ideas and suggestions from people at their level. In response, CEO Fred Smith developed a biweekly employee newsletter to correct the problem.

6-6 REWARDING PERFORMANCE

Performance appraisals can provide input for reward decisions. If companies celebrate teamwork, values, and customer focus, they must reward behaviors demonstrating these ideas. Despite their importance, reward decisions are among the most difficult and complicated decisions managers make. They should remember that people do not simply work for money.[67] While pay and rewards for performance have value, so too do trust, fun, and meaningful work. In fact, some compensation professionals have advanced the idea of Total Rewards that include extrinsic rewards like compensation and benefits as well as intrinsic ones like work-life benefits, performance and recognition, and career-development opportunities.[68]

Reward and punishment decisions affect entire organizations, not just the people receiving the consequence. Reward allocation involves sequential decisions about which people to reward, how to reward them, and when to reward them. These decisions shape all employees' behavior, either directly or through vicarious learning, especially when new programs are implemented. People watch what happens to peers who make mistakes and adjust their own behavior accordingly.

6-6a Individual versus Team Reward Systems

While motivation and reward systems outside the United States are often group focused, many U.S. organizations use systems that are focused on rewarding employees as individuals.[69] These systems foster independent behavior and encourage creativity, problem solving, and distinctive contributions to the organization. Different types of employees may prefer different rewards. For example, adventure seekers may prefer travel awards, while nesters prefer days off.[70]

Individual reward systems directly affect individual behavior and encourage competition within a work team.[71] Too much competition, however, may create a dysfunctional work environment. At the Western Company of North America (now part of BJ Services Company), individual success in the MBO program was tied too tightly to rewards, and individual managers became divisively competitive. Some managers took last-minute interdepartmental financial actions to meet their objectives. By doing so, they caused other managers to miss their objectives. These actions raise ethical questions about how far individual managers should go in serving their own self-interest at the expense of their peers.

Team reward systems solve the problems caused by individual competitive behavior in that they encourage cooperation, joint efforts, and the sharing of information and expertise. The collectivist orientations of Japanese and Chinese cultures position the individual as an element of the team, not as a separate individual.

Some organizations have experimented with individual and group alternative reward systems. At the individual level, these include skill-based and pay-for-knowledge systems that emphasize skills or knowledge possessed by an employee beyond the requirements for the basic job. At the group level, gain-sharing plans emphasize collective cost reduction by allowing workers to share in the gains achieved by reducing production costs. In such plans, everyone shares equally in the collective gain. Avnet, Inc. found that collective profit sharing improved performance. The most effective incentives are those that celebrate the group's accomplishments collectively rather than those that single out individuals.[72]

> **Reward systems shape productive behavior.**

6-6b The Power of Earning

Both individual and team reward systems can shape productive behavior, so effective performance management boosts both individual and team achievements in an organization. Performance management and reward systems assume a demonstrable connection between performance and rewards; that is, organizations get the performance they reward, not the performance they say they want.[73]

When there is no apparent link between performance and rewards, people may begin to believe they are entitled to rewards regardless of their performance. The notion of entitlement at work counteracts the *power of earning*.[74] People who believe they are entitled to rewards without earning them are not motivated to behave constructively. Merit raises in some organizations, for example, have come to be viewed as entitlements, thus reducing their positive value in the organizational reward system. Entitlement engenders passive, irresponsible behavior, whereas earning engenders active, responsible behavior. The power of earning rests on a direct link between performance and rewards. Managers play a critical role in helping to establish this link by establishing performance goals, providing employees with feedback and assistance toward goal completion, evaluating their performance, then recommending rewards based on performance. These "contingent reward leadership" behaviors strengthen the line-of-sight that helps employees more clearly see the connection between the pay they receive and their performance of established goals.[75]

6-7 CORRECTING POOR PERFORMANCE

Often a challenge for supervisors, correcting poor performance can be conceived as a three-step process. First, supervisors must identify the cause or primary responsibility for the poor performance. Second, if the primary responsibility is the employee's (and not the organization's) supervisors must determine the source of the personal problem. Third, they must develop a plan for correcting the poor performance.

A number of problems trigger poor performance. These include poorly designed work systems, poor selection processes, inadequate training and skills development, lack of personal motivation, and personal problems intruding on the work environment. Not all poor performance is self-motivated, though; some is induced by the work system. Therefore, a good diagnosis should precede corrective action, and work systems should be the first factor considered. It may be that an employee is subject to a work design or selection system that keeps him from exhibiting good performance.

If the poor performance can't be attributed to work design or organizational process problems, then supervisors should examine the employee. The problem may lie in (1) some aspect of the person's relationship to the organization or supervisor, (2) some area of the employee's personal life, or (3) a training or developmental deficiency. In the latter two cases, poor performance can be treated as a symptom rather than as a motivated consequence. In such cases, identifying financial problems, family difficulties, or health disorders may help the employee solve problems before they become too extensive.

Poor performance may also stem from an employee's displaced anger or conflict with the organization or supervisor. In such cases, the employee may be unaware of the internal reactions causing the problem. Such angry motivations can generate sabotage, work slowdowns, and work stoppages. The supervisor might be attributing the cause of the problem to the employee while the employee is attributing it to the supervisor or organization. Supervisors must treat the poor performance as a symptom with a deeper cause and resolve the underlying anger or conflict.

6-7a Performance and Kelley's Attribution Theory

Recall from Chapter 3 that humans want to know why people behave the way they do. The same is true for managers. According to Harold Kelley's *attribution theory*, managers make attributions, or inferences, concerning employees' behavior and performance.[76] The attributions may not always be accurate. Supervisors and employees who share perceptions and attitudes tend to evaluate each other highly.[77] Those who do not share perceptions and attitudes are more likely to blame each other for performance problems.

Kelley's attribution theory proposes that individuals make attributions based on information gathered in the form of three informational cues: consensus, distinctiveness, and consistency.[78] **Consensus** is an informational cue indicating the extent to which peers in the same situation behave in a similar fashion. **Distinctiveness** is a cue indicating the degree to which an individual behaves the same way in other situations. **Consistency** is a cue indicating the frequency of behavior over time. We form attributions based on whether these cues are low or high.

Certain combinations of cues suggest an internal attribution, while other combinations suggest that the cause of the poor performance is external. Suppose you have received several complaints from customers regarding one of your customer service representatives, Niki. You have not received complaints about your other service representatives (low consensus). Reviewing Niki's records, you find that she also received customer complaints during her previous job as a sales clerk (low distinctiveness). The complaints have been coming in steadily for three months (high consistency). In this case, you would most likely make an internal attribution and conclude that the complaints must stem from Niki's behavior. The combination of low consensus, low distinctiveness, and high consistency suggests internal attributions.

Other combinations of these cues, however, point to external attributions. High consensus, high distinctiveness, and low consistency, for example, produce external attributions. Suppose one of your employees, Sanjay, is performing poorly on collecting overdue accounts. You find that the behavior is widespread within your work team (high consensus) and that Sanjay is performing poorly only on this aspect of the job (high distinctiveness), and that most of the time he handles this aspect of the job well (low consistency). You will probably decide that something about the work situation caused the poor performance.

FIGURE 6.4 **INFORMATIONAL CUES AND ATTRIBUTIONS**

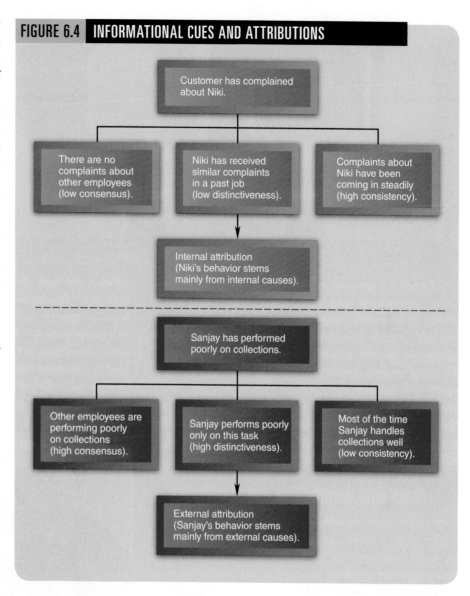

On the basis of the informational cues, the supervisor makes either an internal (personal) attribution or an external (situational) attribution. Internal attributions might include low effort, lack of commitment, or lack of ability. External attributions are outside the employee's control and might include equipment failure or unrealistic goals. These examples are illustrated visually in Figure 6.4. Be warned, however, that the process of determining the cause of a behavior is not always as simple and clear-cut as these examples suggest, because biases sometimes interfere.

consensus An informational cue indicating the extent to which peers in the same situation behave in a similar fashion.

distinctiveness An informational cue indicating the degree to which an individual behaves the same way in other situations.

consistency An informational cue indicating the frequency of behavior over time.

FIGURE 6.5 ATTRIBUTION MODEL

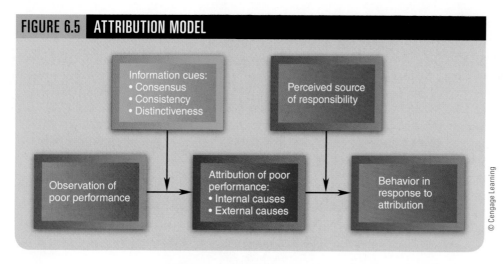

© Cengage Learning

Figure 6.5 presents an attribution model of supervisors' responses to poor performance. Supervisors may choose from a wide range of responses. They can, for example, express personal concern, reprimand the employee, or provide training. Supervisors who attribute the cause of poor performance to a person (an internal cause) will respond more harshly than supervisors who blame the work situation (an external cause). Supervisors should avoid both common attribution errors discussed in Chapter 3: the fundamental attribution error and the self-serving bias.

6-7b Coaching, Counseling, and Mentoring

Supervisors and coworkers are often more effective guides than formally as-signed mentors from higher up in the organizational hierarchy.[79] Consequently, they have important coaching, counseling, and mentoring responsibilities to their subordinates. Success in the mentoring relationship depends on openness and trust.[80] This relationship may help address performance-based deficiencies or personal problems.[81] In either case, supervisors can play a helpful role in employee problem-solving activities without accepting responsibility for the employees' problems. They may refer the employee to trained professionals.

Coaching and counseling are among the career and psychosocial functions of a mentoring relationship.[82] **Mentoring** is a work relationship that encourages development and career enhancement for people moving through the career cycle. Research has found a positive relationship between supervisory mentoring and OCBs. Employees who receive mentoring from their immediate supervisors are more likely to

mentoring A work relationship that encourages development and career enhancement for people moving through the career cycle.

engage in individually-focused OCBs (OCB-Is). OCB-Is are those helping behaviors that directly benefit co-workers as opposed to those that benefit the organization as a whole.[83] Mentor relationships typically go through four phases: initiation, cultivation, separation, and redefinition. Mentoring offers protégés many career benefits.[84] The relationship can significantly enhance the early development of a newcomer and the midcareer development of an experienced employee. Some companies, such as IBM, offer mentoring at all levels of employment.[85] Peer relationships can also enhance career development.[86] Executive coaching is increasingly used to outsource the business mentoring functions. Informational, collegial, and special peers aid the individual's development by sharing information, career strategies, job-related feedback, emotional support, and friendship.

Greg Nelson/Sports Illustrated/Getty Images

A coach that provides constructive criticism to his/her employees will see positive results more often than not.

A_KUDR/Shutterstock.com

FASTFACT

CEOs Need Mentors, Too

While most CEOs of large corporations have benefitted from mentoring and other developmental activities during their rise to the top of organizations, a new study reveals these top-level employees may also benefit from mentoring once they reach the top. A two-year study surveyed forty-five CEOs who had formal mentoring arrangements from veterans outside their own companies. Of those, 71% believed their company performance had improved as a result; 69% made better decisions; 76% felt more capable about fulfilling stakeholder expectations; and 84% credited mentoring with helping them avoid costly mistakes and become proficient more quickly.

SOURCE: S. deJanasz and M. Peiperl, "CEOs Need Mentors Too," *Harvard Business Review* (April 2015): 100–103.

STUDY TOOLS 6

LOCATED AT BACK OF THE TEXTBOOK

☐ Rip out chapter review card

LOCATED AT WWW.CENGAGE.COM/LOGIN

☐ Track your knowledge and understanding of key concepts in business using 4LTR Press Online

☐ Review key term flashcards and create your own using StudyBits

☐ Create and complete practice quizzes based off of your notes and StudyBits

☐ Complete Online activities such as Matching and Fill-in-the-Blank exercises

☐ View chapter highlight box content, including the chapter videos, key exhibits and executive profiles.

7 | Stress and Well-Being at Work

LEARNING OUTCOMES

7-1 Define stress, distress, and strain.

7-2 Compare four different approaches to stress.

7-3 Explain the psychophysiology of the stress response.

7-4 Identify work and nonwork causes of stress.

7-5 Describe the consequences of stress.

7-6 Discuss individual factors that influence a person's response to stress and strain.

7-7 Identify the stages and elements of preventive stress management for individuals and organizations.

After finishing this chapter go to **PAGE 116** for **STUDY TOOLS.**

7-1 WHAT IS STRESS?

Stress is an important topic in organizational behavior, due in part to its influence on competitive pressures that impact workers and managers alike. Poor leadership, work–family conflicts, and sexual harassment are among the leading causes of work stress.[1] Although experts do not always agree on its definition, **stress**, or the *stress response*, can be described as the unconscious preparation to fight or flee that a person experiences when faced with any demand.[2] A **stressor**, or demand, is a person or event that triggers the stress response. While stress is a neutral concept, it carries a negative connotation for some people, as though it should be avoided. This is unfortunate because stress is a great asset in managing legitimate emergencies and achieving peak performance. **Distress**, or **strain**, refers to the adverse psychological, physical, behavioral, and organizational consequences that *may* occur as a result of stressful events.

> **Stress is a great asset in managing legitimate emergencies and achieving peak performance.**

Danielala/Shutterstock.com

7-2 FOUR APPROACHES TO STRESS

The *stress response* was discovered by Walter B. Cannon, a medical physiologist, early in the twentieth century.[3] Later, however, researchers defined stress differently than Cannon did, so we will review four different approaches to define stress: the homeostatic/medical, cognitive appraisal, person–environment fit, and psychoanalytic approaches. These four approaches to stress will give you a more complete understanding of what stress really is.

7-2a The Homeostatic/Medical Approach

When Walter B. Cannon first developed the concept of stress, he called it the *emergency response* or the *militaristic response*, arguing that it was rooted in "the fighting emotions." His early writings showed emotions such as fear and rage cause the *fight-or-flight* response.[4] In Cannon's *homeostatic/medical approach*, stress occurs when deep emotions or environmental demands upset an individual's natural steadystate balance, what he calls **homeostasis**.[5] Cannon believed the body was designed with natural defense mechanisms to keep it in homeostasis. He was especially interested in the role of the sympathetic nervous system in activating a person under stressful conditions.

7-2b The Cognitive Appraisal Approach

Richard Lazarus was more concerned with the psychology of stress, emphasizing the psychological and cognitive aspects of the stress response in his *cognitive appraisal approach*.[6] Like Cannon, Lazarus saw stress as a result of a person–environment interaction, yet he emphasized the individual's cognitive appraisal in classifying persons or events as stressful or not. When appraising stressful workplace events, an important distinction can be made between "hindrance" and "threat" stressors. Whereas hindrance stressors tend to block goal achievement, threat stressors pose immediate personal harm or loss.[7] Individuals differ in their appraisals of events and people. Perception and cognitive appraisal are important processes in determining what is stressful. One study found higher instances of major depression when job demands were objectively assessed.[8] Another study found culture-specific differences in the perception of job stress between China and the United States.[9] American employees reported lack of control as a source of stress, while Chinese employees reported job evaluations as a significant source. In addition to cognitive appraisal, Lazarus introduced the ideas of problem-focused and emotion-focused coping. The former emphasizes managing the stressor, while the latter emphasizes managing the response. Whether individuals use problem- or

stress The unconscious preparation to fight or flee that a person experiences when faced with any demand.

stressor The person or event that triggers the stress response.

distress The adverse psychological, physical, behavioral, and organizational consequences that may arise as a result of stressful events.

strain Distress.

homeostasis A steady state of bodily functioning and equilibrium.

emotion-focused coping strategies depends on motivation. For example, students planning and preparing for exams would more likely use problem-focused coping.[10] Those who evaluate themselves positively and consider themselves capable and in control of their own lives tend to favor emotion-focused coping when faced with stressors.[11]

7-2c The Person–Environment Fit Approach

Robert Kahn was concerned with the social psychology of stress, so his *person–environment fit* approach emphasized the idea that confusing and conflicting expectations of a person in a social role create stress for that person.[12] He extended the approach to consider a person's fit in the environment. A good person–environment fit occurs when one's skills and abilities match a clearly defined, consistent set of role expectations. Stress occurs when the role expectations are confusing and/or conflict with one's skills and abilities. After a period of this type of stress, one can expect to experience symptoms of strain such as depression.

7-2d The Psychoanalytic Approach

Freudian psychoanalytic theory can help us understand the role of unconscious personality factors as causes of stress within a person.[13] Applying this *psychoanalytic* approach, Harry Levinson argued that two elements of the personality interact to cause stress. The first element is the **ego-ideal**—the embodiment of a person's perfect self. The second element is the **self-image**—how the person really sees herself, both positively and negatively. Although not sharply defined, the ego-ideal encompasses admirable attributes of parental personalities, desired and/or imaginable qualities, and the absence of any negative or distasteful qualities. Stress results from the discrepancy between the idealized self (ego-ideal) and the real self-image; the greater the discrepancy, the more stress a person experiences.

 ## THE STRESS RESPONSE

Whether activated by an ego-ideal/self-image discrepancy, a poorly defined social role, a cognitive appraisal suggesting threat, or a lack of balance, the resulting stress response is characterized by a predictable sequence of mind and body events. The stress response begins with the release of chemical messengers, primarily adrenaline, into the bloodstream. These messengers activate the sympathetic nervous system and the endocrine (hormone) system. These two systems work together to trigger four mind–body changes that prepare the person for fight or flight. (Refer to "The Psychophysiology of Stress" on page 116.)

As the body responds, the person shifts from a neutral posture to an offensive posture. The stress response can be very effective in preparing a person to handle legitimate emergencies through peak performance. Thus, it is neither inherently bad nor necessarily destructive. Perceptions of interactional injustice in the workplace can trigger the physiological stress response, with high levels of cortisol being released into the bloodstream of individuals who perceive they are being treated unfairly.[14]

 ## SOURCES OF WORK STRESS

Work stress is caused by factors in the work environment as well as by nonwork (external) pressures that spill over into the workplace. The two major categories of sources of both types of work stress are shown in Table 7.1. An example of an external pressure is when a working mother or father is called at work to come pick up a sick child from day care. One of the most complex work-related causes of stress is role conflict. An innovative study by Pam Perrewé and her colleagues examined the dysfunctional physical and psychological consequences of role conflict.[15] The researchers found political skill to be an antidote for role conflict, one of a range of preventive stress-management strategies discussed later in the chapter.

7-4a Work Demands

Role demands include role ambiguity as well as role conflict. But there are also three other categories of work demands: task demands, interpersonal demands, and physical demands. Table 7.1 does not present an exhaustive list of work demands but rather aims to show major causes of work stress in each of the four major domains of the work environment.

TASK DEMANDS Dramatic changes at work lead to uncertainty in a person's daily tasks and activities, provoking on-the-job pressure and stress.[16] Globalization and large-scale business trends lead to change, as do smaller-scale shifts in company policy. In recent years, the global economic recession has led many companies to make

ego-ideal The embodiment of a person's perfect self.

self-image How a person sees himself or herself, both positively and negatively.

TABLE 7.1	WORK AND NONWORK DEMANDS	
WORK DEMANDS		
Task Demands		**Role Demands**
Change		Role conflict:
Lack of control		Interrole
Career progress		Intrarole
New technologies		Person–role
Temporal pressure		Role ambiguity
Interpersonal Demands		**Physical Demands**
Emotional toxins		Extreme environments
Sexual harassment		Strenuous activities
Poor leadership		Hazardous substances
		Global travel
NONWORK DEMANDS		
Home Demands		**Personal Demands**
Family expectations		Workaholism
Child-rearing/day care arrangements		Civic and volunteer work
Parental care		Traumatic events

© Cengage Learning

Lack of control is another major task-related source of stress, especially in positions that are difficult and psychologically demanding. The lack of control may be caused by the inability to

- influence the timing of tasks and activities;
- select tools or methods for accomplishing the work;
- make decisions that influence work outcomes; or
- exercise direct action to affect the work outcomes.

Concerns over career progress and time pressures (or work overload) are two additional task demands triggering stress at work. Career stress has occurred in many organizations over the past two decades as middle-manager ranks have been thinned by mergers, acquisitions, and downsizing.[19] Leaner organizations, unfortunately, mean overload for the retained employees. Fewer people doing the same amount of work or more creates time pressure, a leading cause of stress often associated with work overload. Time pressure may also result from poor time-management skills. But not all task demands are negative. Challenge stressors that promote personal growth and achievement are positively related to job satisfaction and organizational commitment.[20]

stressful changes, such as downsizing. At least 20 million jobs were lost by the end of 2009 due to the crisis.[17] Even during periods of growth, when hundreds of thousands of jobs are created every month, there may be significant numbers of jobs lost within certain sectors of the U.S. economy. For those who do not lose their jobs, underemployment, monotony, and boredom may be problematic.

Technological innovation creates change and uncertainty for many employees, requiring additional training, education, and skill development. New technologies create both career stress and so-called technostress for those who wonder if smart machines will replace them.[18] Although they enhance the organization's productive capacity, new technologies may be viewed as the enemy by workers who must ultimately learn to use them. This creates a real dilemma for management. Intended to make work easier and more convenient, information technology may have the paradoxical effect of incurring stress rather than relieving it.

> **New technologies create both career stress and so-called technostress for those who wonder if smart machines will replace them.**

ROLE DEMANDS The social–psychological demands of the work environment may be every bit as stressful as task demands. Role stress may be particularly harmful to the job satisfaction and affective commitment of newcomers to the organization.[21] People encounter two major categories of role stress at work: role conflict and role ambiguity.[22] *Role conflict* results from inconsistent or incompatible expectations. The conflict may be an interrole, intrarole, or person–role conflict.

Interrole conflict is caused by opposing expectations related to two separate roles assumed by the same individual, such as employee and parent. For example, the employee with a major sales presentation due on Monday and a sick child at home Sunday night is likely to experience interrole conflict. Work–family conflicts such as these can lead individuals to withdrawal behaviors.[23] High levels of strain may also lead to increased work–family conflicts for women and men.[24] *Intrarole conflict* is caused by opposing expectations related to a single role. For example, the manager who

presses employees for both very fast and high-quality work may be viewed at some point as creating a conflict for employees.

Ethics violations are likely to cause *person–role conflicts*. Employees expected to behave in ways that violate personal values, beliefs, or principles experience this type of conflict. Person–role conflicts and ethics violations create a sense of divided loyalty for an employee. For example, if a distributor tells an organic farmer to cut costs by using a synthetic pesticide, the farmer may find that his personal beliefs are compromised by his role as a producer. Organizations with high ethical standards, such as Johnson & Johnson, are less likely to create ethical conflicts for employees.

The second major cause of role stress is *role ambiguity*, which is the confusion a person experiences in relation to the expectations of others. Role ambiguity may be caused by misunderstanding what is expected, not knowing how to do it, or not knowing the result of failure to do it. For example, a new magazine employee asked to copyedit a manuscript may experience confusion because she mistakes copyediting for proofreading, she doesn't know what formatting style to use, or she doesn't know what will happen if she misses her deadline.

A twenty-one-nation study examined middle managers' experiences in role conflict, role ambiguity, and role overload. The results indicated that role stress varies more by country than it does by demographic and organizational factors. For example, non-Western managers experience less role ambiguity and more role overload than do their Western counterparts.[25] Another study, this time of 2,273 Norwegian employees, found that role conflict, role ambiguity, and conflict with coworkers increased under laissez-faire leadership, suggesting that a hands-off leadership style is destructive.[26] On the other hand, a study of U.S. military personnel found that when role clarity was high in a supportive work group, psychological strain was low.[27]

INTERPERSONAL DEMANDS *Emotional toxins*, such as sexual harassment and poor leadership in the organization, are examples of interpersonal demands, often generated at work by abrasive personalities.[28] Employees' ability to recharge and replace physical and psychological resources depleted during the work day is necessary for well-being. This recovery of resources often takes place once employees leave the workplace. Though considered less severe than other forms of interpersonal demands, workplace incivility experienced one day often remains with the individual and negatively affects the employee's ability to detach from the work and replenish resources needed for the next work day.[29] Another

consequence of interpersonal demands can be *emotional dissonance*, which can spread through a work environment and cause a range of disturbances and stress.[30] Organizations are increasingly less tolerant of sexual harassment, a gender-related interpersonal demand that creates a stressful working environment for both the person being harassed and for others. The vast majority of sexual harassment is directed at women in the workplace and is a chronic yet preventable problem.[31]

Poor organizational leadership and demanding managerial styles are leading causes of work stress for employees. But much depends on an employee's individual characteristics. Employees who feel secure under strong, directive leadership may be anxious under an open, self-directed style of management. Those comfortable with participative leaders may feel restrained by a directive style. In every case, however, trust is an important characteristic of the leader–follower interpersonal relationship, so a threat to a worker's reputation with his supervisor may be especially stressful.[32] Functional diversity in project groups also causes difficulty in the establishment of trusting relationships. Lack of trust increases job stress, which in turn leads to lower cohesiveness within the group.[33]

PHYSICAL DEMANDS Extreme environments, strenuous activities, hazardous substances, and global travel create physical demands for people at work. One cross-cultural study that examined the effects of ambient temperature on role stress concluded that uncomfortable temperatures diminish human well-being, leading to the development of the term *sweatshop* for inhumane working conditions.[34] The unique physical demands of work are often occupation-specific, such as the risk of

Office work has physical hazards, such as eye-strain, neck stiffness, and lower back pain.

Andrey_Popov/Shutterstock.com

A_KUDR/Shutterstock.com

FASTFACT

The Stressful Side of Summer

Summer is typically a time for relaxation, but 33% of Americans say they experience more stress during the summer than at any other time of the year. The longer days give people the impression that they have to do more to fill the days. And many people do fill those days. For 69%, attending three social events in one week is a regular occurrence. Cramming summer days with increased activities leads to increased stress and reduced sleep since cooler temperatures are better for sleeping.

SOURCE: K. Lally, "Summer Stress Can Lead to Sleeplessness," *Washington Post* (June 30, 2014).

Brocreative/Shutterstock.com

gravity-induced loss of consciousness for military pilots flying high-performance fighters or jet lag and loss of sleep for globetrotting CEOs.[35] Despite the fact that there are many positive aspects to business travel, the associated demands are increasingly recognized as sources of stress.[36]

Office work has its physical hazards as well. Noisy, crowded offices, such as those of some stock brokerages, can prove stressful, and even harmful. Working with a computer can also be stressful, especially if the ergonomic design of the workstation is not correct. Eyestrain, neck stiffness, and arm and wrist problems may result. Office designs that use partitions rather than full walls may create stress by offering little privacy and little protection from interruptions. *Stress audits* provide companies with detailed assessments of possible workplace stressors. Identification and alleviation of overlooked stress factors can save a company money and boost productivity.

7-4b Nonwork Demands

Nonwork demands also create stress, which may carry over into the work environment.[37] *Nonwork demands* may broadly be identified as impositions from an individual's personal life environment (home) and self-imposed restrictions.

HOME DEMANDS The wide array of home and family arrangements in contemporary American society has created great diversity in the arena of home demands. Traditional and nontraditional families may experience demands that create role conflicts or overloads that are difficult to manage. For example, the loss of good day care for children may be especially stressful for dual-career and single-parent families.[38] The tension between work and family may lead to a real struggle for balance in life. This struggle led Rocky Rhodes, cofounder

of Silicon Graphics, to establish four priorities for his life: God, family, exercise, and work.[39] These priorities helped him reallocate his time for better balance in his life. Moreover, as a result of the maturing of the American population, an increasing number of people face the added demand of parental care. Even when a person dedicates herself to reducing stress by integrating opposing social and work-related roles into a balanced, "whole" identity, the process is not an easy one.[40]

PERSONAL DEMANDS Self-imposed personal demands are the second major category of nonwork demands identified in Table 7.1. **Workaholism**, a form of addiction, may be the most notable of these stress-inducing demands.[41] Some of the early warning signs of workaholism include overcommitment to work, inability to enjoy vacations and respites from work, preoccupation with work problems when away from the workplace, and insistence on working at home over weekends.

Another type of personal demand comes from civic activities, volunteer work, and organizational commitments to religious or public service organizations. These demands become more or less stressful depending on their compatibility with work and family life, and their capacity to provide alternative satisfactions for the individual. Finally, traumatic events, such as the devastating earthquake and tsunami in Japan in March 2011, are stressful for people who experience them.[42] Not all traumatic events are as catastrophic as natural disasters, of course, but job loss, failed exams, and romantic break-ups are all traumatic and may lead to distress if not addressed and resolved.

workaholism An imbalanced preoccupation with work at the expense of home and personal life satisfaction.

7-5 THE CONSEQUENCES OF STRESS

Stress may be positive or negative. Positive stress can create a healthy, thriving work environment, while negative stress, or distress, can erode morale and performance.

7-5a Positive Stress

Some managers and executives thrive under pressure because they practice what world-class athletes already know—that bringing mind, body, and spirit to peak condition requires recovering energy, which is as important as expending energy.[43] Hence, world-class athletes and managers get high marks on any stress test because they use stress-induced energy in positive, healthy, and productive ways. The consequences of healthy, normal stress (*eustress*; see Chapter 5) include a number of performance and health benefits.[44] An organization striving for high-quality products and services needs a healthy workforce to support the effort. Eustress is a characteristic of healthy people; distress is not.

The *Yerkes-Dodson law*, shown in Figure 7.1, indicates that stress leads to improved performance up to an optimum point.[45] Beyond that point, stress has a detrimental effect on performance. Therefore, healthy amounts of stress are desirable to improve performance by arousing a person to action. The greatest performance benefits from stress are achieved in the midrange of the Yerkes-Dodson curve, and after that, as Joseph McGrath has suggested, increasing difficulty of the task is probably what causes performance to decline.[46] Thus, the stress response invokes heightened strength and physical force for limited periods of exertion. This is how stress provides a basis for peak performance in athletic competition, and it can do the same for any type of job performance. In addition, psychological well-being reduces stress and thereby contributes positively to job performance.[47]

Specific stressful activities, including aerobic exercise, weight training, and flexibility training, improve health and enhance a person's ability to manage stressful demands or situations. Cannon argued that the stress response better prepares soldiers for combat.[48] In the outdoors, in survival or combat situations, stress provides one with the necessary energy boost to manage the situation successfully.

The various individual and organizational forms of distress often associated with the word *stress* are the result of prolonged activation of the stress response, mismanagement of the energy induced by the response, or unique vulnerabilities in a person. We next examine the forms of individual distress and then the forms of organizational distress.

7-5b Individual Distress

An extreme preoccupation with work may result in acute individual distress. In its most extreme form, individual distress can lead to a phenomenon described by the Japanese word *karoshi*, or death by overwork.[49] Work-related psychological disorders are among the ten leading health disorders and diseases in the United States, according to the National Institute for Occupational Safety and Health.[50] The most common symptoms of psychological distress are depression, burnout, and psychosomatic disorders—physical ailments with psychological origins. These psychological distresses usually lead to *emotional exhaustion*, a form of psychological fatigue caused by energy depletion.[51] Emotional exhaustion may also be caused by the requirement for sustained emotional expression on the job.[52] A recent study of

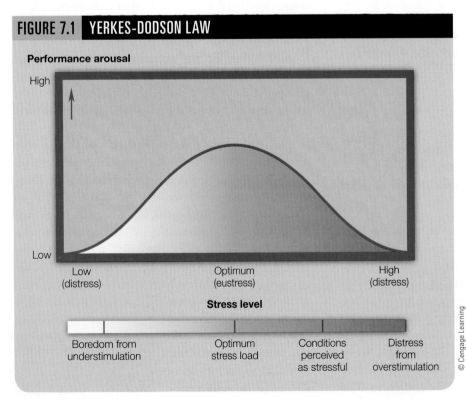

FIGURE 7.1 YERKES-DODSON LAW

Performance arousal

High

Low

| Low (distress) | Optimum (eustress) | High (distress) |

Stress level

| Boredom from understimulation | Optimum stress load | Conditions perceived as stressful | Distress from overstimulation |

© Cengage Learning

257 Australian police officers found that emotional exhaustion at work had the potential to spill over to home life, causing work–family conflict.[53]

Burnout is a psychological response to job stress that Christina Maslach characterizes along three dimensions: emotional exhaustion, depersonalization, and reduced perceptions of personal accomplishment. Emotional exhaustion is at the heart of the burnout experience. The conventional belief is that emotional drain leads to reduced job performance, creating a direct link between burnout and performance. A study by the National Institute questions this assumption and suggests that the influence of motivation has been overlooked in understanding the burnout–performance relationship. Its authors believe that motivation is directly connected to the psychological processes of voluntary goal-directed action, specifically its arousal, direction, intensity, and persistence. Because motivation is considered a direct antecedent of performance, this study suggests that motivation mediates the burnout–performance relationship. Hence, their model is burnout-motivation-performance.[54]

Burnout is not the same as *rust-out*, which is a form of psychological distress caused by a lack of challenge, inspiration, and/or opportunity on the job.[55] For example, a fast-food line cook who has flipped burgers at minimum wage for three years may experience rust-out for all the previously mentioned reasons, resulting in apathy, resentment, and diminished performance.

A number of medical illnesses have a stress-related component.[56] The most significant are heart disease, strokes, backaches, peptic ulcers, and headaches. Ford Motor Company found that cardiovascular diseases, the leading cause of death in the United States since 1910, constituted only 1.5% of the medical incidents among 800 salaried employees at its headquarters but accounted for 29% of the reported medical costs.[57]

Behavioral problems are another form of individual distress. These problems include workplace aggression, substance abuse, and accidents. Workplace aggression may be triggered by perceptions of injustice in the workplace.[58] Interpersonal conflicts can be a form of nonphysical aggression. One study found that conflicts with workmates, neighbors, and other "nonintimates" account for about 80% of our bad moods.[59] Ethnic and cultural differences are too often a basis for interpersonal conflicts and may escalate into physical violence in the workplace. For example, some U.S. employees of Arab descent experienced ethnic slurs and bullying at work after the terrorist attacks of 9/11.

Substance abuse ranges from legal behaviors such as alcohol abuse, excessive smoking, and the overuse of prescription drugs to illegal behaviors such as heroin and cocaine use. The abuse of certain substances, such as tobacco and heroin, can lead to addiction—a physical and/or psychological dependency. Abuse and addiction are behavioral problems that can impair job performance and often lead to significant individual distress.

Stress Hormones Reduce Capacity to Feel Others' Pain

Human beings are normally empathetic. When disaster strikes anywhere in the world, we overwhelmingly respond, offering our financial and emotional support. Yet, we feel no connection with the homeless person sleeping on the sidewalk. Why the disconnect? The physiological stress response may offer some clues. Stanford neuroscientist Dr. Robert Sapolsky, along with Lauren Martin and Jeffrey Mogil, found that the hormones secreted during stress not only impair judgment and our ability to control impulses, these "stress hormones" also have the ability to adversely affect our capacity to feel for someone else in pain, a basic version of empathy called *emotional contagion*. The effect, however, depends on how familiar we are with the person experiencing pain. In one study, research subjects were presented with harmful stimuli designed to illicit increased levels of experienced pain. When subjects were in the "stressed" conditions, they showed emotional contagion for a friend, but not a stranger. However, when the scientists blocked the secretion of stress hormones, the subjects showed emotional contagion for strangers, demonstrating the effects of stress on brain functioning and our ability to feel for others.

SOURCE: R. M. Sapolsky, "When Stress Rises, Empathy Suffers," *Wall Street Journal* (January 16, 2015).

Accidents, both on and off the job, are still another behavioral form of distress that can sometimes be traced to work-related stressors. For example, an unresolved problem at work may preoccupy or distract an employee, causing an accident either at the office or on the road. These three forms of individual distress—psychological disorders, medical illnesses, and behavioral problems—cause a burden of personal suffering. They also cause a collective burden of suffering reflected in organizational distress.

7-5c Organizational Distress

Studies performed at the University of Michigan on *organizational stress* identified a variety of indirect costs of mismanaged stress for an organization, such as low morale, dissatisfaction, breakdowns in communication, and disruption of working relationships. Subsequent research at the Survey Research Center at Michigan established *behavioral costing guidelines*, which specify the direct costs of organizational distress.[60] New research suggests that even positive performance stereotypes can have an adverse effect on organizational health.[61] Three major costs of organizational distress are participation problems, performance decrements, and compensation awards.

Participation problems include absenteeism, tardiness, strikes and work stoppages, and turnover. In the case of absenteeism, the organization may compensate by hiring temporary personnel who take the place of the absentee, possibly elevating personnel costs. When considering turnover, a distinction should be made between dysfunctional and functional turnover. *Dysfunctional turnover* occurs when an organization loses a valuable employee. Replacement costs, including recruiting and retraining, range from five to seven months of the individual monthly salary. *Functional turnover*, in contrast, benefits the organization by creating opportunities for new members, new ideas, and fresh approaches. Functional turnover occurs when an organization loses an employee who has little or no value to the organization; thus the loss of that employee is considered a positive result. The up-or-out promotion policy for members of some organizations is designed to create functional turnover.

participation problem A cost associated with absenteeism, tardiness, strikes and work stoppages, and turnover.

performance decrement A cost resulting from poor quality or low quantity of production, grievances, and unscheduled machine downtime and repair.

compensation award An organizational cost resulting from court awards for job distress.

Performance decrements are the costs resulting from poor quality or low quantity of production, grievances, and unscheduled machine downtime and repair. As in the case of medical illness, stress is not the only causal agent in these performance decrements. Stress does play a role, however, whether the poor quality or low quantity of production is motivated by distressed employees or by an unconscious response to stress on the job. Some employees in California have the option of taking a "stress leave" rather than filing a grievance against the boss.

Compensation awards are the organizational costs resulting from court awards for job distress.[62] In a federal lawsuit against Allstate, Frank Deus claimed that the company created a high-strain job for him that resulted in incapacitating depression.[63] A jury awarded him a $1.5 million judgment that was later overturned. Job stress–related claims have skyrocketed and threaten to bankrupt the workers' compensation system in some states, although claims and costs are down in other states.[64] Employers need not panic because fair procedures go a long way toward avoiding legal liability, and legal rulings are setting realistic limits on employers' obligations.[65]

7-6 INDIVIDUAL DIFFERENCES IN THE STRESS–STRAIN RELATIONSHIP

Individual differences play a central role in the stress–strain relationship. The *weak organ hypothesis* in medicine, also known as the *Achilles' heel phenomenon*, suggests that a person breaks down at her weakest point. Individual differences, such as gender and Type A behavior pattern, enhance vulnerability to strain under stressful conditions. Other individual differences, such as personality hardiness and self-reliance, reduce vulnerability to strain under stressful conditions. One study of personality and emotional performance found that individuals high on extraversion experienced elevated heart rates when asked to express personality-incongruent emotions such as anger and that neuroticism was more generally associated with increased heart rate and poor performance.[66] Extraversion and neuroticism thus seem to affect the stress–strain relationship.

7-6a Gender Effects

While prevailing stereotypes suggest that women are the weaker sex, the truth is that the life expectancy for American women is almost six years longer than for American men. The weaker sex stereotype is further challenged by research in public accounting, which finds that female public accountants have no higher turnover rates than males even though they report more stress.[67] Moreover, research finds that women's behavioral responses to stress are not only different from men's responses but that they are also strengths in women rather than weaknesses.[68]

Some literature suggests that there are differences in the stressors to which the two sexes are subject.[69] For example, sexual harassment is a gender-related source of stress for many working women. Men sometimes experience sexual harassment as well, though, and are more likely than women to abuse alcohol as a coping mechanism. This may be because harassment is not a normative occurrence for men.[70]

There is substantive evidence that vulnerabilities constitute the important differences between the sexes.[71] Males are more vulnerable at an earlier age to fatal health problems such as cardiovascular disorders, whereas women report more nonfatal but long-term and disabling health problems. Although we can conclude that gender indeed creates a differential vulnerability between the two sexes, it may actually be more important to examine the differences *among* women or *among* men.

7-6b Type A Behavior Pattern

Type A behavior pattern is a combination of personality and behavioral characteristics that include competitiveness, time urgency, social status insecurity, aggression, hostility, and a quest for achievements. Type A behavior pattern is also labeled *coronary-prone behavior* because it is linked with coronary heart disease.[72] There are two primary hypotheses concerning which part of the Type A behavior pattern is lethal. One suggests that the problem is time urgency, while the other suggests that it is hostility and aggression. The weight of evidence suggests that hostility and aggression, not time urgency, are the lethal agents.[73]

The alternative to the Type A behavior pattern is the Type B behavior pattern. People with Type B personalities are relatively free of Type A behaviors and characteristics. Type B people are less coronary prone, but if they do have a heart attack, they do not appear to recover as well as those with Type A personalities. Organizations can also be characterized as Type A or Type B.[74] Type A individuals in Type B organizations and Type B individuals in Type A organizations experience stress related to a misfit between their personality type and the predominant type of the organization.

Type A behavior can be modified. The first step is for Type A people to recognize that they are prone to the Type A pattern and possibly to spend time with

> **Type A behavior pattern**
> A complex of personality and behavioral characteristics, including competitiveness, time urgency, social status insecurity, aggression, hostility, and a quest for achievements.

Goldman Sachs Is a Great Place to Work for Type A Employees

Individuals with Type A personalities are known for their quest for numbers and hurried lifestyles. Conventional wisdom suggests that the last thing Type A employees need is a Type A workplace. Goldman Sachs employees defy conventional wisdom. Walk into Goldman's lower Manhattan offices, and you might see groups of employees participating in meditation sessions, being implored to "let go of the day's stresses." These meditation sessions are part of Goldman's "resiliency week" that is designed to help its employees focus on stress management, happiness, and work-life balance in the midst of routinely long workweeks and grueling work hours. Goldman Sachs employees, like other large investment firms, command high salaries, some averaging $380,000 per year. But ask employees why Goldman Sachs is No. 45 on *Fortune's* 100 Best Companies to Work, and they may tell you it's the inclusive culture, the ability to balance work with family, and the emphasis on managing stress. The pay's not bad, either.

Goldman Sachs offers stress relief sessions to employees.

Samuel Borges Photography/Shutterstock.com

SOURCE: C. Matthews. "Why People Love Working at Goldman Sachs: It's Not Just the Money," *Time* (January 16, 2014); A. Vandermey. "Yes, Goldman Sachs Really Is a Great Place to Work," *Fortune* (February 3, 2014): 97–104.

Type B individuals. Type B people often recognize Type A behavior and can help Type A individuals judge situations realistically. Type A individuals can also pace themselves, manage their time well, and try not to do multiple things at once. Focusing only on the task at hand and its completion rather than worrying about other tasks can help Type A individuals cope more effectively.

7-6c Personality Hardiness

People who have hardy personalities resist strain reactions when subjected to stressful events more effectively than do people who are not hardy.[75] The components of **personality hardiness** are commitment, control, and challenge. Commitment is an engagement with one's environment that leads to the experience of activities as interesting and enjoyable. Employees with high levels of commitment are less likely to leave the organization or experience promotion-related stress.[76] Control is an ability to influence the processes and outcomes of events that lead to the experience of activities as personal choices. Challenge is the conception of change as a stimulus to personal development, which leads to the welcome experience of new activities.

The hardy personality appears to use these three components actively to engage in transformational coping when faced with stressful events.[77] **Transformational coping** is the active process of modifying one's perception of an event in order to reduce stress. This is accomplished by viewing the event in broader terms, by altering the course and outcome through action, and/or by achieving greater understanding of the process. The alternative to transformational coping is *regressive coping*, characterized by a passive avoidance of events and decreased interaction with the environment. Regressive coping may lead to short-term stress reduction at the cost of healthy, long-term life adjustment.

personality hardiness A personality characterized by commitment, control, and challenge and, hence, resistant to distress.

transformational coping A way of managing stressful events by changing them into less subjectively stressful events.

self-reliance A healthy, secure, interdependent pattern of behavior related to how people form and maintain supportive attachments with others.

counterdependence An unhealthy, insecure pattern of behavior that leads to separation in relationships with other people.

overdependence An unhealthy, insecure pattern of behavior that leads to preoccupied attempts to achieve security through relationships.

Hardy	Not Hardy
Commitment	Alienation
Control	Powerlessness
Challenge	Threat

7-6d Self-Reliance

There is increasing evidence that social relationships have an important impact on health and life expectancy.[78] **Self-reliance**, a healthy, secure interdependent pattern of behavior, is a personality attribute strongly related to social relationships. The concept of self-reliance was originally based on *attachment theory*, a psychological approach to normal human development that identifies three distinct patterns of attachment.[79] Research suggests that these patterns become behavioral strategies during adulthood in professional as well as personal relationships.[80] A secure pattern of attachment and *interdependent* behavior results in self-reliance. The connection between self-reliance and the word *interdependent* may appear paradoxical because a person appears independent while maintaining a host of supportive attachments.[81] But self-reliant people respond to stressful, threatening situations by reaching out to others appropriately. Indeed, self-reliance is a flexible, responsive strategy of forming and maintaining multiple, diverse relationships. Self-reliant people are confident, enthusiastic, and persistent in facing challenges. Their flexibility allows them to form healthy partner relationships that buffer work-related stress.[82]

Interpersonal attachment is emotional and psychological connectedness to another person. In contrast, the two insecure patterns of attachment are counterdependence and overdependence. **Counterdependence** is an unhealthy, insecure pattern of behavior that leads to separation in relationships with other people. When faced with stressful and threatening situations, counterdependent people withdraw. Counterdependence may be characterized as a rigid, dismissing denial of the need for other people in difficult and stressful times. Counterdependent people exhibit a fearless, aggressive, and active response to challenges, but they are not truly self-reliant.

Overdependence is also an unhealthy, insecure pattern of behavior. Overdependent people respond to stressful and threatening situations by clinging to other people in any way possible. Overdependence may be characterized as a desperate, preoccupied attempt to achieve a sense of security through relationships. Overdependent people exhibit an active but disorganized and anxious response to challenges. This quality prevents a person from being able to organize and maintain healthy relationships; therefore, it creates distress. Interestingly, both counterdependence and overdependence can be exhibited by military personnel who are experiencing adjustment difficulties during the first thirty days of basic training.[83] The recruits who have the most difficulty adjusting to new jobs demonstrate severe overdependence. They often find it difficult to function on their own during training.

7-7 PREVENTIVE STRESS MANAGEMENT

Stress is an inevitable part of work and personal life. **Preventive stress management** is an organizational philosophy according to which people and organizations should take joint responsibility for promoting health and preventing distress and strain. This philosophy is rooted in public health practices first used in preventive medicine. A framework for understanding preventive stress management is presented in Figure 7.2, which includes three stages of prevention that apply in a preventive medicine context as well as an organizational context.

Primary prevention is intended to reduce, modify, or eliminate the stress-causing demand or stressor. The idea behind primary prevention is to eliminate or alleviate the source of a problem. True organizational stress prevention is largely primary in nature because it reduces the demands the organization places on the employee. **Secondary prevention** is intended to modify the individual's or the organization's response to a demand or stressor. Employees must learn to manage the inevitable, unalterable work stressors and demands to avert distress and strain while improving health and well-being. **Tertiary prevention** is intended to heal individual or organizational symptoms of distress and strain. The symptoms may range from early warning signs (such as headaches or absenteeism) to more severe forms of distress (such as hypertension, work stoppages, and strikes). An innovative approach used by the data recovery company DriveSavers bolsters treatment and prevention with a full-time grief counselor.[84] The stages of prevention can be applied to organizational

> **preventive stress management** An organizational philosophy according to which people and organizations should take joint responsibility for promoting health and preventing distress and strain.
>
> **primary prevention** The stage in preventive stress management designed to reduce, modify, or eliminate the demand or stressor causing stress.
>
> **secondary prevention** The stage in preventive stress management designed to alter or modify the individual's or the organization's response to a demand or stressor.
>
> **tertiary prevention** The stage in preventive stress management designed to heal individual or organizational symptoms of distress and strain.

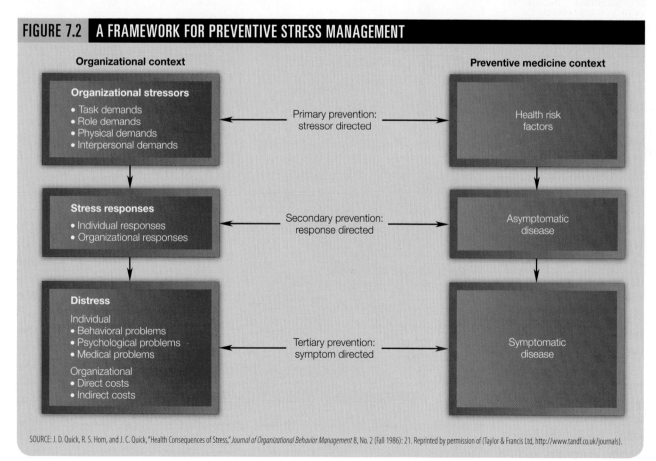

FIGURE 7.2 A FRAMEWORK FOR PREVENTIVE STRESS MANAGEMENT

SOURCE: J. D. Quick, R. S. Horn, and J. C. Quick, "Health Consequences of Stress," *Journal of Organizational Behavior Management* 8, No. 2 (Fall 1986): 21. Reprinted by permission of (Taylor & Francis Ltd, http://www.tandf.co.uk/journals).

prevention, individual prevention, and comprehensive health promotion.

7-7a Organizational Stress Prevention

Some organizations maintain low-stress, healthy environments, while others cultivate high-stress environments that may place their employees' health at risk. The experience of organizational justice and fairness is emerging as one contextual factor that leads to a positive, low-stress work environment.[85] One comprehensive approach to organizational health and preventive stress management was pioneered in the U.S. Air Force by Colonel Joyce Adkins, who developed an Organizational Health Center (OHC) with the Air Force Materiel Command.[86] The OHC's goal is to keep workers happy, healthy, and on the job while increasing efficiency and productivity to their highest levels. This goal is achieved by focusing on workplace stressors, organizational and individual forms of distress, and managerial and individual strategies for preventive stress management. Adkins's comprehensive, organizational health approach addresses primary, secondary, and tertiary prevention. Most organizational prevention, however, is primary prevention, including job redesign, goal setting, role negotiation, and career management.

Two organizational stress prevention methods—team building and social support at work—are secondary prevention. We discuss team building in Chapter 9, but we should note here that under stress, team structure may influence team effectiveness. Specifically, teams experiencing quantitative demands are more effective when more tightly structured, while teams experiencing qualitative demands are more effective when more loosely structured.[87] Finally, companies such as

Kraft Foods (a subsidiary of Altria Group, Inc.) and Hardee's Food Systems (part of CKE Restaurants, Inc.) have developed specific violence prevention programs to combat the rise in workplace violence. Violence in organizations is a category of dysfunctional behaviors that is often motivated by stressful events and whose negative consequences need to be prevented.[88] Ethical decision-making may also be affected by worker anxiety. Studies have shown that anxiety increases threat perception, which in turn often leads individuals to focus narrowly on their own self-interests rather than ethical principles.[89]

JOB REDESIGN The job strain model illustrated in Figure 7.3 suggests that the combination of stringent demands and restricted control leads to a high-strain job. A major goal in job redesign should be to increase worker

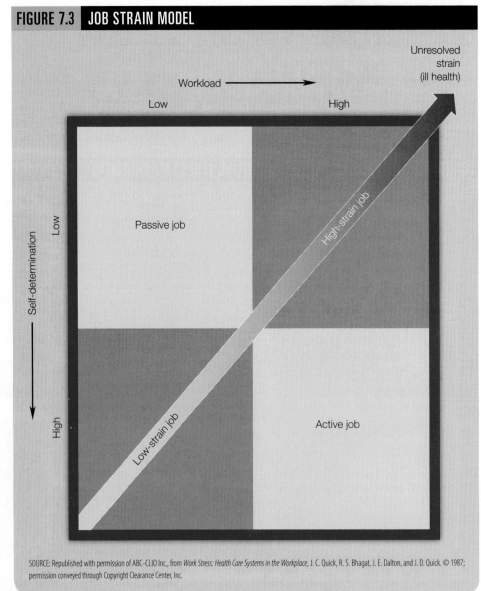

FIGURE 7.3 JOB STRAIN MODEL

SOURCE: Republished with permission of ABC-CLIO Inc., from *Work Stress: Health Care Systems in the Workplace*, J. C. Quick, R. S. Bhagat, J. E. Dalton, and J. D. Quick. © 1987; permission conveyed through Copyright Clearance Center, Inc.

Blablo101/Shutterstock.com

HOT TREND

Reducing Workplace Stress by Order of Management

American workers log more hours on the job than workers in nearly every other country except Korea. Yet American's long work hours have not translated into huge productivity gains. In fact, Germany topped the list of countries with the most productive workers. France, a country with extremely generous vacation policies, came in second in terms of productivity per hours worked.

Along with people issues, American workers site juggling work and personal lives, lack of job security, and workload as the major causes of workplace stress. Despite acknowledgment of these work demands as sources of stress, many American workers do not take their allowed vacation. When they do take vacation, they cannot seem to completely detach. The result for many employers is a workplace filled with employees experiencing high levels of stress, anxiety, and increased depression. Employers are taking steps to reverse this trend, however, by revamping their employee wellness programs, some with free massages, gym memberships, nutrition counseling, and medication courses. Even more companies are offering employees cash incentives to exercise. Employers are slated to spend 15% more per employee on wellness programs and are implementing new policies to reduce employee stress levels. For instance, Citigroup employees are urged to take all of their vacation and forbidden to work on Saturdays. Weekend work requires manager approval.

SOURCE: G. Colvin, "The New Trend? Reducing Stress in the Workplace—By Order of Management," *Fortune* 170 (2014): 42.; J. Stillman, "Which Country Has the Most Productive Workers?" *Inc.* (July 25, 2014).

control. In many cases, this reduces distress and strain without reducing productivity.

Increasing worker control is a strategy of preventive stress management that can be accomplished in a number of ways, the most common being to increase job decision latitude. Increased latitude might include greater authority over the sequencing of work activities, the timing of work schedules, the selection and sequencing of work tools, or the selection of work teams. A second objective of job redesign should be to reduce uncertainty and increase predictability in the workplace.

GOAL SETTING Preventive stress management can also be achieved through goal-setting activities. These activities are designed to increase task motivation while reducing role conflict and ambiguity. Goal setting focuses a person's attention while directing energy into a productive channel. Implicit in much of the goal-setting literature is the assumption that people participate in determining their work goals.

ROLE NEGOTIATION The organizational development technique of role negotiation has value as a stress-management method because it allows individuals to modify their work roles.[90] Role negotiation begins with the definition of a focal role within the organizational context. The person in the focal role identifies the expectations understood for the role, and organizational supervisors specify their own expectations of the person in the focal role. A negotiation of integrated role expectation follows. In the process of such negotiation, points of confusion and conflict become opportunities for clarification and resolution. The final result of the role negotiation process should be a clear, well-defined focal role with which the incumbent and organizational members are all comfortable.

SOCIAL SUPPORT SYSTEMS Team building is one way to develop supportive social relationships in the workplace. However, team building is primarily task oriented, not socioemotional, in nature. Although employees may receive much of their socio-emotional support from personal relationships outside the workplace, some socioemotional support within the workplace is also necessary for psychological well-being.

Social support systems can be enhanced through the work environment in a number of ways. Implementing support systems that help employees identify with the company may buffer the negative effects of workplace stressors and improve employees' ability to adjust.[91] Interpersonal communication is the key to unlocking social support for preventive stress management.[92] Figure 7.4 identifies key elements in a person's work and nonwork social support system. These relationships provide emotional caring, information, evaluative feedback, modeling, and instrumental support.

7-7b Individual Prevention

Clinical research shows that individuals may use a number of self-directed interventions to help prevent distress and enhance positive well-being.[93] Such individual

FIGURE 7.4   SOCIAL SUPPORT AT WORK AND HOME

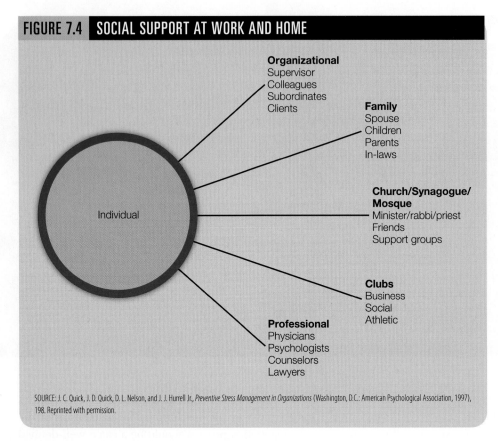

Organizational
Supervisor
Colleagues
Subordinates
Clients

Family
Spouse
Children
Parents
In-laws

Church/Synagogue/Mosque
Minister/rabbi/priest
Friends
Support groups

Clubs
Business
Social
Athletic

Professional
Physicians
Psychologists
Counselors
Lawyers

Individual

SOURCE: J. C. Quick, J. D. Quick, D. L. Nelson, and J. J. Hurrell Jr., *Preventive Stress Management in Organizations* (Washington, D.C.: American Psychological Association, 1997), 198. Reprinted with permission.

prevention can be of a primary, secondary, or tertiary nature. The *primary prevention* activities we discuss are learned optimism, time management, and leisure time activities. The *secondary prevention* activities we discuss are physical exercise, relaxation, and diet. The *tertiary prevention* activities we discuss are opening up and professional help.

POSITIVE THINKING The power of *positive thinking* too often goes unappreciated. When one cultivates an optimistic frame of mind, bad life events are bathed in a positive light, preventing future and healing past distress.[94] An optimistic style of thought must be practiced habitually in order to be effective. It is usually learned over time, though some are predisposed to it. *Pessimism* is an alternative style of thought that focuses on the negative. It can lead to depression, health problems, and low levels of achievement. By contrast, positive thinking enhances physical health and achievement and decreases susceptibility to depression.

Positive thinking does not mean ignoring stressors and challenges. It means viewing them through a different lens. Optimistic people avoid distress by framing the difficult times in their lives as temporary, limited in scope, and often unavoidable. They face adversity with hope, and take credit for the good events in their lives, which they see as more pervasive and generalized.

Optimists are also more motivated and more likely to use proactive coping skills to achieve goals and pursue development opportunities.[95] *Learned optimism* begins with identifying pessimistic thoughts and then distracting oneself from these thoughts or disputing them with evidence and alternative thoughts. It is one of the five dimensions of *positive organizational behavior (POB)*. The other four dimensions are confidence/self-efficacy, hope, subjective well-being/happiness, and emotional intelligence.[96]

TIME MANAGEMENT Temporal pressure is one of the major sources of stress, as listed in Table 7.1. It applies to people both at work and in school. Symptoms of poor time management include constant rushing, missed deadlines, work overload, the sense of being overwhelmed, insufficient rest time, and indecision. Effective time managers employ the macro-level GP^3 *method* of time management.[97] The GP^3 method is to (1) set *goals* that are challenging yet attainable; (2) *prioritize* these goals in terms of their relative importance; (3) *plan* for goal attainment through specific tasks, activities, scheduling, and delegation; and (4) *praise* oneself for specific achievements along the way. Setting concrete goals and prioritizing these goals are the most important first steps in time-management skills, ensuring that the most important work and study activities receive enough time and attention. This system of time management enables a person to track his success over time and goes a long way toward reducing unnecessary stress and confusion.

LEISURE TIME ACTIVITIES People with a high need for achievement are often characterized by an unremitting urge to strive for excellence. Leisure time provides employees an opportunity for rest and recovery from strenuous activities at home and work. When asked what they do with their leisure time, many individuals say that they clean the house or mow the lawn. These activities are fine, as long as the individual gets the stress-reducing benefit of pleasure from them. Some say our work ethic is a cultural barrier to pleasure. We work longer hours, and two-income families are the norm. Leisure is increasingly a luxury among working people. The key to the effective use of leisure time is enjoyment. Leisure time can be used for spontaneity, joy, and connection with others in our lives. Although vacations can be a relief from job burnout, they may incur fade-out effects.[98] Hence, leisure time and vacations must be periodic, recurring activities.

PHYSICAL EXERCISE Different types of physical exercise are important secondary stress prevention activities for individuals. Colleges and universities often implement physical exercise through physical education classes, while military organizations implement it through fitness standards and regulated training. Kenneth Cooper, among others, has long advocated aerobic exercise to improve a person's responsiveness to stressful activities.[99] Research at the Aerobics Center in Dallas has found that aerobically fit people (1) have lower levels of adrenaline in their blood at rest; (2) have a slower, stronger heart beat; and (3) recover from stressful events more quickly.

Flexibility training is an important type of exercise because muscular contractions are associated with the stress response. One component of the stress response is the contraction of the flexor muscles, which prepares a person to fight or flee. Flexibility training enables a person to stretch and relax these muscles to prevent the accumulation of unnecessary muscular tension.[100] In addition, flexibility exercises help maintain joint mobility, increase strength, and play an important role in the prevention of injury.

RELAXATION TRAINING Herbert Benson was one of the first people to identify the relaxation response as the natural counterresponse to stress.[101] In studying Western and Eastern peoples, Benson found that Jews and Christians have elicited this response through their time-honored traditions of prayer, whereas those with backgrounds in Eastern religions have elicited it through meditation. The relaxation response does not require a theological or religious component, however. Reading, massage, and secular yoga practice can all elicit the relaxation response. If you have an unwinding ritual, you may already elicit the relaxation response regularly.

DIET Diet may play an indirect role in stress and stress management. Large amounts of sugar in one's diet can stimulate the stress response, and foods high in cholesterol can adversely affect blood chemistry. Good dietary practices contribute to overall health. In his nonsurgical, nonpharmacological approach to reversing heart disease, Dean Ornish proposes a very stringent "reversal diet" for individuals with identifiable blockage of the arteries.[102] He recommends a somewhat less stringent "prevention diet" as one of four methods for opening up the arteries of healthy individuals. Another element in his program is an emotional one—openness in relationships with other people.

OPENING UP Traumatic, distress-inducing events are an unfortunate fact of life. One of the most therapeutic responses to such events is to confide in other people.[103] Discussing difficult experiences with another person is not always easy, but mental and physical health improves through self-disclosure. Confessions need not be made in person, or to another person at all. Writing in a private diary and posting anonymously on the Internet are also therapeutic. In a study comparing those who wrote once a week about traumatic events with those who wrote about nontraumatic events, significant health benefits and reduced absenteeism were found in the first group.[104] Whatever form it takes, the process of opening up and confessing appears to counter the detrimental effects of stress.

PROFESSIONAL HELP Confession and opening up may occur in professional healing relationships. Psychological counseling, career counseling, physical therapy, medical treatment, surgical intervention, and other therapeutic techniques are available to people who need help. *Employee assistance programs (EAPs)* may be very

> **Mental and physical health improves through self-disclosure.**

Adam Gregor/Shutterstock.com

Confession and opening up may occur in professional healing relationships.

helpful in referring employees to appropriate caregivers. Even soldiers who experience battle stress reactions severe enough to take them out of action can experience healing through EAPs and then participate in subsequent combat missions.[105] The early detection of distress and strain reactions, coupled with prompt professional treatment, can be instrumental in averting permanent physical and psychological damage, such as posttraumatic stress disorder.

7-7c Comprehensive Health Promotion

Whereas organizational stress prevention programs are aimed at eliminating health risks at work, comprehensive health promotion programs are aimed at establishing a "strong and resistant host" by teaching individual prevention and lifestyle change.[106] Physical fitness and exercise programs characterize corporate health promotion programs in the United States and Canada.[107] A health and wellness survey of accredited medical schools in the United States, Canada, and Puerto Rico found that these programs place significant emphasis on physical well-being and minor emphasis on spiritual well-being.[108] A new approach to comprehensive health promotion places emphasis on the organization and *organizational wellness*.[109] Still, social and cognitive processes are key considerations in the successful implementation of stress prevention programs.[110]

Johnson & Johnson developed a comprehensive health promotion program with a wide array of educational modules for individuals and groups. Each of these educational modules addresses a specific topic, such as Type A behavior, stress, diet (through cooperative activities with the American Heart Association), and risk assessment (through regular health evaluations for participants). Upon implementation of this health promotion program, Johnson & Johnson found that the health status of employees improved, even if they didn't participate in the program.

The Psychophysiology of Stress

In preparing to fight or flee, the body

1. redirects blood to the brain and large-muscle groups;
2. increases alertness through improved vision, hearing, and other sensory processes;
3. releases glucose (blood sugar) and fatty acids into the bloodstream to sustain the body during the stressful event; and
4. suppresses the immune system as well as restorative and emergent processes (such as digestion).

STUDY TOOLS 7

LOCATED AT BACK OF THE TEXTBOOK

☐ Rip out chapter review card

LOCATED AT WWW.CENGAGE.COM/LOGIN

☐ Track your knowledge and understanding of key concepts in business using 4LTR Press Online

☐ Review key term flashcards and create your own using StudyBits

☐ Create and complete practice quizzes based off of your notes and StudyBits

☐ Complete Online activities such as Matching and Fill-in-the-Blank exercises

☐ View chapter highlight box content, including the chapter videos, key exhibits and executive profiles.

Effects of Stress on the Body

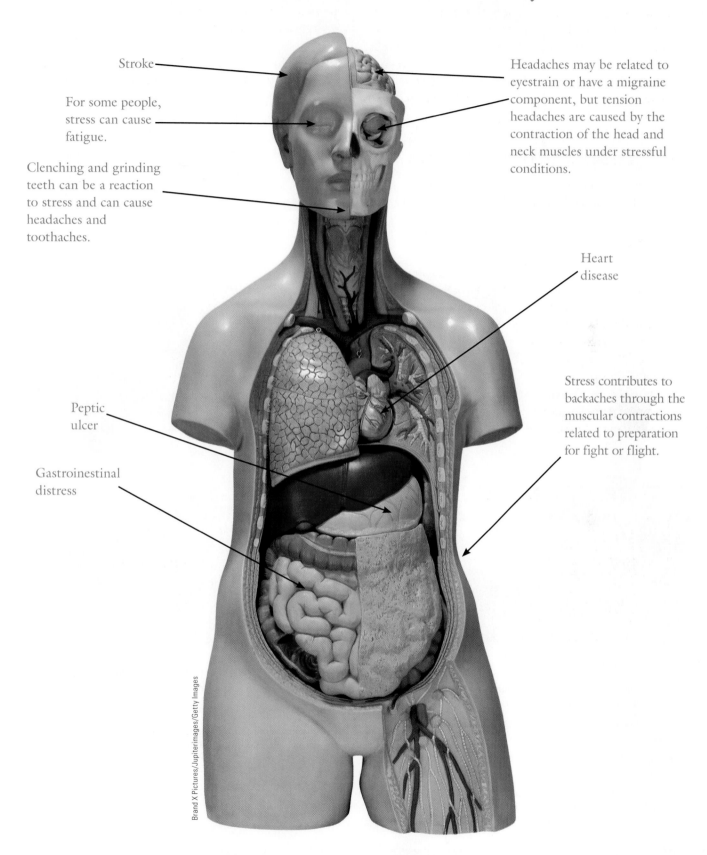

Stroke

For some people, stress can cause fatigue.

Clenching and grinding teeth can be a reaction to stress and can cause headaches and toothaches.

Headaches may be related to eyestrain or have a migraine component, but tension headaches are caused by the contraction of the head and neck muscles under stressful conditions.

Heart disease

Stress contributes to backaches through the muscular contractions related to preparation for fight or flight.

Peptic ulcer

Gastroinestinal distress

Brand X Pictures/Jupiterimages/Getty Images

8 | Communication

8:At82/Shutterstock.com

LEARNING OUTCOMES

8-1 Describe the interpersonal communication process and the role of listening in the process.

8-2 Describe the five communication skills of effective supervisors.

8-3 Explain five communication barriers and the gateways through them.

8-4 Distinguish between civility and incivility, and defensive and nondefensive communication.

8-5 Explain the impact of nonverbal communication.

8-6 Explain positive, healthy communication.

8-7 Identify how new communication technologies and social media affect the communication process.

After finishing this chapter go to **PAGE 134** for **STUDY TOOLS.**

8-1 INTERPERSONAL COMMUNICATION

Communication evokes a shared, or common, meaning in another person. **Interpersonal communication** occurs between two or more people in an organization. It is central to health and well-being, both at home and on the job. Reading, listening, managing and interpreting information, and serving clients are among the interpersonal communication skills identified by the Department of Labor as necessary for success in the workplace.[1] In Chapter 7, we noted that interpersonal communication is the key to unlocking social support for preventive stress management.[2] It is also important in building and sustaining human relationships at work. Recent advances in information technology and data management cannot replace interpersonal communication. Figure 8.1 illustrates the key elements of interpersonal communication: the communicator, the receiver, the perceptual screens, and the message.

8-1a An Interpersonal Communication Model

The **communicator** is the person sending the message. The **receiver** is the person accepting the message. **Perceptual screens** are the windows through which we interact. The communicator's and the receiver's respective perceptual screens influence the quality, accuracy, and clarity of the message. They can allow the message to transmit smoothly, or they can cause static and distortion. Perceptual screens are built upon the sender's

> **Interpersonal communication is central to health and well-being, both at home and on the job.**

Danielala/Shutterstock.com

and receiver's individual attributes, such as age, gender, values, beliefs, past experiences, cultural influences, and individual needs. The degree to which these screens are open significantly influences both sent and received messages.

The **message** contains the thoughts and feelings that the communicator intends to evoke in the receiver. The message has two primary components. The *thought*, or conceptual component, of the message (its content) is contained in the words, ideas, symbols, and concepts chosen to relay the message. The *feeling*, or emotional component, of the message (its affect) is contained in the intensity, demeanor, and gestures of the communicator. The emotional component of the message adds overtones of joy, anger, fear, or pain to the conceptual component. This addition often enriches and clarifies the message.

Feedback may or may not be activated in communication. It occurs when the receiver provides the communicator with a response to the message. More broadly, feedback occurs when information is fed back to the sender that completes two-way communication.

The **language** of the message is important. *Language* is a broad term

---

communication The evoking of a shared or common meaning in another person.

interpersonal communication Communication between two or more people in an organization.

communicator The person sending a message.

receiver The person accepting a message.

perceptual screen A window through which one interacts with others. It influences the quality, accuracy, and clarity of the communication.

message The thoughts and feelings that the communicator is attempting to evoke in the receiver.

feedback Information fed back that completes two-way communication.

language The words, their pronunciations, and the methods of combining them used and understood by a group of people.

FIGURE 8.1 | A BASIC INTERPERSONAL COMMUNICATION MODEL

© Cengage Learning

denoting the words, their pronunciations, and the methods of combining them used and understood by a group of people. Culture and situation dictate the specific language utilized in a message.

Data are the uninterpreted, unanalyzed elements of a message. **Information** is data with meaning to the person who interprets or analyzes them. Since messages are conveyed through a *medium*, such as a telephone or face-to-face discussion, they differ in **richness** according to the ability of that medium to transmit meaning to a receiver.[3] Despite the popularity of text messaging as a communication medium, e-mail remains the preferred method of workplace communication. A recent survey found that workers are almost three times as likely to send an e-mail to a colleague rather than a text message to communicate work-related as well as non-work-related information.[4] Table 8.1 compares different media with regard to data capacity and richness. Such attributes of communication media affect how influence-seeking behavior is generated and perceived in organizations.[5]

data Uninterpreted and unanalyzed elements of a message.

information Data that have been interpreted, analyzed, and have meaning to some user.

richness The ability of a medium to convey meaning to a receiver.

reflective listening Carefully listening to a message and immediately repeating it back to the speaker.

TABLE 8.1	COMMUNICATION MEDIA: INFORMATION RICHNESS AND DATA CAPACITY

Medium	Information Richness	Data Capacity
Face-to-face discussion	Highest	Lowest
Telephone	High	Low
Electronic mail	Moderate	Moderate
Blog	Moderate	Moderate
Individualized letter	Moderate	Moderate
Personalized note or memo	Moderate	Moderate
Formal written report	Low	High
Flyer or bulletin	Low	High
Formal numeric report	Lowest	Highest

SOURCE: Adapted from E. A. Gerloff, "Information Richness: A New Approach to Managerial Behavior and Organizational Design," by R. L. Daft and R. H. Lengel in *Research in Organizational Behavior* 6 (1984): 191–233. Reprinted by permission of JAI Press Inc.

8-1b Reflective Listening

Even though it isn't explicitly noted in the communication model, good listening is paramount to effective communication. **Reflective listening** is the skill of carefully listening to a message and immediately repeating it back to the speaker. This technique helps the communicator clarify the intended message and correct inaccuracies or misunderstandings. Reflective listening emphasizes the role of the receiver, or audience, in interpersonal communication. Managers can use this

This Is Your Brain on Human Contact

According to Harvard Medical School assistant clinical professor and NeuroBusiness Group CEO Dr. Srini Pillay, our brains respond differently when we interact with individuals face-to-face than virtually. The human brain contains "mirror neurons" that help the brain mirror other's behavior, resulting in feelings of familiarity that the brain doesn't register when communicating by telephone or e-mail. During face-to-face interactions, the brain tucks away information about who we are and what we feel so that it is easily accessible during future interactions. Even if future interactions are by telephone, it is best to first meet face-to-face.

SOURCE: S. Dembling, "This is Your Brain on Human Contact," *Entrepreneur* 42 (2014): 28

technique to understand other people and help them solve problems at work.[6] Reflective listening better enables the listener to comprehend the communicator's meaning, reduce perceptual distortions, and overcome interpersonal barriers that lead to communication failures. Especially useful in problem solving, reflective listening can be learned in a short time. Given its positive effects on behavior and emotion in the corporate environment, reflective listening is a valuable skill to possess.[7]

Reflective listening can be characterized as personal, feeling oriented, and responsive.[8] First, it emphasizes the *personal* elements of the communication process. The reflective listener demonstrates empathy and concern for the communicator as a person, not an object. Second, reflective listening emphasizes the *feelings* communicated in the message—the receiver must pay special attention to the feeling component as she repeats the message. Third, reflective listening emphasizes a rational and considerate *response*. Receivers should distinguish their own feelings and thoughts from those of the speaker. In other words, the conversation's focus must remain at all times on the ideas and emotions of the speaker in order for the receiver to effectively respond to them. Empathy and emotional self-control are key emotional competencies in good reflective listening.

Reflective listening necessitates four levels of verbal response: affirming contact, paraphrasing expressed thoughts and feelings, clarifying implicit thoughts and feelings, and reflecting core feelings not fully expressed. Nonverbal behaviors, such as eye contact and silence, are also important in reflective listening. Each of these responses can be illustrated through an example: the interaction between a software engineer, who has just discovered a major problem in a large information system she is building for a difficult customer, and her supervisor.

AFFIRMING CONTACT The receiver (in this case, the supervisor of the software engineer) affirms contact with the communicator (the software engineer) by making periodic statements such as "I see," "Okay," and "Yes, I understand." The purpose of an affirmation response is to communicate attentiveness, not necessarily agreement. Affirming contact is especially reassuring to a speaker in the early stages of expression, and even more so when there may be some associated anxiety or discomfort. As the problem is more fully explored and expressed, it is increasingly important for the receiver to employ other reflective responses.

PARAPHRASING THE EXPRESSED After an appropriate length of time, the receiver (the supervisor in our example) might paraphrase the expressed thoughts and feelings of the speaker (the engineer). Paraphrasing is useful because it tells the speaker what the receiver heard and what the receiver's thoughts and feelings are about what he heard. This verbal response enables the speaker and receiver to build greater empathy, openness, and acceptance into their relationship while ensuring the accuracy of the communication process.

In the case of the software engineer, the supervisor may find paraphrasing the engineer's message particularly useful for both of them in developing a clearer understanding of the system problem. He might say, "I can tell that you're very upset about this problem. Even though you're not quite sure how it happened, it sounds like you have a few good leads." It is difficult to solve a problem until it is clearly understood.

CLARIFYING THE IMPLICIT People often communicate *implicit* thoughts and feelings—that is, thoughts and feelings that are not clearly or fully expressed—along with their explicitly expressed message. The receiver may or may not assume that this implicit component of the message is within the awareness of the speaker. For example, the software engineer may be anxious about how to approach a difficult customer with the system problem. This may be implicit in her discussion with her supervisor because of a previous discussion about this customer. If her feelings of anxiety are not expressed, the supervisor may want to clarify them. He might say, "You seem particularly stressed . . . were you worried about the client's reaction?" This would help the engineer shift the focus of her attention from the main problem, which is in the software, to the important issue of discussing the matter with the customer.

REFLECTING CORE FEELINGS Next, the receiver should look beyond the speaker's explicit and implicit messages to understand the speaker's *core feelings*, the speaker's deepest and most important emotions, beliefs, and values. If the software engineer had not been aware of any anxiety in her relationship with the difficult customer, her supervisor's ability to sense the tension and bring it to the engineer's awareness would exemplify the reflection of core feelings. Emotional intelligence is especially important here.

However, the receiver runs a risk of overreaching if a secure, empathetic relationship with the speaker has not already been established or if strongly repressed feelings are reflected back. Even if the receiver is correct, the speaker may not want those feelings brought to her awareness. Therefore, it is important to exercise caution and care in reflecting core feelings to a speaker.

SILENCE Long periods of silence may cause discomfort or embarrassment, but a certain amount of silence can help both speaker and listener in reflective listening. From the speaker's perspective, silence may be useful in moments of thought or confusion about how to express difficult ideas or feelings. The software engineer may need some patient silence from her supervisor as she thinks through what to say next. Listeners can use brief periods of silence to sort their own thoughts and feelings from those of the speaker. In the case of the software engineer's supervisor, any personal feelings toward the difficult customer should not intrude on the engineer's immediate problem. Silence provides time to identify and isolate the listener's personal responses and exclude them from the dialogue.

EYE CONTACT Eye contact is a nonverbal behavior that may promote openness in communication between two people. During a dialogue, the absence of appropriate eye contact tends to close communication. However, the presence of inappropriate eye contact can also hinder a relationship. Cultural and individual differences influence what constitutes appropriate and inappropriate eye contact. For example, direct eye contact initiated by women and children is discouraged in India. In fact, too much direct eye contact, regardless of the individual or culture, can have an intimidating effect.

Moderate direct eye contact communicates openness and affirmation without causing either speaker or listener to feel intimidated. Periodic aversion of the eyes allows for a sense of privacy and control, even in intense interpersonal communication. The software engineer and the supervisor make eye contact throughout their discussion, though each looks away periodically to ease the tension of intimacy.

dialog

Igor kisselev/Shutterstock.com

two-way communication
An interactive form of communication in which there is an exchange of thoughts, feelings, or both.

one-way communication
Communication in which a person sends a message to another person and no feedback, questions, or interaction follows.

ONE-WAY VERSUS TWO-WAY COMMUNICATION
Reflective listening encourages **two-way communication**, an interactive form of communication in which there is an exchange of thoughts, feelings, or both, and through which shared meaning often occurs. Problem solving and decision making are often examples of two-way communication. **One-way communication** occurs when a person sends a message to another person and no feedback, questions, or interaction follows. Giving instructions and giving directions are examples of one-way communication.

One-way communication tends to be efficient, although how efficient it is depends on the amount and complexity of information communicated and the medium chosen. Even though it is faster than two-way communication, one-way communication is often less accurate. This is especially true for complex tasks that require clarification for completion. When time and accuracy are both important to the successful completion of a task and two-way communication is not an option (such as in combat or emergency situations), extensive training prior to execution enhances accuracy and efficiency.[9] Firefighters and military combat personnel engage extensively in such training to minimize the need for communication during emergencies. These highly trained professionals rely on abbreviated one-way communication as shorthand for more complex information. However, this communication works only within the range of situations for which the professionals are specifically trained.

It is difficult to draw generalizations about individual preference for one-way or two-way communication. Communicators with a stronger need for feedback or who are comfortable with conflict or confusing questions may find two-way communication more satisfying. By contrast, receivers who believe that a message is straightforward may be satisfied with one-way communication and be impatient with lengthy two-way communication.

8-2 COMMUNICATION SKILLS FOR EFFECTIVE MANAGERS

Interpersonal communication is a critical foundation for effective performance and individual well-being in organizations. Power is intertwined in the language of communication between managers and their employees.[10] This power dynamic is especially critical when leaders are articulating an organizational vision and attempting to achieve buy-in from employees.[11] One large study of managers in a variety of industries found that those with the most effective work units engaged in routine communication with their employees, whereas the managers with the highest promotion rates engaged in networking activities with superiors.[12] A study of banking managers found that higher performing managers were more effective, less apprehensive communicators than lower performing managers.[13] Oral communication and managerial cooperation are important contextual performance skills that have positive effects on the psychosocial quality of the work environment.[14]

Research on manager–employee communication identifies five communication skills that distinguish good supervisors from bad ones.[15] A good supervisor is an expressive speaker, an empathetic listener, a persuasive leader, a sensitive person, and an informative manager. Some supervisors are effective without possessing all of these skills, however, and some organizations value one or two skills over the others. But because dyadic relationships are at the core of much organization-based communication, possessing all five skills makes a supervisor that much more effective in communicating to employees.[16]

> Good supervisors keep their employees well informed by appropriately and selectively disseminating information.

8-2a Expressiveness

Effective supervisors express their thoughts, ideas, and feelings openly and aren't afraid to voice opinions in meetings. They tend toward extroversion. Supervisors who are not talkative or who tend toward introversion may at times leave their employees wondering what they're thinking about certain issues. Supervisors who speak out let the people they work with know where they stand, what they believe, and how they feel.

8-2b Empathy and Sensitivity

In addition to being expressive speakers, good supervisors are willing, empathetic, reflective listeners. Empathetic listeners are able to hear the emotional dimensions of the messages people send them, as well as the content of the ideas and issues. Good supervisors are approachable and willing to listen to suggestions and complaints. In a recent study of physicians, those with higher perceptions of control were more open in their communication, and patients found them more empathetic.[17] Good supervisors are emotionally intelligent.

Good supervisors are also sensitive to the feelings, self-images, and psychological defenses of their employees. They know how and when to communicate with employees to maximize psychological health. For example, employees' accomplishments, honors, and achievements should be announced in public, while criticism should be delivered in private. The best supervisors are sensitive to the self-esteem of others.

8-2c Persuasiveness

All supervisors must exercise power and influence in organizations if they want to ensure high performance and achieve positive results. Effective supervisors tend to be persuasive leaders, distinguished by their use of persuasive language to influence others. They are not deceitful or autocratic; they encourage results earnestly instead of manipulating others.

Of course, sometimes emergencies and high-risk situations necessitate the abandonment of sensitive and subtle persuasion. In cases such as a fire at an oil rig or a life-threatening trauma in an emergency room, a supervisor must be direct and assertive.

8-2d Informative Managing Style

Finally, good supervisors keep their employees well informed by appropriately and selectively disseminating information. Failing to effectively filter information may lead to either information overload or a lack of sufficient information for task accomplishment. Good supervisors give advance notice of organizational changes and explain the rationale for organizational policies. Good supervisors are also transparent, communicating openly and honestly with employees. Such transparency leads to increased trust among employees, which, in turn, results in increased employee engagement.[18]

A person may become a good supervisor even in the absence of one of these communication skills. For example, a manager with special talents in planning, organizing, or decision making may compensate for a shortcoming in expressiveness or sensitivity. No matter their perceived skill level or effectiveness, when supervisors and employees engage in open communication and forward planning, they have a greater number of agreements about the employee's performance and behavior.[19]

8-3 BARRIERS AND GATEWAYS TO COMMUNICATION

Barriers to communication are factors that distort, disrupt, or even halt successful communication. They may be temporary and easily resolved or long-lasting and deeply rooted. Roughly 20% of all such barriers to communication can be prevented or solved by communication policy guidelines.[20] **Gateways to communication** are the openings that break down communication barriers. Awareness and recognition of communication barriers are the first steps in opening the gateways. Obvious barriers are physical separation (employees in different geographic locations or buildings) and status differences (related to the organizational hierarchy). One apparent gateway for the separation of geographically dispersed teams is to improve the frequency of face-to-face interaction. Geographically dispersed teams can also increase their performance by targeting their use of information and communication technologies (ICTs) to address specific coordination needs. For example, if teams are responsible for performing nonroutine tasks, their performance can be enhanced by using ICTs to provide task knowledge.[21] Not so obvious are the barriers caused by gender differences, cultural diversity, and language.

8-3a Gender Differences

Communication barriers can be attributed in part to differences in conversational styles.[22] When individuals of different economic backgrounds converse, the receiver's understanding may not be the same as the speaker's meaning. In a similar vein, men and women tend to have different conversational styles. For example, women often prefer to converse face to face, whereas men are comfortable conversing while sitting side by side, concentrating on a focal point in front of them. Hence, conversational differences may result in a barrier of communication between men and women. Male–female conversation is really cross-cultural communication. In a work context, one study found that female employees sent less information to their supervisors and experienced less information overload than did male employees.[23]

An important gateway through the gender barrier is the development of an awareness and appreciation of gender-specific differences in conversational style. These differences

barriers to communication Factors that distort, disrupt, or even halt successful communication.

gateways to communication Openings that break down communication barriers.

can enrich organizational communication and empower professional relationships.[24] A second gateway is to actively seek clarification of the person's meaning rather than freely interpreting meaning from one's own frame of reference.

8-3b Cultural Diversity

Culturally influenced values and patterns of behavior can be very confusing barriers to communication. Significant differences in work-related values exist among people in the United States versus those in Germany, the United Kingdom, Japan, and other nations.[25] These differences in value impact motivation, leadership, and teamwork in work organizations.[26] Habitual patterns of interaction can obstruct communication in any given culture. For example, the German culture places greater value on authority and hierarchical differences than does the United States. It is therefore more difficult for German workers to engage in open communication with their supervisors than it is for U.S. workers.[27]

When a person from one culture views people from another culture through the lens of a stereotype, she discounts the individual differences that exist within that foreign culture. For example, a stereotype of Americans common throughout Asia is that they are aggressive and arrogant, and thus insensitive and unapproachable. Stereotypes of Asians common throughout America are that they are studious, subservient, and assimilative. Individuals who depend on the accuracy of cultural stereotypes may unknowingly create barriers in communicating with people from other cultures.

One gateway through the barrier of diversity is increasing cultural awareness and sensitivity. Part of that knowledge is paying attention to message context when communicating cross-culturally. Whereas Westerners are categorized as being low-context communicators who emphasize message content, Easterners, such as Japanese, Korean, and Chinese, are categorized as high-context communicators who focus more on the context of the message rather than the explicit content.[28] Further, companies can provide seminars for expatriate managers as part of their training for overseas assignments. Bernard Isautier, president and CEO of Petro Kazakstan, believes that understanding and communication are two keys to harmonious workplace diversity, an essential ingredient for success in international markets.[29] A second gateway is developing or acquiring a guide for understanding and interacting with members of other cultures. One approach to initiating diversity training is to describe a nation by way of a suitable metaphor.[30] For example, Irish pubs, the Spanish

Breaking Gender Communication Barriers in Meetings

Men and women communicate differently. In no other workplace context is this difference more pronounced than in meetings. Many women find it difficult to present their ideas in business meetings, often feeling that their ideas are drowned out or ignored. Many women are unable to find their way into conversations in the first place. Even women who are subject-matter experts are not immune to this phenomenon. The result is the inability of women to contribute to their full potential. Researchers interviewed 65 top executives, males and females, to get an idea of how gender plays out in high-level business meetings. They found that women and men use different communication strategies before, during, and after meetings. For example, women will typically arrive at meetings on time, sit through the agenda items, then leave promptly after the meeting ends. Men will come to meetings early to test out ideas and gather support. Once the meeting has ended, men will likely hang around to finalize the discussion and move on to other issues. During meetings, men will repackage ideas, using different words to express yet amplify the same idea. Though this tactic may be effective, many women strongly opposed "simply repeating others' ideas in different words." Women are also encouraged to prepare for "off-the-cuff" remarks by doing their homework about the issues and arming themselves with cogent comments and questions to help them be part of the conversation. Companies have a responsibility to ensure that everyone has a voice during meetings. Sixty-eight percent of women interviewed reported that no one had provided them with feedback about their performance in meetings. Managers should be proactive about pulling women into the conversation, asking them questions, or encouraging them directly to contribute their ideas.

It's becoming the norm for successful businesswomen to have the lead when it comes to running a meeting.

SOURCE: K. Heath, J. Flynn, and M. D. Holt, "Women, Find Your Voice," *Harvard Business Review* 92 (2014): 118-121.

bullfight, and American football are consensually derived metaphors for culturally specific conversational styles that can enable those outside the culture to understand members within.

8-3c Language

Language can be another barrier to communication. Growing numbers of businesspeople are bilingual or multilingual, but even subtle distinctions in dialects within the same language can be barriers. For example, the word *chemist* means a molecular scientist in the United States and a drugstore worker in Great Britain. Language barriers are created across disciplines and professional boundaries by technical terminology. Although acronyms and professional jargon may be very useful tools of communication within a discipline, they may serve only to confuse and derail any attempt at clear understanding by those unfamiliar with the profession. When doing business, it's best to use simple, direct, declarative language. One should speak in brief sentences and employ terms or words already used by one's audience. As much as possible, one should speak in the language of the listener. Above all else, one should not use jargon or technical language except with those who are already familiar with it.

8-4 CIVILITY AND INCIVILITY

While **incivility** can create a barrier between people and jar people's emotions, **civility** may be a gateway to communication that smoothes troubled waters at work. Those who practice incivility are often called bullies, creeps, jerks, tyrants, tormentors, despots, backstabbers, egomaniacs, and even worse. There are, however, some instances in which incivility can have

incivility Discourteous communication and rude behavior that are disrespectful, hurtful, or injurious.

civility Communication and behavior that respect the integrity and dignity of the individual.

positive effects when it is strategically used. In this section, we examine the full range of consequences of incivility and the blessings of civility. In addition, we examine defensive and nondefensive communication that may spring from civil and uncivil communication behavior.

8-4a Consequences of Incivility

Workplace incivility can jar the emotions and cause a range of adverse outcomes both in the workplace and at home. Discourteousness, rudeness, impatience, and lack of respect are very common forms of incivility. The consequences of incivility depend on its source. Research suggests that vulnerability to the negative effects of workplace civility may also depend on ethnicity and cultural values.[31] Much incivility originates with superiors and those in powerful positions within the organization. This type of incivility is often tolerated even though it leads to a decline in satisfaction with the supervisor. Coworkers may display incivility too. As we would expect, someone subject to coworker incivility experiences less satisfaction with the coworker and that may generalize to all coworkers. In fact, observing incivility at work may destroy perceptions of professional conduct and cause the observer concern about whether he or other coworkers will receive similar treatment.[32] In addition, coworker incivility can trigger the perception of being treated unfairly at work and may even lead to depression. So the emotional and psychological adverse effects of coworker incivility are quite real along with additional costs from unfair treatment and depression.

Before rushing to judgment that all incivility is destructive, we need to point out that there is a place in the workplace for what may appear uncivil. Take, for example, swearing. Annoyance swearing is a problem because of the emotional jarring and stressful impact on others, often disrupting social support within a team as well as the team's well-being. Social swearing, on the other hand, can be a stress release for an individual provided the language is not aimed at someone else. It may even be something in which others can empathize and vicariously share while building relationships and camaraderie.

8-4b Blessings of Civility

The blessings of civility are found in its gracious and positive nature. Civil communication and behavior carry the potential to avoid hurt feelings, prevent harm and damage to working relationships, and contribute to well-being in the workplace. Civility should not be confused with the avoidance of difficult or complicated workplace issues, which must be confronted and addressed. There are several ways to create a more civil workplace: bring difficult issues out in the open, write things down before speaking, set enforcement guidelines for incivility, and be consistent in enforcing those guidelines. Civility ensures respect for the integrity and dignity of every member of the workplace.

8-4c Defensive and Nondefensive Communication

In the workplace, defensive language creates barriers between people, whereas nondefensive communication helps to open and deepen relationships.[33] **Defensive communication** includes aggressive, malevolent messages as well as passive, withdrawn messages. **Nondefensive communication** is assertive, direct, and powerful. Though it can be misinterpreted as aggressiveness, assertiveness is indeed nondefensive. Corporations today are increasingly engaged in situations such as courtroom battles and media exchanges that are fertile ground for defensive communication yet benefit greatly from nondefensive language and emotionally intelligent communication.

Defensive communication leads to a wide range of problems, including injured feelings, communication barriers, alienation in working relationships, destructive and retaliatory behaviors, nonproductive efforts, and problem-solving failures. When such problems arise in organizations, people are prone to blame everyone else for what is not working.[34] Defensive reactions such as counterattack and sheepish withdrawal derail communication. These responses tend to lend heat, not light, to the process of communication. Defensive communication often evokes still more defensive communication.

Nondefensive communication, in contrast, provides a positive and productive basis for asserting and defending oneself against aggression without further damaging the communication process. An assertive, nondefensive style restores order, balance, and effectiveness in working relationships. Further discussion of nondefensive communication and defensive communication in the workplace follows.

8-4d Defensive Communication at Work

The two basic patterns of defensiveness are dominant defensiveness and subordinate defensiveness. Subordinate

defensive communication Messages that are aggressive, malevolent, passive, or withdrawn.

nondefensive communication Messages that are assertive, direct, and powerful.

defensiveness is characterized by passive or submissive behavior. The psychological attitude of the subordinately defensive person is "You are right, and I am wrong." People with low self-esteem may be prone to this form of defensive behavior, as may people at lower organizational levels. Individuals who are subordinately defensive do not adequately assert their thoughts and feelings. Their input is likely to be lost, even if it is critical to organizational performance.[35] Passive-aggressive behavior is a form of defensiveness that begins as subordinate defensiveness and ends up as dominant defensiveness. It is behavior that appears very passive, though it actually masks underlying aggression and hostility.

In contrast, dominant defensiveness is characterized by overtly aggressive and domineering behavior. It is offensive in nature, sometimes culminating in verbal or physical harassment. The psychological attitude of the dominantly defensive person is "I am right, and you are wrong." People who are egotistical or overcompensating for low self-esteem may exhibit this pattern of behavior, as may people in higher-level positions within the organizational hierarchy.

8-4e Defensive Tactics

Defensive tactics are subversive actions that employ defensive communication. Unfortunately, these tactics are common in many work organizations. Until defensiveness and defensive tactics are recognized for what they are at an organizational level, it is difficult to address them or respond to them in nondefensive ways. In many cases, defensive tactics raise ethical dilemmas for victims and their supervisors. At what point does simple defensiveness become unethical behavior? Consider the following defensive tactics.

Power plays are tactics used to control and manipulate others. Restricting the choices of employees, enforcing either/or conditions, intentionally ignoring or insulting others, bullying, and displaying overt aggression are all power plays. The underlying dynamic in power plays is that of domination and control. The aggressor attempts to gain the upper hand in the relationship by making the victim feel inferior and thus vulnerable to control.

Labeling is often used to portray another person as abnormal or deficient. Medical and legal labels are often used out of context for this purpose. The words *paranoid*, *retarded*, and *insane* have specific, clinical meanings that are discarded in defensive labeling. Similar to labeling is publicly raising doubts about a person's abilities, values, sexual orientation, or other personal aspects. This tactic breeds confusion and uncertainty, though it tends to lack the specificity and clarity of labeling.

Disseminating misleading information, a form of deception, is the selective presentation of information intentionally designed to produce an inaccurate impression in the listener's mind. This obfuscated information can be used to scapegoat, or pass the buck, which shifts responsibility for an error or problem to the wrong person. If information cannot be altered, defensive individuals may simply blame others for their own wrongdoing.

Finally, *hostile jokes* are a passive-aggressive defensive tactic. Because a jocular framing is used to mask aggressive and even overtly mean sentiments, hostile jokes often go uncited. They should not be confused with good humor, which is both therapeutic and nondefensive. Jokes made at the expense of others are destructive to self-esteem and workplace communication.

8-4f Nondefensive Communication

Nondefensive communication is a healthy alternative to defensive communication in working relationships. An individual who consistently communicates nondefensively may be characterized as centered, assertive, controlled, informative, realistic, and honest. Nondefensive communication is powerful because the speaker exhibits self-control and self-possession without rejecting the listener. It should be self-affirming without being self-aggrandizing—a sometimes difficult balance to maintain.

> An individual who consistently communicates nondefensively may be characterized as centered, assertive, controlled, informative, realistic, and honest.

Converting defensive patterns of communication to nondefensive ones builds relationships at work. Behaviors that build relationships simultaneously reduce adverse responses, such as blame and anger, when negative events occur at work.[36]

To strengthen nondefensive patterns, the subordinately defensive person must learn to be more assertive. One way to do this is to report what one intends to do and invite confirmation instead of asking for permission to do something. Another way is to stop using self-deprecating phrases such as "I'm just following orders." One should drop the *just* and thereby convert the message into a self-assertive, declarative statement.

To strengthen nondefensive patterns, the dominantly defensive person must learn to be less aggressive. This may be especially difficult because it requires

Seattle Seahawks Defensive Line Use Nondefensive Communication to Address Mistakes

The NFL Seattle Seahawks arguably have the best defense in professional football. The Seahawks finished the 2014 regular season leading the NFL in fewest points and fewest yards allowed per game. It is not only the size and agility of the players that help explain why the Seahawks have performed so well defensively. When the players don't perform so well as a unit, they don't shy away from confronting each other about the mistakes. When the defensive unit wasn't performing at the level they had when they won the Super Bowl a year ago, one veteran member of the defense suggested that linemen and linebackers combine their meetings so that they could confront each other directly and candidly about

John Biever/Sports Illustrated/Getty Images

mistakes they made rather than talk behind each other's backs. No room for passive-aggressive behavior there. Defensive players admit that at times, the brutal honesty is a bit awkward, but others outside the league say that the defense's honesty policy has made the Seahawks locker room one of the healthiest and one of the best in the NFL.

SOURCE: K. Clark. "Why the Seahawks Like Confrontation," *Wall Street Journal* (January 8, 2015): D6.; B. Condatta. "Statistics Bear Out that Seahawks' Defense Among Best, and Most Consistent Ever," *The Seattle Times* (December 30, 2014), http://www.seattletimes.com/sports/seahawks/statistics-bear-out-that-seahawksrsquo-defense-among-best-and-most-consistent-ever/.

overcoming the sense of certitude. Those who are working to overcome dominant defensiveness should be particularly sensitive to feedback from others about their behavior. To change this behavior, one should stop giving and denying permission. Instead, one should give others free rein (except in situations where permission is essential to clearance or the security of the task). Alternatively, instead of becoming inappropriately angry, one should provide information about the adverse consequences of a particular course of action.

8-5 NONVERBAL COMMUNICATION

Whereas defensive and nondefensive communication focus on the language used in delivering a message, most of a message's meaning (an estimated 65 to 90%) is conveyed through nonverbal communication.[37] **Nonverbal communication** includes all elements of communication that do not involve words or language such as gestures and the use of space.[38] The four basic types of nonverbal communication that managers need to understand are proxemics, kinesics, facial and eye behavior, and paralanguage. Managers also need to understand that nonverbal communication is influenced by both psychological and physiological processes.[39]

The interpretation of nonverbal communication is specific to the context of the interaction and the actors. That is, the particular meaning of any nonverbal cue relies on its sender, receiver, and the environment in which the cue occurs. For example, some federal and state judges attempt to curb nonverbal communication in the courtroom. Though it may mean nothing outside the courtroom, some nonverbal behavior may unfairly influence jurors' decisions if displayed during a trial. Beyond the contextual element, nonverbal behavior is also culturally bound. (Recall from Chapter 2 the difference in meaning the "thumbs-up" sign has in Australia versus the United States.)

8-5a Proxemics

The study of an individual's perception and use of space, including territorial space, is called **proxemics**.[40]

nonverbal communication All elements of communication that do not involve words or language.

proxemics The study of an individual's perception and use of space.

FIGURE 8.2 ZONES OF TERRITORIAL SPACE IN U.S. CULTURE

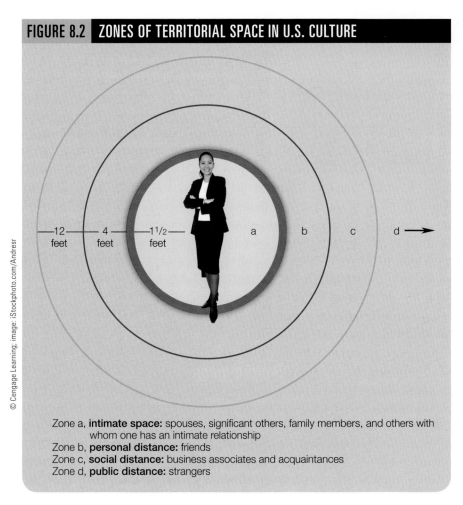

—12— 4 —1½—
feet feet feet a b c d →

© Cengage Learning; image: iStockphoto.com/Andresr

Zone a, **intimate space:** spouses, significant others, family members, and others with
whom one has an intimate relationship
Zone b, **personal distance:** friends
Zone c, **social distance:** business associates and acquaintances
Zone d, **public distance:** strangers

Territorial space refers to bands of concentric space radiating outward from the body. These bands are commonly known as *comfort zones.* Figure 8.2 illustrates the four zones of territorial space common to U.S. culture.

Territorial space varies greatly around the world. Both the sizes of comfort zones and their acceptable modes of interaction are culturally defined. And people often become uncomfortable when operating in territorial spaces different from those with which they are familiar.

According to leading proxemics researcher Edward Hall, Americans working in the Middle East tend to back away to a comfortable distance when conversing with Arabs because Arabs' comfortable conversation distance is closer than that of Americans. As a result, Arabs sometimes perceive Americans as cold and aloof. One Arab wondered, "What's the matter? Does he find me somehow offensive?"[41] The circumference of personal space tends to be larger in cultures with cool climates, such as the United States, Great Britain, and northern Europe, and smaller in cultures with warm climates, such as southern Europe, the Caribbean, India, and South America.[42]

Our relationships shape our use of territorial space. For example, we hold hands with or put an arm around significant others to pull them into *intimate space.* Conversely, we can use territorial space to shape our interactions. A four-foot-wide desk pushes business interactions into the *social distance* zone. Not comfortable with that definition of space, one SBC manager met with her seven first-line supervisors crowded around her four-foot desk, putting them elbow to elbow with each other. As a result of being placed in one another's intimate space, they appeared to act more like friends and frequently talked about their children, favorite television shows, and other personal concerns. When the manager moved the staff meetings to a larger room and thus relocated the supervisors into each others' social distance zones, the personal exchanges ceased, and they acted more like business associates again.

Seating dynamics, another aspect of proxemics, is the art of seating people in certain positions according to their purpose in communication. Figure 8.3 depicts some common seating dynamics. To encourage cooperation, one should seat the adjoining party beside oneself, facing the same direction. To facilitate direct and open communication, one should seat the other party across a corner of one's desk or in another place where he will be at right angles. This allows for more honest disclosure. To take a competitive stand with someone, one must position the person directly across from oneself. Suppose a manager holds a meeting around a conference table, and two of the attendees are disrupting the meeting by chatting loudly. Where should they be seated? If the manager places the two disruptive attendees on either side of herself, the talking should be stifled (unless one is so bold as to lean in front of the manager to keep chatting).

8-5b Kinesics

Kinesics is the study of body movement and posture.[43] Like proxemics, kinesics is bound

territorial space Bands of concentric space radiating outward from the body.

kinesics The study of body movement and posture.

FIGURE 8.3 | SEATING DYNAMICS

X O

O

Cooperation

X

Communication

O X O

X

Competition

Noncommunication

O

© Cengage Learning

As mentioned earlier, eye contact can enhance reflective listening. Along with smiling, eye contact is an easy way to express honesty and positive emotion.[47] However, eye contact must be understood in a cultural context. A direct gaze indicates dedication, truthfulness, and forthrightness in the United States. This may not be true in other cultures. For example, Barbara Walters was uncomfortable interviewing Libyan head of state Muammar al-Gaddafi because he refused to look directly at her. However, in Libya it is a serious offense for a man to look directly at a woman.[48] In many Asian cultures, it is considered polite to bow in deference to a superior rather than to look into the supervisor's eyes.

to culture. With this in mind, we can interpret some common U.S. gestures. Rubbing one's hands together while inhaling sharply indicates anticipation. Stress is indicated by balled fists, clenched teeth, hand wringing, and rubbing the temples. Nervousness may be indicated by drumming fingers, pacing, or jingling coins in one's pocket. Kinesics also includes insulting gestures like giving someone "the finger."

8-5c Facial and Eye Behavior

The face is a rich source of nonverbal communication. Facial expression and eye behavior are used to communicate an emotional state, reveal behavioral intentions, and cue the receiver. It may even give unintended clues to emotions the sender is trying to hide.[44] Unintended facial movements can undermine the illusion of truthfulness, especially in stressful situations.[45]

Culture, environment, and specific actors must be taken into consideration when interpreting smiles, frowns, raised eyebrows, and other expressions. One study of Japanese and U.S. students illustrated the point. The students were shown a stress-inducing film, and their facial expressions were videotaped. When alone, the students had almost identical expressions. When in the presence of others, however, the Japanese students masked their facial expressions of unpleasant feelings much better than the American students did.[46]

communicative disease
Loneliness and social isolation resulting from the absence of heartfelt communication in relationships.

8-5d Paralanguage

Paralanguage consists of variations in speech, such as pitch, loudness, tempo, tone, duration, laughing, and crying.[49] People make assumptions about the communicator by deciphering paralanguage cues. A female's high-pitched, breathy voice may lead coworkers to stereotype her as a "dumb blonde." Rapid, loud speech may be taken as a sign of nervousness or anger. Interruptions such as "mmm" and "okay" may be used to speed up the speaker so that the receiver can get in a few words. Clucking of the tongue and the tsk-tsk sound are used to shame someone. All these cues relate to how something is said.

8-6 POSITIVE, HEALTHY COMMUNICATION

The absence of heartfelt communication in relationships leads to loneliness and social isolation. This condition has been labeled **communicative disease** by James Lynch.[50] Communicative disease has adverse effects on the heart and cardiovascular system and can ultimately lead to premature death. According to Lynch, the only cure for communicative disease is to reengage in thoughtful, heartwarming conversation with friends and loved ones. Yet, even though feelings may be more important to the communication process than cognition, a stable balance between the two is integral. This balance between head and heart is achieved when a person displays positive emotional competence and can maintain a healthy internal conversation between his thoughts and emotions.

Positive, healthy communication is an important aspect of *working together*—that is, cooperating to reach a shared goal—in both the interpersonal and intrapersonal settings.[51] Such communication requires trust and truthfulness. However, it does not exclude honest competition within the workplace, which in fact is consistent with the concept of working together. Sincere, well-managed competition can bring out the best in all those involved.

Healthy communication is at the core of personal integrity and managerial success, as is evident in the lives of most successful executives, including those in the executive branch of the U.S. government.[52] President Ronald Reagan was nicknamed "the great communicator" for his ability to connect with the American people. He conveyed strong ethical character, personal integrity, and simplicity in his communication. Reagan exemplified Lynch's concept of heartfelt communication because his language in speeches and interviews seemed to stem from core values and sincere aspirations. Communication from the heart is communication anchored in personal integrity and ethical character.

Personal integrity is a product of emotional competence and a stable balance of head and heart, as mentioned earlier. Psychologist Karol Wasylyshyn has shown that one method of developing personal integrity is to coach an executive in developing her capacity to talk through challenging issues, both personally and professionally.[53] James Campbell Quick and Marilyn Macik-Frey developed a similar coaching program that works to cultivate executives' inner selves through deep, interpersonal communication.[54] This executive coaching model relies on what Lynch might call a "healing dialogue" between executive and coach. In addition to improving interpersonal communication between executives and employees, this model can enhance positive, healthy communication in a wider range of human relationships.

8-7 COMMUNICATING THROUGH NEW TECHNOLOGIES AND SOCIAL MEDIA

Nonverbal behaviors can be important in establishing trust in working relationships, but modern technologies may challenge our ability to maintain that trust. Too much emphasis on technology tools in communication may have an adverse impact on rich interpersonal communication and relationships. On the positive side, lawyers and legal consultants use Facebook and Twitter to do background checks on potential jurors.[55] Brian J. Dunn, the CEO of Best Buy, uses social media to spot trends and communicate with customers and employees.[56] Finally, information technology can encourage or discourage moral dialogue, and these types of conversations are central to addressing ethical issues at work.[57]

8-7a Written Communication

Even though many organizations are working toward paperless offices and paperless interfaces with their customers, written communication is far from dead—many types of written communication are still necessary to business. Manuals and reports are generally the longest forms of written communication found in the office. Policy manuals are important in organizations because they establish guidelines for decision making and codes of conduct. Operations and procedures manuals explain how to perform various tasks and resolve problems that may occur at work. Reports, such as annual company finance reports, may summarize the results of a committee's or department's work or provide information on progress toward certain objectives.

Letters and memorandums (memos) are briefer than manuals and reports and are more frequently used in larger organizations. Letters are used to communicate formally with individuals and businesses outside the organization. They vary substantially in length and topic. Memos are also used for formal, internal communication within an organization. They are sometimes used as historical records of specific events or occurrences that individuals within the organization can refer back to later.

The shortest kind of written communication is the form, which may be used to collect information inside or outside the organization.

8-7b Communication Technologies

Computer-mediated communication influences virtually all behavior in the work environment. E-mail, voice mail, instant messaging, and facsimile (fax) machines have been common in the business world for more than a decade. Recently, large information databases have become relatively commonplace. These databases provide a tremendous amount of information at the push of a button. An example of an information database is the electronic card catalog system used in university libraries throughout the world. These systems, sometimes linked with each other to form massive networks of data, store information about books' and journals' contents, distributions, and availability.

2nix Studio/Shutterstock.com

The newest technology to impact the work environment is the smartphone, which is nearly as ubiquitous at work as standard cell phones are in our personal lives. Smartphones combine the capabilities of advanced cell phones with computer-like applications and connectivity. Examples include the Apple iPhone, the HTC Thunder-Bolt, and the Nokia N9. The smartphone's introduction was particularly transformative for sales jobs involving travel. While they are widely used, not all reactions to smartphones are positive. For example, one oil producer did not want his daily commute disturbed by outside interference; he used driving as a time for thought and relaxation. Some estimates suggest that using a phone while driving is as risky as driving while under the influence of alcohol. For this reason, some states have outlawed cell phone talking or texting while driving a motor vehicle.

8-7c How Do Communication Technologies Affect Behavior?

Information communication technology (ICT) is an extensive category of new developments in interpersonal communication that allow fast, even immediate, access to information. E-mail, teleconferencing, and Wi-Fi are all classified as ICT. It can facilitate the instant exchange of information in minutes or seconds across geographic

Blablo101/Shutterstock.com

information communication technology (ICT) An extensive category of new developments in interpersonal communication that allow fast, even immediate, access to information.

boundaries and time zones. With adequate ICT implementation, schedules and office hours become irrelevant in that considerations of time and distance that once beleaguered international and intranational business become far less important in the exchange. Given its impact on the way business is done, ICT has a significant influence on people's behavior.

Computer-mediated communication is impersonal in nature. Instant messaging, e-mail, and other forms of online communication can therefore depreciate the richness of personal interaction. Studies show that using these technologies may increase one's likelihood to flame—that is, to make rude, needlessly argumentative or obscene comments by means of computer-mediated communication.[58] Employees' interpersonal skills such as tact and graciousness subside online, and managers tend to be more blunt when using electronic media. People who normally participate in discussions quietly and politely may become more intimate, impolite, or uninhibited when they communicate using computer conferencing or electronic mail.[59]

Another effect of computer-mediated communication is that the nonverbal cues we rely on to decipher a message are absent. Gesturing, touching, facial expressions, and eye contact are not possible, so the emotional aspect of the message is difficult to discern. Even in teleconferencing, where users can see each others' faces, it is often difficult to perceive nonverbal cues.[60] Clues to

HOT TREND

Avoid E-mail Overload

The ever-present nature of e-mail has the potential to lead to e-mail overload. Here are five ways to prevent that from happening. First, don't try to solve problems using e-mail. Huddling the right people into a brief 7–15 minute meeting at the same time each week is more productive than spending 90 minutes e-mailing back and forth. Keep your e-mail subject lines specific to prevent others from wasting precious time searching inboxes for messages. Next, insist that e-mails are "Twitter-tight," not exceeding specified maximum number of words or characters. Fourth, avoid e-mails with multiple parts. Opt instead to one topic per e-mail. Finally, close e-mails quickly. Try putting a simple yes-or-no response in the subject line followed by "EOM" meaning "end of message." That way, recipients will not have to open the e-mail.

SOURCE: V. Harnish. "Five Ways to Liberate Your Team From Email Overload," *Fortune* 169 (2014): 52.

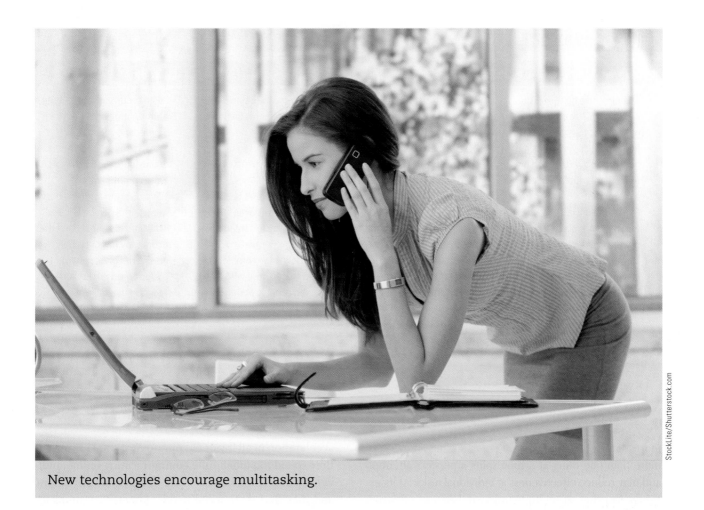

New technologies encourage multitasking.

power such as organizational position and departmental membership may not be available, so the social context of the exchange is often altered.

Communication via technology also changes group dynamics by equalizing participation. As a result, charismatic or higher-status members may lose some power.[61] Studies of group decision making have shown that computer-mediated groups took longer to reach consensus than face-to-face groups. In addition, they were less cooperative, more uninhibited, and there was less influence from any one dominant person. Another study found that ICTs, especially e-mail and e-meetings, reduce tension caused by intercultural communication.[62] Groups that communicate via computer seem to experience a breakdown of social and organizational barriers.

The potential for information overload is particularly great when individuals are first introduced to new communication technologies. Both the sheer volume of information available and its speed of delivery are staggering. An individual can easily become overwhelmed by information and must learn to be selective about its access.

While modern ICT may make work easier and increase employees' productivity, it can also prove precarious for managers. In the wake of mobile e-mail, instant messaging, and texting, managers are more accessible to coworkers, subordinates, and the boss today than they've ever been. Researchers coined the term *workplace telepressure* to describe the pressure employees feel when they perceive asynchronous communication methods as having the same requirements for response time as synchronous communication methods have. Typically, sending an e-mail will give individuals flexibility and additional time to respond, unlike communicating face-to-face. Face-to-face communications require an immediate response. Viewing ICTs as having the same properties as face-to-face communication may cause employees to prioritize these communication methods similarly, making it more difficult for employees to disengage.[63]

Further, many new technologies encourage *polyphasic activity*, or multitasking (i.e., doing more than one thing at a time). Managers can simultaneously make phone calls, send instant messages, and work on memos. Polyphasic activity has its advantages in terms of getting

TABLE 8.2 CHANNEL ETIQUETTE

Facebook	Twitter	YouTube	LinkedIn
> Take sensitive queries into a private sphere online or offline. > Remember all wall posts are public; don't write anything there that is not for wider consumption. > Ensure that all updates are frequent and relevant but not too frequent. > Use language relevant to the channel and to the target demographics. > Show appreciation, and acknowledge positive comments. > Follow up and respond to any feedback.	> Begin with an introduction if used for outreach or active engagement. > Develop a tone of voice and personality. > Keep requests for re-tweets to a minimum. > Keep tweets as short and sweet as possible (less than 140 characters). > Avoid pure self-promotion. Twitter is a knowledge-sharing and conversation channel.	> Develop a thick skin. Many comments are not constructive, so do not take such comments to heart or argue; defensive reactions only fan the flames. > Use video replies because these can be powerful and a good way to spread a message. > Acknowledge comments, and thank those who are being positive about a brand.	> Join groups and contribute information about relevant experience. > Answer questions, and contribute to share pages and communities. > Avoid asking for references unless the person is someone already known or if the company has genuinely delivered great service. > Support unsolicited contacts with a full explanation of who is contacting and why; don't assume that contacts will view the underlying profile.

© Cengage Learning

more done—but only up to a point. Paying attention to more than one thing at a time splits a person's attention and may reduce effectiveness at individual tasks. At its extreme, focusing on multiple tasks can become a destructive habit, making it psychologically difficult for a person to let go of work.

Finally, new technologies may make people less patient with face-to-face communication. The speed of electronic media may lead to expectations of acceleration in all forms of communication. However, if they spend too much time communicating online, individuals may come to miss social interaction with others, and may find their social needs unmet. Communicating via computer often means the end of small talk. In the name of speed, amenity is sacrificed for efficiency. Managers can use new technologies more efficiently and effectively by keeping in mind the suggestions presented in Table 8.2.

STUDY TOOLS 8

LOCATED AT BACK OF THE TEXTBOOK

☐ Rip out chapter review card

LOCATED AT WWW.CENGAGE.COM/LOGIN

☐ Track your knowledge and understanding of key concepts in business using 4LTR Press Online

☐ Review key term flashcards and create your own using StudyBits

☐ Create and complete practice quizzes based off of your notes and StudyBits

☐ Complete Online activities such as Matching and Fill-in-the-Blank exercises

☐ View chapter highlight box content, including the chapter videos, key exhibits and executive profiles.

ORGB
ONLINE

ACCESS TEXTBOOK CONTENT ONLINE—
INCLUDING ON SMARTPHONES!

Includes Videos & Other
Interactive Resources!

Access ORGB ONLINE at www.cengagebrain.com

9 | Work Teams and Groups

LEARNING OUTCOMES

9-1 Define group and work team.

9-2 Explain the benefits organizations and individuals derive from working in teams.

9-3 Identify the factors that influence group behavior.

9-4 Describe how groups form and develop.

9-5 Explain how task and maintenance functions influence group performance.

9-6 Discuss the factors that influence group effectiveness.

9-7 Describe how empowerment relates to self-managed teams.

9-8 Explain the importance of upper echelons and top management teams.

After finishing this chapter go to **PAGE 151** for **STUDY TOOLS.**

9-1 GROUPS AND WORK TEAMS

A **group** is formed when two or more people have common interests, objectives, and continuing interaction. A **work team** is a group of people with complementary skills who are committed to a common mission, performance goals, and approach for which they hold themselves mutually accountable.[1] All work teams are groups, but not all groups are work teams. Groups emphasize individual leadership, personal accountability, and exclusive work products. Work teams emphasize shared leadership, mutual accountability, and collective work products.

Work teams are task-oriented groups, though in some organizations the word *team* has a negative connotation for union members. Work teams make valuable contributions to the organization and are important to the need satisfaction of members.

Several kinds of work teams exist. Some are like baseball teams in that members have set responsibilities, others are like football teams in that members have coordinated action, and still others are like doubles tennis teams in that members have primary yet flexible responsibilities. Another analogy for work teams is that some operate like groundskeeping crews in that all members work synergistically toward a single goal.[2] Although each type of team may have a useful role in the organization, the individual expert should not be overlooked.[3] At the right time and in the right context, individual members must be allowed to shine.

Teams and groups do not all work face-to-face. Advanced computer and telecommunications technologies enable organizations to be more flexible through the use of *virtual teams*.[4] Organizations use virtual teams to access expertise and the best employees around the world. Whether traditional or virtual, groups and teams continue to play a vital role in organizational behavior and performance at work.

9-2 WHY WORK TEAMS?

Teams are very useful in performing work that is complicated, fragmented, and/or more voluminous than one person can handle. Harold Geneen, while chairman of ITT, said, "If I had enough arms and legs and time, I'd do it all myself." Obviously, no one person in an organization can do everything by himself, not only because of the limitations of arms, legs, and time, but also expertise, knowledge, and other resources. However, individual limitations can be overcome through teamwork and collaboration. World-class U.S. corporations, such as Motorola Inc., are increasingly deploying work teams in their global affiliates to meet the competition and gain advantage.[5] Motorola's "Be Cool" team in the Philippines has a family atmosphere (and may even begin a meeting with a prayer) yet is committed to improving individual and team performance.

9-2a Benefits to Organizations

Teams make the most significant contributions to organizations when members can put aside individual interests in favor of unity. This joint action is called **teamwork**. Complex, collaborative work tasks and activities tend to require considerable amounts of teamwork. When knowledge, talent, and abilities are dispersed across numerous workers and require an integrated effort for task accomplishment, teamwork is often the only solution.

A recent movement toward team-oriented work environments has championed empowerment through collaboration rather than self-reliance and competition. Teams with experience working together may produce valuable innovations, and individual contributions within teams are valuable as well.[6] Larry Hirschhorn labeled this structure "the new team environment," founded on a significantly more empowered workforce in the industrial sectors of the American economy. (See Table 9.1 for a comparison of new and old environments.) In this new environment, teams must bring together members with different specialties and knowledge to work on complex problems. The ability to do so improves team performance and psychological well-being.[7]

> **Work teams emphasize shared leadership, mutual accountability, and collective work products.**

Daniela/Shutterstock.com

group Two or more people with common interests, objectives, and continuing interaction.

work team A group of people with complementary skills who are committed to a common mission, performance goals, and approach for which they hold themselves mutually accountable.

teamwork Joint action by a team of people in which individual interests are subordinated to team unity.

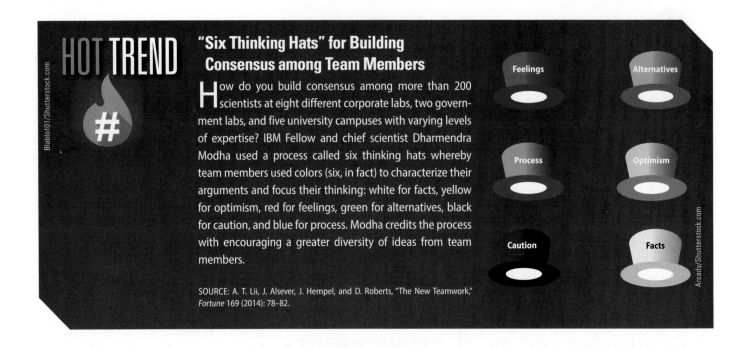

Biablo101/Shutterstock.com

HOT TREND

"Six Thinking Hats" for Building Consensus among Team Members

How do you build consensus among more than 200 scientists at eight different corporate labs, two government labs, and five university campuses with varying levels of expertise? IBM Fellow and chief scientist Dharmendra Modha used a process called six thinking hats whereby team members used colors (six, in fact) to characterize their arguments and focus their thinking: white for facts, yellow for optimism, red for feelings, green for alternatives, black for caution, and blue for process. Modha credits the process with encouraging a greater diversity of ideas from team members.

SOURCE: A. T. Lii, J. Alsever, J. Hempel, and D. Roberts, "The New Teamwork," *Fortune* 169 (2014): 78–82.

Arcady/Shutterstock.com

9-2b Social Benefits to Individuals

On an individual level, team or group members derive benefits from the collective experience of teamwork. These individual benefits are best organized into two categories. One set of benefits accrues from achieving psychological intimacy, while the other comes from achieving integrated involvement.[8]

Psychological intimacy is emotional and psychological closeness to other team or group members. It results in feelings of affection and warmth, unconditional positive regard, opportunity for expression, security and emotional support, and nurturing. Failure to achieve psychological intimacy may result in feelings of emotional isolation and loneliness. This can be especially problematic for chief executives, who sometimes report experiencing loneliness at the top. However, although psychological intimacy is valuable for emotional health and well-being, it need not necessarily be achieved in the work setting. Many executives satisfy their need for intimacy with a rich home life.

Integrated involvement is closeness achieved through tasks and activities. It results in enjoyment of work, social identity and self-definition, being valued for one's skills and abilities, opportunities for power and influence, conditional positive regard, and support for one's beliefs and values. Failure to achieve integrated involvement may result in social isolation. Whereas psychological intimacy is based more in emotion, integrated involvement is based in behavior and activity. Integrated involvement contributes to social psychological health and well-being.

psychological intimacy
Emotional and psychological closeness to other team or group members.

integrated involvement
Closeness achieved through tasks and activities.

TABLE 9.1 NEW TEAM ENVIRONMENT VERSUS OLD WORK ENVIRONMENT	
New Team Environment	**Old Work Environment**
Person comes up with initiatives. Team has considerable authority to chart its own steps.	Person follows orders. Team depends on the manager to chart its course.
Members form a team because people learn to collaborate in the face of their emerging right to think for themselves. People both rock the boat and work together.	Members were a team because people conformed to direction set by the manager. No one rocked the boat.
People cooperate by using their thoughts and feelings. They link up through direct talk.	People cooperated by suppressing their thoughts and feelings. They wanted to get along.

SOURCE: L. Hirschhorn, *Managing in the New Team Environment: Skills, Tools, and Methods* (San Jose: Authors Choice Press). © 2002. Reprinted with permission.

9-3 GROUP BEHAVIOR

Group behavior has been a subject of interest in social psychology for a long time, and many different aspects of group behavior have been studied over the years. We now look at four of those aspects: norms of behavior, group cohesion, social loafing, and loss of individuality. Group behavior topics related to decision making, such as polarization and groupthink, are addressed in Chapter 10.

9-3a Norms of Behavior

The standards that a work group uses to evaluate the behavior of its members are its **norms of behavior**. These norms may be written or unwritten, verbalized or not verbalized, implicit or explicit. As long as individual members of the group understand them, the norms can be effective in influencing behavior. They may specify what members of a group should do (such as a specified dress code) or not do (such as executives not behaving arrogantly with employees).

Norms may exist in any aspect of work group life. They may evolve informally or unconsciously, or they may arise in response to specific challenges, such as firefighters' disciplined behavior in responding to a three-alarm fire in a manner that protects the group.[9] *Morality norms* are more important than *competence norms* when it comes to making decisions about improving the status of one's work group.[10] *Performance norms* are among the most important group norms from the organization's perspective. Even when group members work in isolation on creative projects, they display conformity to group norms.[11] Group norms of cooperative behavior within a team can lead to members working for mutual benefit, which in turn facilitates team performance.[12] On the other hand, verbal expressions of negativity can be detrimental to team performance and a violation of group norms.[13] Organizational culture and corporate codes of ethics, such as Johnson & Johnson's credo (recall Figure 2.3), reflect behavioral norms expected within work groups. Finally, norms that create awareness of and help regulate emotions are critical to groups' effectiveness.[14]

9-3b Group Cohesion

The interpersonal glue that makes the members of a group stick together is **group cohesion**. Group cohesion can enhance job satisfaction for members and improve organizational productivity.[15] Highly cohesive groups are able to manage their membership better than work groups low in cohesion. In one study of 381 banking teams in Hong Kong and the United States, increased job complexity and task autonomy led to increased group cohesiveness, which translated into better performance.[16] A recent study found that when there is a fit between the group's values and those of the organization, groups will report more cohesion and exhibit higher levels of organizational citizenship behavior (OCB).[17] In addition to improved performance, highly cohesive groups can lead to the maintenance of close relationships among the members. We will discuss group cohesion in further detail when we examine the common characteristics of well-developed groups.

9-3c Social Loafing

Social loafing occurs when one group member comes to rely on the efforts of other group members and fails to contribute her own time, effort, thoughts, or other resources to a group.[18] This may create a real drag on the group's efforts and achievements. Some scholars argue that social loafing, also known as *free riding*, is a rational response to feelings of inequity or situations in which individual efforts are hard to observe. Team member personality factors may mitigate the negative effects of social loafing on team performance. Team members who possess high levels of conscientiousness and agreeableness tend to compensate for social loafers so that team performance is not reduced.[19] However, social loafing shortchanges the group, which loses potentially valuable resources possessed by individual members.[20]

One method for countering social loafing is a member self-evaluation system. If members must formally review their contributions to the group, they are less likely to loaf. Identifying individual contributions to the group product also counters loafing. If each group member is responsible for a specific input, an individual's failure to contribute will be noticed by everyone.

9-3d Loss of Individuality

Social loafing may be detrimental to group achievement, but it does not have the potentially explosive effects of **loss of individuality**. Loss of individuality is a social process through which group members lose self-awareness and its accompanying senses of accountability, inhibition, and responsibility for individual behavior.[21]

norms of behavior The standards that a work group uses to evaluate the behavior of its members.

group cohesion The interpersonal glue that makes members of a group stick together.

social loafing The failure of a group member to contribute personal time, effort, thoughts, or other resources to the group.

loss of individuality A social process in which individual group members lose self-awareness and its accompanying sense of accountability, inhibition, and responsibility for individual behavior.

People may engage in morally reprehensible acts and even violent behavior as committed members of their group or organization when their individuality is lost. Loss of individuality was one of several contributing factors to the riot that destroyed sections of Los Angeles following the Rodney King verdict in April 1992. Yet loss of individuality is not always negative or destructive. The loosening of normal ego control mechanisms in the individual sometimes leads to prosocial behavior and even heroic acts in dangerous situations.[22]

9-4 GROUP FORMATION AND DEVELOPMENT

After its formation, a group goes through predictable stages of development. If each of the stages is successfully negotiated, the group emerges as a mature and tightly knit entity. One logical group development model proposed by Warren Bennis and Herbert Shepard delineates four stages following the group's formation: mutual acceptance, decision making, motivation and commitment, and control and sanctions.[23]

According to this group development model, a group addresses three issues: interpersonal issues, task issues, and authority issues.[24] The *interpersonal issues* include matters of trust, personal comfort, and security. Trust, in particular, is a key issue for any company in its working relationships. The *task issues* include the mission or purpose of the group, the methods the group employs, and the outcomes expected of the group. The *authority issues* include decisions about who is in charge, how power and influence are managed, and who has the right to tell whom to do what. This section addresses group formation, each stage of group development, and the characteristics of a mature group.

9-4a Group Formation

Formal and informal groups coalesce in organizations for different reasons. Formal groups are sometimes called *official* or *assigned* groups, and informal groups may be called *unofficial* or *emergent* groups. Formal groups such

> **Diversity is an important consideration in the formation of groups.**

as project task forces, boards of directors, and temporary committees come together to perform specific tasks. An example of a formal group was the task force assembled by the University of Texas at Arlington to design the Goolsby Leadership Academy. Chaired by the associate dean of business, the task force was composed of seven members with diverse academic expertise and business experience. The task force established a five-year plan to inaugurate the select undergraduate program, which cultivates advanced leadership skills in its Goolsby Fellows and Associates.

Informal groups evolve in the work setting to gratify a variety of member needs not met by formal groups. For example, organizational members' inclusion and affirmation needs might be satisfied through informal athletic or specialized interest groups. Athletic teams representing a department, unit, or company may achieve semiofficial status, such as the AT&T National Running Team that uses the corporate logo on its race shirts.

Diversity is an important consideration in the formation of groups, as it can enhance performance and lead to new ways of thinking. Team members will defer more often to members with task-related diversity, such as education and tenure, for their expertise and perceived contributions to task performance.[25] One study of gender diversity among U.S. workers found that men and women in gender-balanced groups had higher job satisfaction than those in homogeneous groups.[26] Organizations have been challenged to blend culturally and linguistically diverse peoples into effective work groups since America's founding. This task was especially demanding during the early years of the 1900s, when waves of immigrant workers arrived from numerous European nations.

In addition to ethnic, gender, and cultural diversity, there is interpersonal diversity, which may be indicated by different needs for inclusion, control of people and events, and affirmation from others. Successful interpersonal relationships are made stronger when group members are emotionally intelligent.

iStockphoto.com/Mattjeacock

FIGURE 9.1 TUCKMAN'S FIVE-STAGE MODEL OF GROUP DEVELOPMENT

Forming	Storming	Norming	Performing	Adjourning
Little agreement Unclear purpose Guidance and direction	Conflict Increased clarity of purpose Power struggles Coaching	Agreement and consensus Clear roles and responsibilities Facilitation	Clear vision and purpose Focus on goal achievement Delegation	Task completion Good feeling about achievements Recognition

© Cengage Learning

9-4b Stages of Group Development

All groups go through stages of development, some more successfully than others. Mature groups are able to work through the interpersonal, task, and authority issues inevitable at the highest echelons of the business world. The path to maturity does not always go smoothly, however. Immature groups often experience personality clashes and other fault lines (i.e., potential breaking points within the group) at various stages of development.[27]

Bruce Tuckman's five-stage model of group development proposes that team behavior progresses through five stages: forming, storming, norming, performing, and adjourning.[28] These stages and their properties are illustrated in Figure 9.1.

Dependence on guidance and direction is the defining characteristic of the *forming* stage. At this point, team members are unclear about individual roles and responsibilities and tend to rely heavily on the leader to answer questions about the team's purpose, objectives, and external relationships. Moving from this stage requires that team members feel they are part of the team. During this time, it may also be beneficial for leaders to encourage team members to get to know each other on an interpersonal level before focusing on task performance.[29]

Team members compete for position in the *storming* stage. As the name suggests, this is a period of considerable conflict as power struggles, cliques, and factions within the group begin to surface. Clarity of purpose increases, but uncertainties still exist. This is also the stage in which members assess one another with regard to trustworthiness, emotional comfort, and evaluative acceptance. The group leader's coaching style is key during this stage of development, as team members may challenge her. The supervisor's ability to control her own emotions is important during this phase.

Agreement and consensus are characteristic of team members in the *norming* stage. It is during this period that roles and responsibilities become clear and are accepted. The group's focus will turn from interpersonal relations to decision making and task accomplishment. Insignificant decisions may be delegated to individuals or small teams, while larger decisions will be discussed and decided by the entire group. The group may address questions of authority, such as the necessity of a primary spokesperson and the delegation of roles within the group. Wallace Supply Company, an industrial distributor of pipes, valves, and fittings, found employee teams particularly valuable in raising and answering questions of authority.[30] The teams concluded that leadership ought to be facilitative and that certain responsibilities could be delegated to teams themselves.

As a team moves into the *performing* stage, it becomes more strategically aware of its mission and purpose. In this stage of development, the group has successfully worked through interpersonal, task, and authority issues and can stand on its own with little interference from the leader. Disagreements are resolved positively with necessary changes to structure and processes attended to by the team. A mature group is able to control its members through the judicious application of positive and negative sanctions based on the evaluation of specific behaviors. Recent research shows that evaluation biases stemming from liking someone operate in face-to-face groups but not in electronic groups, such as virtual teams.[31] Members at this stage do not need to be instructed but may ask for assistance from the leader in regard to personal or interpersonal development.

The final stage of group development is the *adjourning* stage. When the task is completed, everyone on the team can move on to new and different things. Team members retain a sense of accomplishment and feel good knowing that their purpose was fulfilled. The leader's role at this point is primarily to recognize the group's achievements. But unless the group is a task force or other informal team, most groups in organizations remain at the performing stage and do not disband as the adjourning stage suggests.

9-4c Punctuated Equilibrium Model

Though it is still highly cited in team and group research, Tuckman's model may be unrealistic from an organizational perspective. Research has shown that many teams experience relational conflicts at different times and in different contexts. Connie Gersick proposes that groups do not necessarily progress linearly from one step to another in a predetermined sequence but alternate between periods of inertia with little visible progress toward goal achievement. Progress is punctuated by bursts of energy as work groups develop. It is in these bursts that the majority of work is accomplished.[32] For example, a task force given nine months to complete a task may use the first four months to choose its norms, explore contextual issues, and determine how it will communicate. The final five months would then be dedicated to executing the task itself.

9-4d Characteristics of a Mature Group

A mature group has four characteristics: a clear purpose and mission, well-understood norms and standards of conduct, a high level of group cohesion, and a flexible status structure.

PURPOSE AND MISSION The group's purpose and mission may be assigned (as in the example of the Goolsby Leadership Academy task force) or emerge from within the group (as in the example of the AT&T National Running Team). In the case of an assigned mission, the group may embrace the mission as stated or reexamine, revise, or question it. The importance of mission is exemplified by IBM's Process Quality Management, which requires that a process team of no more than twelve people develop a clear understanding of the group's mission as the first step in the process.[33] The IBM approach demands that all members agree to go in the same direction. The mission statement is converted into a specific agenda, clear goals, and a set of critical success factors. Stating the purpose and mission in the form of specific goals enhances productivity and performance far more effectively than individual goal setting.[34]

BEHAVIORAL NORMS *Behavioral norms*, which evolve over time, are well-understood standards of behavior within a group.[35] They are benchmarks against which team members are evaluated by other team members. For example, team altruism is the result of norms established as a result of one or more individual team members engaging in altruistic behaviors, often with different motivations ranging from prosocial to impression management.[36] Although some norms become written rules, such as an attendance policy or an ethical code, other norms remain informal, such as dress codes and norms about after-hours socializing. Additionally, behavioral norms may evolve around performance and productivity.[37] For example, productivity norms can influence the performance of sports teams in office leagues as well as in the professional realm.[38]

A group's productivity norm may or may not be consistent with the organization's productivity standards. A high-performance team sets productivity standards above organizational expectations, average teams set productivity standards consistent with organizational expectations, and noncompliant or counterproductive teams set productivity standards below organizational expectations, sometimes with the intent of damaging the organization or creating change. Usually, however, behavioral norms affect organizational culture in a beneficial way for all.

GROUP COHESION Group cohesion enables a group to exercise effective control over its members in relation to its behavioral norms and standards. Mature teams have the capacity to share the deep acting strategies employed by individual team members, resulting in members behaving more similarly when expressing emotions.[39] Among the threats to a group's cohesion are goal conflict, unpleasant

Enhancing Team Cohesion

Putting a collection of individuals together is much simpler than getting that collection of individuals to behave as a team. Getting people to work as a team requires that they have a shared identity and understand the *why* of their existence as a collective unit. While organizations may deem individuals who do the same work under the same conditions and in the same locations as sharing a sense of common purpose, it is often not enough. Groups and teams need a compelling mission that is persuasive enough to bring members together and inspire them to support each other's efforts. For instance, "Our job is to make sure those buildings are as clean as we would want them for our family" is a goal that can bring people together. Helping individuals shape their own identities through their allegiance to their teams is a powerful way to enhance cohesion.

SOURCE: G. Halvorson, "Getting to Us," *Harvard Business Review* 92 (2014): 38.

The 2014-2015 Golden State Warriors worked together as a team to successfully win an NBA World Championship last season.

productive, but highly cohesive groups with low productivity standards were unproductive despite their high level of cohesion. Nevertheless, no matter what the productivity was, member satisfaction, commitment, and communication were greater in highly cohesive groups.

Group cohesion is influenced by a number of factors, most notably time, size, the prestige of the team, external pressure, and internal competition. Usually cohesion evolves gradually throughout group development. In other words, the more time a group spends together, the more cohesive it will be. Also, smaller groups—those of five or seven members, for example—tend to be more cohesive than those of more than twenty-five, although cohesion does not decline much with size after forty or more members.

experiences, and domination of a subgroup. Groups with low levels of cohesion have greater difficulty exercising control over their members and enforcing their standards of behavior; hence, they are more vulnerable to such threats. Specifically, work-related tensions and anxieties increase in highly cohesive teams and decrease in teams low in cohesion, as depicted in Figure 9.2. This relationship suggests that cohesion has a calming effect on team members.

In addition, actual productivity was found to vary significantly less in highly cohesive teams, making them much more predictable. The actual productivity levels, though, were primarily determined by the productivity norms within each work group. Thus, highly cohesive groups with high production standards were very

FIGURE 9.2 COHESIVENESS AND WORK-RELATED TENSION*

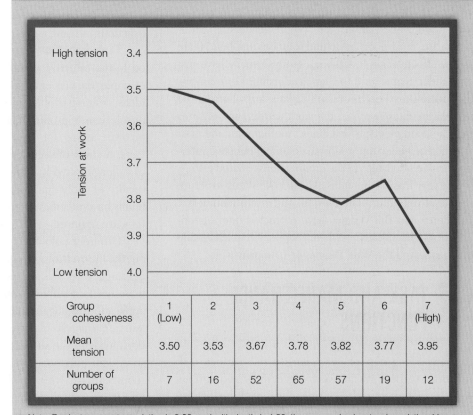

Group cohesiveness	1 (Low)	2	3	4	5	6	7 (High)
Mean tension	3.50	3.53	3.67	3.78	3.82	3.77	3.95
Number of groups	7	16	52	65	57	19	12

Note: Product–moment correlation is 0.28, and critical ratio is 4.20; the group cohesion–tension relationship is highly significant at the .001 level.

*The measure of tension at work is based on group mean response to the question "Does your work ever make you feel 'jumpy' or nervous?" A low numerical score represents relatively high tension.

SOURCE: S. E. Seashore, *Group Cohesiveness in the Industrial Work Group*, 1954. Research conducted by Stanley E. Seashore at the Institute for Social Research, University of Michigan. Reprinted by permission.

Prestige or social status may enhance a group's cohesion as well. More prestigious groups, such as the U.S. Air Force Thunderbirds or the U.S. Navy Blue Angels, are highly cohesive. However, even groups of very low prestige may be highly cohesive as a result of other factors tending toward cohesion, such as the aforementioned factors of longer time together and smaller group size. Finally, external pressure and internal competition are two other factors influencing group cohesion. Although the mechanics' union, pilots, and other internal constituencies at Eastern Airlines had various differences of opinion, they all pulled together in a cohesive fashion in resisting Frank Lorenzo when he came in to reshape the airline before its demise. Whereas external pressures tend to enhance it, internal competition usually decreases cohesion within a team. One study found that company-imposed pressure disrupted group cohesion by increasing internal competition and reducing cooperative interpersonal activity.[40]

STATUS STRUCTURE Status structure is the set of authority and task relations among a group's members. It may be hierarchical or egalitarian, depending on the group. Successful resolution of the authority issue within a team results in a well-understood status structure of leader–follower relationships. Where leadership problems arise, it is important to find solutions and build team leader effectiveness.[41] Although groups usually have just one leader, teams tend to share leadership. For example, one person may be the team's taskmaster, who sets the agenda, initiates much of the work activity, and ensures that the team meets its deadlines. Another team member may take a leadership role in maintaining effective interpersonal relationships in the group. Hence, shared leadership is very feasible in teams. An effective status structure results in role interrelatedness among group members.[42] Bill Perez and Bill Wrigley have promoted interrelatedness through a tag-team style of cooperation in leadership that has served the Wm. Wrigley Jr. Company well.

9-5 TASK AND MAINTENANCE FUNCTIONS

An effective group or team carries out various task functions to perform its work successfully and various maintenance functions to ensure member satisfaction and a sense of team spirit.[43] Teams that successfully fulfill these functions afford their members the potential for the

status structure The set of authority and task relations among a group's members.

task function An activity directly related to the effective completion of a team's work.

TABLE 9.2 TASK AND MAINTENANCE FUNCTIONS IN TEAMS OR GROUPS

Task Functions	Maintenance Functions
Initiating activities	Supporting others
Seeking information	Following others' leads
Giving information	Gatekeeping communication
Elaborating concepts	Setting standards
Coordinating activities	Expressing member feelings
Summarizing ideas	Testing group decisions
Testing ideas	Consensus testing
Evaluating effectiveness	Harmonizing conflict
Diagnosing problems	Reducing tension

© Cengage Learning

social benefits of psychological intimacy and integrated involvement we discussed at the beginning of the chapter. Table 9.2 presents nine task and nine maintenance functions in teams or groups.

Task functions are those activities directly related to the effective completion of the team's work. For example, the task of initiating activity involves suggesting ideas, defining problems, and proposing approaches and/or solutions to problems. The task of seeking information involves asking for ideas, suggestions, information, or facts. A study of security analysts found that the quality of colleagues' work helped to improve and maintain the quality of individual member performance.[44] Effective teams have members who fulfill various task functions as they are required.

Different task functions vary in importance throughout the life cycle of a group. For example, during the engineering test periods for new technologies, the engineering team needs members who focus on testing the practical applications of suggestions and those who diagnose problems and suggest solutions. The effective use of task functions leads to the success of the group. In one case, the successful initiation and coordination of an emergency room team's activities by the senior resident saved the life of a knife wound victim.[45] The victim was stabbed one-quarter inch below the heart, and the team acted quickly to stem the bleeding, begin intravenous fluids, and monitor the victim's vital signs. A recent study found that team member familiarity increases team performance up to a point by reducing team coordination errors (TCEs). Too much team familiarity may lead to increased TCEs as teams begin to rely on habitual routines and implicit coordination rather than explicit coordination methods. The relationship between team familiarity and the occurrence of TCEs is moderated by leader experience.[46]

Maintenance functions are those activities essential to the effective, satisfying interpersonal relationships within a group or team. Following another group member's lead may be as important as being a leader. Communication gatekeepers within a group ensure balanced contributions from all members. Because task activities build tension within teams or groups, tension-reduction activities are important to drain off negative or destructive feelings. In a study of twenty-five work groups over a five-year period, humor and joking behavior were found to enhance the social relationships in the groups.[47] The researchers concluded that performance improvements in the twenty-five groups indirectly resulted from improved relationships attributable to the humor and joking behaviors. Maintenance functions enhance togetherness, cooperation, and teamwork, enabling members to achieve psychological intimacy while furthering the success of the team. Emotional competencies such as empathy self-control are beneficial for maintaining group relationships. Jody Grant's supportive attitude and comfortable demeanor as chair and CEO of Texas Capital Bancshares enabled him to build a vibrant bank in the aftermath of the great Texas banking crash. Grant was respected for his expertise *and* his ability to build relationships. Both task and maintenance functions are important for successful groups and teams.

 ## 9-6 FACTORS THAT INFLUENCE GROUP EFFECTIVENESS

Work team effectiveness in the new team environment requires management's attention to both work team structure and work team process.[48] In addition to how the team is structured and what the team does, diversity and creativity are emerging as two areas with significant impact on team performance.

9-6a Work Team Structure

Work team structure issues include goals and objectives, operating guidelines, performance measures, and role specification. A work team's goals and objectives specify what must be achieved, while the operating guidelines set the organizational boundaries and decision-making limits within which the team must function. The goal-setting process discussed in Chapter 6 applies to work teams, too. In addition to these two structural elements, the work team needs to know what performance measures are being used to assess its task accomplishment. For example, a medical emergency team's performance measures might include the success rate in saving critically injured patients and the average number of hours a patient is in the emergency room before being transferred to a hospital bed.

Finally, work team structure requires a clearly specified set of roles for the executives and managers who oversee the work of the team, for the work team leaders who exercise influence over team members, and for team members. These role specifications should include information about required role behaviors, such as decision making and task performance, as well as restrictions or limits on role behaviors, such as the limitations on managerial interventions in work team activities and decision making. Expectations as well as experience may be especially important for newcomer role performance in work teams.[49]

9-6b Work Team Process

Work team process is the second important dimension of effectiveness. Two of the important process issues in work teams are the managing of cooperative behaviors and the managing of competitive behaviors. Both sets of behaviors are helpful in task accomplishment, and they should be viewed as complementary. *Cooperative teamwork skills* include open communication, trust, personal integrity, positive interdependence, and mutual support. On the other hand, *positive competitive teamwork skills* include the ability to enjoy competition, play fair, and be a good winner or loser; to have access to information for monitoring where the team and members are in the competition; and not to overgeneralize or exaggerate the results of any specific competition. In a study of reward structures in seventy-five four-member teams, competitive rewards enhanced speed of performance, while cooperative rewards enhanced accuracy of performance.[50]

Work team process issues have be-come more complex in the global workplace, where teams are composed of members from many cultures and backgrounds. This complexity is increased by the presence of virtual work teams operating on the global landscape. In addition to the process issues of cooperation, competition, and diversity, three other process issues are related to topics we discuss elsewhere in the text. These are empowerment, which is discussed in the next major section of this chapter; team decision making, which is discussed in Chapter 10; and conflict management and resolution, which are discussed in Chapter 13.

maintenance function An activity essential to effective, satisfying interpersonal relationships within a team or group.

9-6c Diversity

Diversity also plays a large role in how effective work groups and teams are. Diversity in a group is healthy, and members may contribute to the collective effort through one of four basic styles: the contributor, the collaborator, the communicator, or the challenger.[51] The *contributor* is data driven, supplies necessary information, and adheres to high performance standards. The *collaborator* sees the big picture and is able to keep a constant focus on the mission and urge other members to join efforts for mission accomplishment. The *communicator* listens well, facilitates the group's process, and humanizes the collective effort. The *challenger* is the devil's advocate who questions everything from the group's mission, purpose, and methods to its ethics. Members may exhibit one or more of these four basic styles over a period of time. In addition, an effective group must have an *integrator*, especially when the group is a cross-functional one, where different perspectives carry the seeds of conflict.[52] However, cross-functional teams are not necessarily a problem. Effectively managing cross-functional teams of artists, designers, printers, and financial experts enabled Hallmark Cards to cut its new product development time in half.[53]

DISSIMILARITY Recent research in diversity has focused on the effect of dissimilarity within a team. This issue is often studied in relation to social identity theory and self-categorization theory. Since creativity concerns new ideas, some amount of dissimilarity is necessary within a team in order for creativity, novelty, and innovation to blossom. Although creativity is discussed in some detail in Chapter 10, we address it briefly here in the context of teams.

We defined diversity in Chapter 1 in terms of individual differences. Recent relational demography research finds that demographic dissimilarity influences employees' absenteeism, commitment, turnover intentions, beliefs, work group relationships, self-esteem, and OCB.[54] Thus, dissimilarity may have positive or negative effects in teams and on team members. Racial dissimilarity may also impact the extent to which team members communicate with each other and develop a sense of group identity.[55] While value dissimilarity may be positively related to task and relationship conflict, it is negatively related

to team involvement.[56] This fact highlights the importance of managing dissimilarity in teams, being open to diversity, and turning conflicts about ideas into positive outcomes.

Functional background is one way to look at dissimilarity in teams. One study of 262 professionals in thirty-seven cross-functional teams found that promoting social identification with functional background helped individuals perform better as team members.[57] Another study of multifunctional management teams in a *Fortune* 100 company found that functional background predicted team involvement.[58] Finally, in a slightly different study of 129 members on twenty multidisciplinary project teams, informational dissimilarity had no adverse effects when there was member task and goal congruence.[59]

STRUCTURAL DIVERSITY Structural diversity concerns the number of *structural holes*, or disconnections between members, within a work team. One research study examined structural diversity and performance of nineteen teams in a wood-products company. The investigators were interested in demographic diversity among team members as well as the structural diversity, or presence of structural holes, in the teams. Neither race nor gender was a demographic factor that influenced the proportion of structural holes within the teams. However, age diversity significantly improved structural integrity. Hence, greater variance in age within a team leads to more member-to-member connections and fewer member-to-member disconnections.

Are disconnections of team members good or bad for the team? What are the consequences of having more or

Diversity in a group is healthy.

Dean Drobott/Shutterstock.com

Getting Virtual Teams Right

Today, virtual teams are a necessity of doing business. With increased technology, most professionals can perform their jobs from anywhere in the world. Despite its benefits, 66% of IT projects outsourced to virtual teams failed to satisfy their client's requirements. Research finds that most people consider virtual communication less productive than face-to-face interaction, nearly half feeling confused and overwhelmed by the technology. It's not all bad news. A more recent study found that well-managed virtual teams can actually outperform traditional ones and have the potential for productivity gains upwards of 43%. High-performing virtual teams share the following characteristics:

> Team members are suited to work in virtual teams, possessing good communication skills, high emotional intelligence, and the ability to work independently. Team size is manageable, with no more than ten people, and roles are clearly defined.

> Teams are led by individuals who foster trust among team members, encouraging dialogue, and clarifying goals and deadlines.

> Though dispersed geographically, virtual teams come together and meet face-to-face at several critical times during the relationship—at kickoff, during onboarding, and to celebrate milestones.

> Teams have the right technology that integrates a variety of communications media as appropriate for different types of collaboration. This includes conference calling, direct calling and text messaging, and discussion forums.

SOURCE: K. Ferrazzi, "Managing Yourself," *Harvard Business Review* 92 (2014): 120–123.

Rawpixel/Shutterstock.com

fewer structural holes between team members? Teams with few structural holes may have problems with creativity, while teams with a high proportion of structural holes may have difficulty coordinating. These observations led the researchers to conclude that there is a curvilinear relationship between structural diversity, or structural integrity, and team performance. The teams with moderate structural diversity achieve the best performance. This research is important because it points out that managers should look at the overall structure and network of relationships within their work teams in addition to the individual characteristics of team members in attempting to achieve the best performance from these teams.[60]

9-6d Creativity

Creativity is often thought of in an individual context rather than a team context. However, there is such a thing as team creativity. In a study of fifty-four research and development teams, team creativity scores were explained by aggregation processes across both people and time.[61] In another study of creative behavior, a Korean electronics company found that individual dissimilarity in age and performance, as well as functional diversity within the team, positively affected individual employees' creative behavior.

Some think that the deck is stacked against teams as agents of creativity. Leigh Thompson, a management and organizations professor at Northwestern University, thinks differently and suggests that team creativity and divergent thinking can be enhanced through greater diversity in teams, electronic brainstorming, training facilitators, membership change in teams, and building a playground.[62] Human capital diversity in teams can be a source of team social capital, which has the potential to enhance the level of team creativity through increased access to a variety of individuals with varying knowledge and experiences.[63] These practices can overcome social loafing, conformity, and downward norm setting in teams and organizations. Team members might exercise care in timing the insertion of their novel ideas into the team process so as to maximize the positive impact and benefits.[64]

EMPOWERMENT AND SELF-MANAGED TEAMS

To be successful, teams require a culture of empowerment in the organization in which they are implemented. This is especially true of *self-managed teams*, discussed shortly, which are designed to take on responsibilities and address issues traditionally reserved for management.

Empowerment may be thought of as an attribute of a person or of an organization's culture.[65] As an organizational culture attribute, empowerment encourages participation, an essential ingredient for teamwork.[66] *Quality action teams (QATs)* at FedEx are the primary *quality improvement process (QIP)* technique used by the company to engage management and hourly employees in four- to ten-member problem-solving teams.[67] The teams are empowered to act and solve problems as specific as charting the best route from the Phoenix airport to the local distribution center or as global as making major software enhancements to the online package-tracking system.

Empowerment may give employees the power of a lightning strike, but empowered employees must be properly focused through careful planning and preparation before they strike.[68]

To be successful, teams require a culture of empowerment in the organization in which they are implemented.

9-7a Empowerment Skills

Empowerment through employee self-management is an alternative to empowerment through teamwork.[69] Whether through self-management or teamwork, empowerment requires the development of certain skills if it is to be enacted effectively.

Competence skills are the first set of skills required for empowerment. Mastery and experience in one's chosen discipline and profession provide an essential foundation for empowerment. New employees and trainees should experience only limited empowerment until they demonstrate the capacity to accept more responsibility.

Empowerment also requires certain *process skills*. The most critical process skills include negotiating skills, especially with allies, opponents, and adversaries.[70] Allies are the easiest people to negotiate with because they agree with you about the team's mission and you can trust their actions and behavior. Opponents require a different negotiating strategy; although you can predict their actions and behavior, they do not agree with your concept of the team's mission. Adversaries are dangerous,

self-managed team A team that makes decisions that were once reserved for managers.

difficult people to negotiate with because you cannot predict their actions or behaviors and they do not agree with your concept of the team's mission.

A third set of empowerment skills involves the development of *cooperative and helping behaviors*.[71] Cooperative people engage in encouraging, helpful behavior to maximize the gains for everyone on the team. The alternative orientations to cooperation are competitive, individualistic, and egalitarian approaches. *Competitive people* are motivated to maximize their personal gains regardless of the expense to other people. This motivation can be very counterproductive to the team. *Individualistic people* are motivated to act autonomously, though not necessarily to maximize their personal gains. They are less prone to contribute to the efforts of the team. *Egalitarian people* are motivated to equalize the outcomes for each team member, which may or may not be beneficial to the team's well-being. Paradoxically, the team members who need the most help often get the least help because helping behaviors often target the most expert team members, a dynamic that actually compromises overall team performance.[72]

Communication skills are a final set of essential empowerment skills.[73] These skills include self-expression skills and skills in reflective listening. Empowerment cannot occur in a team unless members are able to express themselves in emotionally intelligent ways as well as listen carefully to one another.

9-7b Self-Managed Teams

Self-managed teams, also called *self-directed teams* or *autonomous work groups*, are teams that make decisions that were once reserved for managers. Self-managed teams are one way to implement empowerment in organizations. Even though self-managed teams are self-directed, that fact does not negate the influence of managers. In fact, managers have an important role in providing leadership and influence.[74] There is strong support for the use of soft-influence tactics in managers' communication with self-directed teams, which yields more positive results.[75]

A one-year study of self-managed teams suggests that they have a positive impact on employee attitudes but not on absenteeism or turnover.[76] Evaluative research is helpful in achieving a better understanding of this relatively new way of approaching teamwork and the design of work. Such research helps establish expectations for self-managed teams. Nevertheless, there are risks, such as groupthink in self-managed teams, that must be prevented or managed if the team is to achieve full development and function.[77]

It is noteworthy that one evaluation of empowerment, teams, and *Total Quality Management (TQM)* programs found that companies associated with these popular management techniques did not have higher economic performance.[78] Other evaluations of self-managed teams are more positive. Southwest Industries, a high-technology aerospace manufacturing firm, embarked on a major internal reorganization in the early 1990s that included the creation of self-managed teams to fit its high-technology production process. Southwest's team approach resulted in a 30% increase in shipments, a 30% decrease in lead time, a 40% decrease in total inventory, a decrease in machinery downtime, and almost a one-third decrease in production costs.[79] An overall positive history has resulted in U.S.-based multinational corporations increasingly using self-managed teams in their global operations.

9-8 UPPER ECHELONS: TEAMS AT THE TOP

Self-managed teams at the top of the organization—top-level executive teams—are referred to as **upper echelons**. Organizations are often a reflection of these upper echelons.[80] *Upper echelon theory* argues that the background characteristics of the top management team can predict organizational characteristics and set standards for values, competence, ethics, and unique characteristics throughout the organization.

Furthermore, upper echelons are one key to the strategic success of the organization.[81] The ability to exert power and influence throughout the entire organization makes the top management team a key to the organization's success. This ability may be compromised if the top team sends mixed signals about teamwork and if executive pay systems foster competition, politics, and individualism.[82]

For example, when Lee Iacocca became CEO at the Chrysler Corporation, his top management team was assembled to bring about strategic realignment within the corporation by building on Chrysler's historical engineering strength. The dramatic success of Chrysler during the early 1980s was followed by struggle and accommodation during the late 1980s. This raises the question of how long a CEO and the top management team can sustain organizational success.

Hambrick and Fukutomi addressed this question by examining the dynamic relationship between a CEO's tenure and the success of the organization.[83] They found five *seasons* in a CEO's tenure: (1) response to a mandate, (2) experimentation, (3) selection of an enduring theme, (4) convergence, and (5) dysfunction. A summary of each season is shown in Table 9.3. All else being equal, the seasons model has significant implications for organizational performance. Specifically, organizational performance increases during a CEO's tenure to a peak, after which performance declines. This relationship is depicted in Figure 9.3. The peak has been found

upper echelon A top-level executive team in an organization.

TABLE 9.3	THE FIVE SEASONS OF A CEO'S TENURE				
	1	**2**	**3**	**4**	**5**
Critical CEO Characteristics	**Response to Mandate**	**Experimentation**	**Selection of an Enduring Theme**	**Convergence**	**Dysfunction**
COMMITMENT TO A PARADIGM	Moderately strong	Could be strong or weak	Moderately strong	Strong; increasing	Very strong
TASK KNOWLEDGE	Low but rapidly increasing	Moderate; somewhat increasing	High; slightly increasing	High; slightly increasing	High; slightly increasing
INFORMATION DIVERSITY	Many sources; unfiltered	Many sources but increasingly unfiltered	Fewer sources; moderately filtered	Few sources; highly filtered	Very few sources; highly filtered
TASK INTEREST	High	High	Moderately high	Moderately high but diminishing	Moderately low and diminishing
POWER	Low; increasing	Moderate; increasing	Moderate; increasing	Strong; increasing	Very strong; increasing

SOURCE: D. Hambrick and G. D. S. Fukutomi, "The Seasons of a CEO's Tenure," *Academy of Management Review* (1991): 729. Permission conveyed through Copyright Clearance Center, Inc.

FIGURE 9.3 EXECUTIVE TENURE AND ORGANIZATIONAL PERFORMANCE

SOURCE: D. Hambrick, "The Seasons of an Executive's Tenure," keynote address, the Sixth Annual Texas Conference on Organizations, Lago Vista, Texas, April 1991.

The presence of a so-called wild turkey in the top management team can be a particularly positive force. The wild turkey is a devil's advocate who challenges the thinking of the CEO and other top executives and provides a counterpoint during debates. If not shouted down or inhibited, the wild turkey helps the CEO and the team sustain peak performance and retard the CEO's dysfunction and decline. For example, former Secretary of State Colin Powell enhanced President George W. Bush's administration by exercising an independent voice. Often taking a more moderate position on policy issues than either the secretary of defense or the vice president, Powell brought variance and value to President Bush's administration.

to come at about seven years—somewhere in the middle of the executive's seasons. As indicated by the dotted lines in the figure, the peak may be extended, depending on several factors, such as diversity in the executive's support team.

9-8a Diversity at the Top

From an organizational health standpoint, diversity and depth in the top management team enhance the CEO's well-being.[84] From a performance standpoint, the CEO's top management team can influence the timing of the performance peak, the degree of dysfunction during the closing season of the CEO's tenure, and the rate of decline in organizational performance. Thus, diversity and heterogeneity in the top management team help sustain high levels of organizational performance at the peak and help maintain the CEO's vitality. A study of 207 U.S. firms in eleven industries found that functional diversity of top management teams had a positive effect on firm performance as the proportion of leaders in the same location increased.[85]

Leaders must develop communication strategies to bring together team members who are functionally, intellectually, demographically, and temperamentally diverse so that they can act in ways that complement one another. It is out of dissimilarity that strength is developed, and it is out of similarity that connections are built. Therefore, top management should strive for a balance of dissimilarity and similarity within work teams.

We conclude that the leadership, composition, and dynamics of the top management team have an important influence on the organization's performance, leading, in some cases, to a change from having only one CEO to having more than one. Current research has shown a dramatic increase in the number of co-CEO arrangements in both public and private corporations.[86] While

The wild turkey is a devil's advocate who challenges the thinking of the CEO and provides a counterpoint during debates.

Mike Neale/Shutterstock.com

A_KUDR/Shutterstock.com

FASTFACT

Achieving Diverse Work Teams Goes Beyond Checking Boxes

Three additional forms of diversity should be considered when assembling productive and long-lasting work teams. Using cognitive diversity will enhance creativity. Age/experience diversity will ensure the right balance between what's been done before and what is possible. Proximity diversity, the mix of virtual and traditional interactions, is an important predictor of success. The best managers use legally mandated criteria only as a starting point to achieving a much larger, more effective way of achieving true workplace diversity.

SOURCE: K. Rich, "Diversity's Central Paradox," *Forbes* 195 (2015): 34.

more common in Europe than in the United States, a historical U.S. example of a co-CEO arrangement includes a three-member team created by Walter Wriston while he was chairman at Citicorp (now part of Citigroup).

9-8b Multicultural Top Teams

Homogeneous groups, in which all members share similar backgrounds, are giving way to *token groups*, in which all but one member come from the same background; *bicultural groups*, in which two or more members represent each of two distinct cultures; and *multicultural groups*, in which members represent three or more ethnic backgrounds.[87] On the negative side, diversity within a group may increase the uncertainty, complexity, and inherent confusion in group processes, making it more difficult for the group to achieve its full productivity.[88] On the positive side, most organizations report benefits

> **Most organizations report benefits from increased diversity.**

from increased diversity, such as Merck, which attributes its long-term success to its leadership model that promotes diversity. Chair, President, and CEO Ray Gilmartin values diversity in Merck's top management team because he believes that it sparks innovation when employees with different perspectives work together to offer solutions. Diversities of age and educational specialization within top management teams were found in other studies to have a positive effect on team performance, especially when members needed to participate in cognitive tasks.[89] A recent study found that the performance of top management teams was greatly increased when the CEO had numerous shared experiences with executives from other companies and cultures.[90] The advantages of culturally diverse groups appear to include the generation of more and better ideas while limiting the risk of groupthink, to be discussed in Chapter 10.

STUDY TOOLS 9

LOCATED AT BACK OF THE TEXTBOOK

☐ Rip out chapter review card

LOCATED AT WWW.CENGAGE.COM/LOGIN

☐ Track your knowledge and understanding of key concepts in business using 4LTR Press Online

☐ Review key term flashcards and create your own using StudyBits

☐ Create and complete practice quizzes based off of your notes and StudyBits

☐ Complete Online activities such as Matching and Fill-in-the-Blank exercises

☐ View chapter highlight box content, including the chapter videos, key exhibits and executive profiles.

10 | Decision Making by Individuals and Groups

Dirk Ercken/Shutterstock.com

LEARNING OUTCOMES

10-1 Identify the steps in the decision-making process.

10-2 Describe various models of decision making.

10-3 Discuss the individual influences that affect decision making.

10-4 Explain how groups make decisions.

10-5 Describe the role culture plays in decision making.

10-6 Explain how organizations can improve the quality of decisions through participation.

After finishing this chapter go to **PAGE 169** for **STUDY TOOLS.**

10-1 THE DECISION-MAKING PROCESS

Decision making is a critical activity in the lives of managers. The decisions a manager faces can range from very simple, routine matters for which the manager has an established decision rule (**programmed decisions**) to new and complex decisions that require creative solutions (**nonprogrammed decisions**).[1] Scheduling lunch hours for one's work group, for example, is a programmed decision. The manager performs this programmed decision activity daily, using an established procedure with the same clear goal in mind each time. In contrast, decisions like buying out another company are nonprogrammed, providing a unique, unstructured situation and requiring considerable judgment. Regardless of the type of decision made, it is helpful to understand as much as possible about how individuals and groups make decisions.

> The first step is recognizing the problem; that is, the manager realizes that a decision must be made.

Danielala/Shutterstock.com

Decision making is a process involving a series of steps, as shown in Figure 10.1. The first step is recognizing the problem; that is, the manager realizes that a decision must be made. Identifying the real problem is important; otherwise, the manager may be reacting to symptoms rather than dealing with the root cause of the problem. Next, a manager must identify the objective of the decision. In other words, the manager must determine what is to be accomplished by the decision. The third step in the decision-making process is gathering information relevant to the problem. The manager must accumulate sufficient information about why the problem occurred. This involves conducting a thorough diagnosis of the situation and going on a fact-finding mission.

The fourth step is listing and evaluating alternative courses of action. During this step, a thorough "what-if" analysis should be conducted to determine the various factors that could influence the outcome. It is important to generate a wide range of options and creative solutions in order to be able to move on to the next step. Next, the manager selects the alternative that best meets the decision objective. If the problem has been diagnosed correctly and sufficient alternatives have been identified, this step is much easier. After the solution is implemented, the situation must then be monitored to see whether the decision met its objective. Consistent monitoring and periodic feedback are essential parts of the follow-up process.

Decision making can be stressful. Managers must make decisions with significant risk and uncertainty, and often without all of the necessary information. They must trust and rely on others in their decision-making process, yet they are ultimately responsible for the final decision. Sometimes decisions are painful and involve exiting businesses, firing people, and admitting wrong.

Blue Man Group has a history of making effective decisions. Its theatrical productions blend comedy, music, and multimedia in a unique brand of entertainment. It has grown wildly famous and successful by making sound business choices, even though none of the founders has any formal training in music, acting, or business. The group

Zingerman's Deli Grows but Stays Local

Susan Montgomery/Shutterstock.com

The owners of Ann Arbor, Michigan–based Zingerman's Deli had a lot of success in their first ten years and faced a decision on how to grow. Should they franchise? They decided against franchising because they would lose control and, more importantly, what they loved about their business was the local relationships they developed. Instead, they took a long look at what they were good at: fresh bread, so they started a bakehouse; coffee, so they created a coffee-roasting company; ice cream and cheese, so a creamery was started; great food, so they started a dine-in restaurant. And finally, they had great customer service, so they started a training module for independent businesses in the area. The result of the decision to stay local is nine separate local businesses, each with its own partnership. The partners meet weekly to make decisions. Staying local has worked for Zingerman's, with 550 jobs created in Ann Arbor and sales of $40 million per year.

SOURCES: www.zingermansdeli.com; M. F. Dunbar, "Interview with Michael Shuman," *Conscious Company* 1 (2015): 45–47.

programmed decision
A simple, routine matter for which a manager has an established decision rule.

nonprogrammed decision A new, complex decision that requires a creative solution.

FIGURE 10.1 THE DECISION-MAKING PROCESS

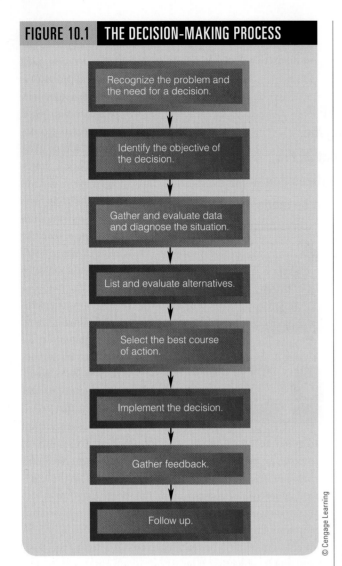

Recognize the problem and the need for a decision.

↓

Identify the objective of the decision.

↓

Gather and evaluate data and diagnose the situation.

↓

List and evaluate alternatives.

↓

Select the best course of action.

↓

Implement the decision.

↓

Gather feedback.

↓

Follow up.

© Cengage Learning

has turned down offers to sell credit cards, soft drinks, breath mints, and paint, all related to the color blue. With each new opportunity, the three founders use the same evaluation: "Okay, that's all good and well, that's a nice thought—but is it Blue Man?" The group has also completed a detailed 132-page operating manual, a task many businesses never complete. Finally, the founders make decisions by unanimous agreement.[2]

10-2 MODELS AND LIMITS OF DECISION MAKING

effective decision A timely decision that meets a desired objective and is acceptable to those individuals affected by it.

rationality A logical, step-by-step approach to decision making, with a thorough analysis of alternatives and their consequences.

The success of any organization depends on managers' abilities to make **effective decisions**. An

effective decision is timely, is acceptable to the individuals affected by it, and meets the desired objective.[3] This section describes three models of decision making: the rational model, the bounded rationality model, and the Z model. The section will conclude with a discussion of the limits of decision-making techniques.

10-2a Rational Model

Rationality refers to a logical, step-by-step approach to decision making with a thorough analysis of alternatives and their consequences. The *rational model* of decision making comes from classic economic theory and assumes the following:

1. The outcome will be completely rational.
2. The decision maker has a consistent system of preferences, which is used to choose the best alternative.
3. The decision maker is aware of all the possible alternatives.
4. The decision maker can calculate the probability of success for each alternative.[4]

In the rational model, the decision maker strives to *optimize*, that is, to select the best possible alternative.

Given the assumptions of the rational model, it is unrealistic. There are time constraints and limits to human knowledge and information-processing capabilities. In addition, a manager's preferences and needs change often. The rational model is thus an ideal that managers strive for in making decisions, and it captures the way a decision should be made, but it does not reflect the reality of managerial decision making.[5]

10-2b Bounded Rationality Model

Recognizing the deficiencies of the rational model, Herbert Simon suggested that there are limits on how rational a decision maker can actually be. His decision theory, the *bounded rationality model*, earned a Nobel Prize in economics in 1978. Simon's theory rests on the idea that there are constraints that force a decision maker to be less than completely rational. The bounded rationality model has four assumptions:

1. Managers select the first alternative that is satisfactory.
2. Managers recognize that their conception of the world is simple.
3. Managers are comfortable making decisions without determining all the alternatives.
4. Managers make decisions by rules of thumb, or heuristics.

Bounded rationality assumes that managers **satisfice**; that is, they select the first alternative that is "good enough," because the costs of optimizing in terms of time and effort are too great.[6] Further, the theory assumes that managers develop shortcuts, called **heuristics**, to make decisions in order to save mental activity. Heuristics are rules of thumb that allow managers to make decisions based on what has worked in past experiences.

Does the bounded rationality model portray the managerial decision process more realistically? Research indicates that it does. One of the reasons managers face limits to their rationality is that they must make decisions under risk and time pressure. The situation they find themselves in is highly uncertain, and the probability of success is not known.

Herbert Simon felt his theory would be incomplete until the role of emotion in decision making was understood, and researchers are beginning to untangle the complex role that emotion plays in the process.[7]

Managers often sacrifice because of time constraints.

10-2c Z Model

Isabel Briggs Myers, co-creator of the Myers-Briggs Type Indicator, also developed the Z *problem-solving model*, which capitalizes on the strengths of the four separate preferences (Sensing, Intuiting, Thinking, and Feeling). By using the Z problem-solving model, managers can use both their preferences and nonpreferences to make decisions more effectively. The Z model is presented in Figure 10.2. According to this model, good problem solving has four steps:

1. *Examine the facts and details.* Use Sensing to gather information about the problem.
2. *Generate alternatives.* Use Intuiting to develop possibilities.
3. *Analyze the alternatives objectively.* Use Thinking to logically determine the effects of each alternative.
4. *Weigh the impact.* Use Feeling to determine how the people involved will be affected.

Using the Z model can help an individual develop his nonpreferences. Another way to use the Z model is to rely on others to perform nonpreferred activities. For example, an individual who is an NF (Intuition-Feeling person) might want to turn to a trusted NT (Intuition-Thinking person) for help in analyzing alternatives objectively.

10-2d Escalation of Commitment

Each decision-making model carries its own unique limits. There is, however, one limitation that they all share: the decision maker's unwillingness to abandon a bad decision. Continuing to support a failing course of action is known as **escalation of commitment**.[8] In situations characterized by escalation of commitment, individuals who make decisions that turn out to be poor choices tend to hold fast to those choices, even when substantial costs are incurred.[9] An example of escalation is the price wars that often occur between airlines. The airlines reduce their prices in response to competitors until at a certain stage both airlines are in no-win situations. They continue to compete despite the heavy losses they incur. The desire to win is a motivation to continue to escalate, and each airline continues to reduce prices (lose money) based on the belief that the other airline will pull out of the price war.

Another example of escalation of commitment is the Drug Abuse Resistance Education Program (D.A.R.E.). Despite growing scientific evidence that the program does not produce reductions in drug use among young people, it continues to receive billions of dollars in donations and taxpayer funds.[10]

Why does escalation of commitment occur? One ex-

bounded rationality A theory that suggests that there are limits to how rational a decision maker can actually be.

satisfice To select the first alternative that is "good enough," because the costs in time and effort are too great to optimize.

heuristics Shortcuts in decision making that save mental activity.

escalation of commitment The tendency to continue to support a failing course of action.

Rangizzi/Shutterstock.com

FIGURE 10.2 THE Z PROBLEM-SOLVING MODEL

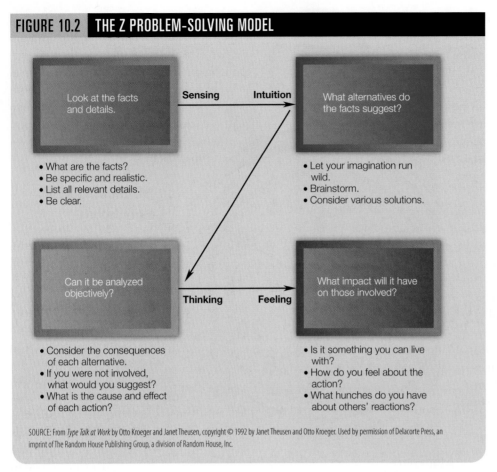

- **Look at the facts and details.**
  - What are the facts?
  - Be specific and realistic.
  - List all relevant details.
  - Be clear.

Sensing → **Intuition**

- **What alternatives do the facts suggest?**
  - Let your imagination run wild.
  - Brainstorm.
  - Consider various solutions.

- **Can it be analyzed objectively?**
  - Consider the consequences of each alternative.
  - If you were not involved, what would you suggest?
  - What is the cause and effect of each action?

Thinking → **Feeling**

- **What impact will it have on those involved?**
  - Is it something you can live with?
  - How do you feel about the action?
  - What hunches do you have about others' reactions?

SOURCE: From *Type Talk at Work* by Otto Kroeger and Janet Theusen, copyright © 1992 by Janet Theusen and Otto Kroeger. Used by permission of Delacorte Press, an imprint of The Random House Publishing Group, a division of Random House, Inc.

planation is offered by cognitive dissonance theory, as we discussed in Chapter 4. This theory assumes that people dislike inconsistency and that when it exists among their attitudes or between their attitudes and behavior, they strive to reduce the dissonance.[11] Other reasons why people may hang on to a losing course of action are optimism and control. Some people are overly optimistic and overestimate the likelihood that positive things will happen to them. Other people operate under an illusion of control—that they have special skills to control the future that other people don't have.[12] Some individuals "throw good money after bad." They think, "Well, I've invested this much … what's a few dollars more?" The closer a project is to completion, the more likely escalation is to occur.[13]

Hanging on to a poor decision can be costly to organizations. While many foreign automakers saw promise in the *green movement* and shifted their development toward hybrid vehicles in 2002, General Motors stuck with a cost-cutting strategy that streamlined its operations and focused on production of SUVs and trucks. Between 2005 and 2008 GM lost $82 billion, and even these losses did not change the ailing company's strategy.[14] In 2009 CEO Rick Wagoner finally attempted to de-escalate, announcing that GM's focus on SUVs and trucks was no longer a viable strategy. It was too late, however, and despite a multibillion-dollar loan from the U.S. government, GM declared bankruptcy.

Recent research on de-escalation found that individuals with higher self-esteem and those who are given an opportunity to affirm an important value are more likely to deescalate.[15] Organizations can use this information to deal with escalation of commitment in several ways. One method of reducing escalation is to split the responsibility for project decisions by allowing different individuals to make decisions at different project stages. Mindfulness meditation, which enhances present-moment awareness, reduces the tendency to think in terms of sunk-costs. Just a brief fifteen-minute breath meditation may help reduce escalation of commitment.[16] Still another suggestion is to provide individuals with a graceful exit from poor decisions so that their images are not threatened. There can be a reward of some type for those who admit to poor decisions before escalating their commitment to them or having groups make an initial investment decision. This way participants in group decision making may experience a diffusion of responsibility for the failed decision rather than feeling personally responsible; thus, they can pull out of a bad decision without threatening their image.[17]

We have seen that there are limits to how rational a manager can be in making decisions. On reason is that most managerial decisions involve considerable risk, and individuals react differently to risk situations, a subject we address in the next section.

 ## 10-3 INDIVIDUAL INFLUENCES ON DECISION MAKING

No decision is made in a vacuum. In many ways, decisions reflect the people who make them, so it is appropriate to examine the individual influences on decision making: comfort with risk, **cognitive style**, personality, intuition, and creativity.

10-3a Risk and the Manager

Many decisions involve some element of risk. For managers, decisions regarding hiring, promotions, delegation, acquisitions and mergers, overseas expansions, and new product development are among many that make risk a part of the job. As individuals, managers, of course, differ in terms of their willingness to take risks—that is, their degree of **risk aversion**. Some choose options that entail fewer risks, preferring familiarity and certainty, while others are *risk takers* and will accept greater potential for loss in decisions as well as tolerating greater uncertainty. Those prone to making risky decisions are more likely to take the lead in group discussions.[18]

Research indicates that women are more risk averse than men and that older, more experienced managers are more risk averse than younger managers. There is also some evidence that successful managers take more risks than unsuccessful managers.[19] However, the tendency to take risks or avoid them is only part of behavior toward risk. Risk taking is influenced not only by an individual's tendency but also by organizational factors. In commercial banks, loan decisions that require the assessment of risk are made every day.

Upper-level managers face a tough task in managing risk-taking behavior. By discouraging lower-level managers from taking risks, they may stifle creativity and innovation. If upper-level managers are going to encourage risk taking, however, they must allow employees to fail without fear of punishment. One way to accomplish this is to consider failure as "enlightened trial and error."[20] The key is establishing a consistent attitude toward risk within the organization.

Obviously, when individuals take risks, losses may occur. Suppose an oil producer thinks there is an opportunity to uncover oil by reentering an old drilling site. She gathers a group of investors and shows them the logs, and they chip in to finance the venture. The reentry is drilled to a certain depth, and nothing is found. Convinced they did not drill deep enough, the producer goes back to the investors and requests additional financial backing to continue drilling. The investors consent, and she drills deeper, only to find nothing. She approaches the investors, and after lengthy discussion, they agree to provide more money to drill deeper. Why do decision makers sometimes throw good money after bad? Why do they continue to provide resources to what looks like a losing venture?

cognitive style An individual's preferred method for gathering information and evaluating alternatives.

risk aversion The tendency to choose options that entail fewer risks and less uncertainty.

FASTFACT

The Time You Take to Make a Decision Signals Doubt

People make assumptions about the time others take to make a decision. For example, in the blind auditions on the television show *The Voice*, any of four coaches hit a buzzer and turn their chair to show interest in a singer. The singer then picks among those who turned to choose a coach—a risky decision. A study showed that coaches who were first to turn their chair were more frequently chosen by contestants, and those who turned last were much less likely to be chosen. So contestants tended to choose the coach who signaled the most confidence and avoided the coach who signaled the most doubt. Interestingly, a survival analysis showed that the contestants who chose the coach who turned first were eliminated early in the competition.

SOURCE: P. P. Van de Calseyde, G. Keren, and M. Zeelenberg, "Decision Time as Information in Judgment and Choice," *Organizational Behavior and Human Decision Processes* 125 (2014): 113–122.

10-3b Personality, Attitudes, and Values

In addition to all of the individual differences variables (discussed in Chapters 3 and 4)—personality characteristics, attitudes, and values—managers must use both their logic and their creativity to make effective decisions. Most of us are more comfortable using either logic or creativity, and we show that preference in everyday decision making.

Our brains have two lateral halves (Figure 10.3). The right side is the center for creative functions, while the left side is the center for logic, detail, and planning. There are advantages to both kinds of thinking, so the ideal situation is to be brain-lateralized, that is, be able to use either logic or creativity or both, depending on the situation.[21] There are ways to develop the side of the brain that you use less often. To develop your right side, or creative side, you can ask what-if questions, engage in play, and follow your intuition. To develop the left side, you can set goals for completing tasks and work to attain those goals. For managers, it is important to see the big picture, craft a vision, and plan strategically, all of which require right-brain skills. But it is equally important to be able to understand day-to-day operations and flowchart work processes, which are left-hemisphere brain skills.

Two particular individual influences that can enhance decision-making effectiveness will be highlighted next: intuition and creativity.

intuition A fast, positive force in decision making that is utilized at a level below consciousness and involves learned patterns of information.

FIGURE 10.3 | FUNCTIONS OF THE LEFT AND RIGHT BRAIN HEMISPHERES

Two Brains, Two Cognitive Styles

Left hemisphere	Right hemisphere
Verbal	Nonverbal, visuospatial
Sequential, temporal, digital	Simultaneous, spatial, analogical
Logical, analytic	Gestalt, synthetic
Rational	Intuitive
Western thought	Eastern thought

SOURCE: Based on ideas from S. P. Springer and G. Deutsch, *Left Brain, Right Brain* (New York: W. H. Freeman and Company, 1993), 272.

10-3c Intuition

There is evidence that managers often use their **intuition** to make decisions.[22] Henry Mintzberg, in his work on managerial roles, found that in many cases managers do not appear to use a systematic, step-by-step approach to decision making. Rather, Mintzberg argued, managers make judgments based on "hunches."[23] Daniel Isenberg studied the way senior managers make decisions

HOT TREND

Some People Intuitively Think of Others When Making Decisions

People differ by social value orientation. Some individuals are selfish in decision making, looking out for self-interest; but others are prosocial, looking out for other people. Neurocognitive researchers wanted to know whether the brain processing of each group differed when making decisions of various kinds. Using a simulation in which participants made decisions that affected their own payoffs and those of a recipient, subjects' blood flow to different regions of the brain was monitored. Functional magnetic resonance imaging (fMRI) showed that for selfish individuals, regions of the brain that determine cognitive control and value integration were taxed when a decision resulted in benefit to the other person. This means that selfish individuals had to work harder during prosocial decisions because they had to actively reflect to make the decision. In contrast, prosocial decision makers made prosocial decisions more quickly and intuitively.

SOURCE: K. Kuss, A. Falk, P. Trautner, C. Montag, B. Weber, and K. Fliessbach, "Neuronal Correlates of Social Decision Making Are Influenced by Social Value Orientation—An fMRI Study," *Frontiers in Behavioral Neuroscience* 9 (2015): 40.

Blablo101/Shutterstock.com

and found that intuition was used extensively, especially as a mechanism to evaluate decisions made more rationally.[24] Robert Beck studied the way managers at Bank of America made decisions about the future direction of the company following the deregulation of the banking industry. Beck described their use of intuition as an antidote to analysis paralysis, or the tendency to analyze decisions rather than developing innovative solutions.[25]

Dr. Gary Klein, a renowned cognitive psychologist, has written a book on the power of intuition. Dr. Klein and colleagues insist that skilled decision makers rely on patterns of learned information in making quick and efficient decisions. In a series of studies conducted with the U.S. Navy, firefighters, and the U.S. Army, they found that decision makers normally rely on intuition in unfamiliar, challenging situations. These decisions were superior to those made after careful evaluation of information and potential alternatives.[26]

Just what is intuition? In Jungian theory, intuiting (N) is a preferred method used for gathering data. This is only one way that the concept of intuition has been applied to managerial decision making, but it is perhaps the most widely researched form of the concept of intuition. There are, however, many definitions of *intuition* in the managerial literature. Chester Barnard, one of the early influential management researchers, argued that intuition's main attributes were speed and the inability of the decision maker to determine how the decision was made.[27] Other researchers have contended that intuition occurs at an unconscious level and that this is why the decision maker cannot verbalize how the decision was made.[28]

Intuition has been variously described as follows:

- The ability to know or recognize quickly and readily the possibilities of a situation.[29]

- Smooth automatic performance of learned behavior sequences.[30]

- Simple analyses frozen into habit and into the capacity for rapid response through recognition.[31]

These definitions share some common assumptions. First, there seems to be a notion that intuition is fast. Second, intuition is used at a level below consciousness. Third, there seems to be agreement that intuition involves learned patterns of information. Fourth, intuition appears to be a positive force in decision making.

The use of intuition may lead to more ethical decisions as intuition allows an individual to take on another's role with ease, and role taking is a fundamental part of developing moral reasoning. You may recall from Chapter 4 the role of cognitive moral development in ethical decision making. One study found a strong link between cognitive moral development and intuition. The development of new perspectives through intuition leads to higher moral growth, and thus to more ethical decisions.[32]

One question that arises is whether managers can be taught to use their intuition. Weston Agor, who has conducted workshops on developing intuitive skills in managers, has attained positive results in organizations such as the city government of Phoenix and entertainment powerhouse Walt Disney Enterprises. After giving intuition tests to more than 10,000 executives, he has concluded that in most cases, higher management positions are held by individuals with higher levels of intuition. But, just as the brain needs both hemispheres to work, Agor cautions that organizations need both analytical and intuitive minds to function at their peak. Lee Iacocca, in his autobiography, spends pages extolling intuition: "To a certain extent, I've always operated by gut feeling."[33] Agor suggests relaxation techniques, using images to guide the mind, and taking creative pauses before making a decision.[34] A review of the research on intuition suggests that, although intuition itself cannot be taught, managers can be trained to rely more fully on the promptings of their intuition.[35]

Intuition, with its many definitions, is an elusive concept. Some researchers view so-called rational methods as preferable to intuition, yet satisfaction with a rational decision is usually determined by how the decision feels intuitively.[36] Intuition appears to have a positive effect on managerial decision making, but it is not without controversy. Some writers argue that intuition has its place and that instincts should be trusted, but not as a substitute for reason. With new technologies, managers can analyze a lot more information in a lot less time, making the rational method less time-consuming than it once was.[37]

10-3d Creativity

In some ways, creativity is as elusive a concept as intuition. (We know it when we encounter it and when we feel its absence.) Even though creativity is highly individual, it is also collective. Personal creativity plays a role in the decisions made in organizations

Illumination is essential to the creative process.

Sarunyu_foto/Shutterstock.com

every day. For our purposes in this text, we can define **creativity** as a process influenced by individual and organizational factors that results in the production of novel and useful ideas, products, or both.[38]

The four stages of the creative process are preparation, incubation, illumination, and verification.[39] *Preparation* means seeking out new experiences and opportunities to learn because creativity grows from a base of knowledge. *Incubation* is a process of reflective thought and is often conducted subconsciously. During incubation, the individual engages in other pursuits while the mind considers the problem and works on it. *Illumination* occurs when the individual senses an insight for solving the problem. Finally, *verification* is conducted to determine if the solution or idea is valid. Verification is accomplished by thinking through the implications of the decision, presenting the idea to another person, or trying out the decision. Momentary quieting of the brain through relaxation can increase coherence, or the ability of different parts of the brain to work together.[40] Both individual and organizational influences affect the creative process.

INDIVIDUAL INFLUENCES Several individual variables are related to creativity. One group of factors involves the cognitive processes that creative individuals tend to use. One such cognitive process is *divergent thinking*, meaning the individual's ability to generate several potential solutions to a problem.[41] In addition, associational abilities and the use of imagery are associated with creativity.[42] Unconscious processes such as dreams are also essential cognitive processes related to creative thinking.[43]

Personality factors have also been related to creativity in studies of individuals from several different occupations. These characteristics include intellectual and artistic values, breadth of interests, high energy, concern with achievement, independence of judgment, intuition, self-confidence, and a creative self-image.[44] Tolerance of ambiguity, intrinsic motivation, risk taking, and a desire for recognition are associated with creativity as well.[45] Not surprisingly, people who have a high level of motivation are more creative, since they are more likely to try to think of different ways to get things done. Also, people who are able to see and understand others' perspectives are more creative since they have skills at seeing situations from more than one viewpoint.[46]

There is evidence that people who are in a good mood are more creative.[47] Positive affect is related to creativity in work teams because being in a positive mood allows team members to explore new ways of thinking.[48] Positive emotions enhance creativity by broadening one's cognitive patterns and resources. These positive emotions initiate thoughts and actions that are novel and unscripted.[49] Moreover, it is a cyclical process: thinking positively makes us more creative, and being more creative makes us think positively.[50]

Yet, conversely, it has been found that people in negative moods perform better at tasks involving considerable cognitive demands. Apparently, when an individual experiences negative moods or emotions, it is a signal to him that all is not well and thus leads to more attention and vigilance in cognitive activity.

ORGANIZATIONAL INFLUENCES The organizational environment in which people work can either support creativity or impede creative efforts. Creativity killers include focusing on how work is going to be evaluated, being closely monitored while you are working, and competing with other people in win–lose situations. In contrast, creativity facilitators include feelings of autonomy, being part of a team with diverse skills, and having creative supervisors and coworkers.[51] High-quality, supportive relationships with supervisors are related to creativity.[52] Plus, high-quality, cohesive social networks can have a positive impact on creative decision making. Such social networks encourage creative decision making by facilitating shared *sense-making* of relevant information and *consensus building*.[53] In addition, flexible organizational structures and participative decision making have been associated with creativity.

An organization can present impediments to creativity by means of internal political problems, harsh criticism of new ideas, destructive internal competition, and avoidance of risk.[54] Even the physical environment can hamper creativity. Companies like Oticon, a Danish hearing aid manufacturer, and Ethicon Endo-Surgery, a division of Johnson & Johnson, use open-plan offices that eliminate walls and cubicles so that employees can interact more frequently. When people mix, ideas mix as well.[55] Organizations can therefore enhance individuals' creative decision making by providing a supportive environment, participative decision making, and a flexible structure.

INDIVIDUAL–ORGANIZATION FIT Research has indicated that creative performance is highest when there is a match, or fit, between the individual and organizational influences on creativity. When individuals who desire to be creative are matched with an organization that values creative ideas, the result is more creative performance.[56]

creativity A process influenced by individual and organizational factors that results in the production of novel and useful ideas, products, or both.

Adobe's Kickbox Stimulates Creative Ideas

Adobe, the digital marketing and media company, developed an approach to creativity called Kickbox, and it was so successful within Adobe that it is now open sourced. The instructions are free, so any company can create its own kickbox. It is a red cardboard box that includes a pen, sticky notes, a timer, a small notebook for bad ideas, a spiral notebook, a sea salt and caramel chocolate bar, and a $10 Starbucks gift card. Also included: a $1,000 prepaid Citibank card that employees can spend without having to justify their expense to management.

Inside the box is a six-step model to develop a creative idea: inception, ideate, improve, investigate, and infiltrate. Each step has detailed instructions on how to complete the step. It's a highly systematic process, and more than 1,000 employees at Adobe have used a Kickbox. Of these, twenty-three have received major investments from Adobe to move their ideas ahead.

Adobe's VP of Creativity, Mark Randall, came up with the Kickbox idea. He surveyed employees to see what kept them from pursuing creative ideas. The number-one response was "convincing management." Kickbox eliminates that barrier and unboxes creativity and innovation.

SOURCES: D. Burkus, "Inside Adobe's Innovation Kit," *Harvard Business Review*, accessed online at https://hbr.org/2015/02/inside-adobes-innovation-kit; M. Wilson, "Adobe's Kickbox: The Kit to Launch Your Next Big Idea," *Fast Company*, February 9, 2015, accessed online at http://www.fastcodesign.com/3042128/adobes-kickbox-the-kit-to-launch -your-next-big-idea.

Source: Adobe Systems Incorporated

A common mistaken assumption regarding creativity is that either you have it or you do not. Research refutes this myth and has shown that individuals can be trained to be more creative.[57] The Disney Institute, for example, features a wide range of programs offered to companies, and one of their best sellers is creativity training. Part of creativity training involves learning to open up *mental locks* that keep us from generating creative alternatives to a decision or problem. Following are some mental locks that diminish creativity:

- Searching for the "right" answer
- Trying to be logical
- Following the rules
- Avoiding ambiguity
- Striving for practicality
- Being afraid to look foolish
- Avoiding problems outside our own expertise
- Fearing failure
- Believing we are not really creative
- Not making play a part of work[58]

Note that many of these mental locks stem from values within organizations.

Organizations can facilitate creative decision making in many ways. Rewarding creativity, allowing employees to fail, making work more fun, and providing creativity training are a few suggestions. Another way companies can encourage creativity is by exposing employees to new ideas through job rotation. As employees move through different jobs, they can be exposed to

Sir Richard Branson believes that letting your employees be creative is vital to success.

Helga Esteb/Shutterstock.com

different information, projects, and teams, either within or outside the company. Finally, managers can encourage employees to surround themselves with stimuli that they have found to enhance their creative processes. These may be music, artwork, books, or anything else that encourages creative thinking.[59]

We have seen that both individual and organizational factors can produce creativity. Leaders can play key roles in modeling creative behavior. Sir Richard Branson, founder and chair of the U.K.-based Virgin Group, believes that if you do not use your employees' creative potential, you are doomed to failure. At Virgin Group, the culture encourages risk taking and rewards innovation rather than following rules and regulations. "Analyzing ideas to death" is avoided. Branson says an employee should be able to have an idea in the morning and implement it that afternoon.[60]

Culture also affects creativity. Tight cultures are those with strong social norms and strong sanctions for violating the norms. Pakistan, Norway, and Malaysia are culturally tight. Loose cultures are less predictable and lack clear norms and enforcement of behavior. Hungary, Brazil, and Australia are looser cultures. Individuals from loose cultures are more likely to take on and succeed in foreign, unfamiliar creative tasks than individuals from tight cultures. However, tight cultures are more successful with innovation within their own cultures.[61]

10-4 THE GROUP DECISION-MAKING PROCESS

Managers use groups to make decisions for several reasons. One is **synergy**, which occurs when group members stimulate new solutions to problems through the process of mutual influence and encouragement within the group. Another reason for using a group is to gain commitment to a decision. Groups also bring more knowledge and experience to the problem-solving situation.

Group decisions can sometimes be predicted by comparing the views of the initial group members with the final group decision. These simple relationships are known as **social decision schemes**. One social decision scheme is the *majority-wins rule*, in which the group supports

synergy A positive force that occurs in groups when group members are stimulated to produce new solutions to problems through the process of mutual influence and encouragement within the group.

social decision schemes Simple rules used to determine final group decisions.

whatever position is taken by the majority of its members. Another scheme, the *truth-wins rule*, predicts that the correct decision will emerge as an increasing number of members realize its appropriateness. The *two-thirds-majority rule* means that the decision favored by two-thirds or more of the members is supported. Finally, the *first-shift rule* states that members support a decision represented by the first shift in opinion shown by a member.

Research indicates that these social decision schemes can predict a group decision as much as 80% of the time.[62] Current research is aimed at discovering which rules are used in particular types of tasks. For example, studies indicate that the majority-wins rule is used most often in judgment tasks (i.e., when the decision is a matter of preference or opinion), whereas the truth-wins rule predicts decisions best when the task is an intellective one (i.e., when the decision has a correct answer).[63]

10-4a Advantages and Disadvantages of Group Decision Making

Group decision making has advantages and disadvantages. The advantages of group decision making include (1) more knowledge and information through the pooling of group member resources, (2) increased acceptance of and commitment to the decision because the members had a voice in it, and (3) greater understanding of the decision because members were involved in the various stages of the decision process. The disadvantages of group decision making include (1) pressure within the group to conform and fit in, (2) domination of the group by one forceful member or a dominant clique who may ramrod the decision, and (3) the amount of time required because a group makes decisions more slowly than an individual.[64]

Given these advantages and disadvantages, should decisions be made by an individual or a group? Substantial empirical research indicates that effectively making that determination depends on the type of task involved. For judgment tasks requiring an estimate or a prediction, groups are usually superior to individuals because of the breadth of experience that multiple individuals bring to the problem.[65] On tasks that have a correct solution, other studies have indicated that the most competent individual outperforms the group.[66] This finding has been called into question, however. Much of the previous research on groups was conducted in the laboratory, where group members interacted only for short periods of time. Researchers wanted to know how a longer group experience would affect decisions. Their study showed that groups who worked together for longer periods of time outperformed the most competent member 70% of the time. As groups gained experience, the best members became less important to the group's success.[67] This study demonstrated that experience in the group is an important variable to consider when evaluating the individual versus group decision-making question.

Given the emphasis on teams in the workplace, many managers believe that groups produce better decisions than individuals, yet the evidence is mixed. More research needs to be conducted in organizational settings to help answer this question.

10-4b Limits of Group Decision Making

There are two potential liabilities in group decision making: groupthink and group polarization.

GROUPTHINK One liability of a cohesive group is its tendency to develop the dysfunctional process of **groupthink**. Irving Janis, the originator of this concept, describes groupthink as "a deterioration of mental efficiency, reality testing, and moral judgment" resulting from pressures within the group.[68] One of the conditions that leads to the development of groupthink is high cohesiveness. Cohesive groups tend to favor solidarity because members identify strongly with the group.[69] High-ranking teams that make decisions without outside help are especially prone to groupthink because they are likely to have shared mental models; that is, they are more likely to think alike.[70] Homogeneous groups (ones with little to no diversity among members) are more likely to suffer from groupthink.[71]

Two other conditions that encourage groupthink are (1) having to make a highly consequential decision and (2) time constraints.[72] A highly consequential decision is one that will have a great impact on the group members and on outside parties. Time restraints may cause group members to rush through the decision-making process. Both conditions can influence members to desire concurrence in decisions so much that they fail to evaluate one another's suggestions critically. A group suffering from groupthink shows recognizable symptoms. Table 10.1 presents these symptoms and makes suggestions on how to avoid groupthink.

An incident cited as a prime example of groupthink is the 1986 space

groupthink A deterioration of mental efficiency, reality testing, and moral judgment resulting from pressures within the group.

TABLE 10.1 SYMPTOMS OF GROUPTHINK AND HOW TO PREVENT IT

Symptoms of Groupthink

> *Illusions of invulnerability.* Group members feel that they are above criticism. This symptom leads to excessive optimism and risk taking.
> *Illusions of group morality.* Group members feel they are moral in their actions and therefore above reproach. This symptom leads the group to ignore the ethical implications of their decisions.
> *Illusions of unanimity.* Group members believe there is unanimous agreement on the decisions. Silence is misconstrued as consent.
> *Rationalization.* Group members concoct explanations for their decisions to make them appear rational and correct. The results are that other alternatives are not considered, and there is an unwillingness to reconsider the group's assumptions.
> *Stereotyping the enemy.* Competitors are stereotyped as evil or stupid. This leads the group to underestimate its opposition.
> *Self-censorship.* Members do not express their doubts or concerns about the course of action. This prevents critical analysis of the decisions.
> *Peer pressure.* Any members who express doubts or concerns are pressured by other group members who question their loyalty.
> *Mindguards.* Some members take it upon themselves to protect the group from negative feedback. Group members are thus shielded from information that might lead them to question their actions.

Guidelines for Preventing Groupthink

> Ask each group member to assume the role of the critical evaluator who actively voices objections or doubts.
> Have the leader avoid stating his or her position on the issue prior to the group decision.
> Create several groups that work on the decision simultaneously.
> Bring in outside experts to evaluate the group process.
> Appoint a devil's advocate to question the group's course of action consistently.
> Evaluate the competition carefully, posing as many different motivations and intentions as possible.
> Once consensus is reached, encourage the group to rethink its position by reexamining the alternatives.

SOURCE: From Breckler/Wiggins/Olson. *Social Psychology Alive!*, 1E. © 2008 Nelson Education Ltd. Reproduced by permission. www.cengage.com/permissions

shuttle *Challenger* disaster, in which the shuttle exploded, killing all seven crew members. A presidential commission concluded that flawed decision making was the primary cause of the accident. In 2003, the shuttle *Columbia* exploded over Texas upon reentering the earth's atmosphere, killing all seven crew members. Within days of the *Columbia* disaster, questions began to surface about the decision-making process that led flight engineers to assume that damage caused to the shuttle upon takeoff was minor and to continue the mission. The subsequent investigation of the disaster led observers to note that NASA's decision-making process appeared just as flawed in 2003 as it was in 1986, exhibiting all the classic symptoms of groupthink. The final accident report blamed the NASA culture that downplayed risk and suppressed dissent for the decision.[73]

Consequences of groupthink include an incomplete survey of alternatives, failure to evaluate the risks of the preferred course of action, biased information processing, and a failure to work out contingency plans. Furthermore, groupthink may be a contributor to corruption in organizations. Beech-Nut sold millions of dollars of phony apple juice, and investigations indicated that employees were aware that the company had been using cheap concentrate. Employees rationalized their actions by saying that other companies were selling fake juice and that it was safe to consume. Ultimately, after incurring $25 million in fines and legal costs, the company was almost destroyed.[74]

Table 10.1 presents Janis's guidelines for avoiding groupthink. Many of these suggestions center around ensuring that decisions are evaluated completely, with opportunities for discussion from all group members. This strategy encourages members to evaluate one another's ideas critically. Groups that are educated about the value of diversity tend to perform better as a result. Less successful are groups that are homogenous and not educated about the value of diversity.[75]

Janis has used the groupthink framework to conduct historical analyses of several political and

The 1986 explosion of space shuttle Challeneger is an oft cited example of groupthink.

military fiascoes, including the Bay of Pigs invasion, the Vietnam War, and Watergate. One review of the decision situation in the *Challenger* incident proposed that two variables, time and leadership style, are important to include.[76] When a decision must be made quickly, there is more potential for groupthink. Leadership style can either promote groupthink (if the leader makes his or her opinion known up front) or avoid groupthink (if the leader encourages open and frank discussion).

There are few empirical studies of groupthink, and most of these involved students in a laboratory setting. More applied research may be seen in the future, however, as a questionnaire has been developed to measure the constructs associated with groupthink.[77] Janis's work on groupthink has led to several interdisciplinary efforts at understanding policy decisions.[78] The work underscores the need to examine multiple explanations for failed decisions. Teams that experience cognitive (task-based) conflict are found to make better decisions than teams that experience affective (emotion-based) conflict. As such, one prescription for managers has been to encourage cognitive conflict while minimizing affective conflict. However, these two forms of conflict can also occur together and more research is needed on how one can be encouraged while minimizing the other.[79]

GROUP POLARIZATION Another group phenomenon was discovered by a graduate student. His study showed that groups and individuals within the group made riskier decisions and accepted greater levels of risk following a group discussion of the issue. Subsequent studies uncovered another shift—toward caution. Thus, group discussion produced shifts both toward more risky positions and toward more cautious positions.[80] Further research revealed that individual group member attitudes simply became more extreme following group discussion. Individuals who were initially against an issue became more radically opposed, and individuals who were in favor of the issue became more strongly supportive following discussion. These shifts came to be known as **group polarization**.[81]

group polarization The tendency for group discussion to produce shifts toward more extreme attitudes among members.

Everett Historical/Shutterstock.com

The tendency toward polarization has important implications for group decision making. Groups whose initial views lean a certain way can be expected to adopt more extreme views following interaction between members. Several ideas have been proposed to explain why group polarization occurs. One explanation is the *social comparison approach*. Prior to group discussion, individuals believe they hold better views than the other members. During group discussion, they see that their views are not so far from average, so they shift to more extreme positions.[82] A second explanation is the *persuasive arguments view*. It contends that group discussion reinforces the initial views of the members, so they take a more extreme position.[83] Both explanations are supported by research. It may be that both processes, along with others, cause the group to develop more polarized attitudes.

In sum, group polarization leads groups to adopt extreme attitudes. In some cases, this can be disastrous. For instance, if individuals are leaning toward a dangerous decision, they are likely to support it more strongly following discussion. A recent study found that after discussing hiring decisions as a group, employers were less accurate in their ratings and were more susceptible both to contrast effects and halo effects.[84]

Both groupthink and group polarization are potential liabilities of group decision making, but several techniques can be used to help prevent or control these two liabilities.

10-4c Techniques for Group Decision Making

Once a manager has determined that a group decision approach should be used, he can determine the technique that is best suited to the decision situation. Seven techniques will be briefly summarized: brainstorming, nominal group technique, devil's advocacy, dialectical inquiry, quality circles and quality teams, and self-managed teams.

BRAINSTORMING Brainstorming is a good technique for generating alternatives. The idea behind **brainstorming** is to generate as many ideas as possible, suspending evaluation until all of the ideas have been suggested. Participants are encouraged to build on the suggestions of others, and imagination is emphasized.

Evidence suggests, however, that group brainstorming is less effective than a comparable number of individuals working alone. This may be because in groups, participants engage in discussions that can make them lose their focus.

To overcome the production blocking of group brainstorming, electronic brainstorming was developed.

In this technique, group members use computers to simultaneously produce as many ideas as possible during a short period of time.[85] Studies show that electronic brainstorming is slightly more effective than traditional brainstorming. One of the limitations of electronic brainstorming is that people may spend more time generating their own ideas rather than looking at the ideas of others. This limitation can be overcome if participants are told in advance that others in the brainstorming group are creative. This entices them to pay attention to others' ideas and can improve the quality and quantity of ideas produced in electronic brainstorming.[86]

NOMINAL GROUP TECHNIQUE A structured approach to decision making that focuses on generating alternatives and choosing one is called **nominal group technique (NGT)**, which involves the following discrete steps:

1. Individuals silently list their ideas.

2. Ideas are written on a chart one at a time until all ideas are listed.

3. Discussion is permitted but only to clarify the ideas. No criticism is allowed.

4. A written vote is taken.

NGT is a good technique to use when group members fear criticism from others.[87]

DEVIL'S ADVOCACY In the **devil's advocacy** decision method, a group or individual is given the role of critic. This devil's advocate has the task of coming up with the potential problems of a proposed decision. By identifying potential pitfalls in advance, organizations can often avoid costly mistakes in decision making.[88] As we discussed in Chapter 9, a devil's advocate who challenges the CEO and top management team can help sustain the vitality and performance of the upper echelon.

DIALECTICAL INQUIRY **Dialectical inquiry** is essentially a debate between two opposing sets of recommendations. Although it sets up a conflict, it is a constructive approach because it brings out the

brainstorming A technique for generating as many ideas as possible on a given subject while suspending evaluation until all the ideas have been suggested.

nominal group technique (NGT) A structured approach to group decision making that focuses on generating alternatives and choosing one.

devil's advocacy A technique for preventing groupthink in which a group or individual is given the role of critic during decision making.

dialectical inquiry A debate between two opposing sets of recommendations.

benefits and limitations of both sets of ideas.[89] However, when using this technique, it is important to guard against a win–lose attitude and to concentrate on reaching the most effective solution for all concerned. Research has shown that the way a decision is framed (i.e., win–win versus win–lose) is very important. A decision's outcome could be viewed as a gain or a loss depending on the way the decision is framed.[90]

10-4d Factors in Selecting the Appropriate Technique

Before choosing a group decision-making technique, the manager should carefully evaluate the group members and the decision situation. Only then can the best method for accomplishing the objectives of the group decision-making process be selected. If the goal is generating a large number of alternatives, for example, brainstorming would be a good choice. If group members are reluctant to contribute ideas, the nominal group technique would be appropriate. The need for expert input would be best facilitated by the Delphi technique, which uses a panel of experts. To guard against groupthink, devil's advocacy or dialectical inquiry would be effective. Decisions that concern quality or production would benefit from the advice of quality circles or the empowered decisions of quality teams. Moreover, recent research results suggest that if individuals within a team are made accountable for the process of decision making (rather than the end decision itself), then such teams are more likely to gather diverse information, share information, and eventually make better decisions.[91] Finally, a manager who wants to provide total empowerment to a group should consider self-managed teams.

10-4e Special Decision-Making Groups

Even though in organizations many types of groups make collective decisions, quality-oriented groups and self-managed teams have higher levels of involvement and authority in group decision making.

QUALITY CIRCLES AND QUALITY TEAMS A **quality circle** is a small group of employees who work voluntarily on company time, typically one hour per week, to address work-related problems such as

quality circle A small group of employees who work voluntarily on company time, typically one hour per week, to address work-related problems such as quality control, cost reduction, production planning and techniques, and even product design.

quality team A team that is part of an organization's structure and is empowered to act on its decisions regarding product and service quality.

quality control, cost reduction, production planning and techniques, and even product design. Quality circles also extend participative decision making into teams. Managers often listen to recommendations from quality circles and implement the suggestions. Involvement in the decision-making process is the primary reward.

Quality circles are not empowered to implement their own recommendations. They operate in parallel fashion to the organization's structure, and they rely on voluntary participation.[92] In Japan, quality circles have been integrated into the organization instead of being added on. This may be one reason for Japan's success with this technique. In contrast, the U.S. experience is not as positive. It has been estimated that 60 to 75% of the quality circles in U.S. firms have failed. Reasons for the failures have included a lack of top management support and a lack of problem-solving skills among quality circle members.[93]

Quality teams, in contrast, are included in total quality management and other quality improvement efforts as part of a change in the organization's structure. Quality teams are generated from the top down and are empowered to act on their own recommendations. Whereas quality circles emphasize the generation of ideas, quality teams make data-based decisions about improving product and service quality. Various decision-making techniques are employed in quality teams. Brainstorming, flowcharts, and cause-and-effect diagrams help pinpoint problems that affect quality.

Quality circles and quality teams are methods for using groups in the decision-making process. Self-managed teams take the concept of participation one step further.

SELF-MANAGED TEAMS Another group decision-making method is the use of self-managed teams, discussed in Chapter 9. The decision-making activities of self-managed teams are more broadly focused than those of quality circles and quality teams. Self-managed teams make many of the decisions that were once reserved for managers, such as work scheduling, job assignments, and staffing.

Many organizations have claimed success with self-managed teams. At Northern Telecom (now Nortel Networks), revenues rose 63%, and sales increased 26% following the implementation of self-managed teams.[94] Research evidence shows that self-managed teams can lead to higher productivity, lower turnover among employees, and flatter organization structure.[95]

Self-managed teams, like any cohesive group, can fall victim to groupthink. The key to stimulating innovation and better problem solving in these groups is welcoming dissent among members. Dissent breaks down complacency and sets in motion a process that results in better decisions. Team members must know that dissent is permissible so that they won't fear embarrassment or ridicule.[96]

 ## 10-5 DIVERSITY AND CULTURE IN DECISION MAKING

Styles of decision making vary greatly among cultures. Many of the dimensions proposed by Hofstede that were presented in Chapter 2 affect decision making. Uncertainty avoidance, for example, can affect the way people view decisions. In the United States, a culture with low uncertainty avoidance, decisions are seen as opportunities for change. In contrast, cultures such as those of Indonesia and Malaysia attempt to accept situations as they are rather than try to change them.[97] Power distance also affects decision making. In more hierarchical cultures, such as India, top-level managers make nearly all decisions. In countries with low power distance, lower-level employees make many decisions. The Swedish culture exemplifies this type.

The individualist/collectivist dimension has implications for decision making. Japan, with its collectivist culture, favors group decisions. The United States has a more difficult time with group decisions because it is an individualistic culture. Time orientation affects the frame of reference of the decision. In China, with its long-term view, decisions are made with the future in mind. In the United States, many decisions are made considering only the short term.

The masculine/feminine dimension can be compared to the Jungian thinking/feeling preferences for decision making. Masculine cultures, as in many Latin American countries, value quick, assertive decisions. Feminine cultures, as in many Scandinavian countries, value decisions that reflect concern for others.

Recent research examining the effects of cultural diversity on decision making has found that when individuals in a group are racially dissimilar, they engage in more open information sharing, encourage dissenting perspectives, and arrive at better decisions than racially similar groups.[98] Other kinds of diversity, such as functional background, have been studied as well. Top management teams that have members who come from a variety of functional backgrounds (e.g., marketing, accounting, information systems) engage in greater debate in decision making than top management teams in which the members come from similar backgrounds. This diversity results in better financial performance for the firm.[99] Research also indicates that strategic decision

making in firms can vary widely by culture. For example, one such source of variation stems from the differential emphasis placed on environmental scanning in different cultures. Furthermore, strategic decision making might appear rational but is also informed by firm level and national characteristics.[100]

 ## 10-6 PARTICIPATION IN DECISION MAKING

Effective management of people can improve a company's economic performance. Firms that capitalize on this fact share several common practices. Chief among them is participation of employees in decision making.[101] Many companies do this through highly empowered self-managed teams. Even in situations where formal teams are not feasible, decision authority can be handed down to frontline employees who have the knowledge and skills to make a difference. At Hampton Inn hotels, for example, guest services personnel are empowered to do whatever is necessary to make guests happy—without consulting their superiors.

10-6a The Effects of Participation

Participative decision making occurs when individuals who are affected by decisions influence the making of those decisions. Participation buffers employees from the negative experiences of organizational politics.[102] Participation in decisions such as how technology is developed has also been found to affect employee's attitudes toward the technology and how they use it.[103] In addition, participative management has been found to increase employee creativity, job satisfaction, and productivity.[104] GE Capital is one company that believes in participation. Each year it holds so-called dreaming sessions, in which employees from all levels of the company attend strategy and budget meetings to discuss where the company is heading.

As our economy becomes increasingly based on knowledge work and as new technologies make it easier for decentralized decision makers to connect, participative decision making will undoubtedly increase.[105] Consider the city and county of San Francisco, a combined city/county government organization. Needing to adopt a single messaging system to meet the requirements of more than 20,000 employees, it faced a huge challenge in getting all the

> **participative decision making** Decision making in which individuals who are affected by decisions influence the making of those decisions.

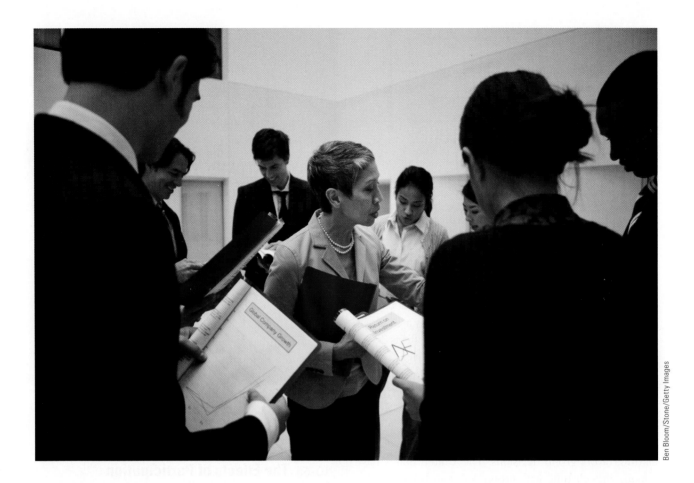

Ben Bloom/Stone/Getty Images

users to provide input into the decision. Technology helped craft a system that balanced the needs of all the groups involved, and IT planners developed a twenty-eight-page spreadsheet to pull together the needs and desires of all sixty departments into a focused decision matrix. Within two years, 90% of the users had agreed on and moved to a single system, reducing costs and complexity.[106]

10-6b Foundations for Participation and Empowerment

What conditions must be in place in order for participative decision making to work? The organizational foundations include a supportive organizational culture and a team-oriented work design. A supportive work environment is essential because of the uncertainty within the organization. Lower-level organizational members must be able to make decisions and take action on them. As operational employees are encouraged to take part in making decisions, however, fear, anxiety, or even terror can be created among middle managers in the organization.[107] Thus, senior leadership must create an

> If participative decision making is to work, employees must be able to comprehend how it provides a personal benefit to them.

organizational culture that is supportive and reassuring for these middle managers as the power dynamics of the system change.

A second organizational foundation for participative decision making concerns the design of work. A team-oriented work design is a key organizational foundation because it leads to broader tasks and a greater sense of responsibility. For example, Volvo builds cars using a team-oriented work design in which each person does many different tasks; therefore, each person retains direct responsibility for the finished product.[108] These work designs create a context for effective participation.

The three individual prerequisites for participative decision making are

1. the capability to become psychologically involved in participative activities,

2. the motivation to act autonomously, and

3. the capacity to see the relevance of participation for one's own well-being.[109]

First, people must be psychologically equipped to become involved in participative activities if they are to be effective team members. Not all people are so predisposed. For example, Germany has an authoritarian tradition that runs counter to participative decision making at the individual and group levels. As a result, General Motors encountered significant difficulties implementing quality circles in its German plants because workers expected to be directed by supervisors, not to engage in participative problem solving. New initiatives to establish supervisory/worker boards in German corporations are intended to change this authoritarian tradition.

The second individual prerequisite is the motivation to act autonomously. People with dependent personalities are predisposed to be told what to do and to rely on external motivation rather than internal, intrinsic motivation.[110] These dependent people are not often effective contributors to decision making.

Finally, if participative decision making is to work, employees must be able to comprehend how it provides a personal benefit to them. The personal payoff for the individual need not be short term. It may be a long-term benefit that results in workers receiving greater rewards through enhanced organizational profitability.

10-6c What Level of Participation?

Participative decision making is complex, and one of the things managers must understand is that employees can be involved in some, or all, of the stages of the decision-making process. For example, employees could be variously involved in identifying problems, generating alternatives, selecting solutions, planning implementations, or evaluating results. Research shows that greater involvement in all five of these stages has a cumulative effect. Employees who are involved in all five processes have higher satisfaction and performance levels. And, all decision processes are not created equal. If employees can't be provided with full participation in all stages, they should be involved in the stages that seem to have the highest payoffs: generating alternatives, planning implementations, and evaluating results.[111] Styles of participation in decision making may need to change as the company grows or as its culture changes.

STUDY TOOLS 10

LOCATED AT BACK OF THE TEXTBOOK
☐ Rip out chapter review card

LOCATED AT WWW.CENGAGE.COM/LOGIN
☐ Track your knowledge and understanding of key concepts in business using 4LTR Press Online

☐ Review key term flashcards and create your own using StudyBits

☐ Create and complete practice quizzes based off of your notes and StudyBits

☐ Complete Online activities such as Matching and Fill-in-the-Blank exercises

☐ View chapter highlight box content, including the chapter videos, key exhibits and executive profiles.

11 | Power and Political Behavior

Orhan Cam/Shutterstock.com

LEARNING OUTCOMES

11-1 Describe the concept of power.

11-2 Identify forms and sources of power in organizations.

11-3 Describe the role of ethics in using power.

11-4 Identify symbols of power and powerlessness in organizations.

11-5 Define organizational politics and understand the role of political skill and major influence tactics.

11-6 Identify ways to manage political behavior in organizations.

After finishing this chapter go to **PAGE 185** for **STUDY TOOLS.**

11-1 THE CONCEPT OF POWER

Power is the ability to influence another person. As an exchange relationship, it occurs in transactions between an agent and a target. The *agent* is the person using the power, and the *target* is the recipient of the attempt to use power.[1] Because power is an ability, individuals can learn to use it effectively, employing either influence or authority or both. **Influence** is the process of affecting the thoughts, behavior, and feelings of another person. **Authority** is the right to influence another person.[2] It is important to understand the subtle differences among these terms. For instance, a manager may have authority but no power. She may have the right, by virtue of her position as boss, to tell someone what to do. But she may not have the skill or ability to influence other people.

In a relationship between the agent and the target, there are many influence attempts that the target will consider legitimate. Working forty hours per week, greeting customers, solving problems, and collecting bills are actions that, when requested by the manager, are considered legitimate by a customer service representative. Requests such as these fall within the employee's **zone of indifference**—the range in which attempts to influence the employee are perceived as legitimate and are acted on without a great deal of thought.[3] The employee accepts that the manager has the authority to request such behaviors and complies with the requests. Some requests, however, fall outside the zone of indifference, so there the manager must work to enlarge the employee's zone of indifference. Enlarging the zone is accomplished with power (an ability) rather than with authority (a right).

Suppose the manager asks an employee to purchase a birthday gift for the manager's wife or to overcharge a customer for a service call. The employee may think that the manager has no right to ask these things. These requests fall outside the zone of indifference. They're viewed as extraordinary, and the manager has to operate from outside the authority base to induce the employee to fulfill them. In some cases, no power base is enough to induce the employee to comply, especially if the employee considers the behaviors requested by the manager to be unethical.

> Individuals have many forms of power to use in their work settings.

Danielala/Shutterstock.com

11-2 FORMS AND SOURCES OF POWER IN ORGANIZATIONS

Individuals have many forms of power to use in their work settings. Some of them are interpersonal, that is, used in interactions with others. One of the earliest and most influential theories of power comes from John French and Bertram Raven, who tried to determine both the forms and the sources of power managers use to influence other people.

11-2a Interpersonal Forms of Power

French and Raven identified five forms of interpersonal power that managers use: reward, coercive, legitimate, referent, and expert power.[4]

Reward power is power based on an agent's ability to control rewards that a target wants, such as salary increases, bonuses, and promotions. Reward power can lead to better performance, but only as long as the employee sees a clear and strong link between performance and rewards. To use reward power effectively, then, the manager should be explicit about the behavior being rewarded and should make the connection clear between the behavior and the reward.

Coercive power is power that is based on an agent's ability to cause the target to have an unpleasant experience. To coerce someone into doing something means to force the person to do it, often with threats of punishment. Managers using coercive power may verbally abuse employees or withhold support from them.

Legitimate power, which is similar to authority, is power that is based on position and mutual

---

power The ability to influence another person.

influence The process of affecting the thoughts, behavior, and feelings of another person.

authority The right to influence another person.

zone of indifference The range in which attempts to influence a person will be perceived as legitimate and will be acted on without a great deal of thought.

reward power Power based on an agent's ability to control rewards that a target wants.

coercive power Power that is based on an agent's ability to cause an unpleasant experience for a target.

legitimate power Power that is based on position and mutual agreement; agent and target agree that the agent has the right to influence the target.

Fast Fact: Gender Diversity on Boards Benefits Everyone

Catalyst conducted a global census of women's share of board seats in stock market index companies across twenty countries. A sample of their findings by country and percentage of board seats held by women:

> Norway, 35.5%

> United Kingdom, 22.8%

> Canada, 20.8%

> United States, 19.2%

> Germany 18.5%

> India, 9.5%

> Japan, 3.1%

Having women on corporate boards is associated with better financial performance, increased innovation, and a stronger talent pipeline. A gender-balanced board of directors is linked with better corporate social performance, which benefits business and society through stronger, more sustainable enterprises.

Source: catalyst.org, "Companies Behaving Responsibly: Gender Diversity on Boards," January 13, 2015, accessed at http://catalyst.org/system/files/companies behaving responsibly_gender_diversity_on_boards.pdf.

agreement. The agent and target agree that the agent has the right to influence the target. Just because a manager thinks he has the right to influence his employees doesn't mean that he will have legitimate power in their eyes. For legitimate power to be effective, the employees must also believe the manager has the right to tell them what to do. For example, in Native American societies, the chief has legitimate power because tribe members believe in his right to influence the decisions in their lives.

Referent power is an elusive power that is based on interpersonal attraction. The agent has referent power over the target because the target identifies with or wants to be like the agent. Charismatic individuals are often

referent power An elusive power that is based on interpersonal attraction.

expert power The power that exists when an agent has specialized knowledge or skills that the target needs.

thought to have referent power. Interestingly, the agent need not be superior to the target in any way. People who use referent power well are most often individualistic and respected by the target.

Expert power is the power that exists when an agent has specialized knowledge or skills that the target needs. For expert power to work, three conditions must be in place. First, the target must trust that the expertise given is accurate. Second, the knowledge involved must be relevant and useful to the target. Third, the target's perception of the agent as an expert is crucial. Using easy-to-understand language signals the target that the expert has an appreciation for real-world concerns and increases the target's trust in the expert.[5]

Which type of interpersonal power is most effective? Research has focused on this question since French and Raven introduced their five forms of power. Some of the results are surprising. Reward power and coercive power have similar effects.[6] Both lead to compliance. That is, employees will do what the manager asks them to, at least temporarily, if the manager offers a reward or threatens them with punishment. Reliance on these sources of power is dangerous, however, because it may require the manager to be physically present and watchful in order to apply rewards or punishment when the behavior occurs. Constant surveillance creates an uncomfortable situation for managers and employees and eventually results in a dependency relationship: employees will not work unless the manager is present.

Legitimate power also leads to compliance. When told "Do this because I'm your boss," most employees will comply. However, the use of legitimate power has not been linked to organizational effectiveness or to employee satisfaction.[7] In organizations where managers rely heavily on legitimate power, organizational goals are not necessarily met.

Referent power is linked with organizational effectiveness. It is the most dangerous power, however, because it can be too extensive and intensive in altering the behavior of others. Charismatic leaders need an accompanying sense of responsibility for others. An example of a good use of referent power is Christopher Reeve's power as spokesperson for research on spinal injuries and stem cell research.

Expert power has been called the power of the future.[8] Of the five forms of power, it has the strongest relationship with performance and satisfaction. It is through expert power that vital skills, abilities, and knowledge are passed on within the organization. Employees internalize what they observe and learn from managers they perceive to be experts.

The results on the effectiveness of these five forms of power pose a challenge in organizations. The least effective power bases—legitimate, reward, and coercive—are the ones most likely to be used by managers.[9] Managers inherit these power bases as part of the position when they take a supervisory job. In contrast, the most effective power bases—referent and expert—are ones that must be developed and strengthened through interpersonal relationships with employees. Indra Nooyi, CEO of Pepsi, has both referent and expert power. Her expertise lies not only in leading the company and exceeding analyst's expectations, but also in her emotional intelligence. Nooyi wrote the parents of each of her direct reports so that they would know they had succeeded as a parent, thanking them for the gift of their children. She believes leaders should work hard to bond the employees to the company and to win hearts as well as minds.[10] Expert power and social networks help CEOs influence their top management teams in ways that are profitable for the firm.

Indra Nooyi has referent and expert power as a leader.

11-2b Intergroup Sources of Power

Groups or teams within an organization can also use power from several sources. One source of intergroup power is control of *critical resources*.[11] When one group controls an important resource that another group desires, the first group holds power. Controlling resources needed by another group allows the power-holding group to influence the actions of the less powerful group. This process can continue in an upward spiral. Groups seen as powerful tend to be given more resources from top management.[12]

Groups also have power to the extent that they control **strategic contingencies**—activities that other groups depend on in order to complete their tasks.[13] The dean's office, for example, may control the number of faculty positions to be filled in each department of a college. The departmental hiring plans are thus contingent on approval from the dean's office. In this case, the dean's office controls the strategic contingency of faculty hiring, and thus has power.

Three factors can give a group control over a strategic contingency.[14] One is the *ability to cope with uncertainty*. If a group can help another group deal with uncertainty, it has power. One group that has gained power in recent years in most organizations is the legal department. Faced with increasing government regulations and fears of litigation, many other departments seek guidance from the legal department.

Another factor that can give a group control power is a *high degree of centrality* within the organization. If a group's functioning is important to the organization's success, it has high centrality. The sales force in a computer firm, for example, has power because of its immediate effect on the firm's operations and because other groups (accounting and servicing groups, for example) depend on its activities.

The third factor that can give a group power is *nonsubstitutability*—the extent to which a group performs a function that is indispensable to an organization. A team of computer specialists may be powerful because of its expertise with a system. It may have specialized experience that another team cannot provide.

The strategic contingencies model thus shows that groups hold power over other groups when they can reduce uncertainty, when their functioning is central to the organization's success, and when the group's activities are difficult to replace.[15] The key to all three of these factors, as you can see, is dependency. When one group controls something that another group needs, it creates a dependent relationship—and gives one group power over the other.

11-3 USING POWER ETHICALLY

Managers can work at developing all five forms of power for future use. The key to using them well is to use them ethically, as Table 11.1 shows. Coercive power, for example, requires careful administration if it is to be used in an ethical manner.

> **strategic contingencies**
> Activities that other groups depend on in order to complete their tasks.

Dario Pignatelli/Bloomberg/Getty Images

TABLE 11.1 GUIDELINES FOR THE ETHICAL USE OF POWER

Form of Power	Guidelines for Use
Reward power	Verify compliance. Make feasible, reasonable requests. Make only ethical requests. Offer rewards desired by subordinates. Offer only credible rewards.
Coercive power	Inform subordinates of rules and penalties. Warn before punishing. Administer punishment consistently and uniformly. Understand the situation before acting. Maintain credibility. Fit punishment to the infraction. Punish in private.
Legitimate power	Be cordial and polite. Be confident. Be clear and follow up to verify understanding. Make sure request is appropriate. Explain reasons for request. Follow proper channels. Exercise power consistently. Enforce compliance. Be sensitive to subordinates' concerns.
Referent power	Treat subordinates fairly. Defend subordinates' interests. Be sensitive to subordinates' needs and feelings. Select subordinates similar to oneself. Engage in role modeling.
Expert power	Maintain credibility. Act confident and decisive. Keep informed. Recognize employee concerns. Avoid threatening subordinates' self-esteem.

SOURCE: G. A. Yuki, *Leadership in Organizations*, 1st ed., © 1981. Reprinted by permission of Pearson Education, Inc., Upper Saddle River, N.J.

Employees should be informed of the rules in advance, and any punishment should be used consistently, uniformly, and privately. The key to using all five types of interpersonal power ethically is to be sensitive to employees' concerns and to communicate well.

To French and Raven's five power sources we can add a source that is very important in today's organizations. **Information power** is access to and control over important information. Consider, for example, the CEO's administrative assistant. He has information about the CEO's schedule that people need if they are going to get in to see the CEO. Central to the idea of information power is the person's position within the communication networks in the organization, both formal and informal. Also important is the idea of *framing*, which is the "spin" that managers put on information. Managers not only pass information on to subordinates, they also

information power Access to and control over important information.

interpret this information and influence the subordinates' perceptions of it. Information power may flow upward from subordinates to managers as well as downward from managers to subordinates. For instance, in manufacturing plants, database operators often control information about plant metrics and shipping performance that is vital to managerial decision making. Information power can also flow laterally. Salespeople convey information from the outside environment (their customers) that is essential for marketing efforts.

Determining whether a power-related behavior is ethical is complicated. One helpful method for establishing criteria in this respect is to ask three questions[16]:

1. *Does the behavior produce a good outcome for people both inside and outside the organization?* This question represents the criterion of *utilitarian outcomes*. The behavior should result in the greatest good for the greatest number of people. If the power-related behavior serves only the individual's self-interest and fails to help the organization reach its goals, it is considered unethical. A salesperson might be tempted to deeply discount a product in order to make a sale that would win a contest. Doing so would be in her self-interest but would not benefit the organization.

2. *Does the behavior respect the rights of all parties?* This question emphasizes the criterion of *individual rights*. Free speech, privacy, and due process are individual rights that are to be respected, and power-related behaviors that violate these rights are considered unethical.

3. *Does the behavior treat all parties equitably and fairly?* This question represents the criterion of *distributive justice*. Power-related behavior that treats one party arbitrarily or benefits one party at the expense of another is unethical. Granting a day of vacation to one employee in a busy week in which coworkers must struggle to cover for him might be considered unethical.

Nut Rage on Korean Air Flight—From an Executive Vice President

Heather Cho, daughter of the Korean Air chair, was mad. Cho, the executive vice president in charge of service for the airline, was on a 747 flight when she was served her macadamia nuts in the wrapper, instead of on a plate, as expected in first class. In a rage, she ordered the pilot of the Boeing 747 to return to the gate so the steward could be kicked off the plane. Cho berated the chief steward and flight attendant loudly, cursing and shoving the flight attendant who knelt before her in apology. The incident was referred to as "nut rage" in the media and created lots of controversy, especially in Korea, due to resentment over wealth and privileges of the families that control Korea's top companies.

Cho resigned in shame a few days after the incident and was later convicted of violating aviation law. The judge ordered her to spend a year in jail.

SOURCE: D. Kirk, "For Korean Air 'Nut Rage' Lady—No Mercy for Being 'Nutrageous,'" *Forbes*, February 12, 2015, accessed at http://www.forbes.com/sites/donaldkirk/2015/02/12/korean-air-nut-rage-exec-goes-to-prison-no-mercy-for-nutrageous-behavior/.

Jung Yeon-JE/AFP/Getty Images

To be considered ethical, power-related behavior must meet all three criteria. If the behavior fails to meet the criteria, then alternative actions should be considered.

Unfortunately, most power-related behaviors are not easy to analyze. Conflicts may exist among the criteria; for example, a behavior may maximize the greatest good for the greatest number of people but may not treat all parties equitably. Individual rights may need to be sacrificed for the good of the organization. A CEO may need to be removed from power for the organization to be saved. Still, these criteria can be used on a case-by-case basis to sort through the complex ethical issues surrounding the use of power. The ethical use of power is one of the hottest topics in the current business arena due to the abuse of power by top executives such as Bernie Madoff, who was convicted of running a $50 billion Ponzi scheme that financially ruined people and businesses around the world.

11-3a Positive versus Negative Power

We turn now to a theory of power that takes a strong stand on the "right" versus "wrong" kind of power to use in organizations. David McClelland has spent a great deal of his career studying the need for power and the ways managers use power. As was discussed in Chapter 5, he believes that there are two distinct faces of power, one negative and one positive.[17] The negative face of power is **personal power**—power used for personal gain. Managers who use personal power are commonly described as "powerhungry." Former Illinois Governor

Rod Blagojevich allegedly used his power as an elected official to try to sell President Obama's Senate seat in exchange for money, ambassadorships, and even a salary for his wife. People who approach relationships with an exchange orientation often use personal power to ensure that they get at least their fair share—and often more—in the relationship. They are most interested in their own needs and interests. One way to encourage ethical behavior in organizations is to encourage *principled dissent*. This term refers to valid criticism that can benefit the organization rather than mere complaints about working conditions. Much like whistle-blowers, who can serve as checks on powerful people within the organization, dissenters can pinpoint wrongdoings, encourage employee voice in key issues, and create a climate conducive to the ethical use of power.[18]

Individuals who rely on personal power at its extreme might be considered *Machiavellian*—willing to do whatever it takes to get one's own way. Niccolo Machiavelli was an Italian statesman during the sixteenth century who wrote *The Prince*, a guide for acquiring and using power.[19] Among his methods for using power was manipulating others, believing that it was better to be feared than loved. Machiavellians (or high Machs) are willing to manipulate others for personal gain and are unconcerned with others' opinions or welfare.

The positive face of power is **social power**—power used to create

> **personal power** Power used for personal gain.
>
> **social power** Power used to create motivation or to accomplish group goals.

motivation or to accomplish group goals. McClelland clearly favors the use of social power by managers. People who approach relationships with a communal orientation focus on the needs and interests of others. In other words, they rely on social power.[20] McClelland has found that managers who use power successfully have four power-oriented characteristics:

1. *Belief in the authority system.* They believe that the institution is important and that its authority system is valid. They are comfortable influencing and being influenced. The source of their power is the authority system of which they are a part.

2. *Preference for work and discipline.* They like their work and are very orderly. They have a basic value preference for the Protestant work ethic, believing that work is good for a person over and beyond its income-producing value.

3. *Altruism.* They publicly put the company and its needs before their own needs. They are able to do this because they see their own well-being as integrally tied to the company's well-being.

4. *Belief in justice.* They believe justice is to be sought above all else. People should receive that to which they are entitled and that which they earn.

McClelland takes a definite stand on the proper use of power by managers. When power is used for the good of the group, rather than for individual gain, it is positive.

11-4 SYMBOLS OF POWER

Organization charts show who has authority, but they do not reveal much about who has power. Two very different ideas about the symbols of power come from Rosabeth Moss Kanter and Michael Korda.

11-4a Kanter's Symbols of Power

powerlessness A lack of power.

Kanter offers a scholarly approach to determining who has power and who feels powerless, providing several characteristics of powerful people in organizations[21]:

1. *Ability to intercede for someone in trouble.* An individual who can pull someone out of a jam has power.

2. *Ability to get placements for favored employees.* Getting a key promotion for an employee is a sign of power.

3. *Exceeding budget limitations.* A manager who can go above budget limits without being reprimanded has power.

4. *Procuring above-average raises for employees.* One faculty member reported that her department head distributed 10% raises to the most productive faculty members although the budget allowed for only 4% increases. "I don't know how he did it; he must have pull," she said.

5. *Getting items on the agenda at meetings.* If a manager can raise issues for action at meetings, it's a sign of power.

6. *Access to early information.* Having information before anyone else does is a signal that a manager is plugged into key sources.

7. *Having top managers seek out their opinion.* When top managers have a problem, they may ask for advice from lower-level managers. The managers they turn to have power.

A theme that runs through Kanter's list is doing things for others—for people in trouble, for employees, for bosses. There is an active, other-directed element in her symbols of power. You can use Kanter's symbols of power to identify powerful people in organizations. They can be particularly useful in finding a mentor who can effectively use power.

11-4b Kanter's Symbols of Powerlessness

Kanter also wrote about symptoms of **powerlessness**—a lack of power—in managers at different levels of the organization. First-line supervisors, for example, often display three symptoms of powerlessness: overly close supervision, inflexible adherence to the rules, and a tendency to do the job themselves rather than training their employees

iStockphoto.com/Urbancow

to do it. Staff professionals such as accountants and law-yers display different symptoms of powerlessness. When they feel powerless, they tend to resist change and try to protect their turf. Top executives can also feel powerless. They show symptoms such as focusing on budget cutting, punishing others, and using dictatorial, top-down communication. Acting in certain ways can lead employees to believe that a manager is powerless. By making *external attributions* (blaming others or circum-stances) for negative events, a manager looks as if she has no power.[22]

11-4c Korda's Symbols of Power

Michael Korda offers a semiserious look at some tan-gible symbols of power: office furnishings, time power, and standing by.[23] Furniture is not just physically useful; it also conveys a message about power. Locked file cabi-nets are signs that the manager has important and con-fidential information in the office. A rectangular (rather than round) conference table enables the most impor-tant person to sit at the head of the table. The size of one's desk may convey the amount of power, too, as most executives prefer large, expensive desks.

Time power means using clocks and watches as power symbols. Korda says that the biggest compliment a busy ex-ecutive can pay a visitor is to remove his watch and place it facedown on the desk, thereby communicating "my time is yours." He also notes that the less powerful the executive, the more intricate the watch. Moreover, managers who are really secure in their power wear no watch at all, since they believe nothing important can happen without them. A full calendar is also proof of power. Personal planners are left open on the desk to display busy schedules.

Standing by is a game in which people are obliged to keep their cell phones, pagers, and so forth with them at all times so executives can reach them. The idea is that the more you can impose your schedule on other people, the more power you have. In fact, Korda defines *power* as follows: There are more people who inconvenience themselves on your behalf than there are people on whose behalf you would inconvenience yourself. Closely tied to this is the ability to make oth-ers perform simple tasks for you, such as getting your coffee or fetching the mail.

While Kanter's symbols focus on the ability to help others, Korda's symbols focus on status—a person's rela-tive standing in a group based on prestige and having other people defer to him.[24] By identifying powerful people and learning from their modeled behavior, you can learn the keys to power use in the organization.

POLITICAL BEHAVIOR IN ORGANIZATIONS

Like the word *power*, the phrase *politics in organi-zations* may conjure up negative images. However, **organizational politics** is not necessarily negative; it is the use of power and influence in organizations. Because organizations are arenas in which people have competing interests, effective managers must recon-cile competing interests. Organizational politics are central to managing. As people try to acquire power and expand their power base, they use various tactics and strategies. Some are sanctioned (acceptable to the organization); others are not. **Political behavior** re-fers to actions not officially sanctioned by an organi-zation that are taken to influence others in order to meet one's personal goals.[25] Sometimes personal goals are aligned with team or organizational goals, and they can be achieved in support of others' interests. But other times personal goals and the interests of others collide, and individuals pursue politics at the expense of others' interests.[26]

Politics is a controversial topic among managers. Some managers take a favorable view of political behav-ior; others see it as detrimental to the organization. Some workers who perceive their workplace as highly political actually find the use of political tactics more satisfying and report greater job satisfaction when they engage in political behavior. Some people may therefore thrive in political environments, while others may find office poli-tics distasteful and stressful.[27] It's important to remem-ber, however, that political behavior is not inherently constructive or destructive.[28]

Most people are also amazingly good at recognizing political behavior at all levels of the firm. Employees are not only keenly aware of political behavior at their level but can also spot political behavior at both their supervi-sor's level and the topmost levels of the organization.[29]

Many organizational conditions encourage political activity. Among them are unclear goals, autocratic de-cision making, ambiguous lines of authority, scarce re-sources, and uncertainty.[30] Moreover, even suppos-edly objective activities may involve politics. One such activity is the perfor-mance appraisal process. A study of sixty executives who had extensive experi-ence in employee evaluation

organizational politics
The use of power and influence in organizations.

political behavior Actions not officially sanctioned by an organization that are taken to influence others in order to meet one's personal goals.

indicated that political considerations were nearly always part of the performance appraisal process.[31]

The effects of political behavior in organizations can be quite negative when the political behavior is strategically undertaken to maximize self-interest. If people within the organization are competitively pursuing selfish ends, they're unlikely to be attentive to the concerns of others. As a consequence, the workplace can seem less helpful, more threatening, and more unpredictable. When people focus on their own concerns rather than on organizational goals, we see the negative face of power described earlier by David McClelland as personal power. And when employees view the organization's political climate as extreme, they experience more anxiety, tension, fatigue, and burnout. They are also dissatisfied with their jobs and are more likely to leave.[32]

However, not all political behavior is destructive. Though positive political behavior still involves self-interest, when it is aligned with organizational goals, the self-interest is perceived positively by employees. Political behavior is also viewed positively when it is seen as the only means by which to accomplish something. Job satisfaction and satisfaction with coworkers and supervisors is affected by any kind of political behavior.[33]

11-5a Influence Tactics

Influence is the process of affecting the thoughts, behavior, or feelings of another person. That other person could be the boss (upward influence), an employee (downward influence), or a coworker (lateral influence). There are eight basic types of influence tactics. They are listed and described in Table 11.2.[34] Research has shown that the four tactics used most frequently are consultation, rational persuasion, inspirational appeals, and ingratiation. Upward appeals and coalition tactics are used moderately. Exchange tactics are used least often.

Influence tactics are used for *impression management*, which was described in Chapter 3. In impression management, individuals use influence tactics to control others' impressions of them. One way in which people engage in impression management is through image building. Another way is to use impression management to get support for important initiatives or projects.

Ingratiation is an example of one tactic often used for impression management. Ingratiation can take many forms, including flattery, opinion conformity, and subservient behavior.[35] *Exchange* is another influence tactic that may be used for impression management. Offering to do favors for someone in an effort to create a favorable impression is an exchange tactic.

Which influence tactics are most effective? It depends on the target of the influence attempt and the objective. Individuals use different tactics for different purposes, and they use different tactics for different people. Influence attempts with subordinates, for example, usually involve assigning tasks or changing behavior. With peers, the objective is often to request help. With superiors, influence attempts are often made to request approval, resources, political support, or personal benefits. *Rational persuasion* and *coalition tactics* are used most often to get support from peers and superiors to change company policy. *Consultation* and *inspirational appeals* are particularly effective for gaining support and resources for a new project.[36] Overall, the most effective tactic in terms of achieving objectives is rational persuasion. *Pressure* is the least effective tactic.

Influence tactics are often used on bosses to get them to evaluate employees more favorably or to give the employees a promotion. Two tactics—rational persuasion and ingratiation—appear to work effectively in this way. Employees who use these tactics receive higher performance evaluations than employees who don't.[37] When supervisors believe an employee's motive for doing favors for the boss is simply to be a good citizen, they are likely to reward that employee. However, when the motive is seen as "brownnosing" (ingratiation), supervisors respond negatively.[38] And, as it becomes more obvious that the employee has something to gain by impressing the boss, the likelihood that ingratiation will succeed decreases. So, how does one use ingratiation effectively?

Results from a study conducted among supervisors and subordinates of a large state agency indicate that subordinates with higher scores on political skill used ingratiation regularly and received higher performance ratings, whereas individuals with lower scores on political skill who used ingratiation frequently received lower performance ratings.[39] Additionally, another research study demonstrated that supervisors rated subordinate ingratiation behavior as less manipulative if the subordinate was highly politically skilled.[40] These results indicate that political skill might be one factor that enables people to use ingratiation effectively.

Still, well-disguised ingratiation is hard to resist. Attempts that are not obvious usually succeed in increasing the target's liking for the ingratiator.[41] Most people have trouble remaining neutral when someone flatters them or agrees with them. However, witnesses to the ingratiation are more likely to question the motive behind the flattery or agreement. Observers are more skeptical than the recipients of the ingratiation.

TABLE 11.2　INFLUENCE TACTICS USED IN ORGANIZATIONS

Tactics	Description	Examples
Pressure	The person uses demands, threats, or intimidation to convince you to comply with a request or to support a proposal.	"If you don't do this, you're fired. You have until 5:00 to change your mind, or I'm going without you."
Upward appeals	The person seeks to persuade you that the request is approved by higher management or appeals to higher management for assistance in gaining your compliance with the request.	"I'm reporting you to my boss. My boss supports this idea."
Exchange	The person makes an explicit or implicit promise that you will receive rewards or tangible benefits if you comply with a request or support a proposal or reminds you of a prior favor to be reciprocated.	"You owe me a favor. I'll take you to lunch if you'll support me on this."
Coalition	The person seeks the aid of others to persuade you to do something or uses the support of others as an argument for you to agree also.	"All the other supervisors agree with me. I'll ask you in front of the whole committee."
Ingratiation	The person seeks to get you in a good mood or to think favorably of him or her before asking you to do something.	"Only you can do this job right. I can always count on you, so I have another request."
Rational persuasion	The person uses logical arguments and factual evidence to persuade you that a proposal or request is viable and likely to result in the attainment of task objectives.	"This new procedure will save us $150,000 in overhead. It makes sense to hire John; he has the most experience."
Inspirational appeals	The person makes an emotional request or proposal that arouses enthusiasm by appealing to your values and ideals or by increasing your confidence that you can do it.	"Being environmentally conscious is the right thing. Getting that account will be tough, but I know you can do it."
Consultation	The person seeks your participation in making a decision or planning how to implement a proposed policy, strategy, or change.	"This new attendance plan is controversial. How can we make it more acceptable? What do you think we can do to make our workers less fearful of the new robots on the production line?"

SOURCE: First two columns from G. Yukl and C. M. Falbe, "Influence Tactics and Objectives in Upward, Downward, and Lateral Influence Attempts," *Journal of Applied Psychology* 75 (1990): 132–140. Copyright © 1990 by the American Psychological Association. Reprinted with permission.

There is evidence that men and women view politics and influence attempts differently. Men tend to view political behavior more favorably than do women. When both men and women witness political behavior, they view it more positively if the agent is of their gender and the target is of the opposite gender.[42] Women executives often view politics with distaste and expect to be recognized and promoted only on the merit of their work. A lack of awareness of organizational politics is a barrier that holds women back in terms of moving into senior executive ranks.[43] Moreover, women may have fewer opportunities to develop political skills because of a lack of mentors and role models and because they are often excluded from informal networks.[44]

Different cultures prefer different influence tactics at work. One study found that American managers dealing with a tardy employee tended to rely on pressure tactics such as, "If you don't start reporting on time for work, I will have no choice but to start docking your pay." In contrast, Japanese managers relied on influence tactics that either appealed to the employee's sense of duty ("It is your duty as a responsible employee of this company to begin work on time.") or emphasized a consultative approach ("Is there anything I can do to help you overcome the problems that are preventing you from coming to work on time?").[45]

Influence can also stem from the way a person's personality fits into his work environment. A recent study found that extraverts have more influence in team-oriented work environments, whereas conscientious employees have more influence in environments where individuals work alone on technical tasks.[46]

It is important to note that influence tactics do have some positive effects. When investors form coalitions and put pressure on firms to increase their research and development efforts, it works.[47] However, some influence tactics, including pressure, coalition building, and exchange, can have strong ethical implications. There is a fine line between being an impression manager and being seen as a manipulator.

How can a manager use influence tactics well? First, a manager can develop and maintain open lines of communication in all directions: horizontally, vertically, and laterally. Then, the manager can treat the targets of influence attempts—whether managers, employees, or peers—with basic respect. Finally, the manager can understand that influence relationships are reciprocal—they are two-way relationships. As long as the influence attempts are directed toward organizational goals, the process of influence can be advantageous to all involved.

11-5b Political Skill

Researchers at Florida State University have generated an impressive body of research on political skill.[48] They have found that political skill is a distinct interpersonal attribute that is important for managerial success. Researchers suggest therefore that political skill should be considered in hiring and promotion decisions. Leaders' political skills have a positive effect on team performance, trust for the leader, and support for the leader.[49] Furthermore, political skill buffers the negative effects of stressors such as role conflict in work settings. This set of research findings points to the importance of developing political skill for managerial success.[50]

So what exactly is **political skill**? It is the ability to get things done through positive interpersonal relationships outside the formal organization. Politically skilled individuals have the ability to accurately understand others and use this knowledge to influence others in order to meet personal or organizational goals.

> **political skill** The ability to get things done through favorable interpersonal relationships outside formally prescribed organizational mechanisms.

Blablo101/Shutterstock.com

HOT TREND

#

Having an Eye for Emotions Pays Off

One of the competencies of emotional intelligence (EI) is emotion recognition ability (ERA)—the ability to recognize the meaning of emotions from facial and vocal expressions. Could it be that individuals who have this ability earn higher annual incomes? A study found it to be so and also identified the links between ERA and income. ERA is an important ability that allows employees to develop political skills. Political skills, in turn, lead to better interpersonal facilitation, getting things done through people. And better interpersonal facilitation leads to higher income. It appears that emotional recognition ability is an EI competency that pays off.

Source: T. Momm, G. Blickle, Y. Liu, A. Wihler, M. Kholin, and J. I. Menges, "It Pays to Have an Eye for Emotions: Emotion Recognition Ability Indirectly Predicts Annual Income," *Journal of Organizational Behavior* 36 (2015): 147–163.

Political skill is made up of four key dimensions: social astuteness, interpersonal influence, networking ability, and sincerity.

Social astuteness refers to the accurate perception and evaluation of social situations. Socially astute individuals manage social situations in ways that present them in the most favorable light. *Interpersonal influence* refers to a subtle and influential personal style that is effective in getting things done. Individuals with interpersonal influence are very flexible in adapting their behavior to differing targets of influence or differing contexts in order to achieve one's goals. *Networking ability* is an individual's capacity to develop and retain diverse and extensive social networks. Individuals with political skills can thrive in the challenging central position of a network in which colleagues turn to you for information.[51] Finally, *sincerity* refers to an individual's ability to portray forthrightness and authenticity in all of his or her dealings. Individuals who can appear sincere inspire more confidence and trust, thus making them very successful in influencing other people. These four dimensions of political skill can each be learned.

High self-monitors and politically savvy individuals score higher on an index of political skill. Individuals who are emotionally intelligent are better able to develop political skills at work.[52] Recruiting new members to the organization is important, and political skill can make a better recruiter. Even in college football, the recruiter's political skill, combined with the head coach's winning record, leads to more success in recruiting NCAA football players.[53] Individuals who have political skill have been shown to be more likely to engage in OCBs, have more total promotions, have higher perceived career success, and greater life satisfaction.[54]

11-6 MANAGING POLITICAL BEHAVIOR IN ORGANIZATIONS

Politics cannot and should not be eliminated from organizations. Managers should, however, take a proactive stance and manage the political behavior that inevitably occurs.[55] The first step in managing political behavior is to recognize it. Some behaviors to watch for include networking, finding key players to support initiatives, making friends with powerful people, bending the rules, and self-promoting. Lesser-used tactics include misinformation, spreading rumors, and blackmailing.[56]

To diffuse these behaviors, open communication is an important tool. Uncertainty tends to increase political behavior, and communication that reduces uncertainty is important. One way to open communication is to clarify the sanctioned and nonsanctioned political behaviors in the organization. For example, managers may want to encourage social power as opposed to personal power.[57]

Another key is to clarify expectations regarding performance. This can be accomplished through the use of specific, quantifiable goals and through the establishment of a clear connection between goal accomplishment and rewards.[58] Participative management is yet another key. Often, people engage in political behavior when they feel excluded from decision-making processes in the organization. By including them, managers will encourage positive input and eliminate behind-the-scenes maneuvering. Also, encouraging cooperation among work groups is helpful in managing political

Political skill is the ability to get things done through positive interpersonal relationships outside the organization.

behavior. Managers can instill a unity of purpose among work teams by rewarding cooperative behavior and by implementing activities that emphasize the integration of team efforts toward common goals.[59]

Managing scarce resources well is also important. An obvious solution to the problem of scarce resources is to increase the resource pool, but few managers have this luxury. However, clarifying the resource allocation process and making the connection between performance and resources explicit can discourage dysfunctional political behavior. Providing a supportive organizational climate allows employees to discuss controversial issues promptly and openly, thus preventing an issue from festering and potentially causing friction among employees.[60]

Managing political behavior at work is important, since the perception of dysfunctional political behavior can lead to job dissatisfaction.[61] When employees perceive that there are dominant interest groups or cliques at work, they are less satisfied with pay and promotions. When they believe that the organization's reward practices are influenced by who you know rather than how well you perform, they are less satisfied.[62] Furthermore, when employees believe that their coworkers are exhibiting increased political behavior, they are less satisfied with their coworkers. Open communication, clear expectations about performance and rewards, participative decision-making practices, work group cooperation, effective management of scarce resources, and a supportive organizational climate can help managers prevent the negative consequences of political behavior.

11-6a Managing Up: Managing the Boss

One of the least discussed aspects of power and politics is the relationship between you and your boss. This is a crucial relationship because your boss is your most important link with the rest of the organization.[63] The employee–boss relationship is one of mutual dependence;

Golden Pixels LLC/Shutterstock.com

you depend on your boss to give you performance feedback, provide resources, and supply critical information. Your boss depends on you for performance, information, and support. Because it's a mutual relationship, you should take an active role in managing it. Too often, the management of this relationship is left to the boss; but if the relationship doesn't meet the employee's needs, chances are the employee hasn't taken the responsibility to manage it proactively.

Table 11.3 shows the basic steps to take in managing your relationship with your boss. The first step is to try to understand as much as you can about your boss. What are her goals and objectives? What kind of pressures does she face in the job? Many individuals naively expect the boss to be perfect and are disappointed when they find that this is not the case. What are the boss's strengths, weaknesses, and blind spots? Because this is an emotionally charged relationship, it is difficult to be objective; but this is a critical step in forging an effective working relationship. What is the boss's preferred work style? Does she prefer everything in writing or hate detail? Does the boss prefer that you make appointments or is dropping in acceptable? The point is to gather as much information about your boss as you can and to try to put yourself in her shoes.

The second step in managing this important relationship is to assess yourself and your own needs much in the same way you analyzed your boss's. What are your strengths, weaknesses, and blind spots? What is your work style? How do you normally relate to authority figures? Some of us have tendencies toward counterdependence; that is, we rebel against the boss as an authority and view him as a hindrance to our performance. Or, in contrast, we might take an overdependent stance, passively accepting the employee–boss relationship and treating the boss as an all-wise, protective parent. What is your tendency? Knowing how you react to authority figures can help you understand your interactions with your boss.

Once you have done a careful self-analysis and tried to understand your boss, the next step is to work to develop an effective relationship. Both parties' needs and styles must be accommodated. A fundraiser for a large volunteer organization related a story about a new boss, describing him as cold, aloof, unorganized, and inept. She made repeated attempts to meet with him and clarify expectations, and his usual reply was that he didn't have the time. Frustrated, she almost looked for a new job. "I just can't reach him!" was her refrain. Then she stepped back to consider her boss's and her own styles. Being an Intuitive-Feeling type of person, she prefers constant feedback and reinforcement from others. Her boss, an Intuitive-Thinker type, works comfortably without feedback from others and has a tendency to fail to praise or reward others. She sat down with him and cautiously discussed the differences in their needs. This discussion became the basis for working out a comfortable relationship. "I still don't like him, but I understand him better," she said.

Another aspect of managing the relationship involves working out mutual expectations. One key activity is to develop a plan for work objectives and have the boss agree to it.[64] It is important to do things right, but it is also important to do the right things. Neither party to the relationship is a mind reader, so clarifying the goals is a crucial step. Keeping the boss informed is also a priority. No one likes to be caught off guard.

The employee–boss relationship must be based on dependability and honesty. This means giving and receiving positive and negative feedback. Most of us are reluctant to give any feedback to the boss, but positive feedback is welcomed at

TABLE 11.3 MANAGING YOUR RELATIONSHIP WITH YOUR BOSS
Make sure you understand your boss and her context, including:
Her goals and objectives.
The pressures on her.
Her strengths, weaknesses, and blind spots.
Her preferred work style.
Assess yourself and your needs, including:
Your own strengths and weaknesses.
Your personal style.
Your predisposition toward dependence on authority figures.
Develop and maintain a relationship that:
Fits both your boss's and your own needs and styles.
Is characterized by mutual expectations.
Keeps your boss informed.
Is based on dependability and honesty.
Selectively uses your boss's time and resources.

SOURCE: Reprinted by permission of *Harvard Business Review*. From "Managing Your Boss," by J. J. Gabarro and J. P. Kotter (May–June 1993): 155.

the top. Negative feedback, while tougher to initiate, can clear the air. If given in a problem-solving format, it can even bring about a closer relationship.[65]

Finally, remember that your boss is on the same team you are. The golden rule is to make your boss look good because you expect the boss to do the same for you.

11-6b Sharing Power: Empowerment

As modern organizations grow flatter, eliminating layers of management, empowerment becomes more and more important. Jay Conger defines **empowerment** as "creating conditions for heightened motivation through the development of a strong sense of personal self-efficacy."[66] This means sharing power in such a way that individuals learn to believe in their ability to do the job. The driving idea of empowerment is that the individuals closest to the work and to the customers should make the decisions and that this makes the best use of employees' skills and talents. You can empower yourself by developing your sense of self-efficacy.

Four dimensions comprise the essence of empowerment: meaning, competence, self-determination, and impact.[67] *Meaning* is a fit between the work role and the employee's values and beliefs. It is the engine of empowerment through which employees become energized about their jobs. If employees' hearts are not in their work, they cannot feel empowered. *Competence* is the belief that one has the ability to do the job well. Without competence, employees will feel inadequate and lack a sense of empowerment. *Self-determination* is having control over the way one does work. Employees who feel they're just following orders from the boss cannot feel empowered. *Impact* is the belief that one's job makes a difference within the organization. Without a sense of contributing to a goal, employees cannot feel empowered. Effective empowerment results in employees with better job performance, strong organizational commitment, and lower levels of job stress. To make this happen, it helps if the supervisor who is empowering employees has a high-quality relationship with his or her own boss.[68] The quality of the dyadic relationship between bosses and supervisors has direct impacts on frontline employees.

Empowerment is easy to advocate for but difficult to put into practice. Conger offers some guidelines on how leaders can empower others in the organization. First, managers should express confidence in employees and set high performance expectations. Positive expectations can go a long way toward enabling good performance, as the Pygmalion effect shows (Chapter 3). Second, managers should create opportunities for employees to participate in decision making. This means participation in the forms of both voice and choice. Employees should not just be asked to contribute their opinions about an issue; they should also have a vote in the decision that is made. One method for increasing participation is using *self-managed teams*, which, as discussed in Chapter 9, are the ultimate in empowered teams because they take on decisions and activities that traditionally belong to managers.

> **empowerment** Sharing power in such a way that individuals learn to believe in their ability to do the job.

Toyota Diversifies Its Power Positions

Toyota is facing the realities of the global marketplace by diversifying its senior management positions. This shift represents a major change for the company's top management team, which has been dominated by Japanese men since the company's founding. Julie Hamp, head of communications for North America, became the first female executive in Toyota's seventy-seven-year history when she was promoted to chief communications officer. Frenchman Didier Leroy became executive vice president in charge of developed markets, the first foreigner to become EVP. Christopher Reynolds became Toyota's first African American managing officer when he was promoted to be Toyota's chief legal officer.

By diversifying its leadership, the company is hoping to increase its power in the world marketplace. To understand foreign markets and design appropriate strategies, they need senior leaders who understand those markets.

SOURCES: Y. Kubota, "Toyota Opts to Diversify Senior Posts," *Wall Street Journal*, March 4, 2015, accessed at http://www.wsj.com/articles/toyota-taps-first-foreign-vice-president-1425451312; B. Snyder, "Toyota Promotes Its First Female Exec Ever," *Fortune*, March 4, 2015, accessed at http://fortune.com/tag/mpw-2/.

Chesnot/Getty ImagesNews/Getty Images

Third, managers should remove bureaucratic constraints that stifle autonomy. Often, companies have antiquated rules and policies that prevent employees from managing themselves. An example is a collection agency, where a manager's signature was once required to approve long-term payment arrangements for delinquent customers. Collectors, who spoke directly with customers, were the best judges of whether the payment arrangements were workable, and having to consult a manager made them feel closely supervised and powerless. The rule was dropped, and collections increased. Fourth, managers should set inspirational or meaningful goals. When individuals feel they "own" a goal, they are more willing to take personal responsibility for it.

Empowerment is a matter of degree. Jobs can be thought of in two dimensions: job content and job context. *Job content* consists of the tasks and procedures necessary for doing a particular job. *Job context* is broader. It is the reason the organization needs the job and includes the way the job fits into the organization's mission, goals, and objectives. These two dimensions are depicted in Figure 11.1, the employee empowerment grid.

Both axes of the grid contain the major steps in the decision-making process. As shown on the horizontal axis, decision-making authority over job content increases in terms of greater involvement in the decision-making process. Similarly, the vertical axis shows that authority over job context increases with greater involvement in that decision-making process. Combining job content and job context authority in this way produces five points that vary in terms of the degree of empowerment.[69]

No Discretion (point A) represents the traditional, assembly-line job—highly routine and repetitive with no decision-making power. Recall from Chapter 7 that if these jobs have a demanding pace and if workers have no discretion, distress will result.

Task Setting (point B) is the essence of most empowerment programs in organizations today. In this case, the worker is empowered to make decisions about the best way to get the job done but has no decision responsibility for the job context.

Participatory Empowerment (point C) represents a situation that is typical of autonomous work groups that have some decision-making power over both job

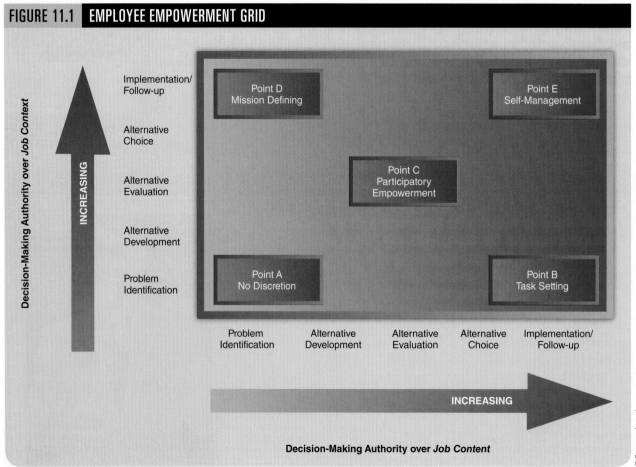

FIGURE 11.1 | **EMPLOYEE EMPOWERMENT GRID**

© Cengage Learning

content and job context. Their involvement is in identifying problems, developing alternatives, and evaluating alternatives, but the actual choice of alternatives is often beyond their power. Participatory empowerment can lead to job satisfaction and productivity.

Mission Defining (point D) is an unusual case of empowerment and is seldom seen. Here, employees have power over job context but not job content. An example would be a unionized team that is asked to decide whether their jobs could be better done by an outside vendor. Deciding to outsource would dramatically affect the mission of the company but would not affect job content, which is specified in the union contract. Assuring these employees of continued employment regardless of their decision would be necessary for this case of empowerment.

Self-Management (point E) represents total decision-making control over both job content and job context. It is the ultimate expression of trust. One example is TXI Chaparral Steel (part of Texas Industries), where employees redesign their own jobs to add value to the organization.

Empowerment should begin with job content and proceed to job context. Because the workforce is so diverse, managers should recognize that some employees are more ready for empowerment than others. Hence, managers must diagnose situations and determine the degree of empowerment to extend to employees. Managers can also empower entire teams of employees with appropriate interventions. When they do empower a team, individuals learn more and they are more committed to their teams.[70] Empowered individuals are also valuable to organizations because they are more motivated, satisfied, and creative.[71]

Unfortunately, the empowerment process carries with it a risk of failure. When you delegate responsibility and authority, you must be prepared to allow employees to fail, and failure is not something most managers tolerate well. At Merck, some say that CEO Ray Gilmartin empowered scientists too much and that their failures cost Merck its profitability and reputation as one of *Fortune*'s Most Admired Companies. One example of this empowerment involved a diabetes drug that early research showed caused tumors in mice. Scientists argued that in spite of early studies showing the drug wasn't viable, research should continue, and it did … until the drug was finally axed, costing the company considerably in terms of time and money.[72]

STUDY TOOLS 11

LOCATED AT BACK OF THE TEXTBOOK

☐ Rip out chapter review card

LOCATED AT WWW.CENGAGE.COM/LOGIN

☐ Track your knowledge and understanding of key concepts in business using 4LTR Press Online

☐ Review key term flashcards and create your own using StudyBits

☐ Create and complete practice quizzes based off of your notes and StudyBits

☐ Complete Online activities such as Matching and Fill-in-the-Blank exercises

☐ View chapter highlight box content, including the chapter videos, key exhibits and executive profiles.

12 | Leadership and Followership

mypokcik/Shutterstock.com

LEARNING OUTCOMES

12-1 Discuss the differences between leadership and management and between leaders and managers.

12-2 Explain the role of trait theory in describing leaders.

12-3 Describe the role of foundational behavioral research in the development of leadership theories.

12-4 Describe and compare the four contingency theories of leadership.

12-5 Discuss the recent developments in leadership theory of leader–member exchange and inspirational leadership.

12-6 Discuss how issues of emotional intelligence, trust, gender, and servant leadership are informing today's leadership models.

12-7 Define followership and identify different types of followers.

12-8 Synthesize historical leadership research into key guidelines for leaders.

After finishing this chapter go to **PAGE 203** for **STUDY TOOLS.**

Leadership in organizations is the process of guiding and directing the behavior of people in the work environment. In the first section, we discuss the ways that leadership differs from *management*. **Formal leadership** is officially sanctioned leadership based on the authority of a formal position. **Informal leadership** is unofficial leadership accorded to a person by other members of the organization. Though one of the most researched topics in organizational behavior, leadership remains one of the least understood social processes in organizations.

12-1 LEADERSHIP VERSUS MANAGEMENT

John Kotter describes leadership and management as two distinct yet complementary systems of action in organizations.[1] Specifically, he believes that effective leadership produces useful change in organizations while good management controls complexity in the organization and its environment.

> Healthy organizations need both effective leadership and good management.

Daniela/Shutterstock.com

The *management process* involves (1) planning and budgeting, (2) organizing and staffing, and (3) controlling and problem solving. Done effectively, the management process reduces uncertainty and stabilizes an organization. Alfred P. Sloan's integration and stabilization of General Motors after its early years of growth are an example of good management. In contrast, the *leadership process* involves (1) setting a direction for the organization; (2) aligning people with that direction through communication; and (3) motivating people to action, partly through empowerment and partly through basic need gratification. The leadership process creates uncertainty and change in an organization. Effective leaders not only control the future of the organization but also act as enablers of change in organizations. They disturb existing patterns of behaviors, promote novel ideas, and help organizational members make sense of the change process.[2] Sheryl Sandberg, chief operating officer of Facebook, knows about creating change. Since joining the company in 2007, she has helped lead the company to great success by creating an advertising platform that's attracted the world's largest brands.[3]

Abraham Zaleznik proposes that leaders have distinct personalities that stand in contrast to the personalities of managers.[4] Therefore, although both leaders and managers make valuable contributions to an organization, their contributions are different. Whereas **leaders** agitate for change and new approaches, **managers** advocate stability and the status quo. As a result, there is a dynamic tension between leaders and managers that makes it difficult for each to understand the other. Leaders and managers differ along four separate dimensions of personality: attitudes toward goals, conceptions of work, relationships with other people, and sense of self. The differences

A_KUDR/Shutterstock.com

FASTFACT

How CEOs Describe Themselves

What do top leaders say about themselves, and what can we learn from them? The Center for Creative Leadership surveyed one hundred CEOs who were attending the Center's training program. Here's how they described themselves.

> Strongest traits: humor, honesty, loyalty

> Weakest traits: impatience, poor listening, judgmental

> How they'd describe themselves: passionate, focused, driven

Their self-described strengths paint a picture of an ethical leader who bonds with others through laughter. The weaknesses they acknowledge reflect self-awareness. The way they describe themselves reveals a quest for success.

SOURCE: Center for Creative Leadership, accessed at http://www.leadingeffectively.com/9-things-ceos-say-about-themselves/.

leadership The process of guiding and directing the behavior of people in the work environment.

formal leadership Officially sanctioned leadership based on the authority of a formal position.

informal leadership Unofficial leadership accorded to a person by other members of the organization.

leader An advocate for change and new approaches to problems.

manager An advocate for stability and the status quo.

Effective leaders, like Sheryl Sandberg of Facebook, act as enablers of change.

Scott Olson/Getty Images

with the visionary abilities of leaders in a synergistic way. The unprecedented success of both Coca-Cola and Microsoft suggests that their leaders, the late Robert Goizueta and Bill Gates, respectively, were strategic leaders.[5]

12-2 EARLY TRAIT THEORIES

The first studies of leadership attempted to identify what physical attributes, personality characteristics, and abilities distinguished leaders from other members of a group.[6] The physical attributes that were considered were height, weight, physique, energy, health, appearance, and age. Although this line of research yielded some interesting findings, it provided insufficient evidence for concluding that leaders can be distinguished on the basis of physical attributes.

Leader *personality* characteristics that have been examined include originality, adaptability, introversion–extroversion, dominance, self-confidence, integrity, conviction, mood optimism, and emotional control. There is some evidence that leaders may be more adaptable and self-confident than the average group member. With regard to leader *abilities*, attention has been devoted to such constructs as social skills, intelligence, scholarship, speech fluency, cooperativeness, and insight. In this area, there is some evidence that leaders are more intelligent, verbal, and cooperative and have a higher level of scholarship than the average group member.

Nonetheless, these findings are neither strong nor uniform. For each attribute or trait claimed to distinguish leaders from followers, there were always at least one or two studies with contradictory findings. For some, the trait theories are invalid, though interesting and intuitively of some relevance. It is generally agreed that the trait theories have had very limited success in being able to identify universal, distinguishing attributes of leaders.

between these two personality types are summarized in Table 12.1.

It has been proposed that some people are *strategic leaders* who combine the stability of managers

TABLE 12.1 | LEADERS AND MANAGERS

Personality Dimension	Manager	Leader
Attitudes toward goals	Has an impersonal, passive, functional attitude; believes goals rise out of necessity and reality	Has a personal and active attitude; believes goals arise from desire and imagination
Conceptions of work	Views work as an enabling process that combines people, ideas, and things; seeks moderate risk through coordination and balance	Looks for fresh approaches to old problems; seeks high-risk positions, especially with high payoffs
Relationships with others	Avoids solitary work activity, preferring to work with others; avoids close, intense relationships; avoids conflict	Is comfortable in solitary work activity; encourages close, intense working relationships; is not conflict averse
Sense of self	Is once born; makes a straightforward life adjustment; accepts life as it is	Is twice born; engages in a struggle for a sense of order in life; questions life

SOURCE: Reprinted by permission of *Harvard Business Review*. From "Managers and Leaders: Are They Different?" by A. Zaleznik (January 2004).

Blablo101/Shutterstock.com

HOT TREND

Narcissistic CEOs, Big Signatures

Does a large signature mean the CEO is a narcissist? A recent study indicates that it may. Researchers compared the signatures of 605 CEOs of U.S. companies from annual reports and proxy filings. They then analyzed the size of the signatures using a custom software program and found that the large signatures predicted overinvestment, lower sales growth, and lower ROA. Despite lower financial performance, CEOs with large signatures enjoyed higher compensation but shorter tenures.

Narcissism is egotism, conceit, and disregard for others. Narcissistic leaders hold high opinions of themselves, belittle others, and ignore feedback about their behavior. And narcissism is on the rise, making it more likely that you may encounter narcissists in the workplace. The best strategy may be to try and avoid working for one.

pio3/Shutterstock.com

SOURCE: C. Ham, N. Seybert, and S. Wang, "Narcissism Is a Bad Sign: CEO Signature Size, Investment, and Performance" (June 1, 2014). UNC Kenan-Flagler Research Paper No. 2013-1, accessed at http://ssrn.com/abstract=2144419; P. Korkki, "Bosses Who Love Themselves," *New York Times*, March 7, 2015, accessed at http://www.nytimes.com/2015/03/08/business/the-perils-of-narcissists-in-the-workplace.html?_r=0.

12-3 BEHAVIORAL THEORIES

Behavioral theories emerged as a response to the deficiencies of the trait theories. Trait theories attempted to tell us what leaders were like but didn't address how leaders behaved. Three research studies built the foundations of many modern leadership theories: the Lewin, Lippitt, and White studies; the Ohio State studies; and the Michigan studies.

12-3a Foundational Behavioral Research

The earliest research on leadership style, conducted by Kurt Lewin and his students, identified three basic styles: autocratic, democratic, and laissez-faire.[7] A leader uses one of these three basic styles when approaching a group of followers in a leadership situation. The specific situation is not an important consideration because the leader's style does not vary with the situation. The leader with an **autocratic style** uses strong, directive actions to control the rules, regulations, activities, and relationships in the work environment. Followers have little discretionary influence over the nature of the work, its accomplishment, or other aspects of the work environment. The leader with a **democratic style** uses interaction and collaboration with followers to direct work and the work environment. Followers have a high degree of discretionary influence, although the leader has ultimate authority and responsibility. The leader with a **laissez-faire style** entails a hands-off approach. A laissez-faire leader abdicates the authority and responsibility of the position, and this style often results in chaos. Laissez-faire leadership also causes role ambiguity for followers because the leader fails to clearly define goals, responsibilities, and outcomes. It leads to higher interpersonal conflict at work.[8]

The leadership research program at The Ohio State University also measured specific leader behaviors. The initial results suggested that there were two important underlying dimensions of leader behaviors—initiating structure and consideration.[9] **Initiating structure** is leader behavior aimed at defining and organizing work relationships and roles, as well as establishing clear patterns of organization, communication, and ways of getting things done. **Consideration** is leader behavior aimed at

autocratic style A style of leadership in which the leader uses strong, directive actions to control the rules, regulations, activities, and relationships in the work environment.

democratic style A style of leadership in which the leader uses interaction and collaboration with followers to direct the work and work environment.

laissez-faire style A style of leadership in which the leader has a hands-off approach.

initiating structure Leader behavior aimed at defining and organizing work relationships and roles, as well as establishing clear patterns of organization, communication, and ways of getting things done.

consideration Leader behavior aimed at nurturing friendly, warm working relationships as well as encouraging mutual trust and interpersonal respect within the work unit.

An employee-oriented leadership style leads to a work environment that focuses on relationships.

Mark Bowden/E+//Getty Images

nurturing friendly, warm working relationships, as well as encouraging mutual trust and interpersonal respect within the work unit. These two leader behaviors are independent of each other; that is, a leader may be high on both, low on both, or high on one and low on the other.[10]

Finally, studies conducted at the University of Michigan suggest that the leader's style has very important implications for the emotional atmosphere of the work environment and, therefore, for the followers who work under that leader. Two styles of leadership were identified: production oriented and employee oriented.[11] A *production-oriented style* leads to a work environment where the focus is on getting things done. The leader in this environment uses direct, close supervision or many written and unwritten rules and regulations to control behavior.

In contrast, an *employee-oriented leadership* style leads to a work environment that focuses on relationships. The leader exhibits less direct, or less close, supervision and establishes fewer written or unwritten rules and regulations for behavior. Employee-oriented leaders display concern for people and their needs.

Leadership Grid An approach to understanding a leader's or manager's concern for results (production) and concern for people.

organization man manager (5,5) A middle-of-the-road leader.

authority-compliance manager (9,1) A leader who emphasizes efficient production.

country club manager (1,9) A leader who has great concern for people and little concern for production, attempts to avoid conflict, and seeks to be well liked.

team manager (9,9) A leader who builds a highly productive team of committed people.

Taken together, these three groups of studies (the Lewin studies, the Ohio State studies, and the Michigan studies) form the building blocks of many recent leadership theories. What the studies have in common is that two basic leadership styles were identified, with one focusing on *tasks* (autocratic, production oriented, initiating structure) and one focusing on *people* (democratic, employee oriented, consideration).

12-3b The Leadership Grid: A Contemporary Extension

Robert Blake and Jane Mouton's **Leadership Grid**, originally called the Managerial Grid, was developed with a focus on attitudes.[12] The two underlying dimensions of the grid are labeled Concern for Results and Concern for People. These two attitudinal dimensions are independent of each other, and, in different combinations, they form various leadership styles. Blake and Mouton originally identified five distinct managerial styles, and further development of the grid has led to the seven distinct leadership styles shown in Figure 12.1.

The **organization man manager (5,5)** is a middle-of-the-road leader who has a medium concern for people and production. This leader attempts to balance a concern for people and production without a commitment to either. The **authority-compliance manager (9,1)** has great concern for production and little concern for people. This leader desires tight control in order to get tasks done efficiently and considers creativity and human relations unnecessary. Authority-compliance managers may become so focused on running an efficient organization that they actually use tactics such as bullying. Some authority-compliance managers may intimidate, verbally and mentally attack, and otherwise mistreat subordinates. This form of abuse is quite common, with one in six U.S. workers reporting that they have been bullied by a manager.[13] The inverse position is the **country club manager (1,9)**, who has great concern for people and little concern for production, attempts to avoid conflict, and seeks to be well liked. This leader's goal is to keep people happy through good interpersonal relations, which are more important to her than the task. (This style is not a sound human relations approach but rather a soft Theory X approach.)

The **team manager (9,9)** builds a highly productive team of committed people. This leader works to motivate employees to reach their highest levels of accomplishment, is flexible, is responsive to change, and

FIGURE 12.1 THE LEADERSHIP GRID

1,9 Country Club Management:
Thoughtful attention to the needs of the people for satisfying relationships leads to a comfortable, friendly organization atmosphere and work tempo.

9,9 Team Management:
Work accomplishment is from committed people; interdependence through a "common stake" in organization purpose leads to relationships of trust and respect.

5,5 Middle-of-the-Road Management:
Adequate organization performance is possible through balancing the necessity to get work out while maintaining morale of people at a satisfactory level.

1,1 Impoverished Management:
Exertion of minimum effort to get required work done is appropriate to sustain organization membership.

9,1 Authority-Compliance Management:
Efficiency in operations results from arranging conditions of work in such a way that human elements interfere to a minimum degree.

Opportunistic Management

In Opportunistic Management, people adapt and shift to any grid style needed to gain the maximum advantage. Performance occurs according to a system of selfish gain. Effort is given only for an advantage for personal gain.

9+9: Paternalism/Maternalism Management:
Reward and approval are bestowed to people in return for loyalty and obedience; failure to comply leads to punishment.

SOURCE: B. Dumaine, "Buffett's Mr. Fix-It," *Fortune* (August 16, 2010): 78–86; M. M. Rose, "NetJets Returns to Profit in the First Quarter," *The Columbus Dispatch* (April 22, 2010), http://www.dispatch.com/live/content/business/stories/2010/04/22/netjets-returns-to-profit-in-first-quarter.html, accessed August 22, 2010.

understands the need for change. The **impoverished manager (1,1)** exerts just enough effort to get by. This leader has little concern for people or production, avoids taking sides, and stays out of conflicts; he is often referred to as a laissez-faire leader. Two new leadership styles have been added to these five original leadership styles within the grid. The **paternalistic father-knows-best manager (9+9)** promises reward for compliance and threatens punishment

impoverished manager (1,1) A leader who exerts just enough effort to get by.

paternalistic father-knows-best manager (9+9) A leader who promises reward and threatens punishment.

for noncompliance. The **opportunistic what's-in-it-for-me manager (Opp)** uses whichever style will maximize self-benefit.

It's important to highlight that the grid evaluates the *team manager* (9,9) as the very best style of managerial behavior. This is the basis on which the grid has been used for team building and leadership training in an organization's development. As an organizational development method, the grid aims to transform the leader in the organization to lead in the "one best way," which, according to the grid, is the team approach. The team style is one that combines optimal concern for people with optimal concern for results.

SAME BASIC IDEA, VERY DIFFERENT MANIFESTATION	
Ohio State	**Blake-Mouton**
Descriptive	Normative
Nonevaluative	Prescriptive
No attitude	Attitudinal overtones

 ## 12-4 CONTINGENCY THEORIES

Contingency theories involve the belief that leadership style must be appropriate for the particular situation. By their nature, contingency theories are if-then theories: If the situation is *x*, then the appropriate leadership behavior is *y*. We examine four such theories, including Fiedler's contingency theory, path–goal theory, normative decision theory, and situational leadership theory.

12-4a Fiedler's Contingency Theory

Fiedler's contingency theory of leadership proposes that the fit between the leader's need structure and the favorableness of the leader's situation determines the team's effectiveness in work accomplishment. This theory assumes that leaders are either task oriented or relationship oriented, depending upon how the leaders obtain their primary need gratification.[14] Task-oriented leaders are primarily gratified by accomplishing tasks and getting work done. Relationship-oriented leaders are primarily gratified by developing good, comfortable interpersonal relationships. Accordingly,

opportunistic what's-in-it-for-me manager (Opp) A leader who uses whichever style will maximize self-benefit.

least preferred coworker (LPC) The person a leader has least preferred to work with.

task structure The degree of clarity, or ambiguity, in the work activities assigned to the group.

Fiedler assessed a leader's style by his/her description of the least preferred co-worker.

the effectiveness of both types of leaders depends on the favorableness of their situation. The theory classifies the favorableness of the leader's situation according to the leader's position power, the structure of the team's task, and the quality of the leader–follower relationships.

THE LEAST PREFERRED COWORKER Fiedler classifies leaders using the Least Preferred Coworker (LPC) Scale, a projective technique in which a leader is asked to choose the person he least prefers to work with (the **least preferred coworker**, or **LPC**).[15] The leader is asked to describe this LPC using sixteen eight-point bipolar adjective sets. Two of these bipolar adjective sets follow (the leader marks the one most descriptive of the LPC):

> Efficient : : : : : : : : : Inefficient
> Cheerful : : : : : : : : : Gloomy

Leaders who describe their LPC in positive terms (i.e., pleasant, efficient, cheerful, and so on) are classified as high LPC, or relationship-oriented, leaders. Those who describe their LPC in negative terms (i.e., unpleasant, inefficient, gloomy, and so on) are classified as low LPC, or task-oriented, leaders.

The LPC score is a controversial element in contingency theory.[16] It has been critiqued conceptually and methodologically because it is a projective technique with low measurement reliability.

SITUATIONAL FAVORABLENESS The leader's situation has three dimensions: task structure, position power, and leader–member relations. Based on these three dimensions, the situation is either favorable or unfavorable for the leader. **Task structure** refers to the degree of clarity, or ambiguity, in the work activities assigned to the group. **Position power** refers to the authority associated with the leader's formal position in the organization.

Leader–member relations, the quality of interpersonal relationships among a leader and the group members, is measured by the *Group-Atmosphere Scale*, composed of nine eight-point bipolar adjective sets. Two of these bipolar adjective sets follow:

Friendly : : : : : : : : Unfriendly
Accepting : : : : : : : : Rejecting

A favorable leadership situation, according to Fiedler, is one with a structured task for the work group, strong position power for the leader, and good leader–member relations. In contrast, an unfavorable leadership situation is one with an unstructured task, weak position power for the leader, and moderately poor leader–member relations. Between these two extremes, the leadership situation has varying degrees of moderate favorableness for the leader.

	Favorable	Moderate	Unfavorable
Task structure	Structured		Unstructured
Position power	Strong		Weak
Leader–member relations	Good		Poor

LEADERSHIP EFFECTIVENESS   The contingency theory suggests that low LPC and high LPC leaders are both effective if placed in the right situation.[17] Specifically, low LPC (task-oriented) leaders are most effective in either very favorable or very unfavorable leadership situations. In contrast, high LPC (relationship-oriented) leaders are most effective in situations of intermediate favorableness. Figure 12.2 shows the nature of these relationships and suggests that leadership effectiveness is determined by the degree of fit between the leader and the situation. Recent research has shown that relationship-oriented leaders encourage team learning and innovation, which helps products get to market faster. This means that most relationship-oriented leaders perform well in leading new product development teams. In short, the right team leader can help get new products out the door faster, while a mismatch between the leader and the situation can have the opposite effect.[18]

> **position power** The authority associated with the leader's formal position in the organization.
>
> **leader–member relations** The quality of interpersonal relationships among a leader and the group members.

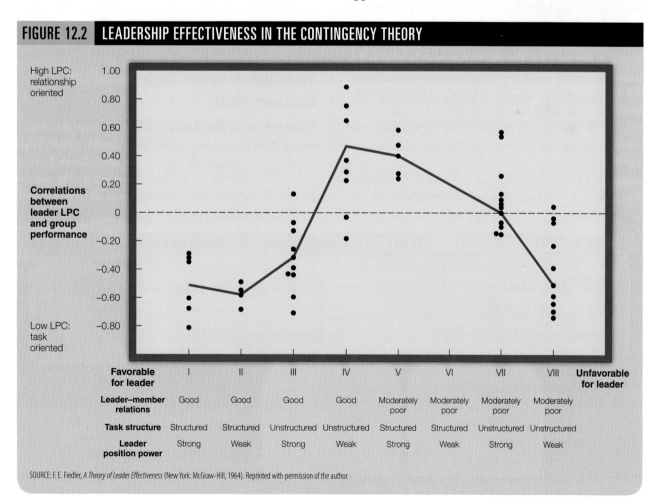

FIGURE 12.2 LEADERSHIP EFFECTIVENESS IN THE CONTINGENCY THEORY

High LPC: relationship oriented

Correlations between leader LPC and group performance

Low LPC: task oriented

Favorable for leader	I	II	III	IV	V	VI	VII	VIII	Unfavorable for leader
Leader–member relations	Good	Good	Good	Good	Moderately poor	Moderately poor	Moderately poor	Moderately poor	
Task structure	Structured	Structured	Unstructured	Unstructured	Structured	Structured	Unstructured	Unstructured	
Leader position power	Strong	Weak	Strong	Weak	Strong	Weak	Strong	Weak	

SOURCE: F. E. Fiedler, *A Theory of Leader Effectiveness* (New York: McGraw-Hill, 1964). Reprinted with permission of the author.

What, then, is to be done if there is a misfit? What happens when a low LPC leader is in a moderately favorable situation or when a high LPC leader is in a highly favorable or highly unfavorable situation? It is unlikely that the leader can be changed, according to the theory, because the leader's need structure is an enduring trait that is hard to change. Fiedler recommends that the situation be changed to fit the leader's style.[19] A moderately favorable situation would be re-engineered to be more favorable and therefore more suitable for the low LPC leader. A highly favorable or highly unfavorable situation would be changed to one that is moderately favorable and more suitable for the high LPC leader.

12-4b Path–Goal Theory

Robert House developed a path–goal theory of leader effectiveness based on an expectancy theory of motivation.[20] From the perspective of path–goal theory, the basic role of the leader is to clear the follower's path to the goal. The leader uses the most appropriate of four leader behavior styles to help followers clarify the paths that lead them to work and personal goals. The key concepts in the theory are shown in Figure 12.3.

A leader selects from the four leader behavior styles, shown in Figure 12.3, the one that is most helpful to followers at a given time. The directive style is used when the leader must give specific guidance about work tasks, schedule work, and let followers know what is expected. The *supportive style* is used when the leader needs to express concern for followers' well-being and social status. The *participative style* is used when the leader must engage in joint decision-making activities with followers. The *achievement-oriented style* is used when the leader

must set challenging goals for followers and show strong confidence in those followers.

In selecting the appropriate leader behavior style, the leader must consider both the followers and the work environment. A number of characteristics are included in Figure 12.3. Let us consider two scenarios. In scenario one, the followers are inexperienced and are working on an ambiguous, unstructured task. The leader in this situation might best use a directive style. In scenario two, the followers are highly trained professionals, and the task is difficult but achievable. The leader in this situation might best use an achievement-oriented style.

In path–goal theory, the leader always chooses the leader behavior style that helps followers achieve their goals. The theory assumes that leaders adapt their behavior and style to fit the characteristics of the followers and the environment in which they work. Actual tests of the path–goal theory and its propositions provide conflicting evidence.[21] The path–goal theory does have intuitive appeal and reinforces the idea that the appropriate leadership style depends on both the work situation and the followers. Research is focusing on which style works best in specific situations. For example, in small organizations, leaders who used visionary, transactional, and empowering behaviors, while avoiding autocratic behaviors, were most successful.[22]

12-4c Vroom-Yetton-Jago Normative Decision Model

Victor Vroom, Phillip Yetton, and Arthur Jago developed and refined the normative decision model, which helps leaders and managers determine the appropriate level of employee participation in decision making. The model recognizes the benefits of authoritative, democratic, and

FIGURE 12.3   THE PATH–GOAL THEORY OF LEADERSHIP

Leader behavior styles
- Directive
- Supportive
- Participative
- Achievement oriented

Follower characteristics
- Ability level
- Authoritarianism
- Locus of control

Workplace characteristics
- Task structure
- Work group
- Authority system

Follower path perceptions
Effort–Performance–Reward linkages

Follower goals
- Satisfaction
- Rewards
- Benefits

© Cengage Learning

Mark Zuckerberg of Facebook: Would I Want to Work for This Person?

Facebook CEO Mark Zuckerberg thinks that hiring top talent is important. He has a rule of thumb for hiring individuals that takes the way we traditionally think about hiring and turns it upside down. Most managers may think, "Do I want this person working for me?" Instead, Zuckerberg says, "I would only hire someone to work directly for me if I would work for that person." His hiring decisions have been pretty good so far. He cites Sheryl Sandberg, Facebook's COO, as one of his successful hires and a person he would enjoy reporting to.

SOURCES: J. Bercovici, "Mark Zuckerberg Shares His Secret to Recruiting the Best Employees," *Inc.*, 4, 2015, accessed at http://www.inc.com/jeff-bercovici/mark-zuckerberg-hiring-rule .html; H. King, "Mark Zuckerberg Has One Rule for Hiring," *CNN Money*, March 5, 2015, accessed at http://money.cnn.com/2015/03/04/ technology/mark-zuckerberg-hiring-advice/.

consultive styles of leader behavior.[23] Five forms of decision making are described in the model:

1. *Decide*. The manager makes the decision alone and either announces it or "sells" it to the group.

2. *Consult individually*. The manager presents the problem to the group members individually, gets their input, and then makes the decision.

3. *Consult group*. The manager presents the problem to the group members in a meeting, gets their input, and then makes the decision.

4. *Facilitate*. The manager presents the problem to the group in a meeting and acts as a facilitator, defining the problem and the boundaries that surround the decision. The manager's ideas are not given more weight than any other group member's ideas. The objective is concurrence.

5. *Delegate*. The manager permits the group to make the decision within prescribed limits, providing needed resources and encouragement.[24]

The key to the normative decision model is that a manager should use the decision method most appropriate for a given decision situation. The manager arrives at the proper method by working through matrices like the one in Figure 12.4. The factors across the top of the model (decision significance, commitment, leader expertise, and so on) are the situational factors in the normative decision model. This matrix is for decisions that must be made under time pressure, but other matrices are also available. For example, there is a different matrix managers can use when their objective is to develop subordinates' decision-making skills. Although the model offers very explicit predictions as well as prescriptions for leaders, its utility is limited to the leader decision-making tasks.

12-4d The Situational Leadership® Model

The Situational Leadership model, developed by Paul Hersey and Kenneth Blanchard, suggests that the leader's behavior should be adjusted to the maturity level of the followers.[25] The model employs two dimensions of leader behavior as used in the Ohio State studies; one dimension is task oriented, and the other is relationship oriented. Follower maturity is categorized into four levels, as shown in Figure 12.5. Follower readiness is determined by the follower's ability and willingness to complete a specific task. Readiness can therefore be low or high depending on the particular task. In addition, readiness varies within a single person according to the task. One person may be willing and able to satisfy simple requests from customers (high readiness) but less able or willing to give highly technical advice to customers (low readiness). It is important that the leader be able to evaluate the readiness level of each follower for each task. The four styles of leader behavior associated with the four readiness levels are depicted in Figure 12.5.

According to the Situational Leadership model, a leader should use a *telling style* (S1) when a follower is unable and unwilling to do a certain task. This style involves providing instructions and closely monitoring performance. As such, the telling style involves considerable

FIGURE 12.4 TIME-DRIVEN MODEL

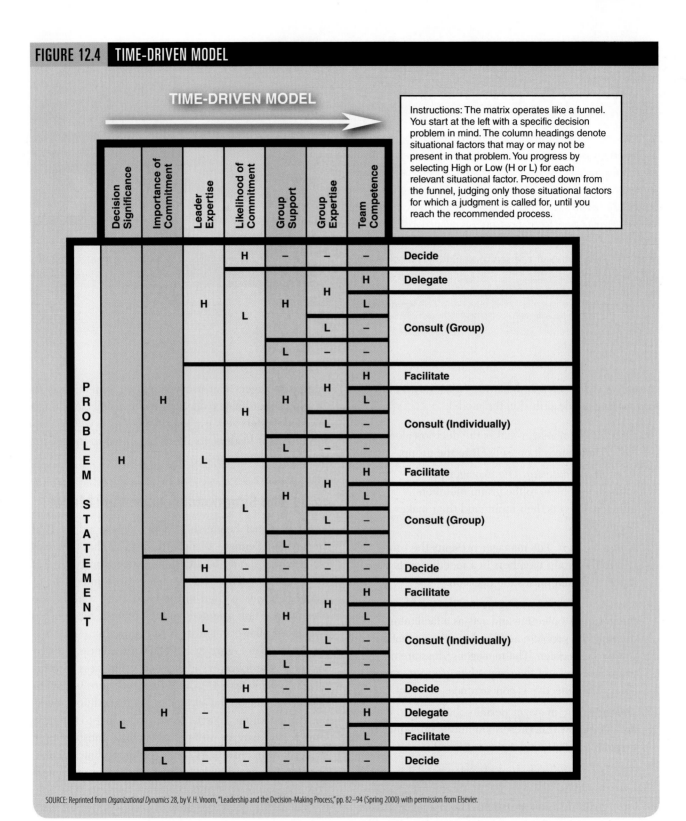

SOURCE: Reprinted from *Organizational Dynamics* 28, by V. H. Vroom, "Leadership and the Decision-Making Process," pp. 82–94 (Spring 2000) with permission from Elsevier.

task behavior and low relationship behavior. When a follower is unable but willing and confident to do a task, the leader can use the *selling style* (S2), in which there is high task behavior and high relationship behavior. In this case, the leader explains decisions and provides opportunities for the employee to seek clarification or help. Sometimes a follower will be able to complete a task but may seem unwilling or insecure about doing so. In these cases, a *participating style* (S3) is warranted, which involves high relationship but low task behavior.

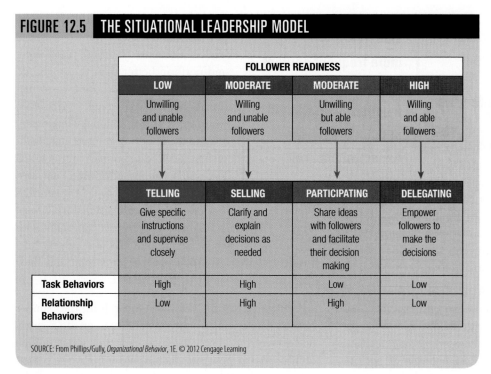

FIGURE 12.5 THE SITUATIONAL LEADERSHIP MODEL

FOLLOWER READINESS			
LOW	**MODERATE**	**MODERATE**	**HIGH**
Unwilling and unable followers	Willing and unable followers	Unwilling but able followers	Willing and able followers

	TELLING	**SELLING**	**PARTICIPATING**	**DELEGATING**
	Give specific instructions and supervise closely	Clarify and explain decisions as needed	Share ideas with followers and facilitate their decision making	Empower followers to make the decisions
Task Behaviors	High	High	Low	Low
Relationship Behaviors	Low	High	High	Low

SOURCE: From Phillips/Gully, *Organizational Behavior*, 1E. © 2012 Cengage Learning

The leader here encourages the follower to participate in decision making. Finally, for tasks in which a follower is able and willing, the leader is able to use a *delegating style* (S4), characterized by low task behavior and low relationship behavior. In this case, follower readiness is high, and low levels of leader involvement (task or relationship) are needed.

One key limitation of the situational leadership model is the absence of central hypotheses that could be tested and would therefore make it a more valid, reliable theory of leadership.[26] However, the theory has intuitive appeal and is widely used for training and development in corporations. In addition, the theory focuses attention on follower maturity as an important determinant of the leadership process.

 12-5 RECENT LEADERSHIP THEORIES

Many newer developments in leadership theory merit discussion here, specifically, leader–member exchange theory and inspirational leadership, which includes transformational, charismatic, and authentic styles.

12-5a Leader–Member Exchange

Leader–member exchange theory, or *LMX*, recognizes that leaders may form different relationships with followers. The basic idea behind LMX is that leaders form two groups of followers: in-groups and out-groups. *In-group members* tend to be similar to the leader and are given greater responsibilities, more rewards, and more attention. They work within the leader's inner circle of communication. As a result, in-group members are more satisfied, have lower turnover, and have higher organizational commitment. In contrast, *out-group members* are outside the circle and receive less attention and fewer rewards. They are managed by formal rules and policies.[27]

Research on LMX is supportive. In-group members are more likely to engage in organizational citizenship behavior, while out-group members are more likely to retaliate against the organization.[28] And the type of stress varies according to the group. In-group members' stress comes from the additional responsibilities placed on them by the leader, whereas out-group members' stress comes from being left out of the communication network.[29] One surprising finding is that more frequent communication with the boss may either help or hurt a worker's performance ratings, depending on whether the worker is in the in-group or the out-group. Among the in-group, more frequent communication generally leads to higher performance ratings, while members of the out-group who communicate more often with the superior tend to receive lower performance ratings.[30]

The higher performance among in-group members occurs because they feel more empowered and engage more in taking charge of situations at work.[31]

In-group members may also be more creative. When employees have a positive relationship with their supervisor, it increases their confidence and self-efficacy, which in turn increase creativity. Followers view communication from leaders differently, and it seems to depend on whether the leader is viewed as "one of us," as shown in neuroscience studies. Followers processed the same statements differently depending on whether the leader was an in-group leader or an out-group leader.[32] This could explain why President Barack Obama may be considered an inspirational speaker but may find it hard to inspire people who see him as associated with an out-group instead of an in-group. Neuroscientific studies show that when in-group leaders speak for "us," followers find them inspirational.[33]

12-5b Inspirational Leadership

Leadership is an exciting area of organizational behavior, one in which new research is constantly emerging. Three new developments are important to understand. These are transformational leadership, charismatic leadership, and authentic leadership. These three theories can be called *inspirational leadership theories* because in each one, followers are inspired by the leader to perform well.

TRANSFORMATIONAL LEADERSHIP *Transactional leaders*, you will recall, are those who use rewards and punishment to strike deals with followers and shape their behavior. In contrast, *transformational leaders* inspire and excite followers to high levels of performance.[34] They rely on their personal attributes instead of their official position to manage followers. There is some evidence that transformational leadership can be learned.[35] Transformational leadership consists of the following four subdimensions: charisma, individualized consideration, inspirational motivation, and intellectual stimulation. We describe *charisma* in detail shortly. *Individualized consideration* refers to how much concern the leader displays for each follower's individual needs and acts as a coach or a mentor. *Inspirational motivation* is the extent to which the leader is able to articulate a vision that is appealing to followers.[36]

Transformational leadership has been shown to increase firm performance. U.S. corporations increasingly operate in a global economy, so there is a greater demand for leaders who can practice transformational leadership by converting their visions into reality and by inspiring followers to perform "above and beyond the call of duty."[37] Howard Schultz, founder and chair of Starbucks Coffee, is the transformational leader and visionary heart of Starbucks. He has grown his firm from a small specialty coffee bar into one of the best-known brands in the world. However, the flagging global economy may challenge Schultz's abilities to continue to develop the new leaders that helped the firm grow so rapidly in the past.[38]

Transformational leadership is very important for individual followers as well. Transformational leadership that is focused on individuals increases

> Employees who enjoy more frequent contact with the boss also have a better understanding of what the boss's expectations are.

task performance and initiative. Employees who work for a transformational leader are more satisfied, motivated, and perform better than those who do not.[39] Leaders can be both transformational and transactional.[40] However, whereas transformational leadership adds to the effects of transactional leadership, even exceptional transactional leadership cannot substitute for transformational leadership.[41] Transformational leadership is effective because transformational leaders encourage followers to set goals congruent with the followers' own authentic interests and values. As a result, followers see their work as important and their goals as aligned with who they are.[42]

CHARISMATIC LEADERSHIP Steve Jobs, the pioneer behind Apple, had an uncanny ability to create a vision and convince others to become part of it. Jobs's unique ability was so powerful that Apple employees coined a term in the 1980s for it—the *reality-distortion field*. This expression is used to describe the persuasive ability and peculiar charisma of managers like Steve Jobs. His reality-distortion field allowed Jobs to convince even skeptics that his plans were worth supporting, no matter how unworkable they may appear. Those close to charismatic managers become passionately committed to possibly insane projects without regard to the practicality of their implementation or competitive forces in the marketplace.[43]

Charismatic leadership results when a leader uses the force of personal abilities and talents to have profound and extraordinary effects on followers.[44] Charismatic leadership falls to those who are chosen (are born with the "gift" of charisma) or who cultivate that gift. Some say charismatic leaders are born, and others say they are taught.

Charismatic leadership carries with it not only great potential for high levels of achievement and performance on the part of followers but also shadowy risks of destructive courses of action that might harm followers or other people. Several researchers have attempted to demystify charismatic leadership and distinguish its two faces.[45] The ugly face of charisma is revealed in the personalized power motivations of Adolf Hitler in Nazi Germany and David Koresh of the Branch Davidian cult in Waco, Texas. Both men led their followers into struggle, conflict, and death. The brighter face of charisma is revealed in the socialized power motivations of former presidents Bill Clinton and Ronald Reagan. While worlds apart in terms of their political beliefs,

charismatic leadership
A leader's use of personal abilities and talents to have profound and extraordinary effects on followers.

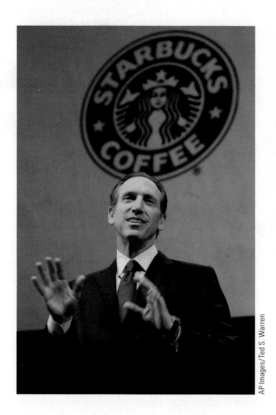

AP Images/Ted S. Warren

were actually quite similar in their use of personal charisma to inspire followers and motivate them to pursue a specific vision. In each case, followers perceived the leader as imbued with a unique vision for America and unique abilities to lead the country there.

Charisma is in the eye of the beholder and relies on the emotional connection between leaders and followers. Both men and women can be perceived as charismatic leaders, and social networks may affect how each gender is perceived in terms of charisma. Men are seen as more charismatic leaders when their work team network is centralized around one individual. Women leaders are seen as charismatic when their work team network involves many connections among different people.[46]

AUTHENTIC LEADERSHIP Recently, a new form of leadership has started to garner attention thanks to the ethical scandals rocking the business environment. In response to concerns about the potential negative side of inspirational forms of leadership, researchers have called for authentic leadership, which includes transformational, charismatic, or transactional leadership as the situation might demand but only in accordance with the leader's conscious and well-developed sense of values.[47] Because authentic leaders act in ways that are consistent with their value systems, they have a highly evolved sense of moral right and wrong. Their life experiences (which can be labeled "moments that matter") lead to such authentic

leadership development, allowing authentic leaders to be their true selves.[48]

Authentic leaders arouse and motivate followers to higher levels of performance by building a workforce characterized by high levels of hope, optimism, resiliency, and self-efficacy.[49] Followers also experience more positive emotions and trust as a result of the authentic leader's transparency and the collective caring climate engendered by such a leader. Researchers contend that this is the kind of leadership embodied by Gandhi, Nelson Mandela, and others like them throughout history. Only time and solid management research will tell if this approach can yield results for organizational leadership.

One recent development in the identification of authentic leaders stems from the arena of emotions. Emotions act as checks on the ugly side of charisma and also provide certain cues to followers. For example, a leader who espouses benevolence (as a value) and does not display compassion (an emotion) might not be very authentic in followers' eyes.[50] Similarly, a leader who displays compassion when announcing a layoff may be seen by followers as more morally worthy and held in high regard.[51]

Authentic leadership produces authentic followers. When employees see a leader display genuine emotion, they are more likely to feel like they are free to be themselves at work.[52] Authentic leaders also encourage followers to report wrongdoing in the organization. Followers of authentic leaders engage in internal whistleblowing because they work in a climate of psychological safety, modeled by the authentic leader.[53] Authentic leadership can be learned. Becoming an authentic leader requires two processes, one social and one intrapersonal. The social process is the development of authentic relationships, and the intrapersonal process is gaining self-awareness and self-management skills.[54]

 # EMERGING ISSUES IN LEADERSHIP

Along with the recent developments in theory, some exciting issues have emerged of which leaders should be aware. These include emotional intelligence, trust, women leaders, and servant leadership.

12-6a Emotional Intelligence

It has been suggested that effective leaders possess emotional intelligence, which is the ability to recognize and manage emotion in oneself and in others. In fact, some researchers argue that emotional intelligence is more important for effective leadership than either IQ or technical skills.[55] Emotional intelligence is made up of several competencies, including self-awareness, empathy, adaptability, and self-confidence. While most people gain emotional intelligence as they age, not everyone starts with an equal amount. Fortunately, emotional intelligence can be learned. With honest feedback from coworkers and ongoing guidance, almost any leader can improve emotional intelligence, and with it, the ability to lead in times of adversity.[56]

Emotional intelligence affects the way leaders make decisions. Under high stress, leaders with higher emotional intelligence tend to keep their cool and make better decisions, while leaders with low emotional intelligence make poor decisions and lose their effectiveness.[57] When Joe Torre was manager of the New York Yankees, he got the most out of his team, worked for a notoriously tough boss, and kept his cool. As manager of the Los Angeles Dodgers, he was still a model of emotional intelligence: compassionate, calm under stress, and a great motivator. He advocates "managing against the cycle," which means staying calm when situations are tough, but turning up the heat on players when things are going well.[58]

12-6b Trust

Trust, the willingness to be vulnerable to the actions of another, is an essential element in leadership.[59] Trust implies that followers believe that their leader will act with the followers' welfare in mind. Trustworthiness is also one of the competencies in emotional intelligence. Among top management team members, trust facilitates strategy implementation. That means that if team members trust each other, they have a better chance of getting buy-in from employees on the direction of the company.[60] And if employees trust their leaders, they will buy in more readily.

Trust in top business leaders may be at an all-time low given the highly publicized failures of many CEOs. Rick Wagoner, CEO of General Motors from 2000 to 2009, lost more money than any CEO in history, yet he continued to express confidence in his company and his strategy. He was fired by the government just before GM went bankrupt.[61] In the midst of the biggest oil spill in history, BP CEO Tony Hayward suggested that the environmental impact of the spill would be "very, very modest" and later

If employees trust their leaders, they will buy in more readily.

complained to reporters that he would like his life back. As people around the Gulf region scrambled for their livelihoods, Hayward took a day off to go yacht racing.

Effective leaders understand both *whom* to trust and *how* to trust. At one extreme, leaders often make the mistake of trusting only a close circle of advisors, listening only to them and gradually cutting themselves off from dissenting opinions. At the opposite extreme, lone-wolf leaders may trust nobody, leading to preventable mistakes. Wise leaders carefully evaluate both the competence and the position of those they trust, seeking out a variety of opinions and input.[62]

12-6c Gender and Leadership

An important, emergent leadership question is whether women and men lead differently. Historical stereotypes persist, and people characterize successful managers as having more male-oriented attributes than female-oriented attributes.[63] Although legitimate gender differences may exist, the same leadership traits may be interpreted differently in a man and a woman because of stereotypes. The real issue should be leader behaviors that are not bound by gender stereotypes.

Early evidence shows that women tend to use a more people-oriented style that is inclusive and empowering. Women managers excel in positions that demand strong interpersonal skills.[64] Even though more and more women are assuming positions of leadership in organizations, interestingly, much of what we know about leadership is based on studies that were conducted on men. We need to know more about the ways women lead.

Recent research looks at the phenomenon of the *glass cliff* (as opposed to the *glass ceiling* effect discussed in Chapter 2). The *glass cliff* represents a trend in organizations wherein more women are placed in difficult leadership situations. Women perceive these assignments as necessary to accept due to the difficulty of attaining leadership positions and lack of alternate opportunities combined with

John Lund/Drew Kelly/Brand X Pictures/Getty Images

Companies with Female CEOs Outperform Those Led by Men

As more women rise to the rank of CEO, the natural question arises as to whether companies led by female or male CEOs fare better. Researchers at Quantopian, a trading platform, used a crowdsourced algorithm to compare the performance of Fortune 1000 companies with female CEOs between 2002 and 2014 with the S&P 500's performance during the same time. The result: Companies led by females produced equity returns 226% better than the S&P 500. One of the CEOs who fared particularly well was Mindy Grossman of HSNi (Home Shopping Network). Since becoming CEO, she boosted sales and increased HSN's customer base by partnering with celebrities and creating concert and movie tie-ins. HSN.com's e-commerce traffic puts it among the top-ten busiest sites.

SOURCES: P. Wechsler, "Women-Led Companies Perform Three Times Better Than the S&P 500," *Fortune*, March 3, 2015, accessed at http://fortune.com/2015/03/03/women-led-companies-perform-three-times-better-than-the-sp-500/; "The World's 100 Most Powerful Women," *Forbes*, accessed at http://www.forbes.com/profile/mindy-grossman/.

Lev radin/Shutterstock.com

---

male in-group favoritism. On the other hand, men perceive that women are better suited to difficult leadership positions because women are better decision makers.[65]

12-6d Servant Leadership

Robert Greenleaf, director of management research at AT&T for many years, believed that leaders should serve employees, customers, and the community, and his essays are the basis for today's view of *servant leadership*. His personal and professional philosophy was that leaders lead by serving others. Other tenets of servant leadership are that work exists for the person as much as the person exists for work and that servant leaders try to find out the will of the group and lead based on that. Servant leadership leads to higher team performance and increased organizational citizenship behaviors in the organization.[66] Servant leaders consider themselves stewards who regard leadership as a trust and desire to leave the organization in better shape for future generations.[67] Although Greenleaf's writings were completed thirty years ago, many have now been published and are becoming more popular.

12-6e Abusive Supervision

Research has investigated not only what makes leaders effective but also negative leadership behaviors. The most common include sexual harassment, physical violence, angry outbursts, public ridicule, taking credit for employees' successes, and scapegoating employees.[68] *Abusive supervision*, as these behaviors are called, is estimated to affect about 13% of U.S. workers and leads to many negative consequences. Abused workers report diminished well-being along with increased deviance behavior, problem drinking, psychological distress, and emotional exhaustion.[69] In addition, abusive supervision increases absenteeism and reduces productivity. In fact, the cost of abusive supervision to U.S. corporations has been estimated at $23.8 billion.[70] It is not clear why supervisors abuse others. Some research suggests that injustice experienced by supervisors increases the likelihood that they will, in turn, abuse others. Other studies suggest that abuse stems from the failure of managers to control themselves and handle stress.[71] Abusive supervisors are more likely to direct their aggression toward employees who are very negative, or toward those who appear weak and unwilling or unable to defend themselves.[72]

12-7 FOLLOWERSHIP

In contrast to leadership, the topic of **followership** has not been extensively researched. Much of the leadership literature suggests that leader and follower roles are highly differentiated. The traditional view casts followers as passive, whereas a more contemporary view casts the follower role as an active one with potential for leadership.[73] The follower role has alternatively been cast as one of self-leadership in

> **followership** The process of being guided and directed by a leader in the work environment.

which the follower assumes responsibility for influencing his own performance.[74] This approach emphasizes the follower's individual responsibility and self-control. Self-led followers perform tasks that are naturally motivating and also do work that must be done but is not naturally motivating. Self-leadership enables followers to be disciplined and effective, essential first steps if one is to become a leader. Organizational programs such as empowerment and self-managed work teams may be used to further activate the follower role.[75]

12-7a Types of Followers

Contemporary work environments are ones in which followers recognize their interdependence with leaders and learn to challenge them while at the same time respecting the leaders' authority.[76] Effective followers are active, responsible, autonomous in their behavior, and critical in their thinking without being insubordinate or disrespectful—in essence, they are highly engaged at work.

Effective followers and four other types of followers are identified based on two dimensions: (1) activity versus passivity and (2) independent, critical thinking versus dependent, uncritical thinking.[77] Figure 12.6 shows these follower types.

Alienated followers think independently and critically, yet are very passive in their behavior. As a result, they become psychologically and emotionally distanced from their leaders. These alienated followers are potentially disruptive and a threat to the health of the organization. *Sheep* are followers who do not think independently or critically and are passive in their behavior. *Yes people* are followers who do not think independently or critically, yet are very active in their behavior. They uncritically reinforce the thinking and ideas of their leaders with enthusiasm, never questioning or challenging the wisdom of the leaders' ideas and proposals. Yes people are the most dangerous to a leader because they are the most likely to give a false positive reaction and give no warning of potential pitfalls. *Survivors* (see the center of the figure) are the least disruptive and the lowest-risk followers in an organization. They perpetually sample the wind, and their motto is "better safe than sorry."

Effective followers are the most valuable to a leader and an organization because of their active contributions. Effective followers share four essential qualities. First, they practice self-management and self-responsibility. A leader can delegate to an effective follower without anxiety about the outcome. Second, they are committed both to the organization and a purpose, principle, or person outside themselves. Effective followers are not self-centered or self-aggrandizing. Third, effective followers invest in their own competence and professionalism and focus their energy for maximum impact. Effective followers look for challenges and ways in which to add to their talents or abilities. Fourth, they are courageous, honest, and credible. Companies can support such qualities among followers by providing training in mindfulness.[78]

Effective followers might be thought of as self-leaders who do not require close supervision. The notion of *self-leadership*, or *superleadership*, blurs the distinction between leaders and followers. Caring leaders are often able to encourage the development of self-leadership in their employees, creating effective, dynamic followers.

FIGURE 12.6 FIVE TYPES OF FOLLOWERS

Independent, critical thinking

Passive — Active

Alienated followers

Effective followers

Survivors

Sheep

Yes people

Dependent, uncritical thinking

SOURCE: Reprinted by permission of *Harvard Business Review*. From "In Praise of Followers" by R. E. Kelley (November–December 1988, p. 145. Copyright © 1988 by Harvard Business School Publishing Corporation; all rights reserved.

12-8 GUIDELINES FOR LEADERSHIP

Leadership is a key to influencing organizational behavior and achieving organizational effectiveness. When artifacts are eliminated, studies of leadership succession show a moderately strong leader influence on organizational performance.[79] With this said, it is important to recognize that other factors also influence organizational performance. These include environmental factors (such as general economic conditions) and technological factors (such as efficiency).

Corporate leaders play a central role in setting the ethical tone and values for their organizations. While many corporate leaders talk about ethics, many never have to actually risk the firm's fortune on an ethical decision. In 1976, when James Burke, head of Johnson & Johnson, challenged his management team to reaffirm the company's historic commitment to ethical behavior, he had no idea he would be asked to demonstrate that commitment in action. But six years later, when poisoned packages of Tylenol appeared on store shelves, Burke did not hesitate to act on what he had pledged. The company pulled the product from the shelves at a cost of $100 million. It also offered a reward for a new design that would revamp the product's packaging. In the end, Tylenol recovered and is once again the leading pain medication in the United States.

Five useful guidelines appear to emerge from the extensive leadership research of the past sixty years:

1. Leaders and organizations should appreciate the unique attributes, predispositions, and talents of each leader. No two leaders are the same, and there is value in this diversity.

2. Although there appears to be no single best style of leadership, there are organizational preferences in terms of style. Leaders should be chosen who challenge the organizational culture, when necessary, without destroying it.

3. Participative, considerate leader behaviors that demonstrate a concern for people appear to enhance the health and well-being of followers in the work environment. This does not imply, however, that a leader must ignore the team's work tasks.

4. Different leadership situations call for different leadership talents and behaviors. Leaders must know when to give advice, when to counsel, when to coach, and when to mentor.[80] To meet the needs of their followers, they must be good diagnosticians.

5. Good leaders are likely to be good followers. Although there are distinctions between their social roles, the attributes and behaviors of leaders and followers may not be as distinct as is sometimes thought.

STUDY TOOLS 12

LOCATED AT BACK OF THE TEXTBOOK
☐ Rip out chapter review card

LOCATED AT WWW.CENGAGE.COM/LOGIN
☐ Track your knowledge and understanding of key concepts in business using 4LTR Press Online

☐ Review key term flashcards and create your own using StudyBits

☐ Create and complete practice quizzes based off of your notes and StudyBits

☐ Complete Online activities such as Matching and Fill-in-the-Blank exercises

☐ View chapter highlight box content, including the chapter videos, key exhibits and executive profiles.

13 | Conflict and Negotiation

iStockphoto.com/MorelSO

LEARNING OUTCOMES

13-1 Describe the nature of conflicts in organizations.

13-2 Explain the role structural and personal factors play in causing conflict in organizations.

13-3 Discuss the nature of group conflict in organizations.

13-4 Describe the factors that influence conflict between individuals in organizations.

13-5 Describe effective and ineffective techniques for managing conflict.

13-6 Identify five styles of conflict management.

After finishing this chapter go to **PAGE 220** for **STUDY TOOLS.**

13-1 THE NATURE OF CONFLICTS IN ORGANIZATIONS

All of us have experienced conflict of various types, yet we probably fail to recognize the variety of conflicts that occur in organizations. *Conflict* is defined as any situation in which incompatible goals, attitudes, emotions, or behaviors lead to disagreement or opposition between two or more parties.[1] Today organizations may face greater potential for conflict than ever before in history. The marketplace, with its increasing competition and globalization, magnifies differences among people in terms of personality, values, attitudes, perceptions, languages, cultures, and national backgrounds.[2] With the increasing diversity of the workforce comes the potential for incompatibility and conflict.

13-1a Importance of Conflict Management Skills for the Manager

Estimates show that managers spend about 21% of their time, or one day every week, dealing with conflict.[3] Not surprisingly, then, conflict management skills are a major predictor of managerial success.[4] A critical indicator of a manager's ability to manage conflict is his or her *emotional intelligence (EI)*, which is the power to control one's emotions and perceive emotions in others, adapt to change, and manage adversity. (Conflict management skills may be more a reflection of EI than of IQ.) People who lack emotional intelligence, especially empathy, or the ability to see life from another person's perspective, are more likely to be causes of conflict than managers of conflict. Management development programs that focus on EI competencies such as impulse control can help with conflict management skills.[5]

13-1b Functional versus Dysfunctional Conflict

Not all conflict is bad. In fact, some types of conflict encourage new solutions to problems and enhance creativity in the organization. In these cases, managers

> Estimates show that managers spend about 21% of their time, or one day every week, dealing with conflict.

Danielala/Shutterstock.com

will want to encourage the conflicts. Thus, the key to conflict management is to stimulate functional conflict and prevent or resolve dysfunctional conflict. The difficulty, however, is distinguishing between dysfunctional and functional conflicts. The consequences of conflict can be positive or negative, as shown in Table 13.1.

Functional conflict is a healthy, constructive disagreement between two or more people. New ideas, learning, and growth among individuals can result from functional conflict. Such conflict is constructive conflict; individuals can develop a better awareness of themselves and others through it. In addition, functional conflict can improve working relationships because when two parties work through disagreements, they feel they have accomplished something together. By releasing tensions and solving problems in working together this way, they experience improved morale.[6] Functional conflict can lead to innovation and positive change for the organization.[7] Because it tends to encourage creativity among individuals, this positive form of conflict often translates into increased productivity.[8] A key to recognizing functional conflict is that it is often cognitive in origin; that is, it arises from someone challenging old policies or thinking of new ways to approach problems. In fact, managers should work to stimulate

> **functional conflict** A healthy, constructive disagreement between two or more people.

TABLE 13.1	CONSEQUENCES OF CONFLICT
Positive Consequences	**Negative Consequences**
> Leads to new ideas	> Diverts energy from work
> Stimulates creativity	> Threatens psychological well-being
> Motivates change	> Wastes resources
> Promotes organizational vitality	> Creates a negative climate
> Helps individuals and groups establish identities	> Breaks down group cohesion
> Serves as a safety valve to indicate problems	> Can increase hostility and aggressive behaviors

© Cengage Learning

A_KUDR/Shutterstock.com

FASTFACT

Workplace Violence Can Be Prevented, Minimized, and Managed

High-risk employees may be triggered at work and pose dangers such as suicides, homicides, assaults, sexual assaults, and wrongful deaths. Although it is impossible to screen out all high-risk employees, it is possible to manage dangerous behavior at work using a three-stage model. In Stage 1, companies can use organizational socialization to create a culture of trust and respect, including stress management and healthy ways of dealing with frustration at work. In Stage 2, supervisors use surveillance to look for incivility, bullying, accidents, and safety violations and for organizational conditions such as unfairness or injustice that could be triggers for violent behavior. Stage 3 calls for containment, caregiving, and resilience. With proper prevention and surveillance, workplace violence can be minimized.

SOURCE: J. C. Quick, A. McFadyen, and D. L. Nelson, "No Accident: Health, Well-Being, Performance . . . and Danger," *Journal of Organizational Effectiveness: People and Performance* 1 (2014): 98–119.

this type of conflict when they suspect their group is suffering from groupthink.[9]

Dysfunctional conflict is an unhealthy, destructive disagreement between two or more people. Its danger is that it takes the focus away from the work to be done and places it on the conflict itself and the parties involved. Excessive conflict drains energy that could be used more productively. A key to recognizing a dysfunctional conflict is that its origin is often emotional or behavioral. For example, disagreements that involve personalized anger and resentment directed at specific individuals rather than specific ideas are dysfunctional.[10] Individuals involved in dysfunctional conflict tend to act before thinking, and they often rely on threats, deception, and verbal abuse to communicate. Moreover, dysfunctional conflict can often lead to aggressive acts or retaliation directed at supervisors, peers, subordinates, or even service providers.[11] In dysfunctional conflict, losses to both parties may exceed any potential gain from the conflict.

13-1c Diagnosing Conflict

Diagnosing conflict as functional or dysfunctional is not easy. The manager must look at the issue, the context of the conflict, and the parties involved. Once the manager has diagnosed the type of conflict, he or she can either work to resolve it (if it is dysfunctional) or to stimulate it (if it is functional).

It is easy to make mistakes in diagnosing conflicts. Sometimes task

dysfunctional conflict
An unhealthy, destructive disagreement between two or more people.

conflict, which is functional, can be misattributed as being personal, and dysfunctional conflict can follow. Developing trust within the work group can keep this misattribution from occurring.[12] A study of group effectiveness found that decision-making groups made up of friends were able to engage more openly in disagreement than groups made up of strangers, allowing the friends' groups to make more effective decisions. When group members (friends) felt comfortable and trusting enough to express conflicting opinions, optimal performance resulted. But decision-making groups made up of friends and strangers exhibited both high levels of conflict *and* low levels of performance, suggesting that open disagreement in these groups was not helpful.

Dysfunctional conflict takes the focus of the team away from the work to be done.

Nick White/Photodisc/Getty Images

This finding should serve as a cautionary tale for managers trying to apply one country's management style and techniques in another cultural setting.[13]

13-2 CAUSES OF CONFLICT IN ORGANIZATIONS

Conflict is pervasive in organizations. To manage it effectively, managers should understand its many sources. These can be classified into two broad categories: *structural factors*, which stem from the nature of the organization and the way in which work is organized, and *personal factors*, which arise from differences among individuals. Figure 13.1 summarizes the causes of conflict within each category.

13-2a Structural Factors

The causes of conflict related to the organization's structure include specialization, interdependence, common resources, goal differences, authority relationships, status inconsistencies, and jurisdictional ambiguities.

SPECIALIZATION When jobs are highly specialized, employees become experts at certain tasks. For example, one software company has one specialist for databases, one for statistical packages, and another for expert systems. Highly specialized jobs can lead to conflict because people have little awareness of the tasks that others perform.

A classic conflict of specialization often occurs between salespeople and engineers. Engineers are technical specialists responsible for product design and quality. Salespeople are marketing experts and liaisons with customers. Salespeople are often accused of making delivery promises to customers that engineers cannot keep because the sales force lacks the technical knowledge necessary to develop realistic delivery deadlines.

INTERDEPENDENCE Work that is interdependent requires groups or individuals to depend on one another to accomplish goals.[14] Depending on other people to get work done is fine when the process works smoothly. When there is a problem, however, it becomes very easy to blame the other party, and conflict escalates. In a garment manufacturing plant, for example, when the fabric cutters get behind in their work, the workers who sew the garments are delayed as well. Considerable frustration may result when the workers at the sewing machines feel their efforts are being blocked by the cutters' slow pace and their pay is affected because they are paid piece-rate.

COMMON RESOURCES Anytime multiple parties must share resources, there is potential for conflict.[15] This potential is enhanced when the shared resources become scarce. For example, managers often share administrative support. Not uncommonly, one administrative assistant supports ten or more managers, each of whom believes his or her work is most important. This puts pressure on the administrative assistant and leads to potential conflicts in prioritizing and scheduling work.

GOAL DIFFERENCES When work groups have different goals, these goals may be incompatible. For example, in one cable television company, the salesperson's goal was to sell as many new installations as possible. This created problems for the service department because its goal was timely installations. With increasing sales, the service department's workload became backed up, and orders were delayed. Often these types of conflicts occur because individuals do not have knowledge of another department's objectives.

AUTHORITY RELATIONSHIPS A traditional boss–employee relationship is hierarchical in nature, with a boss who is superior to the employee. For many employees, such a relationship is not a comfortable one; they don't like

FIGURE 13.1 CAUSES OF CONFLICT IN ORGANIZATIONS

Structural Factors
• Specialization
• Interdependence
• Common resources
• Goal differences
• Authority relationships
• Status inconsistencies
• Jurisdictional ambiguities

Conflict

Personal Factors
• Skills and abilities
• Personalities
• Perceptions
• Values and ethics
• Emotions
• Communication barriers
• Cultural differences

© Cengage Learning

Tsurukame Design/Shutterstock.com

another person having the right to tell them what to do. Some people resent authority more than others, and obviously this creates conflicts. In addition, some bosses are more autocratic than others, compounding the potential for conflict in the relationship. As organizations move toward the team approach and empowerment, there should be less potential for conflict from authority relationships.

STATUS INCONSISTENCIES Some organizations have a strong status difference between management and nonmanagement workers. Managers may enjoy privileges—such as flexible schedules, reserved parking spaces, and longer lunch hours—that are not available to nonmanagement employees and that may result in resentment and conflict.

JURISDICTIONAL AMBIGUITIES Have you ever called a company with a problem and had your call transferred through several different people and departments? This situation illustrates **jurisdictional ambiguity**, that is, unclear lines of responsibility within an organization.[16] The classic situation here involves the hardware/software dilemma. You call the company that made your computer, and it informs you that the problem is caused by the software. You call the software division, and it tells you it's the hardware….

13-2b Personal Factors

Not all conflicts arise out of structural factors in the organization. Some conflicts arise out of differences among individuals. The causes of conflict that arise from individual differences include skills and abilities, personalities, perceptions, values and ethics, emotions, communication barriers, and cultural differences.

SKILLS AND ABILITIES Diversity in skills and abilities may be positive for the organization, but it also holds potential for conflict, especially when jobs are interdependent. Experienced, competent workers may find it difficult to work alongside new and unskilled recruits. Workers can become resentful when their new boss, fresh from college, knows a lot about managing people but is unfamiliar with the technology with which they are working.

PERSONALITIES Individuals do not leave their personalities at the doorstep when they enter the workplace. Personality conflicts are thus realities in organizations. It is naïve to expect that you will like all of your coworkers, just as it is naïve to expect that they will all like you.

jurisdictional ambiguity
The presence of unclear lines of responsibility within an organization.

One personality trait that many people find difficult to deal with is abrasiveness.[17] An abrasive person ignores the interpersonal aspects of work and the feelings of colleagues. These types of people are often achievement oriented and hardworking, but their perfectionist, critical style can leave others feeling unimportant. The working style of abrasive individuals causes stress and strain for those around them.[18]

PERCEPTIONS Differences in perception can also lead to conflict. For example, managers and workers may not have a shared perception of what motivates people. In this case, the reward system can create conflicts if managers provide what they *think* employees want rather than what they actually want.

VALUES AND ETHICS Differences in values and ethics can be sources of disagreement. Older workers, for example, value company loyalty and probably would not take a sick day when they were not really ill. Younger workers, valuing mobility, like the concept of "mental health days," or calling in sick to get away from work. This may not be true for all workers, but it illustrates that differences in values can lead to conflict.

Abercrombie's Look Policy Goes to the Supreme Court

Abercrombie & Fitch has a Look Policy, calling its employees "models" of the company's consistent brand message. Samantha Elauf, a Muslim woman, was denied employment at an Abercrombie Kids store because the hijab she wore did not comply with the company's Look Policy. The case worked its way through the court system and wound up in the Supreme Court, which faces the question of whether it is the company's or the applicant's responsibility to identify a potential religious conflict. The outcome of the case, which focuses on religious discrimination, will have far-reaching effects. Meanwhile, in the face of other similar discrimination accusations, Abercrombie changed its Look Policy to accommodate hijabs or headscarves in the workplace.

SOURCE: C. Zillman, "Abercrombie Prepares for Supreme Court Battle Over Its Muslim Headscarf Policy," *Fortune*, February 24, 2015, accessed at http://fortune.com/2015/02/24/abercrombie-supreme-court-muslim-headscarf-policy/.

Most people have their own sets of values and ethics, although the extent to which they apply these ethics in the workplace varies. Some people have strong desires for approval from others and will work to meet others' ethical standards. Others are relatively unconcerned about approval from others and strongly apply their own ethical standards. Still others operate seemingly without regard to ethics or values.[19] When conflicts about values or ethics do arise, heated disagreement is common because of the personal nature of the differences.

EMOTIONS Conflict is by nature an emotional interaction, and the emotions of the parties involved in conflict play a pivotal role in how they perceive any type of negotiation and therefore how they respond to one another.[20] In fact, emotions are now considered critical elements of negotiation and must be included in an examination of the process and how it unfolds.[21] When negotiators begin to act based on emotions rather than on cognitions, they become much more likely to reach an impasse.[22]

COMMUNICATION BARRIERS Communication barriers such as physical separation and language can create distortions in messages, and these can lead to conflict. Another communication barrier is value judgment, in which a listener assigns worth to a message before it is received. For example, suppose a team member is a chronic complainer. When this individual enters the manager's office, the manager is likely to devalue the message before it is even delivered. Conflict can then emerge.

CULTURAL DIFFERENCES Although cultural differences are assets in organizations, sometimes they can be sources of conflict. Often, these conflicts stem from a lack of understanding of another culture. In one MBA class, for example, Indian students were horrified when American students challenged the professor. Meanwhile, the American students thought the students from India were too passive. Subsequent discussions revealed that professors in India expect to be treated deferentially and with great respect. While students might challenge an idea vigorously, they would rarely challenge the professor. Diversity training that emphasizes education on cultural differences can make great strides in preventing misunderstandings.

 ## 13-3 FORMS OF GROUP CONFLICT IN ORGANIZATIONS

Conflict in an organization can take on any of several different forms that can mainly be sorted into two core groups: conflicts that occur at the group level and conflicts that occur at the individual level. Conflicts at each level can be further classified as either *inter* or *intra*. It is important to note that the prefix *inter* means "between," whereas the prefix *intra* means "within." Conflict at the group level can occur between organizations (interorganizational), between groups (intergroup), or within a group (intragroup).

13-3a Interorganizational Conflict

Conflict that occurs between two or more organizations is called **interorganizational conflict**. Competition can heighten interorganizational conflict. Corporate takeovers, mergers, and acquisitions can also produce interorganizational conflict. What about the interorganizational conflict between the National Football League's players unions and team owners, which was often characterized as a battle between millionaires and billionaires? The players regularly go on strike to extract more of the profits from the owners, while the owners cry that they are not making a dime.

13-3b Intergroup Conflict

When conflict occurs between groups or teams, it is known as **intergroup conflict**. Conflict between groups can have positive effects within each group, such as increased group cohesiveness, increased focus on tasks, and increased loyalty to the group. There are, however, negative consequences as well. Groups in conflict tend to develop an us-against-them mentality whereby each sees the other team as the enemy, becomes more hostile, and decreases its communication with the other group. Groups are even more competitive and less cooperative than individuals. The inevitable outcome is that one group gains and the other group loses.[23]

Competition between groups must be managed carefully so that it does not escalate into dysfunctional conflict. Research has shown that when multiple groups compete for a goal that only one group can achieve, negative consequences such as territoriality, aggression, and prejudice toward other groups can result.[24] To prevent these negative results, managers should encourage and reward cooperative behaviors across groups. Some effective ways of doing this include modifying performance appraisals to include assessing intergroup behavior and using an external supervisor's evaluation of intergroup behavior. Group members will be more likely to help

interorganizational conflict Conflict that occurs between two or more organizations.

intergroup conflict Conflict that occurs between groups or teams in an organization.

HOT TREND

Millennial, Gen X, or Boomer: Who's the Best Manager for Work-Life Balance?

If you could pick a boss who would encourage work-life balance, what generation would that boss come from? Baby Boomer (born 1946–1964)? Generation X (born 1965–1979)? Or Millennials (born 1980–2000)? A study examined employees' perceptions of managers from these different generations to determine which managers displayed more behaviors that promote work-life balance.

Younger managers were more likely to support work-life balance to encourage employee growth and development, whereas older managers were more likely to do so out of a sense of fairness. But results showed that no generation was significantly better than the others at encouraging work-life balance among employees. Few managers were good at encouraging work-life balance, which is concerning because the demand for work-life balance is growing.

SOURCE: A. Gilley, K. Waddell, A. Hall, S. A. Jackson, and J. W. Gilley, "Manager Behavior, Generation, and Influence on Work-Life Balance: An Empirical Investigation," *Journal of Applied Management and Entrepreneurship* 20 (2015): 3–19.

---

other groups when they know that the other group's supervisor will be evaluating their behavior and that they will be rewarded for cooperation.[25] In addition, managers should encourage social interactions across groups so that trust can be developed. Trust allows individuals to exchange ideas and resources with members of other groups and results in innovation when members of different groups cooperate.[26]

13-3c Intragroup Conflict

Conflict that occurs within groups or teams is called **intragroup conflict**. Some conflict within a group is functional, since it can help prevent groupthink, as discussed in Chapter 10.

Even virtual teams are not immune to conflict. The nuances and subtleties of face-to-face communication are often lacking in these teams, and misunderstandings can result. Face-to-face and telephone interactions early on can eliminate later conflicts and allow virtual teams to move on to use electronic communication because trust has been developed. When top management teams make strategic decisions, conflicts within the team frequently arise because so much is at stake. If a crisis occurs,

however, intragroup conflicts may be superseded by the need for urgent decisions and collaboration among the team members.[27]

13-4 INDIVIDUAL CONFLICT IN ORGANIZATIONS

As with groups, conflict can occur between individuals (interpersonal) or within a single individual (intrapersonal).

13-4a Types of Intrapersonal Conflict

When conflict occurs within an individual, it is called **intrapersonal conflict**. There are several types of intrapersonal conflict, including interrole, intrarole, and person–role conflicts. A *role* is a set of expectations placed on an individual by others.[28] The person occupying the focal role is the *role incumbent*, and the individuals who place expectations on the person are *role senders*. Figure 13.2 depicts a set of role relationships.

Interrole conflict occurs when a person experiences conflict among the multiple roles in his or her life. One interrole conflict that many employees experience is *work–home conflict*, in which their role as worker clashes with their role as spouse or parent.[29] Work–home conflict can arise from time constraints, strain, and having responsibilities for people in the workplace and at home.[30] This type of conflict has become even

---

intragroup conflict
Conflict that occurs within groups or teams.

intrapersonal conflict
Conflict that occurs within an individual.

interrole conflict A person's experience of conflict among the multiple roles in his or her life.

FIGURE 13.2 | AN ORGANIZATION MEMBER'S ROLE SET

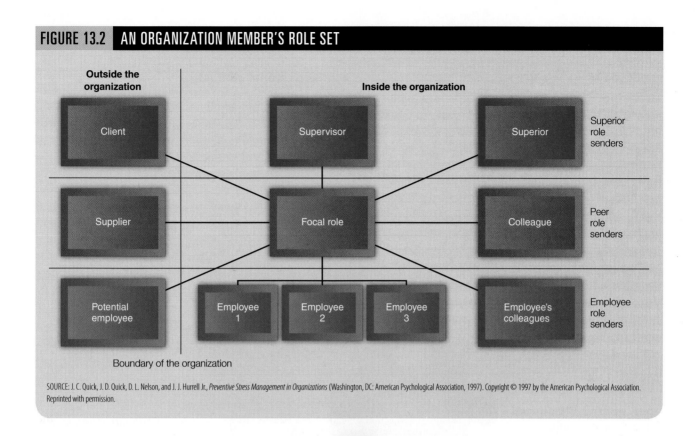

Outside the organization

Inside the organization

| Client | | Supervisor | | Superior | Superior role senders |

| Supplier | | Focal role | | Colleague | Peer role senders |

| Potential employee | Employee 1 | Employee 2 | Employee 3 | Employee's colleagues | Employee role senders |

Boundary of the organization

SOURCE: J. C. Quick, J. D. Quick, D. L. Nelson, and J. J. Hurrell Jr., *Preventive Stress Management in Organizations* (Washington, DC: American Psychological Association, 1997). Copyright © 1997 by the American Psychological Association. Reprinted with permission.

more common with the rise of work-at-home professionals and telecommuting, in which the home becomes the office and the boundary between work and family life is blurred.[31] Ambitious and highly involved employees use office communications (e.g., texting, e-mail, and so on) nights and weekends. After-hours communication usage is associated with increased work–life conflict as reported by the employee and a significant other.[32] Work–home conflict reduces personal well-being, decreases organizational citizenship behavior, and increases stress. People also tend to drink more alcohol on days they experience work–home conflict.[33] Work-home conflicts make it difficult to concentrate at work, and job performance suffers.[34]

Intrarole conflict is conflict within a single role. It often arises when a person receives conflicting messages from role senders about how to perform a certain role. Suppose a manager receives counsel from her department head that she needs to socialize less with nonmanagement employees. She is also told by her project manager that she needs to

be a better team member and that she can accomplish this by socializing more with other nonmanagement team members. This situation is one of intrarole conflict.

Person–role conflict occurs when an individual in a particular role is expected to perform behaviors that clash with his personal values.[35] Salespeople, for example, may be required to offer the most expensive item in the sales line first to the customer, even when it is apparent that the customer does not want or cannot afford it. A computer salesperson may be required to offer a

One intrapersonal conflict that many employees experience is work-home conflict.

intrarole conflict Conflict that occurs within a single role, such as when a person receives conflicting messages from role senders about how to perform a certain role.

person–role conflict Conflict that occurs when an individual in a particular role is expected to perform behaviors that clash with his or her personal values.

large, elaborate system to a student he knows is on a tight budget. This may conflict with the salesperson's values, and he may experience person–role conflict.

Intrapersonal conflicts can have positive consequences. Often, professional responsibilities clash with deeply held values. A budget shortfall may force you to lay off a loyal, hardworking employee. Your daughter may have a piano recital on the same day your largest client is scheduled to be in town visiting the office. In such conflicts, we often have to choose between right and right; that is, there's no wrong response, only one that is better than the other. These decisions pose what may be thought of as *defining moments* that challenge individuals to choose between two or more things in which they believe.[36] Character is formed in defining moments because they cause individuals to shape their identities. They help people crystallize their values and serve as opportunities for personal growth.

13-4b Managing Intrapersonal Conflict

Intrapersonal conflict can be managed with careful self-analysis and diagnosis of the situation. Three actions in particular can help prevent or resolve intrapersonal conflicts. First, when seeking a new job, you should find out as much as possible about the values of the organization.[37] Many person–role conflicts center around differences between the organization's values and the individual's values. Research has shown that when there is a good fit between the values of the individual and the organization, the individual is more satisfied and committed and is less likely to leave the organization.[38]

Second, *role analysis* is a good tool for managing intrarole or interrole conflicts.[39] In role analysis, the individual asks the various role senders what they expect of him. The outcomes are clearer work roles and the reduction of conflict and ambiguity.[40] Role analysis is a simple tool that clarifies the expectations of both parties in a relationship and reduces the potential for conflict within a role or between roles.

Third, political skills can help buffer the negative effects of stress that stem from role conflicts. Effective politicians can negotiate role expectations when conflicts occur. All these forms of conflict can be managed. An understanding of the many forms is a first step.

interpersonal conflict
Conflict that occurs between two or more individuals.

13-4c Managing Interpersonal Conflict

Conflict that occurs between two or more individuals, or **interpersonal conflict**, can arise from many individual differences, including personalities, attitudes, values, and perceptions. To manage interpersonal conflict, it is helpful to understand power networks in organizations and defense mechanisms exhibited by individuals when they are in conflict situations.

POWER NETWORKS According to W.F.G. Mastenbroek, individuals in organizations are organized into three basic types of power networks.[41] Based on these power relationships, certain kinds of conflict tend to emerge. Figure 13.3 illustrates three basic kinds of power relationships in organizations. The first relationship is *equal versus equal*, in which there is a horizontal balance of power among the parties. An example of this type of relationship would be a conflict between individuals from two different project teams. The behavioral tendency is toward *suboptimization*; that is, the focus is on a win–lose approach to problems, and each party tries to maximize its power at the expense of the other party. Conflict within this type of network can lead to depression, low self-esteem, and other distress symptoms.

Alexmillos/Shutterstock.com

"I'm Gonna Call Your Mom!"

A columnist for the *Philadelphia Daily News* heard years of complaints about Comcast and finally got fed up when she heard about a young couple's horror story of six weeks fighting with the company. The couple missed 13 days of work waiting for technicians who never showed up to install Internet and cable service. The columnist came up with an idea and called CEO Brian Roberts's 92-year-old mother. It worked: within a day of the call to the CEO's mom, the couple's service was installed.

SOURCE: "Don't Forget Who's Boss: Mom," *The Week*, February 27, 2015, 31.

Stockphoto-graf/Shutterstock.com

FIGURE 13.3 POWER RELATIONSHIPS IN ORGANIZATIONS

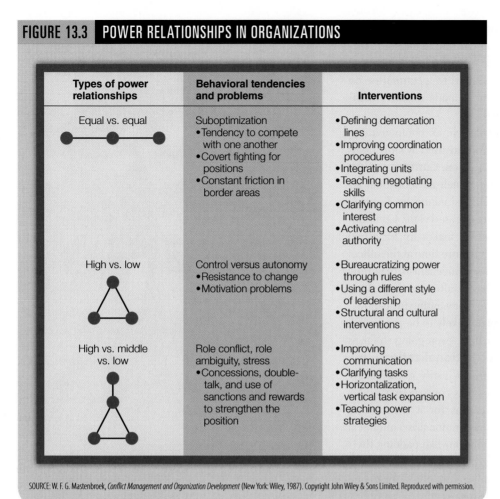

Types of power relationships	Behavioral tendencies and problems	Interventions
Equal vs. equal	Suboptimization • Tendency to compete with one another • Covert fighting for positions • Constant friction in border areas	• Defining demarcation lines • Improving coordination procedures • Integrating units • Teaching negotiating skills • Clarifying common interest • Activating central authority
High vs. low	Control versus autonomy • Resistance to change • Motivation problems	• Bureaucratizing power through rules • Using a different style of leadership • Structural and cultural interventions
High vs. middle vs. low	Role conflict, role ambiguity, stress • Concessions, double-talk, and use of sanctions and rewards to strengthen the position	• Improving communication • Clarifying tasks • Horizontalization, vertical task expansion • Teaching power strategies

SOURCE: W. F. G. Mastenbroek, *Conflict Management and Organization Development* (New York: Wiley, 1987). Copyright John Wiley & Sons Limited. Reproduced with permission.

Interventions such as improving coordination between the parties and working toward common interests can help manage these conflicts.

The second power network is *high versus low*, or a powerful party versus a less powerful party. Conflicts that emerge here take the basic form of the powerful individuals trying to control others, with the less powerful people trying to become more autonomous. Conflict in this network can lead to job dissatisfaction, low organizational commitment, and turnover.[42] Organizations typically respond to these conflicts by tightening the rules. However, the more successful ways of managing these conflicts are to try a different style of leadership, such as a coaching and counseling style, or to change the structure to a more decentralized one.

The third power network is *high versus middle versus low*. This power network illustrates the classic conflicts felt by middle managers. Two particular conflicts are evident for middle managers: *role conflict*, in which conflicting expectations are placed on the manager from bosses and employees, and *role ambiguity*, in which the expectations of the boss are unclear. Improved communication among all parties can reduce role conflict

and ambiguity. In addition, middle managers can benefit from training in positive ways to influence others.

Knowing the typical kinds of conflicts that arise in various kinds of relationships can help a manager diagnose conflicts and devise appropriate ways to manage them.

13-4d Defense Mechanisms

When individuals are involved in conflict with another human being, frustration often results.[43] Conflicts can often arise within the context of a performance appraisal session. Most people do not react well to negative feedback, as was illustrated in a classic study in which more than 50% of employees reacted defensively when given criticism about their work.[44]

When individuals are frustrated, as they often are in interpersonal conflict, they respond by exhibiting *defense mechanisms*.[45] Aggressive mechanisms, such as fixation, displacement, and negativism, are aimed at attacking the source of the conflict. In **fixation**, an individual fixates on the conflict, or keeps up a dysfunctional behavior that obviously will not solve the conflict. An example of fixation occurred in a university where a faculty member became embroiled in a battle with the dean because the faculty member felt he had not received a large enough salary increase. He persisted in writing angry letters to the dean, whose hands were tied because of a low budget allocation to the college. Another aggressive defense mechanism is **displacement**, which means directing anger toward someone who is not the source of the conflict. For example, a manager may respond harshly to an employee after a telephone confrontation with an

fixation An aggressive mechanism in which an individual keeps up a dysfunctional behavior that obviously will not solve the conflict.

displacement An aggressive mechanism in which an individual directs his or her anger toward someone who is not the source of the conflict.

angry customer. **Negativism** is an aggressive mechanism in which a person responds with pessimism to any attempt at solving a problem. Negativism is illustrated by a manager who, when appointed to a committee on which she did not want to serve, made negative comments throughout the meeting.

Compromise mechanisms, such as compensation, identification, and ratiaonalization, are used by individuals to make the best of a conflict situation. **Compensation** is a compromise mechanism in which an individual attempts to make up for a negative situation by devoting himself to another pursuit with increased vigor. Compensation can be seen when a person makes up for a bad relationship at home by spending more time at the office. **Identification** is a compromise mechanism whereby an individual patterns her behavior after another's. One supervisor at a construction firm, not wanting to acknowledge consciously that she was not likely to be promoted, mimicked the behavior of her boss, even going so far as to buy a car just like the boss's. **Rationalization** is trying to justify one's behavior by constructing bogus reasons for it. Employees may rationalize unethical behavior like padding their expense accounts with the argument that "everyone else does it."

Withdrawal mechanisms are exhibited when frustrated individuals try to flee from a conflict using either physical or psychological means. Flight, conversion, and fantasy are examples of withdrawal mechanisms. Physically escaping a conflict is **flight**. An employee taking a day off after a blowup with the boss is an example. **Withdrawal** may take the form of emotionally leaving a conflict, such as exhibiting an "I don't care anymore" attitude. **Conversion** is a process whereby emotional conflicts become expressed in physical symptoms. Most of us have experienced the conversion reaction of a

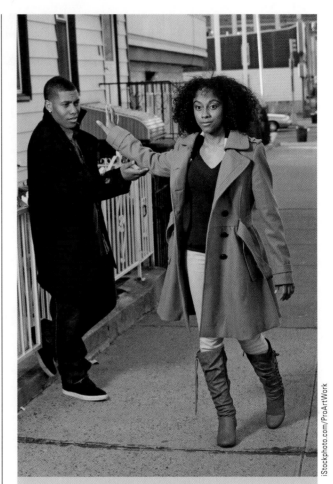

Withdrawal mechanisms are exhibited when frustrated individuals try to flee from a conflict.

iStockphoto.com/ProArtWork

headache following an emotional exchange with another person. **Fantasy** is a withdrawal mechanism that provides an escape from a conflict through daydreaming. In the Internet age, fantasy as an escape mechanism has found new meaning. A study conducted by International Data Corporation (IDC) showed that 30 to 40% of all Internet surfing in the office is nonwork-related and that more than 70% of companies have had sex sites accessed from their networks, suggesting that employees' minds aren't always focused on their jobs.[46]

When employees exhibit withdrawal mechanisms, they often pretend to agree with their bosses or coworkers in order to avoid facing an immediate conflict. Many employees fake a positive response this way because the firm informally rewards agreement and punishes dissent. The long-term consequence of withdrawal and faking a positive response is emotional distress for the employee.[47]

negativism An aggressive mechanism in which a person responds with pessimism to any attempt at solving a problem.

compensation A compromise mechanism in which an individual attempts to make up for a negative situation by devoting himself or herself to another pursuit with increased vigor.

identification A compromise mechanism whereby an individual patterns his or her behavior after another's.

rationalization A compromise mechanism characterized by trying to justify one's behavior by constructing bogus reasons for it.

flight/withdrawal A withdrawal mechanism that entails physically escaping (flight) or psychologically escaping (withdrawal) a conflict.

conversion A withdrawal mechanism in which emotional conflicts are expressed in physical symptoms.

fantasy A withdrawal mechanism that provides an escape from a conflict through daydreaming.

Knowledge of these defense mechanisms can be extremely beneficial to a manager. By understanding the ways in which people typically react to interpersonal conflict, managers can be prepared for employees' reactions and help them uncover their feelings about a conflict.

13-5 CONFLICT MANAGEMENT STRATEGIES AND TECHNIQUES

The overall approach (or strategy) you use in a conflict is important in determining whether the conflict will have a positive or negative outcome. Overall strategies to deal with conflict can be classified as competitive versus cooperative strategies. Table 13.2 depicts the two strategies and four different conflict scenarios. The *competitive strategy* is founded on assumptions of win–lose and entails dishonest communication, mistrust, and a rigid position from both parties.[48] The *cooperative strategy* is founded on different assumptions: the potential for win–win outcomes, honest communication, trust, openness to risk and vulnerability, and the notion that the whole may be greater than the sum of the parts.

To illustrate the importance of the overall strategy, consider the case of two groups competing for scarce resources. Suppose budget cuts have to be made at an insurance company. The claims manager argues that the sales training staff should be cut because agents are fully trained. The sales training manager argues that claims personnel should be cut because the company is processing fewer claims. This could turn into a dysfunctional brawl, with both sides refusing to give ground. The result would be a win–lose, lose–win, or lose–lose scenario. Personnel cuts could be made in one department or the other, or in both departments. In all three cases, the organization winds up in a losing position with the competitive approach.

Even in such intense conflicts as those over scarce resources, a win–win strategy can lead to an overall win for the organization. In fact, conflicts over scarce resources can be productive if the parties have cooperative goals—a strategy that seeks a winning solution for both parties. To achieve a win–win outcome, the conflict must be approached with open-minded discussion of opposing views. Through open-minded discussion, both parties integrate views and create new solutions that facilitate productivity and strengthen their relationship; the result is feelings of unity rather than separation.[49]

In the example of the conflict between the claims manager and sales training manager, open-minded discussion might reveal that there are ways to achieve budget cuts without cutting personnel. Sales support might surrender part of its travel budget, and claims might cut overtime. This represents a win–win situation for the company. The budget has been reduced, and relationships between the two departments have been preserved. Both parties have given up something (note the "Win–" in Table 13.2), but the conflict has been resolved with a positive outcome.

You can see the importance of the broad strategy used to approach a conflict. We now move from broad strategies to more specific techniques.

Effective conflict management techniques include appealing to superordinate goals, expanding resources, changing personnel, changing structure, and confronting and negotiating.

13-5a Ineffective Techniques

There are many specific techniques for dealing with conflict. Before turning to techniques that work, it should be recognized that some actions commonly taken in organizations to deal with conflict are not effective.[50]

Nonaction is doing nothing in hopes that the conflict will disappear. Generally, this is not a good technique because most conflicts do not go away, and the individuals involved in the conflict react with frustration. **Secrecy**, attempting to hide a conflict or an issue that has the potential to create conflict, only creates suspicion. An example is an organizational policy of pay secrecy. In some organizations, discussion of salary is grounds for dismissal. When this is the case, employees suspect that the company has something to hide. **Administrative orbiting** is delaying action on a conflict by buying time, usually by telling the

TABLE 13.2	WIN–LOSE VERSUS WIN–WIN STRATEGIES		
Strategy	**Department A**	**Department B**	**Organization**
Competitive	Lose	Lose	Lose
	Lose	Win	Lose
	Win	Lose	Lose
Cooperative	Win2	Win2	Win

© Cengage Learning

nonaction Doing nothing in hopes that a conflict will disappear.

secrecy Attempting to hide a conflict or an issue that has the potential to create conflict.

administrative orbiting Delaying action on a conflict by buying time.

individuals involved that the problem is being worked on or that the boss is still thinking about the issue. Like nonaction, this technique leads to frustration and resentment.

Due process nonaction is a procedure set up to address conflicts that is so costly, time-consuming, or personally risky that no one will use it. Some companies' sexual harassment policies are examples of this technique. To file a sexual harassment complaint, the accuser must complete detailed paperwork, has to go through appropriate channels, and may be branded a troublemaker. Thus, the company has a procedure for handling complaints (due process), but no one uses it (nonaction).

Character assassination is an attempt to label or discredit an opponent. Character assassination can backfire and make the individual who uses it appear dishonest and cruel. It often leads to name-calling and accusations by both parties, who both end up losers in the eyes of those who witness the conflict. In 2010, Dana Holgorsen was hired as the head football coach at West Virginia University. The only problem was that the school already had a head coach, Bill Stewart. Holgorsen was hired to serve as an assistant for a year under Stewart and then replace him. This arrangement angered Stewart, who contacted journalists to "dig up dirt" on Holgorsen so that he could use it for character assassination. When this became public knowledge, Stewart resigned from his position.[51]

13-5b Effective Techniques

Fortunately, there are effective conflict management techniques. These include appealing to superordinate goals, expanding resources, changing personnel, changing structure, and confronting and negotiating.

SUPERORDINATE GOALS An organizational goal that is more important to both parties in a conflict than their individual or group goals is a **superordinate goal**.[52] Superordinate goals cannot be achieved by an individual or by one group alone. The achievement of these goals requires cooperation by both parties. One effective technique for resolving conflict is to appeal to this superordinate goal—in effect, to focus the parties on a larger issue on which they both agree. This helps them realize their similarities rather than their differences.

due process nonaction A procedure set up to address conflicts that is so costly, time-consuming, or personally risky that no one will use it.

character assassination An attempt to label or discredit an opponent.

superordinate goal An organizational goal that is more important to both parties in a conflict than their individual or group goals.

In the conflict between service representatives and cable television installers that was discussed earlier, appealing to a superordinate goal would be an effective technique for resolving the conflict. Both departments can agree that superior customer service is a goal worthy of pursuit and that this goal cannot be achieved unless cables are installed properly and in a timely manner, and customer complaints are handled effectively. Quality service requires that both departments cooperate to achieve the goal.

EXPANDING RESOURCES One conflict resolution technique is so simple that it may be overlooked. If the conflict's source is common or scarce resources, providing more resources may be a solution. Of course, managers working with tight budgets may not have the luxury of obtaining additional resources. Nevertheless, it is a technique to be considered. In the example of shared administrative support presented earlier in this chapter, one solution to the conflict among managers over administrative support would be to hire more administrative assistants.

CHANGING PERSONNEL In some cases, long-running severe conflict may be traced to a specific individual. For example, managers with lower levels of emotional intelligence demonstrate more negative work attitudes, exhibit less altruistic behavior, and produce more negative work outcomes. A chronically disgruntled manager who exhibits low emotional intelligence might not only frustrate his employees but also impede his department's performance. In such cases, transferring or firing an individual could be the best solution, but only after due process.[53]

CHANGING STRUCTURE Another way to resolve a conflict is to change the structure of the organization. One way of accomplishing this is to create an integrator role. An *integrator* is a liaison between groups with very different interests. In severe conflicts, it may be best that the integrator be a neutral third party.[54] Creating the integrator role is a way of opening dialogue between groups that have difficulty communicating.

Using *cross-functional teams* is another way of changing the organization's structure to manage conflict. In the old methods of designing new products in organizations, many departments had to contribute, and delays resulted from difficulties in coordinating the activities of the various departments. Using a cross-functional team made up of members from different departments improves coordination and reduces delays by allowing many activities to be performed at the same time rather than sequentially.[55] The team approach allows members from different departments to work together and reduces the potential for conflict. However, recent research also suggests that such functional diversity can lead to slower informational processing in teams due to differences in members' perceptions of what might be required to achieve group goals. When putting together cross-functional teams, organizations should emphasize superordinate goals and train team members on resolving conflict. One such training technique could involve educating individual members in other functional areas so that everyone on the team can have a shared language.[56] In teamwork, it is helpful to break up a big task so that it becomes a collection of smaller, less complex tasks and to have smaller teams work on the smaller tasks. This helps to reduce conflict, and organizations can potentially improve the performance of the overall team by improving the outcomes in each subteam.[57]

CONFRONTING AND NEGOTIATING Some conflicts require confrontation and negotiation between the parties. Both of these strategies require skill on the part of the negotiator and careful planning before engaging in negotiations. The process of negotiating involves an open discussion of problem solutions, and the outcome often is an exchange in which both parties work toward a mutually beneficial solution.

Negotiation is a joint process of finding a mutually acceptable solution to a complex conflict. There are two major negotiating approaches: distributive bargaining and integrative negotiation.[58] **Distributive bargaining** is an approach in which the goals of one party are in direct conflict with the goals of the other party. Resources are limited, and each party wants to maximize its share of the resources (get its piece of the pie). It is a competitive, or win–lose, approach to negotiations. Sometimes distributive bargaining causes negotiators to focus so much on their differences that they ignore their common ground. In these cases, distributive bargaining can become counterproductive. The reality is, however, that some situations are distributive in nature, particularly when the parties are interdependent. If a negotiator wants to maximize the value of a single deal and is not worried about maintaining a good relationship with the other party, distributive bargaining may be an option.

In contrast, **integrative negotiation** is an approach in which the parties' goals are not seen as mutually exclusive, but the focus is on both sides achieving their objectives. Integrative negotiation focuses on the merits of the issues and is a win–win approach. (How can we make the pie bigger?) For integrative negotiation to be successful, certain preconditions must be present. These include having a common goal, faith in one's own problem-solving abilities, a belief in the validity of the other party's position, motivation to work together, mutual trust, and clear communication. It also helps if both parties are good at perspective taking, which is the ability to see the other person's point of view.[59]

Cultural differences in negotiation must be acknowledged. Japanese negotiators, for example, when working with American negotiators, tend to see

Mindscanner/Shutterstock.com

distributive bargaining
A negotiation approach in which the goals of the parties are in conflict, and each party seeks to maximize its resources.

integrative negotiation A negotiation approach in which the parties' goals are not seen as mutually exclusive, but the focus is on both sides achieving their objectives.

AP Images/Alex J. Berliner

Awkward confrontation: Angelina Jolie and Sony's Amy Pascal share a stare-down. Two days earlier, leaked Sony emails described Jolie as a minimally talented spoiled brat.

their power as coming from their role (buyer versus seller). Americans, in contrast, view their power as their ability to walk away from the negotiations.[60] Neither culture understands the other very well, so negotiations can resemble a dance in which one person is waltzing while the other is doing a samba. The collectivism–individualism dimension (discussed in Chapter 2) has a great bearing on negotiations. Americans, with their individualism, negotiate from a position of self-interest; Japanese focus on the good of the group. Cross-cultural negotiations can be more effective if you learn as much about other cultures as possible.

Gender may also play a role in negotiation. There appears to be no evidence that men are better negotiators than women or vice versa. It depends on the context of the negotiation. Men achieve better economic outcomes when negotiating for themselves. In contrast, women achieve better outcomes when they are negotiating on behalf of another individual. Often, women lack experience when it comes to negotiating and can benefit from training in negotiation skills.[61]

13-6 CONFLICT MANAGEMENT STYLES

Managers have at their disposal a variety of conflict management styles: avoiding, accommodating, competing, compromising, and collaborating. One way of classifying styles of conflict management is to examine the styles' *assertiveness* (the extent to which you want your goals met) and *cooperativeness* (the extent to which you want to see the other party's concerns met).[62] Figure 13.4 graphs the five conflict management styles using these two dimensions. Table 13.3 lists appropriate situations for using each conflict management style.

13-6a Avoiding

Avoiding is a style low on both assertiveness and cooperativeness. Avoiding is a deliberate decision to take no action on a conflict or to stay out of a

conflict situation. In recent times, Airbus, a European manufacturer of aircraft, has faced massive intraorganizational conflict stemming from major expansions that included French, German, Spanish, and British subsidiaries within the same parent company. Power struggles among executives combined with massive changes in organizational structure are believed to have led to this conflict. Airbus seems to be adopting the avoidance strategy in an effort to let these conflicts subside on their own.[63] Some relationship conflicts, such as those involving political norms and personal tastes, may distract team members from their tasks, in which case, avoiding may be an appropriate strategy.[64] When the parties are angry and need time to cool down, it may be best to use avoidance. There is a potential danger in using an avoiding style too often, however. Research shows that overuse of this style results in negative evaluations from others in the workplace.[65]

13-6b Accommodating

A style in which you are concerned that the other party's goals be met but relatively unconcerned with getting your own way is called accommodating. It is cooperative but unassertive. Appropriate situations

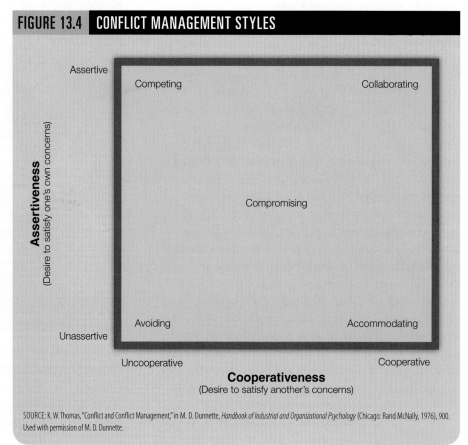

FIGURE 13.4   CONFLICT MANAGEMENT STYLES

SOURCE: K. W. Thomas, "Conflict and Conflict Management," in M. D. Dunnette, *Handbook of Industrial and Organizational Psychology* (Chicago: Rand McNally, 1976), 900. Used with permission of M. D. Dunnette.

TABLE 13.3 USES OF FIVE STYLES OF CONFLICT MANAGEMENT

Conflict-Handling Style	Appropriate Situation
Competing	When quick, decisive action is vital (e.g., emergencies).
	On important issues for which unpopular actions need implementing (e.g., cost cutting, enforcing unpopular rules, discipline).
	On issues vital to company welfare when you know you are right.
	Against people who take advantage of noncompetitive behavior.
Collaborating	To find an integrative solution when both sets of concerns are too important to be compromised.
	When your objective is to learn.
	To merge insights from people with different perspectives.
	To gain commitment by incorporating concerns into a consensus.
	To work through feelings that have interfered with a relationship.
Compromising	When goals are important but not worth the effort or potential disruption of more assertive modes.
	When opponents with equal power are committed to mutually exclusive goals.
	To achieve temporary settlements to complex issues.
	To arrive at expedient solutions under time pressure.
	As a backup when collaboration or competition is unsuccessful.
Avoiding	When an issue is trivial or more important issues are pressing.
	When you perceive no chance of satisfying your concerns.
	When potential disruption outweighs the benefits of resolution.
	To let people cool down and regain perspective.
	When gathering information supersedes immediate decision.
	When others can resolve the conflict more effectively.
	When issues seem tangential or symptomatic of other issues.
Accommodating	When you find you are wrong—to allow a better position to be heard, to learn, and to show your reasonableness.
	When issues are more important to others than to yourself—to satisfy others and maintain cooperation.
	To build social credits for later issues.
	To minimize loss when you are outmatched and losing.
	When harmony and stability are especially important.
	To allow employees to develop by learning from mistakes.

SOURCE: K. W. Thomas, "Toward Multidimensional Values in Teaching: The Example of Conflict Behaviors," *Academy of Management Review* 2 (1977): 309–325. Reproduced by permission of the publisher via Copyright Clearance Center, Inc.

for accommodating include times when you find you are wrong, when you want to let the other party have his way so that that individual will owe you similar treatment later, or when the relationship is important. Overreliance on accommodating has its dangers. Managers who constantly defer to others may find that others lose respect for them. In addition, accommodating managers may become frustrated because their own needs are never met, and they may lose self-esteem.[66] Research has also shown that individuals will overestimate the importance of the relationship and accommodate at the expense of actual outcomes. Research has shown that two females involved in conflict or negotiation overuse accommodation more than two males involved in similar situations.[67]

13-6c Competing

Competing is a style that is very assertive and uncooperative. You want to satisfy your own interests and are willing to do so at the other party's expense. In an emergency or in situations where you know you are right, it may be appropriate to put your foot down. For example, environmentalists forced Shell Oil Company (part of Royal Dutch/Shell Group) to scrap its plans to build a refinery in Delaware after a bitter "To Hell with Shell" campaign.[68] Relying solely on competing strategies is dangerous, though. Managers who do so may become reluctant to admit when they are wrong and may find themselves surrounded by people who are afraid to disagree with them. As noted earlier, task conflict and relationship conflict could occur together in team settings, although task conflict is seen as functional and relationship conflict as dysfunctional for the team. In a recent study, dyads of participants were exposed to task-based conflict. One of the two members of the dyads was trained on using either the competing conflict-handling style or the collaborative style. Results indicated that the competing style led to the most relationship conflict, whereas the collaborative style led to the least relationship conflict.[69]

13-6d Compromising

The compromising style is intermediate in both assertiveness and cooperativeness because each party must give up something to reach a solution to the conflict. Compromises are often made in the final hours of union–management negotiations, when time is of the essence. Compromise may be an effective backup style when efforts toward collaboration are not successful.[70]

It is important to recognize that compromises are not optimal solutions. Compromise means partially surrendering one's position for the sake of coming to terms. For this reason, people often inflate their demands when they begin a compromise. A problem with compromise is that the solutions reached may only be temporary, and often compromises do nothing to improve relationships between the parties in the conflict.

Just like in athletic competition, competing, compromising, and collaborating are all important parts of a successful organization.

13-6e Collaborating

A win–win style that is high on both assertiveness and cooperativeness is known as collaborating. Working toward it involves an open and thorough discussion of the conflict and arriving at a solution that is satisfactory to both parties. Situations where collaboration may be effective include times when both parties need to be committed to a final solution or when a combination of different perspectives can be formed into a solution. Long-term collaboration leads to improved relationships and effective performance.[71] Teams that use collaboration effectively view conflict as a mutual problem that needs common consideration to achieve resolution. Understanding this, team members have confidence that other members will work toward mutually beneficial solutions and ultimately generate diverse ideas to facilitate team performance.[72]

Research on the five styles of conflict management indicates that although most managers favor a certain style, they have the capacity to change styles as the situation demands.[73] A study of project managers found that managers who used a combination of competing and avoiding styles were seen as ineffective by the engineers who worked on their project teams.[74]

AP Images/Adam Creech

STUDY TOOLS 13

LOCATED AT BACK OF THE TEXTBOOK

☐ Rip out chapter review card

LOCATED AT WWW.CENGAGE.COM/LOGIN

☐ Track your knowledge and understanding of key concepts in business using 4LTR Press Online

☐ Review key term flashcards and create your own using StudyBits

☐ Create and complete practice quizzes based off of your notes and StudyBits

☐ Complete Online activities such as Matching and Fill-in-the-Blank exercises

☐ View chapter highlight box content, including the chapter videos, key exhibits and executive profiles.

ORGB ONLINE

STUDY YOUR WAY
WITH STUDYBITS!

WEAK

FAIR

STRONG

UNASSIGNED

Rate and Organize StudyBits

Collect What's Important

Create Flashcards From Your StudyBits

85%

Track/Monitor Your Progress

CORRECT

INCORRECT

INCORRECT

INCORRECT

Personalize Your Quizzes

4LTR
PRESS

Access ORGB ONLINE at www.cengagebrain.com

14 | Jobs and the Design of Work

luriii/Shutterstock.com

LEARNING OUTCOMES

 14-1 Differentiate between job and work.

14-2 Discuss the traditional approaches to job design.

14-3 Identify and describe alternative approaches to job design.

14-4 Identify and describe contemporary issues facing organizations in the design of work.

After finishing this chapter go to **PAGE 237** for **STUDY TOOLS.**

14-1 WORK IN ORGANIZATIONS

A **job** can be defined as a set of specified work and task activities that engage an individual in an organization. A job is not the same as an organizational position or a career. *Organizational position* identifies a job in relation to other parts of the organization; *career* refers to a sequence of job experiences over time. A job is also not the same as *work*, at least not in relation to an organization. **Work**, which can be defined as mental or physical activity that has productive results, is organized into jobs. Thus, a *job* is composed of a set of specific tasks, each of which is an assigned piece of *work* to be done in a specific time period.

Work is one important reason organizations exist. Plus, work is an especially important human endeavor because through work, people become securely attached to reality and securely connected in human relationships. Although *work* has different meanings for different people, from an organization's viewpoint, work is related to the structure of jobs, and jobs fit into the larger structure of an organization. The structure of jobs is the concern of this chapter, and the structure of the organization is the concern of the next chapter. Both chapters emphasize organizations as sets of task and authority relationships through which people get work done.

> It is important to understand and appreciate differences among individuals and cultures with regard to the meaning of work.

Danielala/Shutterstock.com

> For all people, work is organized into jobs, and jobs fit into the larger structure of an organization.

14-1a The Meaning of Work

The **meaning of work** differs from person to person, from culture to culture, and from profession to profession.[1] It is not uncommon for contemporary workers to describe their work and careers as a calling, a sense of fulfilling life's purpose.[2] In an increasingly global workplace, it is important to understand and appreciate differences among individuals and cultures with regard to the meaning of work. One study found six patterns people follow in defining *work*, and these help explain the cultural differences in people's motivation to work.[3]

- *Pattern A* people define *work* as an activity in which value comes from performance and for which

a person is accountable. It is generally self-directed and devoid of negative affect.

- *Pattern B* people define *work* as an activity that provides a person with positive personal affect and identity. Work contributes to society and is not unpleasant.

  - *Pattern C* people define *work* as an activity from which profit accrues to others by its performance and that may be done in various settings other than a working place. Work is usually physically strenuous and somewhat compulsive.

  - *Pattern D* people define *work* as primarily a physical activity a person must do that is directed by others and generally performed in a working place. Work is usually devoid of positive affect and is unpleasantly connected to performance.

  - *Pattern E* people define *work* as a physically and mentally strenuous activity. It is generally unpleasant and devoid of positive affect.

  - *Pattern F* people define *work* as an activity constrained to specific time periods that does not bring positive affect through its performance.

These six patterns were studied in six different countries: Belgium, Germany, Israel, Japan, the Netherlands, and the United States. Table 14.1 summarizes the percentage of workers in each country who defined work according to each of the six patterns. An examination of the table shows that a small percentage of workers in all six countries used either Pattern E or Pattern F to define *work*. Furthermore, there are significant differences among countries in how *work* is defined. In the Netherlands, *work* is defined most positively and with the most balanced personal and collective reasons for doing it. *Work* is defined least positively and with the most collective reason for doing it in

job A set of specified work and task activities that engage an individual in an organization.

work Mental or physical activity that has productive results.

meaning of work The way a person interprets and understands the value of work as part of life.

Biablo101/Shutterstock.com

HOT TREND

Making Work Meaningful

Generating purpose and meaning for workers presents a major challenge for many of today's managers and supervisors. Meaningful work is linked to several workplace outcomes such as increased job satisfaction, employee well-being, and performance. As important as work meaning is to improving these outcomes, it is not easy to infuse meaning into job tasks, especially when those tasks are either mandatory or mundane. The key is to help employees find the deeper meaning of work tasks beyond simply performing the tasks. For the brick worker's supervisor, for example, the challenge is to help the worker see beyond laying bricks to the realization that his bricklaying is instrumental to erecting a building.

SOURCE: L. Stemmet, "Why Are We Doing It . . . What Is the Purpose?" *Human Resources Magazine* 19 (2014): 22–23.

Germany and Japan. Belgium, Israel, and the United States represent a middle position between these two poles.

In another international study, 5,550 people across ten occupational groups in twenty different countries completed the *Work Value Scales (WVS)*.[4] The WVS is composed of thirteen items measuring various aspects of the work environment, such as responsibility and job security. The study found two common basic work dimensions across cultures: *work content*, measured by items such as "the amount of responsibility on the job," and *job context*, measured by items such as "the policies of my company." This finding suggests that people in many cultures distinguish between the nature of the work itself and elements of the context in which work is done. The idea of two work dimensions supports Herzberg's two-factor theory of motivation (see Chapter 5) and his job enrichment method discussed later in this chapter. Although the meaning of *work* differs among countries, new theorizing about crafting a job also suggests that individual employees can alter work meaning and work identity by changing task and relationship configurations in their work.[5]

14-1b Jobs in Organizations

Task and authority relationships define an organization's structure. Jobs, being the basic building blocks of this task–authority structure, are considered the micro-structural element to which employees most directly relate. Jobs are usually designed to complement and support other jobs in the organization. Isolated jobs are rare, although one was identified at Coastal Corporation during the early 1970s. Shortly after Oscar Wyatt moved the company from Corpus Christi, Texas, to Houston, Coastal developed organizational charts and job descriptions because the company had grown so large. In the process, it was discovered that the beloved corporate economist reported to no one. Everyone assumed he worked for someone else. Such peculiarities are rare, however.

Jobs in organizations are interdependent and designed to make a contribution to the organization's overall mission and goals. For salespeople to be successful, the production people must be effective. For production people to be effective, the material department must be effective. These interdependencies require careful planning and design so that all of the pieces of work fit together into a whole. Suppose an envelope salesperson wants to take

TABLE 14.1	WORK DEFINITION PATTERNS BY NATION					
	PATTERN[a]					
SAMPLE	**A**	**B**	**C**	**D**	**E**	**F**
Total Sample (*N* × 4,950)	11%	28%	18%	22%	11%	12%
NATION						
Belgium	8%	40%	13%	19%	11%	9%
Germany	8%	26%	13%	28%	11%	14%
Israel	4%	22%	33%	23%	9%	9%
Japan	21%	11%	13%	29%	10%	17%
The Netherlands	15%	43%	12%	11%	9%	9%
United States	8%	30%	19%	19%	12%	11%

Note: $X^2 = 680.98$ (25 degrees of freedom). P < 0.0001 Significance level

[a]In Pattern A, work is valued for its performance. The person is accountable and generally self-directed. In Pattern B, work provides a person with positive affect and identity. It contributes to society. In Pattern C, work provides profit to others by its performance. It is physical and not confined to a working place. In Pattern D, work is a required physical activity directed by others and generally unpleasant. In Pattern E, work is physically and mentally strenuous. It is generally unpleasant. In Pattern F, work is constrained to specific time periods. It does not bring positive affect through performance.

SOURCE: From G. W. England and I. Harper, "How Working Is Defined: National Contexts and Demographic and Organizational Role Influences," *Journal of Organizational Behavior* 11 (1990), 253–266. This material is used by permission of John Wiley & Sons, Inc.

an order for 1 million envelopes from John Hancock Financial Services. He must coordinate that order with the production department to establish an achievable delivery date. Failure to incorporate this interdependence into his planning could create conflict, resulting in late delivery to John Hancock.

The central concerns of this chapter are designing work and structuring jobs to prevent such problems and to ensure employee well-being. Inflexible jobs that are rigidly structured have an adverse effect, as they cause stress to employees and limit their career growth. In contrast, so-called smart jobs stimulate learning and growth and thus serve as building blocks for a person's career.[6]

The larger issues in the design of organizations are the competing processes of differentiation and integration (see Chapter 15). *Differentiation* is the process of subdividing and departmentalizing the work of an organization. Jobs result from differentiation, which is necessary because no one can do it all (contrary to the famous statement made by Harold Geneen, former chair of ITT: "If I had enough arms and legs and time, I'd do it all myself"). Even small organizations must divide work so that each person is able to accomplish a manageable piece of the whole. At the same time that the organization divides up the work, however, it must also integrate those pieces back into a whole. *Integration* is the process of connecting jobs and departments into a coordinated, cohesive whole. For example, if the envelope salesperson coordinates his order from John Hancock with the production manager, the company will meet the customer's expectations because integration will have occurred.

 ## 14-2 TRADITIONAL APPROACHES TO JOB DESIGN

Failure to differentiate, integrate, or both may result in badly designed jobs, which in turn cause a variety of performance problems in organizations. Good job design helps avoid these problems, improves productivity, and enhances employee well-being. Approaches to job design that were developed during the twentieth century are job enlargement/job rotation, job enrichment, and the job characteristics theory. Each approach offers unique benefits to the organization, the employee, or both, but each also has limitations and drawbacks. Furthermore, an unthinking reliance on a traditional approach can be a serious problem in any company. The later job design approaches were developed to overcome the limitations of traditional job design approaches. For example, job enlargement was intended to overcome the problem of

Work simplification can give an employee a renewed sense of confidence in their work.

boredom associated with scientific management's narrowly defined approach to jobs.

14-2a Scientific Management

Scientific management, an approach to work design first advocated by Frederick Taylor, emphasizes work simplification. **Work simplification** is the standardization and the narrow, explicit specification of task activities for workers.[7] Jobs designed through scientific management have a limited number of tasks, and each task is scientifically designed so that the worker is not required to think or deliberate. According to Taylor, the role of management and the industrial engineer is to calibrate and define each task carefully. The role of the worker is to execute the task. Elements of scientific management, such as time and motion studies, differential piece-rate systems of pay, and the scientific selection of workers, all focus on the efficient use of labor to the economic benefit of the corporation.

14-2b Job Enlargement/Job Rotation

Job enlargement is a method of job design that increases the number of activities in a job to overcome the boredom of overspecialized

work simplification The standardization and the narrow, explicit specification of task activities for workers.

job enlargement A method of job design that increases the number of activities in a job to overcome the boredom of overspecialized work.

work. It is a traditional approach to solving not only the problem of boredom but also the difficulty of coordinating work.[8] **Job rotation**, a variation of job enlargement, exposes a worker to a variety of specialized job tasks over time. Both of these approaches came into being to solve the perceived problems of overspecialization that arose from lack of variety. In other words, jobs designed by scientific management were too narrow and limited in the number of tasks and activities assigned to each worker. The lack of variety led to understimulation and underutilization of the worker.

Variety can be increased by adding to a worker's activities by means of job enlargement or by giving a worker different activities by means of job rotation. For example, job enlargement for a lathe operator in a steel plant might include selecting the steel pieces to be turned and performing all of the maintenance work on the lathe in addition to running it. As an example of job rotation, an employee at a small bank might take new accounts one day, serve as a cashier another day, and process loan applications on a third day.

One of the first studies of the problem of repetitive work was conducted at IBM after World War II. The company implemented a job enlargement program during the war and evaluated the effort after six years.[9] The two most important results were a significant increase in product quality and a reduction in idle time, both for people and for machines. Less obvious and measurable benefits were enhanced worker status and improved manager–worker communication. IBM concluded that job enlargement countered the problems of work specialization. A contemporary study in a Swedish electronics assembly plant used physiological measures of muscle tension.[10] Job enlargement had a positive effect on mechanical exposure variability.

A later study examined the effects of mass production jobs on assembly line workers in the automotive industry.[11] Mass production jobs have six characteristics: mechanically controlled work pace, repetitiveness, minimum skill requirements, predetermined tools and techniques, minute division of the production process, and a requirement for surface mental attention rather than thoughtful concentration. The researchers conducted 180 private interviews with assembly line workers and found generally positive attitudes

toward pay, security, and supervision. They concluded that job enlargement and job rotation would improve other job aspects, such as repetition and a mechanical work pace.

Job rotation and **cross-training** programs are variations of job enlargement. Pharmaceutical company Eli Lilly has found that job rotation can be a proactive means for enhancing work experiences for career development and can have tangible benefits for employees in the form of salary increases and promotions.[12] In cross-training, workers are trained in different specialized tasks or activities of different jobs. While job rotation may be common practice for high-potential employees, they should remain in a position long enough to see the consequences of their decisions.[13]

All three kinds of programs—job enlargement, job rotation, and cross-training horizontally—enlarge jobs; that is, the number and variety of an employee's tasks and activities are increased. Graphic Controls Corporation (now a subsidiary of Tyco International) used cross-training to develop a flexible workforce that enabled the company to maintain high levels of production.[14] Many of today's jobs require that employees manage several work activities as part of their normal business day. However, it is important that employees be able to disengage from one task before moving on to another to achieve high levels of performance.[15]

14-2c Job Enrichment

Job enrichment is designing or redesigning a job by incorporating motivational factors into it. Whereas job enlargement increases the number of job activities through horizontal loading, job enrichment increases the amount of job responsibility through vertical loading. Both approaches to job design are intended, in part, to increase job satisfaction for employees. A study to test whether job satisfaction results from characteristics of the job or of the person found that an interactionist approach is most accurate and that job redesign can contribute to increased job satisfaction for some employees. Another two-year study found that intrinsic job satisfaction and job perceptions are reciprocally related to each other.[16]

Job enrichment builds on Herzberg's two-factor theory of motivation, which distinguished between motivational and hygiene factors for people at work. Whereas job enlargement recommends increasing and varying the number of activities a person does, job enrichment recommends increasing the recognition, responsibility, and opportunity for achievement. For example, enlarging the lathe operator's job means adding maintenance

job rotation A variation of job enlargement in which workers are exposed to a variety of specialized jobs over time.

cross-training A variation of job enlargement in which workers are trained in different specialized tasks or activities.

job enrichment Designing or redesigning a job by incorporating motivational factors into it.

Repetitive Work: A Double-Edged Sword

The United States experienced a sharp decline in the number of manufacturing jobs over the past two decades. Still, one in ten Americans worked in factories in 2010. Factory work is typically highly specialized, a feature associated with reduced mental health and employee well-being. At the same time, designing jobs with repetition built in allows for increased production, an important goal of manufacturing businesses. How do we reconcile both of these competing goals? A new study sought to account for negative and positive effects of work repetitiveness. Investigators tested their hypotheses that repetitive work would negatively affect employee well-being and positively affect performance. As predicted, researchers found that task repetitiveness had a larger positive effect on performance than it had a negative effect on mental strain. Where repetitive work is a reality, researchers suggest using social support to buffer its negative effects. Increasing positive interactions with coworkers could also provide meaning and relief from boredom inherent with repetitive tasks.

One in ten Americans worked in factories as recently as 2010.

SOURCE: C. Kenny, "Why Factory Jobs Are Shrinking Everywhere," *Bloomberg Business* (April 28, 2014), http://www.bloomberg.com/bw/articles/2014-04-28/why-factory-jobs-are-shrinking-everywhere; J. Hausser, S. Schulz-Hardt, T. Schultze, A. Tomaschek, and A. Mojzisch, "Experimental Evidence for the Effects of Task Repetitiveness on Mental Strain and Objective Work Performance," *Journal of Organizational Behavior* 35 (2014): 705–721.

activities, and enriching the job means having the operator meet with customers who buy the products.

Herzberg believed that only certain jobs should be enriched and that the first step is to select the jobs appropriate for job enrichment.[17] He recognized that some people prefer simple jobs. Once jobs are selected for enrichment, management should brainstorm about possible changes, revise the list to include only specific changes related to motivational factors, and screen out generalities and suggestions that would simply increase activities or numbers of tasks. Those whose jobs are to be enriched should not participate in this process, as doing so would present a conflict of interest.

A seven-year implementation study of job enrichment at AT&T found that approach beneficial.[18] Job enrichment required a big change in management style, and AT&T found that it could not ignore hygiene factors in the work environment just because it was enriching existing jobs. Although the AT&T experience with job enrichment was positive, a critical review of job enrichment did not find that to be the case generally.[19] One problem with job enrichment as a strategy for work design is that it is based on an oversimplified motivational theory. Another problem is the lack of consideration for individual differences among employees. Job enrichment, like scientific management's work specialization and job enlargement/job rotation, is a universal approach to the design of work and thus does not differentiate among individuals.

14-2d Job Characteristics Theory

The job characteristics theory, which was initiated during the mid-1960s, is a traditional approach to the design of work that makes a significant departure from the three earlier approaches. It emphasizes the interaction between the individual and specific attributes of the job; therefore, it is a person–job fit model rather than a universal job design model. It originated in a research study of 470 workers in forty-seven different jobs across eleven industries.[20] The study measured and classified relevant task characteristics for these forty-seven jobs and found four core job characteristics: job variety, autonomy, responsibility, and interpersonal interaction. The study also found that core job characteristics did not affect all workers in the same way. A person's values, religious beliefs, and ethnic background influenced how the worker responded to the job. Specifically, workers with rural values and workers with strong religious beliefs preferred jobs high in core characteristics, and workers with urban values and those with weaker religious beliefs preferred jobs low in core characteristics. Another study tested the effect of job and work characteristics on employee turnover intentions and found that employees consider both when deciding to leave a company.[21]

Richard Hackman and his colleagues modified the original model by including three critical psychological states of the individual and refining the measurement of core job characteristics. The result is the **Job Characteristics Model** shown in Figure 14.1.[22] The **Job Diagnostic Survey (JDS)**, the most commonly used job design measure, was developed to diagnose jobs by measuring the five core job characteristics and three critical psychological states shown in the model. The core job characteristics stimulate the critical psychological states in the manner shown in Figure 14.1. This results in varying personal and work outcomes, as identified in the figure. A new proposal to modify the job characteristics model suggests that psychological ownership is an important factor in job design.[23]

FIGURE 14.1   THE JOB CHARACTERISTICS MODEL

SOURCE: J. R. Hackman and G. R. Oldham, "The Relationship Among Core Job Dimensions, the Critical Psychological States, and On-the-Job Outcomes," in *The Job Diagnostic Survey: An Instrument for the Diagnosis of Jobs and the Evaluation of Job Redesign Projects* (New Haven, Conn.: Department of Administrative Services, Yale University, 1974). Reprinted by permission of Greg R. Oldham.

Hackman and his colleagues say that the five core job characteristics interact to determine an overall *Motivating Potential Score (MPS)* for a specific job. The MPS indicates a job's potential for motivating incumbents. An individual's MPS is determined by the following equation:

$$MPS = \frac{\left[\begin{array}{c}\text{Skill}\\\text{variety}\end{array}\right] + \left[\begin{array}{c}\text{Task}\\\text{identity}\end{array}\right] + \left[\begin{array}{c}\text{Task}\\\text{significance}\end{array}\right]}{3} [\text{Autonomy}] \times [\text{Feedback}]$$

Job Characteristics Model
A framework for understanding person–job fit through the interaction of core job dimensions with critical psychological states within a person.

Job Diagnostic Survey (JDS) The survey instrument designed to measure the elements in the Job Characteristics Model.

The Job Characteristics Model includes *growth need strength* (the desire to grow and fully develop one's abilities) as a moderator. People with high growth need strength respond favorably to jobs with high MPSs, and individuals with low growth need strength respond less favorably to such jobs. The job characteristics theory further suggests that core job dimensions stimulate three critical psychological states according to the relationships specified in the model. These critical psychological states are defined as follows:

1. *Experienced meaningfulness of the work*, or the degree to which the employee experiences the job as one that is generally meaningful, valuable, and worthwhile.

2. *Experienced responsibility for work outcomes*, or the degree to which the employee feels personally accountable and responsible for the results of the work he or she does.

3. *Knowledge of results*, or the degree to which the employee knows and understands, on a continuous basis, how effectively he or she is performing the job.

In one early study, Hackman and Oldham administered the JDS to 658 employees working on sixty-two different jobs in seven business organizations.[24] The JDS was useful for job redesign efforts through one or more of five implementing concepts: (1) combining tasks into

A_KUDR/Shutterstock.com

FASTFACT

Employment Engagement Is Good for the Economy

A February 2015 Gallup poll found employee engagement in the United States to be at its highest in three years. That's good for the economy. Organizations with larger percentages of employees who are engaged at work experience lower employee turnover, increased productivity, and increased profitability. As the numbers of "engaged" employees grow, organizations are better positioned to grow. When companies grow, so does the economy.

SOURCE: A. Adkins, "U.S. Employee Engagement Reaches Three-Year High," *Gallup Poll Briefing* (March 9, 2015): 1.

Engaged employees, who care about their work, create a positive working environment.

Monkey Business Images/Shutterstock.com

larger jobs, (2) forming natural work teams to increase task identity and task significance, (3) establishing relationships with customers, (4) loading jobs vertically with more responsibility, and/or (5) opening feedback channels for the job incumbent. For example, if an automotive mechanic received little feedback on the quality of repair work performed, one redesign strategy would be to solicit customer feedback one month after each repair.

A recent sequence of two studies conducted in Egypt aimed to disaggregate *work autonomy*, an important component in job design theory.[25] Study 1 included 534 employees in two Egyptian organizations. Study 2 involved 120 managers in four organizations. The results indicated that separate work method, work schedule, and work criteria autonomy were three separate facets of work autonomy.

An alternative to the Job Characteristics Model is the *Job Characteristics Inventory (JCI)* developed by Henry Sims and Andrew Szilagyi.[26] The JCI primarily measures core job characteristics. It is not as comprehensive as the JDS because it does not incorporate critical psychological states, personal and work outcomes, or employee needs. The JCI does give some consideration to structural and individual variables that affect the relationship between core job characteristics and the individual.[27] One comparative analysis of the JCI and JDS found similarities in the measures and in the models' predictions.[28] The comparative analysis also found two differences. First, the variety scales in the two models appear to have different effects on performance. Second, the autonomy scales in the two models appear to have different effects on employee satisfaction. Overall, the JCI and JDS both support the usefulness of a

person–job fit approach to the design of work over the earlier, universal theories.

ENGAGEMENT Psychological conditions related to job design features are a particular concern of the Job Characteristics Model.[29] One study of more than 200 managers and employees in a Midwestern insurance company found that meaningfulness, safety, and availability were three important psychological conditions that affected employees' **engagement** in their jobs and work roles. The extent to which employees are engaged in their jobs has an impact on workplace behaviors. Employees who identify with supervisor goals are less likely to engage in counterproductive behaviors in the workplace, and this relationship operates through employee engagement. The degree to which work engagement functions as a bridge between goal congruence and deviant behaviors depends on the emotional intelligence of employees. Employees with highly developed emotional intelligence skills will be more likely to respond positively to goal congruence.[30] Gallup's Q12 survey was used to improve engagement for a clinical nutrition group at St. Mary's/Duluth Clinic Health System with successful results.[31] Despite its importance to company success, however, only one-third of employees in a recent study reported that they were engaged in their work.[32]

Full engagement requires the strategic management of one's energy in response to the environment.[33] Being fully engaged in one's work role and job can be highly appropriate and yet demand energy, time, and effort. To achieve

> **engagement** The expression of oneself as one performs in work or other roles.

balance and afford opportunity for recovery, there is a commensurate need to strategically and appropriately disengage from one's job and work role on a periodic basis. The effective management of energy in response to one's job and work role leads to both high performance and personal renewal. Thus, while the design of work is important, the human spirit's response to job characteristics and work design features is equally important.

14-3 ALTERNATIVE APPROACHES TO JOB DESIGN

Because each of the traditional job design approaches has limitations, several alternative approaches have emerged over the past couple of decades. This section examines four alternatives that are in the process of being tried and tested. First, it examines the social information-processing model. Second, it reviews ergonomics and the interdisciplinary framework of Michael Campion and Paul Thayer. Their framework builds on traditional job design approaches. Third, this section examines the international perspectives of the Japanese, Germans, and Scandinavians. Finally, it focuses on the health and well-being aspects of work design. Healthy work enables individuals to adapt, function well, and balance work with private life activities.[34] An emerging fifth approach to the design of work through teams and autonomous work groups was addressed in Chapter 9.

14-3a Social Information Processing

The traditional approaches to the design of work emphasize objective core job characteristics. In contrast, the **social information-processing (SIP) model** emphasizes the interpersonal aspects of work design. Specifically, the SIP model says that what others tell us about our jobs is important.[35] The SIP model has four basic premises about the work environment.[36] First, other people provide cues we use to understand the work environment. Second, other people help us judge what is important in our jobs. Third, other people tell us how they see our jobs. Fourth, other people's positive and negative feedback helps us understand our feelings about our jobs. This is very consistent with the dynamic model of the job design process that views it as a social one involving job-holders, supervisors, and peers.[37]

People's perceptions and reactions to their jobs are shaped by information from other people in the work environment.[38] In other words, what others believe about a person's job may be important to understanding the person's perceptions of, and reactions to, the job. This does not mean that objective job characteristics are unimportant; rather, it means that others can modify the way these characteristics affect us. For example, one study of task complexity found that the objective complexity of a task must be distinguished from the subjective task complexity experienced by the employee.[39] Although objective task complexity may be a motivator, the presence of others in the work environment, social interaction, or even daydreaming may be important additional sources of motivation. The SIP model makes an important contribution to the design of work by emphasizing the importance of other people and the social context of work. For example, relational job design may motivate employees to take prosocial action and make a positive difference in other people's lives.[40] In addition, the relational aspects of the work environment may be more important than objective core job characteristics. Therefore, the subjective feedback of other people about how difficult a particular task is may be more important to a person's motivation to perform than an objective estimate of the task's difficulty.

14-3b Ergonomics and Interdisciplinary Framework

Michael Campion and Paul Thayer used **ergonomics** based on engineering, biology, and psychology to develop an interdisciplinary framework for the design of work. Actually, they say that four approaches—the mechanistic, motivational, biological, and perceptual/motor approaches—are necessary because no one approach can solve all performance problems caused by poorly designed jobs. Table 14.2 describes the benefits and limitations of each approach; we will take a closer look at the biological and perceptual/motor approaches below. One ergonomics study of eighty-seven administrative municipal employees found lower levels of upper body pain along with other positive outcomes thanks to the workstation redesign.[41]

The interdisciplinary framework allows the job designer or manager to consider trade-offs and alternatives among the approaches based on desired outcomes. If a manager finds poor performance a problem, for example, the manager should analyze the job to ensure

social information-processing (SIP) model A model that suggests that the important job factors depend in part on what others tell a person about the job.

ergonomics The science of adapting work and working conditions to the employee or worker.

TABLE 14.2 SUMMARY OF OUTCOMES FROM VARIOUS JOB DESIGN APPROACHES

Job Design Approach (Discipline)	Positive Outcomes	Negative Outcomes
Mechanistic Approach (mechanical engineering)	Decreased training time Higher personnel utilization levels Lower likelihood of error Less chance of mental overload Lower stress levels	Lower job satisfaction Lower motivation Higher absenteeism
Motivational Approach (industrial psychology)	Higher job satisfaction Higher motivation Greater job involvement Higher job performance Lower absenteeism	Increased training time Lower personnel utilization levels Greater chance of errors Greater chance of mental overload and stress
Biological Approach (biology)	Less physical effort Less physical fatigue Fewer health complaints Fewer medical incidents Lower absenteeism Higher job satisfaction	Higher financial costs because of changes in equipment or job environment
Perceptual Motor Approach (experimental psychology)	Lower likelihood of error Lower likelihood of accidents Less chance of mental stress Decreased training time Higher personnel utilization levels	Lower job satisfaction Lower motivation

SOURCE: Reprinted from *Organizational Dynamics*, 15(3), Michael A. Campion, Paul W. Thayer, "Job Design: Approaches, Outcomes, and Trade-Offs," Winter/1987. Copyright © 1987, with permission from Elsevier.

a design aimed at improving performance. The interdisciplinary framework is important because badly designed jobs cause far more performance problems than managers realize.[42]

The *biological approach* to job design emphasizes the person's interaction with physical aspects of the work environment and is concerned with the amount of physical exertion, such as lifting and muscular effort, required by the position. For example, an analysis of medical claims at TXI's Chaparral Steel Company identified lower back pain as the most common physical problem experienced by steel workers and managers alike. As a result, the company instituted an education and exercise program under expert guidance to improve employees' lower back care. Program graduates received back cushions for their chairs with "Chaparral Steel Company" embossed on them.[43]

The *perceptual/motor approach* to job design also emphasizes the person's interaction with physical aspects of the work environment and is based on engineering that considers human factors such as strength or coordination, ergonomics, and experimental psychology. It places an important emphasis on human interaction with computers, information, and other operational systems. This approach addresses how people mentally process information acquired from the physical work environment through perceptual and motor skills. The approach emphasizes perception and fine motor skills as opposed to the gross motor skills and muscle strength emphasized in the *mechanistic approach*. The perceptual/motor approach is more likely to be relevant to operational and technical work, such as keyboard operations and data entry jobs, which may tax a person's concentration and attention, than to managerial, administrative, and custodial jobs, which are less likely to strain concentration and attention.

One study using the interdisciplinary framework to improve jobs evaluated 377 clerical, 80 managerial, and 90 analytical positions.[44] The jobs were improved by combining tasks and adding ancillary duties. The improved jobs provided greater motivation for the incumbents and were better from a perceptual/motor standpoint. The jobs were poorly designed from a mechanical engineering standpoint, however, and they were unaffected from a biological standpoint. Again, the interdisciplinary framework considers trade-offs and alternatives when evaluating job redesign efforts. Table 14.2 presents a summary of the positive and negative outcomes of redesign.

14-3c International Perspectives on the Design of Work

Each culture has a unique way of understanding and designing work.[45] As organizations become more global and international, an appreciation of the perspectives of others is increasingly important. A study of 2,359 call centers in sixteen countries found that an organization's management strategy and operational context influences variation in work design.[46] The Japanese, Germans, and

Japanese success with lean production has drawn the attention of managers.

Scandinavians in particular have distinctive perspectives on the design and organization of work.[47] Each of these cultures has a perspective forged within its unique cultural and economic system, and each is distinct from the approaches used in North America.

THE JAPANESE APPROACH The Japanese began harnessing their productive energies during the 1950s by drawing on the product quality ideas of W. Edwards Deming.[48] In addition, the central government became actively involved in the economic resurgence of Japan, and it encouraged companies to conquer industries rather than to maximize profits.[49] Such an industrial policy, built on the Japanese cultural ethic of collectivism, has implications for how work is done. Whereas Frederick Taylor and his successors in the United States emphasized the job of an individual worker, the Japanese system emphasizes the strategic level and encourages collective and cooperative working arrangements.[50] Also, the Japanese emphasize performance, accountability, and other- or self-directedness in defining work, whereas Americans emphasize the positive affect, personal identity, and social benefits of work.

Japanese success with lean production has drawn the attention of managers. **Lean production** methods are similar to the production concept of **sociotechnical systems (STS)**, although there are some differences.[51] In particular, STS gives greater emphasis to (1) teamwork and self-managed and autonomous work groups, (2) the ongoing nature of the design process, and (3) human values in the work process. The approaches are similar, however, in that both differ from Taylor's scientific management and both emphasize job variety, feedback to work groups and teams, support of human resources, and control of production variance close to the point of origin. One three-year evaluation of lean teams, assembly lines, and workflow formalization as lean production practices conducted in Australia found that employees in all lean production groups were negatively affected, with the assembly line employees experiencing the worst effects.[52]

THE GERMAN APPROACH The German approach to work has been shaped by Germany's unique educational system, cultural values, and economic system. The Germans are a highly educated and well-organized people. For example, their educational system has a multitrack design with technical and university alternatives. The German economic system puts a strong emphasis on free enterprise, private property rights, and management–labor cooperation. A comparison of voluntary and mandated management–labor cooperation in Germany found that productivity was superior under voluntary cooperation.[53] The Germans value hierarchy and authority relationships and, as a result, are generally disciplined.[54] Germany's workers are highly unionized, and their discipline and efficiency have enabled Germany to be highly productive while its workers labor substantially fewer hours than do Americans.

The traditional German approach to work design was **technocentric**, an approach that placed technology and engineering at the center of job design decisions. Recently, German industrial engineers have moved to a more **anthropocentric** approach, which places human considerations at the center of job design decisions. The former approach uses a natural scientific process in the design of work, whereas the latter relies on a more humanistic process, as shown in Figure 14.2. In the anthropocentric approach, work is evaluated using the criteria of practicability and worker satisfaction at the individual level and the criteria of endurability and acceptability at the group level. Figure 14.2 also identifies problem areas and disciplines concerned with each aspect of the work design.

THE SCANDINAVIAN APPROACH The Scandinavian cultural values and economic system stand in contrast

lean production Using committed employees with ever expanding responsibilities to achieve zero waste and 100% good product, delivered on time, every time.

sociotechnical systems (STS) Giving equal attention to technical and social considerations in job design.

technocentric Placing technology and engineering at the center of job design decisions.

anthropocentric Placing human considerations at the center of job design decisions.

FIGURE 14.2 HIERARCHICAL MODEL OF CRITERIA FOR THE EVALUATION OF HUMAN WORK

Scientific approaches of labor sciences	Levels of evaluation of human work	Problem areas and assignment to disciplines
View from natural science — Primarily oriented to individuals ← Primarily oriented to groups — View from cultural studies	Practicability	Technical, anthropometric, and psychophysical problems (ergonomics)
	Endurability	Technical, physiological, and medical problems (ergonomics and occupational health)
	Acceptability	Economical and sociological problems (occupational psychology and sociology, personnel management)
	Satisfaction	Sociopsychological and economic problems (occupational psychology and sociology, personnel management)

SOURCE: H. Luczak, "'Good Work' Design: An Ergonomic, Industrial Engineering Perspective," in J. C. Quick, L. R. Murphy, and J. J. Hurrell, eds., *Stress and Well-Being at Work* (Washington, D.C.: American Psychological Association, 1997). Copyright © 1997 by the American Psychological Association. Reprinted with permission.

to the German system. The social democratic tradition in Scandinavia has emphasized social concern rather than industrial efficiency. Accordingly, the Scandinavians place great emphasis on a work design model that encourages a high degree of worker control and good social support systems for workers.[55] Lennart Levi believes that circumstantial and inferential scientific evidence provides a sufficiently strong basis for legislative and policy actions for redesigns aimed at enhancing worker well-being. An example of such an action for promoting good working environments and occupational health was Swedish Government Bill 1976/77:149, which stated, "Work should be safe both physically and mentally *but also* provide opportunities for involvement, job satisfaction, and personal development." In 1991, the Swedish Parliament set up the Swedish Working Life Fund to fund research, intervention programs, and demonstration projects in work design. For example, a study of Stockholm police on shift schedules found that going from a daily, counterclockwise rotation to a clockwise rotation was more compatible with human biology and resulted in improved sleep, less fatigue, lower systolic blood pressure, and lower blood levels of triglycerides and glucose.[56] Hence, the work redesign improved the police officers' health.

14-3d Work Design and Well-Being

An international group of scholars, including American social scientists, has been concerned about designing work and jobs that are both healthy and productive.[57] Economic and industry-specific upheavals in the United States during the 1990s led to job loss and unemployment, and the adverse health impact of these factors has received attention.[58] Attention has also been devoted to the effects of specific work design parameters on psychological health.[59] For example, by mixing cognitively challenging and "mindless" work throughout the day, one may reduce pressures from chronic overwork and enhance creativity. In addition, task/job design can be improved by enhancing core job characteristics and not patterning service work after assembly line work. Frank Landy believes that organizations should redesign jobs to increase worker control and reduce worker uncertainty, while at the same time managing conflict and task/job demands. In instances where organizations allow employees to craft their own jobs by adjusting task demands or resources, it is important to realize the potential negative effects of job crafting practices on the workloads of other coworkers.[60]

Task uncertainty was shown to have an adverse effect on morale in a study of 629 employment security work units in California and Wisconsin.[61] More important, the study showed that morale was better predicted by considering both the overall design of the work unit and the task uncertainty. This study suggests that if one work design parameter, such as task uncertainty, is a problem in a job, its adverse effects on people may be mitigated by other work design parameters. For example, higher pay may offset an employee's frustration with a difficult coworker, or a friendly, supportive working environment may offset frustration with low pay. See Table 14.3 for more information on increasing control, reducing uncertainty, and managing conflict.

TABLE 14.3 ADJUSTING WORK DESIGN PARAMETERS

Increase control by:	Reduce uncertainty by:	Manage conflict through:
> Giving workers the opportunity to control several aspects of the work and the workplace	> Providing employees with timely and complete information needed for their work	> Participative decision making
> Designing machines and tasks with optimal response times and/or ranges	> Making clear and unambiguous work assignments	> Supportive supervisory styles
> Implementing performance-monitoring systems as a source of relevant feedback to workers	> Improving communication at shift change time	> Having sufficient resources available to meet work demands, thus preventing conflict
	> Increasing employee access to information sources	

© Cengage Learning

14-4 CONTEMPORARY ISSUES IN THE DESIGN OF WORK

A number of contemporary issues related to specific aspects of the design of work have an effect on increasing numbers of employees. Rather than addressing job design or worker well-being in a comprehensive way, these issues—telecommuting, alternative work patterns, technostress, and skill development—address one or another aspect of a job. One study found that employees stay motivated when their work is relationally designed to provide opportunities for respectful contact with those critical to their work.[62] Telecommuting and alternative work patterns such as job sharing can increase employee flexibility. Flexible work arrangements have also been linked to increased employee retention in developing countries. For example, one study of Malaysian banking employees found that allowing workers to participate in flexible work arrangements increased the likelihood that they would remain in their jobs once minimum salary requirements had been met.[63] Companies use job sharing, flextime, and other approaches to the design of work as ways to manage a growing business while contributing to a better balance of work and family life for employees.

14-4a Telecommuting

Telecommuting, as noted in Chapter 2, is when employees work at home or in other locations geographically separate from their company's main location. An estimated 28 million Americans telecommute.

Telecommuting may entail working in a combination of home, satellite office, and main office locations. This flexible arrangement is designed to achieve a better fit between the needs of the individual employee and the organization's task demands. A recent study found that telecommuting had positive benefits on task performance primarily through increased employee perceptions of autonomy.[64]

Telecommuting has been around since the 1970s but was slower to catch on than some expected.[65] This was due to confusion and scheduling errors.[66] Actually, with a greater emphasis on managing the work rather than the worker, managers can enhance control, effectively decentralize, and even encourage teamwork through telecommuting. A number of companies, such as AT&T

AT&T has a telecommuting plan in place for a number of its employees.

Rob Wilson/Shutterstock.com

in Phoenix and Verizon Communications, have programs in telecommuting for a wide range of employees. These flexible arrangements help some companies respond to changing demographics and a shrinking labor pool. The Travelers Group (now part of Citigroup) was one of the first companies to try telecommuting and was considered an industry leader in the practice. Because of its confidence in its employees, Travelers reaped significant rewards from telecommuting, including higher productivity, reduced absenteeism, expanded opportunities for workers with disabilities, and an increased ability to attract and retain talent.[67]

Pacific Bell (now part of AT&T) tried telecommuting on a large scale.[68] In 1990, Pacific Bell had 1,500 managers who telecommuted. For example, an information systems designer might work at home four days a week and spend one day a week at the main office location in meetings, work exchanges, and coordination with others. Of 3,000 Pacific Bell managers responding to a mail survey, 87% said telecommuting would reduce employee stress, 70% said it would increase job satisfaction while reducing absenteeism, and 64% said it would increase productivity.

However, telecommuting is neither a cure-all nor a universally feasible alternative. A recent study showed that the employees who were most satisfied with telecommuting were those who were comfortable with technology and had more experience within the organization.[69] Many telecommuters feel a sense of social isolation. Some executives are concerned that while telecommuters are more productive, their lack of visibility may hold back their careers. Furthermore, not all forms of work are amenable to telecommuting. For example, firefighters and police officers must be at their duty stations to be successful in their work. Employees for whom telecommuting is not a viable option within a company may feel jealous of those able to telecommute.

14-4b Alternative Work Patterns

Job sharing is an alternative work pattern in which more than one person occupies a single job. As an alternative to telecommuting and a way of addressing demographic and labor pool concerns, job sharing is found throughout a wide range of managerial and professional jobs as well as production and service jobs. It is not common among senior executives.

The *four-day workweek* is a second type of alternative work schedule. Information systems personnel at the United Services Automobile Association (USAA) in San Antonio, Texas, work four ten-hour

All Roles Can Flex

Australian telecommunications and information services firm, Telstra Corporation, employs more than 34,000 employees in more than 15 countries including the UK, the United States, Hong Kong, New Zealand, and China. Like other organizations, Telstra has had to respond to the changing workplace demographics and increasing employee requests for flexible work arrangements. Like other organizations, Telstra met employee requests with empathy yet reiterating the stark reality that certain jobs had to be performed during specific hours during the workday. That was before Telstra piloted its "All Roles Flex" job design approach in 2013. "All Roles Flex" assumes that every job can be performed with flexibility built in. In fact, Telstra expects its managers to use the assumption that all job roles can flex as the starting point for job design. Rather than provide reasons why a job cannot be performed flexibly, Telstra's managers are asked to demonstrate why a job cannot be done flexibly. Telstra's unconventional approach to flexible work arrangements has resulted in increased employee engagement and 84% of its employees saying they have the flexibility they need in their jobs. Telstra's job design approach has also been good for diversifying its workforce. Since implementing "All Roles Flex," Telstra has seen an increase in its ability to recruit women into mid- and senior-level positions.

SOURCE: D. Thodey, "All Roles Flex," *McKinsey Quarterly* 4 (2014): 108; "Telstra Corporation Limited," *MarketLine Company Profile* (March 2015): 1–33.

days and enjoy a three-day weekend. This arrangement provides the benefit of more time for those who want to balance work and family life through weekend travel. However, the longer workdays may be a drawback for employees with many family or social activities on weekday evenings. Hence, the four-day workweek has both benefits and limitations.

In **flextime**, a third alternative work pattern, employees set their own daily work schedules. Companies in highly concentrated urban areas, such as Houston, Los Angeles, and New York City, may allow employees to set their own daily work schedules as long as they start their eight hours at any thirty-minute interval between 6:00 A.M. and 9:00 A.M. This arrangement is designed to ease traffic and commuting pressures. It is

job sharing An alternative work pattern in which more than one person occupies a single job.

flextime An alternative work pattern that enables employees to set their own daily work schedules.

also responsive to individual biorhythms, allowing early risers to go to work early and nighthawks to work late. Even in companies without formal programs, flextime may be an individual option arranged between supervisor and subordinate. For example, a first-line supervisor who wants to complete a college degree may negotiate a work schedule accommodating both job requirements and course schedules.

Flextime has been applied in numerous ways in work organizations, but may be offered more often to high performers who assure their bosses that work quality and productivity will not suffer.[70] Although flextime can lead to reduced absenteeism, on the cautionary side, one study found that a woman on a flexible work schedule was perceived to have less job–career dedication and less advancement motivation, though no less ability.[71]

14-4c Technology at Work

New technologies and electronic commerce are here to stay and are changing the face of work environments, dramatically in some cases. For instance, increased technology can blur the lines between work and home. A common practice for many employers is to provide employees with company-sponsored cell phones. Whether the daily use of cell phones outside normal work hours leads to work-home interference depends on perceived supervisor expectations and employee engagement.[72] Many government jobs are expected to change, and even disappear, with the advent of e-government using the Internet. The concept involves work being where people are, rather than people moving to where the work is. New technologies make connectivity, collaboration, and communication easy. Critical voice mails and messages can be delivered to and from the central office, a client's office, the airport, the car, or home. Wireless Internet access and online meeting software such as WebEx make it possible for employees to participate in meetings anywhere, any time.

As a force for change, new technology is a double-edged sword that can be used to improve job performance or to create stress. On the positive side, modern technologies are helping to revolutionize the way jobs are designed and the way work gets done. The **virtual office** is a mobile platform of computer, telecommunication, and information technology and services that allows mobile workforce members to conduct business virtually anywhere, anytime. While virtual offices have benefits, they may also lead to a lack of social connection or to **technostress**, which is stress caused by new and advancing technologies, most often information technologies, in the workplace.[73] For example, the widespread use of web forums or blogs as a source for rumors of layoffs may cause feelings of uncertainty and anxiety (technostress). However, the same electronic bulletin boards can be an important source of information and thus reduce uncertainty for workers.

New information technologies enable organizations to monitor employee work performance, even when the employee is not aware of the monitoring.[74] These new technologies also allow organizations to tie pay to performance because performance is electronically monitored.[75] Three guidelines can help make electronic workplace monitoring, especially of performance, less stressful: First, workers should participate in the introduction of the monitoring system. Second, performance standards should be seen as fair. Third, performance records should be used to improve performance, not to punish the performer. In the extreme, new technologies that allow for virtual work in remote locations take employees beyond such monitoring.[76]

14-4d Skill Development

Problems in work system design are often seen as the source of frustration for those dealing with technostress.[77] However, system and technical problems are not the only sources of technostress in new information technologies. Some experts see a growing gap between the skills demanded by new technologies and the skills possessed by employees in jobs using these technologies.[78] Although technical skills are important and are emphasized in many training programs, the largest sector of the economy is actually service-oriented, and service jobs require interpersonal skills. Managers also need a wide range of nontechnical skills to be effective in their work.[79] Therefore, any discussion of jobs and the design of work must recognize the importance of incumbent skills and abilities to meet the demands of the work. Organizations must consider the talents and skills of their employees when they engage in job design efforts. The two issues of employee skill development and job design are interrelated. The knowledge and information requirements for jobs of the future are especially high.

virtual office A mobile platform of computer, telecommunication, and information technology and services.

technostress The stress caused by new and advancing technologies in the workplace.

STUDY TOOLS 14

LOCATED AT BACK OF THE TEXTBOOK

☐ Rip out chapter review card

LOCATED AT WWW.CENGAGE.COM/LOGIN

☐ Track your knowledge and understanding of key concepts in business using 4LTR Press Online

☐ Review key term flashcards and create your own using StudyBits

☐ Create and complete practice quizzes based off of your notes and StudyBits

☐ Complete Online activities such as Matching and Fill-in-the-Blank exercises

☐ View chapter highlight box content, including the chapter videos, key exhibits and executive profiles.

15 | Organizational Design and Structure

Raywoo/Shutterstock.com

LEARNING OUTCOMES

15-1 Define differentiation and integration as organizational design processes.

15-2 Discuss the basic design dimensions managers must consider in structuring an organization.

15-3 Describe five structural configurations for organizations.

15-4 Describe four contextual variables that influence organizational structure.

15-5 Explain the forces reshaping organizations.

15-6 Identify and describe emerging organizational structures.

15-7 Identify factors that can adversely affect organizational structure.

After finishing this chapter go to **PAGE 256** for **STUDY TOOLS.**

Organizational design is the process of constructing and adjusting an organization's structure to achieve its business strategy and goals. The design process begins with the organization's goals. These goals are broken into tasks, or pieces of work, as the basis for jobs, as discussed in Chapter 14. Jobs are grouped into departments, and departments are linked to form the **organizational structure**.

15-1 KEY ORGANIZATIONAL DESIGN PROCESSES

Differentiation, which will be defined in more detail shortly, can be described as the design process of breaking organizational goals into tasks. *Integration*, also defined in more detail shortly, can then be considered the design process of linking the tasks together to form a structure that supports goal accomplishment. These two processes are the keys to successful organizational design. The organizational structure is designed to prevent chaos through an orderly set of reporting relationships and communication channels. Understanding the key design processes and organizational structure helps a person understand the larger working environment and may prevent confusion in the organization.

The *organization chart* is the most visible representation of the organization's structure and underlying components. Figure 15.1 is the organizational chart for the World Trade Organization. Most organizations have a series of organization charts showing reporting relationships throughout the system. The underlying components are (1) formal lines of authority and responsibility (the organizational structure designates reporting relationships by the way jobs and departments are grouped) and (2) formal systems of communication, coordination, and integration (the organizational structure designates the expected patterns of formal interaction among employees).[1]

15-1a Differentiation

Differentiation is the process of deciding how to divide the work in an organization.[2] Differentiation ensures that all essential organizational tasks are assigned to one or more jobs and that the tasks receive the attention they need. Many dimensions of differentiation have been considered in organizations. Lawrence and Lorsch found four dimensions of differentiation in one study: (1) manager's goal orientation, (2) time orientation, (3) interpersonal orientation, and (4) formality of structure.[3] Three different forms of differentiation are horizontal, vertical, and spatial.

HORIZONTAL DIFFERENTIATION Horizontal differentiation is the degree of differentiation between organizational subunits and is based on employees' specialized knowledge, education, or training. For example, two university professors who teach specialized subjects in different academic departments are subject to horizontal differentiation. Horizontal differentiation increases with specialization and departmentalization.

Specialization refers to the particular grouping of activities performed by an individual.[4] The degree of specialization, or the division of labor, in the organization gives an indication of how much training is needed for various jobs, what the scope of various jobs is, and what individual characteristics are needed for job holders. Specialization can lead to the development of a specialized vocabulary, as well as other behavioral norms. As the two college professors specialize in their subjects, abbreviations or acronyms take on unique meanings. For example, OB means "organizational behavior" to a professor of management but "obstetrics" to a professor of medicine.

Usually, the more specialized the jobs within an organization, the more departments are differentiated within that organization (in other words, the greater is the *departmentalization*). Departmentalization can be by function, product, service, client, geography, process, or some combination of these. A large organization may departmentalize its structure using some or all of these methods at different levels of the organization. For example, the U.S. Army Reserve changed its departmentalization first from divisional

> Differentiation and integration are the keys to successful organizational design.

Danielala/Shutterstock.com

organizational design
The process of constructing and adjusting an organization's structure to achieve its business strategy and goals.

organizational structure
The linking of departments and jobs within an organization.

differentiation The process of deciding how to divide the work in an organization.

FIGURE 15.1 ORGANIZATION

WTO structure

All WTO members may participate in all councils, committees, etc., except Appellate Body, Dispute Settlement panels, Textiles Monitoring Body, and plurilateral committees.

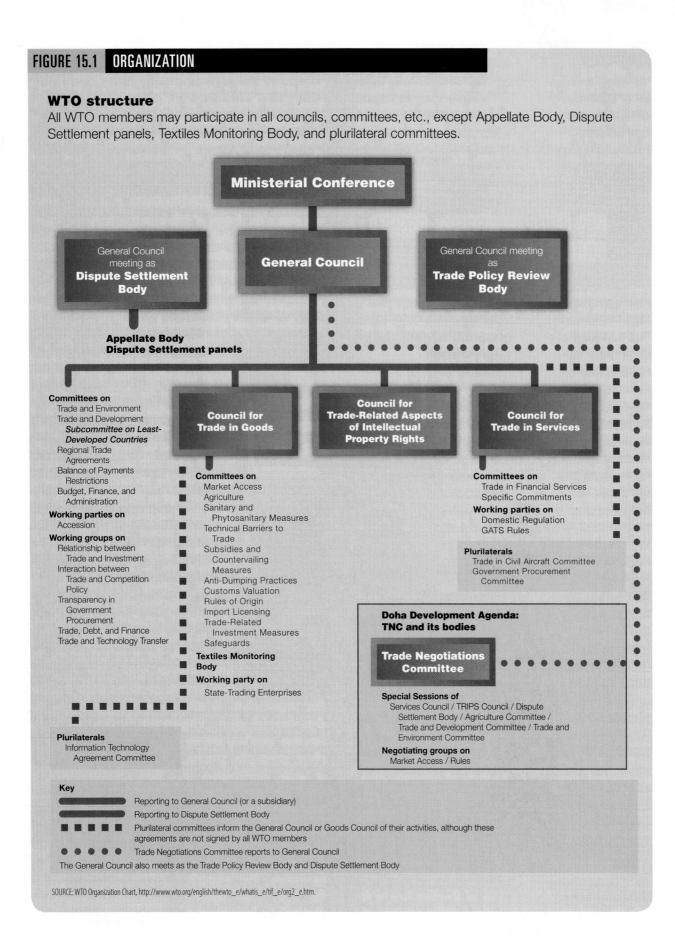

Ministerial Conference

General Council meeting as **Dispute Settlement Body**

General Council

General Council meeting as **Trade Policy Review Body**

Appellate Body
Dispute Settlement panels

Committees on
Trade and Environment
Trade and Development
Subcommittee on Least-Developed Countries
Regional Trade Agreements
Balance of Payments Restrictions
Budget, Finance, and Administration

Working parties on
Accession

Working groups on
Relationship between Trade and Investment
Interaction between Trade and Competition Policy
Transparency in Government Procurement
Trade, Debt, and Finance
Trade and Technology Transfer

Plurilaterals
Information Technology Agreement Committee

Council for Trade in Goods

■ **Committees on**
Market Access
Agriculture
Sanitary and Phytosanitary Measures
Technical Barriers to Trade
Subsidies and Countervailing Measures
Anti-Dumping Practices
Customs Valuation
Rules of Origin
Import Licensing
Trade-Related Investment Measures
Safeguards
■ **Textiles Monitoring Body**
■ **Working party on**
State-Trading Enterprises

Council for Trade-Related Aspects of Intellectual Property Rights

Council for Trade in Services

Committees on
Trade in Financial Services
Specific Commitments
Working parties on
Domestic Regulation
GATS Rules

Plurilaterals
Trade in Civil Aircraft Committee
Government Procurement Committee

Doha Development Agenda: TNC and its bodies

Trade Negotiations Committee

Special Sessions of
Services Council / TRIPS Council / Dispute Settlement Body / Agriculture Committee / Trade and Development Committee / Trade and Environment Committee
Negotiating groups on
Market Access / Rules

Key

Reporting to General Council (or a subsidiary)

Reporting to Dispute Settlement Body

■ ■ ■ ■ ■ Plurilateral committees inform the General Council or Goods Council of their activities, although these agreements are not signed by all WTO members

● ● ● ● ● Trade Negotiations Committee reports to General Council

The General Council also meets as the Trade Policy Review Body and Dispute Settlement Body

SOURCE: WTO Organization Chart, http://www.wto.org/english/thewto_e/whatis_e/tif_e/org2_e.htm.

to an operational strategic reserve and then to an operational force structure.[5]

VERTICAL DIFFERENTIATION Vertical differentiation is the difference in authority and responsibility in the organizational hierarchy. Vertical differentiation occurs, for example, between a chief executive and a maintenance supervisor. Tall, narrow organizations have greater vertical differentiation, and flat, wide organizations have less vertical differentiation. The height of the organization is also influenced by level of horizontal differentiation and span of control. The *span of control* refers to and defines the number of subordinates a manager can and should supervise.[6]

Tall structures—those with narrow spans of control—tend to be characterized by closer supervision and tighter controls. In addition, the communication becomes more burdensome, since directives and information must be passed through more layers. The banking industry has often had tall structures. *Flat structures*—those with wider spans of control—have simpler communication chains and reduced promotion opportunities due to fewer levels of management. Sears is an example of an organization that has gone to a flat structure. With the loss of more than a million middle management positions, many organizations are now flatter. The degree of vertical differentiation affects organizational effectiveness, but there is no strong evidence that flatter or taller organizations are better.[7] Organizational size, type of jobs, skills and personal characteristics of employees, and degree of freedom must all be considered in determining organizational effectiveness.[8]

SPATIAL DIFFERENTIATION Spatial differentiation is the geographic dispersion of an organization's offices, plants, and personnel. A salesperson who works in New York for a company based in Portland experiences spatial differentiation. An increase in the number of locations increases the complexity of organizational design because of spatial differentiation but may be necessary for organizational goal achievement or organizational protection. For example, if an organization wants to expand into a different country, it may be best to form a separate subsidiary that is partially owned and managed by citizens of that country. Few U.S. citizens think of Shell Oil Company as being a subsidiary of Royal Dutch/Shell Group, a company whose international headquarters is in the Netherlands. Spatial differentiation may give an organization political and legal advantages in a country because it is identified as a local company.

IMPLICATIONS OF DIFFERENTIATION Horizontal, vertical, and spatial differentiation indicate the amount of width, height, and breadth an organizational structure needs. Just because an organization is highly differentiated along one of these dimensions does not mean it must be highly differentiated along the others. The university environment, for example, is generally characterized by great horizontal differentiation but relatively little vertical and spatial differentiation. By contrast, a company such as Coca-Cola is characterized by a great deal of all three types of differentiation.

The more structurally differentiated an organization is, the more complex it is.[9] *Complexity* refers to the number of activities, subunits, or subsystems within the organization. Lawrence and Lorsch suggest that an organization's complexity should mirror the complexity of its environment. As the complexity of an organization increases, its need for mechanisms to link and coordinate the differentiated parts also increases. If these links do not exist, the departments or differentiated parts of the organization can lose sight of the organization's larger mission, and the organization runs the risk of chaos. Chaos is not inevitable, however, as research suggests that environmental complexity may be viewed as a "puzzle" that, if understood correctly, increases competence and increases organizational learning.[10]

15-1b Integration

To be effective, organizations must design and build linkage and coordination mechanisms. This process of coordinating the different parts of the

Songquan Deng/Shutterstock.com

organization is known as **integration**. Integration mechanisms are designed to achieve unity among individuals and groups in various jobs, departments, and divisions in the accomplishment of organizational goals and tasks.[11] Effective integration helps keep the organization in a state of *dynamic equilibrium*, a condition in which all the parts of the organization are interrelated and balanced.

To integrate activities up and down the organizational chain of command, a variety of structural devices can be used to achieve *vertical linkages*. These devices include hierarchical referral, rules and procedures, plans and schedules, positions added to the structure of the organization, and management information systems.[12] On an organization chart, the vertical lines indicate these vertical linkages, showing the lines of hierarchical referral up and down the organization. When employees do not know how to solve a problem, they can refer it upward for consideration and resolution. Work that needs to be assigned is usually delegated downward.

Rules and procedures, as well as plans and schedules, provide standing information for employees without direct communication. These vertical integrators, such as an employee handbook, communicate to employees standard information, or information that they can understand on their own. Such integrators allow managers to have wider spans of control because they do not have to inform each employee of what is expected and when it is expected. Vertical integrators encourage managers to use *management by exception*—to make decisions when employees bring problems up the hierarchy. Military organizations depend heavily on vertical linkages, having a well-defined chain of command. Certain duties are expected to be carried out, and proper paperwork is to be in place. In times of crisis, however, much more information is processed, and the proper paperwork becomes secondary to getting the job done. Vertical linkages help individuals understand their roles in the organization, especially in times of crisis.

Adding positions to the hierarchy is used as a vertical integrator when a manager becomes overloaded by hierarchical referral or problems arise in the chain of command. Positions such as "assistant to" may be added, or another level may be added. Such additions often reflect an organization's growth and increasing complexity. This action tends to reduce the span of control, thus allowing more communication and closer supervision.

Generally, the taller the organization, the more vertical integration mechanisms are needed. This is because the chains of command and communication are longer. Additional length requires more linkages to minimize the potential for misunderstandings and miscommunications.

integration The process of coordinating the different parts of an organization.

McDonald's Changes Its Structure to Respond Better to Customers

McDonald's processes are among the most highly standardized of all fast-food restaurants. However, a review of its task environment led the fast-food giant to create a new U.S. organizational structure that pushed decision-making about menu items and other marketing decisions closer to its customers. The new structure was highlighted by the creation of four zones organized around local consumer tastes and preferences: Northeast, South, Central, and West. The new zone structure replaced its three-division structure that rolled out new products from north to south, despite regional preferences. For example, when the restaurant introduced sweet tea to its menu, it did so for customers in Minnesota and Louisiana alike since both states fell in what was formerly McDonald's Central division. According to U.S. president Mike Andres, the new zones gave local markets more autonomy to roll out locally relevant products. Andres wrote in his communication to employees about the reorganization, "You've told us there are too many layers, redundancies in planning and communication, competing priorities, barriers to efficient decision making, and too much talking to ourselves instead of to and about our customers." The new zone structure was McDonald's response to employee and customer concerns.

SOURCE: J. Jargon, "McDonald's Plans to Change U.S. Structure: Organizational Moves Intended to Bring Fast-Food Chain Closer to Consumers," *The Wall Street Journal* (October 30, 2014).

Horizontal integration mechanisms provide the communication and coordination that are necessary for links across jobs and departments in the organization. The need for horizontal integration mechanisms increases as the complexity of the organization increases. These linkages are built into the design of the organization by including liaison roles, task forces, integrator positions, and teams.

A *liaison role* is created when a person in one department or area of the organization has the responsibility for coordinating with another department (e.g., a liaison between the engineering and production departments). *Task forces* are temporary committees composed of representatives from multiple departments who assemble to address a specific problem affecting these departments.[13]

A stronger device for integration is to develop a person or department designed to be an *integrator*. In most organizations, the integrator has a good deal of responsibility but not much authority. Such an individual must have the ability to get people together to resolve differences within the perspective of organizational goals.[14]

The strongest method of horizontal integration is through *teams*. Horizontal teams cut across existing lines of organizational structure to create new entities that make organizational decisions. An example of this may occur in product development with the formation of a team that includes marketing, research, design, and production personnel. Ford used such a cross-functional team to develop the Taurus automobile, which was designed to restore the company's market share in the United States. The information exchanged by such a product development team should lead to a product that is acceptable to a wider range of organizational groups, as well as to customers.[15]

The use of these linkage mechanisms varies from organization to organization, as well as within areas of the same organization. In general, the flatter the organization, the more necessary are horizontal integration mechanisms.

 15-2 BASIC DESIGN DIMENSIONS

Differentiation, then, is the process of dividing work in the organization, and integration is the process of coordinating work in the organization. From a structural perspective, every manager and organization looks for the best combination of differentiation and integration for accomplishing the goals of the organization. There are many ways to approach this process. One way is to establish a desired level of each structural dimension on a high-to-low continuum and then develop a structure that meets the desired configuration. These structural dimensions include the following:

1. **Formalization**. The degree to which an employee's role is defined by formal documentation (procedures, job descriptions, manuals, and regulations).

2. **Centralization**. The extent to which decision-making authority has been delegated to lower levels of an organization. An organization is centralized if the decisions are made at the top of the organization and decentralized if decision making is pushed down to lower levels in the organization.

3. **Specialization**. The degree to which organizational tasks are subdivided into separate jobs. The division of labor and the degree to which formal job descriptions spell out job requirements indicate the level of specialization in the organization.

4. **Standardization**. The extent to which work activities are described and performed routinely in the same way. Highly standardized organizations have little variation in the defining of jobs.

5. **Complexity**. The number of activities within the organization and the amount of differentiation needed within the organization.

6. **Hierarchy of authority**. The degree of vertical differentiation through reporting relationships and the span of control within the structure of the organization.[16]

An organization that is high in formalization, centralization, specialization, standardization, and complexity and has a tall hierarchy of authority is said to be highly *bureaucratic*. Bureaucracies are not inherently bad; however, they are often tainted by abuse and red tape. There are cases, however, where centralized structures can be beneficial. For example, one study found that a more centralized structure is effective

formalization The degree to which the organization has official rules, regulations, and procedures.

centralization The degree to which decisions are made at the top of the organization.

specialization The degree to which jobs are narrowly defined and depend on unique expertise.

standardization The degree to which work activities are accomplished in a routine fashion.

complexity The degree to which many different types of activities occur in the organization.

hierarchy of authority The degree of vertical differentiation across levels of management.

for increased job satisfaction when perceptions of interactional and procedural justice are present.[17] A recent study of 1,000 U.S. firms found that centralized firms had the highest levels of research investments and owned more patents per R&D dollars.[18]

An organization that is on the opposite end of each of these continua is very flexible and loose. Control is very hard to implement and maintain in such an organization, but at certain times such a structure is appropriate. The research and development departments in many organizations are often more flexible than other departments in order to stimulate creativity. An important organizational variable for such flexible structures is trust.

Another approach to the process of accomplishing organizational goals is to describe what is and is not important to the success of the organization rather than worry about specific characteristics. Henry Mintzberg argued that the following questions can guide managers in designing formal structures that fit each organization's unique set of circumstances:

1. How many tasks should a given position in the organization contain, and how specialized should each task be?

2. How standardized should the work content of each position be?

3. What skills, abilities, knowledge, and training should be required for each position?

4. What should be the basis for the grouping of positions within the organization into units, departments, divisions, and so on?

5. How large should each unit be, and what should the span of control be (i.e., how many individuals should report to each manager)?

6. How much standardization should be required in the output of each position?

7. What mechanisms should be established to help individuals in different positions and units adjust to the needs of other individuals?

8. How centralized or decentralized should decision-making power be in the chain of authority? Should most of the decisions be made at the top of the organization (centralized) or be made down in the chain of authority (decentralized)?[19]

The manager who can answer these questions has a good understanding of how the organization should implement the basic structural dimensions. These basic design dimensions act in combination with one another and are not entirely independent characteristics of an organization.

15-3 FIVE STRUCTURAL CONFIGURATIONS

Differentiation, integration, and the basic design dimensions combine to yield various structural configurations. Very early organization structures were often either based on product or function. The *matrix organization* structure merged these two ways of organizing.[20] Mintzberg moved beyond these early approaches and proposed five structural configurations: the simple structure, the machine bureaucracy, the professional bureaucracy, the divisionalized form, and the adhocracy.[21] Table 15.1 shows the prime coordinating mechanism, the key part of the organization, and the type of decentralization for each of these structural configurations. The five basic parts of the organization, for Mintzberg, are the upper echelon, or strategic apex; the middle level, or middle line; the operating core, where work is accomplished; the technical staff, or technostructure; and the support staff. Figure 15.2 depicts these five basic parts with a small strategic apex, connected by a flaring middle line to a large, flat operating core. Each configuration affects people in the organization somewhat differently, and all organizational structures should support the firm's strategic goals.

TABLE 15.1	**FIVE STRUCTURAL CONFIGURATIONS OF ORGANIZATIONS**		
Structural Configuration	**Prime Coordinating Mechanism**	**Key Part of Organization**	**Type of Decentralization**
Simple structure	Direct supervision	Upper echelon	Centralization
Machine bureaucracy	Standardization of work processes	Technical staff	Limited horizontal decentralization
Professional bureaucracy	Standardization of skills	Operating level	Vertical and horizontal decentralization
Divisionalized form	Standardization of outputs	Middle level	Limited vertical decentralization
Adhocracy	Mutual adjustment	Support staff	Selective decentralization

SOURCE: Mintzberg, Henry, *Structuring of Organizations*, 1st Edition, © 1979. Reprinted by permission of Pearson Education, Inc., Upper Saddle River, N.J.

FIGURE 15.2 MINTZBERG'S FIVE BASIC PARTS OF AN ORGANIZATION

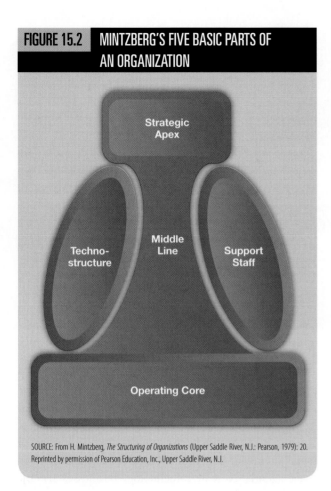

SOURCE: From H. Mintzberg, *The Structuring of Organizations* (Upper Saddle River, N.J.: Pearson, 1979): 20. Reprinted by permission of Pearson Education, Inc., Upper Saddle River, N.J.

15-3a Simple Structure

The **simple structure** is a centralized form of organization that emphasizes a small technical and support staff, strong centralization of decision making in the upper echelon, and a minimal middle level. This structure has a minimum of vertical differentiation of authority and minimal formalization. It achieves coordination through direct supervision, often by the chief executive in the upper echelon. An example of a simple structure is a small, independent landscape practice in which one or two landscape architects supervise the vast majority of work with no middle-level managers.

15-3b Machine Bureaucracy

The **machine bureaucracy** is a moderately decentralized form of organization that emphasizes a support staff differentiated from the line operations of the organization, limited horizontal decentralization of decision making, and a well-defined hierarchy of authority. The technical staff is powerful in a machine bureaucracy. There is strong formalization through policies, procedures, rules, and regulations. Coordination is achieved through the standardization of work processes. An example of a

Hospitals exemplify professional bureaucracies; the expertise of doctors, nurses and technicians is emphasized as the operating core of the organization.

machine bureaucracy is an automobile assembly plant with routinized operating tasks. The strength of the machine bureaucracy is efficiency of operation in stable, unchanging environments. The weakness of the machine bureaucracy is its slow responsiveness to external changes and to individual employee preferences and ideas.

15-3c Professional Bureaucracy

The **professional bureaucracy** is a decentralized form of organization that emphasizes the expertise of the professionals in the operating core of the organization. The technical and support staffs serve the professionals. There is both vertical and horizontal differentiation in the professional bureaucracy. Coordination is achieved through the standardization of the professionals' skills. Examples of organizations, where professional bureaucracies can be found, are hospitals and universities. The doctors, nurses, and professors are given wide latitude to pursue their work based on professional training and indoctrination through professional training programs. Large accounting firms may also fall into the category of professional bureaucracies.

simple structure A centralized form of organization that emphasizes a small technical and support staff, strong centralization of decision making in the upper echelon, and a minimal middle level.

machine bureaucracy A moderately decentralized form of organization that emphasizes support staff differentiated from the line operations of the organization, limited horizontal decentralization of decision making, and a well-defined hierarchy of authority.

professional bureaucracy A decentralized form of organization that emphasizes the expertise of the professionals in the operating core of the organization.

HOT TREND

Retailers Respond to Declining Sales with Downsizing

Staples, one the United States' largest retailers, plans to close up to 225 stores over the next two years, and will shrink the floor space for those stores that remain. Like other retailers, Staples' decision to downsize is in response to increased online purchases and declining foot traffic in brick-and-mortar stores and other retail establishments. Retailers of electronics, appliances, and office supplies have been hit especially hard by the shift to online shopping since these items tend to move more quickly than other goods. Nearly half of Staples' $23 billion annual revenue was the result of Internet sales. By reducing the size of its stores, Staples expects to improve its overall profitability through reduced rents in addition to maintenance, wages, and other operating expenses.

SOURCE: D. Fitzgerald, "Staples' Solution: Smaller Stores," *Wall Street Journal* (March 7, 2014): B1.

15-3d Divisionalized Form

The **divisionalized form** is a loosely coupled, composite structural configuration composed of divisions, each of which may have its own structural configuration.[22] Each division is designed to respond to the market in which it operates. There is vertical decentralization from the upper echelon to the middle of the organization, and the middle level of management is the key part of the organization. This form of organization may have one division that is a machine bureaucracy, one that is an *adhocracy* (discussed next), and one that is a simple structure. The divisionalized organization uses standardization of outputs as its coordinating mechanism.

15-3e Adhocracy

The **adhocracy** is a selectively decentralized form of organization that emphasizes the support staff and mutual adjustment among people. It is designed to fuse interdisciplinary experts into smoothly functioning ad hoc project teams. Liaison devices are the primary mechanism for integrating the project teams through a process of mutual adjustment. There is a high degree of horizontal specialization based on formal training and expertise. Selective decentralization of the project teams occurs within the adhocracy. An example of this form of organization is the National Aeronautics and Space Administration (NASA), which is composed of many talented experts who work in small teams on a wide range of projects related to America's space agenda. New high-technology businesses also often select an adhocracy design.

15-4 CONTEXTUAL VARIABLES

The basic design dimensions and the resulting structural configurations play out in the context of the organization's internal and external environments. Four **contextual variables** influence the success of an organization's design: size, technology, environment, and strategy and goals. These variables provide a manager with key considerations for the right organizational design, although they do not determine the structure. The amount of change in the contextual variables throughout the life of the organization influences the amount of change needed in the basic dimensions of the organization's structure.[23] For example, competitive pressures in many industries have led to *outsourcing*, labeled one of the greatest shifts in organization structure in a century.[24]

15-4a Size

The total number of employees is the appropriate definition of size when discussing the design of organizational structure. This is logical because people and their interactions are the building blocks of structure. Other

---

divisionalized form A loosely coupled, composite structural configuration composed of divisions, each of which may have its own structural configuration.

adhocracy A selectively decentralized form of organization that emphasizes the support staff and mutual adjustment among people.

contextual variables A set of four characteristics that influence the success of an organization's design: size, technology, environment, and strategy and goals.

measures, such as net assets, production rates, and total sales, are usually highly correlated with the total number of employees. However, these may not reflect the actual number of interpersonal relationships that are necessary to effectively structure an organization.

Although there is some argument over the degree of influence that size has on organizational structure, there is no argument that it does influence design options. In one study, Meyer found the size of the organization to be the most important of all variables influencing the organization's structure and design, whereas other researchers argue that the decision to expand the organization's business causes an increase in size as the structure is adjusted to accommodate the planned growth.[25] Downsizing is a planned strategy to reduce the size of an organization, and it is often accompanied by related restructuring and revitalization activities.[26] Researchers predicted and found that firms experienced the most significant post-downsizing performance improvements when they downsized their workforces on either a large or small scale. Intermediate downsizing led to the least positive performance improvements.[27]

How much influence size exerts on the organization's structure is not as important as the relationship between size and the design dimensions of structure. In other words, when exploring structural alternatives, the manager needs to know certain facts about designing structures for large versus small organizations. For example, formalization, specialization, and standardization all tend to be greater in larger organizations because they are necessary to control activities within the organization. Larger organizations are more likely to use documentation, rules, written policies and procedures, and detailed job descriptions than to rely on personal observation by the manager. McDonald's has several volumes of manuals that describe how to make all its products, how to greet customers, how to maintain facilities, and so on. This level of standardization, formalization, and specialization helps McDonald's maintain the same quality of product no matter where a restaurant is located. In contrast, at a small, locally owned café, your hamburger and French fries may taste a little different every time you visit—evidence of a lack of standardization.

Formalization and specialization also help large and growing organizations decentralize decision making. For example, when Australian management consulting firm Nous Group's staff grew from 20 employees in the early 2000s to 150 employees in 2014, the organization pushed decision-making down to lower-level managers and to other personnel according to their job descriptions, policies, standard operating procedures, and norms.[28] Because of the complexity and number of decisions in a large organization, formalization and specialization are used to set parameters for decision making at lower levels. Can you imagine the chaos if the president of the United States, commander-in-chief of all military forces, had to make operational-level decisions in the war on terrorism? By decentralizing decision making, a large organization adds horizontal and vertical complexity, but not necessarily spatial complexity. However, it is more common for a large organization to have more geographic dispersion. For example, the San Diego County Government in California created a regionalized structure to decentralize decision making, share common resources and competencies, and meet its unique client needs.[29]

Hierarchy of authority is another dimension of design related to complexity. As size increases, complexity increases; thus, more levels are added to the hierarchy of authority. This keeps the span of control from getting too large. However, there is a balancing force because formalization and specialization are added. The more formalized, standardized, and specialized the roles within the organization, the wider the span of control can be.

15-4b Technology

An organization's technology is an important contextual variable in determining the organization's structure.[30] Technology is defined as the tools, techniques, and actions used by an organization to transform inputs into outputs.[31] The inputs of the organization include human resources, machines, materials, information, and money. The outputs are the products and services that the organization offers to the external environment. Determining the relationship between technology and structure is complicated because different departments may employ very different technologies. As organizations become larger, there is greater variation in technologies across units in the organization. Joan Woodward, Charles Perrow, and James Thompson have developed ways to understand traditional organizational technologies.

Woodward introduced one of the best-known classification schemes for technology, identifying three types: unit, mass, or process production. *Unit technology* is small-batch manufacturing technology and, sometimes, made-to-order production. Examples include the arms manufacturer Smith & Wesson and the production of fine furniture. *Mass technology* is large-batch manufacturing technology. Examples include automotive assembly lines and latex glove production. *Process production* is a continuous-production process.

Examples include oil refining and beer making. Woodward classified unit technology as the least complex, mass technology as more complex, and process technology as the most complex. The more complex the organization's technology, the more complex the administrative component or structure of the organization needs to be.

Perrow proposed an alternative to Woodward's scheme based on two variables: task variability and problem analyzability. *Task variability* considers the number of exceptions encountered in doing the tasks within a job. *Problem analyzability* examines the types of search procedures followed to find ways to respond to task exceptions. For example, for some exceptions encountered while doing a task, the appropriate response is easy to find. If you are driving down a street and see a sign that says, "Detour—Bridge Out," it is very easy to respond to the task variability, so analyzability is low (i.e., limited analysis is needed). By contrast, when Thomas Edison was designing the first electric light bulb, the problem analyzability was very high for his task.

Perrow went on further to identify the four key aspects of structure that could be modified to technology: (1) the amount of discretion that an individual can exercise to complete a task, (2) the power of groups to control the unit's goals and strategies, (3) the level of interdependence among groups, and (4) the extent to which organizational units coordinate work using either feedback or planning. Figure 15.3 summarizes Perrow's findings about types of technology and basic design dimensions.[32]

Thompson offered yet another view of technology and its relationship to organizational design. This view is based on the concept of **technological interdependence**, which is the degree of interrelatedness of the organization's various technological elements, and the pattern of an organization's work flows. Thompson's research suggests that greater technological interdependence leads to greater organizational complexity and that the problems of greater complexity may be offset by decentralized decision making.[33]

The research of these three early scholars on the influence of technology on organizational design can be combined into one integrating concept—*routineness* in the process of changing inputs into outputs in an organization. This routineness has a very strong relationship with organizational structure. The more routine and repetitive the tasks of the organization, the higher the degree of formalization that is possible, the more centralized, specialized, and standardized the organization can be, and the more hierarchical levels with wider spans of control that are possible.

technological interdependence The degree of interrelatedness of the organization's various technological elements.

Technology is an important contextual variable in determining an organization's structure.

iStockphoto.com/Alvinburrows

FIGURE 15.3   SUMMARY OF PERROW'S FINDINGS

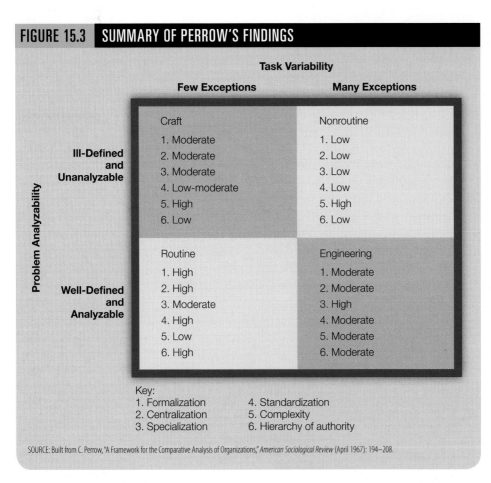

	Task Variability	
	Few Exceptions	**Many Exceptions**
Ill-Defined and Unanalyzable	Craft 1. Moderate 2. Moderate 3. Moderate 4. Low-moderate 5. High 6. Low	Nonroutine 1. Low 2. Low 3. Low 4. Low 5. High 6. Low
Well-Defined and Analyzable	Routine 1. High 2. High 3. Moderate 4. High 5. Low 6. High	Engineering 1. Moderate 2. Moderate 3. High 4. Moderate 5. Moderate 6. Moderate

(left axis: Problem Analyzability)

Key:
1. Formalization
2. Centralization
3. Specialization
4. Standardization
5. Complexity
6. Hierarchy of authority

SOURCE: Built from C. Perrow, "A Framework for the Comparative Analysis of Organizations," *American Sociological Review* (April 1967): 194–208.

15-4c Environment

The third contextual variable for organizational design is **environment**. The environment of an organization is most easily defined as anything outside the boundaries of that organization. Different aspects of the environment have varying degrees of influence on the organization's structure. In one study of 318 CEOs between 1996 and 2000, strategic decision speed was found to moderate the relationship between the environment, the structure of an organization, and performance.[34] The general environment includes all conditions that might have an impact on the organization, such as economic factors, political considerations, ecological changes, sociocultural demands, and governmental regulation.

TASK ENVIRONMENT When aspects of the general environment become more focused in areas of direct interest to the organization, those aspects become part of the **task environment**, or specific environment. The task environment is that part of the environment that is directly relevant to the organization. Typically, this level of environment includes stakeholders such as unions, customers, suppliers, competitors, government regulatory agencies, and trade associations. The *domain* of the organization refers to the area the organization claims for itself with respect to how it fits into its relevant environments. The domain is particularly important because it is defined by the organization,

> **environment** Anything outside the boundaries of an organization.
>
> **task environment** The part of the environment that is directly relevant to the organization.

Top Air Carriers Align Structural Elements for Success

What do Delta Airlines, Emirates, Alaska Airlines, Ryanair, WestJet, Japan Airlines, and Southwest Airlines have in common? Other than the obvious, each of these air carriers was recognized as one of the top-ten global air carriers based on total profit between 2009 and 2013. Contributing to each organization's success is the alignment of culture, structure, processes, systems, employee value proposition, and incentives with their chosen strategy. In an era of heightened industry competition, air carriers must design their organizations to achieve strong performance.

SOURCE: J. Thomas, M. Bell, and T. Lindenau, "Behind the Curtain," *Airline Business* 31 (2015): 42–43.

A_KUDR/Shutterstock.com

Digital Media Pro/Shutterstock.com

and it influences how the organization perceives and acts within its environments.[35] For example, Walmart and Neiman Marcus both sell clothing, but their domains are very different.

The organization's perceptions of its environment and the actual environment may not be the same. The environment that the manager perceives is the environment that the organization responds to and organizes for.[36] Therefore, two organizations may be in relatively the same environment from an objective standpoint, but if the managers perceive differences, the organizations may enact very different structures to deal with this same environment. For example, one company may decentralize and use monetary incentives for managers that lead it to be competitively aggressive, while another company may centralize and use incentives for managers that lead it to be less intense in its rivalry.[37]

ENVIRONMENTAL UNCERTAINTY **Environmental uncertainty** is the amount and rate of change in the organization's environment. The perceived level of environmental uncertainty is the environmental variable that most influences organizational design. The level of environmental uncertainty can also impact the degree to which internal practices are standardized to match multinational firm policies and practices. For instance, customization of HRM practices in high uncertainty environments led to increased financial performance and customer satisfaction.[38] Some organizations have relatively static environments with little uncertainty, whereas others are so dynamic that no one is sure what tomorrow may bring. Binney & Smith, for example, has made basically the same product for more than fifty years with very few changes in the product design or packaging. The environment for its Crayola products is relatively static. In fact, customers rebelled when the company tried to get rid of some old colors and add new ones.

In contrast, in the last two decades, competitors in the airline industry have encountered deregulation, mergers, bankruptcies, changes in cost and price structures, changes in customer and employee demographics, and changes in global competition. In such uncertain conditions, fast-response organizations must use expertise coordination practices to ensure that distributed expertise is managed and applied in a timely manner.[39]

The amount of uncertainty in the environment influences the structural dimensions. Burns and Stalker labeled two structural extremes that are appropriate for the extremes of environmental uncertainty: **mechanistic structure** and **organic structure**.[40] The mechanistic and organic structures occupy opposite ends of a continuum of organizational design possibilities. Although the general premise of environmental uncertainty and structural dimensions has been upheld by research, the organization must make adjustments for the realities of its perceived environment when designing its structure.[41] Some research suggests that the type of structure, either mechanistic or organic, depends on a manager's level of organizational design experience and formal training.[42]

If the organization's environment is uncertain, dynamic, and complex and resources are scarce, the manager needs an organic structure that is better able to adapt to its environment. Such a structure allows the manager to monitor the environment from a number of internal perspectives, thus helping the organization maintain flexibility in responding to environmental changes.[43]

15-4d Strategy and Goals

Strategies and goals are the fourth contextual variable that influences how the design dimensions of structure should be enacted. Strategies and goals provide legitimacy to the organization, as well as employee direction, decision guidelines, and criteria for performance.[44] In addition, strategies and goals help the organization fit into its environment.

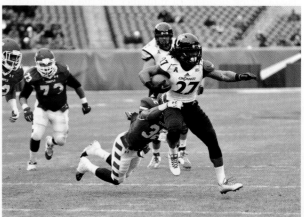

To win the game, you need a reliable team, a solid strategy and a clear path (with the competition behind you).

environmental uncertainty The amount and rate of change in the organization's environment.

mechanistic structure An organizational design that emphasizes structured activities, specialized tasks, and centralized decision making.

organic structure An organizational design that emphasizes teamwork, open communication, and decentralized decision making.

For example, when Apple introduced its line of personal computers to the market, its strategies were very innovative. The structure of the organization was relatively flat and very informal. Apple had Friday afternoon beer and popcorn discussion sessions, and eccentric behavior was easily accepted. As the personal computer market became more competitive, however, the structure of Apple changed to help it differentiate its products and to help control costs. The innovative strategies and structures devised by Steve Jobs, one of Apple's founders, were no longer appropriate. So the board of directors recruited John Scully, a marketing expert from PepsiCo, to help Apple better compete in the market it had created. In 1996 and 1997, Apple reinvented itself again and brought back Jobs to try to restore its innovative edge. After his return, Apple became a major player in the digital music market with its introduction of several models of the iPod and the iPhone.

Limitations exist, however, on the extent to which strategies and goals influence structure. Because the structure of the organization includes the formal information-processing channels in the organization, it stands to reason that the need to change strategies might not be communicated throughout the organization without going through those formal channels. In such a case, the organization's structure influences its strategic choice. Changing the organization's structure might not unlock value but instead drive up costs and difficulties. Therefore, strategic success may hinge on choosing an organization design that works reasonably well, then fine-tuning the structure through a strategic system.[45] The link between strategy and structure extends to acquisitions. Different acquisition strategies, whether unrelated, vertical, or related, will require different levels of centralization and integration. Acculturation processes will also depend on the type of acquisition strategy the organization implements.[46]

The inefficiency of the structure to perceive environmental changes can even lead to organizational failure. In the airline industry, several carriers failed to adjust quickly enough to deregulation and the highly competitive marketplace. Only those airlines that were generally viewed as lean structures with good information-processing systems have flourished in the turbulent years since deregulation. Examples of how different design dimensions can affect the strategic decision process are listed in Table 15.2.

The four contextual variables—size, technology, environment, and strategy and goals—combine to influence the design process. However, the existing structure of the organization influences how the organization interprets and reacts to information about each of the variables. Each of the contextual variables has management researchers who claim that it is the most important variable in determining the best structural design. Because of the difficulty in studying the interactions of the four contextual dimensions and the complexity of organizational structures, the argument about which variable is most important continues.

What is apparent is that there must be some level of fit between the structure and the contextual dimensions of the organization. The better the fit, the more likely the organization will achieve its short-run goals.

TABLE 15.2 EXAMPLES OF HOW STRUCTURE AFFECTS THE STRATEGIC DECISION PROCESS

Formalization

As the level of formalization increases, so does the probability of the following:
1. The strategic decision process will become reactive to crisis rather than proactive through opportunities.
2. Strategic moves will be incremental and precise.
3. Differentiation in the organization will not be balanced with integrative mechanisms.
4. Only environmental crises that are in areas monitored by the formal organizational systems will be acted upon.

Centralization

As the level of centralization increases, so does the probability of the following:
1. The strategic decision process will be initiated by only a few dominant individuals.
2. The decision process will be goal-oriented and rational.
3. The strategic process will be constrained by the limitations of top managers.

Complexity

As the level of complexity increases, so does the probability of the following:
1. The strategic decision process will become more politicized.
2. The organization will find it more difficult to recognize environmental opportunities and threats.
3. The constraints on good decision processes will be multiplied by the limitations of each individual within the organization.

SOURCE: Republished with permission of Academy of Management, from "The Strategic Decision Process and Organizational Structure" (Table), J. Fredrickson, *Academy of Management Review* (1986): 284; permission conveyed through Copyright Clearance Center, Inc.

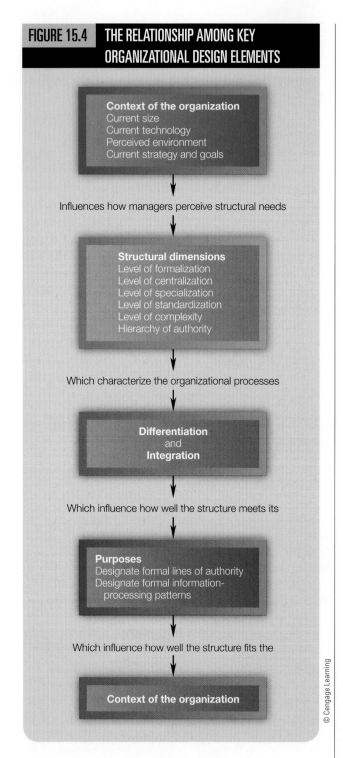

FIGURE 15.4 **THE RELATIONSHIP AMONG KEY ORGANIZATIONAL DESIGN ELEMENTS**

Context of the organization
Current size
Current technology
Perceived environment
Current strategy and goals

Influences how managers perceive structural needs

Structural dimensions
Level of formalization
Level of centralization
Level of specialization
Level of standardization
Level of complexity
Hierarchy of authority

Which characterize the organizational processes

**Differentiation
and
Integration**

Which influence how well the structure meets its

Purposes
Designate formal lines of authority
Designate formal information-
processing patterns

Which influence how well the structure fits the

Context of the organization

© Cengage Learning

In addition, the better the fit, the more likely the organization will process information and design appropriate organizational roles for long-term prosperity, as indicated in Figure 15.4. Some design elements are theorized to fit better during different phases of firm operations. For instance, existing firms engaged in entrepreneurial activities have traditionally favored decentralization and formalization only during opportunity discovery. Recent research suggests that these design elements may also facilitate entrepreneurship during opportunity realization.[47]

organizational life cycle
The differing stages of an organization's life from birth to death.

15-5 FORCES RESHAPING ORGANIZATIONS

Managers and researchers traditionally examine organizational design and structure within the framework of basic design dimensions and contextual variables. In recent decades, though, several forces reshaping organizations are causing managers to go beyond the traditional frameworks to examine ways to make organizations more responsive to customer needs. Some of these forces include shorter organizational life cycles, globalization, and rapid changes in information technology. Together, these forces increase the demands on process capabilities within the organization and emerging organizational structures. Thus to retain their health and vitality, organizations must function as open systems that are responsive to their task environment.[48]

15-5a Life Cycles in Organizations

Organizations are dynamic entities. As such, they ebb and flow through different stages. Usually, researchers think of these stages as **organizational life cycles**. The whole organization has a life cycle that begins at birth, moves through growth and maturity to a stage of decline, and possibly experiences revival.[49]

Organizational subunits may have very similar life cycles. Because of changes in technology and product design, many organizational subunits, especially those that are product based, are experiencing shorter life cycles. Hence, the subunits that compose the organization are changing more rapidly than in the past. These shorter life cycles enable the organization to respond quickly to external demands and changes.

When a new organization or subunit is born, the structure is organic and informal. If the organization or subunit is successful, it grows and matures. This usually leads to formalization, specialization, standardization, complexity, and a more mechanistic structure. If the environment changes, however, the organization must be able to respond. A mechanistic structure is not able to respond to a dynamic environment as well as an organic one. If the organization or subunit does respond, it becomes more organic and revives; if not, it declines and possibly dies. New research suggests that it may be wise to temporarily cycle through mechanistic and organic designs in order to meet the often conflicting demands of organizations.[50]

Shorter life cycles put more pressure on the organization to be both flexible and efficient at the same time. Further, as flexible organizations use design to their competitive advantage, discrete organizational life cycles may give way to a kaleidoscope of continuously emerging, efficiency-seeking organizational designs.[51] The manager's challenge in this context becomes one of creating congruency among various organizational design dimensions to fit continuously changing markets and locations. Many fast-growing organizations face critical transition points through their life cycles that present growth and structural challenges. The organization should attempt to resolve these before moving on to the next phase of growth and development.[52]

15-5b Globalization

Another force that is reshaping organizations is the process of globalization, in which organizations operate worldwide rather than in just one country or region. One potential problem with globalization is that corporations can become pitted against sovereign nations when rules and laws conflict across national borders. Also, globalization makes spatial differentiation even more of a reality for organizations. Besides the obvious geographic differences, there may be deep cultural and value-system differences between the various countries that an organization operates in. This adds another type of complexity to the structural design process and necessitates the creation of integrating mechanisms so that people are able to understand and interpret one another, as well as coordinate with one another.

The choice of structure for managing an international business is generally based on choices concerning the following three factors:

1. *The level of vertical differentiation.* A hierarchy of authority must be created that clarifies the responsibilities of both domestic and foreign managers.

2. *The level of horizontal differentiation.* Foreign and domestic operations should be grouped in such a way that the company effectively serves the needs of all customers.

3. *The degree of formalization, specialization, standardization, and centralization.* The global structure must allow decisions to be made in the most appropriate area of the organization. However, controls must be in place that reflect the strategies and goals of the parent firm.[53]

15-5c Changes in Information-Processing Technologies

Many of the changes in information-processing technologies have allowed organizations to move into new product and market areas more quickly. However, just as shorter life cycles and globalization have caused new concerns for designing organizational structures, so has the increased availability of advanced information-processing technologies. New business technologies are increasingly changing and shaping future business processes, initiatives, and organizational designs.[54]

Organizational structures are already feeling the impact of advanced information-processing technologies. More integration and coordination are evident because managers worldwide can be connected through computerized networks. The basic design dimensions have also been affected as follows:

1. The hierarchy of authority has been flattened.

2. The basis of centralization has been changed. Now managers can use technology to acquire more information and make more decisions, or they can use technology to push information and decision making lower in the hierarchy and thus decrease centralization.

3. Less specialization and standardization are needed because people using advanced information-processing technologies have more sophisticated jobs that require a broader understanding of how the organization gets work done.[55]

Advances in information processing are leading to knowledge-based organizations that incorporate virtual enterprising, dynamic teaming, and knowledge networking.[56]

15-5d Demands on Organizational Processes

Because of the forces reshaping organizations, managers find themselves trying to meet what seem to be conflicting goals: an efficiency orientation that results in on-time delivery *and* a quality orientation that results in customized, high-quality goods or services.[57] Traditionally, managers have seen efficiency and customization as conflicting demands.

To meet these conflicting demands, organizations need to become "dynamically stable."[58] To do so, an organization must have managers who see their roles as architects who clearly understand the "how" of the organizing process. Thus, managers must combine long-term thinking with flexible and quick responses that help improve process and know-how. In addition, the organizational structure must help define, at least to some degree, roles for managers who hope to successfully address the conflicting demands of dynamic stability.

 ## 15-6 EMERGING ORGANIZATIONAL STRUCTURES

The demands placed on managers and on process capabilities in turn place demands on structures. Consequently, the emphasis in organizations is shifting to organizing around processes (see Table 15.3). For example, Procter & Gamble increased its level of innovation by creating teams dedicated to conducting market research, developing technology, creating business plans, and testing assumptions for specific projects.[59]

TABLE 15.3	STRUCTURAL ROLES OF MANAGERS TODAY VERSUS MANAGERS OF THE FUTURE
Roles of Managers Today	1. Strictly adhering to boss–employee relationships.
	2. Getting things done by giving orders.
	3. Carrying messages up and down the hierarchy.
	4. Performing a prescribed set of tasks according to a job description.
	5. Having a narrow functional focus.
	6. Going through channels, one by one by one.
	7. Controlling subordinates.
Roles of Future Managers	1. Having hierarchical relationships subordinated to functional and peer relationships.
	2. Getting things done by negotiating.
	3. Solving problems and making decisions.
	4. Creating the job by developing entrepreneurial projects.
	5. Having broad cross-functional collaboration.
	6. Emphasizing speed and flexibility.
	7. Coaching their workers.

SOURCE: T. R. Horton and P. C. Reid (1991). "What Fate for Middle Managers?" *Management Review*, 80(1), 22.
© 1991. Thomas R. Horton. American Management Association, New York. All rights reserved.

This process orientation emerges from the combination of three streams of applied organizational design: high-performance, self-managed teams; managing processes rather than functions; and the evolution of information technology. Information technology and advanced communication systems have in turn led to *internetworking*. In a study of 469 firms, deeply internetworked firms were found to be more focused and specialized, less hierarchical, and more engaged in external partnering.[60] Three emerging organizational structures associated with these changes are network organizations, virtual organizations, and the circle organization. Virtuality in organizations is often broken down into four interlocking components: geographic dispersion, electronic interdependence, dynamic structure, and national diversity.[61]

Network organizations are weblike structures that contract some or all of their operating functions to other organizations and then coordinate their activities through managers and other employees at their headquarters. Information technology is the basis for building the weblike structure of the network organization and business unit managers that are essential to the success of these systems. This type of organization has arisen in the age of electronic commerce and brought into practice transaction-cost economics, interorganizational collaborations, and strategic alliances. Network organizations can be global in scope.[62]

Virtual organizations are temporary network organizations consisting of independent enterprises. Many dot-coms are virtual organizations designed to come together swiftly to exploit an apparent market opportunity. They may function much like a theatrical troupe that comes together for a "performance."[63] Trust—a complex phenomenon involving ethics, morals, emotions, values, and natural attitudes—can be particularly challenging for virtual organizations. However, trust and trustworthiness are important connective issues in virtual environments. Three key ingredients for the development of trust in virtual organizations are (1) technology that can communicate emotion; (2) a sharing of values, vision, and organizational identity; and (3) a high standard of ethics.[64]

The *circle organization* is a third emerging structure, crafted by Harley-Davidson in its drive to achieve teamwork without teams.[65] The three organizational parts, shown in Figure 15.5, are those that (1) create demand, (2) produce product, and (3) provide support. As the figure indicates, these three parts are linked by the *leadership and strategy council (LSC)*. The circle organization is a more open system than most and an organic structure

Seven Designs for Organizations of the Future

These examples of disruptive organizational designs can help organizations become efficient, innovative, adaptable, and reactive, especially during times of change and uncertainty.

1. Self-Management and Self-Organization—First tested in the 1960s. Characterized by increased autonomy and responsibility of employees and teams for all organizational processes. Whole Foods and W. L. Gore are examples.

2. Intrapreneurship—A subset of the organization functions autonomously from a budgetary, process, and operational standpoint until it gains recognition in the marketplace, after which the unit will either rejoin the organization or become a separate branch. Cisco used a form of this design to inject agility into its organization.

3. Virtual Ephermal Structures—Interim structures made up of dedicated virtual teams that use a collaborative platform to support promising niche markets and jumpstart new businesses.

Google is well-known for its operating model and the efficiency with which it operates.

4. The Neuroscienced Organization—A neurocognitive approach to manage human capital by developing an understanding of how people behave in unplanned situations. Success depends on each employee's ability to be open-minded, view situations differently, and adapt accordingly. Juniper Networks is an example.

5. The Acculturated Organization—Built on the premise that culture isn't created; culture happens by focusing on operating the organization using practical principles of fostering creativity, adaptability, collaboration, trust, and keeping things simple. S7Signals, the startup that developed the top cloud-based project management platform, is an example.

6. The Transparent Organization—Based on the notion that a high degree of transparency throughout the organization increases the quality of insights since individuals know that their contributions will be seen. In that way, executives support and assist lower-level employees instead of vice versa. HCL Technologies uses this design.

7. The Agora Organization—More fluid than self-management; perpetually changing structure fueled by creativity and long-lasting values instilled by its founders. Google is the most well-known example.

SOURCE: C. Demailly, "Shaping the Organization of the Future," *People & Strategy* 37 (2014): 54–56.

FIGURE 15.5 HARLEY-DAVIDSON'S CIRCLE ORGANIZATION

Create Demand

Produce Product

Provide Support

Leadership and Strategy Council (LSC)

SOURCE: Reprinted by permission of Harvard Business School Press from R. Teerlink and L. Ozley, *More Than a Motorcycle: The Leadership Journey at Harley-Davidson* (Boston, Mass.: Harvard Business School Press, 2000): 139. Copyright © 2000 by the Harvard Business School Publishing Corporation; all rights reserved.

for customer responsiveness. One innovation in this organizational scheme is the so-called circle coach, who possesses acute communication, listening, and influencing skills so as to be highly respected by circle members and the company's president.

15-7 FACTORS THAT CAN ADVERSELY AFFECT STRUCTURE

This chapter has identified the purposes of structure, the processes of organizational design, and the dimensions and contexts that must be considered in structure. In addition, it has looked at forces and trends in organizational design. Two cautionary notes are important for the student of organizational behavior. First, an organizational structure may be weak or deficient if it is out of alignment with its contextual variables, in which case one or more of the following four symptoms appears:

- Decision making is delayed because the hierarchy is overloaded and too much information is being funneled through one or two channels.

- Decision making is of poor quality because information linkages are not providing the correct information to the right person in the right format.

- The organization does not respond innovatively to a changing environment, especially when coordinated effort is lacking across departments.

- A great deal of conflict is evident as some departments work against one another rather than for the strategies and goals of the organization as a whole; the structure is often at fault.

Second, the personality of the chief executive may adversely affect the structure of the organization.[66] Managers' personal, cognitive biases and political ideologies may affect their good judgment and decision making.[67] Five dysfunctional combinations of personality and organization have been identified: the paranoid, the depressive, the dramatic, the compulsive, and the schizoid.[68] Each of these personality–organization constellations can create problems for the people who work in the organization. For example, in a paranoid constellation, people are suspicious of each other, hence distrust in working relationships may interfere with effective communication and task accomplishment. In a depressive constellation, people feel depressed and inhibited in their work activities, which can lead to low levels of productivity and task accomplishment.

STUDY TOOLS 15

LOCATED AT BACK OF THE TEXTBOOK

☐ Rip out chapter review card

LOCATED AT WWW.CENGAGE.COM/LOGIN

☐ Track your knowledge and understanding of key concepts in business using 4LTR Press Online

☐ Review key term flashcards and create your own using StudyBits

☐ Create and complete practice quizzes based off of your notes and StudyBits

☐ Complete Online activities such as Matching and Fill-in-the-Blank exercises

☐ View chapter highlight box content, including the chapter videos, key exhibits and executive profiles.

ORGB
ONLINE
PREPARE FOR TESTS ON THE STUDYBOARD!

 CORRECT

 INCORRECT

 INCORRECT

 INCORRECT

Personalize Quizzes from Your StudyBits

Take Practice Quizzes by Chapter

CHAPTER QUIZZES

Chapter 1

Chapter 2

Chapter 3

Chapter 4

4LTR PRESS

Access ORGB ONLINE at www.cengagebrain.com

16 | Organizational Culture

LEARNING OUTCOMES

16-1 Identify the three levels of organizational culture and evaluate the roles they play in an organization.

16-2 Evaluate the four functions of organizational culture within an organization.

16-3 Explain the relationship between organizational culture and performance.

16-4 Describe five ways leaders reinforce organizational culture.

16-5 Describe the three stages of organizational socialization and the ways culture is communicated in each step.

16-6 Discuss how managers assess their organization's culture.

16-7 Explain actions managers can take to change organizational culture.

16-8 Identify the challenges organizations face developing positive, cohesive cultures.

After finishing this chapter go to **PAGE 273** for **STUDY TOOLS.**

The concept of organizational culture has its roots in cultural anthropology. Just as there are cultures in larger human society, there are cultures within organizations. Like societal cultures, they are shared, communicated through symbols, and passed down from generation to generation of employees.

The concept of cultures in organizations was alluded to as early as the Hawthorne studies, which described work group culture. The topic came into its own during the early 1970s, when managers and researchers began to search for keys to survival for organizations in a competitive and turbulent environment. Then, in the early 1980s, several books on corporate culture were published, including Terry Deal and Allan Kennedy's *Corporate Cultures*,[1] William Ouchi's *Theory Z*,[2] and Thomas Peters and Robert Waterman's *In Search of Excellence*.[3] These books found wide audiences, and research began in earnest on the elusive topic of organizational cultures. Executives indicated that these cultures were real and could be managed.[4]

> **Organizational cultures are shared, communicated through symbols, and passed down from generation to generation of employees.**

Danielala/Shutterstock.com

16-1 LEVELS OF ORGANIZATIONAL CULTURE

Many definitions of *organizational culture* have been proposed. Most of them agree that there are several levels of culture and that these levels differ in terms of their visibility and their ability to be changed. Culture has been viewed both as what defines the values of the organization and as a toolkit as to how to behave in an organization. As such, culture influences outcomes that an organization desires to achieve, as well as the processes necessary to achieve those outcomes.[5] The definition adopted in this chapter is that **organizational (corporate) culture** is a pattern of basic assumptions that are considered valid and that are taught to new members as the way to perceive, think, and feel in the organization.[6]

In his comprehensive book on organizational culture and leadership, Edgar Schein suggests that organizational culture has three levels. His view of culture is presented in Figure 16.1. The levels range from visible *artifacts* and creations to testable *values* to invisible and even preconscious basic *assumptions*. To achieve a complete understanding of an organization's culture, all three levels must be studied.

16-1a Artifacts

Symbols of culture in the physical and social work environments are called **artifacts**. They are the most visible and accessible level of culture. The key to understanding culture through artifacts lies in figuring out their meanings. Artifacts are also the most frequently studied manifestation of organizational culture, perhaps because of their accessibility. Examples of the artifacts of culture include personal enactment, ceremonies and rites, stories, rituals, and symbols.[7]

The corporate culture of Google is apparent in the offices of Google headquarters located in Mountain View, California. The lobby is replete with lava lamps, pianos, and displays of live searches on the Google search engine from around the world. The hallways house bikes and exercise machines, while office spaces are laid back, with couches and dogs who follow their owners to work.[8] The artifacts at Google reinforce the notion that the company cares about employees and wants them to be creative and comfortable.

PERSONAL ENACTMENT Culture can be understood, in part, through an examination of the behavior of organization members. When this behavior reflects the organization's values, it is called *personal enactment*. In particular, personal enactment by the top managers provides insight into the organization's values. When Charles Sharf became CEO at Visa, the credit card company had a reputation among merchants for being difficult to work with. Recognizing that the payment world is much more competitive, Sharf eliminated 50 percent of the cumbersome rulebook for merchants. He keeps the original 1,538-page rulebook as a doorstop in his office, reminding him that Visa needs to be easier to do business with.

Eskimo Joe's, a restaurant chain based in Stillwater, Oklahoma, and one of the largest T-shirt sellers in the United States, could probably have become a national franchise years ago. But founder Stan Clark, who began as co-owner of the once tiny bar, says his intent is to become better, not bigger. Clark still meets

> **organizational (corporate) culture** A pattern of basic assumptions that are considered valid and that are taught to new members as the way to perceive, think, and feel in the organization.
>
> **artifacts** Symbols of culture in the physical and social work environments.

FIGURE 16.1 LEVELS OF ORGANIZATIONAL CULTURE

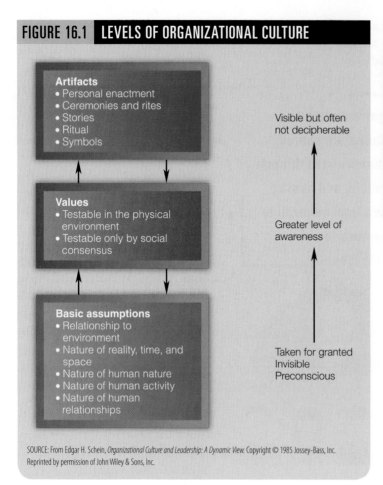

Artifacts
- Personal enactment
- Ceremonies and rites
- Stories
- Ritual
- Symbols

Visible but often not decipherable

Values
- Testable in the physical environment
- Testable only by social consensus

Greater level of awareness

Basic assumptions
- Relationship to environment
- Nature of reality, time, and space
- Nature of human nature
- Nature of human activity
- Nature of human relationships

Taken for granted Invisible Preconscious

SOURCE: From Edgar H. Schein, *Organizational Culture and Leadership: A Dynamic View.* Copyright © 1985 Jossey-Bass, Inc. Reprinted by permission of John Wiley & Sons, Inc.

ZUMA Press, Inc./Alamy

Warren Buffett is known for hosting celebrations that appear more as rock concerts than ceremonies for his annual shareholders meeting.

personally with new hires for the restaurant's serving staff, ensuring that they receive a firm grounding in his philosophy of food and fun.[9]

Modeled behavior is a powerful learning tool for employees, as Bandura's social learning theory demonstrated.[10] As we saw in Chapter 5, individuals learn vicariously by observing others' behavior and patterning their own behavior similarly. In this way, culture can be an important leadership tool. Managerial behavior can clarify what is important and coordinate the work of employees, in effect negating the need for close supervision.[11]

CEREMONIES AND RITES Relatively elaborate sets of activities that are repeatedly enacted on important occasions are known as organizational ceremonies and rites.[12] These occasions provide opportunities to reward and recognize employees whose behavior is congruent with the values of the company. Ceremonies and rites send a message that individuals who both espouse and exhibit corporate values are heroes to be admired.

The ceremonies also bond organization members together. Southwestern Bell (now AT&T) emphasized the importance of management training to the company. Training classes were kicked off by a high-ranking executive (a

rite of renewal), and completion of the classes was signaled by a graduation ceremony (a rite of passage). Six kinds of rites in organizations have been identified, as shown in Table 16.1.[13]

Berkshire Hathaway, Inc., is an Omaha-based company that owns and operates a number of insurance firms and several other subsidiaries. Chair and CEO Warren Buffett is known for his business acumen and for ensuring good returns on shareholder investments. Berkshire's annual shareholder meeting is a ceremony of celebration and appears more like a major rock music festival than a corporate meeting. Each meeting starts with a short film poking fun at the CEO and his cantankerous sidekick, Charlie Munger. Attendees watch the short film eagerly to see who will make cameo appearances and were recently rewarded with an appearance by the cast from *Entourage*. Others who have made cameos include Arnold Schwarzenegger, Donald Trump, and the women of *Desperate Housewives*. One year Jimmy Buffett sang "Margaritaville" at the meeting, with some of the lyrics changed to "wasting away in Berkshire-Hathaway-a-ville!" Bill Gates, who is on the board of directors, often makes it to the meeting and has been seen playing ping-pong with Warren Buffett. More than 40,000 shareholders, employees, and Buffett relatives attend the star-studded event annually.[14]

STORIES Some researchers have argued that the most effective way to reinforce organizational values is through stories.[15] As they are retold, stories give meaning and identity to organizations and are especially helpful in orienting new employees. Part of the strength of organizational stories is that the listeners are left to draw their own conclusions—a powerful communication tool.[16]

TABLE 16.1   SIX RITES IN ORGANIZATIONS

Rite	Role	Example
1. *Rites of passage*	Show that an individual's status has changed	Retirement dinners
2. *Rites of enhancement*	Reinforce the achievement of individuals	Awarding certificates to sales contest winners
3. *Rites of renewal*	Emphasize change in the organization and commitment to learning and growth	Opening a new corporate training center
4. *Rites of integration*	Unite diverse groups or teams within the organization and renew commitment to the larger organization	Company functions such as annual picnics
5. *Rites of conflict reduction*	Dealing with conflicts or disagreements that arise naturally in organizations	Grievance hearings and the negotiation of union contracts
6. *Rites of degradation*	Used to visibly punish persons who fail to adhere to values and norms of behavior	Publicly replacing a CEO for unethical conduct or for failure to achieve organizational goals

© Cengage Learning

Some corporate stories even transcend cultural and political boundaries. Visit the website of Walmart China, and you will read the true story of Jeff, a pharmacist in Harrison, Arkansas, a small town deep in the Ozarks. When Jeff received an early morning weekend call telling him that a diabetic patient needed insulin, he quickly opened his pharmacy and filled the prescription.[17] While Arkansas and Beijing are worlds apart, stories such as this one help transfer Walmart's corporate "personality" to its new Asian associates. Research by Joanne Martin and her colleagues has indicated that certain themes appear in stories across different types of organizations[18]:

1. *Stories about the boss.* These stories may reflect whether the boss is "human" or how the boss reacts to mistakes.

2. *Stories about getting fired.* Events leading to employee firings are recounted.

3. *Stories about how the company deals with employees who have to relocate.* These stories relate to the company's actions toward employees who have to move—whether the company is helpful and takes family and other personal concerns into account.

4. *Stories about whether lower-level employees can rise to the top.* Often these stories describe a person who started out at the bottom and eventually became the CEO. QuikTrip is well known for promoting from within, one reason it has been voted one of *Fortune's* 100 Best Companies to Work For seven years running. In fact, two-thirds of QuikTrip's top 100 managers started at entry-level positions in the organization.[19]

5. *Stories about how the company deals with crisis situations.* These stories show how the company overcomes obstacles. Employees at SAS, a software company in North Carolina, love to tell stories of how the company has never once laid off an employee, even during the global recession. Such stories illustrate that even during financial crisis, SAS cares more about employees than about the bottom line.[20]

6. *Stories about how status considerations work when rules are broken.* When Tom Watson, Sr., was CEO of IBM, he was once confronted by a security guard because he was not wearing an ID badge.

These are the themes that can emerge when stories are passed down. The information from these stories serves to guide the behavior of organization members.

To be effective cultural tools, however, stories must be credible. You can't tell a story about your flat corporate hierarchy and then have reserved parking spaces for managers. Stories that aren't backed by reality can lead to cynicism and mistrust.

Effective stories are not only motivational; they can also reinforce culture and create renewed energy. Storytelling reinforces the culture at Southwest Airlines and reminds employees of their purpose in interactions with customers. Southwest's internal corporate videos are full of stories about employees who go above and beyond to serve customers. In one video, a Southwest customer and her family took her husband to the airport for a six-month deployment in Kuwait. A customer service agent saw the family and asked whether they wanted to go to the departure gate with the soldier. Then, at the departure gate, another employee asked whether the family would like to go onto the plane with him. As passengers cheered, the soldier's children were able to give him one last hug. Stories like this one remind Southwest employees that they matter to millions of customers.[21]

RITUALS Everyday, repetitive, organizational practices are rituals. They are usually unwritten, but they send a clear message about "the way we do things around here." While some companies insist that people address each other by their titles and surnames to reinforce a professional image, others prefer that employees operate on a first-name basis—from the top manager on down. Hewlett-Packard values open communication, so its employees address one another by first names only.

Mark Zuckerberg, the founder of Facebook, used to end company meetings with a ritual—pumping his fist into the air and leading employees in a chant of "Domination!" He later replaced this ritual by quoting movie lines aimed at reminding employees that they are engaged in something greater and more meaningful than making money.[22] As everyday practices, rituals reinforce the organizational culture. Insiders who commonly practice the rituals may be unaware of their subtle influence, but outsiders recognize it easily.

SYMBOLS Symbols communicate organizational culture through unspoken messages. They are representative of organizational identity and membership to employees. Some Nike employees proudly display tattoos of the Nike swoosh above their ankles. Symbols are used to build solidarity in the organizational culture.[23]

Personal enactment, rites and ceremonies, stories, rituals, and symbols serve to reinforce the values that are the next level of culture.

16-1b Values

Values are the second, deeper, level of culture. They reflect a person's inherent beliefs of what should or should not be. Values are often consciously articulated, both in conversation and in a company's mission statement or annual report. However, there may be a difference between a company's **espoused values** (what the members say they value) and its **enacted values** (values reflected in the way the members actually behave).[24] Values also may be reflected in the behavior of individuals, which is an artifact of culture. One study investigating the gender gap in a Canadian sports organization found that coaches and athletes had come to believe that the inequity between espoused and enacted values was normal, or natural. Some even completely denied it existed even though such inequities were widely prevalent. This was because even though the organization espoused gender equity as a value, its practices did not enact gender equity.[25]

How a firm promotes and publicizes its values may also affect how workers feel about their jobs and themselves. A study of 180 managers evaluated their employers' effectiveness in communicating concern for employees' welfare. Managers in organizations that consistently communicated concern for workers' well-being and that focused on treating employees fairly reported feeling better about themselves and their role in the organization.[26] The lesson? *Treat* employees like valuable team members, and they are more likely to *feel* like valuable team members.

Some organizational cultures are characterized by values that support healthy lifestyle behaviors. When the workplace culture values workers' health and psychological needs, there is enhanced potential for high performance and improved well-being.[27] Clif Bar, the energy bar maker, even has a twenty-two-foot rock-climbing wall in its corporate office.

16-1c Assumptions

Assumptions are the deeply held beliefs that guide behavior and tell members of an organization how to perceive situations and people. At the deepest and most fundamental level of an organization's culture, according to Edgar Schein, they are the essence of culture. Assumptions are so strongly held that a member behaving in a fashion that would violate them is unthinkable. Another characteristic of assumptions is that they are often unconscious. Organization members may not be aware of their assumptions and may be reluctant or unable to discuss them or change them.

While unconscious assumptions often guide a firm's actions and decisions, some companies are quite explicit in their assumptions about employees. Some companies operate under the assumption that work/life balance creates more satisfied and productive companies, and capSpire is a company that makes this explicit. capSpire is a global consulting and technology solutions company that has an unlimited vacation policy. They were awarded the national

espoused values What members of an organization say they value.

enacted values Values reflected in the way individuals actually behave.

assumptions Deeply held beliefs that guide behavior and tell members of an organization how to perceive situations and people.

FASTFACT

Japan Considers Making Vacations Mandatory

Japanese workers often work long days of thirteen hours or more and sleep as little as thirty-five hours a week—a schedule that leads sometimes to *karoshi*, which means death by overwork. With the related concept of *kaizen*, or continuous improvement, workers seldom if ever take a vacation. The Japanese government is considering legislation that would make five days of paid vacation mandatory each year. There is growing evidence that young people work long and intense hours and have died young. Grieving families have started nonprofit organizations to influence business and government to stop the madness.

SOURCE: A. Peters, "In Japan, It Soon May Be Illegal Not to Take Vacation," *Fast Company*, March 11, 2015, accessed at http://www.fastcoexist.com/3043444/in-japan-it-soon-may-be-illegal-not-to-take-vacation.

Alfred P. Sloan Award for their use of creative ideas to promote quality family lives and productive careers.[28]

16-2 FUNCTIONS OF ORGANIZATIONAL CULTURE

In an organization, culture serves four basic functions. First, culture provides a sense of identity to members and increases their commitment to the organization.[29] When employees internalize the values of the company, they find their work intrinsically rewarding and identify with their fellow workers. As a result, motivation is enhanced, and employees are more committed.[30]

Second, culture provides a way for employees to interpret the meaning of organizational events.[31] Leaders can use organizational symbols such as corporate logos to help employees understand the changing nature of their organizational identity. Sometimes symbols should remain the same to ensure that some things stay constant despite changing conditions. Other times symbols may have to change to reflect the new culture in the organization.

Third, culture reinforces the values of the organization.

And, fourth, culture serves as a control mechanism for shaping behavior. Norms that guide behavior are part of culture. Thus, if the norm the company wants to promote is teamwork, then its culture must reinforce

that norm. The company's culture must be characterized by open communication, cooperation between teams, and integration of teams.[32] Culture can also be used as a powerful tool to discourage dysfunctional and deviant behaviors in organizations. Norms can send clear messages that certain behaviors are unacceptable.[33]

16-3 THE RELATIONSHIP OF CULTURE TO PERFORMANCE

The effects of organizational culture are hotly debated by organizational behaviorists and researchers. It seems that although managers attest strongly to the positive effects of culture in organizations, it is difficult to quantify these effects. John Kotter and James Heskett have reviewed three theories about the relationship between organizational culture and performance and the evidence that either supports or refutes these theories.[34] The three are the strong-culture perspective, the fit perspective, and the adaptation perspective.

16-3a The Strong-Culture Perspective

The strong-culture perspective states that organizations with strong cultures perform better than other organizations.[35] A **strong culture** is an organizational culture with a consensus on the values that drive the company and with an intensity that is recognizable even to outsiders. Thus, a strong culture is deeply held and widely shared. It is also highly resistant to change.

> **strong culture** An organizational culture with a consensus on the values that drive the company and with an intensity that is recognizable even to outsiders.

Employees that enjoy themselves and their work will lead to a strong culture.

A good example is IBM, which has a strong culture of conservatism, workforce loyalty, and emphasis on customer service.

Strong cultures are thought to facilitate performance for three reasons. First, these cultures are characterized by goal alignment; that is, all employees share common goals. Second, strong cultures create a high level of motivation because of the values shared by the members. Third, strong cultures provide control without the oppressive effects of a bureaucracy.

Two perplexing questions about the strong-culture perspective are (1) what can be said about evidence showing that strong economic performance can create strong cultures, rather than the reverse, and (2) what if the strong culture leads the firm down the wrong path? Sears, for example, is an organization with a strong culture, but since the 1980s, it focused inward, ignoring competition and consumer preferences and damaging its performance.[36]

16-3b The Fit Perspective

The fit perspective argues that a culture is good only if it fits the industry or the firm's strategy. For example, a culture that values a traditional hierarchical structure and stability would not work well in the computer manufacturing industry, which demands fast response and a lean, flat organization. Three particular industry characteristics may affect culture: the competitive environment, customer requirements, and societal expectations.[37]

A study of twelve large U.S. firms indicated that cultures consistent with industry conditions help managers make better decisions. It also indicated that cultures need not change as long as the industry doesn't change. If the industry does change, however, many cultures change too slowly to avoid negative effects on firms' performance.[38]

The fit perspective is useful in explaining short-term performance but not long-term performance. It also indicates that it is

adaptive culture An organizational culture that encourages confidence and risk taking among employees, has leadership that produces change, and focuses on the changing needs of customers.

TABLE 16.2	**ADAPTIVE VERSUS NONADAPTIVE ORGANIZATIONAL CULTURES**	
	Adaptive Organizational Cultures	**Nonadaptive Organizational Cultures**
Core values	Most managers care deeply about customers, stockholders, and employees. They also strongly value people and processes that can create useful change (e.g., leadership up and down the management hierarchy).	Most managers care mainly about themselves, their immediate work group, or some product (or technology) associated with that work group. They value the orderly and risk-reducing management process much more highly than leadership initiatives.
Common behavior	Managers pay close attention to all their constituencies, especially customers, and initiate change when needed to serve their legitimate interests, even if that entails taking some risks.	Managers tend to behave somewhat insularly, politically, and bureaucratically. As a result, they do not change their strategies quickly to adjust to or take advantage of changes in their business environments.

SOURCE: Reprinted with the permission of The Free Press, a Division of Simon & Schuster, Adult Publishing Group, from *Corporate Culture and Performance* by John P. Kotter and James L. Heskett. Copyright © 1992 by Kotter Associates, Inc. and James L. Heskett. All rights reserved.

difficult to change culture quickly, especially if the culture is widely shared and deeply held. But it doesn't explain how firms can adapt to environmental change.

16-3c The Adaptation Perspective

The third theory about culture and performance is the adaptation perspective. Its theme is that only cultures that help organizations adapt to environmental change are associated with excellent performance. An **adaptive culture** is a culture that encourages confidence and risk taking among employees,[39] has leadership that produces change,[40] and focuses on the changing needs of customers. To test the adaptation perspective, Kotter and Heskett interviewed industry analysts about the cultures of twenty-two firms. The contrast between adaptive cultures and nonadaptive cultures was striking. The results of the study are summarized in Table 16.2.

Adaptive cultures facilitate change to meet the needs of three groups of constituents: stockholders, customers, and employees. Nonadaptive cultures are characterized by cautious management that tries to protect its own interests. Adaptive firms showed significantly better long-term economic performance in Kotter and Heskett's study. When strong cultures focus intensely on adaptability, they can perform better financially.[41] Given that high-performing cultures are adaptive ones, it is important to know how managers can develop adaptive cultures.

THE LEADER'S ROLE IN SHAPING AND REINFORCING CULTURE

According to Edgar Schein, leaders play crucial roles in shaping and reinforcing culture.[42] The five most important elements in managing culture are (1) what leaders pay attention to, (2) how leaders react to crises, (3) how leaders behave, (4) how leaders allocate rewards, and (5) how leaders hire and fire individuals.

16-4a What Leaders Pay Attention To

Leaders in an organization communicate their priorities, values, and beliefs through the themes that consistently emerge from their focus. These themes are reflected in what they notice, comment on, measure, and control. If leaders are consistent in their focus, employees receive clear signals about what is important in the organization. If, however, leaders are inconsistent, employees spend a lot of time trying to decipher and find meaning in the inconsistent signals.

16-4b How Leaders React to Crises

The way leaders deal with crises communicates a powerful message about culture. Emotions are heightened during a crisis, and learning is intense. Difficult economic times present crises for many companies and illustrate their different values. Some organizations avoid laying off workers at all costs. Others, despite their claim that employees are important, quickly institute major layoffs at the first signal of an economic downturn. Employees may perceive that the company shows its true colors in a crisis and thus pay careful attention to the reactions of their leaders.

16-4c How Leaders Behave

Through role modeling, teaching, and coaching, leaders reinforce the values that support the organizational culture. Employees often emulate leaders' behavior and look to the leaders for cues to appropriate behavior. Many companies encourage employees to be more entrepreneurial, using more initiative and innovation. A study showed that if managers want employees to be more entrepreneurial, they must demonstrate such behaviors themselves.[43] This is the case with any cultural value. Employees observe the behavior of leaders to find out what the organization values.

16-4d How Leaders Allocate Rewards

To ensure that values are accepted, leaders should reward behavior that is consistent with the values. Some companies, for example, may claim that they use a pay-for-performance system that distributes rewards on the basis of performance. When the time comes for raises, however, the increases are awarded according to length of service with the company. Imagine the feelings of a high-performing newcomer who receives only a tiny raise after hearing company leaders espouse the value of rewarding individual performance.

Some companies may claim to value teamwork. They form cross-functional teams and empower these teams to make important decisions. However, when performance is appraised, the criteria for rating employees focus on individual performance. This sends a confusing signal to employees about the company's culture: Is individual performance valued, or is teamwork the key?

IDEO's Creative Culture of Helping

IDEO, the award-winning global design firm, doesn't buy into pitting designers against each other. Instead, what gets encouraged, recognized, and rewarded at IDEO is helping. People pop in on meetings just to help, and there's trust in the intention of fellow designers. Help is imbedded in brainstorming sessions, formal design reviews, and all kinds of support and encouragement. One key to the helping culture is slack in the organization. For people to help each other, there must be time. Designers can't be overloaded with their own work. And helpfulness is considered in promotion decisions. Giving and receiving help is part of the culture at IDEO and is reflected in one of IDEO's key values: "Make Others Successful."

SOURCE: T. Amabile, C. M. Fisher, and J. Pillemer, "IDEO's Culture of Helping," *Harvard Business Review*, January 2014, accessed at https://hbr.org/2014/01/ideos-culture-of-helping/ar/1

Source: IDEO

16-4e How Leaders Hire and Fire Individuals

A powerful way that leaders reinforce culture is through the selection of newcomers to the organization. With the advent of electronic recruitment practices, applicant perceptions of organizational culture are shaped by what the organization advertises on its recruitment website. Typical perception-shaping mechanisms are organizational values, policies, awards, and goals.[44] Just as newcomers learn culture from perusing corporate websites, leaders shape and communicate culture by the way they hire employees. Many CEOs have a set of questions they like to use in interviews. Mitch Rothschild is CEO of Vitals, a website that connects patients and doctors. Vitals is a small company that prides itself on moving quickly, so Rothschild wants to get a sense of whether a candidate is comfortable with change. The question "What percentage of your life do you control?" helps him understand whether the candidate believes he or she can make change happen. Rothschild is looking for a high number because at Vitals there is a need for rapid change.[45]

The way a company fires an employee and the rationale behind the firing also communicates the culture. Some companies deal with poor performers by trying to find a place within the organization where they can perform better and make a contribution. Other companies seem to operate under the philosophy that those who cannot perform are out quickly.

The reasons for terminations may not be directly communicated to other employees, but curiosity leads to speculation. Suppose an employee caught in the act of unethical behavior is simply reprimanded, with no other penalty, even though such behavior is clearly against the organization's values. Other employees may view this as a failure to reinforce the values within the organization.

In summary, leaders play a critical role in shaping and reinforcing organizational culture. Managers need to create a positive culture through what they pay attention to, how they react to crises, how they behave, the way they allocate rewards, and how they hire and fire employees. Transformational leaders create a more adaptive culture, which in turn increases business unit performance.[46]

organizational socialization The process by which newcomers are transformed from outsiders to participating, effective members of the organization.

anticipatory socialization The first socialization stage, which encompasses all of the learning that takes place prior to the newcomer's first day on the job.

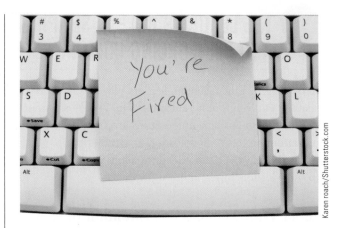

Karen roach/Shutterstock.com

16-5 ORGANIZATIONAL SOCIALIZATION

We have seen that leaders play key roles in shaping an organization's culture. Another process that perpetuates culture is the way it is passed on from generation to generation of employees. Newcomers learn the culture through **organizational socialization**—the process by which newcomers are transformed from outsiders to participating, effective members of the organization.[47] As we saw earlier, cultural socialization begins with the careful selection of newcomers who are likely to reinforce the organizational culture.[48] Once selected, newcomers pass through the stressful socialization process.

16-5a The Stages of the Socialization Process

The organizational socialization process is generally described as having three stages: anticipatory socialization, encounter, and change and acquisition. Figure 16.2 presents a model of the process and the key concerns at each stage of it.[49] It also describes the outcomes of the process, which will be discussed in the next section of the chapter.

ANTICIPATORY SOCIALIZATION The first stage of the socialization process, **anticipatory socialization**, encompasses all of the learning that takes place prior to the newcomer's first day on the job, including the newcomer's expectations. The two key concerns at this stage are realism and congruence.

Realism is the degree to which a newcomer holds realistic expectations about the job and organization. One thing newcomers should receive information about during entry into the organization is the culture. Information about values at this stage can help newcomers begin to

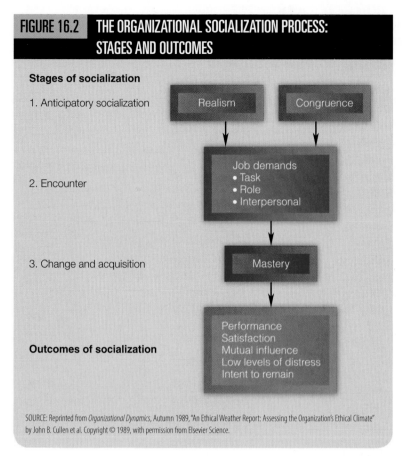

FIGURE 16.2 THE ORGANIZATIONAL SOCIALIZATION PROCESS: STAGES AND OUTCOMES

Stages of socialization

1. Anticipatory socialization

Realism   Congruence

2. Encounter

Job demands
• Task
• Role
• Interpersonal

3. Change and acquisition

Mastery

Outcomes of socialization

Performance
Satisfaction
Mutual influence
Low levels of distress
Intent to remain

SOURCE: Reprinted from *Organizational Dynamics*, Autumn 1989, "An Ethical Weather Report: Assessing the Organization's Ethical Climate" by John B. Cullen et al. Copyright © 1989, with permission from Elsevier Science.

construct a scheme for interpreting their organizational experiences. Later, a deeper understanding of the organization's culture will be possible through time and experience in the organization. When organizations give realistic job previews that not only highlight major stressors but also teach various coping strategies to deal with them, newcomers feel less stressed and report higher levels of adjustment six and nine months postentry.[50]

There are two types of *congruence* between an individual and an organization: congruence between the individual's abilities and the demands of the job, and the fit between the individual's values and the organization's values. Organizations disseminate information about their values through their web pages, annual reports, and recruitment brochures.[51] *Value congruence* is particularly important for organizational culture. It is also important in terms of newcomer adjustment. Newcomers whose values match the company's values are more satisfied with their new jobs, adjust more quickly, and say they intend to remain with the firm longer.[52]

ENCOUNTER The second stage of socialization, **encounter**, is when newcomers learn the tasks associated with the job, clarify their roles, and establish new relationships at work. This stage commences on the first day at work and is thought to encompass the first six to nine months on the new job. Newcomers face task demands, role demands, and interpersonal demands during this period.

Task demands involve the actual work performed. Learning to perform tasks is related to the organization's culture. In some organizations, where creativity is valued, newcomers are given considerable latitude to experiment with new ways to do their job. In others, newcomers are expected to learn the established procedures for their tasks. Early experiences with trying to master task demands can affect employees' entire careers. Auditors, for example, are often forced to choose between being thorough and being fast in completing their work. By pressuring auditors in this way, firms often set themselves up for problems later, when these pressures may lead auditors to make less-than-ethical decisions.

Role demands involve the expectations placed on newcomers. Newcomers may not know exactly what is expected of them (role ambiguity) or may receive conflicting expectations from other individuals (role conflict). The way newcomers approach these demands depends in part on the culture of the organization. Are newcomers expected to operate with considerable uncertainty, or is the manager expected to clarify the newcomers' roles? Some cultures even put newcomers through considerable stress in the socialization process, including humility-inducing experiences, so newcomers will be more open to accepting the firm's values and norms. Long hours, tiring travel schedules, and an overload of work are examples of some socialization practices.

Interpersonal demands arise from relationships at work. Politics, leadership style, and group pressure are interpersonal demands. All of them reflect the values and assumptions that operate within the organization. Most organizations have basic assumptions about the nature of human relationships. For example, the Korean *chaebol* LG Group strongly values harmony in relationships and in society, and its decision-making policy emphasizes unanimity.

In the encounter stage, the expectations formed in

encounter The second socialization stage, in which newcomers learn the tasks associated with the job, clarify their roles, and establish new relationships at work.

anticipatory socialization may clash with the realities of the job. It is a time of facing the task, role, and interpersonal demands of the new job.

CHANGE AND ACQUISITION In the third and final stage of socialization, **change and acquisition**, newcomers begin to master the demands of the job. They become proficient at managing their tasks, clarifying and negotiating their roles, and engaging in relationships at work. The time when the socialization process is completed varies widely depending on the individual, the job, and the organization. The end of the process is signaled by newcomers being considered by themselves and others as organizational insiders.

16-5b Outcomes of Socialization

Newcomers who are successfully socialized should exhibit good performance, high job satisfaction, and the intention to stay with the organization. In addition, they should exhibit low levels of distress symptoms.[53] A high level of organizational commitment is also a mark of successful socialization.[54] This commitment is facilitated throughout the socialization process by the communication of values that newcomers can buy into. Successful socialization is also signaled by mutual influence; that is, the newcomers have made adjustments in the job and organization to accommodate their knowledge and personalities. Newcomers are expected to leave their mark on the organization and not be completely conforming.

When socialization is effective, newcomers understand and adopt the organization's values and norms. This ensures that the company's culture, including its central values, survives. It also provides employees a context for interpreting and responding to things that happen at work, and it ensures a shared framework of understanding among employees.[55] Newcomers adopt the company's norms and values more quickly when they receive positive support from organizational insiders. Sometimes this is accomplished through informal social gatherings.[56]

Socialization is not just the responsibility of the organization and the manager but of the employees as well. Newcomers who are more curious and adaptable adjust to their new jobs more effectively, leading to better performance.[57] Additionally, newcomers who have proactive personalities adjust more effectively to the organization because they are more likely to seek out the information they need to become socialized.[58]

change and acquisition
The third socialization stage, in which the newcomer begins to master the demands of the job.

16-6 ASSESSING ORGANIZATIONAL CULTURE

Although some organizational scientists argue for assessing organizational culture with quantitative methods, others say that organizational culture must be assessed with qualitative methods.[59] Quantitative methods, such as questionnaires, are valuable because of their precision, comparability, and objectivity. Qualitative methods, such as interviews and observations, are valuable because of their detail, descriptiveness, and uniqueness.

Two widely used quantitative assessment instruments are the Organizational Culture Inventory (OCI) and the Kilmann-Saxton Culture-Gap Survey. Both assess the behavioral norms of organizational cultures, as opposed to the artifacts, values, or assumptions of the organization.

16-6a Organizational Culture Inventory

The OCI focuses on behaviors that help employees fit into the organization and meet the expectations of co-workers. Using Maslow's motivational need hierarchy as its basis, it measures twelve cultural styles. The two underlying dimensions of the OCI are task/people and security/satisfaction. There are four satisfaction cultural styles and eight security cultural styles.

A self-report instrument, the OCI contains 120 questions. It provides an individual assessment of culture and may be aggregated to the work group and to the organizational level.[60] It has been used in firms throughout North America, Western Europe, New Zealand, and Thailand, as well as in U.S. military units, the Federal Aviation Administration, and nonprofit organizations.

16-6b Kilmann-Saxton Culture-Gap Survey

The Kilmann-Saxton Culture-Gap Survey focuses on what actually happens and on the expectations of others in the organization.[61] Its two underlying dimensions are (1) technical/human orientation and (2) short-term versus long-term time. With these two dimensions, the actual operating norms and the ideal norms in four areas are assessed. The areas are *task support* (short-term technical norms), *task innovation* (long-term technical norms), *social relationships* (short-term human orientation norms), and *personal freedom* (long-term human orientation norms). Significant gaps in any of the four areas are used as a point of departure for cultural change to improve performance, job satisfaction, and morale.

Like the OCI, the Gap Survey, as a self-report instrument, provides an individual assessment of culture and may be aggregated to the work group. It has been used in firms throughout the United States and in not-for-profit organizations.

16-6c Triangulation

A study of a rehabilitation center in a 400-bed hospital incorporated **triangulation**—the use of multiple methods to measure organizational culture—to improve inclusiveness and accuracy in measuring the organizational culture.[62] Triangulation has been used by anthropologists, sociologists, and other behavioral scientists to study organizational culture. Its name comes from the navigational technique of using multiple reference points to locate an object. In the rehabilitation center study, the three methods used to triangulate on the culture were (1) obtrusive observations by eight trained observers, which provided an outsider perspective; (2) self-administered questionnaires, which provided quantitative insider information; and (3) personal interviews with the center's staff, which provided qualitative contextual information.

The study showed that each of the three methods made unique contributions to the discovery of the rehabilitation center's culture. The complete picture could not have been drawn with just a single technique. Triangulation can lead to a better understanding of the phenomenon of culture and is the best approach to assessing organizational culture.

CHANGING ORGANIZATIONAL CULTURE

With rapid environmental changes such as globalization, workforce diversity, and technological innovation, the fundamental assumptions and basic values that drive the organization may need to be altered.

Changing an organization's culture is feasible but difficult.[63] One reason for the difficulty is that assumptions—the deepest level of culture—are often unconscious. As such, they are often resistant to confrontation and debate. Another reason for difficulty is that culture is deeply ingrained and behavioral norms and rewards are well learned.[64] In a sense, employees must unlearn the old norms before they can learn new ones. Managers who want to change the culture should look first to the ways culture is maintained. Research among hospitals found that change was welcomed in private hospitals with a collaborative culture whereas it was met with opposition in public hospitals with an autocratic culture.[65]

A model for cultural change that summarizes the interventions managers can use is presented in Figure 16.3. In this model, the numbers represent the steps managers can take. There are two basic approaches to changing the existing culture: (1) helping current members buy into a new set of values (steps 1, 2, and 3) or (2) adding newcomers

> **triangulation** The use of multiple methods to measure organizational culture.

HOT TREND #

GE Changes Its Culture by Crowdsourcing Its Employees

General Electric realized that cultures have a life cycle and that its culture needed to shift with the times. Employees felt that GE needed to become more decentralized and easier to do business with. The company simplified its operating mantra and created a new culture template called "GE Beliefs," including stay lean to go fast, learn and adapt to win, and empower and inspire each other, among other beliefs. For the first time in company history, these beliefs were crowdsourced from GE employees. Management wanted to drive a culture that employees wanted to see. One of the changes resulting from the culture shift is that annual events are now passé at GE. Strategic planning processes and employee appraisals have moved from yearly events to more continuous, real-time processes. The changes reinforce the new culture characterized by speed, simplicity, and customer focus.

SOURCE: R. Krishnamoorthy, "GE's Culture Challenge After Welch and Immelt," *Harvard Business Review*, January 26, 2015, accessed at https://hbr.org/2015/01/ges-culture-challenge-after-Welch-and-Immelt.

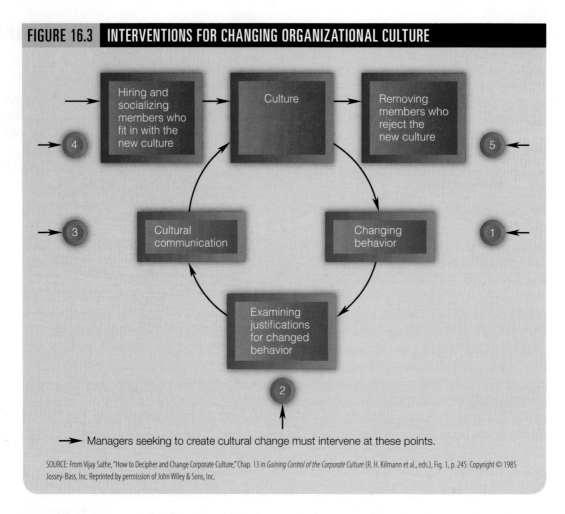

FIGURE 16.3 INTERVENTIONS FOR CHANGING ORGANIZATIONAL CULTURE

→ Managers seeking to create cultural change must intervene at these points.

SOURCE: From Vijay Sathe, "How to Decipher and Change Corporate Culture," Chap. 13 in *Gaining Control of the Corporate Culture* (R. H. Kilmann et al., eds.), Fig. 1, p. 245. Copyright © 1985 Jossey-Bass, Inc. Reprinted by permission of John Wiley & Sons, Inc.

and socializing them into the organization while removing current members as appropriate (steps 4 and 5).[66]

The first step is to change behavior in the organization. Even if behavior does change, however, this change is not sufficient for cultural change to occur. Behavior is an artifact (level 1) of culture. Individuals may change their behavior but not the values that drive it. They may rationalize, "I'm only doing this because my manager wants me to."

Therefore, managers must use step 2, which is to examine the justifications for the changed behavior. Are employees buying into the new set of values, or are they just complying?

The third step, cultural communication, is extremely important. All of the artifacts (personal enactment, stories, rites and ceremonies, rituals, and symbols) must send a consistent message about the new values and beliefs. It is crucial that the communication be credible; that is, managers must live the new values and not just talk about them. Leaders should pay attention to the informal social networks more so than structural positions in leading organizational change. These informal network communication channels combined with employees' values, and beliefs that managers are

highly committed to the change effort, can go a long way in making the change a success.[67]

The two remaining steps (4 and 5) involve shaping the workforce to fit the intended culture. First, the organization can revise its selection strategies to more accurately reflect the new culture. Second, the organization can identify individuals who resist the cultural change or who are no longer comfortable with the values in the organization. Reshaping the workforce should not involve a ruthless pursuit of nonconforming employees; it should be a gradual and subtle change that takes considerable time. Changing personnel in the organization is a lengthy process; it cannot be done effectively in a short period of time without considerable problems.

Evaluating the success of cultural change may be best done by looking at behavior. Cultural change can be assumed to be successful if the behavior is intrinsically motivated—that is, on "automatic pilot." If the new behavior were to persist even if rewards were not present, and if the employees have internalized the new value system, then the behavior is probably intrinsically motivated. If employees automatically respond to a crisis in ways consistent with the corporate culture, then the cultural change effort can be deemed successful.

Given the current business environment, managers may want to focus on three particular cultural modifications: (1) support for a global view of business, (2) reinforcement of ethical behavior, and (3) empowerment of employees to excel in product and service quality.

16-8 CHALLENGES TO DEVELOPING A POSITIVE, COHESIVE CULTURE

Developing an organizational culture is challenging in its own right, but certain factors pose additional challenges to managers in their pursuit of positive, cohesive cultures: mergers and acquisitions, globalization, ethics, and empowerment and quality.

16-8a Merger or Acquisition

One particular situation that may require cultural change is a merger or acquisition. The blending of two distinct organizational cultures may prove difficult despite good-faith efforts. One merger to watch is the marriage of H.J. Heinz and Kraft Foods, which will create one of the world's largest food companies (Kraft Heinz). The mega-merger combines two companies that are each more than 100 years old, selling the most familiar brands of ketchup, hot dogs, pickles, mustard, and other packaged foods. The merger will doubtlessly entail cost cutting and potential layoffs and the combining of two old corporate cultures. The question is whether a new culture will emerge that can be responsive to changing consumer tastes, as people move away from packaged foods to less processed, healthier options.

Sometimes mergers and acquisitions combine both organizational cultures and national cultures. Sweden's Volvo Construction Equipment acquired South Korea's Samsung Heavy Industry's construction division, and employees from both firms encountered challenges. They expressed concerns about differences in the two corporate cultures and national cultures and how "we" are different from "them." Complaints arose about why "they" did not understand "us." Careful attention to cultural differences and thoughtful post-acquisition integration efforts are necessary to help manage acculturation stress.[68]

Alterations in culture may also be required when an organization employs people from different countries. Research indicates that some organizational cultures actually enhance differences in national cultures.[69] One study compared foreign employees working in a multinational organization with employees working in different organizations within their own countries. The assumption was that the employees from various countries working for the same multinational organization would be more similar than employees working in diverse organizations in their native countries. The results were surprising in that there were significantly greater differences among the employees of the multinational than among managers working for different companies within their native countries. In the multinational, Swedes became more Swedish, Americans became more American, and so forth. It appears that employees enhance their national culture traditions even when working within a single organizational culture.[70] This is more likely to occur when diversity is moderate. When diversity is very high, employees are more likely to develop a shared identity in the organization's culture instead of relying on their own national culture.[71]

16-8b Developing a Global Organizational Culture

The values that drive the organizational culture should support a global view of the company and its efforts. Management should embody the shared values and reward employees who support the global view. Finally, the values should be consistent over time. Consistent values give an organization a unifying theme that competitors may be unable to emulate.[72] Because global corporations suffer from the conflicting pressures of centralization and decentralization, an overarching corporate culture that integrates the decentralized subsidiaries in locations around the world can be an asset in the increasingly competitive global marketplace.

16-8c Developing an Ethical Organizational Culture

The culture of an organization can have profound effects on the ethical behavior of organization members.[73] Organizations in which supervisors and top managers act as role models of ethical behavior and create an openness to discuss ethical issues have fewer incidents of unethical behavior.[74] When a company's culture promotes ethical norms, individuals behave accordingly. Thus, managers can encourage ethical behavior by being good role models for employees. They can institute the philosophy that ethical behavior makes good business sense and puts the company in congruence with the larger values of society.[75] Managers can also communicate that rationalizations for unethical behavior are not tolerated.

BY THE NUMBERS

3
levels of organizational culture

120
questions on the OCI

6
types of rites in organizations

>40,000
attendees at Berkshire Hathaway's annual meeting

1984
year when AT&T was broken up by the U.S. government

pio3/Shutterstock.com

Trust is another key to managing effectively ethical behavior, especially in cultures that encourage whistle-blowing (as we saw in Chapter 2). Employees must trust that whistle-blowers will be protected, that procedures used to investigate ethical problems will be fair and that management will take action to solve problems that are uncovered.

Many companies have implemented a code of ethics to help their employees discern right from wrong, but the impact of these codes is not always as positive as might be expected. The implementation of formal ethics guidelines might be expected to improve ethical behavior, yet some studies have shown the exact opposite—institution of formal ethics codes can actually lead to less ethical behavior among employees. There appear to be two main reasons for this: In some cases employees see the code of ethics as simply a management showpiece, leading to cynicism and resentment. In other cases, a heavy reliance on a strict set of rules may reduce the perceived need for employees to think about and be involved in ethical decision making, leading to inferior choices in the long run.[76]

16-8d Developing a Culture of Empowerment and Quality

Throughout this book, we have seen that successful organizations promote cultures that empower employees and excel in product and service quality. Empowerment serves to unleash employees' creativity and productivity,

Southwest Airlines' Culture of Sustainability

When Southwest Airlines undertook a major redesign of their 737-700 aircraft, they replaced their leather seats with environmentally responsible products and reduced the weight of each plane by 600 pounds. Instead of discarding the 80,000 leather seat covers, they upcycled by reusing the leather to have positive impacts. Southwest donated the leather to organizations around the globe. Young adults apprenticed in leatherwork at SOS Children's Villages Kenya and produced 2,100 pairs of shoes. The shoes were then donated to SOS Villages and Cura Orphanage, a home for children who have lost their parents to AIDS. Young people also learned how to make soccer balls, which were donated to Alive and Kicking, an organization that uses sports to raise awareness of HIV/AIDS and malaria prevention. Upcycling means converting waste materials to products of better value—which Southwest has done through Project LUVseat (repurpose with purpose).

Source: Southwest Airlines Co

SOURCES: http://www.swamedia.com/luvseat; "Southwest Airlines," *Conscious Company*, Winter 2015, 107–111.

and cultures that emphasize empowerment are preferred by employees. Companies that value empowerment and continuous improvement have cultures that promote high product and service quality.[77] However, to cultivate such a culture, organizations must eliminate traditional hierarchical notions of power. Moreover, it is essential that managers trust their employees. When an organization strives to develop a culture of trust, employees feel accountable for their performance, and thus sales performance and customer service performance improve.[78] The high level of quality of a Harley-Davidson motorcycle is not merely an artifact of better shop practices. The company's management has worked to foster a unique congenial and trusting relationship with its unions, ensuring that continuous improvement is an organizational priority rather than simply the latest management fad. Today's Harley hog costs less to produce and is more reliable than any before it, due in large part to the firm's incessant drive to produce a better product.[79] Involving employees in decision making, removing obstacles to their performance, and communicating the value of product and service quality reinforce the values of empowerment and quality in the organizational culture.

STUDY TOOLS 16

LOCATED AT BACK OF THE TEXTBOOK

☐ Rip out chapter review card

LOCATED AT WWW.CENGAGE.COM/LOGIN

☐ Track your knowledge and understanding of key concepts in business using 4LTR Press Online

☐ Review key term flashcards and create your own using StudyBits

☐ Create and complete practice quizzes based off of your notes and StudyBits

☐ Complete Online activities such as Matching and Fill-in-the-Blank exercises

☐ View chapter highlight box content, including the chapter videos, key exhibits and executive profiles.

17 | Career Management

M. Unal Ozmen/Shutterstock.com

LEARNING OUTCOMES

17-1 Explain occupational and organizational choice decisions.

17-2 Identify foundations for a successful career.

17-3 Explain the career stage model.

17-4 Explain the major tasks facing individuals in the establishment stage of the career stage model.

17-5 Identify the issues confronting individuals in the advancement stage of the career stage model.

17-6 Describe how individuals can navigate the challenges of the maintenance stage of the career stage model.

17-7 Explain how individuals withdraw from the workforce.

17-8 Explain how career anchors help form a career identity.

After finishing this chapter go to **PAGE 291** for **STUDY TOOLS.**

A **career** is a pattern of work-related experiences that spans the course of a person's life.[1] The two elements in a career are the objective element and the subjective element.[2] The *objective element* of the career is the observable, concrete environment. For example, you can manage a career by getting training to improve your skills. In contrast, the *subjective element* involves your perception of the situation. Rather than getting training (an objective element), you might change your aspirations (a subjective element). Thus, both objective events and the individual's perception of those events are important in defining a career.

Career management is a lifelong process of learning about self, jobs, and organizations, setting personal career goals, developing strategies for achieving the goals, and revising the goals based on work and life experiences.[3] Whose responsibility is career management? It is tempting to place the responsibility solely on individuals, but it is also the organization's duty to form partnerships with individuals in managing their careers. Careers are made up of exchanges between individuals and organizations; in other words, give-and-take is a part of the relationship between an organization and an individual when a career is involved.

Whether we approach it as managers or as employees, career management is an integral activity in our lives. It is important to understand careers for three reasons:

> **Whether we approach it as managers or as employees, career management is an integral activity in our lives.**

1. If we know what to look forward to over the course of our careers, we can take a proactive approach to planning and managing them.

2. As managers, we need to understand the experiences of our employees and colleagues as they pass through the various stages of careers over their life spans.

3. Career management is good business. It makes good financial sense to have highly trained employees keep up with their fields so that organizations can protect valuable investments in human resources.

17-1 OCCUPATIONAL AND ORGANIZATIONAL CHOICE DECISIONS

The time of the fast track to the top of the hierarchical organization is past. Also gone is the idea of lifetime employment in a single organization. Today's environment demands leaner organizations, and the paternalistic attitude that organizations should take care of employees no longer exists. Individuals now take on more responsibility for managing their own careers. So the concept of the career is undergoing a paradigm shift, as shown in Table 17.1. The old career is giving way to a new career characterized by discrete exchange, occupational excellence, organizational empowerment, and project allegiance.[4] Moreover, one recent study found that both individuals and organizations are actively involved in the management of the new career of employees. As such, the new career involves a type of participatory management technique on the part of the individual, but the organization responds to each individual's needs and thus is more flexible in its career development programs.[5]

Discrete exchange occurs when an organization gains productivity while a person gains work experience. It is a short-term arrangement that recognizes that job skills change in value and that renegotiation of the relationship must occur as conditions change. This idea contrasts sharply with the mutual loyalty contract of the old career paradigm in which employee loyalty was exchanged for job security.

Occupational excellence means continuously honing skills that can be marketed across organizations. The individual identifies more with the occupation ("I am an engineer") than the organization ("I am an IBMer"). In

> **career** The pattern of work-related experiences that spans the course of a person's life.
>
> **career management** A lifelong process of learning about self, jobs, and organizations; setting personal career goals; developing strategies for achieving the goals; and revising the goals based on work and life experiences.

TABLE 17.1   THE NEW VERSUS OLD CAREER PARADIGMS

New Career Paradigm	Old Career Paradigm
Discrete exchange means: > explicit exchange of specified rewards in return for task performance > basing job rewards on the current market value of the work being performed > engaging in disclosure and renegotiation on both sides as the employment relationship unfolds > exercising flexibility as each party's interests and market circumstances change	**The mutual loyalty contract meant:** > implicit trading of employee compliance in return for job security > allowing job rewards to be routinely deferred into the future > leaving the mutual loyalty assumptions as a political barrier to renegotiation > assuming employment and career opportunities are standardized and prescribed by the firm
Occupational excellence means: > performance of current jobs in return for developing new occupational expertise > employees identifying with and focusing on what is happening in their adopted occupation > emphasizing occupational skill development over the local demands of any particular firm > getting training in anticipation of future job opportunities; having training lead jobs	**The one-employer focus meant:** > relying on the firm to specify jobs and their associated occupational skill base > employees identifying with and focusing on what is happening in their particular firm > forgoing technical or functional development in favor of firm specific learning > doing the job first to be entitled to new training: making training follow jobs
Organizational empowerment means: > strategic positioning is dispersed to separate business units > everyone is responsible for adding value and improving competitiveness > business units are free to cultivate their own markets > new enterprise, spinoffs, and alliance building are broadly encouraged	**The top-down firm meant:** > strategic direction is subordinated to "corporate headquarters" > competitiveness and added value are the responsibility of corporate experts > business unit marketing depends on the corporate agenda > independent enterprise is discouraged, and likely to be viewed as disloyalty
Project allegiance means: > shared employer and employee commitment to the overarching goal of the project > a successful outcome of the project is more important than holding the project team together > financial and reputational rewards stem directly from project outcomes > upon project completion, organization and reporting arrangements are broken up	**Corporate allegiance meant:** > project goals are subordinated to corporate policy and organizational constraints > being loyal to the work group can be more important than the project itself > financial and reputational rewards stem from being a "good soldier" regardless of results > social relationships within corporate boundaries are actively encouraged

© Cengage Learning

contrast, the old one-employer focus meant that training was company specific and not meant to prepare the person for future job opportunities. A research study that focused on ethnographic data (interviews and stories) was conducted among software engineers in three European firms and two U.S. firms. The study showed that software engineers did not have much regard for their immediate supervisors, the organization, or formal dress codes. The only thing they did believe in was occupational excellence so that they could be better at what they do. In this regard, the authors of the study note that software engineers represent a unique group in terms of career development and that they fit well within the model of the "new career."[6]

Organizational empowerment means that power flows down to business units and in turn to employees. Employees are expected to add value and help the organization remain competitive by being innovative and creative. The old top-down approach meant that control and strategizing were done only by the top managers, and individual initiative could even be viewed as disloyalty or disrespect.

Project allegiance means that both individuals and organizations are committed to the successful completion of a project. The firm's gain is the project outcome; the individual's gain is experience and shared success. Upon project completion, the project team breaks up as individuals move on to new projects. Under the old paradigm, *corporate allegiance* was paramount, not project allegiance. The needs of projects were overshadowed by corporate policies and procedures. Work groups were long term, and keeping the group together was often a more important goal than project completion.

17-1a Preparing for the World of Work

When viewed from one perspective, you might say that we spend our youth preparing for the world of work. Educational and personal life experiences help an individual develop the skills and maturity needed to enter a career. Preparation for work is a developmental process that gradually unfolds over time.[7] As the time approaches for beginning a career, individuals face two difficult decisions: occupational choice and organizational choice.

17-1b Occupational Choice

In choosing an occupation, individuals assess their needs, values, abilities, and preferences and attempt to match them with an occupation that provides a fit. Personality plays a role in the selection of occupation. John Holland's theory of occupational choice contends that there are six types of personalities and that each personality is characterized by a set of interests and values.[8]

Holland also states that occupations can be classified using this typology. For example, realistic occupations include mechanic, restaurant server, and mechanical engineer. Artistic occupations include architect, voice coach, and interior designer. Investigative occupations include physicist, surgeon, and economist. Real estate agent, human resource manager, and lawyer are enterprising occupations. Social occupations include counselor, social worker, and member of the clergy. Conventional occupations include word processor, accountant, and data entry operator. Holland's typology has been used to predict career choices with a variety of international participants, including Australians, Germans, Indians, Mexicans, New Zealanders, Pakistanis, South Africans, and Taiwanese.[9]

An assumption that drives Holland's theory is that people choose occupations that match their personalities. People who fit Holland's social types are those who prefer jobs that are highly interpersonal in nature. They may see careers in physical and math sciences, for example, as not affording the opportunity for interpersonal relationships.[10] Therefore, to fulfill the desire for interpersonal work, they may gravitate toward jobs in customer service.

Although personality is a major influence on occupational choice, it is not the only influence. There are a host of other influences, including social class, parents' occupations, economic conditions, and geography.[11] Once a choice of occupation has been made, another major decision individuals face is the choice of organizations. Individuals are often attracted to organizations whose mission matches their passions and values.

17-1c Organizational Choice and Entry

There are several theories of how individuals choose organizations, ranging from theories that postulate very logical and rational choice processes to those that offer seemingly irrational processes. *Expectancy theory*, discussed in Chapter 5, can be applied to organizational choice.[12] According to expectancy theory, individuals choose organizations that maximize positive outcomes and avoid negative outcomes. Job candidates calculate the probability that an organization will provide a certain outcome and then compare the probabilities across organizations.

Other theories propose that people select organizations in a much less rational fashion. Job candidates may *satisfice*, that is, select the first organization that meets one or two important criteria and then justify their choice by distorting their perceptions.[13] The method of selecting an organization varies greatly among individuals and may reflect a combination of the expectancy theory and theories that postulate less rational approaches.

Entry into an organization is further complicated by the conflicts that occur between individuals and organizations during the process. Figure 17.1 illustrates these potential conflicts. The arrows in the figure illustrate four types of conflicts that can occur as individuals choose organizations and organizations choose individuals. The first two conflicts (1 and 2) occur between individuals and organizations. The first is a conflict between the organization's effort to attract candidates and the individual's choice of an organization. The individual needs complete and accurate information to make a good choice, but the organization may not provide it. Since the

> **Organizational empowerment means that power flows down to business units and in turn to employees.**

FIGURE 17.1 CONFLICTS DURING ORGANIZATIONAL ENTRY

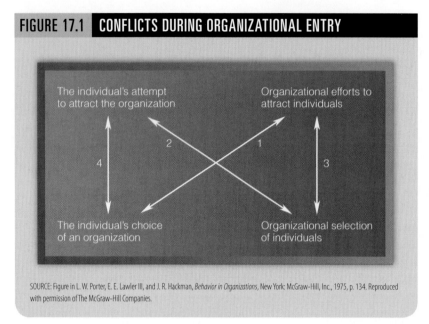

SOURCE: Figure in L. W. Porter, E. E. Lawler III, and J. R. Hackman, *Behavior in Organizations*, New York: McGraw-Hill, Inc., 1975, p. 134. Reproduced with permission of The McGraw-Hill Companies.

organization is trying to attract a large number of qualified candidates, it presents itself in an overly attractive way.

The second conflict is between the individual's attempt to attract several organizations and the organization's need to select the best candidate. Individuals want good offers, so they do not disclose their faults. They describe their preferred job in terms of the organization's opening instead of describing a job they would really prefer.

The third and fourth conflicts are internal to the two parties. The third is a conflict between the organization's desire to recruit a large pool of qualified applicants and the organization's need to select and retain the best candidate. In recruiting, organizations tend to give only positive information, and this sometimes results in mismatches between the individual and the organization. The fourth conflict is internal to the individual; it concerns his or her need to make a good choice from among more than one desirable job offer. This situation can occur when individuals present themselves as overly attractive and consequently receive more job offers than they would have otherwise received, some of which might be a poor fit in terms of their skills and career goals.[14]

The organizational choice and entry process is very complex due to the nature of these conflicts. Partial responsibility for preventing these conflicts rests with the individual. Individuals should conduct thorough research of the organization through published reports and industry

realistic job preview (RJP)
Both positive and negative information given to potential employees about the job they are applying for, thereby giving them a realistic picture of the job.

analyses. In addition, they should conduct a careful self-analysis and be as honest as possible with organizations to ensure a good match. The job interview process can be stressful, but also fun if it is engaged properly. Of course, the organization bears part of the responsibility for avoiding a mismatch by conducting an effective job interview.

REALISTIC JOB PREVIEWS The conflicts just discussed may result in unrealistic expectations on the part of the candidate. People entering the world of work may expect, for example, that they will receive explicit directions from their boss, only to find that they are left with ambiguity about how to do the job. They may expect that promotions will be based on performance but find that promotions are based mainly on political considerations. Some new hires also expect to be given managerial responsibilities right away, but they rarely are.

Giving potential employees a realistic picture of the job they are applying for is known as a **realistic job preview (RJP)**. When candidates are given both positive and negative information, they can make more effective job choices. Traditional recruiting practices often produce unrealistically high expectations, which produce low job satisfaction, whereas RJPs tend to create expectations that are much closer to reality and thus encourage many candidates to withdraw from further consideration.[15]

Time Warner Cable gives applicants RJPs through videos on its website. In the videos, current Time Warner employees discuss the nature of their jobs and the skills necessary for dealing with the challenges and frustrations that are involved with various jobs within the company.[16] Alcoa, a global leader in metals technology, engineering, and manufacturing, posts RJP information on its website about what it's like to be an entry-level employee at the company, and also provides a self-assessment of job fit so that candidates can decide whether to go forward with the next steps of the recruiting process. The Texas Department of Aging and Disability Services website shows videos of actual direct-support workers on the job, describing the rewards and challenges of working with people who have developmental disabilities.[17] Other companies' websites use photo and video tours of their offices and locations, videos of meetings, and testimonials from current employees about what it's like to work there.

RJPs can also be thought of as inoculation against disappointment. If new recruits know what to expect in the new job, they can prepare for the experience. Newcomers who are not given RJPs may find that their jobs don't measure up to their expectations. They may then believe that their employer was deceitful in the hiring process, become unhappy and mishandle job demands, and ultimately leave the organization.[18]

Job candidates who receive RJPs view the organization as honest and also have a greater ability to cope with the demands of the job.[19] RJPs perform another important function: uncertainty reduction.[20] Knowing what to expect, both good and bad, gives a newcomer a sense of control that is important to job satisfaction and performance.

With today's emphasis on ethics, organizations need to do all they can to be seen as operating consistently and honestly. Realistic job previews are one way in which companies can provide ethically required information. Ultimately, RJPs result in more effective matches, lower turnover, and higher organizational commitment and job satisfaction.[21] There is much to gain in providing realistic job information. The U.S. Army hopes to increase its recruitment and retention for Officer Candidate School by using a realistic job preview. By helping potential candidates understand what they will encounter in OCS, the Army looks to establish trust and honesty, reduce role ambiguity, and promote realistic expectations.[22]

In summary, the needs and goals of individuals and organizations can clash during entry into an organization. To avoid potential mismatches, individuals should conduct a careful self-analysis and provide accurate information about themselves to potential employers. They also need to ask appropriate questions. While applicants often focus on asking questions about organizational rewards and not employee contributions, they should seek both in obtaining a realistic job preview.[23] Organizations should present realistic job previews to show candidates both the positive and negative aspects of the job, along with the potential career paths available to the employee.

17-2 FOUNDATIONS FOR A SUCCESSFUL CAREER

In addition to planning and preparation, building a career takes attention and self-examination. One way you can build a successful career is by becoming your own career coach. Another is by developing your emotional

Olivier Le Moal/Shutterstock.com

intelligence, which is an important attribute if you want to climb the corporate ladder.

17-2a Becoming Your Own Career Coach

The best way to stay employed is to see yourself as being in business for yourself, even if you work for someone else. Know what skills you can package for other employers and what you can do to ensure that your skills are state of the art. Organizations need employees who have acquired multiple skills and are adept at more than one job. Employers want employees who have demonstrated competence in dealing with change.[24] To be successful, think of organizational change not as a disruption to your work but instead as the central focus of your work. You will also need to develop self-reliance, as discussed in Chapter 7, to deal effectively with the stress of change. Self-reliant individuals take an interdependent approach to relationships and are comfortable both giving and receiving support from others.

The people who will be most successful in the new career paradigm are individuals who are flexible, team oriented (rather than hierarchical), energized by change, and tolerant of ambiguity. Those who will become frustrated in the new career paradigm are individuals who are rigid in their thinking and learning styles and who have high needs for control. A commitment to continuous, lifelong learning will prevent you from becoming a professional dinosaur.[25] An intentional and purposeful commitment to taking charge of your professional life will be necessary in managing the new career.

Behaving in an ethical manner, standing by your values, and building a professional image of integrity are also very important. Major corporations such as Google conduct extensive reference checks on their applicants—not just with the references supplied in the application, but also with friends of such references. Behaving ethically is not just a benefit to your job application, since an ethical foundation can also help you withstand pressures that might endanger your career. One study suggests that executives succumb to the temptation of fraud because they feel pressure to keep up with inflated expectations and changes in cultural norms, short-term versus long-term orientations, the composition of the board of directors, and senior leadership in the organization.[26]

17-2b Emotional Intelligence and Career Success

Almost 40 percent of new managers fail within the first eighteen months on the job. What are the reasons for the failure? Newly hired managers flame out because they fail to build good relationships with peers and subordinates, are confused about what their bosses expect, lack internal political skills, or are unable to achieve the two or three most important objectives of the new job.[27] You'll note that these failures are all due to a lack of interpersonal skills.

In Chapter 13, we introduced the concept of *emotional intelligence (EI)* as an important determinant of conflict management skills. Daniel Goleman argues that emotional intelligence is a constellation of the qualities that mark a star performer at work. These attributes include self-awareness, self-control, trustworthiness, confidence, and empathy, among others. Goleman's belief is that emotional competencies are twice as important to people's success today as raw intelligence or technical know-how. He also argues that the further up the corporate ranks you go, the more important emotional intelligence becomes.[28] Employers, either consciously or unconsciously, look for emotional intelligence during the hiring process. And emotional intelligence applies across careers. EI predicts success in medical school and success as a doctor. Physicians who show interpersonal sensitivity and effective communication skills improve therapeutic outcomes for their patients.[29] Neither gender seems to have cornered the market on EI. Both men and women who can demonstrate high levels of EI are seen as particularly gifted and may be promoted more rapidly.[30]

Emotional intelligence is important to career success in many cultures. A recent study in Australia found that high levels of emotional intelligence are associated with job success. EI improves one's ability to work with other team members and to provide high-quality customer service, and workers with high EI are more likely to take steps to develop their skills. Several U.S. studies have confirmed that high emotional intelligence is an important attribute for the upwardly mobile worker.[31]

The good news is that emotional intelligence can be developed and does tend to improve throughout life. Accordingly, some companies are providing training in emotional intelligence competencies. When American Express began sending managers through an emotional competence training program, it found that trained managers outperformed those who lacked this training. In the year after completing the course, managers trained in emotional competence grew their businesses by an average of 18.1 percent compared to 16.2 percent for those businesses whose managers were untrained.[32]

17-3 THE CAREER STAGE MODEL

A common way of understanding careers is viewing them as a series of stages through which individuals pass during their working lives.[33] Figure 17.2 presents the career stage model, which will form the basis for our discussion in the remainder of this chapter.[34] The career stage model shows that individuals pass through four stages in their careers: establishment, advancement, maintenance, and withdrawal. It is important to note that the age ranges shown are approximations; that is, the timing of the career transitions varies greatly among individuals.

Establishment is the first stage of a person's career. The activities that occur in this stage center around learning the job and fitting into the organization and occupation. **Advancement** is a high achievement-oriented stage in which people focus on increasing their competence. The **maintenance** stage finds the individual trying to maintain productivity while evaluating progress toward career goals. The **withdrawal** stage involves contemplation of retirement or possible career change.

Along the horizontal axis in Figure 17.2 are the corresponding life stages for each career stage. These life stages are based on the pioneering research on adult development conducted by Levinson and his colleagues.

establishment The first stage of a person's career in which the person learns the job and begins to fit into the organization and occupation.

advancement The second, high achievement-oriented career stage in which people focus on increasing their competence.

maintenance The third stage in an individual's career in which the individual tries to maintain productivity while evaluating progress toward career goals.

withdrawal The final stage in an individual's career in which the individual contemplates retirement or possible career changes.

FIGURE 17.2 THE CAREER STAGE MODEL

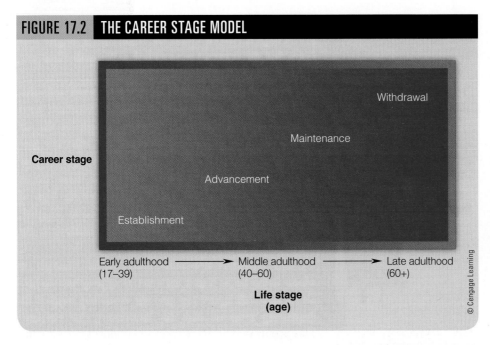

Career stage

Withdrawal

Maintenance

Advancement

Establishment

Early adulthood (17–39) ⟶ Middle adulthood (40–60) ⟶ Late adulthood (60+)

Life stage (age)

© Cengage Learning

The transition from school to work is a part of the establishment stage. Many graduates find the transition to be a memorable experience. The following description was provided by a new graduate who went to work at a large public utility:

We all tried to one-up each other about jobs we had just accepted … bragging that we had the highest salary, the best management training program, the most desirable coworkers, the most upward mobility … and believed we were destined to become future corporate leaders…. Every Friday after work we met for happy hour to visit and relate the events of the week. It is interesting to look at how the mood of those happy hours changed over the first few months … at first, we jockeyed for position in terms of telling stories about how great these new jobs were, or how weird our bosses were…. Gradually, things quieted down at happy hour. The mood went from "Wow, isn't this great" to "What in the world have we gotten ourselves into?" There began to be general agreement that business wasn't all it was cracked up to be.[37]

Levinson conducted extensive biographical interviews to trace the life stages of men and women. He interpreted his research in two books, *The Seasons of a Man's Life* and *The Seasons of a Woman's Life*.[35] Levinson's life stages are characterized by an alternating pattern of stability and transition.[36] Throughout the discussion of career stages that follows, we weave in the transitions of Levinson's life stages. Work and personal life are inseparable, and to understand a person's career experiences, we must also examine the unfolding of the person's personal experiences.

You can see that adult development provides unique challenges for the individual and that there may be considerable overlap between the stages. Now let us examine each career stage in detail.

 17-4 THE ESTABLISHMENT STAGE

During the establishment stage, the individual begins a career as a newcomer to the organization. This is a period of great dependence on others, as the individual is learning about the job and the organization. The establishment stage usually occurs during the beginning of the early adulthood years (ages eighteen to twenty-five). During this time, Levinson notes, an important personal life transition into adulthood occurs: the individual begins to separate from his or her parents and becomes less emotionally and financially dependent on them. Following this period is a fairly stable time of exploring the adult role and settling down.

Establishment is thus a time of big transitions in both personal and work life. At work, three major tasks face the newcomer: negotiating effective psychological contracts, managing the stress of socialization, and making a transition from organizational outsider to organizational insider.

17-4a Psychological Contracts

A **psychological contract** is an implicit agreement between the individual and the organization that specifies what each is expected to give and receive in the relationship.[38] Individuals expect to receive salary, status, advancement opportunities, and challenging work to meet their needs. Organizations expect to receive time, energy, talents,

> **psychological contract**
> An implicit agreement between an individual and an organization that specifies what each is expected to give and receive in the relationship.

Genentech Gets Employees Goats—Literally

Source: Facebook

Biotech company Genentech has been on *Fortune*'s Best Companies to Work For list for 17 years running. The company offers great perks such as compressed work weeks, fully paid sabbaticals, onsite fitness and medical centers, and paid time off for volunteering for its 12,000-plus employees. Genentech's intranet displayed a story saying that goats instead of gardeners would be used for the company's landscaping. Employees were asked to sign up and adopt a goat, based on scientific research showing that goats are better grazers when they have a lot of human interaction. Goats were rented and brought onsite, and more than 300 employees signed up to adopt a goat. The post appeared on April Fools Day and was a prank. Genentech employees do serious work but appreciate a sense of humor.

SOURCE: http://fortune.com/best-companies/genentech-9/

and loyalty in order to meet their goals. Working out the psychological contract with the organization begins with entry, but the contract is modified as the individual proceeds through the career.

Psychological contracts also exist between individuals.[39] During the establishment stage, newcomers form attachment relationships with many people in the organization. This process of working out effective psychological contracts within each relationship is important. Newcomers need social support in many forms and from many sources. Table 17.2 shows the type of psychological contracts, in the form of social support, that newcomers may work out with key insiders in the organization.

One common newcomer concern, for example, is whose behavior to watch for cues to appropriate behavior. Senior colleagues can provide modeling support by displaying behavior that the newcomer can emulate. This is only one of many types of support that newcomers need, though. Newcomers should contract with others to receive each of the needed types of support so that they can adjust to the new job. Organizers can also help newcomers form relationships early and should encourage the psychological contracting process between newcomers and insiders. Broken or breached psychological contracts can have detrimental outcomes. When a breach occurs, employees might experience negative emotional reactions that can lead to loss of trust, reduced

TABLE 17.2	**NEWCOMER–INSIDER PSYCHOLOGICAL CONTRACTS FOR SOCIAL SUPPORT**		
Type of Support	**Function of Supportive Attachments**	**Newcomer Concern**	**Examples of Insider Response/Action**
Protection from stressors	Direct assistance in terms of resources, time, labor, or environmental modification	What are the major risks/threats in this environment?	*Supervisor* cues newcomer to risks/threats.
Informational	Provision of information necessary for managing demands	What do I need to know to get things done?	*Mentor* provides advice on informal political climate in organization.
Evaluative	Feedback on both personal and professional role performances	How am I doing?	*Supervisor* provides day-to-day performance feedback during first week on new job.
Modeling	Evidence of behavioral standards provided through modeled behavior	Whom do I follow?	Newcomer is apprenticed to *senior colleague.*
Emotional	Empathy, esteem, caring, or love	Do I matter? Who cares if I'm here or not?	*Other newcomers* empathize with and encourage individual when reality shock sets in.

SOURCE: Table from D. L. Nelson, J. C. Quick, and J. R. Joplin, "Psychological Contracting and Newcomer Socialization: An Attachment Theory Foundation," from *Journal of Social Behavior and Personality* 6 (1991): 65.

job satisfaction, lower commitment to the organization, and higher turnover intentions.[40] The influence of a broken psychological contract is often felt even after an employee leaves a job. For example, laid-off employees who feel that a psychological contract breach has occurred are not only unhappy with their former firms but may also be both more cynical and less trusting of their new employers.[41]

17-5 THE ADVANCEMENT STAGE

The advancement stage is a period when many individuals strive for achievement. They seek greater responsibility and authority and strive for upward mobility. Usually around age thirty, an important life transition occurs, leading people to reassess their goals and make changes in their career dreams.[42] The transition at age thirty is followed by a period of stability during which the individual tries to find a role in adult society and wants to succeed in the career. During this stage, several issues are important: exploring career paths, finding a mentor, working out dual-career partnerships, and managing conflicts between work and personal life.

17-5a Career Paths and Career Ladders

Career paths are sequences of job experiences along which employees move during their careers.[43] At the advancement stage, individuals examine their career dreams and the paths they must follow to achieve those dreams. For example, suppose a person's dream is to become a top executive in the pharmaceutical industry. She majors in chemistry in college and takes a job with a nationally recognized firm. After she has adjusted to her job as a quality control chemist, she reevaluates her plan and decides that further education is necessary. Now she plans to pursue an MBA degree part time, hoping to gain expertise in management. From there, she hopes to be promoted to a supervisory position within her current firm. If this does not occur within five years, she will consider moving to a different pharmaceutical company. An alternate route would be to try to transfer to a sales position, from which she might advance into management.

The career paths of many women have moved from working in large organizations to starting their own businesses. Currently, there are 9.1 million women-owned firms in the United States. From 1997 to 2014, the number of woman-owned firms grew at 1.5 times the national average. What is the motivation for this exodus to entrepreneurship? The main reasons are to seek additional challenge and self-fulfillment and to have more self-determination and freedom.[44]

A **career ladder** is a structured series of job positions through which an individual progresses in an organization. For example, at Southwestern Bell, it is customary to move through a series of alternating line and staff supervisory assignments to advance toward upper management. Supervisors in customer service might be assigned next to the training staff and then rotate back as line supervisors in network services to gain experience in different departments.

Some companies use the traditional concept of career ladders to help employees advance in their careers. Other organizations take a more contemporary approach to career advancement. Sony, for instance, encourages creativity from its engineers by using nontraditional career

Blablo101/Shutterstock.com

HOT TREND

Unleashing the Power of Women at Kimberly-Clark

At Kimberly-Clark, a talent strategy called "Unleash Your Power" has earned accolades and helped the company increase the number of women in director-level and higher positions by a whopping 71 percent over four years. The idea behind the program is to build an inclusive workforce that looks, thinks, and behaves like the customers who purchase the company's personal care products such as Kleenex and Huggies. The accelerated development program supports movement within the company and access to hot jobs. High potential employees can swap jobs in another country for a three- to six-month assignment. Peer-to-peer mentoring is used, along with reverse mentoring in which Millennials mentor more seasoned employees. And because Kimberly-Clark is a global company, local leaders customize the program to meet their needs. In Malaysia, the focus is on retention. In the United States, employee resource groups are used. Thanks to the comprehensive "Unleash Your Power" program, the company has seen solid results for attracting, developing, and retaining women.

SOURCES: http://www.kimberly-clark.com/ourcompany/overview/recognition. aspx; http://catalyst.org/knowledge/kimberly-clark-corporation-unleash-your-power -strengthening-business-women-leaders

career path A sequence of job experiences that an employee moves along during his or her career.

career ladder A structured series of job positions through which an individual progresses in an organization.

paths in which people have the freedom to move on to interesting and challenging job assignments without notifying their supervisors. If they join a new project team, their current boss is expected to let them move on. This self-promotion philosophy at Sony is seen as a key to high levels of innovation and creative new product designs.

There has been heightened interest in international assignments in response to globalization and global staffing issues. One problem in this regard has been that most expatriate assignments are not successful. Therefore, organizations have been facing the challenge of properly training and preparing individuals for such assignments. One proposed solution is alternative international work assignments such as commuter work assignments, virtual assignments, short-term assignments, and so on, which can be used to help individuals gain international work experience in preparation for higher levels in the organization.[45]

Another approach used by some companies to develop skills is the idea of a *career lattice*—an approach to building competencies by moving laterally through different departments in the organization or by moving through different projects. Top management support for the career lattice is essential because in traditional terms an employee who has made several lateral moves might not be viewed with favor. However, the career lattice approach is an effective way to develop an array of skills to ensure one's employability.[46]

17-5b Finding a Mentor

Exploring career paths is one important activity in advancement. Another crucial activity during advancement is finding a mentor. A **mentor** is an individual who provides guidance, coaching, counseling, and friendship to a protégé. Mentors are important to career success because they perform both career and psychosocial functions.[47]

The *career functions* provided by a mentor include sponsorship, facilitating exposure and visibility, coaching, and protection. *Sponsorship* means actively helping the individual get job experiences and promotions. *Facilitating exposure and visibility* means providing opportunities for the protégé to develop relationships with key figures in the organization in order to advance. *Coaching* involves providing advice in both career and job performance. *Protection* is

mentor An individual who provides guidance, coaching, counseling, and friendship to a protégé.

At IBM, mentoring isn't optional; it's an important performance metric, and senior managers are evaluated on specific mentoring goals.

JuliusKielaitis/Shutterstock.com

provided by shielding the protégé from potentially damaging experiences. Career functions are particularly important to the protégé's future success. One study found that the amount of career coaching received by protégés was related to more promotions and to higher salaries four years later.[48]

The mentor also performs *psychosocial functions*: role modeling, acceptance and confirmation, counseling, and friendship. *Role modeling* occurs when the mentor displays behavior for the protégé to emulate. Such modeling facilitates social learning. *Acceptance and confirmation* are important to both the mentor and protégé. When the protégé feels accepted by the mentor, it fosters a sense of pride. Likewise, positive regard and appreciation from the junior colleague provide a sense of satisfaction for the mentor. *Counseling* by a mentor helps the protégé explore personal issues that arise and require assistance. *Friendship* is another psychosocial function that benefits both mentor and protégé alike.

In effective mentoring relationships, there is regular contact between mentor and protégé that has clearly specified purposes. Mentoring should be consistent with the corporate culture and the organization's goals. Both mentors and protégés alike should be trained in ways to manage the relationship. Mentors should be held accountable and rewarded for their role. They should be perceived (accurately) by protégés as having considerable influence within the organization.[49] While

> In effective mentoring relationships, there is regular contact between mentor and protégé that has clearly specified purposes.

it may be tempting to go after the "top dog" as your mentor, personality compatibility is also an important factor in the success or failure of a mentoring relationship. Thus, mentors who are similar to their protégés in terms of personality traits such as extraversion, and whose expectations are largely met by the relationship, are more likely to show interest in continuing the arrangement.[50]

At IBM, mentoring isn't optional; it's an important performance metric, and senior managers are evaluated on specific mentoring goals. From their first day on the job, employees are told that they are expected to have a mentor and given help on getting a mentor and contracting with a mentor. Senior managers are evaluated on the development of their mentees and their own effectiveness as mentors. IBM has goals around cross-cultural and cross-gender mentoring as well.[51]

Mentoring programs are also effective ways of addressing the challenge of workforce diversity. The mentoring process, however, presents unique problems—including the availability of mentors, issues of language and acculturation, and cultural sensitivity—for minority groups such as Hispanic Americans. Negative stereotypes can limit minority members' access to mentoring relationships and the benefits associated with mentoring.[52] To address this problem, companies need to take steps to facilitate access to mentors for minority employees.

Mentoring programs may be informal or formal. *Informal mentoring programs* identify pools of mentors and protégés, provide training in the development of effective mentoring and diversity issues, and then provide informal opportunities for the development of mentoring relationships. *Network groups* are another

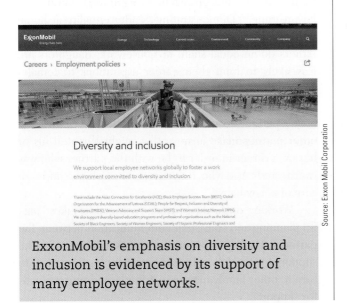

Diversity and inclusion

We support local employee networks globally to foster a work environment committed to diversity and inclusion.

These include the Asian Connection for Excellence (ACE); Black Employee Success Team (BEST); Global Organization for the Advancement of Latinos (GOAL); People for Respect, Inclusion and Diversity of Employees (PRIDE); Veteran Advisory and Support Team (VAST); and Women's Interest Network (WIN). We also support diversity-based education programs and professional organizations such as the National Society of Black Engineers, Society of Women Engineers, Society of Hispanic Professional Engineers and

Source: Exxon Mobil Corporation

ExxonMobil's emphasis on diversity and inclusion is evidenced by its support of many employee networks.

avenue for mentoring. These groups help members identify with a few others who are like them within an organization, build relationships with them, and build social support. Network groups enhance the chance that minorities will find mentors.[53] ExxonMobil's emphasis on diversity and inclusion is evidenced by its support of many employee networks. The networks provide professional development programs, mentor new employees, and engage in community service. Some of the networks at ExxonMobil are the Black Employee Success Team (BEST), Inclusion and Diversity of Employees (PRIDE), and Women's Interest Network (WIN).[54]

Some companies have *formal mentoring programs*. At PricewaterhouseCoopers (PwC) each intern is assigned both a peer mentor to help with day-to-day questions and an experienced mentor to help with larger issues such as career path development. As an international firm, PwC also employs similar methods overseas. In PwC's Czech Republic operations, a team of two mentors—one of whom is called a "counselor"—fills the same guidance role as the two mentors generally fill for U.S. employees.[55]

Mentoring has had a strong impact in shaping the identities of the Big Four accounting firms. In one study, every partner who was interviewed reported having at least one mentor who played a critical role in his or her attainment of the partnership and beyond. These protégés' work identities were shaped through mentoring, and their work goals, language, and even lifestyles reflected the imperatives of the Big Four firm for which they worked.[56] Protégés were schooled on partners' "hot buttons" (what not to talk about), what to wear, to "tuck in the tie," and not to "cut the grass" without wearing a shirt.

In companies without formal mentoring programs, junior employees are often left to negotiate their own mentoring relationships. The barriers to finding a mentor under these circumstances include lack of access to mentors, fear of initiating a mentoring relationship, and fear that supervisors or coworkers might not approve of the mentoring relationship. Individuals may also be afraid to initiate a mentoring relationship because it might be misconstrued as a sexual advance by the potential mentor or by others. Potential mentors may fear this misinterpretation as well. Some are therefore unwilling to develop a relationship because of their own or the protégé's gender. Women report more of these barriers than men, and individuals who lack previous experience report more barriers to finding a mentor.[57]

There are other gender differences found in mentoring relationships. Male protégés report receiving less psychological support than female protégés. Additionally, male mentors report giving more career development support, whereas female mentors report giving more psychological support.[58] Mentoring can be particularly important for women in male-dominated professions. In these environments, women who have male mentors have higher levels of compensation and career progress satisfaction than those without a male mentor.[59] Organizations can encourage junior workers to approach mentors by providing opportunities for them to interact with senior colleagues. The immediate supervisor is not always the best mentor for an individual, so exposure to other senior workers is important. Seminars, multilevel teams, and social events can serve as vehicles for bringing together potential mentors and protégés.

Mentoring relationships go through a series of phases: initiation, cultivation, separation, and redefinition. There is no fixed time length for each phase because each relationship is unique. The *initiation* phase is when the mentoring relationship begins to take on significance for both the mentor and the protégé. In the *cultivation* phase the relationship becomes more meaningful, and the protégé shows rapid progress because of the career support and psychosocial support provided by the mentor. Protégés influence mentors as well. In the *separation* phase the protégé feels the need to assert independence and work more autonomously. Separation can be voluntary, or it can result from an involuntary change (the protégé or mentor may be promoted or transferred). The separation phase can be difficult if it is resisted, either by the mentor (who is reluctant to let go of the relationship) or by the protégé (who resents the mentor's withdrawal of support). Moreover, separation may result from a conflict that disrupts the mentoring relationship rather than proceeding smoothly and naturally.

The *redefinition* phase occurs if separation has been successful. In this phase, the relationship takes on a new identity as the two parties consider each other colleagues or friends. The mentor feels pride in the protégé, and the protégé develops a deeper appreciation for the support from the mentor.

Why are mentors so important? Aside from the support they provide, research shows that mentors are important to the protégé's future success. For example, studies have demonstrated that individuals with mentors have higher promotion rates and higher incomes than individuals who do not have mentors.[60] Professionals who have mentors earn between \$5,600 and \$22,000 more per year than those who do not.[61] Individuals with mentors are also better decision makers.[62] It is not just the presence of the mentor that yields these benefits. The quality of the relationship is the most important element.[63]

17-5c Dual-Career Partnerships

During the advancement stage, many individuals face another transition. They settle into a relationship with a life partner. This lifestyle transition requires adjustment in many respects—learning to live with another person, being concerned with someone besides yourself, dealing with an extended family, and many other demands. The partnership can be particularly stressful if both members are career oriented.

The two-career lifestyle has increased in recent years due in part to the need for two incomes to maintain a preferred standard of living. **Dual-career partnerships** are relationships in which both people have important career roles. This type of partnership can be mutually beneficial, but it can also be stressful. Often these stresses center around stereotypes that providing income is a man's responsibility and taking care of the home is the woman's domain. Thus, men who adhere to traditional gender beliefs may be threatened when the wife's income exceeds their own. However, working women's satisfaction with their marriage is affected by how much the husband helps with child care. Beliefs about who should do what in the partnership complicate the dual-career issue.

One stressor in a dual-career partnership is time pressure. When both partners work outside the home, there may be a time crunch in fitting in work, family, and leisure time.[64] Demonstrating gender equality at home benefits the next generation in their work lives. When fathers do an equal share of housework, daughters are less likely to limit their career aspirations to female-stereotyped jobs.[65] Another issue to work out is whose career takes precedence. For example, what happens if one partner is transferred to another city? Must the other partner make a move that might threaten his or her own career in order to be with the partner who was transferred? And who, if anyone, will stay home and take care of a new baby?

Working out a dual-career partnership takes careful planning and consistent communication between the partners. Each partner must serve as a source of social support for the other. In addition, couples may need to turn to other family members, friends, and professionals for support.

dual-career partnership
A relationship in which both people have important career roles.

17-5d Work–Home Conflicts

An issue related to dual-career partnerships that is faced throughout the career cycle but often first encountered in the advancement phase is the conflict between work and personal life. Such conflict negatively affects an individual's overall quality of life and may even lead to emotional exhaustion. Dealing with customer complaints all day, failed sales calls, or missed deadlines can magnify negative events at home, and vice versa.[66]

Responsibilities at home will likely clash at times with responsibilities at work, so these conflicts must be planned for. Suppose a child gets sick at school. Who will pick up the child and stay home with him? Couples must work together to resolve these conflicts. At Eli Lilly and Co., only 36 percent of workers said it was possible to get ahead in their careers and still devote sufficient time to family. This is surprising because Lilly has a reputation as one of the world's most family-friendly workplaces.[67] A recent study found that an individual's work–home conflict can lead to unfavorable critique and discouragement of goal attainment by that individual's partner, leading to mutual feelings of exhaustion and negativity.[68]

Despite Eli Lilly's reputation as a family-friendly workplace, most employees still have challenges balancing work and family issues.

Work–home conflicts are particular problems for working women.[69] Women have been quicker to share the provider role than men have been to share responsibilities at home.[70] When working women experience work–home conflict, their performance declines, and they suffer more strain. Work–home conflict is a broad topic. It can be narrowed further into work–family conflict, in which work interferes with family, or family–work conflict, in which family or home life interferes with work.[71] Individuals who believe that men and women should share work and home lives equally experience more guilt from work–home conflict than traditionalists, who tend to feel more guilt when home life interferes with work.[72] Cultural differences arise in these types of conflicts. One study showed that while Americans experience more family–work conflict, Chinese experience more work–family conflict.[73] For example, women in management positions in China were very positive about future advancements and carried a strong belief in their ability to succeed. This, in turn, caused them to reevaluate their personal and professional identities. Such an identity transformation is marked by happiness associated with career advancement, even though many women foresaw emotional costs with such career advancement. This study indicated that female Chinese managers experience work–family conflict in part because the Chinese culture emphasizes close social ties and *guanxi*.[74]

WAYS TO MANAGE WORK–HOME CONFLICT To help individuals deal with work–home conflict, companies like Ernst & Young offer **flexible work schedules**, programs that give employees the freedom to set their own hours so that they can attend to personal issues.[75] *Telecommuting* breaks down barriers of time and space by allowing people to work no matter where they are. At Cisco Systems, employees who telecommuted experienced higher productivity, work-life flexibility, and job satisfaction. Furthermore, they reported saving a combined $10.3 million in fuel costs, while the company saved $277 million per year in time and productivity costs.

Company-sponsored child care is another way to help. Companies with on-site day-care centers include Johnson & Johnson, Perdue Farms, and Campbell Soup. Mitchell Gold + Bob Williams, an award-winning furniture maker, believes that treating people right must come first. Its 2,700-square-foot on-site day-care center is education-based rather than activity-based and operates at break-even rates to make it more accessible.[76] Whereas large companies

flexible work schedule
A work schedule that allows employees discretion in order to accommodate personal concerns.

FASTFACT

Intel Offers Bonding Leave for New Moms and Dads

Intel already offers thirteen weeks of paid leave to new mothers, like many other companies. Their new program, bonding leave, adds eight weeks of paid time off for male and female employees who have new children. The bonding leave can be taken within the first year of a child's birth, adoption, or foster care placement. Intel recognizes that both mothers and fathers want time with children, and they want to make life easier for them. The company also wants to do more to attract and retain talented workers.

SOURCE: D. Lumb, "Intel Pledges Time Off for New Moms and Dads," *Fast Company*, January 16, 2015, accessed at http://www.fastcompany.com/3041088/intel-pledges-time-off-for-new-moms-and-dads.

Source: Care.com

Harvard University has partnered with Parents in a Pinch to provide eldercare services for its employees who may have family in need.

may offer corporate day care, small companies can also assist their workers by providing referral services for locating the type of child care the workers need. For smaller organizations, this is a cost-effective alternative. At the very least, companies can be sensitive to work–home conflicts and handle them on a case-by-case basis with flexibility and concern.

A program of increasing interest that organizations can provide is **eldercare**. Often workers find themselves part of the so-called sandwich generation. They are expected to care for both their children and their elderly parents. In many countries, the need for eldercare is expected to increase dramatically over the next decade.[77] Inclusion in this extremely stressful role is reported more often by women than men.[78] The impact of caring for an aging loved one is often underestimated—17 percent of those who provide such care eventually quit their jobs due to time constraints, and another 15 percent cut back their work hours.[79] Caring for an elderly dependent at home not only creates work–home conflicts for an employee but also takes a toll on the employee's own well-being and performance at work. This is most often the case if the organization is not one that provides a supportive climate for discussion of eldercare issues.[80] Harvard University has taken steps to help its faculty and staff dealing with eldercare issues by contracting with Parents in a Pinch, Inc., a firm that specializes in nanny services and also offers eldercare. Fannie Mae's comprehensive approach to eldercare began in 1999.

eldercare Assistance in caring for elderly parents and/or other elderly relatives.

The company, which has more than 6,000 employees, offers an Elderkit planner, reimbursement for emergency backup care, and sessions with a professional eldercare consultant to assist with options for elderly parents.[81]

John Beatrice is one of a growing number of men making work fit their family rather than trying to fit family around career. John remembers his father working most of the night so he could be at John's athletic events during the day, and John wants the same for his family. So while job sharing, flexible scheduling, and telecommuting have traditionally been viewed as meeting the needs of working mothers, John and other men are increasingly taking advantage of such opportunities. In John's case, flexible work hours at Ernst & Young allow him to spend part of his mornings and afternoons coaching a high school hockey team. In John's assessment, flexible work hours actually lead him to work more hours than he would otherwise, and he's happier about doing it. Not surprisingly, John's employer also benefits from the arrangement. After nineteen years, John is more loyal than ever and still loves what he does.[82]

Alternative work arrangements such as flextime, compressed workweeks, work-at-home arrangements, part-time hours, job sharing, and leave options can help employees manage work–home conflicts. Managers must not let their biases get in the way of these benefits. Top managers may be less willing to grant alternative work arrangements to men than to women, to supervisors than to subordinates, and to employees caring for elderly parents rather than children, but it is important that family-friendly policies be applied fairly.[83]

17-6 THE MAINTENANCE STAGE

Maintenance may be a misnomer for this career stage because some people continue to grow in their careers, although the growth is usually not at the rate it was earlier. A career crisis at midlife may accompany the midlife transition. A senior product manager at Borden found himself in such a crisis and described it this way: "When I was in college, I had thought in terms of being president of a company.... But at Borden I felt used and cornered. Most of the guys in the next two rungs above me had either an MBA or fifteen to twenty years of experience in the food business. My long-term plans stalled."[84]

Some individuals who reach a career crisis are burned out, and a month's vacation will help, according to Carolyn Smith Paschal, who owns an executive search firm. She recommends that companies give employees in this stage sabbaticals instead of bonuses. This would help rejuvenate them. Some individuals, on the other hand, reach the maintenance stage with a sense of achievement and contentment, feeling no need to strive for further upward mobility. Whether the maintenance stage is a time of crisis or contentment, however, there are two issues to grapple with: sustaining performance and becoming a mentor.

17-6a Sustaining Performance

Remaining productive is a key concern for individuals in the maintenance stage. This becomes challenging when one reaches a **career plateau**, a point where the probability of moving further up the hierarchy is low. Some people handle career plateauing fairly well, but others may become frustrated, bored, and dissatisfied with their jobs. To keep employees productive, organizations can provide challenges and opportunities for learning. *Lateral moves* are one option. Another option is to involve the employee in *project teams* that provide new tasks and skill development. The key is keeping the work stimulating and involving. Individuals at this stage also need continued affirmation of their value to the organization. They need to know that their contributions are significant and appreciated.[85]

17-6b Becoming a Mentor

During maintenance, individuals can make a contribution by sharing their wealth of knowledge and experience with others. Opportunities to be mentors to new employees can keep senior workers motivated and involved in the organization. It is important for organizations to reward mentors for the time and energy they expend. Some employees adapt naturally to the mentor role, but others may need training on how to coach and counsel junior workers.

Maintenance is a time of transition, like all career stages. It can be managed by individuals who know what to expect and plan to remain productive, as well as by organizations that focus on maximizing employee involvement in work. According to Levinson, during the latter part of the maintenance stage, another life transition occurs. The so-called age-fifty transition is another time of reevaluating the dream and working further on the issues raised in the midlife transition. Following the age-fifty transition is a fairly stable period. During this time, individuals begin to plan seriously for withdrawing from their careers.

17-7 THE WITHDRAWAL STAGE

The withdrawal stage usually occurs later in life and signals that a long period of continuous employment will soon come to a close. Older workers may face discrimination and stereotyping. They are often viewed by others as less productive, more resistant to change, and less motivated. However, older workers are one of the most undervalued groups in the workforce. They can provide continuity in the midst of change and can serve as mentors and role models to younger generations of employees.

Discrimination against older workers is prohibited under the Age Discrimination in Employment Act (go to eeoc.gov/policy/adea.html to read the provisions of this 1967 act). Organizations should strive to create a culture that values older workers' contributions. With their level of experience, strong work ethic, and loyalty, these workers have much to contribute. In fact, older workers have lower rates of tardiness and absenteeism, are more safety conscious, and are more satisfied with their jobs than are younger workers.[86]

17-7a Planning for Change

The decision to retire is an individual one, but the need for planning is universal. A retired sales executive from Boise Cascade said that the best advice is to "plan no unplanned retirement."[87] This means carefully planning not only the transition but also the activities you will be involved in once the transition is made. All options should be open for consideration. One recent trend is to work as a temporary top-level executive. The qualities of a good temporary executive

> **career plateau** A point in an individual's career at which the probability of moving farther up the hierarchy is low.

BY THE NUMBERS

pio3/Shutterstock.com

6
personalities in
Holland's typology

9.1 million
women-owned busi-
nesses in the United
States

$10.3 million
saved by employees
at Cisco in fuel costs
by telecommuting

17 percent
of workers responsible
for eldercare in their
families quit their jobs

11 percent
of retirees fully with-
draw from work

include substantial high-level management experience, financial security that allows the executive to choose only assignments that really interest her, and a willingness to relocate.[88] Some individuals at the withdrawal stage find this an attractive option.

Planning for retirement should include not only financial planning but also a plan for psychologically withdrawing from work. The pursuit of hobbies and travel, volunteer work, or more time with extended family can all be part of the plan. The key is to plan early and carefully, as well as to anticipate the transition with a positive attitude and a full slate of desirable activities.

17-7b Retirement

There are several retirement trends right now, ranging from early retirement to phased retirement to never retiring. Some adults are choosing a combination of these options, leaving their first career for some time off before reentering the workforce either part time or full time doing something they enjoy. For more and more Americans, the idea of a retirement spent sitting beside the swimming pool sounds, for lack of a better word, boring. Factors that influence the decision of when to retire include company policy, financial considerations, family support or pressure, health, and opportunities for other productive activities.

During the withdrawal stage, the individual faces a major life transition that Levinson refers to as the *late adulthood transition* (ages sixty to sixty-five). One's own mortality becomes a major concern, and the loss of family members and friends becomes more frequent. The person works to achieve a sense of integrity in life; that is, the person works to find the encompassing meaning and value in life.

Retirement need not be a complete cessation of work. Many alternative work arrangements can be considered, and many companies offer flexibility in these options. **Phased retirement** is a popular option for retirement-age workers who want to gradually reduce their hours and/or responsibilities. There are many forms of phased retirement, including reduced workdays or workweeks, job sharing, and consulting and mentoring

---

phased retirement
An arrangement that allows employees to reduce their hours and/or responsibilities in order to ease into retirement.

Merrill Edge's Face Retirement Mobile App

Research shows that when we think of our future selves, we consider ourselves in the third-person—as if we are someone else. It may be the reason few people save enough for retirement. Merrill Edge developed an app called Face Retirement to help people overcome the disconnects between their current and future selves.

The app is free, and users input their gender and age along with a selfie. 3D imaging technology creates a lifelike animation that shows what they will look like in older ages. The idea is to make people brave enough to take control of their retirement planning. The app also forecasts costs of living at future ages and provides options for saving and investing, along with the ability to share pictures of future selves on Twitter and Facebook. The intent is to get people to face their retirement in a fun, engaging way.

SOURCES: http://nautil.us/issue/16/nothingness/why-we-procrastinate; http://newsroom.bankofamerica.com/press-releases/consumer-banking/new-merrill-edge-mobile-app-uses-3d-technology-put-retirement-planni.

arrangements. Many organizations cannot afford the loss of large numbers of experienced employees at once. The average retirement age in the United States is 62, and it has been slowly increasing. In fact, Americans who are still working say they expect to work until age 66. This may reflect better health and longer life spans, changes in employer-sponsored retirement plans, or lifestyle choices to simply work longer.[89] Many individuals do not fully retire, but engage in **bridge employment**, which is employment that takes place after a person retires from a full-time position but before the person's permanent withdrawal from the workforce. Bridge employment is related to retirement satisfaction and overall life satisfaction.[90]

Some companies are helping employees transition to retirement in innovative ways. For example, retired individuals can continue their affiliation with the organization by serving as mentors to employees who are embarking on retirement planning or other career transitions. This helps diminish the fear of loss some people have about retirement because the retiree has an option to serve as a mentor or consultant to the organization.

Lawrence Livermore National Labs (LLNL) employs some of the best research minds in the world. And when these great minds retire from full-time work, they have numerous opportunities to continue contributing. LLNL's retiree program website lists a wide variety of requests, ranging from guiding tours and making phone calls to providing guidance on current research and helping researchers make contact with other researchers.[91] Programs like this one help LLNL avoid the typical knowledge drain that takes place when seasoned veteran employees retire.

Now that you understand the career stage model, you can begin to conduct your own career planning. It is never too early to start.

17-8 CAREER ANCHORS

Much of an individual's self-concept rests upon a career. Over the course of the career, **career anchors** are developed—self-perceived talents, motives, and values that guide an individual's career decisions.[92] Edgar Schein developed the concept of career anchors based on a twelve-year study of MBA graduates from the Massachusetts Institute of Technology (MIT). Schein found great diversity in the graduates' career histories but great similarities in the way they explained the career decisions they had made.[93] From extensive interviews with the graduates, Schein developed the five career anchors (see box).

Career anchors emerge over time and may be modified by work or life experiences. The importance of knowing your career anchor is that it can help you find a match between you and an organization. For example, individuals with creativity as an anchor may find themselves stifled in bureaucratic organizations. Textbook sales may not be the place for an individual with a security anchor because of the frequent travel and seasonal nature of the business.

> **bridge employment**
> Employment that takes place after a person retires from a full-time position but before the person's permanent withdrawal from the workforce.
>
> **career anchors** A network of self-perceived talents, motives, and values that guide an individual's career decisions.

STUDY TOOLS 17

LOCATED AT BACK OF THE TEXTBOOK

☐ Rip out chapter review card

LOCATED AT WWW.CENGAGE.COM/LOGIN

☐ Track your knowledge and understanding of key concepts in business using 4LTR Press Online

☐ Review key term flashcards and create your own using StudyBits

☐ Create and complete practice quizzes based off of your notes and StudyBits

☐ Complete Online activities such as Matching and Fill-in-the-Blank exercises

☐ View chapter highlight box content, including the chapter videos, key exhibits and executive profiles.

18 | Managing Change

180°

Bian-k./Shutterstock.com

LEARNING OUTCOMES

18-1 Identify the major external and internal forces for change in organizations.

18-2 Describe how different types of change vary in scope.

18-3 Discuss methods organizations can use to manage resistance to change.

18-4 Explain Lewin's organizational change model.

18-5 Explain how companies determine the need to conduct an organization development intervention.

18-6 Discuss the major group-focused techniques for organization development intervention.

18-7 Discuss the major individual-focused techniques for organization development intervention.

After finishing this chapter go to **PAGE 307** for **STUDY TOOLS.**

18-1 FORCES FOR CHANGE IN ORGANIZATIONS

Change has become the norm in most organizations. Many American companies have experienced plant closings, failures, mergers and acquisitions, and downsizing. *Adaptiveness*, *flexibility*, and *responsiveness* are characteristics of organizations that will succeed in meeting the competitive challenges that businesses face.[1] In the past, organizations could succeed by claiming excellence in one area—quality, reliability, or cost, for example—but this is not the case today. The current environment demands excellence in all areas and vigilant leaders. A recent survey of CEOs who were facing crises found that 50% of them said they believed problems arrived "suddenly" and that they had not prepared adequately for them. More than 10% said they were, in fact, the last to know about problems.[2]

As we saw in Chapter 1, change is what's on managers' minds. The pursuit of organizational effectiveness through downsizing, restructuring, reengineering, productivity management, cycle-time reduction, and other efforts is paramount. Organizations are in a state of tremendous turmoil and transition, and all members are affected. Continued downsizings may have left firms leaner but not necessarily richer. Though downsizing can increase shareholder value by better aligning costs with revenues, firms may suffer from public criticism for their actions. Laying off employees may be accompanied by increases in CEO pay and stock options, linking the misery of employees with the financial success of owners and management.[3]

Organizations must also deal with ethical, environmental, and other social issues. Competition is fierce, and companies can no longer afford to rest on their laurels. Understanding this situation, American Airlines has developed a series of programs to constantly reevaluate and change its operating methods to prevent the company from stagnating. General Electric holds off-site WorkOut sessions with groups of managers and employees, with the goal of making GE a faster, less complex organization that can respond effectively to change. In the WorkOut sessions, employees recommend specific changes, explain why they are needed, and propose ways the changes can be implemented. Top management must make an immediate response: an approval, a disapproval (with an explanation), or a request for more information. The GE WorkOut sessions eliminate the barriers that keep employees from contributing to change.

There are two basic forms of change in organizations. **Planned change** results from a deliberate decision to alter the organization. For example, companies that wish to move from a traditional hierarchical structure to one that facilitates self-managed teams must use a proactive, carefully orchestrated approach. **Unplanned change** is imposed on the organization and is often unforeseen. Changes in government regulations and changes in the economy are two examples. Responsiveness to unplanned change requires tremendous flexibility and adaptability on the part of organizations.

Managers must be prepared to handle both planned and unplanned forms of change in organizations.

Forces for change can come from many sources. Some of these are external, arising from outside the company, whereas others are internal, arising from sources within the organization.

18-1a External Forces

The four major managerial challenges described throughout the book are major external forces for change: globalization, workforce diversity, technological change, and managing ethical behavior.

GLOBALIZATION The power players in the global market are the organizations that can capitalize on emerging markets throughout the world. The prime example is China, which has become the second largest economy in the world. Western firms like Nestlé, Procter & Gamble, and Kentucky Fried Chicken are all trying to pick up market share in China. Companies that understand what makes Chinese culture unique are finding success while others, who ignore these elements, are not. Home Depot, for example, has struggled in China because it did not understand that most Chinese people do not have places to store tools and typically hire

> Organizations are in a state of tremendous turmoil and transition, and all members are affected.

Danielala/Shutterstock.com

planned change Change resulting from a deliberate decision to alter the organization.

unplanned change Change that is imposed on the organization and is often unforeseen.

Biablo101/Shutterstock.com

HOT TREND

Warby Parker—A Brand Made on the Internet

The popular eyewear brand Warby Parker started on the Internet, and the company's success has looked easy. But according to co-CEOs Dave Gilboa and Neil Blumenthal, it is actually painstaking and deliberate. They have produced disruptive change in the eyewear industry by being

Two limited-edition hues. One classic pair of frames.

Downing Summer

Shop the collection ›

Source: Warby Parker

carefully focused on execution and brand. By designing and making their own frames, sold to consumers on the Internet for as little as $95, they have taken a bite out of the luxury eyewear business. Prices include prescription lenses, shipping, and donations to a not-for-profit organization. They're now opening up retail stores and plan to add children's frames and thinner lenses. There's also an investment in future technology that conducts eye exams online, which may render traditional optical stores obsolete. Warby Parker is a company that has changed the way consumers think about buying eyewear.

SOURCE: M. Chafkin, "Most Innovative Companies 2015: #1, Warby Parker," *Fast Company*, March 2015, 69–144.

---

people to work on their homes rather than doing it themselves. In addition to differences in consumers, companies must negotiate different legal requirements, as the Chinese government is still writing the rule of business.[4] Because global business implicitly involves multiple governments and legal systems, it carries unique risks not found by firms competing within a single nation.

The United States is but one nation in the drive to open new markets. Japan and Germany are responding to global competition in sufficient ways, and the emergence of the European Union as a powerful trading group will have a profound impact on world markets. By joining with their European neighbors, companies in smaller countries will begin to make major progress in world markets, thus increasing the fierce competition that already exists.

These changes, among others, have led companies to rethink the borders of their markets and to encourage their employees to think globally. Jack Welch, former CEO of GE, was among the first to call for a *borderless company*, in which there are no mental distinctions between domestic and foreign operations or between managers and employees.[5] GE has locations in 160 countries across the globe and has become a truly multinational corporation. The thought that drives the borderless company is that barriers interfere with people working together and should be removed. Globalizing an organization means rethinking the most efficient ways to use resources, disseminate and gather information, and

develop people. It requires not only structural changes but also changes in the minds of employees. You may think of Costco, the big box retailer, solely as a North American company. But in reality, Costco has more than 500 outlets in the United States, Canada, Mexico, Britain, South Korea, and Japan. Its expansion into Australia has been a big success, with plans to open more stores. Although Wal-Mart has considered expansion into Australia, so far it has no presence there, which bodes well for Costco.[6]

WORKFORCE DIVERSITY Related to globalization is the challenge of workforce diversity. As we have seen throughout this book, workforce diversity is a powerful force for change in organizations. First, increased female participation means that the majority of new workers will be female.[7] Currently, the U.S. labor force is 57.2% female.[8] Second, the workforce will be increasingly more culturally diverse as a result of globalization and changing U.S. demographics such as the dramatic rise in the participation of Hispanic Americans. Third, as the workforce ages, there will be fewer young workers and more older workers. The global workforce is also diversifying.[9] Following a high-profile bribery scandal (during which many top executives resigned), Siemens, the 160-year-old German technology and equipment firm, moved to represent better the diversity of its customers. Siemens hired a chief diversity officer who has since launched several programs focusing on mentoring and increasing diversity in the company's previously all-male managerial ranks. The percentage of women in management at Siemens globally has nearly doubled since 2002 to 15.6.[10]

TECHNOLOGICAL CHANGE Rapid technological innovation is another force for change in organizations, and those who fail to keep pace can quickly fall behind. Technology has enabled the mobile payment market to become competitive. The major players in the market, Google Wallet, PayPal, and Apple Pay, are hoping that consumers will ditch their wallets in favor of cell phones. But retailers are less excited about investing in the technologies.[11] Merchants will have to install new technologies to take advantage of mobile pay, and consumers worry about cyber theft and payment hacks. Apple Pay, the newest of the players, is building its list of participating merchants; however, its use is limited to the newest iPhones (6 or 6 Plus) and leaves out consumers who have earlier versions.

Changes are coming to credit cards too. Magnetic strip cards are being replaced with EMV cards, which have a chip that reduces the possibility of fraud.[12] Merchants will have to replace their existing credit card terminals with new ones, which makes mobile pay businesses happy because the new terminals will also accommodate mobile pay applications.

Technological innovations bring about profound change within organizations because the innovation process promotes associated changes in work relationships and organizational structures.[13] The team approach adopted by many organizations leads to flatter structures, decentralized decision making, and more open communication between leaders and team members.

MANAGING ETHICAL BEHAVIOR Recent scandals have brought ethical behavior in organizations to the forefront of public consciousness. Ethical issues, however, are not always public and monumental. Employees face ethical dilemmas in their daily work lives. The need to manage daily ethical behavior has brought about several changes in organizations, most centering around the idea that an organization must create a culture that encourages ethical behavior.

All public companies issue annual financial reports; Gap Inc. has gone a step further by issuing an annual ethical report. The clothing industry is almost synonymous with the use of sweatshops, but what sets Gap apart is its candid admission that none of its 3,000 suppliers fully complies with the firm's ethical code of conduct. Rather than retreat from these problems, Gap chose to work with its suppliers to improve conditions overseas. The Vendor Engagement & Monitoring team at Gap Inc. includes more than thirty people located in twelve countries, monitoring working conditions in the factories that do not participate in the Better Work Program.[14] The annual report includes extensive descriptions of workers' activities, including which factories were monitored, violations that were found, and which factories are no longer used by Gap because of the violations. It also addresses media reports critical of Gap and its operations.

Gap tries to improve worker conditions by providing training and encouraging suppliers to develop their own conduct codes. For example, in China it has encouraged lunchtime sessions in which workers are advised of their rights. While most facilities respond positively to these efforts, some don't, and Gap pulled its business from 136 factories it concluded were not going to improve. It also terminated contracts with two factories that had verified use of child labor. Gap's approach to overseas labor offers a model for other garment firms.[15]

Society expects organizations to maintain ethical behavior both internally and in relationships with other organizations, as well as with customers, the environment, and society. These expectations may be informal, or they may come in the form of increased regulation. In addition to the pressure from societal expectations, legal developments, changing stakeholder expectations, and shifting consumer demands can also lead to change.[16] And some companies change simply because others are

---

FASTFACT

Panera Goes High Tech

Fast casual chain Panera is making over its technology with Panera 2.0, which enables digital ordering and payment systems. If you are ordering to go, you can place an online or mobile order up to five days in advance and pick it up at a set time without waiting in line. Touch screen kiosks are being installed so eat-in and to-go customers can place their orders. The system works with the My Panera rewards cards, so favorites and previous orders are stored and you only have to customize your order once, then simply reorder. The objective of the technology innovation is to minimize wait time, increase order accuracy, and create a more customized experience for customers.

SOURCES: https://www.panerabread.com/content/dam/panerabread/documents/press/2014/panera-unveils-panera-2.0.pdf; B. Kowitt, "With Digital Ordering, Panera Makes a Big Bet on Tech," *Fortune*, March 27, 2014, accessed at http://fortune.com/2014/03/27/with-digital-ordering-panera-makes-a-big-bet-on-tech/.

A_KUDR/Shutterstock.com

changing.[17] Other powerful forces for change originate from within the organization.

18-1b Internal Forces

Pressures for change that originate inside the organization are generally recognizable by symptoms such as declining effectiveness. A company that experiences its third quarterly loss within a fiscal year undoubtedly experiences a pressure for change. Some companies react by instituting layoffs and massive cost-cutting programs, whereas others look at the bigger picture, view the loss as symptomatic of an underlying problem, and seek out its cause.

A crisis may also stimulate change in an organization. Strikes or walkouts may lead management to change the wage structure. The resignation of a key decision maker may cause the company to rethink the composition of its management team and its role in the organization.

Changes in employee expectations can trigger change in organizations as well. A company that hires a group of young newcomers may find that their expectations are very different from those of older workers. One reason for changed expectations is that the workforce is more educated than ever before. Although this has its advantages, workers with more education demand more of employers. Furthermore, today's workers are concerned with career and family balance issues, such as dependent care. And the many sources of workforce diversity hold potential for a host of other differing expectations among employees.

Still another pressure is a change in the work climate that produces a workforce that is lethargic, unmotivated, and dissatisfied. Such symptoms are common in organizations that have experienced layoffs. Workers who have escaped a layoff may grieve for those who have lost their jobs and may find it difficult to continue to be productive. They may fear that they will be laid off as well, and many feel insecure in their jobs.

chip producers must continually upgrade their manufacturing equipment just to stay competitive. Intel's conversion of an Arizona fab (a chip-making plant) from older to newer technology cost $3 billion.[18] While radical change is more exciting and interesting to discuss, most organizational change—and therefore most research on organizational change—has focused on evolutionary (incremental) rather than revolutionary change.[19] Change can also be on a larger scale, such as the restructuring of an organization (a **strategic change**).[20] In strategic change, the organization moves from an old state to a known new state during a controlled period of time. Sometimes strategic changes work; sometimes they don't. YouTube was a startup that was acquired by Google for $1.65 billion, and Google altered YouTube's strategy by going after premium content providers such as ABC, NBC, and CBS. In addition, a partner program was launched that allowed popular users to share in the advertising revenue their videos generated. This change in strategy has not worked, however. Although it now has one billion viewers, YouTube has yet to become profitable. Some say that a new strategy is needed that focuses on attracting a broader audience beyond young people.[21]

The most massive scope of change is **transformational change**, in which the organization moves to a radically different, and sometimes unknown, future state.[22] In transformational change, the organization's mission, culture, goals, structure, and leadership may all change dramatically.[23] Just over a century ago, two successful bicycle makers decided to leave the safety of their business to devote time to building and selling

incremental change
Change of a relatively small scope, such as making small improvements.

strategic change Change of a larger scale, such as organizational restructuring.

transformational change Change in which the organization moves to a radically different, and sometimes unknown, future state.

18-2 THE SCOPE OF CHANGE

Change can be of a relatively small scope, such as a modification in a work procedure (an **incremental change**). Such changes are a fine-tuning of the organization. For example, Intel and other

Apple's Data Centers in Europe

Apple may be responding to external forces in its move to open data centers in Ireland and Denmark. European politicians have leveled criticism at companies who hold European citizens' data in U.S. facilities, citing security concerns. Other companies are also opening data centers in Europe, trying to get ahead of post-Snowden privacy laws that will require European users' data to be stored in Europe. An added bonus is that Northern Europe's cooler climate will permit free cooling, in which external air circulates to cool the servers, saving money and energy.

SOURCE: D. Lumb, "Why Apple Is Spending $1.9 Billion to Open Data Centers in Denmark and Ireland," *Fast Company*, February 23, 2015, accessed at http://www.fastcompany.com/3042746/fast-feed/why-apple-is-spending-19-billion-to-open-data-centers-in-denmark-and-ireland.

an amazing new invention—the airplane—which transformed travel, warfare, and communications around the world. The Wright brothers transformed not only their bike business but the whole world! Of all the tasks a leader undertakes, many say that changing the form and nature of the organization itself may be the most difficult, an observation supported by research.[24]

One of the toughest decisions faced by leaders is the proper pace of change. Some scholars argue that rapid change is more likely to succeed than slower change because it creates momentum,[25] while others argue that these short, sharp changes are actually rare and not experienced by most firms.[26] Still others observe that change in a large organization may occur incrementally in some parts of the firm and quickly in others.[27] In summary, researchers agree that the pace of change is important, but they can't quite agree on which pace of change is most beneficial.

Very little long-term research has looked at change over a significant time period. One twelve-year study looked at change in the structure of Canadian National Sports Organizations (NSOs). It found that within NSOs, radical transition did not always require a fast pace of change. It also found that successful transitions often involve changing the high-impact elements of an organization (in this case, their decision-making structures) early in the process.[28]

18-2a The Change Agent's Role

The individual or group that introduces and manages change in an organization is known as the **change agent**. Change agents can be internal, such as managers or employees who are appointed to oversee the change process. In her book *The Change Masters*, Rosabeth Moss Kanter notes that at companies like Hewlett-Packard and Polaroid, managers and employees alike are developing the needed skills to produce change and innovation in the organization.[29]

Internal change agents have certain advantages in managing the change process. First, they know the organization's history, its political system, and its culture. Then, because they must live with the results of their change efforts, internal change agents are likely to be very careful about managing change. There are disadvantages, however, to using internal change agents. They may be associated with certain factions within the organization, be accused of favoritism, or be too close to the situation to have an objective view of what needs to be done.

Change leaders within organizations tend to be young, between twenty-five and forty. A high number of change leaders are women. Also, change agents are more flexible than ordinary general managers and much more people oriented. Using a balance of technical and interpersonal skills, they are tough decision makers who focus on performance results. Plus, they know how to energize people and get them aligned in the same direction. In addition, they have the ability to operate in more than one leadership style and can shift from a team mode to command and control, depending on the situation. Finally, change agents are comfortable with uncertainty.[30]

If change is large scale or strategic in nature, it may require a team of leaders with a variety of skills, expertise, and influence that can work together harmoniously.[31]

External change agents bring an outsider's objective view to the organization. They may be preferred by employees because of their impartiality. External change agents face certain problems, however. Not only is their knowledge of the organization's history limited, but they may also be viewed with suspicion by organization members. External change agents have more power in directing changes if employees perceive them as being trustworthy, possessing important expertise, having a track record that establishes credibility, and being similar to them.[32]

Different change agent competencies are required at different stages of the change process. Leadership, communication, training, and participation have varying levels of impact as the change proceeds, meaning change agents must be flexible in how they work through the different phases of the process.[33] Effective change leaders build strong relationships within their leadership team, between the team and organizational members, and between the team and key environmental players. Maintaining all three relationships simultaneously is quite difficult, so successful leaders are continually coupling and uncoupling with the different groups as the change process proceeds. Adaptability is a key skill for both internal and external change leaders.[34]

18-3 RESISTANCE TO CHANGE

People often resist change in a rational response based on self-interest. However, there are countless other reasons people resist change. Many of these center around the notion of *reactance*—that is, a negative reaction that occurs when individuals feel that their personal freedom is threatened.[35] Let us take a look at some expressions of reactance and then at some ways of dealing with it.

> **change agent** The individual or group that undertakes the task of introducing and managing a change in an organization.

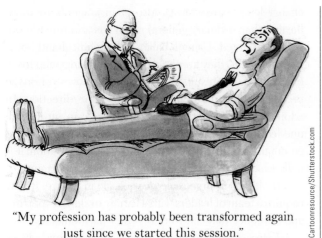

"My profession has probably been transformed again just since we started this session."

Some individuals find constant change as an impediment to successfully completing their daily tasks.

18-3a Major Reasons People Resist Change

Common reasons people resist change include fear of the unknown, fear of loss, fear of failure, fear of disruption of interpersonal relationships, personality factors, politics, and cultural assumptions and values.

FEAR OF THE UNKNOWN Change often brings with it substantial uncertainty. Employees facing a technological change may resist the change simply because it introduces ambiguity into what was once a comfortable situation for them.

FEAR OF LOSS Some employees may fear losing their jobs with impending change, especially when an advanced technology like robotics is introduced. Employees may also fear losing their status because of change.[36] Computer systems experts, for example, may feel that their expertise will be less appreciated when a more user-friendly networked information system is installed. Another common fear is that changes may diminish the positive qualities the individual enjoys in the job. Computerizing the customer service positions at Southwestern Bell (now part of SBC Communications), for example, threatened the autonomy that representatives previously enjoyed.

FEAR OF FAILURE Some employees fear changes because they fear their own failure as a result of those changes. They may question their competence to deal with changes that might mean increased workloads or increased task difficulty. They may also fear that performance expectations will be elevated following the change and that they might not measure up.[37]

Resistance can also stem from the fear that change will not really take place. In other words, there can be fear of failure on the part of the organization, not the individual. In one large library that was undergoing a major automation effort, employees were doubtful that the vendor could deliver the state-of-the-art system that was promised. In this case, the implementation never became a reality; the employees' fears were well founded.[38]

FEAR OF DISRUPTION OF INTERPERSONAL RELATIONSHIPS Employees may resist change that threatens to limit meaningful interpersonal relationships on the job. Librarians facing the automation effort feared that once the computerized system was implemented, they would not be able to interact as they did when they had to go to another floor of the library to get help finding a resource.

PERSONALITY Individuals with an internal locus of control, high growth needs, strong motivation, and a positive outlook are more likely to embrace changes at work.[39] Personality conflicts may impact workers' acceptance of change. A change agent who appears insensitive to employees' concerns and feelings may meet considerable resistance from those who feel that their needs are not being taken into account.

POLITICS Organizational change may also shift the existing balance of power in the organization. Individuals or groups empowered under the current arrangement may be threatened with losing these political advantages in the advent of change.

CULTURAL ASSUMPTIONS AND VALUES Sometimes cultural assumptions and values can be impediments to change, particularly if the assumptions underlying the change are alien to employees. Other times, employees might interpret strategic change initiatives from the standpoint of the organization's value system and ideologies of the management team. In fact, research indicates that employees pay attention to the informal sense-making process prevalent in organizations and leading top-down change initiatives to fail.[40] This form of resistance can be very difficult to overcome because some cultural assumptions are unconscious. As discussed in Chapter 2, some cultures tend to avoid uncertainty. In Mexican and Greek cultures, for example, change that creates a great deal of uncertainty may be met with great resistance.

We have described several sources of resistance to change, but the reasons for resistance are as diverse as the workforce itself and vary with different individuals and organizations. The challenge for managers is introducing change in a positive manner and managing employee resistance.

18-3b Managing Resistance to Change

The traditional view of managing resistance to change was to treat it as something to be overcome, and many organizational attempts to reduce the resistance have only served to intensify it. The contemporary view holds that resistance is simply a form of feedback and that this feedback can be used very productively to manage the change process. When individuals, teams, or organizations are not ready for change, it is an opportunity to gather important diagnostic information that can be used to identify weaknesses in the organization's approach to change and to improve the process.[41] In this view, the idea is to manage resistance by planning for it and being ready with a variety of strategies for using the resistance as feedback and helping employees negotiate the transition. Three key strategies for managing resistance to change are communication, participation, and empathy and support.[42]

Communication about impending change is essential if employees are to adjust effectively.[43] The details and, equally important, the rationale of the change should be provided. Accurate and timely information can help prevent unfounded fears and potentially damaging rumors from developing. Conversely, delaying announcements and withholding information can serve to fuel the rumor mill. Open communication in a culture of trust is a key ingredient for successful change.[44] Managers should pay attention to the informal communication networks in an organization because they can serve as power channels for disseminating change-related information.[45] Educating employees on new work procedures and other potential consequences of change is helpful. In addition, both mentors and mentees derive benefits from going through the process of organizational change together. Mentees are assisted by mentors who help them make sense of the change, and mentors experience satisfaction in having helped the mentee through the change process. Another key ingredient that can help employees adjust to change is a supervisor whom they can trust. When employees trust their supervisors, it serves as a social support mechanism, and they are more committed to the organization even if they feel they can't control the change process.[46]

There is substantial research support underscoring the importance of *participation* in the change process. Employees must be engaged and involved in order for change to work—as supported by the notion "That which we create, we support." Participation helps employees become involved in the change and establishes a feeling of ownership in the process. Mergers and acquisitions are widely prevalent in the current business environment.

Another strategy for managing resistance is to provide *empathy and support* to employees who have trouble dealing with the change. Active listening is an excellent tool for identifying the reasons behind resistance and for uncovering fears. An expression of concerns about the change can provide important feedback that managers can use to improve the change process. Emotional support and encouragement can help an employee deal with the anxiety that is a natural response to change. Employees who experience severe reactions to change can benefit from talking with a counselor. Some companies provide counseling through their employee assistance plans.

The Hartford Financial Services Group encountered some resistance to change in going global. When the company attempted to enter the lucrative British and Dutch insurance markets through acquisitions, the overseas staff resisted changes suggested by Hartford, such as using laptops and introducing new financial products. The introduction of such U.S. business practices is often referred to as "economic imperialism" by employees who feel they are being forced to substitute corporate values for personal or national values.

Hartford needed its European staff to understand that they were part of a transnational company. Its solution was to offer a stock ownership plan that tied the personal fortunes of the staff to the company. This gave employees a considerable interest in Hartford's success and helped them identify with the company.[47]

Managers dealing with resistance to change will choose to communicate in a positive manner with their direct reports.

Docstockmedia/Shutterstock.com

FIGURE 18.1 FORCE FIELD ANALYSIS OF A DECISION TO ENGAGE IN EXERCISE

Forces for change

Weight gain

Minimally passing treadmill test

Feeling lethargic; having no energy

Family history of cardiovascular disease

New, physically demanding job

Equilibrium

Forces for status quo

Lack of time

No exercise facility at work

Spouse/partner hates to exercise

No interest in physical activity or sports

Made a grade of D in a physical education class

© Cengage Learning

18-4 LEWIN'S MODEL FOR MANAGING CHANGE

Kurt Lewin developed a model of the change process that has stood the test of time and continues to influence the way organizations manage planned change. Lewin's model is based on the idea of *force field analysis*.[48] Figure 18.1 shows a force field analysis of a decision to engage in exercise behavior. This model contends that a person's behavior is the product of two opposing forces: one force pushes toward preserving the status quo, and the other force pushes for change. When the two opposing forces are approximately equal, current behavior is maintained. For behavioral change to occur, the forces maintaining the status quo must be overcome. This can be accomplished by increasing the forces for change, by weakening the forces for the status quo, or by a combination of these actions.

Lewin's change model is a three-step process, as shown in Figure 18.2. The process begins with unfreezing, which is a crucial first hurdle in the change process. Unfreezing involves encouraging individuals to discard old behaviors by shaking up the equilibrium state that maintains the status quo. Change management literature has long advocated that certain individuals have personalities that make them more resistant to change. However, recent research indicates that only a small portion of a study's respondents (23%) displayed consistency in their reactions to three different kinds of change: structural, technological, and office relocation. The majority of respondents (77%) reacted differently to these different kinds of change, suggesting that reactions to change might be more situationally driven than was previously thought.[49] Organizations often accomplish unfreezing by eliminating the rewards for current behavior and showing that current behavior is not valued. In essence, individuals surrender by allowing the boundaries of their status quo to be opened in preparation for change.[50]

The second step in the change process is **moving**. In the moving stage, new attitudes, values, and behaviors are substituted for old ones. Organizations accomplish moving by initiating new options and explaining the rationale for the change, as well as by providing training to help employees develop the new skills they need. Employees should be given the overarching vision for the change so that they can establish their roles within the new organizational structure and processes.[51]

unfreezing The first step in Lewin's change model, in which individuals are encouraged to discard old behaviors by shaking up the equilibrium state that maintains the status quo.

moving The second step in Lewin's change model, in which new attitudes, values, and behaviors are substituted for old ones.

FIGURE 18.2 LEWIN'S CHANGE MODEL

Unfreezing	Moving	Refreezing
Reducing forces for status quo	Developing new attitudes, values, and behaviors	Reinforcing new attitudes, values, and behaviors

© Cengage Learning

Refreezing is the final step in the change process. In this step, new attitudes, values, and behaviors are established as the new status quo. The new ways of operating are cemented in and reinforced. Managers should ensure that the organizational culture and formal reward systems encourage the new behaviors. Changes in the reward structure may be needed to ensure that the organization is not rewarding the old behaviors and merely hoping for the new behaviors. A study by Exxon Research and Engineering showed that framing and displaying a mission statement in managers' offices may eventually change the behavior of 2% of the managers. In contrast, changing managers' evaluation and reward systems will change the behavior of 55% of the managers almost overnight.[52]

The approach used by Monsanto to increase opportunities for women within the company is an illustration of how to use Lewin's model effectively. First, Monsanto emphasized unfreezing by helping employees debunk negative stereotypes about women in business. This also helped overcome resistance to change. Second, Monsanto moved employees' attitudes and behaviors through diversity training in which differences were emphasized as positive, and supervisors learned ways of training and developing female employees. Third, Monsanto changed its reward system so that managers were evaluated and paid according to how they coached and promoted women, which helped refreeze the new attitudes and behaviors.

One frequently overlooked issue is whether or not the change is consistent with the company's deeply held core values. Value consistency is critical to making a change stick. Organizations whose members perceive the changes to be consistent with the firm's values adopt the changes much more easily and fully. Conversely, organizations whose members' values conflict with the changes may display "superficial conformity," in which members pay lip service to the changes but ultimately revert to their old behaviors.[53]

 18-5 DETERMINING THE NEED FOR ORGANIZATION DEVELOPMENT INTERVENTIONS

Related to change is the subject of *organization development*, a method that consists of various programs for making organizations more effective. **Organization development (OD)** is defined as a systematic approach to organizational improvement that applies behavioral science theory and research in order to increase individual and organizational well-being and effectiveness.[54] This definition implies certain characteristics. First, as a systematic approach to planned change, OD is a structured cycle of diagnosing organizational problems and opportunities and then applying expertise to them. Second, OD is grounded in solid research and theory. It involves the application of behavioral science knowledge to the challenges that organizations face. Third, OD recognizes the reciprocal relationship between individuals and organizations. It acknowledges that for organizations to change, individuals must change. Finally, OD is goal oriented. It is a process that seeks to improve both individual and organizational well-being and effectiveness.

Prior to deciding on a method of intervention, managers must carefully diagnose the problem they are attempting to address. Diagnosis and needs analysis is a critical first step in any OD intervention. Following this, an intervention method is chosen and applied. Finally, a thorough follow-up of the OD process is conducted. Figure 18.3 presents the OD cycle, a continuous process of moving the organization and its employees toward effective functioning.

New Belgium Brewery Becomes Employee-Owned

You may know New Belgium Brewery as the creator of Fat Tire Amber Ale. It is also a company that has changed over time to become entirely owned by employees. Co-founder and CEO Kim Jordan is an advocate of progressive business thinking, transparency, and environmental stewardship. As the company has grown, employee ownership that started at 10% grew to 32%. In 2012 all of the shareholders, including Jordan, sold their ownership to employees through the employee stock ownership plan. Transparency is important, and the company's books are open to the employee-owners. The result is a democratic culture of highly engaged workers.

SOURCE: D. Eng, "New Belgium's Kim Jordan Is Tasting Success in Craft Brewing," *Fortune*, June 12, 2014, accessed at http://fortune.com/2014/06/12/new-belgium-kim-jordan/.

refreezing The final step in Lewin's change model, in which new attitudes, values, and behaviors are established as the new status quo.

organization development (OD) A systematic approach to organizational improvement that applies behavioral science theory and research in order to increase individual and organizational well-being and effectiveness.

FIGURE 18.3 THE ORGANIZATION DEVELOPMENT CYCLE

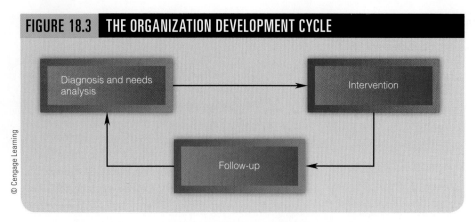

© Cengage Learning

which can be the organization, groups within the organization, or individuals.

18-6 GROUP-FOCUSED TECHNIQUES FOR OD INTERVENTION

Some OD intervention methods emphasize changing the organization itself or changing the work groups within the organization rather than targeting the employees as individuals. Intervention methods in this category include survey feedback, management by objectives, product and service quality programs, team building, and process consultation.

18-5a Diagnosis and Needs Analysis

Before any intervention is planned, a thorough organizational diagnosis should be conducted. Diagnosis is an essential first step for any organization development intervention.[55] The term *diagnosis* comes from two Greek words, *dial* (through) and *gnosis* (knowledge). Thus, the diagnosis should pinpoint specific problems and areas in need of improvement. Six areas to examine carefully are the organization's purpose, structure, reward system, support systems, relationships, and leadership.[56]

Harry Levinson's diagnostic approach asserts that the process should begin by identifying where the pain (the problem) in the organization is, what it is like, how long it has been happening, and what has already been done about it.[57] Then a four-part, comprehensive diagnosis can begin. The first part of the diagnosis involves achieving an understanding of the organization's history. In the second part, the organization as a whole is analyzed to obtain data about its structure and processes. In the third part, interpretive data about attitudes, relationships, and current organizational functioning are gathered. In the fourth part of the diagnosis, the data are analyzed and conclusions are reached. In each stage of the diagnosis, the data can be gathered using a variety of methods, including observation, interviews, questionnaires, and archival records.

A *needs analysis* is another crucial step in managing change. This is an analysis of the skills and competencies that employees must have to achieve the goals of the change. A needs analysis is essential because interventions such as training programs must target these skills and competencies.

Hundreds of alternative OD intervention methods exist. One way of classifying these methods is by the target of change,

18-6a Survey Feedback

Survey feedback is a widely used intervention method whereby employee attitudes are solicited using a questionnaire. Once the data are collected, they are analyzed and fed back to the employees to diagnose problems and plan other interventions. Survey feedback is often used as an exploratory tool and then is combined with some other intervention. The effectiveness of survey feedback in actually improving outcomes (e.g., absenteeism or productivity) increases substantially when this method is combined with other interventions.[58] Furthermore, the effectiveness of this technique is contingent upon trust between management and subordinates, and this can be reinforced through the anonymity and confidentiality of survey responses.

For survey feedback to be an effective method, certain guidelines should be used. Employees must be assured that their responses to the questionnaire will be confidential and anonymous. Feedback should be reported in a group format. Employees must be able to trust that negative repercussions will not result from their responses. Employees should be informed of the purpose of the survey. Failing to do this can set up unrealistic expectations about the changes that might come from the surveys.

In addition, management must be prepared to follow up on the survey results. If some things cannot be changed, the rationale (e.g., prohibitive cost) must be explained to the employees. Without appropriate follow-through, employees will not take the survey process seriously the next time.

survey feedback A widely used intervention method whereby employee attitudes are solicited using a questionnaire.

18-6b Management by Objectives

As an organization-wide technique, **management by objectives (MBO)** involves joint goal setting between employees and managers. The MBO process includes the setting of initial objectives, periodic progress reviews, and problem solving to remove any obstacles to goal achievement.[59] All these steps are joint efforts between managers and employees.

MBO is a valuable intervention because it meets three needs. First, it clarifies what is expected of employees. This reduces role conflict and ambiguity. Second, MBO provides knowledge of results, an essential ingredient in effective job performance. Finally, MBO provides an opportunity for coaching and counseling by the manager. The problem-solving approach encourages open communication and discussion of obstacles to goal achievement.[60]

Companies that have used MBO successfully include the former Tenneco, Mobil (now part of Exxon-Mobil), and General Electric. The success of MBO in effecting organizational results hinges on the linking of individual goals to the goals of the organization.[61] MBO programs should be used with caution, however. An excessive emphasis on goal achievement can result in cut-throat competition among employees, falsification of results, and striving for results at any cost.

18-6c Product and Service Quality Programs

Quality programs—programs that embed product and service quality excellence in the organizational culture—are assuming key roles in the organization development efforts of many companies. The success or failure of a service company may hinge on the quality of customer service it provides.[62] Even manufacturing companies need high-quality customer service in addition to high-quality products. Toyota Motor Corporation constantly finds ways to integrate cutting-edge technological innovations with the growing pains of global expansion. The famed Toyota Way of doing business is focused on two key principles: continuous improvement focused on innovation and respect for people.[63]

18-6d Team Building

Team building programs can improve the effectiveness of work groups. Usually they begin with a diagnostic process through which team members identify problems and continue with the team planning actions to resolve those problems. The OD practitioner in team building serves as a facilitator, and the work itself is completed by team members.[64]

A popular method for team building is the use of outdoor challenges.

Team building is a very popular OD method. A survey of *Fortune* 500 companies indicated that human resource managers considered team building the most successful OD technique.[65] Managers are particularly interested in building teams that can learn. To build *learning teams*, members must be encouraged to seek feedback, discuss errors, reflect on successes and failures, and experiment with new ways of performing. Mistakes should be analyzed for ways to improve, and a climate of mutual support should be developed. Leaders of learning teams are good coaches who promote a climate of psychological safety so that team members feel comfortable discussing problems.[66]

One popular technique for team building is the use of outdoor challenges. Teambuilding, Inc. uses rowing as a team-building exercise. It enlisted the services of an Olympic gold medalist, Dan Lyons, to design a seminar focused on team building using rowing as the central organizing theme. This activity encourages participants to practice leadership, communication, goal setting, conflict management, and motivation. GE Healthcare, ING Direct, and Wyeth Corporate Communications have all used this technique for their team-building programs as well.[67] One of TeamBonding's culinary challenges takes advantage of the popularity of food trucks. In the Food Truck Challenge, teams design the façade of their tabletop food trucks, along

management by objectives (MBO) An organization-wide intervention technique that involves joint goal setting between employees and managers.

quality program A program that embeds product and service quality excellence in the organizational culture.

team building An intervention designed to improve the effectiveness of a work group.

with a logo for their aprons.[68] They create recipes, prepare their signature dishes, and market their creations from one of three cuisines: Southwest, All-American, or Tailgater. A panel of judges does a taste test, and then the teams are evaluated on best taste, best presentation, and culinary champion. The objective of the Food Truck Challenge is to improve teamwork through the power of play.

Teambuilding is particularly challenging in virtual teams, in which members rarely if ever meet face-to-face. Normal processes such as conflict management, decision making, and communication of emotions are challenges with which virtual teams may need help. It takes time in virtual teams to build relationships, and interventions that help build trust among the geographically dispersed team members are valuable. Topics such as intercultural teamwork are helpful, and new members of virtual teams can especially benefit from teambuilding training.[69]

18-6e Process Consultation

Pioneered by Edgar Schein, **process consultation** is an OD method that helps managers and employees improve the processes that are used in organizations.[70] The processes most often targeted are communication, conflict resolution, decision making, group interaction, and leadership.

One of the distinguishing features of process consultation is that an outside consultant is used. The role of the consultant is to help employees help themselves. In this way, the ownership of a successful outcome rests with the employees.[71] The consultant guides the organization members in examining the processes in the organization and in refining them. The steps in process consultation are entering the organization, defining the relationship, choosing an approach, gathering data and diagnosing problems, intervening, and gradually leaving the organization.

Process consultation is an interactive technique between employees and an outside consultant, so it is seldom used as a sole OD method. Most often it is used in combination with other OD interventions.

All the preceding OD methods focus on changing the organization or the work group, whereas the following OD methods are aimed at individual change.

> To build *learning teams*, members must be encouraged to seek feedback, discuss errors, reflect on successes and failures, and experiment with new ways of performing.

18-7 INDIVIDUAL-FOCUSED TECHNIQUES FOR OD INTERVENTION

OD efforts that are targeted at individuals include skills training, leadership training and development, executive coaching, role negotiation, job redesign, health promotion programs, and career planning.

18-7a Skills Training

The key question addressed by **skills training** is, "What knowledge, skills, and abilities are necessary to do this job effectively?" Skills training is accomplished either in formal classroom settings or on the job. The challenge is integrating skills training into OD in today's rapidly changing organizational environments. The job knowledge in most positions requires continual updates to keep pace with rapid change.

Companies such as Google and Genentech are supplementing their traditional skills training with training in mindfulness skills. At Dow Chemical Company, researchers wondered whether mindfulness skills taught online would have as much impact as mindfulness skills taught in a classroom setting. A group of employees participated in an online mindfulness course, and they were compared to a group of employees who were wait-listed for the training. The employees from the mindfulness online intervention reported decreased stress, better resilience and vigor, more work engagement, and higher overall well-being than those who had not yet completed the training.[72]

18-7b Leadership Training and Development

Companies invest millions of dollars in **leadership training and development**, a term that encompasses a variety of techniques that are designed to enhance individuals' leadership skills. One popular technique is to send future leaders to off-site training classes. Research shows that this type of education experience

process consultation An OD method that helps managers and employees improve the processes that are used in organizations.

skills training Increasing the job knowledge, skills, and abilities that are necessary to do a job effectively.

leadership training and development A variety of techniques that are designed to enhance individuals' leadership skills.

Companies like General Mills are including mindfulness training in their leadership development programs.

can have some impact, but participants' enthusiastic return to work may be short-lived due to the challenges and realities of work life. Classroom learning alone thus has a limited effect on leadership skills.

Some leadership training and development programs combine classroom learning with on-the-job experiences. One way of accomplishing development is through the use of *action learning*, a technique that was pioneered in Europe. In action learning, leaders take on unfamiliar problems or familiar problems in unfamiliar settings. The leaders work on the problems and meet weekly in small groups made up of individuals from different organizations. The outcome of action learning is that leaders learn about themselves through the challenges of their comrades. Other techniques that provide action learning for participants are simulation, business games, role-playing, and case studies.[73]

Eli Lilly has an action-learning program that pulls together eighteen future company leaders and gives them a strategic business issue to resolve. For six weeks, the trainees meet with experts, best-practices organizations, and customers, and then present their recommendations to top brass. One action-learning team was charged with coming up with an e-business strategy; their plan was so good that executives immediately implemented it. At Eli Lilly and other firms, action-learning programs provide developmental experiences for leaders and result in useful initiatives for the company.[74]

Companies such as General Mills and Apple are including mindfulness training in their leadership development programs. Google has long done so and integrates mindfulness with emotional intelligence in its training. Mindfulness training benefits the leaders themselves in terms of lower stress, more empathy, and improved well-being. Mindfulness training also has spillover effects for the leaders' employees. When leaders are more mindful, their employees have better job satisfaction and performance, along with improved well-being.[75]

Leadership training and development is an ongoing process that takes considerable time and effort. There are no quick fixes. At IBM, managers are held accountable for leadership development. In fact, IBM's managers will not be considered for promotion into senior executive positions unless they have a record of developing leaders. Top management must be committed to the process of leadership training and development if it wants to create a pipeline of high-potential employees to fill leadership positions.

18-7c Executive Coaching

Executive coaching is a technique in which managers or executives are paired with a coach in a partnership to help the executive perform more efficiently. Although coaching is usually done in a one-on-one manner, it is sometimes attempted in groups. The popularity of executive coaching has increased dramatically in recent years. The International Coach Federation, a group that trains and accredits executive coaches, doubled its membership in just two years of existence to 7,000 members in thirty-five countries.

Coaching is typically a special investment in top-level managers. Coaches provide another set of eyes and ears and help executives see beyond their own blinders. They elicit solutions and ideas from the client rather than making suggestions. Thus they develop and enhance the talents and capabilities within the client. Many coaching arrangements focus on developing the emotional intelligence of the client executive and may use a 360-degree assessment in which the executive, her boss, peers, subordinates, and even family members rate the executive's emotional competencies.[76] This information is then fed back to the executive, and along with the coach, a development plan is put in place.

Good coaches form strong connections with clients, exhibit professionalism, and deliver forthright, candid feedback. The top reasons executives seek out coaches are to make personal behavior changes, enhance their effectiveness, and foster stronger relationships. Does executive coaching pay off? Evidence suggests that successful coaching can result in sustained changes in executives' behavior, increased self-awareness and understanding, and more effective leadership competencies.[77] In one

> **executive coaching** A technique in which managers or executives are paired with a coach in a partnership to help them perform more efficiently.

study, for example, executives who worked with executive coaches were more likely to set specific goals, ask for feedback from their supervisors, and were rated as better performers by their supervisors and subordinates when compared to executives who simply received feedback from surveys.[78] Effective coaching relationships depend on a professional, experienced coach, an executive who is motivated to learn and change, and a good fit between the two.

18-7d Role Negotiation

Individuals who work together sometimes have differing expectations of one another within the working relationship. **Role negotiation** is a technique whereby individuals meet and clarify their psychological contract, that is, their expectations of each other. The outcome of role negotiation is a better understanding between the two parties. When both parties have a mutual agreement on expectations, there is less ambiguity in the process of working together.

18-7e Job Redesign

As an OD intervention method, **job redesign** alters jobs to improve the fit between individual skills and the demands of the job. Chapter 14 outlined several approaches to job design. Many of these methods are used as OD techniques for realigning task demands and individual capabilities or for redesigning jobs to fit new techniques or organizational structures better.

Ford Motor Company has redesigned virtually all of its manufacturing jobs, shifting workers from individual to team-based roles in which they have greater control of their work and can take the initiative to improve products and production techniques. Ford began trying this technique more than a decade ago and found that it not only improved employee job satisfaction but also productivity and product quality.

Another form of job redesign is telecommuting. Companies including American Express, AT&T, and Merrill Lynch have significant numbers of employees who work this way. When the Chinese travel site Ctrip gave employees the option to work from home for nine months, they compared the results of the volunteers who worked from home with the rest who remained in the office. At the end of the nine months, the at-home workers were happier, more productive, and less likely to quit the company. It saved Ctrip $1,900 per employee for the nine months in furniture and space, and people working from home raised their productivity by the equivalent of an extra day per week. Ctrip attributes the productivity increase to the quieter environment at home. Without the distractions in the workplace, employees found it easier to focus on customer calls.[79]

18-7f Health Promotion Programs

As organizations have become increasingly concerned with the costs of distress in the workplace, health promotion programs have become a part of larger OD efforts. In Chapter 7, we examined stress and strain at work. To relieve stress and strain, companies such as AT&T, Caterpillar, Kimberly-Clark, and Johnson & Johnson have successfully integrated health promotion programs into their organizations.

The American Psychological Association recognizes companies for innovative programs that support psychologically healthy work environments. Past winners included *El Nuevo Dial* and Green Mountain Coffee Roasters. *El Nuevo Dial* is the most popular newspaper in Puerto Rico and offers healthcare benefits to its employees at no cost, after-work fitness programs, and quarterly health publications designed to prevent stress and maintain a healthy lifestyle. Green Mountain Coffee Roasters has yoga, meditation, and physical therapy programs to reduce work-related stress and injury. It pays for 90% of healthcare costs of its full-time employees. Furthermore, it reimburses each employee up to $400 per year for participation in wellness programs, health club memberships, or smoking cessation programs.[80]

Although companies have long recognized the importance of maintenance on their machinery, many are only recently learning that their human assets need maintenance as well, and they are supplying that need

Herb Swanson/Bloomberg via Getty Images

Green Mountain Coffee Roasters offers yoga, meditation and physical therapy programs to reduce stress for their employees.

---

role negotiation A technique whereby individuals meet and clarify their psychological contract.

job redesign An OD intervention method that alters jobs to improve the fit between individual skills and the demands of the job.

in the form of employee wellness and health promotion activities. These programs focus on helping employees manage their stress and prevent health problems.

18-7g Career Planning

Matching an individual's career aspirations with the opportunities in the organization is career planning. This proactive approach to career management is often part of an organization's development efforts although it is a joint responsibility of organizations and individuals. Certainly career-planning activities benefit both the organization and its individuals. Through counseling sessions, employees identify their skills and skill deficiencies. The organization then can plan its training and development efforts based on this information. In addition, the process can be used to identify and nurture talented employees for potential promotion.

To sum up, managers can choose from a host of organization development techniques to facilitate organizational change. Large-scale changes in organizations require the use of multiple techniques. For example,

> As organizations have become increasingly concerned with the costs of distress in the workplace, health promotion programs have become a part of larger OD efforts.

implementing a new technology like robotics may require simultaneous changes in the structure of the organization, the configuration of work groups, and individual attitudes.

Since organization development is designed to help organizations manage change, it is important to evaluate the effectiveness of these efforts. The success of any OD intervention depends on a host of factors, including the technique used, the competence of the change agent, the organization's readiness for change, and top management commitment. No single method of OD is effective in every instance. Instead, multiple-method OD approaches are recommended because they allow organizations to capitalize on the benefits of several approaches.[81]

Efforts to evaluate OD effects have focused on outcomes such as productivity. One review of more than 200 interventions indicated that worker productivity improved in 87% of the cases.[82] We can conclude that when properly applied and managed, organization development programs have positive effects on performance.[83]

STUDY TOOLS 18

LOCATED AT BACK OF THE TEXTBOOK

☐ Rip out chapter review card

LOCATED AT WWW.CENGAGE.COM/LOGIN

☐ Track your knowledge and understanding of key concepts in business using 4LTR Press Online

☐ Review key term flashcards and create your own using StudyBits

☐ Create and complete practice quizzes based off of your notes and StudyBits

☐ Complete Online activities such as Matching and Fill-in-the-Blank exercises

☐ View chapter highlight box content, including the chapter videos, key exhibits and executive profiles.

YOUR
FEEDBACK
MATTERS.

www.cengage.com/4ltrpress

ENDNOTES

1

1. H. Schwartz, "The Clockwork or the Snakepit: An Essay on the Meaning of Teaching Organizational Behavior," *Organizational Behavior Teaching Review* 11, No. 2 (1987): 19–26.

2. P. Schilpzand, I. E. Depater, and A. Erez, "Workplace Incivility: A Review of the Literature and Agenda for Future Research," *Journal of Organizational Behavior* (Early View Published Online October 28, 2014).

3. Rath and Strong Management Consultants, "Creating an Energized Organization," http://www.rathstrong.com/whitepaper_creatingenergized.htm, accessed June 27, 2008.

4. H. G. Barkem, J. A. C. Baum, and E. A. Mannix, "Management Challenges in a New Time," *Academy of Management Journal* 45 (2002): 916–930.

5. K. Lewin, "Field Theory in Social Science: Selected Theoretical Papers" (edited by Dorin Cartwright) (New York: Harper, 1951).

6. N. Schmitt, ed., Industrial/Organizational Section in *Encyclopedia of Psychology* (Washington, D.C.: American Psychological Association, and New York: Oxford University Press, 2000).

7. R. M. Yerkes, "The Relation of Psychology to Military Activities," *Mental Hygiene* 1 (1917): 371–376.

8. R. Lopopolo, "Development of the Professional Role Behaviors Survey (PROBES)," *Physical Therapy* 81 (July 2001): 1317–1327.

9. F. W. Taylor, *The Principles of Scientific Management* (New York: Norton, 1911).

10. E. A. Locke and G. P. Latham, *A Theory of Goal Setting and Task Performance* (Englewood Cliffs, N.J.: Prentice-Hall, 1990).

11. A. L. Wilkins and W. G. Ouchi, "Efficient Cultures: Exploring the Relationship between Culture and Organizational Performance," *Administrative Science Quarterly* 28 (1983): 468–481.

12. M. F. R. Kets de Vries and D. Miller, "Personality, Culture, and Organization," *Academy of Management Review* 11 (1986): 266–279.

13. H. Schwartz, *Narcissistic Process and Corporate Decay: The Theory of the Organizational Ideal* (New York: NYU Press, 1990).

14. J. G. March and H. A. Simon, *Organizations* (New York: Wiley, 1958).

15. H. B. Elkind, *Preventive Management: Mental Hygiene in Industry* (New York: B. C. Forbes, 1931).

16. J. C. Quick, "Occupational Health Psychology: Historical Roots and Future Directions," *Health Psychology* 18 (1999): 82–88.

17. R. Eby and D. Mahone, "How to Use Ergonomics as a Loss Control Tool," *Risk Management* (March 1, 1991).

18. "Workplace Initiative Reduces Headaches, Neck and Shoulder Pain," *Occupational Health and Safety* (June 10, 2008), http://www.ohsonline.com/articles/64148.

19. B. M. Staw, L. E. Sandelands, and J. E. Dutton, "Threat-Rigidity Effects in Organizational Behavior: A Multilevel Analysis," *Administrative Science Quarterly* 26 (1981): 501–524.

20. D. Kirkpatrick, "The Net Makes It All Easier—Including Exporting U.S. Jobs," *Fortune* (May 26, 2003): 146.

21. C. Crosby, "Quest for Talent Is Driving Evolution in Outsourcing," *Banking Wire* (June 25, 2008): 59.

22. E. V. Brown, Vice President of Global Business Development, Alberto Culver, Inc., "Commencement Address—College of Business Administration, the University of Texas at Arlington" (December 2003).

23. T. Reay, K. Golden-Biddle, and K. Germann, "Legitimizing a New Role: Small Wins and Microprocesses of Change," *Academy of Management Journal* 49 (2006): 977–998.

24. R. L. A. Sterba, "The Organization and Management of the Temple Corporations in Ancient Mesopotamia," *Academy of Management Review* 1 (1976): 16–26; S. P. Dorsey, *Early English Churches in America* (New York: Oxford University Press, 1952).

25. Sir I. Moncreiffe of That Ilk, *The Highland Clans: The Dynastic Origins, Chiefs, and Background of the Clans and of Some Other Families Connected to Highland History*, rev. ed. (New York: C. N. Potter, 1982); D. Shambaugh, "The Soldier and the State in China: The Political Work System in the People's Liberation Army," *Chinese Quarterly* 127 (1991): 527–568.

26. L. L' Abate, ed., *Handbook of Developmental Family Psychology and Psychopathology* (New York: Wiley, 1993); J. A. Hostetler, *Communitarian Societies* (New York: Holt, Rinehart & Winston, 1974).

27. J. M. Lewis, "The Family System and Physical Illness," in *No Single Thread: Psychological Health in Family Systems* (New York: Brunner/Mazel, 1976).

28. D. Katz and R. L. Kahn, *The Social Psychology of Organizations,* 2nd ed. (New York: John Wiley, 1978); H. J. Leavitt, "Applied Organizational Change in Industry: Structural, Technological, and Humanistic Approaches," in J. G. March, ed., *Handbook of Organizations* (Chicago: Rand McNally, 1965): 1144–1170.

29. J. D. Thompson, *Organizations in Action* (New York: McGraw-Hill, 1967).

30. M. Malone, "The Twitter Revolution," *The Wall Street Journal* (April 18, 2009): A11.

31. P. E. Queen, "Enlightened Shareholder Maximization: Is This Strategy Achievable?" *Journal of Business Ethics*, 127 (2015): 683–694.

32. F. J. Roethlisberger and W. J. Dickson, *Management and the Worker* (Cambridge, Mass.: Harvard University Press, 1939).

33. W. L. French and C. H. Bell, *Organization Development*, 4th ed. (Englewood Cliffs, N.J.: Prentice-Hall, 1990).

34. S. G. Barsade and D. E. Gibson, "Why Does Affect Matter in Organizations?" *Academy of Management Perspectives*, 21 (2007): 36–59.

35. J. P. Kotter, "Managing External Dependence," *Academy of Management Review* 4 (1979): 87–92.

36. H. K. Steensma and D. G. Corley, "Organizational Context as a Moderator of Theories on Firm Boundaries for Technology Sourcing," *Academy of Management Journal* 44 (2001): 271–291.

37. M. Yunus, F. Dalsace, D. Menasce, and B. Faivre-Tavignot, "Reaching the World's Poorest Consumers," *Harvard Business Review*, 93 (March 2015): 46–53.

38. T. B. Lawrence and V. Corwin, "Being There: The Acceptance and Marginalization of Part-Time Professional Employees," *Journal of Organizational Behavior* 24 (2003): 923–943.

39. M. K. Gowing, J. D. Kraft, and J. C. Quick, *The New Organizational Reality: Downsizing, Restructuring and Revitalization* (Washington, D.C.: American Psychological Association, 1998); T. Tang and R. M. Fuller, "Corporate Downsizing: What Managers Can Do to Lessen the Negative Effects of Layoffs," *SAM Advanced Management Journal* 60 (1995): 12–15, 31.

40. L. E. Thurow, *Head to Head: The Coming Economic Battle among Japan, Europe, and America* (New York: William Morrow, 1992).

41. S. Ovide, "Microsoft CEO Nadella Hints at Organizational Changes; Chief Asks Top Staff to Simplify Operations; Defends Xbox Business," *Wall Street Journal* (July 10, 2014).

42. J. E. Patterson, *Acquiring the Future: America's Survival and Success in the Global Economy* (Homewood, Ill.: Dow Jones-Irwin, 1990); H. B. Stewart, *Recollecting the Future: A View of Business, Technology, and Innovation in the Next 30 Years* (Homewood, Ill.: Dow Jones-Irwin, 1989).

43. D. Ciampa, *Total Quality* (Reading, Mass.: Addison-Wesley, 1992).

44. T. J. Douglas and W. Q. Judge Jr., "Total Quality Management Implementation and Competitive Advantage: The Role of Structural

Control and Exploration," *Academy of Management Journal* 44 (2001): 158–169.

45. American Management Association, *Blueprints for Service Quality: The Federal Express Approach* (New York: American Management Association, 1991); P. R. Thomas, L. J. Gallace, and K. R. Martin, *Quality Alone Is Not Enough* (New York: American Management Association, 1992).

46. J. de Mast, "A Methodological Comparison of Three Strategies for Quality Improvement," *International Journal of Quality & Reliability Management* 21 (2004): 198–213.

47. M. Barney, "Motorola's Second Generation," *Six Sigma Forum Magazine* 1, No. 3 (May 2002): 13.

48. S. Shahabudin, "Six Sigma: Issues and Problems," *International Journal of Productivity and Quality Management* 3 (2008): 145–160.

49. J. A. Edosomwan, "Six Commandments to Empower Employees for Quality Improvement," *Industrial Engineering* 24 (1992): 14–15.

50. N. T. Duarte, J. R. Goodson, and T. P. Dougherty, "Managing Innovation in Hospitals and Health Systems: Lessons from the Malcolm Baldrige National Quality Award Winners," *Journal of Healthcare Management*, 7 (2014): 21–34.

51. G. H. W. Bush, "Remarks at the Presentation Ceremony for the Malcolm Baldrige National Quality Awards" (speech, December 13, 1990).

52. See also the five articles in the Special Research Forum on Teaching Effectiveness in the Organizational Sciences, *The Academy of Management Journal* 40 (1997): 1265–1398.

53. L. Proserpio and D. A. Gioia, "Teaching the Virtual Generation," *Academy of Management Learning & Education* 6 (2007): 69–80.

54. R. M. Steers, L. W. Porter, and G. A. Bigley, *Motivation and Leadership at Work* (New York: McGraw-Hill, 1996).

55. H. Levinson, *Executive Stress* (New York: New American Library, 1975).

56. D. L. Whetzel, "The Department of Labor Identifies Workplace Skills," *Industrial/Organizational Psychologist* 29 (1991): 89–90.

57. D. A. Whetton and K. S. Cameron, *Developing Management Skills*, 3rd ed. (New York: HarperCollins, 1995).

58. E. R. Kemery and L. T. Stickney, "A Multifaced Approach to Teamwork Assessment in an Undergraduate Business Program," *Journal of Management Education* 38 (2014): 462–479.

59. C. Argyris and D. A. Schon, *Organizational Learning: A Theory of Action Perspective* (Reading, Mass.: Addison-Wesley, 1978).

60. A. Y. Kolb and D. A. Kolb, "Learning Styles and Learning Spaces: Enhancing Experiential Learning in Higher Education," *Academy of Management Learning & Education* 4 (2005): 193–212.

2

1. M. A. Hitt, R. E. Hoskisson, and J. S. Harrison, "Strategic Competitiveness in the 1990s: Challenges and Opportunities for U.S. Executives," *Academy of Management Executive* 5 (1991): 7–22.

2. H. G. Barkem, J. A. C. Baum, and E. A. Mannix, "Management Challenges in a New Time," *Academy of Management Journal* 45 (2002): 916–930.

3. S. C. Harper, "The Challenges Facing CEOs: Past, Present, and Future," *Academy of Management Executive* 6 (1992): 7–25; T. R. Mitchell and W. G. Scott, "America's Problems and Needed Reforms: Confronting the Ethic of Personal Advantage," *Academy of Management Executive* 4 (1990): 23–25.

4. K. Sera, "Corporate Globalization: A New Trend," *Academy of Management Executive* 6 (1992): 89–96.

5. K. Ohmae, *Borderless World: Power and Strategies in the Interlinked Economy* (New York: Harper & Row, 1990).

6. C. A. Bartlett and S. Ghoshal, *Managing across Borders: The Transnational Solution* (Boston: Harvard Business School Press, 1989).

7. F. Warner, "Learning How to Speak to Gen Y," *Fast Company* 72 (July 2003): 36–37.

8. K. R. Xin and J. L. Pearce, "Guanxi: Connections as Substitutes for Formal Institutional Support," *Academy of Management Journal* 39 (1996): 1641–1658.

9. P. S. Chan, "Franchise Management in East Asia," *Academy of Management Executive* 4 (1990): 75–85.

10. H. Weihrich, "Europe 1992: What the Future May Hold," *Academy of Management Executive* 4 (1990): 7–18.

11. E. H. Schein, "Coming to a New Awareness of Organizational Culture," *MIT Sloan Management Review* 25 (1984): 3–16.

12. S. S. Sarwano and R. M. Armstrong, "Microcultural Differences and Perceived Ethical Problems: An International Business Perspective," *Journal of Business Ethics* 30 (2001): 41–56.

13. F. Warner, "Learning How to Speak to Gen Y," *Fast Company* 72 (July 2003): 36–37.

14. R. Sharpe, "Hi-Tech Taboos," *The Wall Street Journal* (October 31, 1995): A1.

15. G. Hofstede, *Culture's Consequences: International Differences in Work-Related Values* (Beverly Hills, Calif.: Sage Publications, 1980); G. Hofstede, "Motivation, Leadership, and Organization: Do American Theories Apply Abroad?" *Organizational Dynamics* (Summer 1980): 42–63.

16. G. M. Spreitzer, M. W. McCall, Jr., and J. D. Mahoney, "Early Identification of International Executive Potential," *Journal of Applied Psychology* 82 (1997): 6–29.

17. M. A. Hitt, L. Bierman, K. Uhlenbruck, and K. Shimizu, "The Importance of Resources in the Internationalization of Professional Service Firms: The Good, the Bad, and the Ugly," *Academy of Management Journal* 49 (2006): 1137–1157.

18. A. J. Michel, "Goodbyes Can Cost Plenty in Europe," *Fortune* (April 6, 1992): 16.

19. G. Hofstede, "Gender Stereotypes and Partner Preferences of Asian Women in Masculine and Feminine Countries," *Journal of Cross Cultural Psychology* 27 (1996): 533–546.

20. G. Hofstede, "Cultural Constraints in Management Theories," *Academy of Management Executive* 7 (1993): 81–94.

21. "IBM Offers Employees New 'Learning Accounts' and Global Training Programs," *InformationWeek* (July 26, 2007).

22. J. Sandberg, "Global-Market Woes Are More Personality Than Nationality," *The Wall Street Journal* (January 29, 2008).

23. L. R. Offerman and M. K. Growing, "Organizations of the Future," *American Psychologist* 45 (1990): 95–108.

24. J. Chatman, J. Polzer, S. Barsade, and M. Neale, "Being Different Yet Feeling Similar: The Influence of Demographic Composition and Organizational Culture on Work Processes and Outcomes," *Administrative Science Quarterly* 43 (1998): 749–780.

25. S. Caudron, "Task Force Report Reveals Coke's Progress on Diversity," *Workforce* 82 (2003): 40, http://www.workforceonline.com/section/03/feature/23/42/44/234246.html.

26. S. Prasso, "Google Goes to India," *Fortune* (October 29, 2007).

27. Women in the Labor Force: A Databook, http://www.bls.gov/opub/reports/cps/women-in-the-labor-force-a-databook-2014.pdf.

28. "Degrees Earned by Women," *Indicator* 27 (2008), http://nces.ed.gov/programs/coe/2008/section3/indicator27.asp.

29. Catalyst, *2007 Catalyst Census of Women Corporate Officers and Top Earners of the Fortune 500*, http://catalyst.org/publication/13/2007-catalyst-census-of-women-corporate-officers-and-top-earners-of-the-fortune-500.

30. "The 2015 NAFE Top 50 Companies for Executive Women," *Working Mother*, http://www.workingmother.com/best-companies/american-express-17.

31. U.S. Department of Labor, "Highlights of Women's Earnings in 2005," Report 995 (September 2006): 33; Catalyst, *Catalyst Census of Women Corporate Officers and Top Earners* (2001).

32. A. M. Morrison, R. P. White, E. Van Velsor, and the Center for Creative Leadership, *Breaking the Glass Ceiling: Can Women Reach the Top of America's Largest Corporations?* (Reading, Mass.: Addison-Wesley, 1987).

33. Catalyst, "2014 S&P 500 Board Seats Held by Women by Race/Ethnicity," New York: Catalyst, March 17, 2105.

34. R. Soares, H. Foust-Cummings, C. Francoeur, and R. Labelle, *Companies Behaving Responsibly: Gender Diversity on Boards* (New York: Catalyst, 2015).

35. D. L. Nelson and M. A Hitt, "Employed Women and Stress: Implications for Enhancing Women's Mental Health in the Workplace," in D. C. Quick, L. R. Murphy, and J. J. Hurrell, Jr., eds., *Stress and Well Being at Work* (Washington, D. C.: American Psychological Association, 1992): 164–177.

36. L. L. Martins and C. K. Parsons, "Effects of Gender Diversity Management on Perceptions of Organizational Attractiveness: The Role of Individual Differences in Attitudes and Beliefs," *Journal of Applied Psychology* 92 (2007): 865–875.

37. A. Eyring and B. A. Stead, "Shattering the Glass Ceiling: Some Successful Corporate Practices," *Journal of Business Ethics* 17 (1998): 245–251.

38. Catalyst, *Advancing Women in Business: The Catalyst Guide* (San Francisco: Jossey-Bass, 1998).

39. Department of Health and Human Services, "A Profile of Older Americans: 2012," http://www.aoa.gov/Aging_Statistics/Profile/2012/docs/2012profile.pdf.

40. W. B. Johnston, "Global Workforce 2000: The New World Labor Market," *Harvard Business Review* 69 (1991): 115–127.

41. S. Needleman, "The Last Office Perk: Getting Paid to Volunteer," *The Wall Street Journal* (April 29, 2008): D1, D5.

42. J. Li, C. W. L. Chu, K. C. K. Lam, and S. Liao, "Age Diversity and Firm Performance in an Emerging Economy," *Human Resource Management* 50, No. 2 (March–April 2011): 247–270.

43. S. E. Jackson and E. B. Alvarez, "Working through Diversity as a Strategic Imperative," in S. E. Jackson, ed., *Diversity in the Workplace: Human Resources Initiatives* (New York: Guilford Press, 1992): 13–36.

44. "Managing Generational Diversity," *HR Magazine* 36 (1991): 91–92.

45. K. Tyler, "The Tethered Generation," *HR Magazine* (May 2007): 41–46.

46. S. R. Rhodes, "Age-Related Differences in Work Attitudes and Behavior: A Review and Conceptual Analysis," *Psychological Bulletin* 93 (1983): 338–367.

47. B. L. Hassell and P. L. Perrewe, "An Examination of Beliefs about Older Workers: Do Stereotypes Still Exist?" *Journal of Organizational Behavior* 16 (1995): 457–468.

48. U.S. Bureau of the Census, *Population Profile of the United States, 1997* (Washington, D.C.: U.S. Government Printing Office, 1997).

49. W. J. Rothwell, "HRD and the Americans with Disabilities Act," *Training and Development Journal* (August 1991): 45–47.

50. J. J. Laabs, "The Golden Arches Provide Golden Opportunities," *Personnel Journal* (July 1991): 52–57.

51. Catalyst. "Quick Take: Lesbian, Gay, Bisexual & Transgender Workplace Issues," *Catalyst*, May 15, 2014.

52. B. A. Everly and J. L. Schwarz, "Predictors of the Adoption of LGBT-Friendly HR Policies," *Human Resource Management*, 54 (2015), 367–384.

53. DiversityInc, "The Diversity Top 10 Companies for LGBT Employees," http://www.diversityinc.com/top-10-companies-lgbt-employees/.

54. A. N. Smith and S. V. Simms, "The Impact of Discrimination on Organizations." in A. J. Colella and E. B. King, eds., *Oxford Handbook of Workplace Discrimination* (New York: Oxford University Press, in press).

55. L. Armstrong, "What Men Say behind Closed Doors," *Working Mother* (June–July 2008): 87–90.

56. J. E. Rigdon, "PepsiCo's KFC Scouts for Blacks and Women for Its Top Echelons," *The Wall Street Journal* (November 13, 1991): A1.

57. P. A. Galagan, "Tapping the Power of a Diverse Workforce," *Training and Development Journal* 26 (1991): 38–44.

58. C. L. Holladay, J. L. Knight, D. L. Paige, and M. A. Quinones, "The Influence of Framing on Attitudes toward Diversity Training," *Human Resource Development Quarterly* 14 (2003): 245–263.

59. R. Thomas, "From Affirmative Action to Affirming Diversity," *Harvard Business Review* 68 (1990): 107–117.

60. T. H. Cox, Jr., *Cultural Diversity in Organizations: Theory, Research and Practice* (San Francisco: Berrett-Koehler, 1994).

61. "Business Ethics 100 Best Corporate Citizens 2004," http://www.business-ethics.com/BE100_2004, accessed June 23, 2008.

62. M. R. Fusilier, C. D. Aby, Jr., J. K. Worley, and S. Elliott, "Perceived Seriousness of Business Ethics Issues," *Business and Professional Ethics Journal* 15 (1996): 67–78.

63. J. S. Mill, *Utilitarianism, Liberty, and Representative Government* (London: Dent, 1910).

64. A. Smith, *An Inquiry into the Nature and Causes of the Wealth of Nations,* vol. 10 of The Harvard Classics, ed. C. J. Bullock (New York: P. F. Collier & Son, 1909).

65. A. Smith, *The Theory of Moral Sentiments* (Glasgow Edition, Scotland, 1790).

66. C. Fried, *Right and Wrong* (Cambridge, Mass.: Harvard University Press, 1978).

67. I. Kant, *Groundwork of the Metaphysics of Morals,* trans. H. J. Paton (New York: Harper & Row, 1964).

68. R. C. Solomon, "Corporate Roles, Personal Virtues: Aristotelean Approach to Business Ethics," *Business Ethics Quarterly* 2 (1992): 317–339; R. C. Solomon, *A Better Way to Think about Business: How Personal Integrity Leads to Corporate Success* (New York: Oxford University Press, 1999).

69. J. C. Quick and J. L. Goolsby, "Integrity First: Ethics for Leaders and Followers," *Organizational Dynamics* 42 (2010): 1–7; J. L. Goolsby, D. A. Mack, and J. C. Quick, "Winning by Staying in Bounds: Good Outcomes from Positive Ethics," *Organizational Dynamics* 39 (2010): 248–257.

70. M. Kouchaki and S. D. Desai, "Anxious, Threatened, and Also Unethical: How Anxiety Makes Individuals Feel Threatened and Commit Unethical Acts," *Journal of Applied Psychology*, 100 (2015), 360–375.

71. W. Bulkeley, "Email Software Delves into Employees' Contacts," *The Wall Street Journal* (April 21, 2008): B9.

72. D. Kemp, "Employers and AIDS: Dealing with the Psychological and Emotional Issues of AIDS in the Workplace," *American Review of Public Administration* 25 (1995): 263–278.

73. J. J. Koch, "Wells Fargo's and IBM's HIV Policies Help Protect Employees' Rights," *Personnel Journal* (April 1990): 40–48.

74. U.S. EEOC, "Discrimination Because of Sex under Title VII of the 1964 Civil Rights Act as Amended: Adoption of Interim Guidelines—Sexual Harassment," *Federal Register* 45 (1980): 25024–25025.

75. L. F. Fitzgerald, F. Drasgow, C. L. Hulin, M. J. Gelfand, and V. J. Magley, "Antecedents and Consequences of Sexual Harassment in Organizations: A Test of an Integrated Model," *Journal of Applied Psychology* 82 (1997): 578–589.

76. E. Felsenthal, "Rulings Open Way for Sex-Harass Cases," *The Wall Street Journal* (June 29, 1998): A10; S. J. Adler, "Lawyers Advise Concerns to Provide Precise Written Policy to Employees," *The Wall Street Journal* (October 9, 1991): B1.

77. K. T. Schneider, S. Swan, and L. F. Fitzgerald, "Job-Related and Psychological Effects of Sexual Harassment in the Workplace: Empirical Evidence from Two Organizations," *Journal of Applied Psychology* 82 (1997): 401–415.

78. A. M. O'Leary-Kelly, R. L. Paetzold, and R. W. Griffin, "Sexual Harassment as Aggressive Behavior: An Actor-Based Perspective," *Academy of Management Review* 25 (2000): 372–388.

79. L. M. Goldenhar, N. G. Swanson, J. J. Hurrell, Jr., A. Ruder, and J. Deddens, "Stressors and Adverse Outcomes for Female Construction Workers," *Journal of Occupational Health Psychology* 3 (1998): 19–32; C. S. Piotrkowski, "Gender Harassment, Job Satisfaction and Distress among Employed White and Minority Women," *Journal of Occupational Health Psychology* 3 (1998): 33–42.

80. K. Aquino, L. Sheppard, M. B. Watkins, J. O'Reilly, and A. Smith, "Social Sexual Behavior at Work," *Research in Organizational Behavior,* 34 (2014): 217–236.

81. R. A. Posthuma, C. P. Maertz, Jr., and J. B. Dworkin, "Procedural Justice's Relationship with Turnover: Explaining Past Inconsistent Findings," *Journal of Organizational Behavior* 28 (2007): 381–398.

82. D. Fields, M. Pang, and C. Chio, "Distributive and Procedural Justice as Predictors of Employee Outcomes in Hong Kong," *Journal of Organizational Behavior* 21 (2000): 547–562.

83. H. L. Laframboise, "Vile Wretches and Public Heroes: The Ethics of Whistleblowing in Government," *Canadian Public Administration* (Spring 1991): 73–78.

84. E. J. Epstein, "Was Snowden's Heist a Foreign Espionage Operation," *Wall Street Journal* (May 10, 2014): A13.

85. L. J. Christensen, A. Mackey, and D. Whetton, "Taking Responsibility for Corporate Social Responsibility: The Role of Leaders in Creating, Implementing, Sustaining, or Avoiding Socially Responsible Firm Behaviors," *The Academy of Management Perspectives*, 28 (2014): 164–178.

86. S. Covel, "Tours to Fair-Trade Farms Help Coffee Sellers Spread Word," *The Wall Street Journal* (March 11, 2008): B5.

87. D. B. Turban and D. W. Greening, "Corporate Social Performance and Organizational Attractiveness to Prospective Employees," *Academy of Management Journal* 40 (1996): 658–672.

88. R. Walker, "Sex vs. Ethics," *Fast Company* (June 2008): 74–78.

3

1. K. Lewin, "Formalization and Progress in Psychology," in D. Cartwright, ed., *Field Theory in Social Science* (New York: Harper, 1951).

2. N. S. Endler and D. Magnusson, "Toward an Interactional Psychology of Personality," *Psychological Bulletin* 83 (1976): 956–974.

3. J. R. Terborg, "Interactional Psychology and Research on Human Behavior in Organizations," *Academy of Management Review* 6 (1981): 561–576.

4. C. Spearman, "General Intelligence: Objectively Determined and Measured," *American Journal of Psychology* 15 (1904): 201–293.

5. F. L. Schmidt and J. Hunter, "General Mental Ability in the World of Work: Occupational Attainment and Job Performance," *Journal of Personality and Social Psychology* 86, No. 1 (2004): 162–173; C. Bertua, N. Anderson, and J. F Salgado, "The Predictive Validity of Cognitive Ability Tests: A UK Meta-Analysis," *Journal of Occupational and Organizational Psychology* 78 (2004): 387–409.

6. T. J. Bouchard, Jr., "Twins Reared Together and Apart: What They Tell Us about Human Diversity," in S. W. Fox, ed., *Individuality and Determinism* (New York: Plenum Press, 1984); R. D. Arvey, T. J. Bouchard, Jr., N. L. Segal, and L. M. Abraham, "Job Satisfaction: Environmental and Genetic Components," *Journal of Applied Psychology* 74 (1989): 235–248.

7. G. Allport, *Pattern and Growth in Personality* (New York: Holt, 1961).

8. R. B. Cattell, *Personality and Mood by Questionnaire* (San Francisco: Jossey-Bass, 1973).

9. J. M. Digman, "Personality Structure: Emergence of a Five-Factor Model," *Annual Review of Psychology* 41 (1990): 417–440.

10. T. A. Judge, J. J. Martocchio, and C. J. Thoresen, "Five-Factor Model of Personality and Employee Absence," *Journal of Applied Psychology* 82 (1997): 745–755.

11. H. J. Bernardin, D. K. Cooke, and P. Villanova, "Conscientiousness and Agreeableness as Predictors of Rating Leniency," *Journal of Applied Psychology* 85 (2000): 232–234.

12. D. H. Kluemper, B. D. McLarty, and M. N. Bing, "Acquaintance Ratings of the Big Five Personality Traits: Incremental Validity Beyond and Interactive Effects with Self-Reports in the Prediction of Workplace Deviance," *Journal of Applied Psychology* 100 (2015): 237–248.

13. T. A. Judge and R. Ilies, "Relationships of Personality to Performance Motivation: A Meta-Analytic Review," *Journal of Applied Psychology* 87 (2002): 797–807.

14. G. M. Hurtz and J. J. Donovan, "Personality and Job Performance: The Big Five Revisited," *Journal of Applied Psychology* 85 (2000): 869–879.

15. K. A. Byrne, C. D. Silasi-Mansat, and D. A. Worthy. "Who Chokes Under Pressure? The Big Five Personality Traits and Decision-Making under Pressure," *Personality and Individual Differences* 74 (2015): 22–28.

16. H. Le, I. S. Oh, S. B. Robbins, R. Ilies, E. Holland, and P. Westrick, "Too Much of a Good Thing: Curvilinear Relationships between Personality Traits and Job Performance," *Journal of Applied Psychology* 96 (2011): 113–133.

17. J. F. Salgado, S. Moscoso, and M. Lado, "Evidence of Cross-Cultural Invariance of the Big Five Personality Dimensions in Work Settings," *European Journal of Personality* 17 (2003): S67–S76; C. Rodriguez and T. H. Church, "The Structure and Personality Correlates of Affect in Mexico: Evidence of Cross-Cultural Comparability Using the Spanish Language," *Journal of Cross-Cultural Psychology* 34 (2003): 211–230.

18. H. C. Triandis, "Cultural Influences on Personality," *Annual Review of Psychology* 53 (2002): 133–160.

19. M. Moody, "Adaptive Behavior in Intercultural Environments: The Relationship between Cultural Intelligence Factors and Big Five Personality Traits" (Ph.D. thesis, George Washington University, 2007).

20. M. R. Barrick and M. K. Mount, "The Big Five Personality Dimensions and Job Performance: A Meta-Analysis," *Personnel Psychology* 44 (1991): 1–26.

21. D. D. Clark and R. Hoyle, "A Theoretical Solution to the Problem of Personality-Situational Interaction," *Personality and Individual Differences* 9 (1988): 133–138.

22. D. Byrne and L. J. Schulte, "Personality Dimensions as Predictors of Sexual Behavior," in J. Bancroft, ed., *Annual Review of Sexual Research*, vol. 1 (Philadelphia: Society for the Scientific Study of Sex, 1990).

23. P. Harms, B. Roberts, and D. Wood, "Who Shall Lead? An Integrative Personality Approach to the Study of the Antecedents of Status in Informal Social Organizations," *Journal of Research in Personality* 41 (2007): 689–699.

24. T. A. Judge, E. A. Locke, and C. C. Durham, "The Dispositional Causes of Job Satisfaction: A Core Self-Evaluation Approach," *Research in Organizational Behavior* 19 (1997): 151–188.

25. M. Erez and T. A. Judge, "Relationship of Core Self-Evaluations to Goal Setting, Motivation and Performance," *Journal of Applied Psychology* 86 (2001): 1270–1279; R. F. Piccolo, T. A. Judge, K. Takahashi, N. Watanabe, and E. A Locke, "Core Self-Evaluations in Japan: Relative Effects on Job Satisfaction, Life Satisfaction, and Happiness," *Journal of Organizational Behavior* 26, No. 8 (2005): 965–984.

26. J. B. Rotter, "Generalized Expectancies for Internal vs. External Control of Reinforcement," *Psychological Monographs* 80, No. 609 (1966).

27. M. Erez and T. A. Judge, "Relationship of Core Self-Evaluations to Goal Setting, Motivation and Performance," *Journal of Applied Psychology* 86 (2001): 1270–1279.

28. T. A. Judge and J. E. Bono, "Relationship of Core Self-Evaluations Traits—Self-Esteem, Generalized Self-Efficacy, Locus of Control, and Emotional Stability—With Job Satisfaction and Job Performance: A Meta-Analysis," *Journal of Applied Psychology* 86 (2001): 80–92.

29. *Ibid.*

30. S. S. K. Lam and J. Shaubroeck, "The Role of Locus of Control in Reactions to Being Promoted and to Being Passed Over: A Quasi Experiment," *Academy of Management Journal* 43 (2000): 66–78.

31. G. Chen, S. M. Gully, J. Whiteman, and R. N. Kilcullen, "Examination of Relationships among Trait-Like Individual Differences, State-Like Individual Differences, and Learning Performance," *Journal of Applied Psychology* 85 (2000): 835–847; G. Chen, S. M. Gully, and D. Eden, "Validation of a New General Self-Efficacy Scale," *Organizational Research Methods* 4 (2001): 62–83.

32. A. Bandura, *Self-Efficacy: The Exercise of Control* (San Francisco: Freeman, 1997).

33. D. R. Avery, "Personality as a Predictor of the Value of Voice," *Journal of Psychology* 137 (2003): 435–447.

34. T. A. Judge and J. E. Bono, "Relationship of Core Self-Evaluations Traits—Self-Esteem, Generalized Self-Efficacy, Locus of Control, and Emotional Stability—With Job Satisfaction and Job Performance: A Meta-Analysis," *Journal of Applied Psychology* 86 (2001): 80–92.

35. B. W. Pelham and W. B. Swann, Jr., "From Self-Conceptions to Self-Worth: On the Sources and Structure of Global Self-Esteem," *Journal of Personality and Social Psychology* 57 (1989): 672–680.

36. A. H. Baumgardner, C. M. Kaufman, and P. E. Levy, "Regulating Affect Interpersonally: When Low Esteem Leads to Greater Enhancement," *Journal of Personality and Social Psychology* 56 (1989): 907–921.

37. J. Schimel, T. Pyszczynski, J. Arndt, and J. Greenberg, "Being Accepted for Who We Are: Evidence That Social Validation of the Intrinsic Self Reduces General Defensiveness," *Journal of Personality and Social Psychology* 80 (2001): 35–52.

38. P. Tharenou and P. Harker, "Moderating Influences of Self-Esteem on Relationships between Job Complexity, Performance, and Satisfaction," *Journal of Applied Psychology* 69 (1984): 623–632.

39. R. A. Ellis and M. S. Taylor, "Role of Self-Esteem within the Job Search Process," *Journal of Applied Psychology* 68 (1983): 632–640.

40. J. Brockner and T. Hess, "Self-Esteem and Task Performance in Quality Circles," *Academy of Management Journal* 29 (1986): 617–623.

41. B. R. Schlenker, M. F. Weingold, and J. R. Hallam, "Self-Serving Attributions in Social Context: Effects of Self-Esteem and Social Pressure," *Journal of Personality and Social Psychology* 57 (1990): 855–863.

42. M. K. Duffy, J. D. Shaw, and E. M. Stark, "Performance and Satisfaction in Conflicted Interdependent Groups: When and How Does Self-Esteem Make a Difference?" *Academy of Management Journal* 43 (2000): 772–782.

43. T. Mussweiler, S. Gabriel, and G. V. Bodenhausen, "Shifting Social Identities as a Strategy for Deflecting Threatening Social Comparisons," *Journal of Personality and Social Psychology* 79 (2000): 398–409.

44. M. Snyder and S. Gangestad, "On the Nature of Self-Monitoring: Matters of Assessment, Matters of Validity," *Journal of Psychology and Social Psychology* 51 (1986): 125–139.

45. G. Toegel, N. Anand, and M. Kilduff, "Emotion Helpers: The Role of High Positive Affectivity and High Self-Monitoring Managers," *Personnel Psychology* 60, No. 2 (2007): 337–365.

46. A. Mehra, M. Kilduff, and D. J. Brass, "The Social Networks of High and Low Self-Monitors: Implications for Workplace Performance," *Administrative Science Quarterly* 46 (2001): 121–146.

47. W. H. Turnley and M. C. Bolino, "Achieving Desired Images while Avoiding Undesired Images: Exploring the Role of Self-Monitoring in Impression Management," *Journal of Applied Psychology* 86 (2001): 351–360.

48. M. Kilduff and D. V. Day, "Do Chameleons Get Ahead? The Effects of Self-Monitoring on Managerial Careers," *Academy of Management Journal* 37 (1994): 1047–1060.

49. A. H. Church, "Managerial Self-Awareness in High-Performing Individuals in Organizations," *Journal of Applied Psychology* 82 (1997): 281–292.

50. C. Douglas and W. L. Gardner, "Transition to Self-Directed Work Teams: Implications of Transition Time and Self-Monitoring for Managers' Use of Influence Tactics," *Journal of Organizational Behavior* 25 (2004): 45–67.

51. A. M. Isen and R. A. Baron, "Positive Affect and Organizational Behavior," in B. M. Staw and L. L. Cummings, eds., *Research in Organizational Behavior*, vol. 12 (Greenwich, Conn.: JAI Press, 1990).

52. D. Watson and L. A. Clark, "Negative Affectivity: The Disposition to Experience Aversive Emotional States," *Psychological Bulletin* 96 (1984): 465–490.

53. R. Ilies and T. Judge, "On the Heritability of Job Satisfaction: The Mediating Role of Personality," *Journal of Applied Psychology* 88 (2003): 750–759.

54. J. M. George, "State or Trait," *Journal of Applied Psychology* 76 (1991): 299–307.

55. J. M. George, "Mood and Absence," *Journal of Applied Psychology* 74 (1989): 287–324.

56. S. Lyubomirsky, L. King, and L. E. Diener, "The Benefits of Frequent Positive Affect: Does Happiness Lead to Success?" *Psychological Bulletin* 131, No. 6 (2005): 803–855.

57. S. Barsade, A. Ward, J. Turner, and J. Sonnenfeld, "To Your Heart's Content: A Model of Affective Diversity in Top Management Teams," *Administrative Science Quarterly* 45 (2000): 802–836.

58. J. M. Crant, "The Proactive Personality Scale and Objective Job Performance among Real Estate Agents," *Journal of Applied Psychology* 80 (1995): 532–537.

59. T. W. H. Ng, L. T. Eby, K. L. Sorensen, and D. C. Feldman, "Predictors of Objective and Subjective Career Success: A Meta Analysis," *Personnel Psychology* 58 (2005): 367–408; D. J. Brown, R. T. Cober, K. Kane, P. E. Levey, and J. Shalhoop, "Proactive Personality and the Successful Job Search: A Field Investigation with College Graduates," *Journal of Applied Psychology* 91 (2006): 717–726.

60. J. M. Crant and T. S. Bateman, "Charismatic Leadership Viewed from Above: The Impact of Proactive Personality," *Journal of Organizational Behavior* 21 (2000): 63–75.

61. H. Rorschach, *Psychodiagnostics* (Bern: Hans Huber, 1921).

62. C. G. Jung, *Psychological Types* (New York: Harcourt & Brace, 1923).

63. Consulting Psychologists Press, http://www.cpp.com/products/mbti/index.asp, accessed June 30, 2008.

64. R. Benfari and J. Knox, *Understanding Your Management Style* (Lexington, Mass.: Lexington Books, 1991).

65. O. Kroeger and J. M. Thuesen, *Type Talk* (New York: Delacorte Press, 1988).

66. S. Hirsch and J. Kummerow, *Life Types* (New York: Warner Books, 1989).

67. I. B. Myers and M. H. McCaulley, *Manual: A Guide to the Development and Use of the Myers-Briggs Type Indicator* (Palo Alto, Calif.: Consulting Psychologists Press, 1990).

68. G. P. Macdaid, M. H. McCaulley, and R. I. Kainz, *Myers-Briggs Type Indicator: Atlas of Type Tables* (Gainesville, Fla.: Center for Application of Psychological Type, 1987).

69. J. B. Murray, "Review of Research on the Myers-Briggs Type Indicator," *Perceptual and Motor Skills* 70 (1990): 1187–1202; J. G. Carlson, "Recent Assessment of the Myers-Briggs Type Indicator," *Journal of Personality Assessment* 49 (1985): 356–365.

70. A. Thomas, M. Benne, M. Marr, E. Thomas, and R. Hume, "The Evidence Remains Stable: The MBTI Predicts Attraction and Attrition in an Engineering Program," *Journal of Psychological Type* 55 (2000): 35–42.

71. C. Walck, "Training for Participative Management: Implications for Psychological Type," *Journal of Psychological Type* 21 (1991): 3–12.

72. G. Lawrence and C. Martin, *Building People, Building Programs: A Practitioner's Guide for Introducing the MBTI to Individuals and Organizations* (Center for Applications of Psychological Type, 2001); L. Berens, L. Ernst, M. Smith, *Quick Guide to the 16 Personality Types and Teams: Applying Team Essentials™ to Create Effective Teams* (Denbighshire, UK ,Telos Publications, 2004).

73. J. Michael, "Using the Myers-Briggs Indicator as a Tool for Leadership Development: Apply with Caution," *Journal of Leadership & Organizational Studies* 10 (2003): 68–78.

74. E. C. Webster, *The Employment Interview: A Social Judgment Process* (Schomberg, Canada: SIP, 1982).

75. A. J. Ward, M. J. Lankau, A. C. Amason, J. A. Sonnenfeld, and B. R. Agle, "Improving the Performance of Top Management Teams," *MIT Sloan Management Review* 48, No. 3 (2007): 85–90.

76. N. Adler, *International Dimensions of Organizational Behavior*, 2nd ed. (Boston: PWS-Kent, 1991).

77. L. R. Offerman and M. K. Gowing, "Personnel Selection in the Future: The Impact of Changing Demographics and the Nature of Work," in Schmitt, Borman & Associates, eds., *Personnel Selection in Organizations* (San Francisco: Jossey-Bass, 1993).

78. H. G. Halvorson, "Managing Yourself: A Second Chance to Make the Right Impression," *Harvard Business Review* (2015, January–February): 108–111.

79. J. Park and M. R. Banaji, "Mood and Heuristics: The Influence of Happy and Sad States on Sensitivity and Bias in Stereotyping," *Journal of Personality and Social Psychology* 78 (2000): 1005–1023.

80. M. W. Levine and J. M. Shefner, *Fundamentals of Sensation and Perception* (Reading, Mass.: Addison-Wesley, 1981).

81. R. L. Dipboye, H. L. Fromkin, and K. Willback, "Relative Importance of Applicant Sex, Attractiveness, and Scholastic Standing in Evaluations of Job Applicant Resumes," *Journal of Applied Psychology* 60 (1975): 39–43; I. H. Frieze, J. E. Olson, and J. Russell, "Attractiveness and Income for Men and Women in Management," *Journal of Applied Social Psychology* 21 (1991): 1039–1057.

82. P. Ekman and W. Friesen, *Unmasking the Face* (Englewood Cliffs, N.J.: Prentice-Hall, 1975).

83. J. E. Rehfeld, "What Working for a Japanese Company Taught Me," *Harvard Business Review* (November–December 1990): 167–176.

84. M. W. Morris and R. P. Larrick, "When One Cause Casts Doubt on Another: A Normative Analysis of Discounting in Causal Attribution," *Psychological Review* 102 (1995): 331–355.

85. G. B. Sechrist and C. Stangor, "Perceived Consensus Influences Intergroup Behavior and Stereotype Accessibility," *Journal of Personality and Psychology* 80 (2001): 645–654; A. Lyons and Y. Kashima, "How Are Stereotypes Maintained through Communication? The Influence of Stereotype Sharedness," *Journal of Personality and Social Psychology* 85 (2003): 989–1005.

86. R. Hastings, "The Forgotten Minority: Stereotypes of Asian-Americans Not Only Can Limit Their Workplace Opportunities But Also Can Stifle the Talents They Can Offer Their Employers," *HR Magazine* (July 2007), http://infotrac-college.thomsonlearning.com, accessed June 30, 2008; J. Katz, "How Troublesome Are Stereotypes in International Business?," *CAHRS Working Paper Series 1995*,

http://digitalcommons.ilr.cornell.edu/cahrswp/193, accessed June 30, 2008.

87. A. Feingold, "Gender Differences in Effects of Physical Attractiveness on Romantic Attraction: A Comparison across Five Research Paradigms," *Journal of Personality and Social Psychology* 59 (1990): 981–993.

88. M. Snyder, "When Belief Creates Reality," *Advances in Experimental Social Psychology* 18 (1984): 247–305.

89. M. Biernat, "Toward a Broader View of Social Stereotyping," *American Psychologist* 58 (2003): 1019–1027.

90. E. Burnstein and Y. Schul, "The Informational Basis of Social Judgments: Operations in Forming an Impression of Another Person," *Journal of Experimental Social Psychology* 18 (1982): 217–234.

91. T. DeGroot and S. Motowidlo, "Why Visual and Vocal Cues Can Affect Interviewers' Judgments and Predict Job Performance," *Journal of Applied Psychology* 84 (1999): 986–993; M. C. L. Greene and L. Mathieson, *The Voice and Its Disorders* (London: Whurr, 1989).

92. R. L. Gross and S. E. Brodt, "How Assumptions of Consensus Undermine Decision Making," *MIT Sloan Management Review* 42 (Winter 2001): 86–94.

93. R. Rosenthal and L. Jacobson, *Pygmalion in the Classroom: Teacher Expectations and Pupils' Intellectual Development* (New York: Holt, Rinehart & Winston, 1968).

94. D. Eden, "Pygmalion without Interpersonal Contrast Effects: Whole Groups Gain from Raising Manager Expectations," *Journal of Applied Psychology* 75 (1990): 394–398.

95. R. A. Giacalone and P. Rosenfeld, eds., *Impression Management in Organizations* (Hillsdale, N.J.: Erlbaum, 1990); J. Tedeschi and V. Melburg, "Impression Management and Influence in the Organization," in S. Bacharach and E. Lawler, eds., *Research in the Sociology of Organizations* (Greenwich, Conn.: JAI Press, 1984): 31–58.

96. A. Colella and A. Varma, "The Impact of Subordinate Disability on Leader–Member Exchange Relationships," *Academy of Management Journal* 44 (2001): 304–315.

97. D. H. M. Chng, M. S. Rodgers, E. Shih, and X. Song, "Leaders' Impression Management during Organizational Decline: The Roles of Publicity, Image Concerns, and Incentive Compensation," *The Leadership Quarterly*, published online January 2015.

98. S. Bozzolan, C. H. Cho, and G. Michelon, "Impression Management and Organizational Audiences: The Fiat Group Case," *Journal of Business Ethics* 126(2015): 143-165.

99. R. A. Baron, "Impression Management by Applicants during Employment Interviews: The 'Too Much of a Good Thing' Effect," in R. W. Eder and G. R. Ferris, eds., *The Employment Interview: Theory, Research, and Practice* (Newbury Park, Calif.: Sage Publications, 1989).

100. F. Heider, *The Psychology of Interpersonal Relations* (New York: Wiley, 1958).

101. S. Graham and V. Folkes, *Attribution Theory: Applications to Achievement, Mental Health, and Interpersonal Conflict* (Hillsdale: L. Erlbaum and Associates, 1990).

102. P. D. Sweeney, K. Anderson, and S. Bailey, "Attributional Style in Depression: A Meta-Analytic Review," *Journal of Personality and Social Psychology* 51 (1986): 974–991.

103. P. Rosenthal, D. Guest, and R. Peccei, "Gender Differences in Managers' Causal Explanations for Their Work Performance," *Journal of Occupational and Organizational Psychology* 69 (1996): 145–151.

104. J. Silvester, "Spoken Attributions and Candidate Success in Graduate Recruitment Interviews," *Journal of Occupational and Organizational Psychology* 70 (1997): 61–71.

105. L. Ross, "The Intuitive Psychologist and His Shortcomings: Distortions in the Attribution Process," in L. Berkowitz, ed., *Advances in Experimental Social Psychology* (New York: Academic Press, 1977); M. O'Sullivan, "The Fundamental Attribution Error in Detecting Deception: The Boy-Who-Cried-Wolf Effect," *Personality & Social Psychology Bulletin* 29 (2003): 1316–1327.

106. D. T. Miller and M. Ross, "Self-Serving Biases in the Attribution of Causality: Fact or Fiction?" *Psychological Bulletin* 82 (1975): 313–325.

107. J. R. Schermerhorn, Jr., "Team Development for High-Performance Management," *Training and Development Journal* 40 (1986): 38–41.

108. J. G. Miller, "Culture and the Development of Everyday Causal Explanation," *Journal of Personality and Social Psychology* 46 (1984): 961–978.

109. G. Si, S. Rethorst, and K. Willimczik, "Causal Attribution Perception in Sports Achievement: A Cross-Cultural Study on Attributional Concepts in Germany and China," *Journal of Cross-Cultural Psychology* 26 (1995): 537–553.

4

1. A. H. Eagly and S. Chaiken, *The Psychology of Attitudes* (Orlando, Fla.: Harcourt Brace Jovanovich, 1993).

2. M. Pounds, "Bring Positive Attitude to the Workplace Using Praise," *South Florida Sun-Sentinel* (Fort Lauderdale, FL) (September 27, 2007), http://infotrac-college.thomsonlearning.com, accessed July 2, 2008.

3. M. J. Rosenberg, C. I. Hovland, W. J. McGuire, R. P. Abelson, and J. H. Brehm, *Attitude Organization and Change* (New Haven, Conn.: Yale University Press, 1960).

4. L. Festinger, *A Theory of Cognitive Dissonance* (Evanston, Ill.: Row, Peterson, 1957).

5. R. H. Fazio and M. P. Zanna, "On the Predictive Validity of Attitudes: The Roles of Direct Experience and Confidence," *Journal of Personality* 46 (1978): 228–243.

6. A. Tversky and D. Kahneman, "Judgment under Uncertainty: Heuristics and Biases," in D. Kahneman, P. Slovic, and A. Tversky, eds., *Judgment under Uncertainty* (New York: Cambridge University Press, 1982): 3–20.

7. A. Bandura, *Social Learning Theory* (Englewood Cliffs, N. J.: Prentice-Hall, 1977).

8. I. Ajzen and M. Fishbein, "Attitude–Behavior Relations: A Theoretical Analysis and Review of Empirical Research," *Psychological Bulletin* 84 (1977): 888–918.

9. B. T. Johnson and A. H. Eagly, "Effects of Involvement on Persuasion: A Meta-Analysis," *Psychological Bulletin* 106 (1989): 290–314.

10. K. G. DeBono and M. Snyder, "Acting on One's Attitudes: The Role of History of Choosing Situations," *Personality and Social Psychology Bulletin* 21 (1995): 629–636.

11. I. Ajzen and M. Fishbein, *Understanding Attitudes and Predicting Social Behavior* (Englewood Cliffs, N.J.: Prentice-Hall, 1980).

12. I. Ajzen, "From Intentions to Action: A Theory of Planned Behavior," in J. Kuhl and J. Beckmann, eds., *Action-Control: From Cognition to Behavior* (Heidelberg: Springer, 1985).

13. I. Ajzen, "The Theory of Planned Behavior," *Organizational Behavior and Human Decision Processes* 50 (1991): 1–33.

14. A. Sagie and M. Krausz, "What Aspects of the Job Have Most Effect on Nurses?" *Human Resource Management Journal* 13 (2003): 46–62.

15. J. Kettle, "Factors Affecting Job Satisfaction in the Registered Nurse," *Journal of Undergraduate Nursing Scholarship*, http://juns.nursing.arizona.edu/Default.htm, accessed July 1, 2008.

16. C. P. Parker, B. B. Baltes, S. A. Young, J. W. Huff, R. A. Altman, H. A. LaCost, and J. E. Roberts, "Relationships between Psychological Climate Perceptions and Work Outcomes: A Meta-Analytic Review," *Journal of Organizational Behavior* 24 (2003): 389–416.

17. E. A. Locke, "The Nature and Causes of Job Satisfaction," in M. Dunnette, ed., *Handbook of Industrial and Organizational Psychology* (Chicago: Rand McNally, 1976).

18. P. C. Smith, L. M. Kendall, and C. L. Hulin, *The Measurement of Satisfaction in Work and Retirement* (Skokie, Ill.: Rand McNally, 1969).

19. R. Ilies and T. A. Judge, "On the Heritability of Job Satisfaction: The Mediating Role of Personality," *Journal of Applied Psychology* 88 (2003): 750–759.

20. T. A. Judge, R. F. Piccolo, N. P. Podsakoff, J. C. Shaw, and B. Rich, "The Relationship between Pay and Job Satisfaction: A Meta-Analysis of the Literature," *Journal of Vocational Behavior* 77 (2010): 157–167.

21. D. J. Weiss, R. V. Davis, G. W. England, and L. H. Lofquist, *Manual for the Minnesota Satisfaction Questionnaire* (Minneapolis: Industrial Relations Center, University of Minnesota, 1967).

22. C. D. Fisher, "Why Do Lay People Believe that Satisfaction and Performance

Are Correlated? Possible Sources of a Commonsense Theory," *Journal of Organizational Behavior* 24 (2003): 753–777.

23. M. Christen, G. Iyer, and D. Soberman, "Job Satisfaction, Job Performance, and Effort: A Reexamination Using Agency Theory," *Journal of Marketing* 70 (January 2006): 137–150.

24. L. A. Bettencourt, K. P. Gwinner, and M. L. Meuter, "A Comparison of Attitude, Personality, and Knowledge Predictors of Service-Oriented Organizational Citizenship Behaviors," *Journal of Applied Psychology* 86 (2001): 29–41.

25. D. W. Organ, *Organizational Citizenship Behavior: The Good Soldier Syndrome* (Lexington, Mass.: Lexington Books, 1988).

26. P. M. Podsakoff, S. B. Mackenzie, and C. Hui, "Organizational Citizenship Behaviors and Managerial Evaluations of Employee Performance: A Review and Suggestions for Future Research," G. Ferris, ed., in *Research in Personnel and Human Resources Management* (Greenwich, Conn.: JAI Press, 1993): 1–40.

27. J. Y. M. Lai, L. W. Lam, and S. S. K. Lam, "Organizational Citizenship Behavior in Work Groups: A Team Cultural Perspective," *Journal of Organizational Behavior* 34 (2013): 1039–1056.

28. W. H. Bommer, E. W. Miles, and S. L. Grover, "Does One Good Turn Deserve Another? Coworker Influences on Employee Citizenship," *Journal of Organizational Behavior* 24 (2003): 181–196.

29. J. P. Trougakos, D. J. Beal, B. H. Cheng, I. Hideg, and D. Zweig, "Too Drained to Help: A Resource Depletion Perspective on Daily Interpersonal Citizenship Behaviors," *Journal of Applied Psychology* 100 (2015): 227–236.

30. M. C. Bolino, H. Hsiung, J. Harvey, and J. A. LePine, "Well, I'm Tired of Tryin'! Organizational Citizenship Behavior and Citizen Fatigue," *Journal of Applied Psychology* 100 (2015): 56–74.

31. C. Ostroff, "The Relationship between Satisfaction, Attitudes and Performance: An Organizational Level Analysis," *Journal of Applied Psychology* 77 (1992): 963–974.

32. R. Griffin and T. Bateman, "Job Satisfaction and Organizational Commitment," in C. Cooper and I. Robertson, eds., *International Review of Industrial and Organizational Psychology* (New York: Wiley, 1986).

33. A. R. Wheeler, V. C. Gallagher, R. L. Brouer, and C. J. Sablynski, "When Person-Organization (Mis)Fit and (Dis)Satisfaction Lead to Turnover: The Moderating Role of Perceived Job Mobility," *Journal of Managerial Psychology* 22, No. 2 (2007): 203–219.

34. X. Huang and E. Van De Vliert, "Where Intrinsic Job Satisfaction Fails to Work: National Moderators of Intrinsic Motivation," *Journal of Organizational Behavior* 24 (2003): 133–250.

35. L. Sun, S. Aryee, and K. S. Law, "High-Performance Human Resource Practices, Citizenship Behavior, and Organizational Performance: A Relational Perspective," *Academy of Management Journal* 50 (2007): 558–577.

36. S. L. Robinson, and R. J. Bennett, "A Typology of Deviant Workplace Behaviors: A Multidimensional Scaling Study," *Academy of Management Journal*, 38, No. 2 (1995): 555; P. D. Dunlop and K. Lee, "Workplace Deviance, Organizational Citizenship Behavior, and Business Unit Performance: The Bad Apples Do Spoil the Whole Barrel," *Journal of Organizational Behavior* 25 (2004): 67–80.

37. M. E. Heilman and V. B. Alcott, "What I Think You Think of Me: Women's Reactions to Being Viewed as Beneficiaries of Preferential Selection," *Journal of Applied Psychology* 86 (2001): 574–582; M. E. Heilman, C. J. Block, and P. Stathatos, "The Affirmative Action Stigma of Incompetence: Effects of Performance Information Ambiguity," *Academy of Management Journal* 40 (1997): 603–625.

38. R. T. Mowday, L. W. Porter, and R. M. Steers, *Employee–Organization Linkages: The Psychology of Commitment* (New York: Academic Press, 1982).

39. N. Allen and J. Meyer, "Affective, Continuance, and Normative Commitment to the Organization: An Examination of Construct Validity," *Journal of Vocational Behavior* 49 (1996): 252–276.

40. J. P. Meyer, N. J. Allen, and C. A. Smith, "Commitment to Organizations and Occupations: Extension and Test of a Three-Component Model," *Journal of Applied Psychology* 78 (1993): 538–551.

41. J. P. Curry, D. S. Wakefield, J. L. Price, and C. W. Mueller, "On the Causal Ordering of Job Satisfaction and Organizational Commitment," *Academy of Management Journal* 29 (1986): 847–858; T. N. Bauer, T. Bodner, B. Erdogan, D. M. Truxillo, and J. S. Tucker, "Newcomer Adjustment during Organizational Socialization: A Meta-Analytic Review of Antecedents, Outcomes, and Methods," *Journal of Applied Psychology* 92 (2007): 707–721.

42. B. Benkhoff, "Ignoring Commitment Is Costly: New Approaches Establish the Missing Link between Commitment and Performance," *Human Relations* 50 (1997): 701–726; N. J. Allen and J. P. Meyer, "Affective, Continuance, and Normative Commitment to the Organization: An Examination of Construct Validity," *Journal of Vocational Behavior* 49 (1996): 252–276.

43. M. J. Somers, "Organizational Commitment, Turnover, and Absenteeism: An Examination of Direct and Interaction Effects," *Journal of Organizational Behavior* 16 (1995): 49–58; L. Lum, J. Kervin, K. Clark, F. Reid, and W. Sirola, "Explaining Nursing Turnover Intent: Job Satisfaction, Pay Satisfaction, or Organizational Commitment?" *Journal of Organizational Behavior* 19 (1998): 305–320.

44. F. Stinglhamber and C. Vandenberghe, "Organizations and Supervisors as Sources of Support and Targets of Commitment," *Journal of Organizational Behavior* 24 (2003): 251–270.

45. R. Eisenberger, S. Armeli, B. Rexwinkel, P. D. Lynch, and L. Rhoades, "Reciprocation of Perceived Organizational Support," *Journal of Applied Psychology* 86 (2001): 42–51; J. E. Finegan, "The Impact of Person and Organizational Values on Organizational Commitment," *Journal of Occupational and Organizational Psychology* 73 (2000): 149–169.

46. E. Snape and T. Redman, "Too Old or Too Young? The Impact of Perceived Age Discrimination," *Human Resource Management Journal* 13 (2003): 78–89.

47. J. A. Conger, "The Necessary Art of Persuasion," *Harvard Business Review* 76 (1998): 84–96.

48. J. Cooper and R. T. Croyle, "Attitudes and Attitude Change," *Annual Review of Psychology* 35 (1984): 395–426.

49. B. Martin, D. Wentzel, and T. Tomczak, "Effects of Susceptibility to Normative Influence and Type of Testimonial on Attitudes toward Print Advertising," *Journal of Advertising* (Spring 2008), http://infotrac-college .thomsonlearning.com, accessed July 2, 2009.

50. D. M. Mackie and L. T. Worth, "Processing Deficits and the Mediation of Positive Affect in Persuasion," *Journal of Personality and Social Psychology* 57 (1989): 27–40.

51. J. W. Brehm, *Responses to Loss of Freedom: A Theory of Psychological Reactance* (New York: General Learning Press, 1972).

52. D. DeSteno, R. E. Petty, and D. D. Rucker, "Discrete Emotions and Persuasion: The Role of Emotion-Induced Expectancies," *Journal of Personality & Social Psychology* 86 (2004): 43–56.

53. R. Petty, D. T. Wegener, and L. R. Fabrigar, "Attitudes and Attitude Change," *Annual Review of Psychology* 48 (1997): 609–647.

54. P. Brinol and R. E. Petty, "Overt Head Movements and Persuasion: A Self-Validation Analysis," *Journal of Personality and Social Psychology* 84 (2003): 1123–1139.

55. W. Wood, "Attitude Change: Persuasion and Social Influence," *Annual Review of Psychology* 51 (2000): 539–570.

56. A. Ortony, G. L. Clore, and A. Collins, *The Cognitive Structure of Emotions* (Cambridge, England: Cambridge University Press, 1988).

57. R. S. Lazarus, *Emotion and Adaptation* (New York: Oxford University Press, 1991).

58. X. Hu and S. Kaplan, "Is 'Feeling Good' Good Enough? Differentiating Discrete Positive Emotions at Work," *Journal of Organizational Behavior* 36 (2015): 39–58.

59. P. T. Van Katwyk, S. Fox, P. E. Spector, and E. K. Kelloway, "Using the Job-Related Affective Well-Being Scale to Investigate Affective Responses to Work Stressors," *Journal of Occupational Health Psychology* 52 (2000): 219–230.

60. B. L. Fredrickson, "The Role of Positive Emotions in Positive Psychology: The Broaden-and-Build Theory of Positive Emotions," *American Psychologist* 56 (2001): 218–226.

61. S. S. Kaplan, J. C. Bradley, J. N. Luchman, and D. Haynes, "On the Role of Positive and

Negative Affectivity in Job Performance: A Meta-Analytic Investigation," *Journal of Applied Psychology* 94 (2009): 162–178; B. Lawrence and S. L. Robinson, "Ain't Misbehavin: Workplace Deviance as Organizational Resistance," *Journal of Management* 33, No. 3 (2007): 378–394.

62. B. L. Fredrickson and C. Brannigan, "Positive Emotions," in G. Bonnano and T. Mayne, eds., *Emotions: Current Issues and Future Directions* (New York: Guilford Press, 2001): 123–152.

63. D. Watson and L. A. Clark, "Affects Separable and Inseparable: On the Hierarchical Arrangement of Negative Affects," *Journal of Personality and Social Psychology* 62 (1992): 489–505.

64. A. M. Isen and R. A. Baron, "Positive Affect as a Factor in Organizational Behavior," *Research in Organizational Behavior* 13 (1991): 1–53; A. G. Miner and T. M. Glomb, "State Mood, Task Performance, and Behavior at Work: A Within-Persons Approach," *Organizational Behavior and Human Decision Processes* 112 (2010): 43–57.

65. J. M. George, "Mood and Absence," *Journal of Applied Psychology* 74 (1989): 317–324; L. H. Pelled and K. R. Xin, "Down and Out: An Investigation of the Relationship between Mood and Employee Withdrawal Behavior," *Journal of Management* 25 (1999): 875–895.

66. S. G. Barsade, "The Ripple Effect: Emotional Contagion and Its Influence on Group Behavior," *Administrative Science Quarterly* 47 (2007): 644–675.

67. J. E. Dutton, P. J. Frost, M. C. Worline, J. M. Lilius, and J. M. Kanov, "Leading in Times of Trauma," *Harvard Business Review* 80 (2002): 54–61.

68. T. A. Stewart, "The Highway of the Mind," *Harvard Business Review* 82 (2004): 116.

69. J. D. Mayer, P. Salovey, and D. R. Caruso, "Emotional Intelligence: Theory, Findings, and Implications," *Psychological Inquiry* 15 (2004): 197–215.

70. H. A. Elfenbein, S. G. Barsade, and N. Eisenkraft, "The Social Perception of Emotional Abilities: Expanding What We Know about Observer Ratings of Emotional Intelligence," *Emotion*, published online February 15, 2015.

71. A. R. Hochschild, *The Managed Heart: Commercialization of Human Feeling* (Berkeley: University of California Press, 1983).

72. A. A. Grandey, "When 'The Show Must Go On': Surface Acting and Deep Acting as Determinants of Emotional Exhaustion and Peer-Rated Service Delivery," *Academy of Management Journal* 46 (2003): 86–96; C. M. Brotherridge and A. A. Grandey, "Emotional Labor and Burnout: Comparing Two Perspectives of 'People Work'," *Journal of Vocational Behavior* 60 (2002): 17–39.

73. F. Navran, "Your Role in Shaping Ethics," *Executive Excellence* 9 (1992): 11–12.

74. K. Labich, "The New Crisis in Business Ethics," *Fortune* (April 20, 1992): 167–176.

75. L. S. Paine, *Value Shift: Why Companies Must Merge Social and Financial Imperatives to Achieve Superior Performance* (New York: McGraw-Hill, 2003).

76. D. B. Turban and D. M. Cable, "Firm Reputation and Applicant Pool Characteristics," *Journal of Organizational Behavior* 24 (2003): 733–751.

77. E. A. Lind, J. Greenberg, K. S. Scott, and T. D. Welchans, "The Winding Road from Employee to Complainant: Situational and Psychological Determinants of Wrongful-Termination Claims," *Administrative Science Quarterly* 45 (2000): 557–590.

78. "Stolen Birthrights; Australia's Aborigines," *The Economist* (US) (February 2, 2008), http://infotrac-college.thomsonlearning.com, accessed July 8, 2008; T. Johnston, "Australia Says 'Sorry' to Aborigines for Mistreatment," *The New York Times* (February 13, 2008), http://www.nytimes.com, accessed July 2, 2008.

79. Miriam Schulman, "Little Brother Is Watching You," Makkula Center for Applied Ethics, http://www.scu.edu/ethics/publications/iie/v9n2/brother.html, accessed July 1, 2008.

80. M. Oneal, P. Callahan, and E. Osnos, "Mattel Recalls 18 Million Toys," *Chicago Tribune* (August 15, 2007), http://www.chicagotribune.com/business/chi-toysaug15,0,7223810.story.

81. M. S. Baucus and D. A. Baucus, "Paying the Piper: An Empirical Examination of Longer-Term Financial Consequences of Illegal Corporate Behavior," *Academy of Management Journal* 40 (1997): 129–151.

82. J. O. Cherrington and D. J. Cherrington, "A Menu of Moral Issues: One Week in the Life of *The Wall Street Journal*," *Journal of Business Ethics* 11 (1992): 255–265.

83. B. L. Flannery and D. R. May, "Environmental Ethical Decision Making in the U.S. Metal-Finishing Industry," *Academy of Management Journal* 43 (2000): 642–662.

84. K. R. Andrews, "Ethics in Practice," *Harvard Business Review* (September–October 1989): 99–104.

85. M. Rokeach, *The Nature of Human Values* (New York: Free Press, 1973).

86. M. Rokeach and S. J. Ball-Rokeach, "Stability and Change in American Value Priorities, 1968–1981," *American Psychologist* 44 (1989): 775–784.

87. S. P Eisner, "Managing Generation Y," S.A.M. *Advanced Management Journal* 70, No. 4 (2005): 4–15.

88. M. Henderson and D. Thompson, *Values at Work: The Invisible Threads between People, Performance, and Profit* (Auckland, New Zealand: HarperBusiness, 2003).

89. E. C. Ravlin and B. M. Meglino, "Effects of Values on Perception and Decision Making: A Study of Alternative Work Values Measures," *Journal of Applied Psychology* 72 (1987): 666–673.

90. E. C. Ravlin and B. M. Meglino, "The Transitivity of Work Values: Hierarchical Preference Ordering of Socially Desirable Stimuli," *Organizational Behavior and Human Decision Processes* 44 (1989): 494–508.

91. B. M. Meglino, E. C. Ravlin, and C. L. Adkins, "A Work Values Approach to Corporate Culture: A Field Test of the Value Congruence Process and Its Relationship to Individual Outcomes," *Journal of Applied Psychology* 74 (1989): 424–432.

92. T. A. Judge and R. D. Bretz, Jr., "Effects of Work Values on Job Choice Decisions," *Journal of Applied Psychology* 77 (1992): 261–271.

93. R. H. Doktor, "Asian and American CEOs: A Comparative Study," *Organizational Dynamics* 18 (1990): 46–56.

94. R. L. Tung, "Handshakes across the Sea: Cross-Cultural Negotiating for Business Success," *Organizational Dynamics* (Winter 1991): 30–40.

95. C. Gomez, B. L. Kirkman, and D. L. Shapiro, "The Impact of Collectivism and In-Group/Out-Group Membership on the Evaluation Generosity of Team Members," *Academy of Management Journal* 43 (2000): 1097–1106; J. Zhou and J. J. Martocchio, "Chinese and American Managers' Compensation Award Decisions: A Comparative Policy-Capturing Study," *Personnel Psychology* 54 (2001): 115–145.

96. A. J. Ali and M. Amirshahi, "The Iranian Manager: Work Values and Orientations," *Journal of Business Ethics* 40 (2002): 133–143.

97. R. Neale and R. Mindel, "Rigging Up Multicultural Teamworking," *Personnel Management* (January 1992): 27–30.

98. J. B. Rotter, "Generalized Expectancies for Internal versus External Control of Reinforcement," *Psychological Monographs* 80 (1966): 1–28.

99. L. K. Trevino and S. A. Youngblood, "Bad Apples in Bad Barrels: A Causal Analysis of Ethical Decision-Making Behavior," *Journal of Applied Psychology* 75 (1990): 378–385.

100. H. M. Lefcourt, *Locus of Control: Current Trends in Theory and Research*, 2nd ed. (Hillsdale, N.J.: Erlbaum, 1982).

101. N. Machiavelli, *The Prince*, trans. George Bull (Middlesex, England: Penguin Books, 1961).

102. R. Christie and F. L. Geis, *Studies in Machiavellianism* (New York: Academic Press, 1970).

103. R. A. Giacalone and S. B. Knouse, "Justifying Wrongful Employee Behavior: The Role of Personality in Organizational Sabotage," *Journal of Business Ethics* 9 (1990): 55–61.

104. S. B. Knouse and R. A. Giacalone, "Ethical Decision Making in Business: Behavioral Issues and Concerns," *Journal of Business Ethics* 11 (1992): 369–377.

105. L. Kohlberg, "Stage and Sequence: The Cognitive Developmental Approach to Socialization," in D. A. Goslin, ed., *Handbook of Socialization Theory and Research* (Chicago: Rand McNally, 1969): 347–480.

106. C. I. Malinowski and C. P. Smith, "Moral Reasoning and Moral Conduct: An Investigation Prompted by Kohlberg's Theory," *Journal of Personality and Social Psychology* 49 (1985): 1016–1027; M. Brabeck, "Ethical

Characteristics of Whistleblowers," *Journal of Research in Personality* 18 (1984): 41–53; W. Y. Penn and B. D. Collier, "Current Research in Moral Development as a Decision Support System," *Journal of Business Ethics* 4 (1985): 131–136; L. K. Trevino and S. A. Youngblood, "Bad Apples in Bad Barrels: A Causal Analysis of Ethical Decision-Making Behavior," *Journal of Applied Psychology* 75 (1990): 378–385.

107. C. Gilligan, *In a Different Voice: Psychological Theory and Women's Development* (Cambridge, Mass.: Harvard University Press, 1982).

108. S. Jaffee and J. S. Hyde, "Gender Differences in Moral Orientation: A Meta-Analysis," *Psychological Bulletin* 126 (2000): 703–726.

109. G. R. Franke, D. F. Crown, and D. F. Spake, "Gender Differences in Ethical Perceptions of Business Practices: A Social Role Theory Perspective," J*ournal of Applied Psychology* 82 (1997): 920–934.

5

1. L. W. Porter, G. Bigley, and R. M. Steers, *Motivation and Leadership at Work,* 7th ed. (New York: McGraw-Hill, 2002).

2. J. P. Campbell and R. D. Pritchard, "Motivation Theory in Industrial and Organizational Psychology," in M. D. Dunnette, ed., *Handbook of Industrial and Organizational Psychology* (Chicago: Rand McNally, 1976): 63–130.

3. M. Weber, *The Protestant Ethic and the Spirit of Capitalism* (London: Talcott Parson, tr., 1930).

4. S. Freud, *Civilization and Its Discontents,* trans. and ed. J. Strachey (New York: Norton, 1961).

5. P. D. Dunlop and K. Lee, "Workplace Deviance, Organizational Citizenship Behavior, and Business Unit Performance: The Bad Apples Do Spoil the Whole Barrel," *Journal of Organizational Behavior* 25 (2004): 67–80.

6. T. A. Judge, L. S. Simon, C. Hurst, and K. Kelley, "What I Experienced Yesterday Is Who I Am Today: Relationship of Work Motivations and Behaviors to Within-Individual Variation in the Five-Factor Model of Personality," *Journal of Applied Psychology* 99 (2014): 199–221.

7. A. Smith, *An Inquiry into the Nature and Causes of the Wealth of Nations,* Vol. 10 of *The Harvard Classics,* C. J. Bullock, ed. (New York: Collier, 1909).

8. J. Jennings, *Less Is More: How Great Companies Use Productivity as a Competitive Tool in Business* (New York: Portfolio, 2002).

9. F. W. Taylor, *The Principles of Scientific Management* (New York: Norton, 1911).

10. Hearings before Special Committee of the House of Representatives to Investigate the Taylor and Other Systems of Shop Management under Authority of House Resolution 90, Vol. 3, 1377–1508 contains Taylor's testimony before the committee from Thursday, January 25, through Tuesday, January 30, 1912.

11. J. Breal, "Secret Sauce," *Fast Company* 115 (May 2007): 61–63.

12. F. J. Roethlisberger, *Management and Morale* (Cambridge, Mass.: Harvard University Press, 1941).

13. L. Van Dyne and J. L. Pierce, "Psychological Ownership and Feelings of Possession: Three Field Studies Predicting Employee Attitudes and Organizational Citizenship Behavior," *Journal of Organizational Behavior* 25 (2004): 439–459.

14. A. H. Maslow, "A Theory of Human Motivation," *Psychological Review* 50 (1943): 370–396.

15. W. James, *The Principles of Psychology* (New York: H. Holt & Co., 1890; Cambridge, Mass.: Harvard University Press, 1983); J. Dewey, *Human Nature and Conduct: An Introduction to Social Psychology* (New York: Holt, 1922); S. Freud, *A General Introduction to Psycho-Analysis: A Course of Twenty-Eight Lectures Delivered at the University of Vienna* (New York: Liveright, 1963); A. Adler, *Understanding Human Nature* (Greenwich, Conn.: Fawcett, 1927).

16. E. E. Lawler, III, and J. L. Suttle, "A Causal Correlational Test of the Need Hierarchy Concept," *Organizational Behavior and Human Performance* 7 (1973): 265–287.

17. N. K. Austin, "The Power of the Pyramid: The Foundation of Human Psychology and, Thereby, of Motivation, Maslow's Hierarchy Is One Powerful Pyramid," *Incentive* 176 (July 2002): 10.

18. D. M. McGregor, *The Human Side of Enterprise* (New York: McGraw-Hill, 1960).

19. D. M. McGregor, "The Human Side of Enterprise," *Management Review* (November 1957): 22–28, 88–92.

20. E. E. Lawler, G. E. Lawford, S. A. Mohrman, and G. E. Ledford, Jr., *Strategies for High Performance Organizations—The CEO Report: Employee Involvement, TQM, and Reengineering Programs in* Fortune *1000 Corporations* (San Francisco: Jossey-Bass, Inc., 1998).

21. Y. Berson, N. Halevy, B. Shamir, and M. Erez, "Leading from Different Psychological Distances: A Construal-Level Perspective on Vision Communication, Goal Setting, and Follower Motivation," *The Leadership Quarterly* 26 (2015): 143–155.

22. J. Boorstin, "No Preservatives. No Unions. Lots of Dough," *Fortune* 148 (September 15, 2003): 127–129.

23. C. P. Alderfer, *Human Needs in Organizational Settings* (New York: Free Press, 1972).

24. B. Schneider and C. P. Alderfer, "Three Studies of Need Satisfactions in Organizations," *Administrative Science Quarterly* 18 (1973): 489–505.

25. H. A. Murray, *Explorations in Personality: A Clinical and Experimental Study of Fifty Men of College Age* (New York: Oxford University Press, 1938).

26. D. C. McClelland, *Motivational Trends in Society* (Morristown, N.J.: General Learning Press, 1971).

27. D. C. McClelland, "Achievement Motivation Can Be Learned," *Harvard Business Review* 43 (1965): 6–24.

28. J. P. Chaplin and T. S. Krawiec, *Systems and Theories of Psychology* (New York: Holt, Rinehart & Winston, 1960); M. Stahl, *Managerial and Technical Motivation: Assessing Needs for Achievement, Power, and Affiliation* (Santa Barbara, CA, 1986).

29. J. S. Chun and J. N. Choi, "Members' Needs, Intragroup Conflict, and Group Performance," *Journal of Applied Psychology* 99 (2014): 437–450.

30. E. A. Ward, "Multidimensionality of Achievement Motivation among Employed Adults," *Journal of Social Psychology* 134 (1997): 542–544.

31. A. Sagie, D. Elizur, and H. Yamauchi, "The Structure and Strength of Achievement Motivation: A Cross-Cultural Comparison," *Journal of Organizational Behavior* 17 (1996): 431–444.

32. D. C. McClelland and D. Burnham, "Power Is the Great Motivator," *Harvard Business Review* 54 (1976): 100–111; J. Hall and J. Hawker, *Power Management Inventory* (The Woodlands, Tex.: Teleometrics International, 1988).

33. S. Schachter, *The Psychology of Affiliation* (Stanford, Calif.: Stanford University Press, 1959).

34. F. Herzberg, B. Mausner, and B. Snyderman, *The Motivation to Work* (New York: Wiley, 1959).

35. F. Herzberg, *Work and the Nature of Man* (Cleveland: World, 1966).

36. B. A. Scott, A. S. Garza, D. E. Conlon, and Y. J. Kim, "Why Do Managers Act Fairly in the First Place? A Daily Investigation of 'Hot' and 'Cold' Motives and Discretion," *Academy of Management Journal* 1015 (2015): 37–57.

37. J. Marquez, "Winning Women Back," *Workforce Management* 86, No. 7 (2007): 20–21.

38. R. Griffin, "Organizational Behavior," *Oxford Annotated Bibliographies: Management* (2013), www.oxfordbibliographies.com.

39. D. L. Nelson and B. L. Simmons, "Health Psychology and Work Stress: A More Positive Approach," in J. C. Quick and L. E. Tetrick, eds., *Handbook of Occupational Health Psychology* (Washington, D.C.: American Psychological Association, 2003): 97–119.

40. K. S. Cameron, J. E. Dutton, and R. E. Quinn, eds., *Positive Organizational Scholarship: Foundations of a New Discipline* (San Francisco: Berrett-Keohler, 2003).

41. J. Loehr and T. Schwartz, "The Making of a Corporate Athlete," *Harvard Business Review* 79 (2001): 120–129.

42. J. Loehr and T. Schwartz, *The Power of Full Engagement: Managing Energy, Not Time, Is the Key to High Performance and Personal Renewal* (New York: Free Press, 2003).

43. G. Kholreiser, "Engaging Employees Crucial for Their Morale," *The Nation* (November 29, 2010), http://www .nationmultimedia.com/2010/11/29/business /Engaging-employees-crucial-for-their-morale -30143355.html, accessed May 12, 2011.

44. P. M. Blau, *Exchange and Power in Social Life* (New York: Wiley, 1964); N. Horster, *Principles of Exchange and Power: Integrating the Theory of Social Institutions and the Theory of Value* (New York: P. Lang, 1997).

45. A. Etzioni, "A Basis for Comparative Analysis of Complex Organizations," in A. Etzioni, ed., *A Sociological Reader on Complex Organizations,* 2nd ed. (New York: Holt, Rinehart & Winston, 1969): 59–76.

46. S. S. Masterson and C. L. Stamper, "Perceived Organizational Membership: An Aggregate Framework Representing the Employee–Organization Relationship," *Journal of Organizational Behavior* 24 (2003): 473–490.

47. L. J. Song, A. S. Tsui, and K. S. Long, "Unpacking Employee Responses to Organizational Exchange Mechanisms: The Role of Social and Economic Exchange Perceptions," *Journal of Management* 35 (2009): 56–93.

48. J. S. Adams, "Inequity in Social Exchange," in L. Berkowitz, ed., *Advances in Experimental Social Psychology,* Vol. 2 (New York: Academic Press, 1965): 267–299; J. S. Adams, "Toward an Understanding of Inequity," *Journal of Abnormal and Social Psychology* 67 (1963): 422–436.

49. J. Nelson-Horchler, "The Best Man for the Job Is a Man," *Industry Week* (January 7, 1991): 50–52.

50. P. E. Downes and D. Choi, "Employee Reactions to Pay Dispersion: A Typology of Existing Research," *Human Resource Management Review* 24 (2014): 53–66.

51. R. C. Huseman, J. D. Hatfield, and E. A. Miles, "A New Perspective on Equity Theory: The Equity Sensitivity Construct," *Academy of Management Review* 12 (1987): 222–234.

52. G. Lemmon and S. J. Wayne, "Underlying Motives of Organizational Citizenship Behavior: Comparing Egoistic and Altruistic Motivations," *Journal of Leadership & Organization Studies* 22 (2015): 129–148.

53. K. E. Weick, M. G. Bougon, and G. Maruyama, "The Equity Context," *Organizational Behavior and Human Performance* 15 (1976): 32–65.

54. R. C. Huseman, J. D. Hatfield, and E. W. Miles, "A New Perspective on Equity Theory: The Equity Sensitivity Construct," *The Academy of Management Review* 12 (1987): 222–234.

55. J. Greenberg, "Equity and Workplace Status: A Field Experiment," *Journal of Applied Psychology* 73 (1988): 606–613.

56. J. Greenberg, "Losing Sleep over Organizational Justice: Attenuating Insomniac Reactions to Underpayment Inequity with Supervisory Training in Interactional Justice," *Journal of Applied Psychology* 91 (2006): 58–69.

57. J. Greenberg and B. Alge, "Aggressive Reactions to Workplace Injustice," in R. W. Griffin, A. O'Leary-Kelly, and J. Collins, eds., *Dysfunctional Behavior in Organizations, Vol. 1: Violent Behaviors in Organizations* (Greenwich, CT: JAI, 1998): 119–145.

58. R. A. Cosier and D. R. Dalton, "Equity Theory and Time: A Reformulation," *Academy of Management Review* 8 (1983): 311–319.

59. J. E. Martin and M. W. Peterson, "Two-Tier Wage Structures: Implications for Equity Theory," *Academy of Management Journal* 30 (1987): 297–315.

60. R. J. Sanchez, D. M. Truxillo, and T. N. Bauer, "Development and Examination of an Expectancy-Based Measure of Test-Taking Motivation," *Journal of Applied Psychology* 85 (2000): 739–750.

61. V. H. Vroom, *Work and Motivation* (New York: Wiley, 1964/1970).

62. U. R. Larson, "Supervisor's Performance Feedback to Subordinates: The Effect of Performance Valence and Outcome Dependence," *Organizational Behavior and Human Decision Processes* 37 (1986): 391–409.

63. M. C. Kernan and R. G. Lord, "Effects of Valence, Expectancies, and Goal-Performance Discrepancies in Single and Multiple Goal Environments," *Journal of Applied Psychology* 75 (1990): 194–203.

64. R. J. Sanchez, D. M. Truxillo, and T. N. Bauer, "Development and Examination of an Expectancy-Based Measure of Test-Taking Motivation," *Journal of Applied Psychology* 85 (2000): 739–750.

65. W. VanEerde and H. Thierry, "Vroom's Expectancy Models and Work-Related Criteria: A Meta-Analysis," *Journal of Applied Psychology* 81 (1996): 575–586.

66. E. D. Pulakos and N. Schmitt, "A Longitudinal Study of a Valence Model Approach for the Prediction of Job Satisfaction of New Employees," *Journal of Applied Psychology* 68 (1983): 307–312; F. J. Landy and W. S. Becker, "Motivation Theory Reconsidered," in L. L. Cummings and B. M. Staw, eds., *Research in Organizational Behavior* 9 (Greenwich, Conn.: JAI Press, 1987): 1–38.

67. J. Gibbs, K. Basinger, and D. Fuller, *Moral Maturity: Measuring the Development of Sociomoral Reflection* (Hillsdale, NJ: L. Erlbaum, 1992).

68. N. J. Adler, *International Dimensions of Organizational Behavior,* 4th ed. (Mason, Ohio: South-Western, 2001).

69. G. Hofstede, "Motivation, Leadership, and Organization: Do American Theories Apply Abroad?" *Organizational Dynamics* 9 (1980): 42–63.

70. G. H. Hines, "Cross-Cultural Differences in Two-Factor Theory," *Journal of Applied Psychology* 58 (1981): 313–317.

71. M. C. Bolino and W. H. Turnley, "Old Faces, New Places: Equity Theory in Cross-Cultural Contexts," *Journal of Organizational Behavior* 29 (2008): 29–50; M. C. Bolino and W. H. Turnley, "Erratum: Old Faces, New Places: Equity Theory in Cross-Cultural Contexts," *Journal of Organizational Behavior* 29 (2008): i.

6

1. P. Pavlov, *Conditioned Reflexes* (New York: Oxford University Press, 1927).

2. B. Cannon, "Walter B. Cannon: Reflections on the Man and His Contributions," *Centennial Session,* American Psychological Association Centennial Convention, Washington, D.C., 1992.

3. B. F. Skinner, *The Behavior of Organisms: An Experimental Analysis* (New York: Appleton-Century-Crofts, 1938).

4. B. F. Skinner, *Science and Human Behavior* (New York: Free Press, 1953).

5. F. Luthans and R. Kreitner, *Organizational Behavior Modification and Beyond* (Glenview, Ill.: Scott, Foresman, 1985).

6. A. D. Stajkovic and F. Luthans, "A Meta-Analysis of the Effects of Organizational Behavior Modification on Task Performance, 1975–95," *Academy of Management Journal* 40 (1997): 1122–1149.

7. C. B. Cadsby, F. Song, and F. Tapon, "Sorting and Incentive Effects of Pay for Performance: An Experimental Investigation," *Academy of Management Journal* 50 (2007): 387–405.

8. K. K. Merriman, "Lost in Translation: Cultural Interpretations of Performance Pay," *Compensation and Benefits Review* 42 (2010): 403–410.

9. J. Hale, "Strategic Rewards: Keeping Your Best Talent from Walking Out the Door," *Compensation and Benefits Management* 14 (1998): 39–50.

10. B. F. Skinner, *Contingencies of Reinforcement: A Theoretical Analysis* (New York: Appleton-Century-Crofts, 1969).

11. J. P. Chaplin and T. S. Krawiec, *Systems and Theories of Psychology* (New York: Holt, Rinehart & Winston, 1960).

12. L. Bareket-Bojmel, G. Hochman, and D. Ariely, "It's (Not) All about the Jacksons: Testing Different Types of Short-Term Bonuses in the Field," *Journal of Management* (Advanced online publication May 27, 2014).

13. M. Maccoby, J. Hoffer Gittell, and M. Ledeen, "Leadership and the Fear Factor," *Sloan Management Review* 148 (Winter 2004): 14–18.

14. A. Bandura, *Social Learning Theory* (Englewood Cliffs, N.J.: Prentice-Hall, 1977); A. Bandura, "Self-Efficacy: Toward a Unifying Theory of Behavioral Change," *Psychological Review* 84 (1977): 191–215.

15. J. J. Martocchio and E. J. Hertenstein, "Learning Orientation and Goal Orientation Context: Relationships with Cognitive and Affective Learning Outcomes," *Human Resource Development Quarterly* 14 (2003): 413–434.

16. A. Bandura, "Regulation of Cognitive Processes through Perceived Self-Efficacy," *Developmental Psychology* (September 1989): 729–735.

17. J. M. Phillips and S. M. Gully, "Role of Goal Orientation, Ability, Need for Achievement, and Locus of Control in the Self-Efficacy and Goal-Setting Process," *Journal of Applied Psychology* 82 (1997): 792–802.

18. M. Tims, A. B. Bakker, and D. Derks, "Daily Job Crafting and the Self-Efficacy-Performance

Relationship," *Journal of Managerial Psychology* 29 (2014): 490–507.

19. J. C. Weitlauf, R. E. Smith, and D. Cervone, "Generalization Effects of Coping-Skills Training: Influence of Self-Defense Training on Women's Efficacy Beliefs, Assertiveness, and Aggression," *Journal of Applied Psychology* 85 (2000): 625–633.

20. A. D. Stajkovic and F. Luthans, "Social Cognitive Theory and Self-Efficacy: Going beyond Traditional Motivational and Behavioral Approaches," *Organizational Dynamics* (Spring 1998): 62–74.

21. T. M. Amabile and S. J. Kramer, "The Power of Small Wins," *Harvard Business Review* 38, No. 5 (July 8, 2008): 70–80.

22. V. Gecas, "The Social Psychology of Self-Efficacy," *Annual Review of Sociology* 15 (1989): 291–316.

23. E. A. Locke and G. P. Latham, *A Theory of Goal Setting and Task Performance* (Englewood Cliffs, N.J.: Prentice-Hall, 1990).

24. A. D. Stajkovic, E. A. Locke, and E. S. Blair, "A First Examination of the Relationships between Primed Subconscious Goals, Assigned Conscious Goals, and Task Performance," *Journal of Applied Psychology* 91 (2006): 1172–1180.

25. T. O. Murray, *Management by Objectives: A Systems Approach to Management* (Fort Worth, Tex.: Western Company, n.d.).

26. W. T. Brooks and T. W. Mullins, *High Impact Time Management* (Englewood Cliffs, N.J.: Prentice-Hall, 1989).

27. E. A. Locke, "Toward a Theory of Task Motivation and Incentives," *Organizational Behavior and Human Performance* 3 (1968): 157–189.

28. J. C. Quick, "Dyadic Goal Setting within Organizations: Role Making and Motivational Considerations," *Academy of Management Review* 4 (1979): 369–380.

29. D. McGregor, "An Uneasy Look at Performance Appraisal," *Harvard Business Review* 35 (1957): 89–94.

30. J. R. Hollenbeck, C. R. Williams, and H. J. Klein, "An Empirical Examination of the Antecedents of Commitment to Difficult Goals," *Journal of Applied Psychology* 74 (1989): 18–23.

31. R. C. Rodgers and J. E. Hunter, "The Impact of Management by Objectives on Organizational Productivity," unpublished paper (Lexington: University of Kentucky, 1989).

32. E. A. Locke, K. N. Shaw, L. M. Saari, and G. P. Latham, "Goal Setting and Task Performance: 1969–1980," *Psychological Bulletin* 90 (1981): 125–152.

33. D. B. Fedora, W. D. Davis, J. M. Maslync, and K. Mathiesond, "Performance Improvement Efforts in Response to Negative Feedback: The Roles of Source Power and Recipient Self-Esteem," *Journal of Management* 27 (2001): 79–98.

34. J. C. Quick, "Dyadic Goal Setting and Role Stress," *Academy of Management Journal* 22 (1979): 241–252.

35. G. S. Odiorne, *Management by Objectives: A System of Managerial Leadership* (New York: Pitman, 1965).

36. American Management Association, *Blueprints for Service Quality: The Federal Express Approach* (New York: American Management Association, 1991).

37. P. F. Drucker, *The Practice of Management* (New York: Harper & Bros., 1954).

38. R. D. Prichard, P. L. Roth, S. D. Jones, P. J. Galgay, and M. D. Watson, "Designing a Goal-Setting System to Enhance Performance: A Practical Guide," *Organizational Dynamics* 17 (1988): 69–78.

39. C. L. Hughes, *Goal Setting: Key to Individual and Organizational Effectiveness* (New York: American Management Association, 1965).

40. M. E. Tubbs and S. E. Ekeberg, "The Role of Intentions in Work Motivation: Implications for Goal-Setting Theory and Research," *Academy of Management Review* 16 (1991): 180–199.

41. S. Vatave, "Managing Risk," *Supervision* 65 (2004): 6–9.

42. J. R. Hollenbeck and A. P. Brief, "The Effects of Individual Differences and Goal Origin on Goal Setting and Performance," *Organizational Behavior and Human Decision Processes* 40 (1987): 392–414.

43. R. A. Katzell and D. E. Thompson, "Work Motivation: Theory and Practice," *American Psychologist* 45 (1990): 144–153; M. W. McPherson, "Is Psychology the Science of Behavior?" *American Psychologist* 47 (1992): 329–335.

44. E. A. Locke, "The Ideas of Frederick W. Taylor: An Evaluation," *Academy of Management Review* 7 (1982): 15–16; R. M. Yerkes and J. D. Dodson, "The Relation of Strength of Stimulus to Rapidity of Habit-Formation," *Journal of Comparative Neurology and Psychology* 18 (1908): 459–482.

45. F. L. Schmidt and J. Hunter, "General Mental Ability in the World of Work: Occupational Attainment and Job Performance," *Journal of Personality and Social Psychology* 86 (2004): 162–173.

46. D. L. Joseph, J. Jin, D. A. Newman, and E. H. O'Boyle, "Why Does Self-Reported Emotional Intelligence Predict Job Performance? A Meta-Analytic Investigation of Mixed EI," *Journal of Applied Psychology* 100 (2015): 298–342.

47. R. L. Cardy, *Performance Management: Concepts, Skills, and Exercises* (Armonk, New York, and London, England: M. E. Sharpe, 2004).

48. D. Hartley-Wilkins, "Getting the Best out of Your People: Managing Performance," *Human Resources* (April/May 2010): 26–27.

49. P. Cappelli and N. Rogovsky, "Employee Involvement and Organizational Citizenship: Implications for Labor Law Reform and 'Lean Production,'" *Industrial & Labor Relations Review* 51 (1998): 633–653.

50. L. D. Ordonez, M. E. Schweitzer, A. D. Galinskly, and M. H. Bazerman. "Goals Gone Wild: The Systematic Side Effects of Overprescribing Goal Setting," *Academy of Management Perspectives* 23 (2009): 6–16; E. A. Locke and G. P. Latham, "Has Goal Setting Gone Wild, or Have Its Attackers Abandoned Good Scholarship?" *Academy of Management Perspectives* 23 (2009): 17–23.

51. M. E. Tubbs and M. L. Trusty, "Direct Reports of Motivation for Task Performance Levels: Some Construct-Related Evidence," *Journal of Psychology* 135 (2001): 185–205.

52. S. Ellis, R. Mendel, and M. Aloni-Zohar, "The Effect of Accuracy of Performance Evaluation on Learning from Experience: The Moderating Role of After-Event Reviews," *Journal of Applied Social Psychology* 39, No. 3 (2009): 541–563.

53. R. R. Kilburg, *Executive Coaching: Developing Managerial Wisdom in a World of Chaos* (Washington, D.C.: American Psychological Association, 2000).

54. K. Y. Wilson, "An Analysis of Bias in Supervisor Narrative Comments in Performance Appraisal," *Human Relations* 63 (2010): 1903–1933.

55. H. H. Meyer, E. Kay, and J. R. P. French, "Split Roles in Performance Appraisal," *Harvard Business Review* 43 (1965): 123–129.

56. W. Lam, X. Huang, and E. Snape, "Feedback-Seeking Behavior and Leader-Member Exchange: Do Supervisor-Attributed Motives Matter?" *Academy of Management Journal* 50 (2007): 348–363.

57. W. A. Fisher, J. C. Quick, L. L. Schkade, and G. W. Ayers, "Developing Administrative Personnel through the Assessment Center Technique," *Personnel Administrator* 25 (1980): 44–46, 62.

58. J. S. Goodman, R. E. Wood, and M. Hendrickx, "Feedback Specificity, Exploration, and Learning," *Journal of Applied Psychology* 89 (2004): 248–262.

59. M. B. DeGregorio and C. D. Fisher, "Providing Performance Feedback: Reactions to Alternative Methods," *Journal of Management* 14 (1988): 605–616.

60. G. C. Thornton, "The Relationship between Supervisory and Self-Appraisals of Executive Performance," *Personnel Psychology* 21 (1968): 441–455.

61. A. S. DeNisi and A. N. Kluger, "Feedback Effectiveness: Can 360-Degree Appraisals Be Improved?" *Academy of Management Executive* 14 (2000): 129–140.

62. F. Luthans and S. J. Peterson, "360-Degree Feedback with Systematic Coaching: Empirical Analysis Suggests a Winning Combination," *Human Resource Management* 42 (2003): 243–256.

63. G. Toegel and J. A. Conger, "360-Degree Assessment: Time for Reinvention," *Academy of Management Learning and Education* 2 (2003): 297–311.

64. L. Hirschhorn, "Leaders and Followers in a Postindustrial Age: A Psychodynamic View," *Journal of Applied Behavioral Science* 26 (1990): 529–542.

65. F. M. Jablin, "Superior-Subordinate Communication: The State of the Art," *Psychological Bulletin* 86 (1979): 1201–1222.

66. T. C. Bednall, K. Sanders, and P. Runhaar, "Stimulating Informal Learning Activities through Perceptions of Performance Appraisal Quality and Human Resource Management Strength: A Two-Wave Study," *Academy of Management Learning & Education* 13 (2014): 45–61.

67. J. Pfeffer, "Six Dangerous Myths about Pay," *Harvard Business Review* 76 (1998): 108–119.

68. F. L. Giancola, "Examining the Job Itself as a Source of Employee Motivation," *Compensation and Benefits Review* 43 (2011): 23–29.

69. "Six Employee Types Prefer Different Rewards," *HRFocus* 84, No. 4 (April 2007): 12.

70. M. Erez, "Work Motivation from a Cross-Cultural Perspective," in A. M. Bouvy, F. J. R. Van de Vijver, P. Boski, and P. G. Schmitz, eds., *Journeys into Cross-Cultural Psychology* (Amsterdam, Netherlands: Swets and Zeitlinger, 1994): 386–403.

71. G. T. Milkovich and J. M. Newman, *Compensation,* 4th ed. (Homewood, Ill.: Irwin, 1993).

72. T. Taylor, "The Challenge of Project Team Incentives," *Compensation and Benefits Review* 42 (2010): 411–419.

73. J. M. Bardwick, *Danger in the Comfort Zone* (New York: American Management Association, 1991).

74. D. F. Giannetto, "Get Your Money's Worth from Incentives," *Business Performance Management,* 7 (2009): 12.

75. J. H. Han, K. M. Bartol, and S. Kim, "Tightening Up the Performance-Pay Linkage: Roles of Contingent Reward Leadership and Profit-Sharing in the Cross-Level Influence of Individual Pay-for-Performance," *Journal of Applied Psychology* 100 (2015): 417–430.

76. K. N. Wexley, R. A. Alexander, J. P. Greenawalt, and M. A. Couch, "Attitudinal Congruence and Similarity as Related to Interpersonal Evaluations in Manager-Subordinate Dyads," *Academy of Management Journal* 23 (1980): 320–330.

77. H. H. Kelley, *Attribution in Social Interaction* (New York: General Learning Press, 1971); H. H. Kelley, "The Processes of Causal Attribution," *American Psychologist* 28 (1973): 107–128.

78. B. Raabe and T. A. Beehr, "Formal Mentoring versus Supervisor and Coworker Relationships: Differences in Perceptions and Impact," *Journal of Organizational Behavior* 24 (2003): 271–293.

79. A. M. Young and P. L. Perrewe, "What Did You Expect? An Examination of Career-Related Support and Social Support among Mentors and Protégés," *Journal of Management* 26 (2000): 611–633.

80. K. Doherty, "The Good News about Depression," *Business and Health* 3 (1989): 1–4.

81. K. E. Kram, "Phases of the Mentor Relationship," *Academy of Management Journal* 26 (1983): 608–625.

82. T. D. Allen, L. T. Eby, M. L. Poteet, E. Lentz, and L. Lima, "Career Benefits Associated with Mentoring for Protégés: A Meta-Analysis," *Journal of Applied Psychology* 89 (2004): 127–136.

83. L. T. Eby, M. M. Butts, B. J. Hoffman, and J. B. Sauer, "Cross-Lagged Relations between Mentoring Received from Supervisors and Employee OCBs: Disentangling Causal Direction and Identifying Boundary Conditions," *Journal of Applied Psychology* (Advanced online publication January 19, 2015).

84. S.J. Wells, "Choices Flourish at IBM," *HR Magazine* (May 2009): 52–57.

85. K. E. Kram and L. A. Isabella, "Mentoring Alternatives: The Role of Peer Relationships in Career Development," *Academy of Management Journal* 28 (1985): 110–132.

86. J. Greco, "Hey, Coach!" *Journal of Business Strategy* 22 (2001): 28–32.

7

1. J. Barling, E. K. Kelloway, and M. R. Frone, eds., *Handbook of Work Stress* (Thousand Oaks, CA: Sage Publications, 2005).

2. M. Blake Hargrove, J. C. Quick, D. L. Nelson, and J. D. Quick, "The Theory of Preventive Stress Management: A 33-Year Review and Evaluation," *Stress and Health* 27 (2011): 182–193.

3. S. Benison, A. C. Barger, and E. L. Wolfe, *Walter B. Cannon: The Life and Times of a Young Scientist* (Cambridge, Mass.: Harvard University Press, 1987).

4. W. B. Cannon, *Bodily Changes in Pain, Hunger, Fear, and Rage: An Account of Recent Researches into the Function of Emotional Excitement* (New York: Appleton-Century-Crofts, 1915).

5. W. B. Cannon, *The Wisdom of the Body* (New York: Norton, 1932).

6. R. S. Lazarus, *Psychological Stress and the Coping Process* (New York: McGraw-Hill, 1966).

7. M. R. Tuckey, B. J. Searle, C. M. Boyd, A. H. Winefield, and H. R. Winefield. "Hindrances Are Not Threats: Advancing the Multimensionality of Work Stress," *Journal of Occupational Health Psychology* 20 (2015): 131–147.

8. R. Rau, K. Morling, and U. Rosler, "Is There a Relationship between Major Depression and Both Objectively Assessed and Perceived Demands and Control?" *Work and Stress* 24 (2010): 88–106.

9. C. Liu, P. E. Spector, and L. Shi, "Cross-National Job Stress: A Quantitative and Qualitative Study," *Journal of Organizational Behavior* 28 (2007): 209–239.

10. J. Doron, Y. Stephan, C. Maiano, and C. LeScanff, "Motivational Predictors of Coping with Academic Examinations," *The Journal of Social Psychology* 151 (2011): 87–104.

11. J. D. Kammeyer-Mueller, T. A. Judge, and B. A. Scott, "The Role of Core Self-Evaluations in the Coping Process," *Journal of Applied Psychology* 94 (2009): 177–195.

12. D. Katz and R. L. Kahn, *The Social Psychology of Organizations,* 2nd ed. (New York: Wiley, 1978): 185–221.

13. H. Levinson, "A Psychoanalytic View of Occupational Stress," *Occupational Mental Health* 3 (1978): 2–13.

14. L. Yang, J. Bauer, R. E. Johnson, M. W. Groer, and K. Salomon. "Physiological Mechanisms That Underlie the Effects of Interactional Fairness on Deviant Behavior: The Role of Cortisol Activity," *Journal of Applied Psychology* 99 (2014): 310–321.

15. P. L. Perrewé, K. L. Zellars, G. R. Ferris, A. M. Rossi, C. J. Kacmar, and D. A. Ralston, "Neutralizing Job Stressors: Political Skill as an Antidote to the Dysfunctional Consequences of Role Conflict," *Academy of Management Journal* 47 (2004): 141–152.

16. T. L. Friedman, *The Lexus and the Olive Tree* (New York: Vintage Anchor, 2000).

17. S. Zuboff, *In the Age of the Smart Machine: The Future of Work and Power* (New York: Basic Books, 1988).

18. D. T. Hall and J. Richter, "Career Gridlock: Baby Boomers Hit the Wall," *Academy of Management Executive* 4 (1990): 7–22.

19. N. P. Podsakoff, J. A. LePine, and M. A. LePine, "Differential Challenge Stressor-Hindrance Stressor Relationships with Job Attitudes, Turnover Intentions, Turnover, and Withdrawal Behavior: A Meta-Analysis," *Journal of Applied Psychology* 92 (2007): 438–454.

20. R. L. Kahn, D. M. Wolfe, R. P. Quinn, J. D. Snoek, and R. A. Rosenthal, *Organizational Stress: Studies in Role Conflict and Ambiguity* (New York: Wiley, 1964).

21. C. Vandenberge, A. Panaciio, K. Bentein, K. Mignonac, and P. Roussel, "Assessing Longitudinal Change of and Dynamic Relationships among Role Stressors, Job Attitudes, Turnover Intention, and Well-Being in Neophyte Newcomers," *Journal of Organizational Behavior* 34 (2011): 652–671.

22. L. B. Hammer, T. N. Bauer, and A. A. Grandey, "Work-Family Conflict and Work-Related Withdrawal Behaviors," *Journal of Business and Psychology* 17 (2003): 419–436.

23. M. F. Peterson et al., "Role Conflict, Ambiguity, and Overload: A 21-Nation Study," *Academy of Management Journal* 38 (1995): 429–452.

24. C. Nohe, L. L. Meier, K. Sonntag, and A. Michel, "The Chicken or the Egg? A Meta-Analysis of Panel Studies of the Relationship between Work-Family Conflict and Strain," *Journal of Applied Psychology* 100 (2015): 522–536.

25. S. Pal and P. O. Saksvik, "Work–Family Conflict and Psychosocial Work Environment Stressors as Predictors of Job Stress in a Cross-Cultural Study," *International Journal of Stress Management* 15, No. 1 (2008): 22–42.

26. A. Skogstad, S. Einarsen, T. Torsheim, M. S. Aasland, and H. Hetland, "The Destructiveness of Laissez-Faire Leadership Behavior," *Journal of Occupational Health Psychology* 12 (2007): 80–92.

27. P. D. Bliese and C. A. Castro, "Role Clarity, Work Overload and Organizational Support: Multilevel Evidence of the Importance of Support," *Work and Stress* 14 (2000): 65–74.

28. P. J. Frost, *Toxic Emotions at Work: How Compassionate Managers Handle Pain and Conflict* (Boston: Harvard Business School Press, 2003).

29. T. Nicholson and B. Griffin, "Here Today but Not Gone Tomorrow: Incivility Affects After-Work and Next-Day Recovery," *Journal of Occupational Health Psychology* 20 (2015) 218–225.

30. S. Grebner, N. K. Semmer, L. L. Faso, S. Gut, W. Kalin, and A. Elfering, "Working Conditions, Well-Being, and Job-Related Attitudes among Call Centre Agents," *European Journal of Work and Organizational Psychology* 12 (2003): 341–365.

31. M. P. Bell, J. C. Quick, and C. Cycota, "Assessment and Prevention of Sexual Harassment: An Applied Guide to Creating Healthy Organizations," *International Journal of Selection and Assessment* 10 (2002): 160–167.

32. L. T. Hosmer, "Trust: The Connecting Link between Organizational Theory and Philosophical Ethics," *Academy of Management Review* 20 (1995): 379–403; V. J. Doby and R. D. Caplan, "Organizational Stress as Threat to Reputation: Effects on Anxiety at Work and at Home," *Academy of Management Journal* 38 (1995): 1105–1123.

33. R. T. Keller, "Cross-Functional Project Groups in Research and New Product Development: Diversity, Communications, Job Stress, and Outcomes," *Academy of Management Journal* 33 (2001): 547–555.

34. M. F. Peterson and P. B. Smith, "Does National Culture or Ambient Temperature Explain Cross-National Differences in Role Stress? No Sweat!" *Academy of Management Journal* 40 (1997): 930–946.

35. K. K. Gillingham, "High-G Stress and Orientational Stress: Physiologic Effects of Aerial Maneuvering," *Aviation, Space, and Environmental Medicine* 59 (1988): A10–A20.

36. R. S. DeFrank, "Executive Travel Stress: Perils of the Road Warrior," *Academy of Management Executive* 14 (2000): 58–72; M. Westman, "Strategies for Coping with Business Trips: A Qualitative Exploratory Study," *International Journal of Stress Management* 11 (2004): 167–176.

37. R. S. Bhagat, S. J. McQuaid, S. Lindholm, and J. Segovis, "Total Life Stress: A Multimethod Validation of the Construct and Its Effect on Organizationally Valued Outcomes and Withdrawal Behaviors," *Journal of Applied Psychology* 70 (1985): 202–214.

38. J. C. Quick, J. R. Joplin, D. A. Gray, and E. C. Cooley, "The Occupational Life Cycle and the Family," in L. L'Abate, ed., *Handbook of Developmental Family Psychology and Psychopathology* (New York: John Wiley, 1993).

39. S. Shellenbarger, "Work and Family," *The Wall Street Journal* (January 31, 1996): B1.

40. S. A. Lobel, "Allocation of Investment in Work and Family Roles: Alternative Theories and Implications for Research," *Academy of Management Review* 16 (1991): 507–521.

41. G. Porter, "Organizational Impact of Workaholism: Suggestions for Researching the Negative Outcomes of Excessive Work," *Journal of Occupational Health Psychology* 1 (1996): 70–84.

42. J. W. Pennebaker, C. F. Hughes, and R. C. O'Heeron, "The Psychophysiology of Confession: Linking Inhibitory and Psychosomatic Processes," *Journal of Personality and Social Psychology* 52 (1987): 781–793.

43. J. Loehr and T. Schwartz, "The Making of a Corporate Athlete," *Harvard Business Review* 79 (2001): 120–129.

44. J. D. Quick, R. S. Horn, and J. C. Quick, "Health Consequences of Stress," *Journal of Organizational Behavior Management* 8 (1986): 19–36.

45. R. M. Yerkes and J. D. Dodson, "The Relation of Strength of Stimulus to Rapidity of Habit-Formation," *Journal of Comparative Neurology and Psychology* 18 (1908): 459–482.

46. J. E. McGrath, "Stress and Behavior in Organizations," in M. D. Dunnette, ed., *Handbook of Industrial and Organizational Psychology* (Chicago: Rand McNally, 1976): 1351–1395.

47. T. A. Wright, R. Cropanzano, and D. G. Meyer, "State and Trait Correlates of Job Performance: A Tale of Two Perspectives," *Journal of Business and Psychology* 18 (2004): 365–383.

48. W. B. Cannon, *Bodily Changes in Pain, Hunger, Fear, and Rage* (New York: Appleton, 1915).

49. P. A. Herbig and F. A. Palumbo, "Karoshi: Salaryman Sudden Death Syndrome," *Journal of Managerial Psychology* 9 (1994): 11–16.

50. S. Sauter, L. R. Murphy, and J. J. Hurrell, Jr., "Prevention of Work-Related Psychological Distress: A National Strategy Proposed by the National Institute for Occupational Safety and Health," *American Psychologist* 45 (1990): 1146–1158.

51. R. Cropanzano, D. E. Rupp, and Z. S. Byrne, "The Relationship of Emotional Exhaustion to Work Attitudes, Job Performance, and Organizational Citizenship Behaviors," *Journal of Applied Psychology* 88 (2003): 160–169.

52. A. A. Grandey, "When 'The Show Must Go On': Surface Acting and Deep Acting as Determinants of Emotional Exhaustion and Peer-Rated Service Delivery," *Academy of Management Journal* 46 (2003): 86–96.

53. G. B. Hall, M. F. Dollard, M. R. Tuckey, A. H. Winefield, and B. M. Thompson, "Job Demands, Work–Family Conflict, and Emotional Exhaustion in Police Officers: A Longitudinal Test of Competing Theories," *Journal of Occupational and Organizational Psychology* 83 (2010): 237–250.

54. J. R. B. Halbesleben and W. M. Bowler, "Emotional Exhaustion and Job Performance: The Mediating Role of Motivation," *Journal of Applied Psychology* 92 (2007): 93–106.

55. I. Wylie, "Routing Rust-Out," *Fast Company Magazine* (January 2004): 40, www.fastcompany.com/magazine/78/5things.html.

56. H. Selye, *Stress in Health and Disease* (Boston: Butterworth, 1976).

57. B. G. Ware and D. L. Block, "Cardiovascular Risk Intervention at a Work Site: The Ford Motor Company Program," *International Journal of Mental Health* 11 (1982): 68–75.

58. D. B. Kennedy, R. J. Homant, and M. R. Homant, "Perceptions of Injustice as a Predictor of Support for Workplace Aggression," *Journal of Business and Psychology* 18 (2004): 323–336.

59. N. Bolger, A. DeLongis, R. C. Kessler, and E. A. Schilling, "Effects of Daily Stress on Negative Mood," *Journal of Personality and Social Psychology* 57 (1989): 808–818.

60. B. A. Macy and P. H. Mirvis, "A Methodology for Assessment of Quality of Work Life and Organizational Effectiveness in Behavioral-Economic Terms," *Administrative Science Quarterly* 21 (1976): 212–226.

61. F. K. Cocchiara and J. C. Quick, "The Negative Effects of Positive Stereotypes: Ethnicity-Related Stressors and Implications on Organizational Health," *Journal of Organizational Behavior* 25 (2004): 781–785.

62. J. M. Ivancevich, M. T. Matteson, and E. Richards, "Who's Liable for Stress on the Job?" *Harvard Business Review* 64 (1985): 60–72.

63. Frank S. Deus v. Allstate Insurance Company, civil action no. 88-2099, U.S. District Court, Western District of Louisiana.

64. R. S. DeFrank and J. M. Ivancevich, "Stress on the Job: An Executive Update," *Academy of Management Executive* 12 (1998): 55–66.

65. P. Wilson and M. Bronstein, "Employers: Don't Panic about Workplace Stress," *Personnel Today* (November 4, 2003): 10.

66. J. E. Bono and M. A. Vey, "Personality and Emotional Performance: Extraversion, Neuroticism, and Self-Monitoring," *Journal of Occupational Health Psychology* 12 (2007): 177–192.

67. C. S. Troutman, K. G. Burke, and J. D. Beeler, "The Effects of Self-Efficacy, Assertiveness, Stress, and Gender on Intention," *Journal of Applied Business Research* 16 (2000): 63–75.

68. S. E. Taylor, L. C. Klein, G. P. Lewis, T. L. Gruenewald, R. A. R. Burung, and J. A. Updegraff, "Biobehavioral Responses to Stress in Females: Tend-and-Befriend, Not Fight-or-Flight," *Psychological Review* 107 (2000): 411–429.

69. D. L. Nelson and J. C. Quick, "Professional Women: Are Distress and Disease Inevitable?" *Academy of Management Review* 10 (1985): 206–218; T. D. Jick and L. F. Mitz, "Sex Differences in Work Stress," *Academy of Management Review* 10 (1985): 408–420.

70. K. M. Rospenda, K. Fujishiro, C. A. Shannon, and J. A. Richman, "Workplace Harassment, Stress, and Drinking Behavior over Time: Gender Differences in a National Sample," *Addictive Behaviors* 33 (2008): 964–967.

71. L. Verbrugge, "Recent, Present, and Future Health of American Adults," *Annual Review of Public Health* 10 (1989): 333–361.

72. M. D. Friedman and R. H. Rosenman, *Type A Behavior and Your Heart* (New York: Knopf, 1974).

73. L. Wright, "The Type A Behavior Pattern and Coronary Artery Disease," *American Psychologist* 43 (1988): 2–14.

74. J. M. Ivancevich and M. T. Matteson, "A Type A–B Person–Work Environment Interaction Model for Examining Occupational Stress and Consequences," *Human Relations* 37 (1984): 491–513.

75. S. O. C. Kobasa, "Conceptualization and Measurement of Personality in Job Stress Research," in J. J. Hurrell, Jr., L. R. Murphy, S. L. Sauter, and C. L. Cooper, eds., *Occupational Stress: Issues and Developments in Research* (New York: Taylor & Francis, 1988): 100–109.

76. J. K. Ito and C. M. Brotheridge, "Predictors and Consequences of Promotion Stress: A Bad Situation Made Worse by Employment Dependence," *International Journal of Stress Management* 16, No. 1 (2009): 65–85.

77. J. Borysenko, "Personality Hardiness," *Lectures in Behavioral Medicine* (Boston: Harvard Medical School, 1985).

78. J. S. House, K. R. Landis, and D. Umberson, "Social Relationships and Health," *Science* 241 (1988): 540–545.

79. J. Bowlby, *A Secure Base* (New York: Basic Books, 1988).

80. C. Hazan and P. Shaver, "Love and Work: An Attachment-Theoretical Perspective," *Journal of Personality and Social Psychology* 59 (1990): 270–280.

81. J. C. Quick, D. L. Nelson, and J. D. Quick, *Stress and Challenge at the Top: The Paradox of the Successful Executive* (Chichester, England: Wiley, 1990).

82. "Partner Relationship Could Be a Buffer against Work-Related Stress," Asian News International (June 24, 2009).

83. J. C. Quick, J. R. Joplin, D. L. Nelson, and J. D. Quick, "Self-Reliance for Stress and Combat" (*Proceedings of the 8th Combat Stress Conference,* U.S. Army Health Services Command, Fort Sam Houston, Texas, September 23–27, 1991): 1–5.

84. J. C. Dvorak, "Baffling," *PC Magazine* 3 (November 4, 2003): 61, http://www.pcmag.com/article2/0,4149,1369270,00.asp.

85. O. Janssen, "How Fairness Perceptions Make Innovative Behavior More or Less Stressful," *Journal of Organizational Behavior* 25 (2004): 201–215; T. A. Judge and J. A. Colquitt, "Organizational Justice and Stress: The Mediating Role of Work–Family Conflict," *Journal of Applied Psychology* 89 (2004): 395–404.

86. K. Hickox, "Content and Competitive," *Airman* (January 1994): 31–33.

87. A. Drach-Zahavy and A. Freund, "Team Effectiveness under Stress: A Structural Contingency Approach," *Journal of Organizational Behavior* 28 (2007): 423–450.

88. R. W. Griffin, A. O'Leary-Kelly, and J. M. Collins, eds., *Dysfunctional Behavior in Organizations: Violent and Deviant Behavior* (Stamford, Conn.: JAI Press, 1998).

89. M. Kouchaki and S. D. Desai, "Anxious, Threatened, and Also Unethical: How Anxiety Makes Individuals Feel Threatened and Commit Unethical Acts," *Journal of Applied Psychology* 100 (2015): 360–375.

90. W. L. French and C. H. Bell, Jr., *Organizational Development: Behavioral Science Interventions for Organization Improvement,* 4th ed. (Englewood Cliffs, N.J.: Prentice-Hall, 1990).

91. C. Newton and S. Teo, "Identification and Occupational Stress: A Stress-Buffering Perspective," *Human Resource Management* 53 (2014): 89–113.

92. M. Macik-Frey, J. C. Quick, and J. D. Quick, "Interpersonal Communication: The Key to Unlocking Social Support for Preventive Stress Management," in C. L. Cooper, ed., *Handbook of Stress, Medicine, and Health,* rev. ed. (Boca Raton, FL: CRC Press).

93. J. C. Quick and C. L. Cooper, *FAST FACTS: Stress and Strain,* 2nd ed. (Oxford, England: Health Press, 2003).

94. M. E. P. Seligman, *Learned Optimism* (New York: Knopf, 1990).

95. F. Griva and F. Anagnostopoulos, "Positive Psychological States and Anxiety: The Mediating Effect of Proactive Coping," *Psychological Reports* 107 (2010): 795–804.

96. F. Luthans, "Positive Organizational Behavior: Developing and Managing Psychological Strengths for Performance Improvement," *Academy of Management Executive* 16 (2002): 57–75.

97. W. T. Brooks and T. W. Mullins, *High-Impact Time Management* (Englewood Cliffs, N.J.: Prentice-Hall, 1989).

98. M. Westman and D. Eden, "Effects of a Respite from Work on Burnout: Vacation Relief and Fade-Out," *Journal of Applied Psychology* 82 (1997): 516–527.

99. C. P. Neck and K. H. Cooper, "The Fit Executive: Exercise and Diet Guidelines for Enhancing Performance," *Academy of Management Executive* 14 (2000): 72–84.

100. M. Davis, E. R. Eshelman, and M. McKay, *The Relaxation and Stress Reduction Workbook,* 3rd ed. (Oakland, Calif.: New Harbinger, 1988).

101. H. Benson, "Your Innate Asset for Combating Stress," *Harvard Business Review* 52 (1974): 49–60.

102. D. Ornish, *Dr. Dean Ornish's Program for Reversing Cardiovascular Disease* (New York: Random House, 1995).

103. J. W. Pennebaker, *Opening Up: The Healing Power of Expressing Emotions* (New York: Guilford, 1997).

104. M. E. Francis and J. W. Pennebaker, "Putting Stress into Words: The Impact of Writing on Physiological, Absentee, and Self-Reported Emotional Well-Being Measures," *American Journal of Health Promotion* 6 (1992): 280–287.

105. Z. Solomon, B. Oppenheimer, and S. Noy, "Subsequent Military Adjustment of Combat Stress Reaction Casualties: A Nine-Year Follow-Up Study," in N. A. Milgram, ed., *Stress and Coping in Time of War: Generalizations from the Israeli Experience* (New York: Brunner/Mazel, 1986): 84–90.

106. D. Wegman and L. Fine, "Occupational Health in the 1990s," *Annual Review of Public Health* 11 (1990): 89–103; J. C. Quick, "Occupational Health Psychology: Historical Roots and Future Directions," *Health Psychology* 17 (1999): 82–88.

107. D. Gebhardt and C. Crump, "Employee Fitness and Wellness Programs in the Workplace," *American Psychologist* 45 (1990): 262–272.

108. T. Wolf, H. Randall, and J. Faucett, "A Survey of Health Promotion Programs in U.S. and Canadian Medical Schools," *American Journal of Health Promotion* 3 (1988): 33–36.

109. S. Weiss, J. Fielding, and A. Baum, *Health at Work* (Hillsdale, N.J.: Erlbaum, 1990).

110. J. B. Bennett, R. F. Cook, and K. R. Pelletier, "Toward an Integrated Framework for Comprehensive Organizational Wellness: Concepts, Practices, and Research in Workplace Health Promotion," in J. C. Quick and L. E. Tetrick, eds., *Handbook of Occupational Health Psychology* (Washington, D.C.: American Psychological Association, 2003): 69–95.

8

1. D. L. Whetzel, "The Department of Labor Identifies Workplace Skills," *The Industrial/Organizational Psychologist* (July 1991): 89–90.

2. M. Macik-Frey, J. C. Quick, and J. D. Quick, "Interpersonal Communication: The Key to Unlocking Social Support for Preventive Stress Management," in C. L. Cooper, ed., *Handbook of Stress, Medicine, and Health, rev. ed.* (Boca Raton, FL: CRC Press), in press.

3. *Richness* is a term originally coined by W. D. Bodensteiner, "Information Channel Utilization under Varying Research and Development Project Conditions" (Ph.D. diss., University of Texas at Austin, 1970).

4. T. J. Kiddie, "Text(ing) in Context: The Future of Workplace Communication in the United States," *Business and Professional Communication Quarterly* 77 (2014): 65–88.

5. B. Barry and I. S. Fulmer, "The Medium and the Message: The Adaptive Use of Communication Media in Dyadic Influence," *Academy of Management Review* 29 (2004): 272–292.

6. R. Reik, *Listen with the Third Ear* (New York: Pyramid, 1972).

7. E. Rautalinko and H. O. Lisper, "Effects of Training Reflective Listening in a Corporate Setting," *Journal of Business and Psychology* 18 (2004): 281–299.

8. A. G. Athos and J. J. Gabarro, *Interpersonal Behavior: Communication and Understanding in Relationships* (Englewood Cliffs, N.J.: Prentice-Hall, 1978).

9. A. D. Mangelsdorff, "Lessons Learned from the Military: Implications for Management" (Distinguished Visiting Lecture, University of Texas at Arlington, January 29, 1993).

10. D. A. Morand, "Language and Power: An Empirical Analysis of Linguistic Strategies Used in Superior–Subordinate Communication," *Journal of Organizational Behavior* 21 (2000): 235–249.

11. S. Bates, "How Leaders Communicate Big Ideas to Drive Business Results," *Employment Relations Today* 33 (Fall 2006): 13–19.

12. F. Luthans, "Successful versus Effective Real Managers," *Academy of Management Executive* 2 (1988): 127–132.

13. L. E. Penley, E. R. Alexander, I. E. Jernigan, and C. I. Henwood, "Communication Abilities of Managers: The Relationship of Performance," *Journal of Management* 17 (1991): 57–76.

14. J. A. LePine and L. Van Dyne, "Voice and Cooperative Behavior as Contrasting Forms of Contextual Performance: Evidence of Differential Relationships with Big Five Personality Characteristics and Cognitive Ability," *Journal of Applied Psychology* 86 (2001): 326–336.

15. F. M. Jablin, "Superior-Subordinate Communication: The State of the Art," *Psychological Bulletin* 86 (1979): 1201–1222; W. C. Reddin, *Communication within the Organization: An Interpretive Review of Theory and Research* (New York: Industrial Communication Council, 1972).

16. B. Barry and J. M. Crant, "Dyadic Communication Relationships in Organizations: An Attribution Expectancy Approach," *Organization Science* 11 (2000): 648–665.

17. J. Silvester, F. Patterson, A. Koczwara, and E. Ferguson, "'Trust Me . . .': Psychological and Behavioral Predictors of Perceived Physician Empathy," *Journal of Applied Psychology* 92 (2007): 519–527.

18. K. Mishra, L. Boynton, and A. Mishra, "Driving Employee Engagement: The Expanded Role of Internal Communications," *International Journal of Business Communications* 51 (2014): 183–202.

19. A. Furhham and P. Stringfield, "Congruence in Job-Performance Ratings: A Study of 360 Degree Feedback Examining Self, Manager, Peers, and Consultant Ratings," *Human Relations* 51 (1998): 517–530.

20. J. W. Gilsdorf, "Organizational Rules on Communicating: How Employees Are—and Are Not—Learning the Ropes," *Journal of Business Communication* 35 (1998): 173–201.

21. A. Malhotra and A. Majchrzak, "Enhancing Performance of Geographically Dispersed Teams through Targeted Use of Information and Communication Technologies," *Human Relations* 67 (2014): 389–411.

22. D. Tannen, *That's Not What I Mean! How Conversational Style Makes or Breaks Your Relations with Others* (New York: Morrow, 1986); D. Tannen, *You Just Don't Understand* (New York: Ballentine, 1990).

23. D. G. Allen and R. W. Griffeth, "A Vertical and Lateral Information Processing: The Effects of Gender, Employee Classification Level, and Media Richness on Communication and Work Outcomes," *Human Relations* 50 (1997): 1239–1260.

24. K. L. Ashcraft, "Empowering 'Professional' Relationships," *Management Communication Quarterly* 13 (2000): 347–393.

25. G. Hofstede, *Culture's Consequences: International Differences in Work-Related Values* (Beverly Hills, Calif.: Sage Publications, 1980).

26. G. Hofstede, "Motivation, Leadership, and Organization: Do American Theories Apply Abroad?" *Organizational Dynamics* 9 (1980): 42–63.

27. H. Levinson, *Executive* (Cambridge, Mass.: Harvard University Press, 1981).

28. B. M. Cole, "Lessons from a Martial Arts Dojo: A Prolonged Process Model of High-Context Communication," *Academy of Management Journal* 58 (2015): 567–591.

29. P. Benimadhu, "Adding Value through Diversity: An Interview with Bernard F. Isautier," *Canadian Business Review* 22 (1995): 6–11.

30. M. J. Gannon and Associates, *Understanding Global Cultures: Metaphorical Journeys through 17 Countries* (Thousand Oaks, Calif.: Sage Publications, 1994).

31. J. L. Welbourne, A. Gangadharan, and A. M. Sariol, "Ethnicity and Cultural Values as Predictors of the Occurrence and Impact of Experienced Workplace Incivility," *Journal of Occupational Health Psychology* 20 (2015): 205–217.

32. T. C. Reich and S. Hershcovis, "Observing Workplace Incivility," *Journal of Applied Psychology* 100 (2015): 203–215.

33. T. Wells, *Keeping Your Cool under Fire: Communicating Nondefensively* (New York: McGraw-Hill, 1980).

34. R. D. Laing, *The Politics of the Family and Other Essays* (New York: Pantheon, 1971).

35. H. S. Schwartz, *Narcissistic Process and Corporate Decay: The Theory of the Organizational Ideal* (New York: New York University Press, 1990).

36. W. R. Forrester and M. F. Maute, "The Impact of Relationship Satisfaction on Attribution, Emotions, and Behaviors Following Service Failure," *Journal of Applied Business Research* (2000): 1–45.

37. M. L. Knapp, *Nonverbal Communication in Human Interaction* (New York: Holt, Rinehart & Winston, 1978); J. McCroskey and L. Wheeless, *Introduction to Human Communication* (New York: Allyn & Bacon, 1976).

38. A. M. Katz and V. T. Katz, eds., *Foundations of Nonverbal Communication* (Carbondale, Ill.: Southern Illinois University Press, 1983).

39. M. D. Lieberman, "Intuition: A Social Cognitive Neuroscience Approach," *Psychological Bulletin* (2000): 109–138.

40. E. T. Hall, *The Hidden Dimension* (Garden City, N.Y.: Doubleday Anchor, 1966).

41. E. T. Hall, "Proxemics," in A. M. Katz and V. T. Katz, eds., *Foundations of Nonverbal Communication* (Carbondale, Ill.: Southern Illinois University Press, 1983).

42. R. T. Barker and C. G. Pearce, "The Importance of Proxemics at Work," *Supervisory Management* 35 (1990): 10–11.

43. R. L. Birdwhistell, *Kinesics and Context* (Philadelphia: University of Pennsylvania Press, 1970).

44. K. I. Ruys and D. A. Stapel, "Emotion Elicitor or Emotion Messenger?" *Psychological Science*, 19 (2008): 593–600.

45. M. G. Frank and P. Ekman, "Appearing Truthful Generalizes across Different Deception Situations," *Journal of Personality and Social Psychology* 86 (2004): 486–495.

46. P. Ekman and W. V. Friesen, "Research on Facial Expressions of Emotion," in A. M. Katz and V. T. Katz, eds., *Foundations of Nonverbal Communication* (Carbondale, Ill.: Southern Illinois University Press, 1983).

47. H. H. Tan, M. D. Foo, C. L. Chong, and R. Ng, "Situational and Dispositional Predictors of Displays of Positive Emotions," *Journal of Organizational Behavior* 24 (2003): 961–978.

48. C. Barnum and N. Wolniansky, "Taking Cues from Body Language," *Management Review* 78 (1989): 59.

49. A. M. Katz and V.T. Katz, *Foundations of Nonverbal Communication*, (Carbondale, IL: Southern Illinois University Press, 1983): 181.

50. J. J. Lynch, *A Cry Unheard: New Insights into the Medical Consequences of Loneliness* (Baltimore, MD: Bancroft Press, 2000).

51. J. C. Quick, J. H. Gavin, C. L. Cooper, and J. D. Quick, "Working Together: Balancing Head and Heart," in N. G. Johnson, R. H. Rozensky, C. D. Goodheart, and R. Hammond, eds., *Psychology Builds a Healthy World* (Washington, D.C.: American Psychological Association, 2004): 219–232.

52. J. C. Quick, C. L. Cooper, J. D. Quick, and J. H. Gavin, *The Financial Times Guide to Executive Health* (London, UK: Financial Times–Prentice Hall, 2003).

53. K. M. Wasylyshyn, "Coaching the Superkeepers," in L. A. Berger and D. R. Berger, eds., *The Talent Management Handbook: Creating Organizational Excellence by Identifying, Developing, and Positioning Your Best People* (New York: McGraw-Hill, 2003): 320–336.

54. J. C. Quick and M. Macik-Frey, "Behind the Mask: Coaching through Deep Interpersonal Communication," *Consulting Psychology Journal: Practice and Research* 56 (2004): 67–74.

55. R. Flinn, "Social Media: A New Jury Selection Tool," *Bloomberg Businessweek* (April 21, 2011).

56. B. J. Dunn, "Best Buy's CEO on Learning to Love Social Media," *Harvard Business Review* 88 (December 2010): 43–48.

57. B. Drake and K. Yuthas, "It's Only Words—Impacts of Information Technology on Moral Dialogue," *Journal of Business Ethics* 23 (2000): 41–60.

58. C. Brod, Technostress: *The Human Cost of the Computer Revolution* (Reading, Mass.: Addison-Wesley, 1984).

59. S. Kiesler, "Technology and the Development of Creative Environments," in Y. Ijiri and R. L. Kuhn, eds., *New Directions in Creative and Innovative Management* (Cambridge, Mass.: Ballinger Press, 1988).

60. S. Adams, "Being There," *Forbes* 187 (2011): 94.

61. S. Kiesler, J. Siegel, and T. W. McGuire, "Social Psychological Aspects of Computer-Mediated Communication," *American Psychologist* 39 (1984): 1123–1134.

62. P. Shachaf, "Cultural Diversity and Information and Communication Technology Impacts on Global Virtual Teams: An Exploratory Study," *Information & Management* 45 (2008): 131–142.

63. L. K. Barber and A. M. Santuzzi, "Please Respond ASAP: Workplace Telepressure and Employee Recovery," *Journal of Occupational Health Psychology* 20 (2015): 172–189.

9

1. J. R. Katzenbach and D. K. Smith, "The Discipline of Teams," *Harvard Business Review* 71 (1993): 111–120.

2. S. S. Webber and R. J. Klimoski, "Crews: A Distinct Type of Work Team," *Journal of Business and Psychology* 18 (2004): 261–279.

3. P. F. Drucker, "There's More Than One Kind of Team," *The Wall Street Journal* (February 11, 1992): A16.

4. A. M. Towsend, S. M. DeMarie, and A. R. Hendrickson, "Virtual Teams: Technology and the Workplace of the Future," *Academy of Management Executive* 12 (1998): 17–29.

5. B. L. Kirkman, C. B. Gibson, and D. L. Shapiro, "'Exporting' Teams: Enhancing the Implementation and Effectiveness of Work Teams in Global Affiliates," *Organizational Dynamics* 30 (2001): 12–29.

6. A. Taylor and H. R. Greve, "Superman or the Fantastic Four? Knowledge Combination and Experience in Innovative Teams," *Academy of Management Journal* 49 (2006): 723–740.

7. S. Faraj and A. Yan, "Boundary Work in Knowledge Teams," *Journal of Applied Psychology* 94 (2009): 604–617.

8. P. Shaver and D. Buhrmester, "Loneliness, Sex-Role Orientation, and Group Life: A Social Needs Perspective," in P. Paulus, ed., *Basic Group Processes* (New York: Springer-Verlag, 1985): 259–288.

9. K. L. Bettenhausen and J. K. Murnighan, "The Development and Stability of Norms in Groups Facing Interpersonal and Structural Challenge," *Administrative Science Quarterly* 36 (1991): 20–35.

10. N. Ellemers, S. Pagliaro, M. Barreto, and C. W. Leach, "Is It Better to Be Moral Than Smart? The Effects of Morality and Competence Norms on the Decision to Work at Group Status Improvement," *Journal of Personality and Social Psychology* 95 (2008): 1397–1410.

11. I. Adarves-Yorno, T. Postmes, and S. A. Haslam, "Creative Innovation or Crazy Irrelevance? The Contribution of Group Norms and Social Identity to Creative Behavior," *Journal of Experimental Social Psychology* 43 (2007): 410–416.

12. D. Tjosvold and Z. Yu, "Goal Interdependence and Applying Abilities for Team In-Role and Extra-Role Performance in China," *Group Dynamics: Theory, Research, and Practice* 8 (2004): 98–111.

13. M. S. Cole, F. Walter, and H. Bruch, "Affective Mechanisms Linking Dysfunctional Behavior to Performance in Work Teams: A Moderated Mediation Study," *Journal of Applied Psychology* 93 (2008): 945–958.

14. V. U. Druskat and S. B. Wolff, "Building the Emotional Intelligence of Groups," *Harvard Business Review* 79 (2001): 80–90.

15. I. Summers, T. Coffelt, and R. E. Horton, "Work-Group Cohesion," *Psychological Reports* 63 (1988): 627–636.

16. D. C. Man and S. S. K. Lam, "The Effects of Job Complexity and Autonomy on Cohesiveness in Collectivistic and Individualistic Work Groups: A Cross-Cultural Analysis," *Journal of Organizational Behavior* 24 (2003): 979–1001.

17. Y. Shin and J. N. Choi, "What Makes a Group of Good Citizens? The Role of Perceived Group-Level Fit and Critical Psychological States in Organizational Teams," *Journal of Occupational and Organizational Psychology* 83 (2010): 531–552.

18. K. H. Price, "Working Hard to Get People to Loaf," *Basic and Applied Social Psychology* 14 (1993): 329–344.

19. M. C. Schippers, "Social Loafing Tendencies and Team Performance: The Compensating Effect of Agreeableness and Conscientiousness," *Academy of Management Learning & Education* 13 (2014): 62–81.

20. R. Albanese and D. D. Van Fleet, "Rational Behavior in Groups: The Free-Riding Tendency," *Academy of Management Review* 10 (1985): 244–255.

21. E. Diener, "Deindividuation, Self-Awareness, and Disinhibition," *Journal of Personality and Social Psychology* 37 (1979): 1160–1171.

22. S. Prentice-Dunn and R. W. Rogers, "Deindividuation and the Self-Regulation of Behavior," in P. Paulus, ed., *Psychology of Group Influence* (Hillsdale, N.J.: Erlbaum, 1989): 87–109.

23. B. M. Bass and E. C. Ryterband, *Organizational Psychology*, 2nd ed. (Boston: Allyn & Bacon, 1979).

24. W. G. Bennis and H. A. Shepard, "A Theory of Group Development," *Human Relations* 9 (1956): 415–438.

25. A. Joshi and A. P. Knight, "Who Defers to Whom and Why? Dual Pathways Linking Demographic Differences and Dyadic Deference to Team Effectiveness," *Academy of Management Journal* 58 (2015): 59–84.

26. D. L. Fields and T. C. Bloom, "Employee Satisfaction in Work Groups with Different Gender Composition," *Journal of Organizational Behavior* 18 (1997): 181–196.

27. D. C. Lau and J. K. Murnighan, "Demographic Diversity and Faultlines: The Compositional Dynamics of Organizational Groups," *Academy of Management Review* 23 (1998): 325–340.

28. B. Tuckman, "Developmental Sequence in Small Groups," *Psychological Bulletin* 63 (1965): 384–399; B. Tuckman and M. Jensen, "Stages of Small-Group Development," *Group and Organizational Studies* 2 (1977): 419–427.

29. S. T. Bell and J. A. Belohlav, "The Power of 'We': The Effects of Psychological Collectivism on Team Performance over Time," *Journal of Applied Psychology* 96 (2011): 247–262.

30. D. Nichols, "Quality Program Sparked Company Turnaround," *Personnel* (October 1991): 24. For a commentary on Wallace's hard times and subsequent emergence from Chapter 11 bankruptcy, see R. C. Hill, "When the Going Gets Tough: A Baldrige Award Winner on the Line," *Academy of Management Executive* 7 (1993): 75–79.

31. S. Weisband and L. Atwater, "Evaluating Self and Others in Electronic and Face-to-Face Groups," *Journal of Applied Psychology* 84 (1999): 632–639.

32. C. J. G. Gersick, "Time and Transition in Work Teams: Toward a New Model of Group Development," *The Academy of Management Journal* 31 (1988): 9–41.

33. M. Hardaker and B. K. Ward, "How to Make a Team Work," *Harvard Business Review* 65 (1987): 112–120.

34. C. R. Gowen, "Managing Work Group Performance by Individual Goals and Group Goals for an Interdependent Group Task," *Journal of Organizational Behavior Management* 7 (1986): 5–27.

35. K. L. Bettenhausen and J. K. Murnighan, "The Emergence of Norms in Competitive Decision-Making Groups," *Administrative Science Quarterly* 30 (1985): 350–372; K. L. Bettenhausen, "Five Years of Groups Research: What We Have Learned and What Needs to Be Addressed," *Journal of Management* 17 (1991): 345–381.

36. N. Li, B. L. Kirkman, and C. O. L. H. Porter, "Toward a Model of Work Team Altruism," *Academy of Management Review* 39 (2014): 541–565.

37. J. E. McGrath, *Groups: Interaction and Performance* (Englewood Cliffs, N.J.: Prentice-Hall, 1984).

38. K. L. Gammage, A. V. Carron, and P. A. Estabrooks, "Team Cohesion and Individual

Productivity," *Small Group Research* 32 (2001): 3–18.

39. W. J. Becker and R. Cropanzano, "Good Acting Requires a Good Cast: A Meso-Level Model of Deep Acting in Work Teams," *Journal of Organizational Behavior* 36 (2015): 232–249.

40. S. M. Klein, "A Longitudinal Study of the Impact of Work Pressure on Group Cohesive Behaviors," *International Journal of Management* 12 (1996): 68–75.

41. N. Steckler and N. Fondas, "Building Team Leader Effectiveness: A Diagnostic Tool," *Organizational Dynamics* 23 (1995): 20–35.

42. A. Carter and S. Holmes, "Curiously Strong Teamwork," *BusinessWeek* 4023 (February 26, 2007): 90–92.

43. W. R. Lassey, "Dimensions of Leadership," in W. R. Lassey and R. Fernandez, eds., *Leadership and Social Change* (La Jolla, Calif.: University Associates, 1976): 10–15.

44. B. Broysberg and L. Lee, "The Effect of Colleague Quality on Top Performance: The Case of Security Analysts," *Journal of Organizational Behavior* 29 (2008): 1123–1144.

45. J. D. Quick, G. Moorhead, J. C. Quick, E. A. Gerloff, K. L. Mattox, and C. Mullins, "Decision Making among Emergency Room Residents: Preliminary Observations and a Decision Model," *Journal of Medical Education* 58 (1983): 117–125.

46. J. Sieweke and B. Zhao, "The Impact of Team Familiarity and Team Leader Experience on Team Coordination Errors: A Panel Analysis of Professional Basketball Teams," *Journal of Organizational Behavior* 36 (2015): 382–402.

47. W. J. Duncan and J. P. Feisal, "No Laughing Matter: Patterns of Humor in the Workplace," *Organizational Dynamics* 17 (1989): 18–30.

48. L. Hirschhorn, *Managing in the New Team Environment* (Upper Saddle River, N.J.: Prentice-Hall, 1991): 521A.

49. G. Chen and R. J. Klimoski, "The Impact of Expectations on Newcomer Performance in Teams as Mediated by Work Characteristics, Social Exchanges, and Empowerment," *Academy of Management Journal* 46 (2003): 591–607.

50. B. Beersma, J. R. Hollenbeck, S. E. Humphrey, H. Moon, D. E. Conlon, and D. R. Ilgen, "Cooperation, Competition, and Team Performance: Toward a Contingency Approach," *Academy of Management Journal* 46 (2003): 572–590.

51. G. Parker, *Team Players and Teamwork* (San Francisco: Jossey-Bass, 1990).

52. N. R. F. Maier, "Assets and Liabilities in Group Problem Solving: The Need for an Integrative Function," *Psychological Review* 74 (1967): 239–249.

53. T. A. Stewart, "The Search for the Organization of Tomorrow," *Fortune* (May 18, 1992): 92–98

54. P. Chattopadhyay, M. Tluchowska, and E. George, "Identifying the Ingroup: A Closer Look at the Influence of Demographic Dissimilarity on Employee Social Identity," *Academy of Management Review* 29 (2004): 180–202.

55. M. M. Stewart and P. Garcia-Prieto, "A Relational Demography Model of Workgroup Identification: Testing the Effects of Race, Race Dissimilarity, Racial Identification, and Communication Behavior," *Journal of Organizational Behavior* 29 (2008): 657–680.

56. E. V. Hobman, P. Bordia, and C. Gallois, "Consequences of Feeling Dissimilar from Others in a Work Team," *Journal of Business and Psychology* 17 (2003): 301–325.

57. A. E. Randel and K. S. Jaussi, "Functional Background Identity, Diversity, and Individual Performance in Cross-Functional Teams," *Academy of Management Journal* 46 (2003): 763–774.

58. J. S. Bunderson, "Team Member Functional Background and Involvement in Management Teams: Direct Effects and the Moderating Role of Power Centralization," *Academy of Management Journal* 46 (2003): 458–474.

59. G. S. Van Der Vegt, E. Van De Vliert, and A. Oosterhof, "Informational Dissimilarity and Organizational Citizenship Behavior: The Role of Intrateam Interdependence and Team Identification," *Academy of Management Journal* 46 (2003): 715–727.

60. F. Balkundi, M. Kilduff, Z. I. Barsness, and J. H. Michael, "Demographic Antecedents and Performance Consequences of Structural Holes in Work Teams," *Journal of Organizational Behavior* 28 (2007): 241–260.

61. A. Pirola-Merlo and L. Mann, "The Relationship between Individual Creativity and Team Creativity: Aggregating across People and Time," *Journal of Organizational Behavior* 25 (2004): 235–257.

62. L. Thompson, "Improving the Creativity of Organizational Work Groups," *Academy of Management Executive* 17 (2003): 96–111.

63. J. Han, and D. J. Brass, "Human Capital Diversity in the Creation of Social Capital for Team Creativity," *Journal of Organizational Behavior* 35 (2014): 54–71.

64. C. Ford and D. M. Sullivan, "A Time for Everything: How the Timing of Novel Contributions Influences Project Team Outcomes," *Journal of Organizational Behavior* 25 (2004): 279–292.

65. K. W. Thomas and B. A. Velthouse, "Cognitive Elements of Empowerment: An 'Interpretive' Model of Intrinsic Task Motivation," *Academy of Management Review* 15 (1990): 666–681.

66. R. R. Blake, J. S. Mouton, and R. L. Allen, *Spectacular Teamwork: How to Develop the Leadership Skills for Team Success* (New York: Wiley, 1987).

67. American Management Association, *Blueprints for Service Quality: The Federal Express Approach,* AMA Management Briefing (New York: AMA, 1991).

68. W. C. Byham, *ZAPP! The Human Lightning of Empowerment* (Pittsburgh, PA: Developmental Dimensions, 1989).

69. F. Shipper and C. C. Manz, "Employee Self-Management without Formally Designated Teams: An Alternative Road to

Empowerment," *Organizational Dynamics* (Winter 1992): 48–62.

70. P. Block, *The Empowered Manager: Positive Political Skills at Work* (San Francisco: Jossey-Bass, 1987).

71. V. J. Derlega and J. Grzelak, eds., *Cooperation and Helping Behavior: Theories and Research* (New York: Academic Press, 1982).

72. G. S. Van der Vegt, J. S. Bunderson, and A. Oosterhof, "Expertness Diversity and Interpersonal Helping in Teams: Why Those Who Need the Most Help End Up Getting the Least," *Academy of Management Journal* 49 (2006): 877–893.

73. A. G. Athos and J. J. Gabarro, *Interpersonal Behavior: Communication and Understanding in Relationships* (Englewood Cliffs, N.J.: Prentice-Hall, 1978).

74. C. Douglas and W. L. Gardner, "Transition to Self-Directed Work Teams: Implications of Transition Time and Self-Monitoring for Managers' Use of Influence Tactics," *Journal of Organizational Behavior* 25 (2004): 47–65.

75. C. Douglas, J. S. Martin, and R. H. Krapels, "Communication in the Transition to Self-Directed Work Teams," *Journal of Business Communication* 43 (2006): 295–321.

76. J. L. Cordery, W. S. Mueller, and L. M. Smith, "Attitudinal and Behavioral Effects of Autonomous Group Working: A Longitudinal Field Study," *Academy of Management Journal* 34 (1991): 464–476.

77. G. Moorhead, C. P. Neck, and M. S. West, "The Tendency toward Defective Decision Making within Self-Managing Teams: The Relevance of Groupthink for the 21st Century," *Organizational Behavior and Human Decision Processes* 73 (1998): 327–351.

78. B. M. Staw and L. D. Epstein, "What Bandwagons Bring: Effects of Popular Management Techniques on Corporate Performance, Reputation, and CEO Pay," *Administrative Science Quarterly* 45 (2000): 523–556.

79. R. M. Robinson, S. L. Oswald, K. S. Swinehart, and J. Thomas, "Southwest Industries: Creating High-Performance Teams for High-Technology Production," *Planning Review* 19, published by the Planning Forum (November–December 1991): 10–47.

80. D. C. Hambrick and P. Mason, "Upper Echelons: The Organization as a Reflection of Its Top Managers," *Academy of Management Review* 9 (1984): 193–206.

81. D. C. Hambrick, "The Top Management Team: Key to Strategic Success," *California Management Review* 30 (1987): 88–108.

82. A. D. Henderson and J. W. Fredrickson, "Top Management Team Coordination Needs and the CEO Pay Gap: A Competitive Test of Economic and Behavioral Views," *Academy of Management Journal* 44 (2001): 96–117.

83. D. C. Hambrick and G. D. S. Fukutomi, "The Seasons of a CEO's Tenure," *Academy of Management Review* 16 (1991): 719–742.

84. J. C. Quick, D. L. Nelson, and J. D. Quick, "Successful Executives: How Independent?"

Academy of Management Executive 1 (1987): 139–145.

85. A. A. Cannella, Jr, J. Park, and H. Lee, "Top Management Team Functional Background Diversity and Firm Performance: Examining the Roles of Team Member Colocation and Environmental Uncertainty," *Academy of Management Journal* 51(2008): 768–784.

86. L. G. Love, "The Evolving Pinnacle of the Corporation: An Explanatory Study of the Antecedents, Processes, and Consequences of Co-CEOs," 2003 (The University of Texas at Arlington).

87. N. J. Adler, *International Dimensions of Organizational Behavior* (Mason, Ohio: South-Western, 2001).

88. I. D. Steiner, *Group Process and Productivity* (New York: Academic Press, 1972).

89. E. Kearney, D. Gebert, and S. C. Voelpel, "When and How Diversity Benefits Teams: The Importance of Team Members' Need for Cognition," *Academy of Management Journal* 52 (2009): 581–598.

90. T. Buyl, C. Boone, W. Hendriks, and P. Matthyssens, "Top Management Team Functional Diversity and Firm Performance: The Moderating Role of CEO Characteristics," *Journal of Management Studies* 48 (2011): 151–176.

10

1. H. A. Simon, *The New Science of Management Decision* (New York: Harper & Row, 1960).

2. R. Walker, "Brand Blue," *Fortune* (April 28, 2003): http://www.fortune.com/fortune /smallbusiness/articles/0,15114,426909,00.html.

3. G. Huber, *Managerial Decision Making* (Glenview, Ill.: Scott, Foresman, 1980).

4. H. A. Simon, *Administrative Behavior* (New York: Macmillan, 1957).

5. E. F. Harrison, *The Managerial Decision-Making Process* (Boston: Houghton Mifflin, 1981).

6. R. L. Ackoff, "The Art and Science of Mess Management," *Interfaces* (February 1981): 20–26.

7. J. S. Lerner, Y. Li, P. Valdesolo, and K. S. Kassam, "Emotion and Decision Making," *Annual Review of Psychology* 66 (2015): 799–823.

8. B. M. Staw, "Knee-Deep in the Big Muddy: A Study of Escalating Commitment to a Chosen Course of Action," *Organizational Behavior and Human Performance* 16 (1976): 27–44; B. M. Staw, "The Escalation of Commitment to a Course of Action," *Academy of Management Review* 6 (1981): 577–587.

9. B. M. Staw and J. Ross, "Understanding Behavior in Escalation Situations," *Science* 246 (1989): 216–220.

10. R. L. Schaumberg and S. S. Wiltermuth, "Desire for a Positive Moral Self-Regard Exacerbates Escalation of Commitment to Initiatives with Prosocial Aims," *Organizational Behavior and Human Decision Processes* 123 (2014): 110–123.

11. L. Festinger, *A Theory of Cognitive Dissonance* (Evanston, Ill.: Row, Peterson, 1957).

12. B. M. Staw, "The Escalation of Commitment: An Update and Appraisal," in Z. Shapira, ed., *Organizational Decision Making* (Cambridge, England: Cambridge University Press, 1997).

13. D. M. Boehne and P. W. Paese, "Deciding Whether to Complete or Terminate an Unfinished Project: A Strong Test of the Project Completion Hypothesis," *Organizational Behavior and Human Decision Processes* 81 (2000): 178–194; H. Moon, "Looking Forward and Looking Back: Integrating Completion and Sunk Cost Effects within an Escalation-of-Commitment Progress Decision," *Journal of Applied Psychology* 86 (2000): 104–113.

14. J. A. Sonnenfeld, "How Rick Wagoner Lost GM," *BusinessWeek* (June 1, 2009), http://www .businessweek.com/managing/content/jun2009 /ca2009061_966638.htm.

15. N. Sivanathan, D. C. Molden, A. D. Galinsky, and G. Ku, "The Promise and Peril of Self-Affirmation in the De-Escalation of Commitment," *Organizational Behavior and Human Decision Processes* 107 (2008): 1–14.

16. A. C. Hafenbrack, Z. Kinias, and S. G. Barsade, "Debiasing the Mind through Meditation: Mindfulness and the Sunk-Cost Bias," *Psychological Science* 25 (2014): 369–376.

17. G. Whyte, "Diffusion of Responsibility: Effects on the Escalation Tendency," *Journal of Applied Psychology* 76 (1991): 408–415.

18. D. van Knippenberg, B. van Knippenberg, and E. van Dijk, "Who Takes the Lead in Risky Decision Making? Effects of Group Members' Risk Preferences and Prototypicality," *Organizational Behavior and Human Decision Processes* 83 (2000): 213–234.

19. K. R. MacCrimmon and D. Wehrung, *Taking Risks* (New York: Free Press, 1986).

20. T. S. Perry, "How Small Firms Innovate: Designing a Culture for Creativity," *Research Technology Management* 28 (1995): 14–17.

21. A. Saleh, "Brain Hemisphericity and Academic Majors: A Correlation Study," *College Student Journal* 35 (2001): 193–200.

22. N. Khatri, "The Role of Intuition in Strategic Decision Making," *Human Relations* 53 (2000): 57–86.

23. H. Mintzberg, "Planning on the Left Side and Managing on the Right," *Harvard Business Review* 54 (1976): 51–63.

24. D. J. Isenberg, "How Senior Managers Think," *Harvard Business Review* 62 (1984): 81–90.

25. R. N. Beck, "Visions, Values, and Strategies: Changing Attitudes and Culture," *Academy of Management Executive* 1 (1987): 33–41.

26. K. G. Ross, G. A. Klein, P. Thunholm, J. F. Schmitt, and H. C. Baxter, "The Recognition-Primed Decision Model," *Military Review*, Fort Leavenworth 84 (2004): 6–10.

27. C. I. Barnard, *The Functions of the Executive* (Cambridge, Mass.: Harvard University Press, 1938).

28. R. Rowan, *The Intuitive Manager* (New York: Little, Brown, 1986).

29. W. H. Agor, *Intuition in Organizations* (Newbury Park, Calif.: Sage, 1989).

30. D. J. Isenberg, "How Senior Managers Think" (Thousand Oaks, CA: Sage Publications, 1991).

31. H. A. Simon, "Making Management Decisions: The Role of Intuition and Emotion," *Academy of Management Executive* 1 (1987): 57–64.

32. J. L. Redford, R. H. McPhierson, R. G. Frankiewicz, and J. Gaa, "Intuition and Moral Development," *Journal of Psychology* 129 (1994): 91–101.

33. R. Wild, "Naked Hunch; Gut Instinct Is Vital to Your Business," *Success* (June 1998), http://www.findarticles.com/cf_dls/m3514/n6 _v45/20746158/p1/article.jhtml.

34. W. H. Agor, "How Top Executives Use Their Intuition to Make Important Decisions," *Business Horizons* 29 (1986): 49–53.

35. O. Behling and N. L. Eckel, "Making Sense out of Intuition," *Academy of Management Executive* 5 (1991): 46–54.

36. L. R. Beach, *Image Theory: Decision Making in Personal and Organizational Contexts* (Chichester, England: Wiley, 1990).

37. E. Bonabeau, "Don't Trust Your Gut," *Harvard Business Review* 81 (2003): 116–126.

38. L. Livingstone, "Person-Environment Fit on the Dimension of Creativity: Relationships with Strain, Job Satisfaction, and Performance" (Ph.D. diss., Oklahoma State University, 1992).

39. G. Wallas, *The Art of Thought* (New York: Harcourt Brace, 1926).

40. H. Benson and W. Proctor, *The Break-Out Principle* (Scribner: New York, 2003); G. L. Fricchione, B. T. Slingsby, and H. Benson, "The Placebo Effect and the Relaxation Response: Neural Processes and Their Coupling to Constitutive Nitric Oxide," *Brain Research Reviews* 35 (2001): 1–19.

41. M. D. Mumford and S. B. Gustafson, "Creativity Syndrome: Integration, Application, and Innovation," *Psychological Bulletin* 103 (1988): 27–43.

42. T. Poze, "Analogical Connections—The Essence of Creativity," *Journal of Creative Behavior* 17 (1983): 240–241.

43. I. Sladeczek and G. Domino, "Creativity, Sleep, and Primary Process Thinking in Dreams," *Journal of Creative Behavior* 19 (1985): 38–46.

44. F. Barron and D. M. Harrington, "Creativity, Intelligence, and Personality," *Annual Review of Psychology* 32 (1981): 439–476.

45. R. J. Sternberg, "A Three-Faced Model of Creativity," in R. J. Sternberg, ed., *The Nature of Creativity* (Cambridge, England: Cambridge University Press, 1988): 125–147.

46. A. M. Grant and J. W. Berry, "The Necessity of Others Is the Mother of Invention: Intrinsic and Prosocial Motivations, Perspective Taking, and Creativity," *Academy of Management Journal* 54, No. 1 (2011): 73–96.

47. A. M. Isen, "Positive Affect and Decision Making," in W. M. Goldstein and R. M. Hogarth, eds., *Research on Judgment and Decision Making* (Cambridge, England: Cambridge University Press, 1997).

48. G. L. Clore, N. Schwartz, and M. Conway, "Cognitive Causes and Consequences of Emotion," in R. S. Wyer and T. K. Srull, eds., *Handbook of Social Cognition* (Hillsdale, N.J.: Erlbaum, 1994): 323–417.

49. B. L. Frederickson, "What Good Are Positive Emotions?" *Review of General Psychology* 2 (1998): 300–319; B. L. Frederickson, "The Role of Positive Emotions in Positive Psychology," *American Psychologist* 56 (2001): 218–226.

50. T. M. Amabile, S. G. Barsade, J. S. Mueller, and B. M. Staw, "Affect and Creativity at Work," *Administrative Science Quarterly* 50, No. 3 (2005): 367–403.

51. J. Zhou, "When the Presence of Creative Coworkers Is Related to Creativity: Role of Supervisor Close Monitoring, Developmental Feedback, and Creative Personality," *Journal of Applied Psychology* 88 (2003): 413–422.

52. C. Axtell, D. Holman, K. Unsworth, T. Wall, and P. Waterson, "Shopfloor Innovation: Facilitating the Suggestion and Implementation of Ideas," *Journal of Occupational Psychology* 73 (2000): 265–285.

53. B. Kijkuit and J. van den Ende, "The Organizational Life of an Idea: Integrating Social Network, Creativity and Decision-Making Perspectives," *Journal of Management Studies* 44, No. 6 (2007): 863–882.

54. T. M. Amabile, R. Conti, H. Coon, J. Lazenby, and M. Herron, "Assessing the Work Environment for Creativity," *Academy of Management Journal* 39 (1996): 1154–1184.

55. T. Tetenbaum and H. Tetenbaum, "Office 2000: Tear Down the Wall," *Training* (February 2000): 58–64.

56. L. Livingstone, D. L. Nelson, and S.H. Barr, "Person-Environment Fit and Creativity: An Examination of Supply-Value and Demand-Ability Versions of Fit," *Journal of Management* 23 (1997): 119–146.

57. R. L. Firestein, "Effects of Creative Problem-Solving Training on Communication Behaviors in Small Groups," *Small Group Research* (November 1989): 507–521.

58. R. Von Oech, *A Whack on the Side of the Head* (New York: Warner, 1983).

59. A. G. Robinson and S. Stern, *How Innovation and Improvement Actually Happen* (San Francisco: Berrett Koehler, 1997).

60. M. F. R. Kets de Vries, R. Branson, and P. Barnevik, "Charisma in Action: The Transformational Abilities of Virgin's Richard Branson and ABBS's Percy Barnevik," *Organizational Dynamics* 26 (1998): 7–21.

61. R. Y. J. Chua, Y. Roth, and J. Lemoine, "How Culture Impacts Creativity: Cultural Tightness, Cultural Distance, and Global Creative Work," *Administrative Science Quarterly*, in press, published online December 8, 2014.

62. G. Stasser, L. A. Taylor, and C. Hanna, "Information Sampling in Structured and Unstructured Discussion of Three- and Six-Person Groups," *Journal of Personality and Social Psychology* 57 (1989): 67–78.

63. E. Kirchler and J. H. Davis, "The Influence of Member Status Differences and Task Type on Group Consensus and Member Position Change," *Journal of Personality and Social Psychology* 51 (1986): 83–91.

64. R. F. Maier, "Assets and Liabilities in Group Problem Solving," *Psychological Review* 74 (1967): 239–249.

65. M. E. Shaw, *Group Dynamics: The Psychology of Small Group Behavior*, 3rd ed. (New York: McGraw-Hill, 1981).

66. P. W. Yetton and P. C. Bottger, "Individual versus Group Problem Solving: An Empirical Test of a Best Member Strategy," *Organizational Behavior and Human Performance* 29 (1982): 307–321.

67. W. Watson, L. Michaelson, and W. Sharp, "Member Competence, Group Interaction, and Group Decision Making: A Longitudinal Study," *Journal of Applied Psychology* 76 (1991): 803–809.

68. I. Janis, *Victims of Groupthink* (Boston: Houghton Mifflin, 1972); M. Kostera, M. Proppe, and M. Szatkowski, "Staging the New Romantic Hero in the Old Cynical Theatre: On Managers, Roles, and Change in Poland," *Journal of Organizational Behavior* 16 (1995): 631–646.

69. M. A. Hogg and S. C. Hains, "Friendship and Group Identification: A New Look at the Role of Cohesiveness in Groupthink," *European Journal of Social Psychology* 28 (1998): 323–341.

70. P. E. Jones and H. M. P. Roelofsma, "The Potential for Social Contextual and Group Biases in Team Decision Making: Biases, Conditions, and Psychological Mechanisms," *Ergonomics* 43 (2000): 1129–1152; J. M. Levine, E. T. Higgins, and H. Choi, "Development of Strategic Norms in Groups," *Organizational Behavior and Human Decision Processes* 82 (2000): 88–101.

71. A. L. Brownstein, "Biased Predecision Processing," *Psychological Bulletin* 129 (2003): 545–568.

72. C. P. Neck and G. Moorhead, "Groupthink Remodeled: The Importance of Leadership, Time Pressure, and Methodical Decision-Making Procedures," *Human Relations* 48 (1995): 537–557.

73. J. Schwartz and M. L. Ward, "Final Shuttle Report Cites 'Broken Safety Culture' at NASA," *The New York Times* (August 26, 2003), http://www.nytimes.com/2003/08/26/national/26CND-SHUT.html?ex=1077253200&en=882575f2c 17ed8ff&ei=5070; C. Ferraris and R. Carveth, "NASA and the Columbia Disaster: Decision Making by Groupthink?" in Proceedings of the 2003 Convention of the Association for Business Communication Annual Convention, http://www.businesscommunication.org/conventions/Proceedings/2003/PDF/03ABC03.pdf.

74. V. Anand, B. E Ashforth, and M. Joshi, "Business as Usual: The Acceptance and Perpetuation of Corruption in Organizations," *Academy of Management Executive* 19 (2005): 9–23.

75. A. C. Homan, D. van Knippenberg, G. A. Van Kleef, and K. W. C. De Dreu, "Bridging Faultlines by Valuing Diversity: Diversity Beliefs, Information Elaboration, and Performance in Diverse Work Groups," *Journal of Applied Psychology* 92, No. 5 (2007):1189–1199.

76. G. Moorhead, R. Ference, and C. P. Neck, "Group Decision Fiascoes Continue: Space Shuttle *Challenger* and a Revised Groupthink Framework," *Human Relations* 44 (1991): 539–550.

77. J. R. Montanari and G. Moorhead, "Development of the Groupthink Assessment Inventory," *Educational and Psychological Measurement* 49 (1989): 209–219.

78. P. Hart, "Irving L. Janis' Victims of Groupthink," *Political Psychology* 12 (1991): 247–278.

79. A. C. Mooney, P. J. Holahan, and A. C. Amason, "Don't Take It Personally: Exploring Cognitive Conflict as a Mediator of Affective Conflict," *Journal of Management Studies* 44, No. 5 (2007): 733–758.

80. J. A. F. Stoner, "Risky and Cautious Shifts in Group Decisions: The Influence of Widely Held Values," *Journal of Experimental Social Psychology* 4 (1968): 442–459.

81. S. Moscovici and M. Zavalloni, "The Group as a Polarizer of Attitudes," *Journal of Personality and Social Psychology* 12 (1969): 125–135.

82. G. R. Goethals and M. P. Zanna, "The Role of Social Comparison in Choice of Shifts," *Journal of Personality and Social Psychology* 37 (1979): 1469–1476.

83. A. Vinokur and E. Burnstein, "Effects of Partially Shared Persuasive Arguments on Group-Induced Shifts: A Problem-Solving Approach," *Journal of Personality and Social Psychology* 29 (1974): 305–315; J. Pfeffer, "Seven Practices of Successful Organizations," *California Management Review* 40 (1998): 96–124.

84. J. K. Palmer and J. M. Loveland, "The Influence of Group Discussion on Performance Judgments: Rating Accuracy, Contrast Effects and Halo," *The Journal of Psychology: Interdisciplinary and Applied* 142 (2008): 117–130.

85. P. Paulus, N. W. Kohn, L. E. Arditti, and R. Korde, "Understanding the Group Size Effect in Electronic Brainstorming," *Small Group Research* 44 (2013): 332–352.

86. N. Michinov, E. Jamet, N. Metayer, and B. L. Henaff, "The Eyes of Creativity: Impact of Social Comparison and Individual Creativity on Performance and Attention to Others' Ideas During Electronic Brainstorming," *Computers in Human Behavior* 42 (2015): 57–67.

87. A. Van de Ven and A. Delbecq, "The Effectiveness of Nominal, Delphi and

Interacting Group Decision-Making Processes," *Academy of Management Journal* 17 (1974): 605–621.

88. R. A. Cosier and C. R. Schwenk, "Agreement and Thinking Alike: Ingredients for Poor Decisions," *Academy of Management Executive* 4 (1990): 69–74.

89. D. M. Schweiger, W. R. Sandburg, and J. W. Ragan, "Group Approaches for Improving Strategic Decision Making: A Comparative Analysis of Dialectical Inquiry, Devil's Advocacy, and Consensus," *Academy of Management Journal* 29 (1986): 149–159.

90. G. Whyte, "Decision Failures: Why They Occur and How to Prevent Them," *Academy of Management Executive* 5 (1991): 23–31.

91. L. Scholten, D. van Knippenberg, B. A. Nijstad, and K. W. C. De Dreu, "Motivated Information Processing and Group Decision-Making: Effects of Process Accountability on Information Processing and Decision Quality," *Journal of Experimental Social Psychology* 43, No. 4 (2007): 539–552.

92. E. E. Lawler III and S. A. Mohrman, "Quality Circles: After the Honeymoon," *Organizational Dynamics* (Spring 1987): 42–54.

93. T. L. Tang and E. A. Butler, "Attributions of Quality Circles' Problem-Solving Failure: Differences among Management, Supporting Staff, and Quality Circle Members," *Public Personnel Management* 26 (1997): 203–225.

94. J. Schilder, "Work Teams Boost Productivity," *Personnel Journal* 71 (1992): 67–72.

95. L. I. Glassop, "The Organizational Benefits of Teams," *Human Relations* 55 (2002): 225–249.

96. C. J. Nemeth, "Managing Innovation: When Less Is More," *California Management Review* 40 (1997): 59–68.

97. N. Adler, *International Dimensions of Organizational Behavior*, 3rd ed. (Mason, Ohio: South-Western, 1997).

98. K. W. Phillips and D. L. Lloyd, "When Surface- and Deep-Level Diversity Collide: The Effects on Dissenting Group Members," *Organizational Behavior and Human Decision Processes* 99, No. 2 (2006): 143–160.

99. T. Simons, L. H. Pelled, and K. A. Smith, "Making Use of Difference: Diversity, Debate, and Decision Comprehensiveness in Top Management Teams," *Academy of Management Journal* 42, No. 6 (1999): 662–673.

100. S. Elbanna and J. Child, "The Influence of Decision, Environmental and Firm Characteristics on the Rationality of Strategic Decision-Making," *Journal of Management Studies* 44, No. 4 (2007): 561–591.

101. J. Pfeffer, "Seven Practices of Successful Organizations," *California Management Review* 40 (1998): 96–124.

102. L. A. Witt, M. C. Andrews, and K. M. Kacmar, "The Role of Participation in Decision Making in the Organizational Politics–Job Satisfaction Relationship," *Human Relations* 53 (2000): 341–358.

103. J. He and W. R. King, "The Role of User Participation in Information Systems Development: Implications from a Meta-Analysis," *Journal of Management Information Systems* 25 (2008): 301–331.

104. C. R. Leana, E. A. Locke, and D. M. Schweiger, "Fact and Fiction in Analyzing Research on Participative Decision Making: A Critique of Cotton, Vollrath, Froggatt, Lengnick-Hall, and Jennings," *Academy of Management Review* 15 (1990): 137–146; J. L. Cotton, D. A. Vollrath, M. L. Lengnick-Hall, and K. L. Froggatt, "Fact: The Form of Participation Does Matter—A Rebuttal to Leana, Locke, and Schweiger," *Academy of Management Review* 15 (1990): 147–153.

105. T. W. Malone, "Is Empowerment Just a Fad? Control, Decision Making, and Information Technology," *Sloan Management Review* 38 (1997): 23–35.

106. IBM Customer Success Stories, "City and County of San Francisco Lower Total Cost of Ownership and Build on Demand Foundation" (February 3, 2004), http://www-306.ibm.com/software/success/cssdb.nsf/cs/LWRT-5VTLM2?OpenDocument&Site=lotusmandc.

107. T. L. Brown, "Fearful of 'Empowerment': Should Managers Be Terrified?" *Industry Week* (June 18, 1990): 12.

108. P. G. Gyllenhammar, *People at Work* (Reading, Mass.: Addison-Wesley, 1977).

109. R. Tannenbaum and F. Massarik, "Participation by Subordinates in the Managerial Decision-Making Process," *Canadian Journal of Economics and Political Science* 16 (1950): 408–418.

110. H. Levinson, *Executive* (Cambridge, Mass.: Harvard University Press, 1981).

111. R. F. Maier, "Assets and Liabilities in Group Problem Solving," *Psychological Review* 74 (1967): 239–249.

11

1. G. C. Homans, "Social Behavior as Exchange," *American Journal of Sociology* 63 (1958): 597–606.

2. R. D. Middlemist and M. A. Hitt, *Organizational Behavior: Managerial Strategies for Performance* (St. Paul, Minn.: West Publishing, 1988).

3. C. Barnard, *The Functions of the Executive* (Cambridge, Mass.: Harvard University Press, 1938).

4. J. R. P. French and B. Raven, "The Bases of Social Power," in D. Cartwright, ed., *Group Dynamics: Research and Theory* (Evanston, Ill.: Row Peterson, 1962); T. R. Hinkin and C. A. Schriesheim, "Development and Application of New Scales to Measure the French and Raven (1959) Bases of Social Power," *Journal of Applied Psychology* 74 (1989): 561–567.

5. K. D. Elsbach and G. Elofson, "How the Packaging of Decision Explanations Affects Perceptions of Trustworthiness," *Academy of Management Journal* 43, No. 1 (2000): 80–89.

6. P. M. Podsakoff and C. A. Schriesheim, "Field Studies of French and Raven's Bases of Power: Critique, Reanalysis, and Suggestions for Future Research," *Psychological Bulletin* 97 (1985): 387–411.

7. M. A. Rahim, "Relationships of Leader Power to Compliance and Satisfaction with Supervision: Evidence from a National Sample of Managers," *Journal of Management* 15 (1989): 545–556.

8. C. Argyris, "Management Information Systems: The Challenge to Rationality and Emotionality," *Management Science* 17 (1971): 275–292; J. Naisbitt and P. Aburdene, *Megatrends 2000* (New York: Morrow, 1990).

9. P. P. Carson, K. D. Carson, E. L. Knight, and C. W. Roe, "Power in Organizations: A Look through the TQM Lens," *Quality Progress* (November 1995): 73–78.

10. K. Kruse, "Why Pepsi's CEO Writes to Her Employees' Parents," *Forbes*, February 6, 2014, accessed at http://www.forbes.com/sites/kevinkruse/2014/02/06/indra-nooyi-wholehearted-leader/.

11. J. Pfeffer and G. Salancik, *The External Control of Organizations* (New York: Harper & Row, 1978).

12. T. M. Welbourne and C. O. Trevor, "The Roles of Departmental and Position Power in Job Evaluation," *Academy of Management Journal* 43, No. 4 (2000): 761–771.

13. R. H. Miles, *Macro Organizational Behavior* (Glenview, Ill.: Scott, Foresman, 1980).

14. D. Hickson, C. Hinings, C. Lee, R. E. Schneck, and J. M. Pennings, "A Strategic Contingencies Theory of Intraorganizational Power," *Administrative Science Quarterly* 14 (1971): 219–220.

15. C. R. Hinings, D. J. Hickson, J. M. Pennings, and R. E. Schneck, "Structural Conditions of Intraorganizational Power," *Administrative Science Quarterly* 19 (1974): 22–44.

16. M. Velasquez, D. J. Moberg, and G. F. Cavanaugh, "Organizational Statesmanship and Dirty Politics: Ethical Guidelines for the Organizational Politician," *Organizational Dynamics* 11 (1982): 65–79.

17. D. E. McClelland, *Power: The Inner Experience* (New York: Irvington, 1975).

18. N. Shahinpoor and B. F. Matt, "The Power of One: Dissent and Organizational Life," *Journal of Business Ethics* 74, No. 1 (2007): 37–49.

19. N. Machiavelli, *The Prince*, trans. by G. Bull (Middlesex, England: Penguin Books, 1961).

20. S. Chen, A. Y. Lee-Chai, and J. A. Bargh, "Relationship Orientation as a Moderator of the Effects of Social Power," *Journal of Personality and Social Psychology* 80, No. 2 (2001): 173–187.

21. R. Kanter, "Power Failure in Management Circuits," *Harvard Business Review* (July–August 1979): 31–54.

22. F. Lee and L. Z. Tiedens, "Who's Being Served? 'Self-Serving' Attributions in Social Hierarchies," *Organizational Behavior and*

Human Decision Processes 84, No. 2 (March 2001): 254–287.

23. M. Korda, *Power: How to Get It, How to Use It* (New York: Random House, 1975).

24. S. R. Thye, "A Status Value Theory of Power in Exchange Relations," *American Sociological Review* (2000): 407–432.

25. B. T. Mayes and R. T. Allen, "Toward a Definition of Organizational Politics," *Academy of Management Review* 2 (1977): 672–678.

26. M. Valle and P. L. Perrewe, "Do Politics Perceptions Relate to Political Behaviors? Tests of an Implicit Assumption and Expanded Model," *Human Relations* 53 (2000): 359–386.

27. W. A. Hochwarter, "The Interactive Effects of Pro-Political Behavior and Politics Perceptions on Job Satisfaction and Affective Commitment," *Journal of Applied Social Psychology* 33 (2003): 1360–1378.

28. W. A. Hochwarter, "The Interactive Effects of Pro-Political Behavior and Politics Perceptions on Job Satisfaction and Affective Commitment," *Journal of Applied Social Psychology* 33 (2003): 1360–1378.

29. W. A. Hochwarter, K. M. Kacmar, D. C. Treadway, and T. S. Watson, "It's All Relative: The Distinction and Prediction of Political Perceptions across Levels," *Journal of Applied Social Psychology* 33 (2003): 1955–2016.

30. D. A. Ralston, "Employee Ingratiation: The Role of Management," *Academy of Management Review* 10 (1985): 477–487; D. R. Beeman and T. W. Sharkey, "The Use and Abuse of Corporate Politics," *Business Horizons* (March–April 1987): 25–35.

31. C. O. Longnecker, H. P. Sims, and D. A. Gioia, "Behind the Mask: The Politics of Employee Appraisal," *Academy of Management Executive* 1 (1987): 183–193.

32. M. Valle and P. L. Perrewe, "Do Politics Perceptions Relate to Political Behaviors? Tests of an Implicit Assumption and Expanded Model," *Human Relations* 53, No. 3 (2000): 359–386.

33. D. Fedor, J. Maslyn, S. Farmer, and K. Bettenhausen, "The Contribution of Positive Politics to the Prediction of Employee Reactions," *Journal of Applied Social Psychology* 38, No. 1 (2008): 76–96.

34. D. Kipnis, S. M. Schmidt, and I. Wilkinson, "Intraorganizational Influence Tactics: Explorations in Getting One's Way," *Journal of Applied Psychology* 65 (1980): 440–452; D. Kipnis, S. Schmidt, C. Swaffin-Smith, and I. Wilkinson, "Patterns of Managerial Influence: Shotgun Managers, Tacticians, and Bystanders," *Organizational Dynamics* (Winter 1984): 60–67; G. Yukl and C. M. Falbe, "Influence Tactics and Objectives in Upward, Downward, and Lateral Influence Attempts," *Journal of Applied Psychology* 75 (1990): 132–140.

35. G. R. Ferris and T. A. Judge, "Personnel/Human Resources Management: A Political Influence Perspective," *Journal of Management* 17 (1991): 447–488.

36. G. Yukl, P. J. Guinan, and D. Sottolano, "Influence Tactics Used for Different Objectives with Subordinates, Peers, and Superiors," *Groups & Organization Management* 20 (1995): 272–296.

37. C. A. Higgins, T. A. Judge, and G. R. Ferris, "Influence Tactics and Work Outcomes: A Meta-Analysis," *Journal of Organizational Behavior* 24 (2003): 89–106.

38. K. K. Eastman, "In the Eyes of the Beholder: An Attributional Approach to Ingratiation and Organizational Citizenship Behavior," *Academy of Management Journal* 37 (1994): 1379–1391.

39. K. J. Harris, K. M. Kacmar, S. Zivnuska, and J. D Shaw, "The Impact of Political Skill on Impression Management Effectiveness," *Journal of Applied Psychology* 92, No. 1 (2007): 278–285.

40. D. C. Treadway, G. R. Ferris, A. B. Duke, G. L. Adams, and J. B. Thatcher, "The Moderating Role of Subordinate Political Skill on Supervisors' Impressions of Subordinate Ingratiation and Ratings of Subordinate Interpersonal Facilitation," *Journal of Applied Psychology* 92, No. 3 (2007): 848–855.

41. R. A. Gordon, "Impact of Ingratiation on Judgments and Evaluations: A Meta-Analytic Investigation," *Journal of Personality and Social Psychology* 71 (1996): 54–70.

42. A. Drory and D. Beaty, "Gender Differences in the Perception of Organizational Influence Tactics," *Journal of Organizational Behavior* 12 (1991): 249–258.

43. S. Wellington, M. B. Kropf, and P. R. Gerkovich, "What's Holding Women Back?" *Harvard Business Review* (June 2003): 2–4.

44. P. Perrewe and D. Nelson, "Gender and Career Success: The Facilitative Role of Political Skill," *Organizational Dynamics* 33 (2004): 366–378.

45. R. Y. Hirokawa and A. Miyahara, "A Comparison of Influence Strategies Utilized by Managers in American and Japanese Organizations," *Communication Quarterly* 34 (1986): 250–265.

46. C. Anderson, S. E. Spataro, and F. J. Flynn, "Personality and Organizational Culture as Determinants of Influence," *Journal of Applied Psychology* 93 (May 2008): 702–710.

47. P. David, M. A. Hitt, and J. Gimeno, "The Influence of Activism by Institutional Investors on R&D," *Academy of Management Journal* 44, No. 1 (2001): 144–157.

48. G. R. Ferris, P. L. Perrewe, W. P. Anthony, and D. C. Gilmore, "Political Skill at Work," *Organizational Dynamics* 28 (2000): 25–37.

49. D. C. Treadway, W. A. Hochwarter, G. R. Ferris, C. J. Kacmar, C. Douglas, A. P. Ammeter, and M. R. Buckley, "Leader Political Skill and Employee Reactions," *Leadership Quarterly* 15 (2004): 493–513; K. K. Ahearn, G. R. Ferris, W. A. Hochwarter, C. Douglas, and A. P. Ammeter, "Leader Political Skill and Team Performance," *Journal of Management* 30, No. 3 (2004): 309–327.

50. P. L. Perrewé, K. L. Zellars, G. R. Ferris, A. M. Rossi, C. J. Kacmar, and D. A. Ralston, "Neutralizing Job Stressors: Political Skill as an Antidote to the Dysfunctional Consequences of Role Conflict Stressors," *Academy of Management Journal* 47 (2004): 141–152.

51. K. L. Cullen, A. Gerbasi, and D. Chrobot-Mason, "Thriving in Central Network Positions: The Role of Political Skill," *Journal of Management*, published online February 17, 2015.

52. G. Meisler, "Exploring Emotional Intelligence, Political Skill, and Job Satisfaction," *Employee Relations* 36 (2014): 280–293.

53. D. C. Treadway, G. Adams, T. J. Hanes, P. L. Perrewe, M. J, Magnusen, and G. R. Ferris, "The Roles of Recruiter Political Skill and Performance Resource Leveraging in NCAA Football Recruitment Effectiveness," *Journal of Management* 40 (2014): 1607–1626.

54. S. Y. Todd, K. J. Harris, R. B. Harris, and A. R. Wheeler, "Career Success Implications of Political Skill," *The Journal of Social Psychology* 149, No. 3 (June 2009): 179–204; I. M. Jawahar, J. A. Meurs, G. R. Ferris, and W. A. Hochwarter, "Self-Efficacy and Political Skill as Comparative Predictors of Task and Contextual Performance: A Two-Study Constructive Replication," *Human Performance* 21 (2008): 138–157.

55. K. Kumar and M. S. Thibodeaux, "Organizational Politics and Planned Organizational Change," *Group and Organization Studies* 15 (1990): 354–365.

56. D. Buchanan, "You Stab My back, I'll Stab Yours: Management Experience and Perceptions of Organization Political Behaviour," *British Journal of Management* 19 (March 2008): 49–64.

57. McClelland, *Power*.

58. D.R. Beeman and T.W. Sharkey, "Use and Abuse of Corporate Politics," *Business Horizons* 30 (1987): 26–30.

59. C. P. Parker, R. L. Dipboye, and S. L. Jackson, "Perceptions of Organizational Politics: An Investigation of Antecedents and Consequences," *Journal of Management* 21 (1995): 891–912.

60. S. J. Ashford, N. P. Rothbard, S. K. Piderit, and J. E. Dutton, "Out on a Limb: The Role of Context and Impression Management in Selling Gender-Equity Issues," *Administrative Science Quarterly* 43 (1998): 23–57.

61. J. Zhou and G. R. Ferris, "The Dimensions and Consequences of Organizational Politics Perceptions: A Confirmatory Analysis," *Journal of Applied Social Psychology* 25 (1995): 1747–1764.

62. M. L. Seidal, J. T. Polzer, and K. J. Stewart, "Friends in High Places: The Effects of Social Networks on Discrimination in Salary Negotiations," *Administrative Science Quarterly* 45 (2000): 1–24.

63. J. J. Gabarro and J. P. Kotter, "Managing Your Boss," *Harvard Business Review* (January–February 1980): 92–100.

64. P. Newman, "How to Manage Your Boss," *Peat, Marwick, Mitchell & Company's Management Focus* (May–June 1980): 36–37.

65. F. Bertolome, "When You Think the Boss Is Wrong," *Personnel Journal* 69 (1990): 66–73.

66. J. Conger and R. Kanungo, *Charismatic Leadership: The Elusive Factor in Organizational Effectiveness* (New York: Jossey-Bass, 1988).

67. G. M. Spreitzer, M. A. Kizilos, and S. W. Nason, "A Dimensional Analysis of the Relationship between Psychological Empowerment and Effectiveness, Satisfaction, and Strain," *Journal of Management* 23 (1997): 679–704.

68. N. M. Lorinkova and S. J. Perry, "When Is Empowerment Effective? The Role of Leader-Leader Exchange in Empowering Leadership, Cynicism and Time Theft," *Journal of Management*, published online November 26, 2014.

69. R. C. Ford and M. D. Fottler, "Empowerment: A Matter of Degree," *Academy of Management Executive* 9 (1995): 21–31.

70. M. R. Kukenberger, J. E. Mathieu, and T. Ruddy, "A Cross-Level Test of Empowerment and Process Influences on Members' Informal Learning and Team Commitment," *Journal of Management* 41 (2015): 987–1016.

71. X. Zhang and K. M. Bartol, "Linking Empowering Leadership and Employee Creativity: The Influence of Psychological Empowerment, Intrinsic Motivation, and Creative Process Engagement," *The Academy of Management Journal* 53 (2010): 107–128; S. Seibert, G. Wang, and S. Courtright, "Antecedents and Consequences of Psychological and Team Empowerment in Organizations: A Meta-Analytic Review," *The Journal of Applied Psychology* 96, No. 5 (2011): 981–1003.

72. J. Simons, "Merck's Man in the Hot Seat," *Fortune* (February 23, 2004): 111–114.

12

1. J. P. Kotter, "What Leaders Really Do," *Harvard Business Review* 68 (1990): 103–111.

2. D. A. Plowman, S. Solansky, T. E Beck, L. Baker, M. Kulkarni, and D. V. Travis, "The Role of Leadership in Emergent, Self-Organization," *Leadership Quarterly* 18, No. 4 (2007): 341–356.

3. B. Stone, "Why Facebook Needs Sheryl Sandberg," *Bloomberg Businessweek* (May 12, 2011), http://www.businessweek.com/magazine/content/11_21/b4229050473695.htm.

4. A. Zaleznik, "HBR Classic—Managers and Leaders: Are They Different?" *Harvard Business Review* 70 (1992): 126–135.

5. W. G. Rowe, "Creating Wealth in Organizations: The Role of Strategic Leadership," *Academy of Management Executive* 15 (2001): 81–94.

6. R. M. Stogdill, "Personal Factors Associated with Leadership: A Survey of the Literature," *Journal of Psychology* 25 (1948): 35–71.

7. K. Lewin, R. Lippitt, and R. K. White, "Patterns of Aggressive Behavior in Experimentally Created 'Social Climates,'" *Journal of Social Psychology* 10 (1939): 271–299.

8. S. D. Sidle, "The Danger of Do Nothing Leaders," *The Academy of Management Perspectives* 21, No. 2 (2007): 75–77.

9. A. W. Halpin and J. Winer, "A Factorial Study of the Leader Behavior Description Questionnaire," in R. M. Stogdill and A. E. Coons, eds., *Leader Behavior: Its Description and Measurement,* research monograph No. 88 (Columbus, Ohio: Bureau of Business Research, The Ohio State University, 1957): 39–51.

10. E. A. Fleishman, "Leadership Climate, Human Relations Training, and Supervisory Behavior," *Personnel Psychology* 6 (1953): 205–222.

11. R. Kahn and D. Katz, "Leadership Practices in Relation to Productivity and Morale," in D. Cartwright and A. Zander, eds., *Group Dynamics, Research and Theory* (Elmsford, NY: Row, Paterson, 1960).

12. R. R. Blake and J. S. Mouton, *The Managerial Grid III: The Key to Leadership Excellence* (Houston: Gulf, 1985).

13. W. Vandekerckhove and R. Commers, "Downward Workplace Mobbing: A Sign of the Times?" *Journal of Business Ethics* 45 (2003): 41–50.

14. F. E. Fiedler, *A Theory of Leader Effectiveness* (New York: McGraw-Hill, 1964).

15. F. E. Fiedler, *Personality, Motivational Systems, and Behavior of High and Low LPC Persons,* tech. rep. No. 70-12 (Seattle: University of Washington, 1970).

16. J. T. McMahon, "The Contingency Theory: Logic and Method Revisited," *Personnel Psychology* 25 (1972): 697–710; L. H. Peters, D. D. Hartke, and J. T. Pohlman, "Fiedler's Contingency Theory of Leadership: An Application of the Meta-Analysis Procedures of Schmidt and Hunter," *Psychological Bulletin* 97 (1985): 224–285.

17. F. E. Fiedler, "The Contingency Model and the Dynamics of the Leadership Process," in L. Berkowitz, ed., *Advances in Experimental and Social Psychology,* vol. 11 (New York: Academic Press, 1978).

18. S. Arin and C. McDermott, "The Effect of Team Leader Characteristics on Learning, Knowledge Application, and Performance of Cross-Functional New Product Development Teams," *Decision Sciences* 34 (2003): 707–739.

19. F. E. Fiedler, "Engineering the Job to Fit the Manager," *Harvard Business Review* 43 (1965): 115–122.

20. R. J. House, "A Path–Goal Theory of Leader Effectiveness," *Administrative Science Quarterly* 16 (1971): 321–338; R. J. House and T. R. Mitchell, "Path–Goal Theory of Leadership," *Journal of Contemporary Business* 3 (1974): 81–97.

21. C. A. Schriescheim and V. M. Von Glinow, "The Path–Goal Theory of Leadership: A Theoretical and Empirical Analysis," *Academy of Management Journal* 20 (1977): 398–405; E. Valenzi and G. Dessler, "Relationships of Leader Behavior, Subordinate Role Ambiguity, and Subordinate Job Satisfaction," *Academy of Management Journal* 21 (1978): 671–678; N. R. F. Maier, *Leadership Methods and Skills* (New York: McGraw-Hill, 1963).

22. J. P. Grinnell, "An Empirical Investigation of CEO Leadership in Two Types of Small Firms," *S.A.M. Advanced Management Journal* 68 (2003): 36–41.

23. V. H. Vroom and P. W. Yetton, *Leadership and Decision Making* (Pittsburgh: University of Pittsburgh, 1973).

24. V. H. Vroom, "Leadership and the Decision-Making Process," *Organizational Dynamics* 28 (2000): 82–94.

25. P. Hersey and K. H. Blanchard, "Life Cycle Theory of Leadership," *Training and Development* 23 (1969): 26–34; P. Hersey, K. H. Blanchard, and D. E. Johnson, *Management of Organizational Behavior: Leading Human Resources,* 8th ed. (Upper Saddle River, N.J.: Prentice-Hall, 2001).

26. B. M. Bass, *Bass and Stogdill's Handbook of Leadership: Theory, Research, and Managerial Applications,* 3rd ed. (New York: Free Press, 1990).

27. G. B. Graen and M. Uhl-Bien, "Relationship-Based Approach to Leadership: Development of Leader–Member Exchange (LMX) Theory of Leadership over 25 Years," *Leadership Quarterly* 6 (1995): 219–247; C. R. Gerstner and D. V. Day, "Meta-Analytic Review of Leader–Member Exchange Theory: Correlates and Construct Issues," *Journal of Applied Psychology* 82 (1997): 827–844; R. C. Liden, S. J. Wayne, and R. T. Sparrowe, "An Examination of the Mediating Role of Psychological Empowerment on the Relations between the Job, Interpersonal Relationships, and Work Outcomes," *Journal of Applied Psychology* 85 (2001): 407–416.

28. J. Townsend, J. S. Phillips, and T. J. Elkins, "Employee Retaliation: The Neglected Consequence of Poor Leader–Member Exchange Relations," *Journal of Occupational Health Psychology* 5 (2000): 457–463.

29. D. Nelson, R. Basu, and R. Purdie, "An Examination of Exchange Quality and Work Stressors in Leader–Follower Dyads," *International Journal of Stress Management* 5 (1998): 103–112.

30. K. M. Kacmar, L. A. Witt, S. Zivnuska, and S. M. Gully, "The Interactive Effect of Leader–Member Exchange and Communication Frequency on Performance Ratings," *Journal of Applied Psychology* 88 (2003): 764–772.

31. T. Y. Kim and J. M. Diefendorff, "Leader-Member Exchange and Job Performance: The Effects of Taking Charge and Organizational Tenure," *Journal of Organizational Behavior* 36 (2015): 216–231.

32. H. Liao, D. Liu, and R. Loi, "Looking at Both Sides of the Social Exchange Coin: A Social Cognitive Perspective on the Joint Effects of Relationship Quality and Differentiation on Creativity," *Academy of Management Journal* 53 (2010): 1090–1109.

33. P. Molenberghs, G. Prochilo, N. K. Steffens, and S. A. Haslam, "The Neuroscience of

Inspirational Leadership: The Importance of Collective-Oriented Language and Shared Group Membership," *Journal of Management*, published online January 9, 2015.

34. J. M. Burns, *Leadership* (New York: Harper & Row, 1978); T. O. Jacobs, *Leadership and Exchange in Formal Organizations* (Alexandria, Va.: Human Resources Research Organization, 1971).

35. B. M. Bass, "From Transactional to Transformational Leadership: Learning to Share the Vision," *Organizational Dynamics* 19 (1990): 19–31; B. M. Bass, *Leadership and Performance beyond Expectations* (New York: Free Press, 1985).

36. P. M. Podsakoff, S. B. MacKenzie, and W. H. Bommer, "Transformational Leader Behaviors and Substitutes for Leadership as Determinants of Employee Satisfaction, Commitment, Trust, and Organizational Citizenship Behaviors," *Journal of Management* 22 (1996): 259–298.

37. W. Bennis, "Managing the Dream: Leadership in the 21st Century," *Training* 27 (1990): 43–48; P. M. Podsakoff, S. B. MacKenzie, R. H. Moorman, and R. Fetter, "Transformational Leader Behaviors and Their Effects on Followers' Trust in Leader, Satisfaction, and Organizational Citizenship Behaviors," *Leadership Quarterly* 1 (1990): 107–142.

38. MyPrimeTime, Inc., "Great Entrepreneurs—Biography: Howard Schultz, Starbucks," http://www.myprimetime.com/work/ge/schultz-bio/index.shtml.

39. X. H. F. Wang and J. M. Howell, "Exploring the Dual-Level Effects of Transformational Leadership on Followers," *Journal of Applied Psychology* 95 (2010): 1134–1144.

40. C. P. Egri and S. Herman, "Leadership in the North American Environmental Sector: Values, Leadership Styles, and Contexts of Environmental Leaders and Their Organizations," *Academy of Management Journal* 43 (2000): 571–604.

41. T. A. Judge and J. E. Bono, "Five-Factor Model of Personality and Transformational Leadership," *Journal of Applied Psychology* 85 (2001): 751–765.

42. J. E. Bono and T. A. Judge, "Self-Concordance at Work: Toward Understanding the Motivational Effects of Transformational Leaders," *Academy of Management Journal* 46 (2003): 554–571.

43. The Jargon Dictionary, "The R Terms: Reality-Distortion Field," http://info.astrian.net/jargon/terms/r/reality-distortion_field.html.

44. R. J. House and M. L. Baetz, "Leadership: Some Empirical Generalizations and New Research Directions," in B. M. Staw, ed., *Research in Organizational Behavior,* vol. 1 (Greenwood, Conn.: JAI Press, 1979): 399–401.

45. J. M. Howell, "Two Faces of Charisma: Socialized and Personalized Leadership in Organizations," in J. A. Conger, ed., *Charismatic Leadership: Behind the Mystique of Exceptional Leadership* (San Francisco: Jossey-Bass, 1988).

46. R. A. Brands, J. Menges, and M. Kilduff, "The Leader in Social Network Schema: Perceptions of Network Structure Affect Gendered Attributions of Charisma," *Organization Science* (2015): in press.

47. F. Luthans and B. J. Avolio, "Authentic Leadership: A Positive Development Approach," in K. S. Cameron, J. E. Dutton, and R. E. Quinn, eds., *Positive Organizational Scholarship: Foundations of a New Discipline* (San Francisco: Berrett-Koehler, 2004): 241–261.

48. W. L. Gardner, B. J. Avolio, F. Luthans, D. R. May, and F. O. Walumbwa, "Can You See the Real Me? A Self-Based Model of Authentic Leader and Follower Development," *The Leadership Quarterly* 16 (2005): 343–372.

49. B. J. Avolio, W. L. Gardner, F. O. Walumbwa, F. Luthans, and D. R. May, "Unlocking the Mask: A Look at the Process by Which Authentic Leaders Impact Follower Attitudes and Behaviors," *The Leadership Quarterly* 15 (2004): 801–823.

50. S. Michie and J. Gooty, "Values, Emotions and Authentic Leadership Behaviors: Will the Real Leader Please Stand Up?" *The Leadership Quarterly* 16 (2005): 441–457.

51. S. Michie and D. L. Nelson, "The Effects of Leader Compassion Display on Follower Attributions: Building a Socialized Leadership Image," Paper presented at the *Academy of Management Conference* in Honolulu, Hawaii (2005).

52. D. Yagil and H. Medler-Liraz, "Feel Free, Be Yourself: Authentic Leadership, Emotional Expression, and Employee Authenticity," *Journal of Leadership and Organizational Studies* 21 (2014): 59–70.

53. S. Liu, J. Laio, and H. Wei, "Authentic Leadership and Whistleblowing: Mediating Roles of Psychological Safety and Personal Identification," *Journal of Business Ethics*, published online January 8, 2015.

54. D. V. Day, J. W. Fleenor, L. E. Atwater, R. E. Sturm, and R. A McKee, "Advances in Leader and Leadership Development: A Review of 25 Years of Research and Theory," *The Leadership Quarterly* 25 (2014): 63–82.

55. D. Goleman, "What Makes a Leader?" *Harvard Business Review* 82 (2004): 82–91.

56. D. Goleman, "Never Stop Learning," *Harvard Business Review* 82 (2004): 28–30.

57. C. L. Gohm, "Mood Regulation and Emotional Intelligence: Individual Differences," *Journal of Personality and Social Psychology* 84 (2003): 594–607.

58. J. Useem, "A Manager for All Seasons," *Fortune* (April 30, 2001): 66–72.

59. R. C. Mayer, J. H. Davis, and F. D. Schoorman, "An Integrative Model of Organizational Trust," *Academy of Management Review* 20 (1995): 709–734.

60. R. S. Dooley and G. E. Fryxell, "Attaining Decision Quality and Commitment from Dissent: The Moderating Effects of Loyalty and Competence in Strategic Decision-Making Teams," *Academy of Management Journal* 42 (1999): 389–402.

61. J. Flint, "Why Rick Wagoner Had to Go," *Forbes* (March 30, 2009), http://www.forbes.com/2009/03/30/rick-wagoner-gm-jerry-flint-business-autos-backseat-driver.html.

62. S. A. Joni, "The Geography of Trust," *Harvard Business Review* 82 (2003): 82–88.

63. M. E. Heilman, C. J. Block, R. F. Martell, and M. C. Simon, "Has Anything Changed? Current Characteristics of Men, Women, and Managers," *Journal of Applied Psychology* 74 (1989): 935–942.

64. A. H. Eagly, S. J. Darau, and M. Makhijani, "Gender and the Effectiveness of Leaders: A Meta-Analysis," *Psychological Bulletin* 117 (1995): 125–145.

65. M. K. Ryan, S. A. Haslam, and T. Postmes, "Reactions to the Glass Cliff: Gender Differences in the Explanations for the Precariousness of Women's Leadership Positions," *Journal of Organizational Change Management* 20, No. 2 (2007): 182–197.

66. J. Hu and R. C. Liden, "Antecedents of Team Potency and Team Effectiveness: An Examination of Goal and Process Clarity and Servant Leadership," *Journal of Applied Psychology* 96, No. 4 (2011): 851–862.

67. R. K. Greenleaf, L. C. Spears, and D. T. Frick, eds., *On Becoming a Servant-Leader* (San Francisco: Jossey-Bass, 1996).

68. A. C. H. Schat, M. R. Frone, and E. K. Kelloway, "Prevalence of Workplace Aggression in the U.S. Workforce: Findings from a National Study," in E. K. Kelloway, J. Barling, and J. J. Hurrell, eds., *Handbook of Workplace Violence* (Thousand Oaks, CA: Sage, 2006): 47–89.

69. B. J. Tepper, C. A. Henle, L. S. Lambert, R. A. Giacalone, and M. K. Duffy, "Abusive Supervision and Subordinates' Organization Deviance," *Journal of Applied Psychology* 93 (2008): 721–732; P. A. Bamberger and S. B. Bacharach, "Abusive Supervision and Subordinate Problem Drinking: Taking Resistance, Stress and Subordinate Personality into Account," *Human Relations* 59 (2006): 1–30; B. J. Tepper, "Consequences of Abusive Supervision," *Academy of Management Journal* 43 (2000): 178–190; A. A. Grandey, J. Kern, and M. Frone, "Verbal Abuse from Outsiders Versus Insiders: Comparing Frequency, Impact on Emotional Exhaustion, and the Role of Emotional Labor," *Journal of Occupation Health Psychology* 12 (2007): 63–79.

70. B. J. Tepper, M. K. Duffy, C. A. Henle, and L. S. Lambert, "Procedural Injustice, Victim Precipitation and Abusive Supervision," *Personnel Psychology* 59 (2006): 101–123.

71. S. Thau and M. S. Mitchell, "Self-Gain or Self-Regulation Impairment? Tests of Competing Explanations of the Supervisor Abuse and Employee Deviance Relationship through Perceptions of Distributive Justice," *Journal of Applied Psychology* (in press).

72. B. J. Tepper, "Abusive Supervision in Work Organizations: Review, Synthesis and Research Agenda," *Journal of Management* 33 (2007): 261–289.

73. E. P. Hollander and L. R. Offerman, "Power and Leadership in Organizations: Relationships in Transition," *American Psychologist* 45 (1990): 179–189.

74. H. P. Sims, Jr., and C. C. Manz, *Company of Heros: Unleashing the Power of Self-Leadership* (New York: John Wiley & Sons, 1996).

75. C. C. Manz and H. P. Sims, "Leading Workers to Lead Themselves: The External Leadership of Self-Managing Work Teams," *Administrative Science Quarterly* 32 (1987): 106–128.

76. L. Hirschhorn, "Leaders and Followers in a Postindustrial Age: A Psychodynamic View," *Journal of Applied Behavioral Science* 26 (1990): 529–542.

77. R. E. Kelley, "In Praise of Followers," *Harvard Business Review* 66 (1988): 142–148.

78. S. A. Eisenbeiss and D. van Knippenberg, "On Ethical Leadership Impact: The Role of Follower Mindfulness and Moral Emotions," *Journal of Organizational Behavior* 36 (2014): 182–195.

79. G. A. Yukl, *Leadership in Organizations*, 2nd ed. (Upper Saddle River, N.J.: Prentice-Hall, 1989).

80. D. A. Garvin and J. D. Margolis, "The Art of Giving and Receiving Advice," *Harvard Business Review*, January–February (2015): 61–71.

13

1. Definition adapted from D. Hellriegel, J. W. Slocum, Jr., and R. W. Woodman, *Organizational Behavior* (St. Paul: West, 1992), and from R. D. Middlemist and M. A. Hitt, *Organizational Behavior* (St. Paul, Minn.: West, 1988).

2. D. Tjosvold, *The Conflict-Positive Organization* (Reading, Mass.: Addison-Wesley, 1991).

3. K. Thomas and W. Schmidt, "A Survey of Managerial Interests with Respect to Conflict," *Academy of Management Journal* 19 (1976): 315–318; G. L. Lippitt, "Managing Conflict in Today's Organizations," *Training and Development Journal* 36 (1982): 66–74.

4. M. Rajim, "A Measure of Styles of Handling Interpersonal Conflict," *Academy of Management Journal* 26 (1983): 368–376.

5. M. M. Hopkins and R. D. Yonker, "Managing Conflict with Emotional Intelligence: Abilities That Make a Difference," *Journal of Management Development* 34 (2015): 226–244.

6. Tjosvold, *The Conflict-Positive Organization*, 4.

7. R. A. Cosier and D. R. Dalton, "Positive Effects of Conflict: A Field Experiment," *International Journal of Conflict Management* 1 (1990): 81–92.

8. D. Tjosvold, "Making Conflict Productive," *Personnel Administrator* 29 (1984): 121–130.

9. I. Janis, *Groupthink*, 2nd ed. (Boston: Houghton Mifflin, 1982).

10. A. C. Amason, W. A. Hochwarter, K. R. Thompson, and A. W. Harrison, "Conflict: An Important Dimension in Successful Management Teams," *Organizational Dynamics* 24 (1995): 25–35.

11. T. L. Simons and R. S. Peterson, "Task Conflict and Relationship Conflict in Top Management Teams: The Pivotal Role of Intergroup Trust," *Journal of Applied Psychology* 85 (2000): 102–111.

12. R. Nibler and K. L. Harris, "The Effects of Culture and Cohesiveness on Intragroup Conflict and Effectiveness," *The Journal of Social Psychology* 143 (2003): 613–631.

13. J. D. Thompson, *Organizations in Action* (New York: McGraw-Hill, 1967).

14. G. Walker and L. Poppo, "Profit Centers, Single-Source Suppliers, and Transaction Costs," *Administrative Science Quarterly* 36 (1991): 66–87.

15. R. Miles, *Macro Organizational Behavior* (Glenview, Ill.: Scott, Foresman, 1980).

16. H. Levinson, "The Abrasive Personality," *Harvard Business Review* 56 (1978): 86–94.

17. J. C. Quick and J. D. Quick, *Organizational Stress and Preventive Management* (New York: McGraw-Hill, 1984).

18. F. N. Brady, "Aesthetic Components of Management Ethics," *Academy of Management Review* 11 (1986): 337–344.

19. J. R. Ogilvie and M. L. Carsky, "Building Emotional Intelligence in Negotiations," *The International Journal of Conflict Management* 13 (2002): 381–400.

20. A. M. Bodtker and R. L. Oliver, "Emotion in Conflict Formation and Its Transformation: Application to Organizational Conflict Management," *International Journal of Conflict Management* 12 (2001): 259–275.

21. D. E. Conlon and S. H. Hunt, "Dealing with Feeling: The Influence of Outcome Representations on Negotiation," *International Journal of Conflict Management* 13 (2002): 35–58.

22. J. Schopler, C. A. Insko, J. Wieselquist, M. Pemberton, B. Witcher, R. Kozar, C. Roddenberry, and T. Wildschut, "When Groups Are More Competitive Than Individuals: The Domain of the Discontinuity Effect," *Journal of Personality and Social Psychology* 80 (2001): 632–644.

23. M. Sherif and C. W. Sherif, *Social Psychology* (New York: Harper & Row, 1969).

24. M. A. Zarate, B. Garcia, A. A. Garza, and R. T. Hitlan, "Cultural Threat and Perceived Realistic Group Conflict as Dual Predictors of Prejudice," *Journal of Experimental Social Psychology* 40 (2004): 99–105; J. C. Dencker, A. Joshi, and J. J. Martocchio, "Employee Benefits as Context for Intergenerational Conflict," *Human Resource Management Review* 17, No. 2 (2007): 208–220.

25. C. Song, S. M. Sommer, and A. E. Hartman, "The Impact of Adding an External Rater on Interdepartmental Cooperative Behaviors of Workers," *International Journal of Conflict Management* 9 (1998): 117–138.

26. W. Tsai and S. Ghoshal, "Social Capital and Value Creation: The Role of Intrafirm Networks," *Academy of Management Journal* 41 (1998): 464–476.

27. K. J. Hurt and M. A. Abebe, "The Effect of Conflict Type and Organizational Crisis on Perceived Strategic Decision Effectiveness," *Journal of Leadership and Organizational Studies*, published online February 4, 2015.

28. D. L. Nelson and J. C. Quick, "Professional Women: Are Distress and Disease Inevitable?" *Academy of Management Review* 10 (1985): 206–218; D. L. Nelson and M. A. Hitt, "Employed Women and Stress: Implications for Enhancing Women's Mental Health in the Workplace," in J. C. Quick, J. Hurrell, and L. A. Murphy, eds., *Stress and Well-Being at Work: Assessments and Interventions for Occupational Mental Health* (Washington, D.C.: American Psychological Association, 1992).

29. E. C. Dierdorff and J. K. Ellington, "It's the Nature of Work: Examining Behavior-Based Sources of Work–Family Conflict across Occupations," *Journal of Applied Psychology* 93 (2008): 883–892.

30. M. G. Pratt and J. A. Rosa, "Transforming Work–Family Conflict into Commitment in Network Marketing Organizations," *Academy of Management Journal* 46 (2003): 395–418.

31. W. R. Boswell and J. B. Olson-Buchanan, "The Use of Communication Technologies after Hours: The Role of Work Attitudes and Work–Life Conflict," *Journal of Management* 33, No. 4 (2007): 592–610.

32. R. L. Kahn, D. M. Wolfe, R. P. Quinn, J. D. Noek, and R. A. Rosenthal, *Organizational Stress: Studies in Role Conflict and Ambiguity* (New York: Wiley, 1964).

33. J. R. B. Halbeslaben, "A Meta-Analysis of Work Engagement: Relationships with Burnout, Demands, Resources, and Consequences," in A. Bakker and M. Leiter, eds., *Work Engagement: A Handbook of Essential Theory and Research* (New York: Psychology Press, 2010); M. Wang, S. Liu, Y. Zhan, and J. Shi, "Daily Work–Family Conflict and Alcohol Use: Testing the Cross-Level Moderation Effects of Peer Drinking Norms and Social Support," *Journal of Applied Psychology* 95 (2010): 377–386.

34. C. Nohe, A. Michel, and K. Sonntag, "Family-Work Conflict and Job Performance: A Diary Study of Boundary Conditions and Mechanisms," *Journal of Organizational Behavior* 35 (2014): 339–357.

35. J. L. Badaracco, Jr., "The Discipline of Building Character," *Harvard Business Review* (March–April 1998): 115–124.

36. B. Schneider, "The People Make the Place," *Personnel Psychology* 40 (1987): 437–453.

37. C. A. O'Reilly, J. Chatman, and D. F. Caldwell, "People and Organi-zational Culture: A Profile Comparison Approach to Assessing Person-Organization Fit," *Academy of Management Journal* 34 (1991): 487–516.

38. I. Dayal and J. M. Thomas, "Operation KPE: Developing a New Organization," *Journal of Applied Behavioral Science* 4 (1968): 473–506.

39. R. H. Miles, "Role Requirements as Sources of Organizational Stress," *Journal of Applied Psychology* 61 (1976): 172–179.

40. W. F. G. Mastenbroek, *Conflict Management and Organization Development* (Chichester, England: Wiley, 1987).

41. M. R. Frone, "Interpersonal Conflict at Work and Psychological Outcomes: Testing a Model among Young Workers," *Journal of Occupational Health Psychology* 5 (2000): 246–255.

42. K. Thomas, "Conflict and Conflict Management," in M. D. Dunnette, ed., *Handbook of Industrial and Organizational Psychology* (New York: Wiley, 1976).

43. H. H. Meyer, E. Kay, and J. R. P. French, "Split Roles in Performance Appraisal," *Harvard Business Review* 43 (1965): 123–129.

44. T. W. Costello and S. S. Zalkind, *Psychology in Administration: A Research Orientation* (Englewood Cliffs, N.J.: Prentice-Hall, 1963).

45. Snapshot Spy, "Employee Computer & Internet Abuse Statistics," http://www.snapshotspy.com/employee-computer-abuse-statistics.htm; data sources include U.S. Department of Commerce—Economics and Statistics Administration and the National Telecommunications and Information Administration—Greenfield and Rivet, "Employee Computer Abuse Statistics."

46. P. F. Hewlin, "And the Award for Best Actor Goes to . . . : Facades of Conformity in Organizational Settings," *Academy of Management Review* 28 (2003): 633–642.

47. C. A. Insko, J. Scholper, L. Gaertner, T. Wildschut, R. Kozar, B. Pinter, E. J. Finkel, D. M. Brazil, C. L. Cecil, and M. R. Montoya, "Interindividual–Intergroup Discontinuity Reduction through the Anticipation of Future Interaction," *Journal of Personality and Social Psychology* 80 (2001): 95–111.

48. D. Tjosvold and M. Poon, "Dealing with Scarce Resources: Open-Minded Interaction for Resolving Budget Conflicts," *Group and Organization Management* 23 (1998): 237–255.

49. Miles, *Macro Organizational Behavior*; R. Steers, *Introduction to Organizational Behavior*, 4th ed. (Glenview, Ill.: Harper-Collins, 1991).

50. A. Tyerman and C. Spencer, "A Critical Text of the Sherrif's Robber's Cave Experiments: Intergroup Competition and Cooperation between Groups of Well-Acquainted Individuals," *Small Group Behavior* 14 (1983): 515–531; R. M. Kramer, "Intergroup Relations and Organizational Dilemmas: The Role of Categorization Processes," in B. Staw and L. Cummings, eds., *Research in Organizational Behavior* 13 (1991): 191–228.

51. N. Kercheval, "Dana Holgorsen Becomes West Virginia Coach after Bill Stewart Resigns,"

Bloomberg (June 11, 2011), http://bloomberg.com/news/2011-06-11/dana-holgorsen-becomes-west-virgiinia-coach-after-bill-stewart-resigns.html.

52. A. Carmeli, "The Relationship between Emotional Intelligence and Work Attitudes, Behavior and Outcomes: An Examination among Senior Managers," *Journal of Managerial Psychology* 18 (2003): 788–813.

53. R. Blake and J. Mouton, "Overcoming Group Warfare," *Harvard Business Review* 64 (1984): 98–108.

54. D. G. Ancona and D. Caldwell, "Improving the Performance of New Product Teams," *Research Technology Management* 33 (1990): 25–29.

55. M. A. Cronin and L. R. Weingart, "Representational Gaps, Information Processing and Conflict in Functionally Diverse Teams," *Academy of Management Review* 32, No. 3 (2007): 761–773.

56. C. K. W. DeDreu and L. R. Weingart, "Task versus Relationship Conflict, Team Performance, and Team Member Satisfaction: A Meta-Analysis," *Journal of Applied Psychology* 88 (2003): 741–749.

57. R. J. Lewicki, J. A. Litterer, J. W. Minton, and D. M. Saunders, *Negotiation*, 2nd ed. (Burr Ridge, Ill.: Irwin, 1994).

58. C. K. W. De Dreu, S. L. Koole, and W. Steinel, "Unfixing the Fixed Pie: A Motivated Information-Processing Approach to Integrative Negotiation," *Journal of Personality and Social Psychology* 79 (2000): 975–987.

59. G. Ku, C. S. Wang, and A. D. Galinsky, "Promise and Perversity: Towards a Comprehensive Model of Perspective Taking," *Research in Organizational Behavior*, forthcoming.

60. I. Ayers and P. Siegelman, "Race and Gender Discrimination in Bargaining for a New Car," *American Economic Review* 85 (1995): 304–321.

61. J. Mazei, J. Huffmeier, P. A. Freund, A. F. Stuhlmacher, L. Bilke, and G. Hertel, "A Meta-Analysis on Gender Differences in Negotiation Outcomes and Their Moderators," *Psychological Bulletin* 141 (2015): 85–104.

62. C. K. W. De Dreu and A. E. M. Van Vianen, "Managing Relationship Conflict and the Effectiveness of Organizational Teams," *Journal of Organizational Behavior* 22 (2001): 309–328.

63. S. Steinberg, "Airbus Workers in France, Germany Strike against Massive Job Cuts," (March 1, 2007). http://www.wsws.org/articles/2007/mar2007/airb-m01.shtml.

64. R. A. Baron, S. P. Fortin, R. L. Frei, L. A. Hauver, and M. L. Shack, "Reducing Organizational Conflict: The Role of Socially Induced Positive Affect," *International Journal of Conflict Management* 1 (1990): 133–152.

65. S. L. Phillips and R. L. Elledge, *The Team Building Source Book* (San Diego: University Associates, 1989).

66. J. R. Curhan, M. A. Neale, L. Ross, and J. Rosencranz-Engelmann, "Relational Accom-

modation in Negotiation: Effects of Egalitarianism and Gender on Economic Efficiency and Relational Capital," *Organizational Behavior and Human Decision Processes* 107 (2008): 192–205.

67. T. N. Gladwin and I. Walter, "How Multinationals Can Manage Social and Political Forces," *Journal of Business Strategy*, No. 1 (1980): 54–68.

68. L. A. Dechurch, K. L. Hamilton, and C. Haas, "Effects of Conflict Management Strategies on Perceptions of Intragroup Conflict," *Group Dynamics: Theory, Research, and Practice* 11, No. 1 (2007): 66–78.

69. K. W. Thomas, "Toward Multidimensional Values in Teaching: The Example of Conflict Behaviors," *Academy of Management Review* 2 (1977): 484–490.

70. S. Alper, D. Tjosvold, and K. S. Law, "Conflict Management, Efficacy, and Performance in Organizational Teams," *Personnel Psychology* 53 (2000): 625–642.

71. A. Somech, H. S. Desvililya, and H. Lidogoster, "Team Conflict Management and Team Effectiveness: The Effects of Task Interdependence and Team Identification," *Journal of Organizational Behavior* 30 (2009): 359–378.

72. W. King and E. Miles, "What We Know and Don't Know about Measuring Conflict," *Management Communication Quarterly* 4 (1990): 222–243.

73. J. Barker, D. Tjosvold, and I. R. Andrews, "Conflict Approaches of Effective and Ineffective Project Managers: A Field Study in a Matrix Organization," *Journal of Management Studies* 25 (1988): 167–178.

74. M. Chan, "Intergroup Conflict and Conflict Management in the R&D Divisions of Four Aerospace Companies," *IEEE Transactions on Engineering Management* 36 (1989): 95–104.

14

1. J. S. Bunderson and J. A. Thompson, "The Call of the Wild: Zookeepers, Callings, and the Double-Edged Sword of Deeply Meaningful Work," *Administrative Science Quarterly* 54 (2009): 32–57.

2. B. L. Berkelaar and P. M. Buzzanell, "Bait and Switch or Double-Edged Sword? The (Sometimes) Failed Promises of Calling," *Human Relations* 68 (2014): 157–178.

3. G. W. England and I. Harpaz, "How Working Is Defined: National Contexts and Demographic and Organizational Role Influences," *Journal of Organizational Behavior* 11 (1990): 253–266.

4. L. R. Gomez-Mejia, "The Cross-Cultural Structure of Task-Related and Contextual Constructs," *Journal of Psychology* 120 (1986): 5–19.

5. A. Wrzesniewski and J. E. Dutton, "Crafting a Job: Revisioning Employees as Active Crafters of Their Work," *Academy of Management Review* 26 (2001): 179–201.

6. D. T. Hall and M. Las Heras, "Reintegrating Job Design and Career Theory: Creating Not Just Good Jobs but Smart Jobs," *Journal of Organizational Behavior* 31 (2010): 448–462.

7. F. W. Taylor, *The Principles of Scientific Management* (New York: Norton, 1911).

8. T. Bell, *Out of This Furnace* (Pittsburgh: University of Pittsburgh Press, 1941); J. H. Gittell, D. B. Weinberg, A. L. Bennett, and J. A. Miller, "Is the Doctor in? A Relational Approach to Job Design and the Coordination of Work," *Human Resource Management* 47 (Winter 2008): 729–755.

9. N. D. Warren, "Job Simplification versus Job Enlargement," *Journal of Industrial Engineering* 9 (1958): 435–439.

10. T. Moller, S. E. Mathiassen, H. Franzon, and S. Kihlberg, "Job Enlargement and Mechanical Exposure Variability in Cyclic Assembly Work," *Ergonomics* 47 (2004): 19–40.

11. C. R. Walker and R. H. Guest, *The Man on the Assembly Line* (Cambridge, Mass.: Harvard University Press, 1952).

12. M. A. Campion, L. Cheraskin, and M. J. Stevens, "Career-Related Antecedents and Outcomes of Job Rotation," *Academy of Management Journal* 37 (1994): 1518–1542.

13. H. R. Nalbantian and R. A. Guzzo, "Making Mobility Matter," *Harvard Business Review* (March 2009): 76–84.

14. E. Santora, "Keep Up Production through Cross-Training," *Personnel Journal* (June 1992): 162–166.

15. S. Leroy, "Why Is It So Hard to Do My Work? The Challenge of Attention Residue When Switching between Work Tasks," *Organizational Behavior and Human Decision Processes* 109 (2009): 168–181.

16. R. P. Steel and J. R. Rentsch, "The Dispositional Model of Job Attitudes Revisited: Findings of a 10-Year Study," *Journal of Applied Psychology* 82 (1997): 873–879; C. S. Wong, C. Hui, and K. S. Law, "A Longitudinal Study of the Job Perception–Job Satisfaction Relationship: A Text of the Three Alternative Specifications," *Journal of Occupational & Organizational Psychology* 71 (Part 2, 1998): 127–146.

17. F. Herzberg, "One More Time: How Do You Motivate Employees?" *Harvard Business Review* 46 (1968): 53–62.

18. R. N. Ford, "Job Enrichment Lessons from AT&T," *Harvard Business Review* 51 (1973): 96–106.

19. R. J. House and L. A. Wigdor, "Herzberg's Dual-Factor Theory of Job Satisfaction and Motivation: A Review of the Evidence and a Criticism," *Personnel Psychology* 20 (1967): 369–389.

20. A. N. Turner and P. R. Lawrence, *Industrial Jobs and the Worker* (Cambridge, Mass.: Harvard University Press, 1965).

21. D. H. McKnight, B. Phillips, and B. C. Hardgrave, "Which Reduces IT Turnover Intention the Worst: Workplace Characteristics or Job Characteristics?" *Information & Management* 46 (2009): 167–174.

22. J. R. Hackman and G. R. Oldham, "The Relationship among Core Job Dimensions, the Critical Psychological States, and On-the-Job Outcomes," in *The Job Diagnostic Survey: An Instrument for the Diagnosis of Jobs and the Evaluation of Job Redesign Projects* (New Haven, Conn.: Department of Administrative Sciences, Yale University, 1974).

23. J. L. Pierce, I. Jussila, and A. Cummings, "Psychological Ownership within the Job Design Context: Revision of the Job Characteristics Model," *Journal of Organizational Behavior* 30 (2009): 477–496.

24. J. R. Hackman and G. R. Oldham, "Development of the Job Diagnostic Survey," *Journal of Applied Psychology* 60 (1975): 159–170.

25. E. Sadler-Smith, G. El-Kot, and M. Leat, "Differentiating Work Autonomy Facets in a Non-Western Context," *Journal of Organizational Behavior* 24 (2003): 709–731.

26. H. P. Sims, A. D. Szilagyi, and R. T. Keller, "The Measurement of Job Characteristics," *Academy of Management Journal* 19 (1976): 195–212.

27. H. P. Sims and A. D. Szilagyi, "Job Characteristic Relationships: Individual and Structural Moderators," *Organizational Behavior and Human Performance* 17 (1976): 211–230.

28. Y. Fried, "Meta-Analytic Comparison of the Job Diagnostic Survey and Job Characteristic Inventory as Correlates of Work Satisfaction and Performance," *Journal of Applied Psychology* 76 (1991): 690–698.

29. D. R. May, R. L. Gilson, and L. M. Harter, "The Psychological Conditions of Meaningfulness, Safety, and Availability and the Engagement of the Human Spirit at Work," *Journal of Occupational and Organizational Psychology* 77 (2004): 11–37.

30. D. DClercq, D. Bouckenooghe, U. Raja, and G. Matsyborska, "Unpacking the Goal Congruence-Organizational Deviance Relationship: The Roles of Work Engagement and Emotional Intelligence," *Journal of Business Ethics* 124 (2014): 695–711.

31. R. Wagner, "Nourishing Employee Engagement," *Gallup Management Journal* (February 12, 2004): 1–7, http://gmj.gallup.com/content/default.asp?ci=10504.

32. M. Soyars and J. Brusino, "Essentials of Engagement," *T&D* (March 2009): 62–65.

33. J. Loehr and T. Schwartz, *The Power of Full Engagement: Managing Energy, Not Time, Is the Key to High Performance and Personal Renewal* (New York: Free Press, 2003).

34. M. F. R. Kets de Vries, "Creating Authentizotic Organizations: Well-Functioning Individuals in Vibrant Companies," *Human Relations* 54 (2001): 101–111.

35. G. R. Salancik and J. Pfeffer, "A Social Information Processing Approach to Job Attitudes and Task Design," *Administrative Science Quarterly* 23 (1978): 224–253.

36. J. Pfeffer, "Management as Symbolic Action: The Creation and Maintenance of Organizational Paradigms," in L. L. Cummings and B. M. Staw, eds., *Research in Organizational Behavior*, vol. 3 (Greenwich, Conn.: JAI Press, 1981): 1–52.

37. C. Clegg and C. Spencer, "A Circular and Dynamic Model of the Process of Job Design," *Journal of Occupational & Organizational Psychology* 80 (2007): 321–339.

38. J. Thomas and R. Griffin, "The Social Information Processing Model of Task Design: A Review of the Literature," *Academy of Management Review* 8 (1983): 672–682.

39. D. J. Campbell, "Task Complexity: A Review and Analysis," *Academy of Management Review* 13 (1988): 40–52.

40. A. M. Grant, "Relational Job Design and the Motivation to Make a Prosocial Difference," *Academy of Management Review* 32 (2007): 393–417.

41. D. R. May, K. Reed, C. E. Schwoerer, and P. Potter, "Ergonomic Office Design and Aging: A Quasi-Experimental Field Study of Employee Reactions to an Ergonomics Intervention Program," *Journal of Occupational Health Psychology* 9 (2004): 123–135.

42. M. A. Campion and P. W. Thayer, "Job Design: Approaches, Outcomes, and Trade-Offs," *Organizational Dynamics* 16 (1987): 66–79.

43. J. Teresko, "Emerging Technologies," *Industry Week* (February 27, 1995): 1–2.

44. M. A. Campion and C. L. McClelland, "Interdisciplinary Examination of the Costs and Benefits of Enlarged Jobs: A Job Design Quasi-Experiment," *Journal of Applied Psychology* 76 (1991): 186–199.

45. B. Kohut, *Country Competitiveness: Organizing of Work* (New York: Oxford University Press, 1993).

46. D. Holman, S. Frenkel, O. Sorensen, and S. Wood, "Work Design Variation and Outcomes in Call Centers: Strategic Choice and Institutional Explanations," *Industrial and Labor Relations Review* 62 (July 2009): 510–532.

47. J. C. Quick and L. E. Tetrick, eds., *Handbook of Occupational Health Psychology* (Washington, D.C.: American Psychological Association, 2002).

48. W. E. Deming, *Out of the Crisis* (Cambridge, Mass.: MIT Press, 1986).

49. L. Thurow, *Head to Head: The Coming Economic Battle among Japan, Europe, and America* (New York: Morrow, 1992).

50. M. A. Fruin, *The Japanese Enterprise System—Competitive Strategies and Cooperative Structures* (New York: Oxford University Press, 1992).

51. W. Niepce and E. Molleman, "Work Design Issue in Lean Production from a Sociotechnical System Perspective: Neo-Taylorism or the Next

Step in Sociotechnical Design?" *Human Relations* 51 (1998): 259–287.

52. S. K. Parker, "Longitudinal Effects of Lean Production on Employee Outcomes and the Mediating Role of Work Characteristics," *Journal of Applied Psychology* 88 (2003): 620–634.

53. E. Furubotn, "Codetermination and the Modern Theory of the Firm: A Property-Rights Analysis," *Journal of Business* 61 (1988): 165–181.

54. H. Levinson, *Executive: The Guide to Responsive Management* (Cambridge, Mass.: Harvard University Press, 1981).

55. B. Gardell, "Scandinavian Research on Stress in Working Life" (Paper presented at the IRRA Symposium on Stress in Working Life, Denver, September 1980).

56. L. Levi, "Psychosocial, Occupational, Environmental, and Health Concepts; Research Results and Applications," in G. P. Keita and S. L. Sauter, eds., *Work and Well-Being: An Agenda for the 1990s* (Washington, D.C.: American Psychological Association, 1992): 199–211.

57. L. R. Murphy and C. L. Cooper, eds., *Healthy and Productive Work: An International Perspective* (London and New York: Taylor & Francis, 2000).

58. R. L. Kahn, *Work and Health* (New York: Wiley, 1981); M. Gowing, J. Kraft, and J. C. Quick, *The New Organizational Reality: Downsizing, Restructuring, and Revitalization* (Washington, D.C.: American Psychological Association, 1998).

59. F. J. Landy, "Work Design and Stress," in G. P. Keita and S. L. Sauter, eds., *Work and Well-Being: An Agenda for the 1990s* (Washington, D.C.: American Psychological Association, 1992): 119–158.

60. M. Tims, A. B. Bakker, and D. Derks, "Examining Job Crafting from an Interpersonal Perspective: Is Employee Job Crafting Related to the Well-Being of Colleagues?" *Applied Psychology: An International Review* (published online March 2, 2015).

61. C. Gresov, R. Drazin, and A. H. Van de Ven, "Work-Unit Task Uncertainty, Design, and Morale," *Organizational Studies* 10 (1989): 45–62.

62. A. M. Grant, E. M. Campbell, G. Chen, K. Cottone, D. Lapedis, and K. Lee, "Impact and the Art of Motivation Maintenance: The Effects of Contact with Beneficiaries on Persistence Behavior," *Organizational Behavior and Human Decision Processes* 103 (2007): 53–67.

63. A. Idris, "Flexible Working as an Employee Retention Strategy in Developing Countries," *Journal of Management Research* 14 (2014): 71–86.

64. R. S. Gajendran, D. A. Harrison, and R. Delaney-Klinger, "Are Telecommuters Remotely Good Citizens? Unpacking Telecommuting's Effects on Performance via I-Deals and Job Resources," *Personnel Psychology* (published online August 15, 2014).

65. Y. Baruch, "The Status of Research on Teleworking and an Agenda for Future Research," *International Journal of Management Review* 3 (2000): 113–129.

66. K. E. Pearlson and C. S. Saunders, "There's No Place Like Home: Managing Telecommuting Paradoxes," *Academy of Management Executive* 15 (2001): 117–128.

67. S. Caudron, "Working at Home Pays Off," *Personnel Journal* (November 1992): 40–47.

68. D. S. Bailey and J. Foley, "Pacific Bell Works Long Distance," *HRMagazine* (August 1990): 50–52.

69. M. Virick, N. DaSilva, and K. Arrington, "Moderators of the Curvilinear Relationship between Extent of Telecommuting and Job and Life Satisfaction; The Role of Performance Outcome Orientation and Worker Type," *Human Relations* 63 (2010): 137–154.

70. S. M. Pollan and M. Levine, "Asking for Flextime," *Working Women* (February 1994): 48.

71. S. A. Rogier and M. Y. Padgett, "The Impact of Utilizing a Flexible Work Schedule on the Perceived Career Advancement Potential of Women," *Human Resource Development Quarterly* 15 (2004): 89–106.

72. D. Derks, D. van Duin, M. Tims, and A. B. Bakker, "Smartphone Use and Work-Home Interference: The Moderating Role of Social Norms and Employee Work Engagement," *Journal of Occupational and Organizational Psychology* 88 (2015): 155–177.

73. S. Zuboff, *In the Age of the Smart Machine: The Future of Work and Power* (New York: Basic Books, 1988).

74. B. A. Gutek and S. J. Winter, "Computer Use, Control over Computers, and Job Satisfaction," in S. Oskamp and S. Spacapan, eds., *People's Reactions to Technology in Factories, Offices, and Aerospace: The Claremont Symposium on Applied Social Psychology* (Newbury Park, Calif.: Sage, 1990): 121–144.

75. L. M. Schleifer and B. C. Amick, III, "System Response Time and Method of Pay: Stress Effects in Computer-Based Tasks," *International Journal of Human-Computer Interaction* 1 (1989): 23–39.

76. K. Voight, "Virtual Work: Some Telecommuters Take Remote Work to the Extreme," *The Wall Street Journal Europe* (February 1, 2001): 1.

77. G. Salvendy, *Handbook of Industrial Engineering: Technology and Operations Management* (New York: John Wiley & Sons, 2001).

78. D. M. Herold, "Using Technology to Improve Our Management of Labor Market Trends," in M. Greller, ed., "Managing Careers with a Changing Workforce," *Journal of Organizational Change Management* 3 (1990): 44–57.

79. D. A. Whetten and K. S. Cameron, *Developing Management Skills*, 6th ed. (Upper Saddle River, N.J.: Prentice Hall, 2004).

15

1. J. Child, *Organization* (New York: Harper & Row, 1984).

2. P. Lawrence and J. Lorsch, "Differentiation and Integration in Complex Organizations," *Administrative Science Quarterly* 12 (1967): 1–47.

3. P. Lawrence and J. Lorsch, *Organization and Environment: Managing Differentiation and Integration,* rev. ed. (Cambridge, Mass.: Harvard University Press, 1986).

4. J. Hage, "An Axiomatic Theory of Organizations," *Administrative Science Quarterly* 10 (1965): 289–320.

5. "The Army Reserve at 100: An Emerging Operational Force," *Army Logistician* (November–December, 2008): 15–16.

6. W. Ouchi and J. Dowling, "Defining the Span of Control," *Administrative Science Quarterly* 19 (1974): 357–365.

7. L. Porter and E. Lawler, III, "Properties of Organization Structure in Relation to Job Attitudes and Job Behavior," *Psychological Bulletin* 65 (1965): 23–51.

8. J. Ivancevich and J. Donnelly, Jr., "Relation of Organization and Structure to Job Satisfaction, Anxiety-Stress, and Performance," *Administrative Science Quarterly* 20 (1975): 272–280.

9. R. Dewar and J. Hage, "Size, Technology, Complexity, and Structural Differentiation: Toward a Theoretical Synthesis," *Administrative Science Quarterly* 23 (1978): 111–136.

10. F. C. Vasoncelos and R. Ramirez, "Complexity in Business Environments," *Journal of Business Research* 64 (2011): 236–241.

11. Paul R. Lawrence and Jay W. Lorsch, "Differentiation and Integration in Complex Organizations," *Administrative Science Quarterly* 12, No. 1 (1967): 1–47.

12. J. R. R. Galbraith, *Designing Complex Organizations* (Reading, Mass.: Addison-Wesley-Longman, 1973).

13. W. Altier, "Task Forces: An Effective Management Tool," *Management Review* 76 (1987): 26–32.

14. P. Lawrence and J. Lorsch, "New Managerial Job: The Integrator," *Harvard Business Review* 45 (1967): 142–151.

15. J. Lorsch and P. Lawrence, "Organizing for Product Innovation," *Harvard Business Review* 43 (1965): 110–111.

16. D. Pugh, D. Hickson, C. Hinnings, and C. Turner, "Dimensions of Organization Structure," *Administrative Science Quarterly* 13 (1968): 65–91; B. Reimann, "Dimensions of Structure in Effective Organizations: Some Empirical Evidence," *Academy of Management Journal* 17 (1974): 693–708; S. Robbins, *Organization Theory: The Structure and Design of Organizations,* 3rd ed. (Englewood Cliffs, N.J.: Prentice-Hall, 1990).

17. M. C. Andrews, T. L. Baker, and T. G. Hunt, "The Interactive Effects of Centralization on the Relationship between Justice and Satisfaction," *Journal of Leadership & Organizational Studies* 15 (2008): 135–144.

18. A. Arora, S. Belenzon, and L. A. Rios, "Make, Buy, Organize: The Interplay Between Research, External Knowledge, and Firm Knowledge," *Strategic Management Journal* 35 (2014): 317–337.

19. H. Mintzberg, *The Structuring of Organizations* (Englewood Cliffs, N.J.: Prentice-Hall, 1979).

20. J. A. Kuprenas, "Implementation and Performance of a Matrix Organization Structure," *International Journal of Project Management* 21 (2003): 51–62.

21. Mintzberg, *Structuring of Organizations*.

22. K. Weick, "Educational Institutions as Loosely Coupled Systems," *Administrative Science Quarterly* (1976): 1–19.

23. D. Miller and C. Droge, "Psychological and Traditional Determinants of Structure," *Administrative Science Quarterly* 31 (1986): 540; H. Tosi, Jr. and J. Slocum, Jr., "Contingency Theory: Some Suggested Directions," *Journal of Management* 10 (1984): 9–26.

24. C. B. Clott, "Perspectives on Global Outsourcing and the Changing Nature of Work," *Business and Society Review* 109 (2004): 153–170.

25. M. Meyer, "Size and the Structure of Organizations: A Causal Analysis," *American Sociological Review* 37 (1972): 434–441; J. Beyer and H. Trice, "A Reexamination of the Relations between Size and Various Components of Organizational Complexity," *Administrative Science Quarterly* 24 (1979): 48–64; B. Mayhew, R. Levinger, J. McPherson, and T. James, "Systems Size and Structural Differentiation in Formal Organizations: A Baseline Generator for Two Major Theoretical Propositions," *American Sociological Review* 37 (1972): 26–43.

26. M. Gowing, J. Kraft, and J. C. Quick, *The New Organizational Reality: Downsizing, Restructuring, and Revitalization* (Washington, D.C.: American Psychological Association, 1998).

27. M. Brauer and L. Laamanen, "Workforce Downsizing and Firm Performance: An Organizational Routine Perspective," *Journal of Management Studies* 51 (2014): 1311–1333.

28. L. Donaldson and G. Joffe, "Fit—The Key to Organizational Design," *Journal of Organization Design* 3 (2014): 38–45.

29. J. Werth and D. Fleming, "Creating a 'Super' Agency in San Diego County," *The Public Manager* (Fall 2008): 21–26.

30. J. Woodward, *Industrial Organization: Theory and Practices* (London: Oxford University Press, 1965).

31. C. Perrow, "A Framework for the Comparative Analysis of Organizations," *American Sociological Review* 32 (1967): 194–208; D. Rosseau, "Assessment of Technology in Organizations: Closed versus Open Systems Approaches," *Academy of Management Review* 4 (1979): 531–542.

32. C. Perrow, "A Framework for the Comparative Analysis of Organizations," *American Sociological Review* 32, No. 2 (1967): 194–208.

33. J. D. Thompson, *Organizations in Action* (New York: McGraw-Hill, 1967).

34. J. R. Baum and S. Wally, "Strategic Decision Speed and Firm Performance," *Strategic Management Journal* 24 (2003): 1107–1129.

35. Thompson, *Organizations in Action*.

36. H. Downey, D. Hellriegel, and J. Slocum, Jr., "Environmental Uncertainty: The Construct and Its Application," *Administrative Science Quarterly* 20 (1975): 613–629.

37. G. Dess and D. Beard, "Dimensions of Organizational Task Environments," *Administrative Science Quarterly* 29 (1984): 52–73.

38. J. A. Cogin and I. O. Williamson, "Standardize or Customize: The Interactive Effects of HRM and Environment Uncertainty on MNC Subsidiary Performance," *Human Resource Management* 53 (2014): 701–721.

39. G. G. Dess and D. W. Beard, "Dimensions of Organizational Task Environments," *Administrative Science Quarterly* 29, No. 1 (1984): 52–73.

40. T. Burns and G. Stalker, *The Management of Innovation* (London: Tavistock, 1961); Mintzberg, *Structuring of Organizations*.

41. M. Chandler and L. Sayles, *Managing Large Systems* (New York: Harper & Row, 1971).

42. M. Sanchez-Manzanares, R. Rico, and F. Gil, "Designing Organizations: Does Expertise Matter?" *Journal of Business Psychology* 23 (2008): 87–101.

43. J. Courtright, G. Fairhurst, and L. Rogers, "Interaction Patterns in Organic and Mechanistic Systems," *Academy of Management Journal* 32 (1989): 773–802.

44. R. Daft, *Organization Theory and Design*, 7th ed. (Mason, Ohio: South-Western, 2000).

45. R. S. Kaplan and D. P. Norton, "How to Implement a New Strategy without Disrupting Your Organization," *Harvard Business Review* (March 2006): 100–109.

46. L-H Lin, "Organizational Structure and Acculturation in Acquisitions: Perspectives of Congruence Theory and Task Interdependence," *Journal of Management* 40 (2014): 1831–1856.

47. N. J. Foss, J. Lyngsie, and S. A. Zahra, "Organizational Design Correlates of Entrepreneurship: The Roles of Decentralization and Formalization for Opportunity Discovery and Realization," *Strategic Organization* 13 (2015): 32–60.

48. W. R. Scott, *Organizations: Rational, Natural, and Open Systems*, 4th ed. (Upper Saddle River, N.J.: Prentice-Hall, 1997).

49. D. Miller and P. Friesen, "A Longitudinal Study of the Corporate Life Cycle," *Management Science* 30 (1984): 1161–1183.

50. S. Raisch, "Balanced Structures: Designing Organizations for Profitable Growth," *Long Range Planning* 41 (2008): 483–508.

51. M. H. Overholt, "Flexible Organizations: Using Organizational Design as a Competitive Advantage," *Human Resource Planning* 20 (1997): 22–32; P. W. Roberts and R. Greenwood,

"Integrating Transaction Cost and Institutional Theories: Toward a Constrained-Efficiency Framework for Understanding Organizational Design Adoption," *Academy of Management Review* 22 (1997): 346–373.

52. G. Davidson, "Organisation Structure: The Life Cycle of an Organization," *New Zealand Management* 56 (2008): 58–60.

53. C. W. L. Hill and G. R. Jones, *Strategic Management Theory*, 5th ed. (Boston: Houghton Mifflin, 2000).

54. F. Hoque, "Designing the Right Kind of Organization," *Baseline* (January/February 2009): 46.

55. Cengage Learning, 11e, 2013.

56. C. M. Savage, *5th Generation Management, Revised Edition: Co-creating through Virtual Enterprising, Dynamic Teaming, and Knowledge Networking* (Boston: Butterworth-Heinemann, 1996).

57. S. M. Davis, *Future Perfect* (Perseus Publishing, 1997).

58. A. Boynton and B. Victor, "Beyond Flexibility: Building and Managing a Dynamically Stable Organization," *California Management Review* 8 (Fall 1991): 53–66.

59. B. Brown and S. D. Anthony, "How P&G Tripled Its Innovation Success Rate," *Harvard Business Review* 89 (June 2011): 64–72.

60. P. J. Brews and C. L. Tucci, "Exploring the Structural Effects of Internetworking," *Strategic Management Journal* 25 (2004): 429–451.

61. C. B. Gibson and J. L. Gibbs, "Unpacking the Concept of Virtuality: Geographic Dispersion, Electronic Dependence, Dynamic Structure, and National Diversity on Team Innovation," *Administrative Science Quarterly* 51 (2006): 451–495.

62. J. Fulk, "Global Network Organizations: Emergence and Future Prospects," *Human Relations* 54 (2001): 91–100.

63. The use of the theatrical troupe as an analogy for virtual organizations was first used by David Mack, circa 1995.

64. E. C. Kasper-Fuehrer and N. M. Ashkanasy, "Communicating Trustworthiness and Building Trust in Interorganizational Virtual Organizations," *Journal of Management* 27 (2001): 235–254.

65. R. Teerlink and L. Ozley, *More Than a Motorcycle: The Leadership Journey at Harley-Davidson* (Boston: Harvard Business School Press, 2000).

66. W. A. Cohen and N. Cohen, *The Paranoid Organization and 8 Other Ways Your Company Can Be Crazy: Advice from an Organizational Shrink* (New York: American Management Association, 1993).

67. P. E. Tetlock, "Cognitive Biases and Organizational Correctives: Do Both Disease and Cure Depend on the Politics of the Beholder?" *Administrative Science Quarterly* 45 (2000): 293–326.

68. M. F. R. Kets de Vries and D. Miller, "Personality, Culture, and Organization," *Academy of Management Review* 11 (1986): 266–279.

16

1. T. E. Deal and A. A. Kennedy, *Corporate Cultures* (Reading, Mass.: Addison-Wesley, 1982).

2. W. Ouchi, *Theory Z* (Reading, Mass.: Addison-Wesley, 1981).

3. T. J. Peters and R. H. Waterman, *In Search of Excellence* (New York: Harper & Row, 1982).

4. M. Gardner, "Creating a Corporate Culture for the Eighties," *Business Horizons* (January–February 1985): 59–63.

5. S. J. Hogan and L. V. Coote, "Organizational Culture, Innovation, and Performance: A Test of Schein's Model," *Journal of Business Research* 67 (2014): 1609–1621.

6. Definition adapted from E. H. Schein, *Organizational Culture and Leadership* (San Francisco: Jossey-Bass, 1985): 9.

7. C. D. Sutton and D. L. Nelson, "Elements of the Cultural Network: The Communicators of Corporate Values," *Leadership and Organization Development* 11 (1990): 3–10.

8. See http://www.google.com/about/company/facts/culture/

9. J. Pagel, "Eskimo Joe's Getting Older, But Still Fun at 21," *Amarillo Business Journal* (November 20, 1996), http://www.businessjournal.net/entrepreneur1196.html.

10. A. Bandura, *Social Learning Theory* (Englewood Cliffs, N.J.: Prentice-Hall, 1977).

11. J. A. Chatman, "Leading by Leveraging Culture," *California Management Review* 45 (2003): 20–34.

12. J. M. Beyer and H. M. Trice, "How an Organization's Rites Reveal Its Culture," *Organizational Dynamics* 16 (1987): 5–24.

13. H. M. Trice and J. M. Beyer, "Studying Organizational Cultures through Rites and Ceremonials," *Academy of Management Review* 9 (1984): 653–669.

14. "Recap: The 2014 Berkshire Hathaway Annual Meeting," *The Wall Street Journal*, May 3, 2014, accessed at http://blogs.wsj.com/moneybeat/2014/05/03/live-blog-the-2014-berkshire-hathaway-annual-meeting/.

15. H. Levinson and S. Rosenthal, *CEO: Corporate Leadership in Action* (New York: Basic Books, 1984).

16. V. Sathe, "Implications of Corporate Culture: A Manager's Guide to Action," *Organizational Dynamics* 12 (1987): 5–23.

17. "Wal-Mart Culture Stories—The Sundown Rule," http://www.wal-martchina.com/english/walmart/rule/sun.htm.

18. J. Martin, M. S. Feldman, M. J. Hatch, and S. B. Sitkin, "The Uniqueness Paradox in Organizational Stories," *Administrative Science Quarterly* 28 (1983): 438–453.

19. J. Lofstock, "Applauding the QuikTrip Culture," http://www.quiktrip.com/aboutqt/news.asp.

20. "No layoffs—ever!" CNNMoney.com (August 12, 2011), http://money.cnn.com/galleries/2010/fortune/1001/gallery.bestcompanies_layoffs.fortune/.

21. C. Gallo, "Southwest Airlines Motivates Its Employees with a Purpose Bigger than a Paycheck," *Forbes*, January 21, 2014, accessed at http://www.forbes.com/sites/carminegallo/2014/01/21/southwest-airlines-motivates-its-employees-with-a-purpose-bigger-than-a-paycheck/.

22. J. E. Vascellaro, "Facebook CEO in a Rush to 'Friend' Wall Street," *The Wall Street Journal* (March 3, 2010), http:/online.wsj.com/article/SB10001424052748703787304575075942803630712.html?mod=djem_jiewr_HR_domainid.

23. R. Goffee and G. Jones, "What Holds the Modern Company Together?" *Harvard Business Review* (November–December 1996): 133–143.

24. C. Argyris and D. A. Schon, *Organizational Learning* (Reading, Mass.: Addison-Wesley, 1978).

25. L. Hoeber, "Exploring the Gaps between Meanings and Practices of Gender Equity in a Sport Organization," *Gender Work and Organization* 14, No. 3 (2007): 259–280.

26. D. J. McAllister and G. A. Bigley, "Work Context and the Definition of Self: How Organizational Care Influences Organization-Based Self-Esteem," *Academy of Management Journal* 45 (2002): 894–905.

27. M. Peterson, "Work, Corporate Culture, and Stress: Implications for Worksite Health Promotion," *American Journal of Health Behavior* 21 (1997): 243–252.

28. http://www.capspire.com/careers/life-at-capspire/

29. L. Smircich, "Concepts of Culture and Organizational Analysis," *Administrative Science Quarterly* (1983): 339–358.

30. Y. Weiner and Y. Vardi, "Relationships between Organizational Culture and Individual Motivation: A Conceptual Integration," *Psychological Reports* 67 (1990): 295–306.

31. M. R. Louis, "Surprise and Sense Making: What Newcomers Experience in Entering Unfamiliar Organizational Settings," *Administrative Science Quarterly* 25 (1980): 209–264.

32. T. L. Doolen, M. E. Hacker, and E. M. van Aken, "The Impact of Organizational Context on Work Team Effectiveness: A Study of Production Teams," *IEEE Transactions on Engineering Management* 50 (2003): 285–296.

33. D. D. Van Fleet and R. W. Griffin, "Dysfunctional Organization Culture: The Role of Leadership in Motivating Dysfunctional Work Behaviors," *Journal of Managerial Psychology* 21, No. 8 (2006): 698–708.

34. J. P. Kotter and J. L. Heskett, *Corporate Culture and Performance* (New York: Free Press, 1992); A. S. Boyce, L. R. G. Nieminen, M. A. Gillespie, A. M. Ryan, and D. R. Denison, "Which Comes First, Organizational Culture or Performance? A Longitudinal Study of Causal Priority with Automobile Dealerships," *Journal of Organizational Behavior*, published online January 15, 2015..

35. Deal and Kennedy, *Corporate Cultures.*

36. D. R. Katz, *The Big Store* (New York: Viking, 1987).

37. G. G. Gordon, "Industry Determinants of Organizational Culture," *Academy of Management Review* 16 (1991): 396–415.

38. G. Donaldson and J. Lorsch, *Decision Making at the Top* (New York: Basic Books, 1983).

39. R. H. Kilman, M. J. Saxton, and R. Serpa, eds., *Gaining Control of the Corporate Culture* (San Francisco: Jossey-Bass, 1986).

40. J. P. Kotter, *A Force for Change: How Leadership Differs from Management* (New York: Free Press, 1990); R. M. Kanter, *The Change Masters* (New York: Simon & Schuster, 1983).

41. J. A. Chatman, D. F. Caldwell, C. A. O'Reilly, and B. Doerr, "Parsing Organizational Culture: How the Norm for Adaptability Influences the Relationship Between Culture Consensus and Financial Performance in High-Technology Firms," *Journal of Organizational Behavior* 35 (2015): 785–808.

42. Schein, *Organizational Culture and Leadership.*

43. J. A. Pearce II, T. R. Kramer, and D. K. Robbins, "Effects of Managers' Entrepreneurial Behavior on Subordinates," *Journal of Business Venturing* 12 (1997): 147–160.

44. P. W. Braddy, A. W. Meade, and C. M. Kroustalis, "Organizational Recruitment Website Effects on Viewers' Perceptions of Organizational Culture," *Journal of Business and Psychology* 20, No. 4 (2006): 525–543.

45. A. Bryant, "Mitch Rothschild of Vitals: Pushing beyond Comfort Zones," *New York Times*, January 24, 2015, accessed at http://www.nytimes.com/2015/01/25/business/mitch-rothschild-of-vitalis-juggle-but-dont-tiptoe.html.

46. A. Xenikou and M. Simosi, "Organizational Culture and Transformational Leadership as Predictors of Business Unit Performance," *Journal of Managerial Psychology* 21, No. 6 (2006): 566–579.

47. D. C. Feldman, "The Multiple Socialization of Organization Members," *Academy of Management Review* 6 (1981): 309–318.

48. A. M. Ellis, T. N. Bauer, L. R. Mansfield, B. Erdogan, D. M. Truxillo, and L. S. Simon, "Navigating Uncharted Waters: Newcomer Socialization through the Lens of Stress Theory," *Journal of Management* 41 (2015): 203–235.

49. D. L. Nelson, "Organizational Socialization: A Stress Perspective," *Journal of Occupational Behavior* 8 (1987): 311–324.

50. J. Fan and J. P. Wanous, "Organizational and Cultural Entry: A New Type of Orientation Program for Multiple Boundary Crossings," *Journal of Applied Psychology* 93 (2008): 1390–1400.

51. D. M. Cable, L. Aiman-Smith, P. W. Mulvey, and J. R. Edwards, "The Sources and Accuracy of Job Applicants' Beliefs about Organizational Culture," *Academy of Management Journal* 43 (2000): 1076–1085.

52. J. Chatman, "Matching People and Organizations: Selection and Socialization in Public Accounting Firms," *Administrative Science Quarterly* 36 (1991): 459–484.

53. D. L. Nelson, J. C. Quick, and M. E. Eakin, "A Longitudinal Study of Newcomer Role Adjustment in U.S. Organizations," *Work and Stress* 2 (1988): 239–253.

54. N. J. Allen and J. P. Meyer, "Organizational Socialization Tactics: A Longitudinal Analysis of Links to Newcomers' Commitment and Role Orientation," *Academy of Management Journal* 33 (1990): 847–858.

55. T. N. Bauer, E. W. Morrison, and R. R. Callister, "Organizational Socialization: A Review and Directions for Future Research," *Research in Personnel and Human Resources Management* 16 (1998): 149–214.

56. D. M. Cable and C. K. Parsons, "Socialization Tactics and Person–Organization Fit," *Personnel Psychology* 54 (2001): 1–23.

57. S. H. Harrison, D. M. Sluss, and B. E. Ashforth, "Curiosity Adapted the Cat: The Role of Trait Curiosity in Newcomer Adaption," *Journal of Applied Psychology* 96 (2011): 211–220; M. Wang, Y. Zhan, E. McCune, and D. Truxillo, "Understanding Newcomers' Adaptability and Work-Related Outcomes: Testing the Mediating Roles of Perceived P-E Fit Variables," *Personnel Psychology* 64 (2011): 163–189.

58. A. M. Saks, J. A. Gruman, and H. Cooper-Thomas, "The Neglected Role of Proactive Behavior and Outcomes in Newcomer Socialization," *Journal of Vocational Behavior* 79 (2011): 36–46.

59. D. M. Rousseau, "Assessing Organizational Culture: The Case for Multiple Methods," in B. Schneider, ed., *Organizational Climate and Culture* (San Francisco: Jossey-Bass, 1990).

60. R. A. Cooke and D. M. Rousseau, "Behavioral Norms and Expectations: A Quantitative Approach to the Assessment of Organizational Culture," *Group and Organizational Studies* 12 (1988): 245–273.

61. R. H. Kilmann and M. J. Saxton, *Kilmann-Saxton Culture-Gap Survey* (Pittsburgh: Organizational Design Consultants, 1983).

62. W. J. Duncan, "Organizational Culture: 'Getting a Fix' on an Elusive Concept," *Academy of Management Executive* 3 (1989): 229–236.

63. P. Bate, "Using the Culture Concept in an Organization Development Setting," *Journal of Applied Behavior Science* 26 (1990): 83–106.

64. K. R. Thompson and F. Luthans, "Organizational Culture: A Behavioral Perspective," in B. Schneider, ed., *Organizational Climate and Culture* (San Francisco: Jossey-Bass, 1990).

65. S. Seren and U. Baykal, "Relationships between Change and Organizational Culture in Hospitals," *Journal of Nursing Scholarship* 39, No. 2 (2007): 191–197.

66. V. Sathe, "How to Decipher and Change Corporate Culture," in R. H. Kilman et al., *Managing Corporate Cultures* (San Francisco: Jossey-Bass, 1985).

67. M. E. Johnson-Cramer, S. Parise, and R. L. Cross, "Managing Change through Networks and Values," *California Management Review* 49(3) (2007): 85–109.

68. S. Lee, J. Kim, and B. Park, "Culture Clashes in Cross-Border Mergers and Acquisitions: A Case Study of Sweden's Volvo and South Korea's Samsung," *International Business Review*, November 20, 2014, accessed at http://www.sciencedirect.com/science/article/pii/S0969593114001772.

69. N. J. Adler, *International Dimensions of Organizational Behavior*, 2nd ed. (Boston: PWS Kent, 1991).

70. A. Laurent, "The Cultural Diversity of Western Conceptions of Management," *International Studies of Management and Organization* 13 (1983): 75–96.

71. P. C. Earley and E. Mosakowski, "Creating Hybrid Team Cultures: An Empirical Test of Transnational Team Functioning," *Academy of Management Journal* 43 (2000): 26–49.

72. D. Lei, J. W. Slocum, Jr., and R. W. Slater, "Global Strategy and Reward Systems: The Key Roles of Management Development and Corporate Culture," *Organizational Dynamics* 19 (1990): 27–41.

73. L. K. Trevino and K. A. Nelson, *Managing Business Ethics: Straight Talk about How to Do It Right* (New York: John Wiley & Sons, 1995).

74. M. Kaptein, "Understanding Unethical Behavior by Unraveling Ethical Culture," *Human Relations* (in press).

75. A. Bhide and H. H. Stevenson, "Why Be Honest if Honesty Doesn't Pay?" *Harvard Business Review* (September–October 1990): 121–129.

76. A. Pater and A. van Gils, "Stimulating Ethical Decision Making in a Business Context: Ethics of Ethical and Professional Codes," *European Management Journal* 21 (December 2003): 762–772.

77. J. R. Detert, R. G. Schroeder, and J. J. Mauriel, "A Framework for Linking Culture and Improvement Initiatives in Organizations," *Academy of Management Review* 25 (2000): 850–863.

78. S. D. Salamon and S. L. Robinson, "Trust That Binds: The Impact of Collective Felt Trust on Organizational Performance," *Journal of Applied Psychology* 93 (2008): 593–601.

79. R. Bruce, "A Case Study of Harley-Davidson's Business Practices," http://stroked.virtualave.net/casestudy.shtml.

17

1. J. H. Greenhaus, *Career Management* (Hinsdale, Ill.: CBS College Press, 1987).

2. D. T. Hall, *Careers in Organizations* (Pacific Palisades, Calif.: Goodyear, 1976).

3. Greenhaus, *Career Management;* T. G. Gutteridge and F. L. Otte, "Organizational Career Development: What's Going on Out There?" *Training and Development Journal* 37 (1983): 22–26.

4. M. B. Arthur, P. H. Claman, and R. J. DeFillippi, "Intelligent Enterprise, Intelligent Careers," *Academy of Management Executive* (November 1995): 7–22.

5. M. Lips-Wiersma and D. T. Hall, "Organizational Career Development Is Not Dead: A Case Study on Managing the New Career during Organizational Change," *Journal of Organizational Behavior* 28, No. 6 (2007): 771–792.

6. D. Jemielniak, "Managers as Lazy, Stupid Careerists?" *Journal of Organizational Change Management* 20, No. 4 (2007): 491–508.

7. D. E. Super, *The Psychology of Careers* (New York: Harper & Row, 1957); D. E. Super and M. J. Bohn, Jr., *Occupational Psychology* (Belmont, Calif.: Wadsworth, 1970).

8. J. L. Holland, *The Psychology of Vocational Choice* (Waltham, Mass.: Blaisdell, 1966); J. L. Holland, *Making Vocational Choices: A Theory of Careers* (Englewood Cliffs, N.J.: Prentice-Hall, 1973).

9. F. T. L. Leong and J. T. Austin, "An Evaluation of the Cross-Cultural Validity of Holland's Theory: Career Choices by Workers in India," *Journal of Vocational Behavior* 52 (1998): 441–455.

10. C. Morgan, J. D. Isaac, and C. Sansone, "The Role of Interest in Understanding the Career Choices of Female and Male College Students," *Sex Roles* 44 (2001): 295–320.

11. J. K. Hellerstein and M. S. Morrill, "Dads and Daughters: The Changing Impact of Fathers on Women's Occupational Choices," *Journal of Human Resources* 46, No. 2 (2011): 333–372; S. H. Osipow, *Theories of Career Development* (Englewood Cliffs, N.J.: Prentice-Hall, 1973).

12. J. P. Wanous, T. L. Keon, and J. C. Latack, "Expectancy Theory and Occupational/Organizational Choices: A Review and Test," *Organizational Behavior and Human Performance* 32 (1983): 66–86.

13. P. O. Soelberg, "Unprogrammed Decision Making," *Industrial Management Review* 8 (1967): 19–29.

14. J. P. Wanous, *Organizational Entry: Recruitment, Selection, and Socialization of Newcomers* (Reading, Mass.: Addison-Wesley, 1980).

15. S. L. Premack and J. P. Wanous, "A Meta-Analysis of Realistic Job Preview Experiments," *Journal of Applied Psychology* 70 (1985): 706–719.

16. http://www.timewarnercable.com/corporate/about/careers.

17. http://www.dads.state.tx.us/providers/jobpreview/idd-video.html

18. P. W. Hom, R. W. Griffeth, L. E. Palich, and J. S. Bracker, "An Exploratory Investigation into Theoretical Mechanisms Underlying Realistic

Job Previews," *Personnel Psychology* 41 (1998): 421–451.

19. J. A. Breaugh, "Realistic Job Previews: A Critical Appraisal and Future Research Directions," *Academy of Management Review* 8 (1983): 612–619.

20. G. R. Jones, "Socialization Tactics, Self-Efficacy, and Newcomers' Adjustment to Organizations," *Academy of Management Journal* 29 (1986): 262–279.

21. M. R. Buckley, D. B. Fedor, J. G. Veres, D. S. Wiese, and S. M. Carraher, "Investigating Newcomer Expectations and Job-Related Outcomes," *Journal of Applied Psychology* 83 (1998): 452–461.

22. J. Oliver, R. T. Erk, A. Koch, T. L. Russell, N. E. Babin, S. A. Ardison, and M. C. Young, "Identification and Accessioning of Individuals for Officer Candidate School: Developing Realistic Job Previews," technical report, United States Army Research Institute for Behavioral and Social Sciences (2014), accessed online.

23. A. De Vos and C. Freese, "Sensemaking During Organizational Entry: Changes in Newcomer Information Seeking and the Relationship with Psychological Contract Fulfillment," *Journal of Occupational and Organizational Psychology* 84 (2011): 288–314.

24. P. Buhler, "Managing in the '90s," *Supervision* (July 1995): 24–26.

25. D. T. Hall and J. E. Moss, "The New Protean Career Contract: Helping Organizations and Employees Adapt," *Organizational Dynamics* (Winter 1998): 22–37.

26. S. A. Zahra, R. L. Priem, and A. A. Rasheed, "Understanding the Causes and Effects of Top Management Fraud," *Organizational Dynamics* 36, No. 2 (2007): 122–139.

27. A. Fisher, "Don't Blow Your New Job," *Fortune* (June 22, 1998): 159–162.

28. D. Goleman, *Working with Emotional Intelligence* (New York: Bantam, 1998); A. Fisher, "Success Secret: A High Emotional IQ," *Fortune* (October 26, 1998): 293–298.

29. N. Libbrecht, F. Lievens, B. Carette, and S. Cote, "Emotional Intelligence Predicts Success in Medical School," *Emotion* 14 (2014): 64–73.

30. K. V. Petrides, A. Furnham, and G. N. Martin, "Estimates of Emotional and Psychometric Intelligence," *Journal of Social Psychology* 144 (April 2004): 149–162.

31. C. Chermiss, "The Business Case for Emotional Intelligence," *The Consortium for Research on Emotional Intelligence in Organizations* (2003), http://www.eiconsortium.org /research/business_case_for _ei.htm; L. M. Spencer, Jr., and S. Spencer, *Competence at Work: Models for Superior Performance* (New York: John Wiley & Sons, 1993); L. M. Spencer, Jr., D. C. McClelland, and S. Kelner, *Competency Assessment Methods: History and State of the Art* (Boston Hay/McBer, 1997).

32. J. O. Crites, "A Comprehensive Model of Career Adjustment in Early Adulthood," *Journal*

of *Vocational Behavior* 9 (1976): 105–118; S. Cytrynbaum and J. O. Crites, "The Utility of Adult Development in Understanding Career Adjustment Process," in M. B. Arthur, D. T. Hall, and B. S. Lawrence, eds., *Handbook of Career Theory* (Cambridge: Cambridge University Press, 1989): 66–88.

33. D. E. Super, "A Life-Span, Life-Space Approach to Career Development," *Journal of Vocational Behavior* 16 (1980): 282–298; L. Baird and K. Kram, "Career Dynamics: Managing the Superior/Subordinate Relationship," *Organizational Dynamics* 11 (1983): 46–64.

34. D. J. Levinson, *The Seasons of a Man's Life* (New York: Knopf, 1978); D. J. Levinson, *The Seasons of a Woman's Life* (New York: Knopf, 1996).

35. D. J. Levinson, "A Conception of Adult Development," *American Psychologist* 41 (1986): 3–13.

36. D. L. Nelson, "Adjusting to a New Organization: Easing the Transition from Outsider to Insider," in J. C. Quick, R. E. Hess, J. Hermalin, and J. D. Quick, eds., *Career Stress in Changing Times* (New York: Haworth Press, 1990): 61–86.

37. J. P. Kotter, "The Psychological Contract: Managing the Joining Up Process," *California Management Review* 15 (1973): 91–99.

38. D. M. Rousseau, "New Hire Perceptions of Their Own and Their Employers' Obligations: A Study of Psychological Contracts," *Journal of Organizational Behavior* 11 (1990): 389–400; D. L. Nelson, J. C. Quick, and J. R. Joplin, "Psychological Contracting and Newcomer Socialization: An Attachment Theory Foundation," *Journal of Social Behavior and Personality* 6 (1991): 55–72.

39. H. Zhao, S. Wayne, B. Glibkowski, and J. Bravo "The Impact of Psychological Breach on Work-Related Outcomes," *Personnel Psychology* (2007): 647–680.

40. S. D. Pugh, D. P. Skarlicki, and B. S. Passell, "After the Fall: Layoff Victims' Trust and Cynicism in Reemployment," *Journal of Occupational and Organizational Psychology* 76 (June 2003): 201–212.

41. D. J. Levinson," A conception of adult development," *American Psychologist* 41, No. 1 (Jan 1986): 3–13.

42. J. W. Walker, "Let's Get Realistic about Career Paths," *Human Resource Management* 15 (1976): 2–7.

43. E. H. Buttner and D. P. Moore, "Women's Organizational Exodus to Entrepreneurship: Self-Reported Motivations and Correlates," *Journal of Small Business Management* 35 (1997): 34–46; Center for Women's Business Research Press Release, "Privately Held, 50% or More Women-Owned Businesses in the United States," 2004, http://www.nfwbo.org/pressreleases /nationalstatetrends/total.htm.

44. D. G. Collings, H. Scullion, and M. J. Morley, "Changing Patterns of Global Staffing in the Multinational Enterprise: Challenges to

the Conventional Expatriate Assignment and Emerging Alternatives," *Journal of World Business* 42, No. 2 (2007): 198–213.

45. B. Filipczak, "You're on Your Own," *Training* (January 1995): 29–36.

46. K. E. Kram, *Mentoring at Work: Developmental Relationships in Organizational Life* (Glenview, Ill.: Scott, Foresman, 1985).

47. C. Orpen, "The Effects of Mentoring on Employees' Career Success," *Journal of Social Psychology* 135 (1995): 667–668.

48. J. Arnold and K. Johnson, "Mentoring in Early Career," *Human Resource Management Journal* 7 (1997): 61–70.

49. B. P. Madia and C. J. Lutz, "Perceived Similarity, Expectation–Reality Discrepancies, and Mentors' Expressed Intention to Remain in the Big Brothers/Big Sisters Programs," *Journal of Applied Social Psychology* 34 (March 2004): 598–622.

50. "A Guide to the Mentor Program Listings," *Mentors Peer Resources,* http://www.mentors.ca /mentorprograms.html.

51. http://www.diversityinc.com/mentoring /why-mentoring-is-not-an-option-at-ibm/

52. R. Friedman, M. Kan, and D. B. Cornfield, "Social Support and Career Optimism: Examining the Effectiveness of Network Groups among Black Managers," *Human Relations* 51 (1998): 1155–1177.

53. S. E. Seibert, M. L. Kraimer, and R. C. Liden, "A Social Capital Theory of Career Success," *Academy of Management Journal* 44 (2001): 219–237.

54. http://corporate.exxonmobil.com/en/company /careers/employment-policies/diversity

55. M. A. Covaleski, M. W. Dirsmuth, J. B. Heian, and S. Samuel, "The Calculated and the Avowed: Techniques of Discipline and Struggles over Identity in Big Six Public Accounting Firms," *Administrative Science Quarterly* 43 (1998): 293–327.

56. B. R. Ragins and J. L. Cotton, "Easier Said Than Done: Gender Differences in Perceived Barriers to Gaining a Mentor," *Academy of Management Journal* 34 (1991): 939–951; S. D. Phillips and A. R. Imhoff, "Women and Career Development: A Decade of Research," *Annual Review of Psychology* 48 (1997): 31–43.

57. Ibid.

58. A. Ramaswami, G. F. Dreher, R. Bretz, and C. Wiethoff, "Gender, Mentoring and Career Success: The Importance of Organizational Context," *Personnel Psychology* 63, No. 2 (2010): 385–405.

59. W. Whiteley, T. W. Dougherty, and G. F. Dreher, "Relationship of Career Mentoring and Socioeconomic Origin to Managers' and Professionals' Early Career Progress," *Academy of Management Journal* 34 (1991): 331–351; G. F. Dreher and R. A. Ash, "A Comparative Study of Mentoring among Men and Women in Managerial, Professional, and Technical Positions," *Journal of Applied Psychology* 75 (1990): 539–546; T. A. Scandura, "Mentorship and

Career Mobility: An Empirical Investigation," *Journal of Organizational Behavior* 13 (1992): 169–174.

60. G. F. Dreher and T. H. Cox, Jr., "Race, Gender and Opportunity: A Study of Compensation Attainment and Establishment of Mentoring Relationships," *Journal of Applied Psychology* 81 (1996): 297–309.

61. D. D. Horgan and R. J. Simeon, "Mentoring and Participation: An Application of the Vroom-Yetton Model," *Journal of Business and Psychology* 5 (1990): 63–84.

62. B. R. Ragins, J. L. Cotton, and J. S. Miller, "Marginal Mentoring: The Effects of Type of Mentor, Quality of Relationship, and Program Design on Work and Career Attitudes," *Academy of Management Journal* 43 (2000): 1177–1194.

63. R. T. Brennan, R. C. Barnett, and K. C. Gareis, "When She Earns More Than He Does: A Longitudinal Study of Dual-Earner Couples," *Journal of Marriage and Family* 63 (2001): 168–182.

64. C. R. Masterson and J. M. Hoobler, "Care and Career: A Family Identity-Based Typology of Dual-Earner Couples," *Journal of Organizational Behavior* 36 (2015), accessed online, doi:10.1002/job.1945.

65. A. Croft, T. Schmader, K. Block, and A. S. Baron, "The Second Shift Reflected in the Second Generation," *Psychological Science* (2015), accessed online, doi:10.1177/0956797614533968.

66. B. Morris, "Is Your Family Wrecking Your Career? (And Vice Versa)," *Fortune* (March 17, 1997): 70–80.

67. Ibid.

68. D. L. Nelson, J. C. Quick, M. A. Hitt, and D. Moesel, "Politics, Lack of Career Progress, and Work/Home Conflict: Stress and Strain for Working Women," *Sex Roles* 23 (1990): 169–185.

69. L. E. Duxbury and C. A. Higgins, "Gender Differences in Work–Family Conflict," *Journal of Applied Psychology* 76 (1991): 60–74.

70. R. G. Netemeyer, J. S. Boles, and R. McMurrian, "Development and Validation of Work–Family Conflict and Family–Work Conflict Scales," *Journal of Applied Psychology* 81 (1996): 400–410.

71. B. Livingston and T. A. Judge, "Emotional Responses to Work-Family Conflict: An Examination of Gender Role Orientation among Working Men and Women," *Journal of Applied Psychology* (2008): 207–216.

72. N. Yang, C. C. Chen, J. Choi, and Y. Zou, "Sources of Work–Family Conflict: A Sino–U.S. Comparison of the Effects of Work and Family Demands," *Academy of Management Journal* 43 (2000): 113–123.

73. A. Iris Aaltion and H. Jiehua Huang, "Women Managers' Careers in Information Technology in China: High Flyers with Emotional Costs?" *Journal of Organizational Change Management* 20, No. 2 (2007): 227–244.

74. See http://www.ehow.com/info_7737471 _companies-great-benefits.html.

75. Mitchell Gold Co., "Day Care," http://www. mitchellgold.com/daycare.asp.

76. http://www.mgbwhome.com/OurDaycare. aspx

77. H. Zacher and H. Schultz, "Employees' Eldercare Demands, Strain, and Perceived Support," *Journal of Managerial Psychology* 30 (2015): 183–198.

78. Cincinnati Area Senior Services, "Corporate Elder Care Program," http://www.senserv.org/ elder.htm.

79. E. E. Kossek, J. A. Colquitt, and R. A. Noe, "Caregiving Decisions, Well-Being, and Performance: The Effects of Place and Provider as a Function of Dependent Type and Work–Family Climates," *Academy of Management Journal* 44 (2001): 29–44.

80. http://www.parentsinapinch.com/sitters- and-nannies/

81. B. Schulte, "Aging Population Prompts More Employers to Offer Elder-Care Benefits to Workers," *The Washington Post*, November 16, 2014, accessed at http://www .washingtonpost.com/local/aging-population -prompts-more-employers-to-offer-elder -care-benefits-to-workers/2014/11/16 /25f9c8e6-6847-11e4-a31c-77759fc1eacc _story.html.

82. L. J. Barham, "Variables Affecting Managers' Willingness to Grant Alternative Work Arrangements," *Journal of Social Psychology* 138 (1998): 291–302; J. Kaplan, "Hitting the Wall at Forty," *Business Month* 136 (1990): 52–58.

83. K. E. Kram, "Phases of the Mentoring Relationship," *Academy of Management Review* 26 (1983): 608–625.

84. B. Rosen and T. Jerdee, *Older Employees: New Roles for Valued Resources* (Homewood, Ill.: Irwin, 1985).

85. J. W. Gilsdorf, "The New Generation: Older Workers," *Training and Development Journal* (March 1992): 77–79.

86. J. F. Quick, "Time to Move On?" in J. C. Quick, R. E. Hess, J. Hermalin, and J. D. Quick, eds., *Career Stress in Changing Times* (New York: Haworth Press, 1990): 239–250.

87. D. Machan, "Rent-an-Exec," *Forbes* (January 22, 1990): 132–133.

88. S. Kim and D. C. Feldman, "Working in Retirement: The Antecedents of Bridge Employment and Its Consequences for Quality of Life in Retirement," *Academy of Management Journal* 43 (2000): 1195–1210.

89. http://www.gallup.com/poll/168707/average- retirement-age-rises.aspx

90. T. A. Beehr, "To Retire or Not to Retire: That Is Not the Question," *Journal of Organizational Behavior* 35 (2014): 1093–1108.

91. E. Schein, *Career Anchors* (San Diego: University Associates, 1985).

92. G. W. Dalton, "Developmental Views of Careers in Organizations," in M. B. Arthur, D. T. Hall, and B. S. Lawrence, eds., *Handbook of Career Theory* (Cambridge: Cambridge University Press, 1989): 89–109.

93. D. C. Feldman, "Careers in Organizations: Recent Trends and Future Directions," *Journal of Management* 15 (1989): 135–156.

18

1. M. A. Verespej, "When Change Becomes the Norm," *Industry Week* (March 16, 1992): 35–38.

2. P. Mornell, "Nothing Endures but Change," *Inc.* 22 (July 2000): 131–132, http://www.inc. com/magazine/20000701/19555.html.

3. H. J. Van Buren, III, "The Bindingness of Social and Psychological Contracts: Toward a Theory of Social Responsibility in Downsizing," *Journal of Business Ethics* 25 (2000): 205–219.

4. "The Mystery of the Chinese Consumer," *The Economist* (July 7, 2011), http://www .economist.com/node/18928514?story_id =189285148.

5. See http://www.tata.com/htm/Grou-_MnA _YearWise.htm.

6. http://www.fool.com/investing/general/2014 /01/04/costco-expands-its-global-reach.aspx

7. L. R. Offerman and M. Gowing, "Organizations of the Future: Changes and Challenges," *American Psychologist* (February 1990): 95–108.

8. http://www.fool.com/investing/general/2014 /01/04/costco-expands-its-global-reach.aspx

9. http://www.pewresearch.org/fact-tank/2014 /01/07/number-of-older-americans-in-the -workforce-is-on-the-rise/

10. http://www.siemens.com/about/sustainability /en/core-topics/employees/ management-and -facts/index.php

11. http://www.cnet.com/how-to/apple-pay-vs -google-wallet-vs-paypal/

12. https://www.currencycloud.com/news /blog/currency-cloud-reviews-apple-pay-google -wallet-and-paypal

13. R. M. Kanter, "Improving the Development, Acceptance, and Use of New Technology: Organizational and Interorganizational Challenges," in *People and Technology in the Workplace* (Washington, D.C.: National Academy Press, 1991): 15–56.

14. http://www.gapinc.com/content/attachments /gapinc/GPS_AR13.pdf

15. "Gap Inc. 2003 Social Responsibility Report," *Gap Inc.* (September 17, 2004), http:// ccbn.mobular.net/ccbn/7/645/696/index.html.

16. S. A. Mohrman and A. M. Mohrman, Jr., "The Environment as an Agent of Change," in A. M. Mohrman, Jr., et al., eds., *Large-Scale Organizational Change* (San Francisco: Jossey-Bass, 1989): 35–47.

17. T. D'Aunno, M. Succi, and J. A. Alexander, "The Role of Institutional and Market Forces in Divergent Organizational Change," *Administrative Science Quarterly* 45 (2000): 679–703.

18. M. Jarman, "Intel Opens 'Leading-Edge Fab: Plant to Build Most Powerful Chips," *The Arizona Republic* (October 21, 2007), http:// www.azcentral.com/arizonarepublic/business /articles/1021biz -intel1021.html.

19. Q. N. Huy, "Emotional Balancing of Organizational Continuity and Radical Change: The Contribution of Middle Managers," *Administrative Science Quarterly* 47 (March 1, 2002): 31–69.

20. D. Nadler, "Organizational Frame-Bending: Types of Change in the Complex Organization," in R. Kilmann and T. Covin, eds., *Corporate Transformation* (San Francisco: Jossey-Bass, 1988): 66–83.

21. R. Winkler, "YouTube: 1 Billion Viewers, No Profit," *The Wall Street Journal*, February 15, 2015, accessed at http://www.wsj.com /articles/viewers-dont-add-up-to-profit-for-youtube -1424897967.

22. L. Ackerman, "Development, Transition, or Transformation: The Question of Change in Organizations," *OD Practitioner* (December 1986): 1–8.

23. T. D. Jick, *Managing Change* (Homewood, Ill.: Irwin, 1993): 3.

24. J. M. Bloodgood and J. L. Morrow, "Strategic Organizational Change: Exploring the Roles of Environmental Structure, Internal Conscious Awareness, and Knowledge," *Journal of Management Studies* 40 (2003): 1761–1782.

25. D. Miller and M. J. Chen, "Sources and Consequences of Competitive Inertia. A Study of the U.S. Airline Industry," *Administrative Science Quarterly* 39 (1994): 1–23.

26. S. L. Brown and K. M. Eisenhardt, "The Art of Continuous Change: Linking Complexity Theory and Time-Paced Evolution in Relentlessly Shifting Organizations," *Administrative Science Quarterly* 42 (1997): 1–34.

27. J. Child and C. Smith, "The Context and Process of Organizational Transformation: Cadbury Ltd. in Its Sector," *Journal of Management Studies* 12 (1987): 12–27.

28. J. Amis, T. Slack, and C. R. Hinings, "The Pace, Sequence, and Linearity of Radical Change," *Academy of Management Journal* 47 (2004): 15–39.

29. R. M. Kanter, *The Change Masters* (New York: Simon & Schuster, 1983).

30. J. R. Katzenbach, *Real Change Leaders* (New York: Times Business, 1995).

31. J. L. Denis, L. Lamothe, and A. Langley, "The Dynamics of Collective Leadership and Strategic Change in Pluralistic Organizations," *Academy of Management Journal* 44 (2001): 809–837.

32. M. Beer, *Organization Change and Development: A Systems View* (Santa Monica, Calif.: Goodyear, 1980): 78.

33. K. Whalen-Berry and C. R. Hinings, "The Relative Effect of Change Drivers in Large-Scale Organizational Change: An Empirical Study," in W. Passmore and R. Goodman, eds., *Research in Organizational Change and Development* 14 (New York: JAI Press, 2003): 99–146.

34. Denis et al., "The Dynamics of Collective Leadership and Strategic Change in Pluralistic Organizations."

35. J. W. Brehm, *A Theory of Psychological Reactance* (New York: Academic Press, 1966).

36. J. A. Klein, "Why Supervisors Resist Employee Involvement," *Harvard Business Review* 62 (1984): 87–95.

37. B. L. Kirkman, R. G. Jones, and D. L. Shapiro, "Why Do Employees Resist Teams? Examining the 'Resistance Barrier' to Work Team Effectiveness," *International Journal of Conflict Management* 11 (2000): 74–92.

38. D. L. Nelson and M. A. White, "Management of Technological Innovation: Individual Attitudes, Stress, and Work Group Attributes," *Journal of High Technology Management Research* 1 (1990): 137–148.

39. S. Elias, "Employee Commitment in Times of Change: Assessing the Importance of Attitudes Toward Organizational Change," *Journal of Management* 35 (2009): 37–55; J. B. Avey, T. S. Wernsing, and F. Luthans, "Can Positive Employees Help Positive Organizational Change? Impact of Psychological Capital and Emotions on Relevant Attitudes and Behaviors," *Journal of Applied Behavioral Science* 44 (2008): 48–70.

40. T. Diefenbach, "The Managerialistic Ideology of Organisational Change Management," *Journal of Organizational Change Management* 20, No. 1 (2007): 126–144.

41. A. E. Rafferty, N. L. Jimmieson, and A. A. Armenakis, "Change Readiness: A Multilevel Review," *Journal of Management* 39 (2013): 110–135.

42. T. G. Cummings and E. F. Huse, *Organizational Development and Change* (St. Paul, Minn.: West, 1989).

43. N. L. Jimmieson, D. J. Terry, and V. J. Callan, "A Longitudinal Study of Employee Adaptation to Organizational Change: The Role of Change-Related Information and Change-Related Self Efficacy," *Journal of Occupational Health Psychology* 9 (2004): 11–27.

44. N. DiFonzo and P. Bordia, "A Tale of Two Corporations: Managing Uncertainty during Organizational Change," *Human Resource Management* 37 (1998): 295–303.

45. J. de Vries, C. Webb, and J. Eveline, "Mentoring for Gender Equality and Organisational Change," *Employee Relations* 28, No. 6 (2006): 573–587.

46. A. H. Hon, M. Bloom, and J. M. Crant, "Overcoming Resistance to Change and Enhancing Creative Performance," *Journal of Management* 40 (2014): 919–941.

47. M. Hickins, "Reconcilable Differences," *Management Review* 87 (1998): 54–58.

48. K. Lewin, "Frontiers in Group Dynamics," *Human Relations* 1 (1947): 5–41.

49. C. Bareil, A. Savoie, and S. Meunier, "Patterns of Discomfort with Organizational Change," *Journal of Change Management* 7(1) (2007):13–24.

50. W. Mc Whinney, "Meta-Praxis: A Framework for Making Complex Changes," in A. M. Mohrman, Jr., et al., eds., *Large-Scale Organizational Change* (San Francisco: Jossey-Bass, 1989): 154–199.

51. M. Beer and E. Walton, "Developing the Competitive Organization: Interventions and Strategies," *American Psychologist* 45 (1990): 154–161.

52. B. Bertsch and R. Williams, "How Multinational CEOs Make Change Programs Stick," *Long Range Planning* 27 (1994): 12–24.

53. J. Amis, T. Slack, and C. R. Hinings, "Values and Organizational Change," *Journal of Applied Behavioral Science* 38 (2002): 356–385.

54. W. L. French and C. H. Bell, *Organization Development: Behavioral Science Interventions for Organization Improvement*, 4th ed. (Englewood Cliffs, N.J.: Prentice-Hall, 1990); W. W. Burke, *Organization Development: A Normative View* (Reading, Mass.: Addison-Wesley, 1987).

55. A. O. Manzini, *Organizational Diagnosis* (New York: AMACOM, 1988).

56. M. R. Weisbord, "Organizational Diagnosis: Six Places to Look for Trouble with or without a Theory," *Group and Organization Studies* (December 1976): 430–444.

57. H. Levinson, *Organizational Diagnosis* (Cambridge, Mass.: Harvard University Press, 1972).

58. J. Nicholas, "The Comparative Impact of Organization Development Interventions," *Academy of Management Review* 7 (1982): 531–542.

59. G. Odiorne, *Management by Objectives* (Marshfield, Mass.: Pitman, 1965).

60. E. Huse, "Putting in a Management Development Program that Works," *California Management Review* 9 (1966): 73–80.

61. J. P. Muczyk and B. C. Reimann, "MBO as a Complement to Effective Leadership," *Academy of Management Executive* (May 1989): 131–138.

62. L. L. Berry and A. Parasuraman, "Prescriptions for a Service Quality Revolution in America," *Organizational Dynamics* 20 (1992): 5–15.

63. T. A. Stewart, and A. P. Raman, "Lessons from Toyota's Long Drive," *Harvard Business Review* 85, No. 7/8 (2007): 74–83.

64. W. G. Dyer, *Team Building: Issues and Alternatives*, 2nd ed. (Reading, Mass.: Addison-Wesley, 1987).

65. E. Stephan, G. Mills, R. W. Pace, and L. Ralphs, "HRD in the Fortune 500: A Survey," *Training and Development Journal* (January 1988): 26–32.

66. A. Edmondson, "Psychological Safety and Learning Behavior in Work Teams," *Administrative Science Quarterly* 44 (1999): 350–383.

67. See http://www.teambuildinginc.com /services4_teamconcepts.htm; http://www .teambuildinginc.com/services5.htm.

68. https://www.teambonding.com/programs /team-food-truck-challenge/

69. L. L. Gilson, M. T. Maynard, N. C. J. Young, M. Vartiainen, and M. Hakonen, "Virtual Teams Research: 10 Years, 10 Themes, and 10 Opportunities," *Journal of Management*, published online before print on November 24, 2014, accessed at http://jom.sagepub.com .argo.library.okstate.edu/content/early/2014 /11/21/0149206314559946.full.

70. E. Schein, *Its Role in Organization Development, Process Consultation*, vol. 1 (Reading, Mass.: Addison-Wesley, 1988).

71. H. Hornstein, "Organizational Development and Change Management: Don't Throw the Baby Out with the Bath Water," *Journal of Applied Behavioral Science* 37 (2001): 223–226.

72. K. A. Aikens, J. Astin, K. R. Pelletier, K. Levanovich, C. M. Baase, Y. Y. Park, and C. M. Bodnar, "Mindfulness Goes to Work: Impact of an Online Workplace Intervention," *Journal of Occupational and Environmental Medicine* 56 (2014): 721–731.

73. I. L. Goldstein, *Training in Organizations,* 3rd ed. (Pacific Grove, Calif.: Brooks/Cole, 1993).

74. J. A. Conger and R. M. Fulmer, "Developing Your Leadership Pipeline," *Harvard Business Review* 81 (2003): 76–84.

75. J. Reb, J. Narayanan, and S. Chaturvedi, "Leading Mindfully: Two Studies on the Influence of Supervisor Trait Mindfulness on Employee Well-Being and Performance," *Mindfulness* 5 (2014): 36–45.

76. M. Jay, "Understanding How to Leverage Executive Coaching," *Organization Development Journal* 21 (2003): 6–13; D. Goleman, R. Boyaysis, and A. McKee, *Primal Leadership: Learning to Lead with Emotional Intelligence* (Harvard Business School Press, 2004).

77. K. M. Wasylyshyn, "Executive Coaching: An Outcome Study," *Consulting Psychology Journal* 55 (2003): 94–106.

78. J. W. Smither, M. London, R. Flautt, Y. Vargas, and I. Kucine, "Can Working with an Executive Coach Improve Multisource Feedback Ratings over Time? A Quasi-Experimental Field Study," *Personnel Psychology* 56 (2003): 23–44.

79. N. Bloom, "To Raise Productivity, Let More Employees Work from Home," *Harvard Business Review*, January–February 2014, accessed at https://hbr.org/2014/01/to-raise-productivity-let-more-employees-work-from-home.

80. American Psychological Association, "Psychologically Healthy Workplace Awards," http://apahelpcenter.mediaroom.com/file.php/mr_apahelpcenter/spinsite_docfiles/134/phwa_magazine_2007.pdf.

81. A. M. Pettigrew, R. W. Woodman, and K. S. Cameron, "Studying Organizational Change and Development: Challenges for Future Research," *Academy of Management Journal* 44 (2001): 697–713.

82. R. A. Katzell and R. A. Guzzo, "Psychological Approaches to Worker Productivity," *American Psychologist* 38 (1983): 468–472.

83. Goldstein, *Training in Organizations.*

INDEX

Multicultural group, 151
Multicultural top teams, 151
Multinational organizations, 17
Multitasking, 133–134
Munger, Charles, 261
Murray, Henry, 74
Murray Thematic Apperception Test (TAT), 74
Myers, Isabel Briggs, 41, 155
Myers-Briggs Type Indicator (MBTI), 41–44

N

Nadella, Staya, 9
Name-dropping, 49
Narcissism, 189
National Aeronautics and Space Administration (NASA), 4, 6, 164, 246
Natural liberty, 28
Nature of human activity, 260
Nature of human nature, 260
Nature of human relationships, 260
Nature of reality, 260
Need for achievement, 74–75
Need for affiliation, 75
Need for autonomy, 75
Need for power, 75
Needs analysis, 302
Needs theories of motivation, 71, 72–75
Negative affect, 37, 39, 56, 160
Negative consequences, 88
Negative emotions, 60–61, 62
Negative inequity, 79–80
Negative moods, 61
Negative reinforcement, 86–87
Negative stress, 106–108
Negativism, 214
Negotiation, 20, 217–218
Neiman Marcus, 250
NEO Personality Inventory, 40
Nestlé, 293
Netherlands, 66, 67, 223–224
Network groups, 285
Network organization, 254
Networking ability, 180
Networking technology, 5
Neuroscienced organization, 255
Neuroticism, 108
New Belgium Brewery, 301
New team environment, 138
New Zealand, 83
Nike, 262
Nissan, 17
No discretion (employee empowerment grid), 184
Noise, 105
Nominal group technique (NGT), 165
Nonaction, 215
Nonadaptive culture, 264
Nondefensive communication, 126, 127–128
Nonfinancial reinforcement, 85, 86
Nonprofit sector, 8
Nonprogrammed decisions, 153

Nonsubstitutability, 173
Nonverbal communication, 46, 61, 128–130, 132. *See also* Eye contact
Nonwork demands, 103, 105
Nooyi, Indra, 173
Normative commitment, 58
Normative decision model, 194–195, 196
Norming stage, 141
Norms of behavior, 139, 142
North American Free Trade Agreement (NAFTA), 18
Northern Telecom (Nortel Networks), 166
Northwest Airlines (now Delta), 9
Norway, 21, 104, 162, 172
Nous Group, 247
Nut rage, 175

O

Obama, Barack, 42, 197
Objective element of career, 275
Objective knowledge acquisition, 12–13
OCB (organizational citizenship behavior). *See* Organizational citizenship behavior (OCB)
Occupational choice, 277
Occupational excellence, 275–276
OCI (organizational culture inventory), 268
OD (organizational development), 301–302
Office design, 105, 160
Officer effectiveness reports (1813), 93
Official group, 140
Older workers, 24
Oldham, Greg, 228–229
Olive Garden, 81
One-way communication, 122
Online shopping, 246
On-site day-care center, 287
Opening up, 114, 115
Open-minded discussion, 215
Openness, 14, 36
Open-plan offices, 160
Open-systems view of organization, 5–8
Operant conditioning, 85
Operating level, 244–245
Operational support planning, 91
Opponents, 148
Opportunistic management, 191, 192
Opportunistic what's-in-it-for-me manager (Opp), 191, 192
Opportunities, 3, 8–12
Optimism, 114, 156
Optimization, 154
Organic structure, 250, 252–253
Organization
  clockwork metaphor, 3, 6
  diversity, 8

formal, 6–7
informal, 6–8
network, 254
as open systems, 5–8
snake pit metaphor, 3, 6–7
transnational, 17
virtual, 254
Organization man manager, 190, 191
Organizational behavior, 3–14
  application of knowledge and skills, 14
  attitudes, 53–56
  defined, 3, 12
  diversity of, 8
  individual differences, 35
  interdisciplinary influences, 4–6
  management of, 11–12
  objective knowledge acquisition, 12–13
  personality and, 36–40
  quality at work and, 10–11
  skill development, 13–14
Organizational behavior modification (OBM), 85, 88
Organizational change. *See* Change management
Organizational chart, 239, 240
Organizational choice, 277–279
Organizational citizenship behavior (OCB)
  defined, 72
  dissimilarity and, 146
  employee involvement programs enhancing, 92
  of in-group vs. out-group members, 197
  group-organization fit and, 138
  leadership fostering, 201
  mentoring and, 98
  workplace deviance vs., 57–59
Organizational commitment, 58–59, 90
Organizational context, 5–6
Organizational culture, 259–273
  anthropology, 4
  assessing, 268–269
  behavior norms, 139
  challenges to developing a positive, cohesive culture, 271–273
  changing, 269–271
  decision making, 168
  defined, 259
  functions, 263
  leader's role in shaping and reinforcing, 265–266
  levels of, 259–263
  organizational socialization, 266–268
  relationship to performance, 263–264
Organizational culture inventory (OCI), 268
Organizational design and structure, 239–256
  basic design dimensions, 243–244

contextual variables, 246–252
definitions, 239
emerging organizational structures, 254–255
factors adversely affecting structure, 255–256
five structural configurations, 244–246
forces reshaping organizations, 252–254
key organizational design processes, 239–242
relationship among key organizational design elements, 252
seven designs for organizations of the future, 255
Organizational development cycle, 301
Organizational development (OD), 301–302
Organizational distress, 106, 108
Organizational empowerment, 275, 276
Organizational forms, 5
Organizational Health Center (OHC), 111
Organizational influences, 160
Organizational justice, 30–31, 111
Organizational life cycle, 252–253
Organizational performance, 150
Organizational politics
  defined, 177
  influence tactics, 178–180
  managing political behavior, 181–185
  political skill, 180–181
  resistance to change, 298
Organizational position, 223
Organizational processes, 253–254
Organizational psychology, 4
Organizational reward systems, 85–86
Organizational socialization, 206, 266–268
Organizational stress, 111
Organizational stress prevention, 111, 112–113
Organizational wellness, 116
Ornish, Dean, 115
Other-enhancing techniques, 49
Oticon, 160
Ouchi, William, 259
Outcomes of socialization, 268
Out-group member, 197–198
Outputs, 6
Outsourcing, 5, 246
Overdependence, 110

P

Pacific Bell, 235
Page, Larry, 42
Paid volunteerism, 24
Pakistan, 162

ORGB⁵
Test your knowledge

CHAPTER 1 Organizational Behavior and Opportunity

1. Define *organizational behavior*. What is its focus?

2. Identify the four action steps for responding positively to change.

3. What is an organization? What are its four system components? Give an example of each.

4. Briefly describe the elements of the formal and the informal organization. Give examples of each.

5. Describe how competition and total quality are affecting organizational behavior.

CHAPTER 2 Challenges for Managers

1. What are Hofstede's five dimensions of cultural differences that affect work attitudes?

2. What are the primary sources of diversity in the U.S. workforce?

3. What are the potential benefits and problems of diversity?

4. What are some of the ethical challenges encountered in organizations?

5. Describe the difference between distributive and procedural justice.

CHAPTER 3 Personality, Perception, and Attribution

1. What are individual differences, and why should managers understand them?

2. Define *personality* and describe its origins.

3. Describe two theories of personality and explain what each contributes to our knowledge of personality.

4. What factors influence social perception? What are the barriers to social perception?

5. Describe the errors that affect the attribution process.

CHAPTER 4 Attitudes, Emotions, and Ethics

1. Discuss cultural differences in job satisfaction and organizational commitment.

2. Define *values*. Distinguish between instrumental values and terminal values.

3. What is the relationship between values and ethics?

4. How does locus of control affect ethical behavior?

5. What is Machiavellianism, and how does it relate to ethical behavior?

CHAPTER 5 Motivation at Work

1. What are the five categories of motivational needs described by Maslow? Give an example of how each can be satisfied.

2. What are the Theory X and Theory Y assumptions about people at work? How do they relate to the hierarchy of needs?

3. What three manifest needs does McClelland identify?

4. How do hygiene and motivational factors differ?

5. What are two new ideas in motivation that managers are using?

CHAPTER 6 Learning and Performance Management

1. Define the terms *learning, reinforcement, punishment*, and *extinction*.

2. What are the differences in the way introverted and extraverted and intuitive and sensing people learn?

3. What are the five characteristics of well-developed goals?

4. What are the benefits of 360-degree feedback?

5. What are the two possible attributions of poor performance? What are the implications of each?

CHAPTER 7 Stress and Well-Being at Work

1. Define *stress*, *distress*, and *strain*.

2. Describe four approaches to understanding stress.

3. What are the four changes associated with the stress response?

4. What is a nonwork demand? How does it affect an individual?

5. What are primary prevention, secondary prevention, and tertiary prevention?

CHAPTER 8 Communication

1. Why is reflective listening important in interpersonal communication?

2. What are the five communication skills of effective supervisors and managers?

3. What are the costs of incivility and blessings of civility?

4. How does nonverbal communication affect interpersonal relationships?

5. What is communicative disease?

CHAPTER 9 Work Teams and Groups

1. What is the difference between a group and a team?

2. What are the components of Tuckman's Five-Stage Model?

3. Describe the four characteristics of mature groups.

4. Describe five task and five maintenance functions that effective work teams must perform.

5. What are the benefits and potential drawbacks of self-managed teams?

CHAPTER 10 Decision Making by Individuals and Groups

1. List and describe Jung's four cognitive styles.
2. What are the individual and organizational influences on creativity?
3. What are the individual and organizational foundations of empowerment and teamwork?
4. Describe the advantages and disadvantages of group decision making.
5. Describe the symptoms of groupthink, and identify actions that can be taken to prevent it.

CHAPTER 11 Power and Political Behavior

1. What are the five types of power according to French and Raven? What are their effects?
2. What is information power?
3. What are the intergroup sources of power?
4. What are the four power-oriented characteristics of the best managers?
5. What are the symbols of power according to Kanter?

CHAPTER 12 Leadership and Followership

1. Define leadership and followership.
2. Distinguish between formal leadership and informal leadership.
3. Define transformational, charismatic, and authentic leadership.
4. Describe the differences between autocratic and democratic work environments. How do they differ from a laissez-faire workplace?
5. Define initiating structure and consideration as leader behaviors.

CHAPTER 13 Conflict and Negotiation

1. Discuss the differences between functional and dysfunctional conflict.
2. Identify the structural and personal factors that contribute to conflict.
3. Discuss the four major forms of conflict in organizations.
4. What defense mechanisms do people use in interpersonal conflict?
5. Identify five styles of conflict management.

CHAPTER 14 Jobs and the Design of Work

1. Describe six patterns of working that have been studied in different countries.
2. Describe four traditional approaches to the design of work in America.
3. What are the salient features of the social information-processing (SIP) model of job design?
4. How do the Japanese, German, and Scandinavian approaches to work differ from one another and from the American approach?
5. What are five emerging issues in jobs and the design of work?

CHAPTER 15 Organizational Design and Structure

1. Define differentiation and integration.
2. Describe the six basic dimensions of organizational design.
3. Identify four forces that are reshaping organizations today.
4. Discuss the nature of emerging organizational structures.
5. List four symptoms of structural weakness.

CHAPTER 16 Organizational Culture

1. Explain the three levels of organizational culture.
2. Describe five artifacts of culture and give an example of each.
3. Explain three theories about the relationship between organizational culture and performance.
4. Contrast adaptive and nonadaptive cultures.
5. Describe the three stages of organizational socialization. How is culture communicated in each stage?

CHAPTER 17 Career Management

1. What is a realistic job preview, and why is it important?
2. What are psychological contracts?
3. What stressors are associated with socialization?
4. What are the career functions provided by a mentor?
5. What are the two key issues to deal with during the maintenance career stage?

CHAPTER 18 Managing Change

1. What are the major external and internal forces for change in organizations?
2. Contrast incremental, strategic, and transformational change.
3. Name the four behavioral reactions to change.
4. Describe force field analysis and its relationship to Lewin's change model.
5. What is organization development? Why is it undertaken by organizations?

WHAT'S INSIDE:

definition of organizational behavior; interdisciplinary influences on organizational behavior; formal and informal organizations; the impact of globalization, workforce diversity, ethics and character, and technological innovation on organizations; how organizations deal with change; understanding organizational behavior as a body of objective knowledge and as the practice of skill development.

LEARNING OUTCOMES

1-1 Define organizational behavior.

1-2 Identify four action steps for responding positively in times of change.

1-3 Identify the important system components of an organization.

1-4 Describe the formal and informal elements of an organization.

1-5 Identify factors that contribute to the diversity of organizations in the economy.

1-6 Describe the opportunities that change creates for organizational behavior.

1-7 Demonstrate the value of objective knowledge and skill development in the study of organizational behavior.

CHAPTER OUTLINE

Human Behavior in Organizations
Understanding Human Behavior
Interdisciplinary Influences

Behavior in Times of Change

The Organizational Context
Organizations as Open Systems

The Formal and Informal Organization

Diversity of Organizations

Change Creates Opportunities
Global Competition in Business
Customer Focused for High Quality
Behavior and Quality at Work
Managing Organizational Behavior
   in Changing Times

Learning about Organizational Behavior
Objective Knowledge
Skill Development
Application of Knowledge and Skills

4LTR PRESS ONLINE

Have students access their 4LTR Press Online account to. . .

- Create StudyBits and post to their Study Board

- Review key terms and create flashcards

- Create practice quizzes from their StudyBits

- Complete assessment content: matching, drag and drop, and fill-in-the-blank problems

- View Chapter Highlight Boxes: these include chapter videos and key exhibits/figures

VIDEO

*PROFILE ON HOLDEN OUTERWEAR MANAGING IN A GLOBAL ENVIRONMENT

Run time: 5:28 minutes
Like many other American brands, Holden apparel is made in China. LeBlanc explains that while he would like to manufacture lines in the United States, government regulations, labor costs, and high corporate tax rates are too heavy a burden. Availability of material is another reason for producing goods in China, since most of the fabrics, buttons, and snaps that Holden uses come from Asian suppliers. In addition to such procurement problems, garment making requires skilled labor—something LeBlanc says is rare in the United States. Despite the many challenges Holden faces as a small business competing in a global economy, LeBlanc's knack for navigating global markets is as sharp as his ability to tame even the most challenging downhill courses.

Ask your students:

1. Using the open systems view of organizations, describe Holden Outerwear's internal and external environment.

2. How has globalization influenced Holden's business and created opportunity?

3. What are some challenges of globalization for managers at Holden?

CHAPTER PREP 1

DISCUSSION QUESTIONS

1. How do the formal aspects of your work environment affect you? What informal aspects of your work environment are important?

2. What is the biggest competitive challenge or change facing the businesses in your industry today? Will that be different in the next five years?

3. Describe the next chief executive of your company and what she or he must do to succeed

EXPERIENTIAL EXERCISE

WHAT'S CHANGING AT WORK

This exercise provides an opportunity to discuss changes occurring in your workplace and university. These changes may be for the better or the worse. However, rather than evaluating whether they are good or bad changes, begin by simply identifying the changes that are occurring. Later, you can evaluate whether they are good or bad.

Step 1. The class forms into groups of approximately six members each. Each group elects a spokesperson and answers the following questions. The group should spend at least five minutes on each question. Make sure that each member of the group makes a contribution to each question. The spokesperson for each group should be ready to share the group's collective responses.

 a. *What are the changes occurring in your workplace or university?* Members should focus both on internal changes, such as reorganizations, and on external changes, such as new customers or competitors. Develop a list of the changes discussed in your group.

 b. *What are the forces that are driving the changes?* To answer this question, look for the causes of the changes members of the group are observing. For example, a reorganization may be caused by new business opportunities, by new technologies, or by a combination of factors.

 c. *What signs of resistance to change do you see occurring?* Change is not always easy for people or organizations. Do you see signs of resistance, such as frustration, anger, increased absences, or other forms of discomfort with the changes you observe?

Step 2. Once you have answered the three questions in Step 1, your group needs to spend some time evaluating whether these changes are good or bad. Decide whether each change on the list developed in Step 1a is good or bad, In addition, answer the question "Why?" That is, why is this change good? Why is that change bad?

Step 3. Each group shares the results of its answers to the questions in Step 1 and its evaluation of the changes completed in Step 2. Cross-team questions and discussion follow.

Step 4. Your instructor may allow a few minutes at the end of the class period to comment on his or her perceptions of changes occurring within the university, or businesses with which he or she is familiar.

ASSIGNMENTS

- Have students prepare a memo about an organizational change occurring where they work or in the college or university, using Figure 1.1 to identify how the change is affecting the people, structure, task, and/or technology of the organization.

- Have students research a service or manufacturing company, entrepreneurial venture, or nonprofit organization of their choice and then prepare a brief description of it.

WHAT'S NEW TO ORGB5

- Updated section 1-1, Human Behavior in Organizations
- Updated section 1-3a, Organizations as Open Systems
- Updated "Fast Fact" on "The United State Economy"
- New box feature, "Formal Organizational Elements to Help Make Marriott a Great Place to Work"
- New box feature, "Sustainable Solution Is Good to Go"
- New Hot Trend box, "Four Things That Worry Business"
- Updated "By the Numbers" in section 1-7b

TERMS

opportunities 3
change 3
challenge 3
organizational behavior 3
psychology 4

sociology 4
engineering 4
anthropology 4
management 4
medicine 4
task 5
people 6

technology 6
structure 6
formal organization 6
informal organization 6
hawthorne studies 7
objective knowledge 12
skill development 12

LEARNING OUTCOMES

2-1 Describe the factors that affect organizations competing in the global economy.

2-2 Explain how cultural differences form the basis of work-related attitudes.

2-3 Describe the challenges and positive influences diversity brings to today's business environment.

2-4 Discuss the role of ethics, character, and personal integrity in the organization.

2-5 Explain five issues that pose ethical dilemmas for managers.

2-6 Describe the effects of technological advances on today's workforce.

4LTR PRESS ONLINE

Have students access their 4LTR Press Online account to. . .

- Create StudyBits and post to their Study Board
- Review key terms and create flash-cards
- Create practice quizzes from their StudyBits
- Complete assessment content: matching, drag and drop, and fill-in-the-blank problems
- View Chapter Highlight Boxes: these include chapter videos and key exhibits/figures

VIDEO

*PROFILE ON THEO CHOCOLATE: ETHICS AND SOCIAL RESPONSIBILITY

Run time: 6:44 minutes
Unlike leading candy manufacturers that deliver sweets in high volume, Theo produces award-winning organic chocolate in small batches. The company boasts a bean-to-bar production method that uses cocoa beans grown without pesticides and without harm to farmers or the environment. At Theo Chocolate, the terms *organic* and *fair trade* are no mere marketing buzzwords. Organic means that the cocoa beans are grown naturally and harvested in ways that preserve habitats and the balance of the ecosystem; fair trade is a business approach that ensures equity between buyers, as well as fair treatment of workers.

Ask your students:

1. What practices at Theo Chocolate illustrate the concept of *social responsibility*?

2. What does Vice President Debra Music mean when she says that Theo is a "triple bottom line" company? What happens if Theo's social objectives conflict with the organization's economic objectives?

3. What does *fair trade* mean to the leaders at Theo, and how does this relate to workers' rights and organizational justice?

DISCUSSION QUESTIONS

1. How can managers be encouraged to develop global thinking?

2. Why do you think some companies encourage alternative work arrangements?

3. What effects will the globalization of business have on a company's culture? How can an organization with a strong "made in America" identity compete in the global marketplace?

CHAPTER PREP 2

EXPERIENTIAL EXERCISE

ETHICAL DILEMMAS

Divide the class into five groups. Each group should choose one of the following scenarios and agree on a course of action:

1. Sam works for you. He is technically capable and a good worker, but he does not get along well with others in the work group. When Sam has an opportunity to transfer, you encourage him to take it. What would you say to Sam's potential supervisor when he asks about Sam?

2. Your boss has told you that you must reduce your work group by 30 percent. Which of the following criteria would you use to lay off workers?
    a. Lay off older, higher-paid employees.
    b. Lay off younger, lower-paid employees.
    c. Lay off workers based on seniority only.
    d. Lay off workers based on performance only.

3. You are an engineer, but you are not working on your company's Department of Transportation (DOT) project. One day you overhear a conversation in the cafeteria between the program manager and the project engineer that makes you reasonably sure a large contract will soon be given to the ABC Company to develop and manufacture a key DOT subsystem. ABC is a small firm, and its stock is traded over the counter. You feel sure that the stock will rise from its present $2.25 per share as soon as news of the DOT contract gets out. Would you go out and buy ABC's stock?

4. You are the project engineer working on the development of a small liquid rocket engine. You know that if you could achieve a throttling ratio greater than 8 to 1, your system would be considered a success and continue to receive funding support. To date, the best you have achieved is a 4-to-1 ratio. You have an unproven idea that you feel has a 50 percent chance of being successful. Your project is currently being reviewed to determine if it should be continued. You would like to continue it. How optimistically should you present the test results?

5. Imagine that you are the president of a company in a highly competitive industry. You learn that a competitor has made an important scientific discovery that is not patentable and will give that company an advantage that will substantially reduce the profits of your company for about a year. There is some hope of hiring one of the competitor's employees who knows the details of the discovery. Would you try to hire this person?

Each group should present its scenario and chosen course of action to the class. The class should then evaluate the ethics of the course of action, using the following questions to guide discussion:

1. Are you following rules that are understood and accepted?
2. Are you comfortable discussing and defending your action?
3. Would you want someone to do this to you?
4. What if everyone acted this way?
5. Are there alternatives that rest on firmer ethical ground?

SOURCE: Scenarios adapted from R. A. DiBattista, "Providing a Rationale for Ethical Conduct from Alternatives Taken in Ethical Dilemmas," *Journal of General Psychology* 116 (1989): 207–214; discussion questions adapted with the permission of The Free Press, a Division of Simon & Schuster, Inc. from The *Manager as Negotiator: Bargaining for Cooperation and Competitive Gain* by David A. Lax and James K. Sebenius 0-02-918770-2. Copyright © 1986 by David A. Lax and James K. Sebenius.

ASSIGNMENTS

Have each student find someone whose culture is different from his or her own. This might be a classmate, an international student, or a Native American at the university. Have students ask their interviewees about their cultures using Hofstede's dimensions of (1) individualism/collectivism, (2) high power distance/low power distance, (3) high uncertainty avoidance/low uncertainty avoidance, (4) masculinity/femininity, and (5) long-term orientation/short-term orientation. Have students share this information in class.

WHAT'S NEW TO ORGB5

- Updated section 2-3, The Diverse Workforce
- Updated section 2-3b, Gender Diversity
- New box feature, "Hot Trend: Working Women Work to Preserve Their Identities During Pregnancy"
- Updated section 2-3c, Age Diversity
- New box feature, "Men: The Secret Weapon for Increasing Gender Diversity at the Top"
- New section, 2-3e, Sexual Orientation and Gender Identity
- New box feature, "Can Knowledge of Stereotypes Increase Stereotypical Behavior?"
- New box feature, "Fast Fact: A Slippery Slope Toward Unethical Behavior"
- Section 2-6, Technological Innovation and Today's Workforce, has been removed from the chapter

TERMS

WHAT'S INSIDE:

individual differences and organizational behavior; personality and organizations; application of personality theory in organizations; social perception and how characteristics of the perceiver, the target, and the situation affect it; common barriers to social perception; attributions and their affect on managerial behavior.

CHAPTER OUTLINE

Individual Differences and Organizational Behavior
Skills and Abilities

Personality and Organizations
Trait Theory
Integrative Approach
Personality Characteristics in
    Organizations
Proactive Personality

Application of Personality Theory in Organizations
Common Personality Measurement Tools
Carl Jung and the Myers-Briggs Type
    Indicator® Instrument

Social Perception
Characteristics of the Perceiver
Characteristics of the Target
Characteristics of the Situation

Barriers to Social Perception
Impression Management

Attribution in Organizations
Internal and External Attributions
Attributional Biases

LEARNING OUTCOMES

3-1 Describe individual differences and explain why they are important in understanding organizational behavior.

3-2 Articulate key personality traits and explain how they influence behavior in organizations.

3-3 Discuss how personality theories may be applied in organizations.

3-4 Define social perception and explain the factors that affect it.

3-5 Identify five common barriers to social perception and explain the difficulties they cause.

3-6 Explain the attribution process and how attributions affect managerial behavior.

4LTR PRESS ONLINE

Have students access their 4LTR Press Online account to. . .

- Create StudyBits and post to their Study Board

- Review key terms and create flashcards

- Create practice quizzes from their StudyBits

- Complete assessment content: matching, drag and drop, and fill-in-the-blank problems

- View Chapter Highlight Boxes: these include chapter videos and key exhibits/figures

VIDEO

*PROFILE ON THEO CHOCOLATE: PERSONALITY

Run time: 7:15 minutes
When Theo first started its production, the company offered an exotic line of dark and milk chocolate bars and truffles with unusual names like the 3400 Phinney Bar, and Bread & Chocolate. But pitching chocolate to foodies and green consumers didn't add up to high-volume sales. In particular, consumers perceived Theo's exotic flavors to be off or too funky. To increase product appeal, Theo now offers distinct product lines for two different market segments: a classic line of milk chocolate bars for mainstream customers, and "fantasy flavors" for more adventurous eaters. Appealing to mainstream customers was consistent with Joe Whinney's belief that everyone should be able to enjoy Theo Chocolate.

Ask your students:

1. Describe the personality traits of Theo Chocolate's founders.

2. What is your perception of CEO Joe Whinney? On what do you base your perception?

3. To what do you attribute Joe Whinney's success?

DISCUSSION QUESTIONS

1. What contributions can high self-monitors make in organizations? Low self-monitors?

2. Which has the stronger impact on personality: heredity or environment? Be prepared to support your position.

3. How can managers encourage self-efficacy in employees?

CHAPTER PREP 3

EXPERIENTIAL EXERCISE

IDENTIFYING COGNITIVE STYLES

Purpose: For students to identify and define their cognitive styles

Group size: Any number of students

Activity: Have students read the situation and managers' reactions to the crisis. Students then answer the questions that follow. One variation is to have each student write out his or her own reaction before discussing the reactions of the characters in the scenario. Students can then situate their own responses in the context and reflect on their personal cognitive styles,

Handout: MBTI Temperaments and Leadership Styles, located in the Instructor Manual *Cognitive Styles of Managers:*

Assume that it is Friday, 3:00 p.m. A customer calls to say that a major shipment of computers you sent a week ago has not arrived and that they must have the computers by noon Monday. Failing to deliver the computers will result in losing the client. The manager must either find the shipment or reship the computers and make sure they arrive on time.

Below are descriptions of how four different managers would react to this crisis. Read their reactions and answer the questions that follow.

BILL accepts the reality that the shipment of computers is lost and that he shouldn't waste time tracking it down. He sees no alternative but to put together a new shipment and send it out immediately. He expects all his workers to pitch in and stay late to get the new shipment out.

MONA considers the possibility that the original shipment might be recovered as this would save everyone the trouble of having to prepare a new shipment. She attempts to motivate a team of workers to work together to track down the shipment. At the same time, she puts together another team to work out a backup plan. She works back and forth between the two teams, trying to inconvenience everyone as little as possible.

DENISE tries to track down the original shipment because no matter what happens it will have to be located. She sees putting together another shipment as the only reliable solution. At the same time, she is going to develop a strategy for evaluating shipping operations to ensure that this problem doesn't come up again.

BLAKE writes off the original shipment and feels in reality there's no time to waste looking for it. He polls his workers to see who can work late to put together a new shipment and if no one volunteers, he will do it himself.

ANSWER THE FOLLOWING:

1. Bill's cognitive style is_____.
   What clues were evident in his handling of the crisis?

2. Mona's cognitive style is _____.
   What clues were evident in her handling of the crisis?

3. Denise's cognitive style is_____.
   What clues were evident in her handling of the crisis?

4. Blake's cognitive style is_____.
   What clues were evident in his handling of the crisis?

SOURCE: Adapted from O. Kroeger and J.M. Thuesen, *Type Talk at Work* (New York: Delacorte Press, 1992), 165–166.

ASSIGNMENTS

Assign students to develop a section of a training program focused on helping interviewers develop better social perception skills. Be sure to address barriers to social perception and ways to avoid these barriers in the training process. Have students turn in a written outline for this section of the training program.

WHAT'S NEW TO ORGB5

- Updated 3-2a, Trait Theory
- New box feature, "Hot Trend: High Self-Monitors Are Good Networkers"
- New box feature, "Who Says Introverts Can't Be Leaders"
- Updated 3-4a, Characteristics of the Perceiver
- New box feature, "Is Bossy a Negative Stereotype for Women?"
- New box feature, "Fast Fact: Faking Good Is Our Default Mode of Impression Management"
- Updated 3-5a, Impression Management

TERMS

individual differences 35
interactional psychology 35
personality 36
trait theory 36
integrative approach 37
strong situations 37
locus of control 37
general self-efficacy 38
self-esteem 38
self-monitoring 39
positive affect 39

negative affect 39
projective tests 40
behavioral measures 40
self-report questionnaire 40
myers-briggs type indicator®
(MBTI) instrument 41
extraversion 41
introversion 41
sensing 42
intuition 42
thinking 43
feeling 43
judging 43

perceiving 43
social perception 45
discounting principle 47
selective perception 47
stereotype 47
first-impression 48
projection 48
self-fulfilling prophecies 48
impression management 49
attribution theory 49
fundamental attribution
error 50
self-serving bias 50

WHAT'S INSIDE:

attitudes; attitude formation; job satisfaction; organizational citizenship versus workplace deviance; persuasion and attitude change; emotions at work as part of functioning and decision making; ethical behavior; factors that affect ethical behavior.

CHAPTER OUTLINE

Attitudes
The ABC Model
Cognitive Dissonance

Attitude Formation
Attitudes and Behavior
Work Attitudes

Job Satisfaction

Organizational Citizenship versus Workplace Deviance
Organizational Commitment and Job Satisfaction

Persuasion and Attitude Change
Source Characteristics
Target Characteristics
Message Characteristics
Cognitive Routes to Persuasion

Emotions and Moods at Work
Emotions
Moods
Emotional Contagion at Work
Emotional Intelligence
Emotional Labor

Ethical Behavior

Factors That Affect Ethical Behavior
Values
Locus of Control
Machiavellianism
Cognitive Moral Development

LEARNING OUTCOMES

4-1 Explain the ABC model of an attitude.

4-2 Describe how attitudes are formed.

4-3 Identify sources of job satisfaction and commitment.

4-4 Distinguish between organizational citizenship and workplace deviance behaviors.

4-5 Identify the characteristics of the source, target, and message that affect persuasion.

4-6 Discuss the definition and importance of emotions at work.

4-7 Contrast the effects of individual and organizational influences on ethical behavior.

4-8 Identify the factors that affect ethical behavior.

4LTR PRESS ONLINE

Have students access their 4LTR Press Online account to. . .

- Create StudyBits and post to their Study Board
- Review key terms and create flashcards
- Create practice quizzes from their StudyBits
- Complete assessment content: matching, drag and drop, and fill-in-the-blank problems
- View Chapter Highlight Boxes: these include chapter videos and key exhibits/figures

VIDEO

*PROFILE ON MITCHELL GOLD + BOB WILLIAMS

Run time: 6:22 minutes
In many organizations, hidden talents often remain hidden. But at Mitchell Gold + Bob Williams, managers encourage employees to discover their talents and seize new opportunities. While taking stock of human resources, managers recognized Kim Clay's knack for computers, and they came to her to discuss the creation of a new job position: a computer help desk specialist. Although Clay lacked formal computer training, she was willing to put herself out there and see where the opportunity might lead. Clay's hard work and desire to develop new skills paid off: today Clay is the head of technology for MG + BW.

Ask your students:

1. Which component of attitudes does HR executive Dan Gauthreaux express when he says, "I think you can learn from any job you do and try to make the best of it"?

2. How did Kim Clay's organizational citizenship behavior lead to the creation of a new computer help desk at MG + BW?

3. What role did management play in fostering Kim Clay's organizational commitment? In what ways does this commitment benefit the organization?

DISCUSSION QUESTIONS

1. What jobs do you consider to be most satisfying? Why?

2. How can managers increase their employees' job satisfaction?

CHAPTER PREP 4

3. Suppose you have an employee whose lack of commitment is affecting others in the work group. How would you go about persuading the person to change this attitude?

EXPERIENTIAL EXERCISE

IS THIS BEHAVIOR ETHICAL?

The purpose of this exercise is for students to explore their opinions about ethical issues faced in organizations. The class should be divided into twelve groups. Each group will randomly be assigned one of the following issues, which reflect the twelve ethical themes found in the *The Wall Street Journal* study shown in Table 4.2.

1. Is it ethical to take office supplies from work for home use? Make personal long-distance calls from the office? Use company time for personal business? Or do these behaviors constitute stealing?

2. If you exaggerate your credentials in an interview, is it lying? Is lying in order to protect a coworker acceptable?

3. If you pretend to be more successful than you are in order to impress your boss, are you being deceitful?

4. How do you differentiate between a bribe and a gift?

5. If there are slight defects in a product you are selling, are you obligated to tell the buyer? If an advertised "sale" price is really the everyday price, should you divulge the information to the customer?

6. Suppose you have a friend who works at the ticket office for the convention center where Shania Twain will be appearing. Is it cheating if you ask the friend to get you tickets so that you won't have to fight the crowd to get them? Is buying merchandise for your family at your company's cost cheating?

7. Is it immoral to do less than your best in terms of work performance? Is it immoral to accept workers' compensation when you are fully capable of working?

8. What behaviors constitute emotional abuse at work? What would you consider an abuse of one's position of power?

9. Are high-stress jobs a breach of ethics? What about transfers that break up families?

10. Are all rule violations equally important? Do employees have an ethical obligation to follow company rules?

11. To what extent are you responsible for the ethical behavior of your coworkers? If you witness unethical behavior and don't report it, are you an accessory?

12. Is it ethical to help one work group at the expense of another? For instance, suppose one group has excellent performance and you want to reward its members with an afternoon off. In that case, the other group will have to pick up the slack and work harder. Is this ethical?

Once each group has been assigned its issue, assign the students the following two tasks:

1. First, formulate your group's answer to the ethical dilemma.

2. After you have formulated your group's position, discuss the individual differences that may have contributed to your position. You will want to discuss the individual differences presented in this chapter as well as any others that you feel affected your position on the ethical dilemma.

Lead the class in a discussion of how individual differences may have influenced students' positions on these ethical dilemmas.

SOURCE: Kluwer Academic Publishers, by J. O. Cherrington and D. J. Cherrington, "A Menu of Moral Issues: One Week in the Life of *The Wall Street Journal*" *Journal of Business Ethics* 11 (1992): 255–265. Reprinted with kind permission of Springer Science and Business Media.

ASSIGNMENTS

- Have students write a follow-up to the experiential exercise, describing how their initial thoughts and perceptions evolved (or were confirmed) after going through the value-ranking exercise.

- Assign students to write a brief description of the cognitive dissonance experience exercise in the discussion question section.

WHAT'S NEW TO ORGB5

- Updated section 4-4, Organizational Citizenship versus Workplace Deviance

- New box feature, "Intuit's Emotional Connection with Customers"

- New box feature, "Google's SIYLI Develops Emotional Intelligence and Mindfulness"

- Updated section, 4-6d, "Emotional Intelligence"

- New box feature, "Hot Trend: Mindful Facebooking and Less Burnout"

- New box feature, "Fast Fact: What Is a B Corp?"

TERMS

attitude 53

affect 53

cognitive dissonance 54

social learning 54

job satisfaction 56

organizational citizenship behavior (OCB) 57

workplace deviance behavior (WDB) 58

organizational commitment 58

affective commitment 58

continuance commitment 58

normative commitment 58

emotions 60

emotional contagion 61

ethical behavior 63

values 65

instrumental values 65

terminal values 65

machiavellianism 67

cognitive moral development 67

WHAT'S INSIDE:

motivation and work behavior; Maslow's need hierarchy; McClelland's need theory; Herzberg's two-factor theory; two new ideas in motivation in the past decade; social exchange and equity theory; expectancy theory of motivation; understanding cultural differences in motivation.

CHAPTER OUTLINE

Motivation and Work Behavior
Internal Needs
External Incentives

Maslow's Need Hierarchy
Theory X and Theory Y
ERG Theory

McClelland's Need Theory
Need for Achievement
Need for Power
Need for Affiliation

Herzberg's Two-Factor Theory
Motivation Factors
Hygiene Factors
Critique of the Two-Factor Theory

Two New Ideas in Motivation
Eustress, Strength, and Hope
Positive Energy and Full Engagement

Social Exchange and Equity Theory
Demands and Contributions
Adams's Theory of Inequity
The Resolution of Inequity
New Perspectives on Equity Theory

Expectancy Theory of Motivation
Motivational Problems
Motivation and Moral Maturity

Cultural Differences in Motivation

LEARNING OUTCOMES

5-1 Define motivation and articulate different views of how individuals are motivated at work.

5-2 Explain Maslow's hierarchy of needs and its two main modifications.

5-3 Discuss how the needs for achievement, power, and affiliation influence an individual's behavior in the workplace.

5-4 Describe the two-factor theory of motivation.

5-5 Explain two new ideas in human motivation.

5-6 Describe the role of inequity in motivation.

5-7 Describe the expectancy theory of motivation.

5-8 Describe the cultural differences in motivation.

4LTR PRESS ONLINE

Have students access their 4LTR Press Online account to...

- Create StudyBits and post to their Study Board
- Review key terms and create flashcards
- Create practice quizzes from their StudyBits
- Complete assessment content: matching, drag and drop, and fill-in-the-blank problems
- View Chapter Highlight Boxes: these include chapter videos and key exhibits/figures

VIDEO

*PROFILE ON URBAN ESCAPES

Run time: 6:12 minutes
Founded in 2008 by Maia Josebachvili and Bram Levy, Urban Escapes has earned high praise for its vast array of exciting outdoor adventures. For the Urban Escapes employees working behind the scenes to deliver "Zen Escape Yoga Hikes" and "Boulder and Brew Tours," motivation comes naturally. The company's managers and guides are driven by the freedom and opportunity that only a start-up company can offer. "We gave everyone a lot of ownership in their cities," Josebachvili says of her guides. "Initially, we said every time you want to run a trip, you run it by us. Within a few months, I was like, 'Okay, if you know it's going to work, don't come to us—you got this'. After a year, I felt really good about what they were doing."

Ask your students:

1. Which needs in Maslow's hierarchy are most important to the employees who work for Urban Escapes, and how can managers use this information to develop a highly motivated workforce?

2. According to equity theory, how might an Urban Escapes guide react if he or she feels underpaid or unappreciated?

3. What outcomes or rewards possess high valence for the managers and guides who work at Urban Escapes?

DISCUSSION QUESTIONS

1. What do you think are the most important motivational needs for the majority of people? Do you think your needs differ from those of most people?

2. What important experiences have contributed to your moral and ethical development? Are you working to further your own moral maturity at this time?

EXPERIENTIAL EXERCISE

WHAT'S IMPORTANT TO EMPLOYEES?

This exercise provides students an opportunity to discuss their basic needs and those of other students in the class. Have students do a ranking of the ten possible job reward factors and think about basic needs they may have that are possibly work related and yet would not be satisfied by one or another of these ten job reward factors. Teaching notes are in the Instructor Manual.

Step 1. The class will form into groups of approximately six members each. Each group elects a spokesperson and answers the questions below. The group should spend at least five minutes on the first question and make sure each member of the group makes a contribution. The second question will probably take longer (up to fifteen minutes) for groups to answer. The spokesperson should be ready to share the group's answers.

   a. *What important basic needs do you have that are not addressed by one or another of the ten job reward factors?* Members should focus on the whole range of needs discussed in the different need theories of motivation covered in Chapter 5. Develop a list of the basic needs overlooked by the ten factors.

   b. *What is important to members of your group?* Rank-order all job reward factors (the original ten and any new ones your group came up with in Step 1) in terms of their importance for your group. If group members disagree about the rankings, take time to discuss the differences among group members. Work for consensus and note points of disagreement.

Step 2. Each group will share the results of its answers to the questions in Step 1, Cross-team questions and discussion follow.

Step 3. As the instructor, share the normative data for 1,000 employees and their supervisors found in the Instructor Manual.

Step 4. **(Optional).** Have students discuss the similarities and differences in their group's rankings with the employee and supervisory normative rankings. Spend some time addressing two questions.

   a. *What underlying reasons do you think may account for the differences that exist?*

   b. *How have the needs of employees and supervisors changed over the past twenty years? Are they likely to change In the future?*

SOURCE; "Crossed Wires on Employee Motivation," *Training and Development* 49 (1995): 59–60.

ASSIGNMENTS

■ Assign students to write a memo describing the two coworkers with whom they most closely operate according to Theory X and Theory Y assumptions about human nature. Ask students to be as specific and detailed in their descriptions as they can, using quotes and/or observational examples.

■ Have students develop an oral presentation about the most current management practices in employee motivation. Ask students to find out what at least four different companies are doing in this area. Students should be prepared to compare these practices with the theory and research in the chapter.

■ *Present this scenario to students:* "Assume you are leaving your current job to look for employment elsewhere. What will you look for that you do not have now? If you do not have a job, assume you will be looking for one soon. What will be the most important factors that you will seek?" Tell students to be prepared to discuss answers in class.

WHAT'S NEW TO ORGB5

■ Updated section 5-1a, Internal Needs

■ New box feature, "Intrinsic Factors and External Incentives Work Together to Improve Employee Performance"

■ Updated section 5-2a, Theory X and Theory Y

■ Updated section 5-3a, Need for Achievement

■ New box feature, "Hot Trend: The Best Way to Really Motivate Your Team"

■ New box feature, "Increasing Valence by Connecting Employees with End-Users"

■ New box feature, "Fast Fact: Moral Acts Depend on Language"

TERMS

motivation 71
psychoanalysis 71
self-interest 71
theory X 73
theory Y 73
erg theory 74

manifest needs 74
need for achievement 74
need for power 75
need for affiliation 75
motivation factors 76
hygiene factors 76
eustress 77
inequity 79

equity sensitives 80
benevolents 80
entitleds 80
valence 81
expectancy 81
instrumentality 81
moral maturity 82

WHAT'S INSIDE:

learning in organizations; social and cognitive learning theories at work; guiding and directing work behavior through goal setting; the process of performance management; the effect of performance rewards on organizational culture and motivation; correcting poor performance.

CHAPTER OUTLINE

Behavioral Models of Learning in Organizations
Classical Conditioning
Operant Conditioning
Reinforcement Theory
Punishment

Social and Cognitive Theories of Learning
Bandura's Social Learning Theory
Cognitive Theories of Learning

Goal Setting at Work
Characteristics of Effective Goals
Goals Increase Work Motivation and Task Performance
Goals Reduce Role Stress, Conflict, and Ambiguity
Goals Improve Performance Evaluation

Performance: A Key Construct
Performance Management
Defining Performance
Measuring Performance

Performance Feedback
360-Degree Feedback
Developing People and Enhancing Careers
Key Characteristics of an Effective Appraisal System

Rewarding Performance
Individual versus Team Reward Systems
The Power of Earning

Correcting Poor Performance
Performance and Kelley's Attribution Theory
Coaching, Counseling, and Mentoring

LEARNING OUTCOMES

6-1 Describe behavioral theories of learning.

6-2 Describe social and cognitive theories of learning.

6-3 Explain how goal setting can be used to direct learning and performance.

6-4 Define performance and identify the tools used to measure it.

6-5 Explain the importance of performance feedback and how it can be delivered effectively.

6-6 Identify ways managers can reward performance.

6-7 List several strategies for correcting poor performance.

4LTR PRESS ONLINE

Have students access their 4LTR Press Online account to. . .

- Create StudyBits and post to their Study Board
- Review key terms and create flashcards
- Create practice quizzes from their StudyBits
- Complete assessment content: matching, drag and drop, and fill-in-the-blank problems
- View Chapter Highlight Boxes: these include chapter videos and key exhibits/figures

VIDEO

*PROFILE ON BARCELONA RESTAURANT GROUP

Run time: 7:11 minutes
At Barcelona Restaurant Group it's about more than food: it's about an experience. Cuisine is only 50 percent of the total Barcelona experience; the other half is made up of intangibles such as lighting, clientele, atmospherics, background music, and conversation with managers and wait staff. For Barcelona to be successful, each employee must deliver the European tapas ambience night after night. To achieve consistent quality, Barcelona gauges its performance with the help of multiple feedback loops. First, the establishment participates in a Secret Shoppers program. Next, the restaurant solicits comments from regular patrons, and every comment card and e-mail goes straight to the owner. Finally, managers monitor activities through restaurant surveillance cameras and by walking the floors to interact with customers.

Ask your students:

1. According to Barcelona owner Andy Pforzheimer, why do so many restaurants go out of business?
2. What tactics do leaders at Barcelona use to help measure and control the restaurant's financial performance?
3. How does Barcelona reward managers and chefs?

DISCUSSION QUESTIONS

1. Which learning approach—the behavioral approach or Bandura's social learning theory—do you find more appropriate for people?
2. Given your personality type, how do you learn best? Do you miss learning some things because of how they are taught?

CHAPTER PREP 6

EXPERIENTIAL EXERCISE

POSITIVE AND NEGATIVE REINFORCEMENT

Purpose: To examine the effects of positive and negative reinforcement on behavior change.

1. Select two or three volunteers to receive reinforcement from the class while performing a particular task. Ask the volunteers to leave the room.

2. Identify an object for the student volunteers to locate when they return to the room. (The object should he unobtrusive but clearly visible to the class. Some that have worked well are a small triangular piece of paper that was left behind when a notice was torn off a classroom bulletin board, a smudge on the chalkboard, and a chip in the plaster of a classroom wall.)

3. Specify the reinforcement contingencies that will be in effect when the volunteers return to the room. For negative reinforcement, students should hiss, boo, and throw things (although they should not throw anything harmful) when the first volunteer is moving away from the object; students should cheer and applaud when the second volunteer is getting closer to the object; and if a third volunteer is used, students should use both negative and positive reinforcement.

4. Assign a student to keep a record of the time it takes each of the volunteers to locate the object.

5. Ask Volunteer #1 to come back to the room, and instruct him or her as follows: "Your task is to locate and touch a particular object in the room, and the class has agreed to help you. You may begin."

6. Volunteer #1 continues to look for the object until it is found while the class assists by giving negative reinforcement.

7. Ask Volunteer #2 to come back to the room, and instruct him or her as follows: "Your task is to locate and touch a particular object in the room, and the class has agreed to help you. You may begin."

8. Volunteer #2 continues to look for the object until it is found while the class assists by giving positive reinforcement.

9. Ask Volunteer #3 to come back to the room, and instruct him or her as follows: "Tour task is to locate and touch a particular object in the room, and the class has agreed to help you. You may begin."

10. Volunteer #3 continues to look for the object until it is found while the class assists by giving both positive and negative reinforcement.

11. In a class discussion, have students answer the following questions:
    a. How did the behavior of the volunteers differ when different kinds of reinforcement (positive, negative, or both) were used? *Most of the time the individual receiving positive reinforcement will have a number of gestures and nonverbal indicators of success.*
    b. What were the emotional reactions of the volunteers to the different kinds of reinforcement? *One of the ways to give the volunteers time to reflect and to get out of the spotlight for a moment is to have them go to a board or flip chart and list a series of words that described how they felt. Typical for volunteer #1 will be embarrassment, frustration, quit, etc. Volunteer #3 may have feelings like confusion, frustration, and ambiguity.*
    c. Which type of reinforcement—positive or negative—is most common in organizations? What effect do you think this has on motivation and productivity? *Students' responses will depend on their exposure to specific instances.*

ASSIGNMENTS

- Have students prepare a memo detailing the consequences of behavior in their work or university environment (e.g., grades, awards, suspensions, and scholarships). Their memo should include their classification of these consequences as positive or negative.

- Tell students to be prepared to discuss whether the organization or university should change the way it applies these consequences.

WHAT'S NEW TO ORGB5

- New box feature, "Bosses Being Asked to Accentuate the Positive"
- Updated section 6-1c, Reinforcement Theory
- New box feature, "Deloitte's Performance Management Redesign"
- New box feature, "Hot Trend: Treat Your Career Like a Startup"
- New box feature, "Fast Fact: CEOs Need Mentors Too"

TERMS

WHAT'S INSIDE:

the definition of stress; four approaches to stress; the stress response—fight or flight; sources of work stress; consequences of stress; individual differences in the stress–strain relationship; preventing stress management by promoting health and preventing distress and strain.

CHAPTER OUTLINE

What Is Stress?

Four Approaches to Stress
The Homeostatic/Medical Approach
The Cognitive Appraisal Approach
The Person–Environment Fit Approach
The Psychoanalytic Approach

The Stress Response

Sources of Work Stress
Work Demands
Nonwork Demands

The Consequences of Stress
Positive Stress
Individual Distress
Organizational Distress

Individual Differences in the Stress–Strain Relationship
Gender Effects
Type A Behavior Pattern
Personality Hardiness
Self-Reliance

Preventive Stress Management
Organizational Stress Prevention
Individual Prevention
Comprehensive Health Promotion

LEARNING OUTCOMES

7-1 Define stress, distress, and strain.

7-2 Compare four different approaches to stress.

7-3 Explain the psychophysiology of the stress response.

7-4 Identify work and nonwork causes of stress.

7-5 Describe the consequences of stress.

7-6 Discuss individual factors that influence a person's response to stress and strain.

7-7 Identify the stages and elements of preventive stress management for individuals and organizations.

4LTR PRESS ONLINE

Have students access their 4LTR Press Online account to. . .

- Create StudyBits and post to their Study Board
- Review key terms and create flashcards
- Create practice quizzes from their StudyBits
- Complete assessment content: matching, drag and drop, and fill-in-the-blank problems
- View Chapter Highlight Boxes: these include chapter videos and key exhibits/figures

VIDEO

*PROFILE ON MODERN SHED

Run time: 6:10 minutes
Modern Shed's lead sales consultant, Scott Pearl, relies on disciplined goal setting. After noting that Modem Shed was popular with people who wanted small backyard studios, Pearl determined that selling two 10 ft. × 12 ft. structures per month would be an achievable first sales goal. Today, as Modern Shed seeks to build upon its early success, Pearl is once again setting goals. This time, the marketer is focusing on the company's larger sheds—12 ft. × 16 ft. According to Pearl, Modern Shed's larger dwellings need to make up 25 percent of all products sold. With that in mind, Pearl has a plan for how to achieve the higher target: he will pitch the larger shed as a "nanny solution" for Seattle's well-to-do families.

Ask your students:

1. How might being an outside contractor add stress to Scott Pearl's job?

2. How does Scott Pearl's person–environment fit affect his responses to stressors?

3. Is Scott Pearl's goal setting an example of primary, secondary, or tertiary preventive stress management? Explain.

DISCUSSION QUESTIONS

1. Do you think there is more stress today than in past generations? What evidence is available concerning this question?

2. If an individual claims to have job-related anxiety or depression, do you think the company should be liable?

3. Do you use any stress-prevention methods that are not discussed in the chapter? If so, what are they?

CHAPTER PREP 7

EXPERIENTIAL EXERCISE

WORKPLACE STRESS DIAGNOSIS

The following exercise gives students an opportunity to work within groups to compare the work demands and job stressors found in different work settings. Intervention for preventive stress management should always be based on a good diagnosis. This exercise gives students a start in this direction.

Step 1. Before breaking the students into groups, ask them to rate the degree to which each of the following work demands is a source of stress for them and their coworkers at work. Use a 7-point rating scale for assigning the stressfulness of the work demand, with 7 = *very high source of stress*, 4 = *moderate source of stress*, and 1 = *very little source of stress*.

___ Uncertainty about various aspects of the work environment

___ Lack of control over people, events, or other aspects of work

___ Lack of career opportunities and progress

___ The implementation of new technologies

___ Work overload; that is, too much to do and not enough time

___ Conflicting expectations from one or more people at work

___ Confusing expectations from one or more people at work

___ Dangerous working conditions and/or hazardous substances

___ Sexual harassment by supervisors, coworkers, or others

___ Abrasive personalities and/or political conflicts

___ Rigid, insensitive, unresponsive supervisors or managers

Step 2. Then ask each student to write a brief description of the most stressful event that has occurred in his or her work environment during the past twelve-month period.

Step 3. Break the class into groups of approximately six members each. Each group elects a spokesperson and then compares the information developed by each person in Steps 1 and 2. In the process of this comparison, ask the groups to answer the following questions:

a. What are the similarities between work environments in terms of their most stressful work demands?

b. What are the differences among work environments in terms of their most stressful work demands?

c. Are there similarities in the descriptions of the most stressful events? If so, what are they?

Step 4. Each group will share the results of its answers to the questions in Step 3. Cross-team questions and discussion follow.

Step 5. (Optional). You may ask students to choose one or another of the work environments in which to develop some preventive stress-management strategies. Ask them to complete parts a and b below in their groups.

a. Identify one to three preventive stress-management strategies that you think are the best to use in the work environment. Why have you chosen them?

b. How should the effectiveness of these strategies be evaluated?

ASSIGNMENTS

■ Have students write a memo describing the most challenging demands and/or stressors at their workplace (or university). They should be specific in fully describing the details of these demands and/or stressors. How might they go about changing these demands and/or stressors?

■ Have students interview a medical doctor, a psychologist, or another healthcare professional about the most common forms of health problems and distress seen in his or her work. Tell them to summarize their interviews and compare the results to the categories of distress discussed in the chapter. Encourage students to share in class the responses they obtained from the medical professionals and to discuss the similarities and differences among the responses.

WHAT'S NEW TO ORGB5

■ Updated section 7-2a, The Homeostatic/Medical Approach

■ Updated paragraph on **Interpersonal Demands**

■ New box feature, "Fast Fact: The Stressful Side of Summer"

■ New box feature, "Stress Hormones Reduce Capacity to Feel Others' Pain"

■ New box feature, "Goldman Sachs Is a Great Place to Work for Type A(s)"

■ New box feature, "Hot Trend: Reducing Workplace Stress by Order of Management"

TERMS

stress 101

stressor 101

distress 101

strain 101

homeostasis 101

ego-ideal 102

self-image 102

workaholism 105

participation problem 108

performance decrement 108

compensation award 108

type a behavior pattern 109

personality hardiness 110

transformational coping 110

self-reliance 110

counterdependence 110

overdependence 110

preventive stress management 111

primary prevention 111

secondary prevention 111

tertiary prevention 111

WHAT'S INSIDE:

interpersonal communication; five keys to effective supervisory communication; barriers and gateways to communication; defensive and nondefensive communication; nonverbal communication; positive, healthy communication; communicating through new technologies.

CHAPTER OUTLINE

Interpersonal Communication
An Interpersonal Communication Model
Reflective Listening

Communication Skills for Effective Managers
Expressiveness
Empathy and Sensitivity
Persuasiveness
Informative Managing Style

Barriers and Gateways to Communication
Gender Differences
Cultural Diversity
Language

Civility and Incivility
Consequences of Incivility
Blessings of Civility
Defensive and Nondefensive Communication
Defensive Communication at Work
Defensive Tactics
Nondefensive Communication

Nonverbal Communication
Proxemics
Kinesics
Facial and Eye Behavior
Paralanguage

Positive, Healthy Communication

Communicating through New Technologies and Social Media
Written Communication
Communication Technologies
How Do Communication Technologies Affect Behavior?

LEARNING OUTCOMES

8-1 Describe the interpersonal communication process and the role of listening in the process.

8-2 Describe the five communication skills of effective supervisors.

8-3 Explain five communication barriers and the gateways through them.

8-4 Distinguish between civility and incivility, and defensive and nondefensive communication.

8-5 Explain the impact of nonverbal communication.

8-6 Explain positive, healthy communication.

8-7 Identify how new communication technologies and social media affect the communication process.

4LTR PRESS ONLINE

Have students access their 4LTR Press Online account to…

- Create StudyBits and post to their Study Board
- Review key terms and create flashcards
- Create practice quizzes from their StudyBits
- Complete assessment content: matching, drag and drop, and fill-in-the-blank problems
- View Chapter Highlight Boxes: these include chapter videos and key exhibits/figures

VIDEO

*PROFILE ON PLANT FANTASIES

Run time: 7:12 minutes
Plant Fantasies owner Teresa Carleo doesn't use e-mail, Facebook, or Twitter. At first glance, her preference for traditional communication methods seems out of touch with twenty-first-century trends. However, leaders at Plant Fantasies desire communication that works, and that means matching the right communication channel with the light business situations.

Some tasks at Plant Fantasies involve installing and maintaining gardens; other situations require collaboration with landscape designers or speaking with clients. Not all communication channels are equally suited for each situation.

Ask your students:

1. Using the concept of information richness, explain why leaders at Plant Fantasies place a high value on face-to-face communication.

2. What impact might gender have on the communication styles of Teresa Carleo and Steve Martucci? Give examples.

3. Although leaders at Plant Fantasies prefer face-to-face interaction, they use digital communication technologies in some situations. Which situations at Plant Fantasies require digital communication technology and why?

DISCUSSION QUESTIONS

1. Who is the best communicator you know? Why do you consider that person to be so?

2. Who is the best listener you have ever known? Describe what that person does that makes him or her so good at listening.

3. Have you ever been the object of incivility? Describe how it made you feel and how you reacted.

EXPERIENTIAL EXERCISE

PREPARING FOR AN EMPLOYMENT-SELECTION INTERVIEW

The purpose of this exercise is to help students develop guidelines for an employment selection interview. Such interviews are one of the more important settings in which supervisors and job candidates use applied communication skills. There is always the potential for defensiveness and confusion as well as lack of complete information exchange in this interview. This exercise allows students to think through ways to maximize the value of an employment selection interview, whether as the supervisor or the candidate, so that it is a productive experience based on effective applied communication.

Form the class into groups of students. Each group should work through Steps 1 and 2 of the exercise.

Step 1. *Guidelines for the Supervisor*

Develop a set of guidelines for the supervisor in preparing for and then conducting an employment selection interview. Consider the following questions in developing your guidelines.
a. What should the supervisor do before the interview?
b. How should the supervisor act and behave during the interview?
c. What should the supervisor do after the interview?

Step 2. *Guidelines for the Employee*

Develop another set of guidelines for the employee in preparing for and then being involved in an employment selection interview. Consider the following questions in developing your guidelines.
a. What should the employee do before the interview?
b. How should the employee act and behave during the interview?
c. What should the employee do after the interview?

Once each group has developed the two sets of guidelines, lead the class in a general discussion in which groups share and compare their guidelines. Ask students to consider the following questions during this discussion.

1. What similarities are there among the groups for each set of guidelines?
2. What unique or different guidelines have some of the groups developed?
3. What are essential guidelines for conducting an employment selection interview?

ASSIGNMENTS

■ Ask students: What methods have you found most helpful in overcoming these barriers to communication: physical, status based, cultural, linguistic? Have students write a brief response for each barrier and explain their answers. Students should be prepared to discuss in class.

■ Have students identify a person at work or at the university who is difficult to talk to and arrange an interview in which they practice good reflective listening skins. Direct them to ask the person questions about a topic in which you think he or she is interested. Students should pay particular attention to being patient, calm, and nonreactive. After the interview, summarize what they have learned.

WHAT'S NEW TO ORGB5

■ Updated section 8-1a, An Interpersonal Communication Model
■ New box feature, "Fast Fact: This Is Your Brain on Human Contact"
■ New box feature, "Breaking Gender Communication Barriers in Meetings"
■ Updated section 8-3b, Cultural Diversity
■ New box feature, "Seattle Seahawks Defensive Line Use Non-defensive Communication to Address Mistakes"
■ New box feature, "Hot Trend: Avoid E-mail Overload"
■ Updated section 8-7c, How Do Communication Technologies Affect Behavior?

TERMS

WHAT'S INSIDE:

group behavior; group formation and development; work teams in organizations; diversity and creativity in teams; empowerment and self-managed teams; upper echelons: teams at the top; managerial implications: teamwork for productivity and quality.

CHAPTER OUTLINE

LEARNING OUTCOMES

9-1 Define group and work team.

9-2 Explain the benefits organizations and individuals derive from working in teams.

9-3 Identify the factors that influence group behavior.

9-4 Describe how groups form and develop.

9-5 Explain how task and maintenance functions influence group performance.

9-6 Discuss the factors that influence group effectiveness.

9-7 Describe how empowerment relates to self-managed teams.

9-8 Explain the importance of upper echelons and top management teams.

4LTR PRESS ONLINE

Have students access their 4LTR Press Online account to. . .

- Create StudyBits and post to their Study Board

- Review key terms and create flash-cards

- Create practice quizzes from their StudyBits

- Complete assessment content: matching, drag and drop, and fill-in-the-blank problems

- View Chapter Highlight Boxes: these include chapter videos and key exhibits/figures

VIDEO

*PROFILE ON HOLDEN OUTERWEAR

Run time: 6:41 minutes
At Holden, the use of teams emerged out of necessity. For much of the company's brief history, managers worked independently on design projects. But as the company grew, founder Mikey LeBlanc needed more designers, and he began looking to outside freelancers for help. For the first time, Holden managers formed virtual teams to produce new apparel lines, and many of the team members were outside contractors. The change was especially positive for Nikki Brush, a design and development manager who began working for Holden as an outside freelancer. Brush's freelance work was so good that LeBlanc eventually hired her as a full-time employee.

Ask your students:

1. Is design manager Nikki Brush a part of a group or part of a work team? Explain the difference.

2. What changes in technology made it possible for designer Nikki Brush to be a member of Holden's work teams while she was an outside freelancer?

3. What are the potential disadvantages of teams for Holden's apparel designers? What can managers do to help minimize these downsides?

CHAPTER PREP 9

DISCUSSION QUESTIONS

1. What was the most effective group (or team) that you have been a member of? What made that group (or team) so effective?

2. Name a company you know of that successfully uses teamwork and empowerment. What has that company done that makes it so successful at teamwork and empowerment? Has its team approach made a difference in its performance? How?

3. Think of a person whom you think is a particularly good member of a team. What makes him or her so? Think of someone who is a problematic team member. What makes this person a problem?

EXPERIENTIAL EXERCISE

DESIGN A TEAM

The following exercise gives students an opportunity to design a team. Working in six-person groups, students should address the individual characteristics, team composition, and norms for an effective group whose task is to make recommendations on improving customer relations. The president of a small clothing manufacturer is concerned that his customers are not satisfied enough with the company's responsiveness, product quality, and returned-orders process. He has asked each group to put together a team to address these problems.

Step 1. Form the class into groups of approximately six members each. Each group elects a spokesperson and answers the following questions. The group should spend an equal amount of time on each question.

   a. *What characteristics should the individual members of the task team possess?* Members may consider professional competence, skills, department, and/or personality and behavioral characteristics in the group's discussion.

   b. *What should the composition of the task team be?* Once your group has addressed individual char-

acteristics, consider the overall composition of the task team. Have special and/or unique competencies, knowledge, skills, and abilities been considered in your deliberations?

   c. *What norms of behavior do you think the task team should adopt?* A team's norms of behavior may evolve, or they may be consciously discussed and agreed upon. Take the latter approach.

Step 2. Each group will share the results of its answers to the questions in Step 1. Cross-team questions and discussion follow.

ASSIGNMENTS

- Have students prepare a memo describing their observations about work teams and groups in their workplace or university. Instruct students to address the following questions: Where have you observed teams or groups to be most effective? Why? What changes might be made at work or in the university to make teams more effective?

- Have each student develop an oral presentation about what the most important norms of behavior should be in an academic community or a workplace. The presentation should include how these norms should be established and reinforced.

WHAT'S NEW TO ORGB5

- New box feature, "Hot Trend: Six Thinking Hats for Building Consensus Among Team Members"
- Updated section 9-3c, Social Loafing
- Updated section 9-4d, Characteristics of a Mature Group
- New box feature, "Enhancing Team Cohesion"
- Updated section 9-5, Task and Maintenance Functions
- New box feature, "Getting Virtual Teams Right"
- New box feature, "Fast Fact: Achieving Diverse Work Teams Goes Beyond Checking Boxes"

WHAT'S INSIDE:

the decision-making process; models of decision making; decision making and risk; Jung's cognitive styles; other individual influences on decision making; participation in decision making; the group decision-making process; techniques for group decision making; cultural issues in decision making and how participation levels affect the outcome of group decision-making efforts.

CHAPTER OUTLINE

The Decision-Making Process

Models and Limits of Decision Making
Rational Model
Bounded Rationality Model
Z Model
Escalation of Commitment

Individual Influences on Decision Making
Risk and the Manager
Personality, Attitudes, and Values
Intuition
Creativity

The Group Decision-Making Process
Advantages and Disadvantages of Group Decision Making
Limits of Group Decision Making
Techniques for Group Decision Making
Factors in Selecting the Appropriate Technique
Special Decision-Making Groups

Diversity and Culture in Decision Making

Participation in Decision Making
The Effects of Participation
Foundations for Participation and Empowerment
What Level of Participation?

LEARNING OUTCOMES

10-1 Identify the steps in the decision-making process.

10-2 Describe various models of decision making.

10-3 Discuss the individual influences that affect decision making.

10-4 Explain how groups make decisions.

10-5 Describe the role culture plays in decision making.

10-6 Explain how organizations can improve the quality of decisions through participation.

4LTR PRESS ONLINE

Have students access their 4LTR Press Online account to…

- Create StudyBits and post to their Study Board
- Review key terms and create flash-cards
- Create practice quizzes from their StudyBits
- Complete assessment content: matching, drag and drop, and fill-in-the-blank problems
- View Chapter Highlight Boxes: these include chapter videos and key exhibits/figures

VIDEO

*PROFILE ON PLANT FANTASIES

Run time: 6:37 minutes
In landscaping, success often boils down to big decisions over little details. While some decisions involve plant colors and types, others involve complex negotiation with people. Owner Teresa Carleo notes that it's sometimes difficult to work with landscape architects, since they can come up with designs that the company doesn't agree with. Despite Carleo's confidence in her own decision making, she understands the benefits of empowering others. "More and more, as I'm trying to grow the company, I'm trying to get my team to be more independent of me. I don't want to know every Single thing."

Ask your students:

1. Did Plant Fantasies owner Teresa Carleo use the rational decision-making process to launch Plant Fantasies? Explain.

2. List an example of a programmed decision at Plant Fantasies. Identify a nonprogrammed decision at Plant Fantasies.

DISCUSSION QUESTIONS

1. Why do you think identification of the real problem is the first and most important step in the decision-making process? How does attribution theory explain mistakes that can be made as managers and employees work together to explain why the problem occurred?

2. How can organizations encourage creative decision making?

CHAPTER PREP 10

ASSIGNMENTS

- Have students find two examples of recent decisions made in organizations: one that they consider a good decision and one they consider a bad decision. Instruct them to write a brief description of the decisions and then to write a summary of what went right, what went wrong, and what could be done to improve the decision-making process. Students should be prepared to compare and contrast the two examples in a presentation to the class.

EXPERIENTIAL EXERCISE

MAKING A LAYOFF DECISION

Purpose: In this exercise, students will examine how to weigh a set of facts and make a difficult personnel decision about laying off valued employees during a time of financial hardship. They will also examine their own values and criteria used in the decision-making process.

Problem: Walker Space Institute (WSI) is a medium-sized firm located in Connecticut. The firm essentially has been a subcontractor on many large space contracts that have been acquired by firms like Alliant Techsystems and others.

With the cutback in many NASA programs, Walker has an excess of employees. Stuart Tartaro, the head of one of the sections, has been told by his superior that he must reduce his section of engineers from seven to four. He is looking at the following summaries of their vitae and pondering how he will make this decision.

1. *Roger Allison*, age twenty-six, married, two children. Allison has been with WSI for a year and a half. He is a very good engineer, with a degree from Rensselaer Polytech. He has held two prior jobs and lost both of them because of cutbacks in the space program. He moved to Connecticut from California to take this job. Allison is well liked by his coworkers.

2. *Dave Jones*, age twenty-four, single. Jones is an African American, and the company looked hard to get him because of affirmative action pressure. He is not very popular with his coworkers. Because he has been employed less than a year, not much is known about his work. On his one evaluation (which was average), Jones accused his supervisor of bias against African Americans. He is a graduate of the Detroit Institute of Technology.

3. *William Foster*, age fifty-three, married, three children. Foster is a graduate of "the school of hard knocks." After serving in Desert Storm, he started to go to school but dropped out because of high family expenses. Foster has worked at the company for twenty years. His ratings were excellent for fifteen years. The last five years they have been average. Foster feels his supervisor grades him down because he does not "have sheepskins covering his office walls."

4. *Donald Boyer*, age thirty-two, married, no children. Boyer is well liked by his coworkers. He has been at WSI five years, and he has a B.S. and M.S. in engineering from Purdue University. Boyer's ratings have been mixed. Some supervisors rated him high and some average. Boyer's wife is a doctor.

Tartaro does not quite know what to do. He sees the good points of each of his section members. Most have been good employees. They all can pretty much do one another's work. No one has special training.

He is fearful that the section will hear about the downsizing and morale will drop. Work would fall off. He does not even want to talk to his wife about it, in case she would let something slip. Tartaro has come to you, Edmund Graves, personnel manager at WSI, for some guidelines on this decision—legal, moral, and best personnel practice.

SOURCE: W. F. Glueck, *Cases and Exercises in Personnel* (Dallas: Business Publications, 1978), 24–26.

WHAT'S NEW TO ORGB5

- New box feature, "Zingerman's Deli Grows but Stays Local"
- New box feature, "Fast Fact: The Time You Take to Make a Decision Signals Doubt"
- New box feature, "Hot Trend: Some People Intuitively Think of Others When Making Decisions"
- New box feature, "Adobe's Kickbox Stimulates Creative Ideas"
- Updated section 10-4c, Techniques for Group Decision Making

TERMS

WHAT'S INSIDE:

the concept of power; individuals and groups as sources of power in organizations; the ethics of power; symbols of power and powerlessness; politicking and influence tactics in organizations; managing up (i.e., managing the boss, sharing power, and empowerment).

CHAPTER OUTLINE

The Concept of Power

Forms and Sources of Power in Organizations
Interpersonal Forms of Power
Intergroup Sources of Power

Using Power Ethically
Positive versus Negative Power

Symbols of Power
Kanter's Symbols of Power
Kanter's Symbols of Powerlessness
Korda's Symbols of Power

Political Behavior in Organizations
Influence Tactics
Political Skill

Managing Political Behavior in Organizations
Managing Up: Managing the Boss
Sharing Power: Empowerment

LEARNING OUTCOMES

11-1 Describe the concept of power.

11-2 Identify forms and sources of power in organizations.

11-3 Describe the role of ethics in using power.

11-4 Identify symbols of power and powerlessness in organizations.

11-5 Define organizational politics and understand the role of political skill and major influence tactics.

11-6 Identify ways to manage political behavior in organizations.

4LTR PRESS ONLINE

Have students access their 4LTR Press Online account to…

- Create StudyBits and post to their Study Board
- Review key terms and create flashcards
- Create practice quizzes from their StudyBits
- Complete assessment content: matching, drag and drop, and fill-in-the-blank problems
- View Chapter Highlight Boxes: these include chapter videos and key exhibits/figures

VIDEO

*PROFILE ON BARCELONA RESTAURANT GROUP

Run time: 6:14 minutes
For anyone who has waited tables, restaurant turnover is a familiar experience. Cooks, servers, and bussers have famously short careers, and restaurant managers also suffer burnout. Unlike run-of-the-mill chains, Barcelona's higher standard of service demands letting go employees who aren't up to snuff. At the end of the day, Chief Operating Officer Scott Lawton says, people either possess the necessary intelligence and skills to run a restaurant or they don't. And since the restaurant industry doesn't have time for

learning curves, the success or failure of an establishment boils down to hiring competent self-motivated employees.

Ask your students:

1. Who has authority at Barcelona?

2. What forms of interpersonal power do these individuals possess?

3. Identify Kanter's symbols of power that are evident at Barcelona Restaurant Group.

DISCUSSION QUESTIONS

1. Who is the most powerful person you know personally? What is it that makes the person so powerful?

2. What kinds of membership (alienative, calculative, moral) do you currently have? Is the power used in these relationships congruent?

3. As a student, do you experience yourself as powerful, powerless, or both? On what symbols or symptoms are you basing your perception?

ASSIGNMENTS

Assign students to write a newspaper feature on a person they admire that analyzes the person's use of power in terms of the ideas presented in the chapter.

CHAPTER PREP 11

EXPERIENTIAL EXERCISE

SOCIAL POWER ROLE PLAYS

The French and Raven's (1959) taxonomy of bases of social power is a useful conceptual tool. In an organizational behavior course, we invariably deal with notions of power, influence, and authority, often as a prelude to getting into issues of leadership. The distinctions among legitimate, expert, referent, reward, punishment, and information bases of social power are also very relevant.

Purpose:
This experiential exercise involves students learning the material in an active way.

Goals of the Exercise:
Three things happen with the exercise: (1) students get an opportunity to devise influence attempts based on the French and Raven taxonomy; (2) the class assesses the probable results of using each kind of power; and (3) the class can more clearly focus on understanding social power at work in the class itself. This exercise is most effective one-third of the way into a typical course, when control and influence issues are most salient.

Procedures:
Divide the class into six groups of equal size, each of which is assigned one of the power bases. (It is helpful to have three or four people who do not join a group but remain outside to assist with data collection and tabulation.) The groups are given the same scenario, which involves one person (a teacher) attempting to influence another person (a student). Each group has ten to fifteen minutes to prepare an actual influence plan using the type of power that it has been assigned.

You may wish to tailor the presented situations to your own needs. The following situation has worked well with undergraduate classes.

Situation:
You are an instructor in a college class and have become aware that a potentially good student is repeatedly absent from class and is sometimes unprepared when he is there. He seems to be satisfied with the grade he is getting, but you would like to see him attend regularly, be better prepared, and thus, do better in the class. You even feel that the student might get really excited about pursuing a career in this field, which is an exciting one for you. You are respected and liked by your students, and it kind of

irritates you that this person treats your dedicated teaching with such a cavalier attitude. You want to influence the student to start attending class regularly.

This situation may be particularly useful because it allows you to discuss, at the conclusion of the exercise, your position in the class and how that particular class might respond if you were to use these different kinds of power.

When all groups have completed their planning, each selects one member to play the instructor. In the development of their role play, the group has to decide where the influence attempt is to take place (in the classroom, teacher's office, snack bar, and so forth). The group may also pick, from their own or another group, a "student" who is to be the recipient of the "instructor's" attempt.

While the role play is going on, the students in other groups are asked to think of themselves as the student being influenced. They fill out the "Reaction to Influence Questionnaire." After each presentation, all students outside the playing group record their reactions as if they were the student being addressed by the teacher. As an option, the forms can be collected by the assistants who tabulate the results while the next group is playing the influencer. When all groups have presented, the aggregated response to each question by influence type can be displayed on the board for discussion. (The assistants are helpful since the data comes in fast, and your time is spent coordinating role playing, It's helpful for the assistants to have calculators.) The entire activity, including introductory lecture and post-exercise discussion, can be completed in fifty to seventy minutes.

SOURCE: Adapted with permission from G. Akin, *Exchange 3*, No.4 (1978): 38–39.

WHAT'S NEW TO ORGB5

- New box feature, "Fast Fact: Gender Diversity on Boards Benefits Everyone"
- Updated section 11-2a, Interpersonal Forms of Power
- New box feature, "Nut Rage on Korean Air Flight—From an Executive Vice President"
- New box feature, "Hot Trend: Having an Eye for Emotions Pays Off"
- Updated section 11-5b, Political Skill
- New box feature, "Toyota Diversifies Its Power Positions"
- Updated section 11-6b, Sharing Power: Empowerment

TERMS

LEARNING OUTCOMES

12-1 Discuss the differences between leadership and management and between leaders and managers.

12-2 Explain the role of trait theory in describing leaders.

12-3 Describe the role of foundational behavioral research in the development of leadership theories.

12-4 Describe and compare the four contingency theories of leadership.

12-5 Discuss the recent developments in leadership theory of leader–member exchange and inspirational leadership.

12-6 Discuss how issues of emotional intelligence, trust, gender, and servant leadership are informing today's leadership models.

12-7 Define followership and identify different types of followers.

12-8 Synthesize historical leadership research into key guidelines for leaders.

4LTR PRESS ONLINE

Have students access their 4LTR Press Online account to. . .

- Create StudyBits and post to their Study Board
- Review key terms and create flash-cards
- Create practice quizzes from their StudyBits
- Complete assessment content: matching, drag and drop, and fill-in-the-blank problems
- View Chapter Highlight Boxes: these include chapter videos and key exhibits/figures

VIDEO

*PROFILE ON CAMP BOW WOW

Run time: 6:37 minutes
As the owner of a wildly popular pet franchise, Heidi Ganahl is top dog to an increasing number of employees. "At Camp Bow Wow, leading a franchise company means leading 2,000 employees that work at camps, at Home Buddies, and at Bow Wow Behavior Buddies franchises," Ganahl said of her expanding pet care empire. One challenge Ganahl faces in leading so many talented people is getting everyone to follow a single business model. Since franchise companies attract hundreds of independent business owners into the system, Ganahl also has to work with many strong leaders.

Ask your students:

1. Where does Heidi Ganahl's leadership fall on the Leadership Grid discussed in the chapter? Explain.

2. In what way is Heidi Ganahl's leadership transformational, charismatic, and visionary? Give examples.

3. What is the difference between a manager and a leader, and how has Heidi Ganahl's role shifted toward leadership and away from management as the organization has grown?

CHAPTER PREP 12

DISCUSSION QUESTIONS

1. Do you (or would you want to) work in an autocratic, democratic, or laissez-faire work environment? What might be the advantages of each work environment? The disadvantages?

2. Is your supervisor or professor someone who is high in concern for production? High in concern for people? What is his or her Leadership Grid style?

3. Describe the relationship you have with your supervisor or a professor. What is the best part of the relationship? The worst part? What could you do to make the relationship better?

EXPERIENTIAL EXERCISE

NATIONAL CULTURE AND LEADERSHIP

Purpose: Effective leadership often varies by national culture, as Hofstede's research has shown. This exercise gives you the opportunity to examine your own and your group's leadership orientation compared to norms from ten countries, including the United States.

The complete twenty-nine item questionnaire can be found in the Instructor Manual.

The following shows which items should go with which elements on the scale:

1–5	Uncertainty avoidance
6–11	Individualism
12–17	Power distance
18–24	Paternalism
25–29	Masculinity

This instrument has no scoring mechanism. There are two ways to evaluate the results:

1. Have the students determine their total scores for each of the five sections (higher scores are indicative of strength on that dimension toward the value the dimension's title indicates) and see which of the dimensions scores higher.

They can see, relative to themselves, how the dimensions vary in strength.

2. Take mean scores from the whole class either:
   a. for each separate item, or
   b. for each of the five sections.

Then write these means on the board and discuss the relevance of the variability of the scores.

SOURCE: Adapted from P. Dorfman, *Advances in International Comparative Management*, vol. 3, (Greenwich, Conn.: JAI Press; 1988): 127–150. Reprinted by permission of JAI Press Inc.; D. Marcic and S. M. Puffer, "Dimensions of National Culture and Effective Leadership Patterns: Hofstede Revisited," *Management International* (Minneapolis/St. Paul, West Publishing, 1994): 10–15.

ASSIGNMENTS

- Have students choose a leader they admire and write a description of this person including his or her characteristics and attributes that they admire. Also, have them note any aspects of this leader or his or her behavior that they find less than wholly admirable. Ask students to limit their answers to one page or an outline format.

- Have students interview a supervisor or manager about the best follower the supervisor or manager has worked with. They should ask questions about the characteristics and behaviors that made this person such a good follower. Note in particular how this follower responds to change. Students should be prepared to present interview results in class.

WHAT'S NEW TO ORGB5

- New box feature, "How CEOs Describe Themselves"
- New box feature, "Hot Trend: Narcissistic CEOs, Big Signatures"
- New box feature, "Mark Zuckerberg of Facebook: Would I Want to Work for This Person?"
- Updated section 12-5a, Leader-Member Exchange
- Updated section 12-5b, Inspirational Leadership
- New box feature, "Companies with Female CEOs Outperform Those Led by Men"

TERMS

leadership 187
formal leadership 187
informal leadership 187
leader 187
manager 187
autocratic style 189
democratic style 189
laissez-faire style 189

initiating structure 189
consideration 189
leadership grid 190
organization man manager (5,5) 190
authority-compliance manager (9,1) 190
country club manager (1,9) 190
team manager (9,9) 190
impoverished manager (1,1) 191

paternalistic father-knows-best manager (9+9) 191
opportunistic what's-in-it-for-me manager (Opp) 192
least preferred coworker (LPC) 192
task structure 192
position power 193
leader–member relations 193
charismatic leadership 198
followership 201

WHAT'S INSIDE:

functional and dysfunctional conflict; structural and personal factors that cause conflict in organizations; forms of conflict in organizations; intrapersonal conflict; interpersonal conflict; conflict management strategies and techniques; conflict management styles.

CHAPTER OUTLINE

The Nature of Conflicts in Organizations
Importance of Conflict Management Skills for the Manager
Functional versus Dysfunctional Conflict
Diagnosing Conflict

Causes of Conflict in Organizations
Structural Factors
Personal Factors

Forms of Group Conflict in Organizations
Interorganizational Conflict
Intergroup Conflict
Intragroup Conflict

Individual Conflict in Organizations
Types of Intrapersonal Conflict
Managing Intrapersonal Conflict
Managing Interpersonal Conflict
Defense Mechanisms

Conflict Management Strategies and Techniques
Ineffective Techniques
Effective Techniques

Conflict Management Styles
Avoiding
Accommodating
Competing
Compromising
Collaborating

LEARNING OUTCOMES

13-1 Describe the nature of conflicts in organizations.

13-2 Explain the role structural and personal factors play in causing conflict in organizations.

13-3 Discuss the nature of group conflict in organizations.

13-4 Describe the factors that influence conflict between individuals in organizations.

13-5 Describe effective and ineffective techniques for managing conflict.

13-6 Identify five styles of conflict management.

4LTR PRESS ONLINE

Have students access their 4LTR Press Online account to. . .

- Create StudyBits and post to their Study Board
- Review key terms and create flash-cards
- Create practice quizzes from their StudyBits
- Complete assessment content: matching, drag and drop, and fill-in-the-blank problems
- View Chapter Highlight Boxes: these include chapter videos and key exhibits/figures

VIDEO

*PROFILE ON BARCELONA RESTAURANT GROUP

Run time: 7:00 minutes
At Barcelona, life is all about authentic cuisine, exceptional service, and a good time. But delivering this eclectic dining expedience involves a serious, sometimes confrontational, approach to restaurant management. The company recruits only self-confident individuals who take complete

ownership over the establishment. When Andy Pforzheimer coaches new recruits, he is adamant that his staff be willing to take responsibility for their work and success. The enormous trust Barcelona places in employees is evident during weekly staff meetings. Pforzheimer routinely mixes it up with managers and chefs, and the dialogue gets feisty at times.

Ask your students:

1. Would you characterize the conflict evident at Barcelona Restaurant as functional or dysfunctional? Explain.

2. What forms of conflict are on display at Barcelona? What structural and personal factors are likely causes of this conflict?

3. Which of the five styles of conflict management mentioned in the chapter best characterizes interactions at Barcelona?

DISCUSSION QUESTIONS

1. What causes you the most conflict at work or school?

2. Identify the different intragroup, interrole, intrarole, and person-role conflicts that you experience.

CHAPTER PREP 13

EXPERIENTIAL EXERCISE

THE WORLD BANK GAME: AN INTERGROUP NEGOTIATION

Purpose: To experience the conflict between advantages of cooperation and advantages of competition in a mixed-motive dilemma; to explore some dynamics of trust between groups; to practice negotiation skills.

Group size: No more than ten participants per team. Two teams can be formed to compete against each other, with the instructor serving as banker and the remaining students designated as observers.

Materials:

- Twenty 3 × 5 cards for each team, each card with a marked side (X covering the entire side) and an unmarked side. (Playing cards may be used as substitutes.)
- A copy of the World Bank Record Sheet for each team (found in the Instructor Manual).
- A copy of the World Bank Banker's Instruction Sheet for each banker (also in the Instructor Manual).

Physical Setting: Teams competing against each other are located close to each other, but their meetings are private. Their negotiators also need a private place to meet briefly several times.

Process:

1. The banker forms pairs of teams. (There must be an even number of teams.)
2. Participants should read the World Bank General Instructions, and the banker responds to questions.
3. If there are two teams, the instructor serves as banker. If there are more than two teams, additional bankers (one for each additional pair of teams) are appointed. Bankers are briefed about their roles and given a copy of the world Bank Banker's Instruction Sheet.
4. Teams have ten minutes to organize themselves and plan their strategies. Before play begins, each team must select a negotiator, a representative, a team recorder, and a treasurer.
5. The banker signals the beginning of round one to each team.
6. The banker calls the game to a close at an appropriate time.

Variations:

1. To increase collaboration, the design may be altered as follows: (a) reduce the number of moves in each round to five, (b) require negotiation after each move, or (c) increase the penalty for an attack.
2. To increase competition, the design may be altered as follows: (a) increase the number of moves in each round to ten, (b) make negotiations more difficult and costly by assessing a fee, (c) remove the penalty for an attack, or (d) multiply the payoff threefold for move and fivefold for the final move.
3. To focus on the negotiation process, all negotiations may take place in a neutral location in the presence of all parties to the negotiation (e.g., both teams may observe). The number of negotiators may also be increased to two from each team.

SOURCE: Adapted from N. H. Berkowitz and H. A. Hornstein. "World Bank: An Intergroup Negotiation," in J. W. Pfeiffer and J. E. Jones, eds., *The 1975 Handbook for Group Facilitators* (San Diego: Pfeiffer 1975), 58–62. Copyright © 1975 Pfeiffer/Jossey-Bass. Reprinted with permission of John Wiley & Sons, Inc.

ASSIGNMENTS

- Have students describe three defense mechanisms they have seen people exhibit and analyze why they think these mechanisms were used. Have them briefly describe how they would manage this type of reaction to a conflict.

WHAT'S NEW TO ORGB5

- New box feature, "Fast Fact: Workplace Violence Can Be Prevented, Minimized, and Managed"
- New box feature, "Abercrombie's Look Policy Goes to the Supreme Court"
- New box feature, "Hot Trend: Millennial, Gen X, or Boomer: Who's the Best Manager for Work-Life Balance?"
- New box feature, "I'm Gonna Call Your Mom"

TERMS

WHAT'S INSIDE:

work in organizations; scientific management; job characteristics model; social information processing and ergonomics as alternative approaches to job design; Japanese, German, and Scandinavian approaches to work design; telecommuting, alternative work patterns, and technology at work.

CHAPTER OUTLINE

Work in Organizations
The Meaning of Work
Jobs in Organizations

Traditional Approaches to Job Design
Scientific Management
Job Enlargement/Job Rotation
Job Enrichment
Job Characteristics Theory

Alternative Approaches to Job Design
Social Information Processing
Ergonomics and Interdisciplinary
    Framework
International Perspectives on the Design
    of Work
Work Design and Well-Being

Contemporary Issues in the Design of Work
Telecommuting
Alternative Work Patterns
Technology at Work
Skill Development

LEARNING OUTCOMES

14-1 Differentiate between job and work.

14-2 Discuss the traditional approaches to job design.

14-3 Identify and describe alternative approaches to job design.

14-4 Identify and describe contemporary issues facing organizations in the design of work.

4LTR PRESS ONLINE

Have students access their 4LTR Press Online account to…

- Create StudyBits and post to their Study Board
- Review key terms and create flash-cards
- Create practice quizzes from their StudyBits
- Complete assessment content: matching, drag and drop, and fill-in-the-blank problems
- View Chapter Highlight Boxes: these include chapter videos and key exhibits/figures

VIDEO

*PROFILE ON CAMP BOW WOW

Run time: 6:08 minutes
A few years ago, Sue Ryan, a Camp Bow Wow franchisee, handled all the ins and outs of managing the doggie day camp. Once the job became overwhelming, however, Ryan hired experienced pet care worker Candace Stathis to be camp counselor, and, later, general manager. To keep camp running as efficiently as possible, Stathis maintains a strict schedule for doggie baths, nail trimmings, feedings, and play time. Staying on schedule is no easy task, however, especially during the busy holidays and summer months, or whenever the pets get territorial. Stathis says that while dogs get in occasional tussles, all camp staff members are trained to handle hairy situations.

Ask your students:

1. How do the tasks of managers and camp counselors differ at Camp Bow Wow?

2. How does Camp Bow Wow utilize a form of job rotation to keep camp counselors satisfied with their jobs?

3. Using the job characteristics model, explain why the employees of Camp Bow Wow love their jobs.

DISCUSSION QUESTIONS

1. What do you think managers should learn from the traditional approaches to the design of work used in the United States?

2. Do you think it is possible for American companies to apply approaches to the design of work that were developed in other countries?

3. What do you think is the most important emerging issue in the design of work?

EXPERIENTIAL EXERCISE

A JOB REDESIGN EFFORT

This activity will help you consider ways in which work can be redesigned to improve its impact on people and its benefit to the organization. Consider the following case.

Eddie is a quality control inspector for an automotive manufacturer. His job is to inspect the body, interior, and engine of cars as they roll off the assembly line. Eddie's responsibility is to identify quality problems that either hinder the functioning of these parts of the car or noticeably mar the car's appearance. He is to report the problem so that it can be corrected. Sometimes late in the day, especially on Thursdays and Fridays, Eddie lets assembly problems slip past him. In addition, his back feels sore at the end of the day, and sometimes he is very stiff in the morning. There are times when he is not sure whether he is seeing a serious problem or just a glitch.

As part of a five-person team, your job is to evaluate two alternative approaches to redesigning Eddie's job using theories presented in the chapter. Answer the following questions as a team. Your team should be prepared to present its recommendations to the class as a whole.

Discussion Questions:

1. For this particular job, which are the two best models to use in a redesign effort? Why?

2. Does your team need any additional information before it begins to redesign Eddie's job? If so, what information do you need?

3. Using the two models you chose in Question 1, what would your team specifically recommend to redesign Eddie's job?

ASSIGNMENTS

- Have students interview an employee in your organization or another organization and develop an oral presentation about how the job the employee is doing could be enriched. Make sure they ask questions about all aspects of the employee's work (e.g., what specific tasks are done and with whom the employee interacts on the job).

- Based on the materials in the chapter, have students prepare a memo detailing the advantages and disadvantages of flextime job arrangements. In a second part of the memo, have them identify the specific conditions and characteristics required for a successful flextime program.

WHAT'S NEW TO ORGB5

- New box feature, "Hot Trend: Making Work Meaningful"
- New box feature, "Repetitive Work: A Double-Edged Sword"
- Updated paragraph on key term, **Engagement**
- New box feature, "Fast Fact: Employment Engagement Is Good for the Economy"
- Updated section 14-4, Contemporary Issues in the Design of Work
- Updated section 14-4a, Telecommuting
- New box feature, "All Roles Can Flex"

TERMS

job 223
work 223
meaning of work 223
work simplification 225
job enlargement 225
job rotation 226

cross-training 226
job enrichment 226
Job Characteristics Model 228
Job Diagnostic Survey (JDS) 228
engagement 229
social information-processing (SIP) model 230
ergonomics 230

lean production 232
sociotechnical systems (STS) 232
technocentric 232
anthropocentric 232
job sharing 235
flextime 235
virtual office 236
technostress 236

WHAT'S INSIDE:

key organizational design processes; basic design dimensions; five structural configurations; contextual variables such as size, technology, and environment; forces reshaping organizations; cautionary notes about structure.

CHAPTER OUTLINE

Key Organizational Design Processes
Differentiation
Integration

Basic Design Dimensions

Five Structural Configurations
Simple Structure
Machine Bureaucracy
Professional Bureaucracy
Divisionalized Form
Adhocracy

Contextual Variables
Size
Technology
Environment
Strategy and Goals

Forces Reshaping Organizations
Life Cycles in Organizations
Globalization
Changes in Information-Processing Technologies
Demands on Organizational Processes

Emerging Organizational Structures

Factors That Can Adversely Affect Structure

LEARNING OUTCOMES

15-1 Define differentiation and integration as organizational design processes.

15-2 Discuss the basic design dimensions managers must consider in structuring an organization.

15-3 Describe five structural configurations for organizations.

15-4 Describe four contextual variables that influence organizational structure.

15-5 Explain the forces reshaping organizations.

15-6 Identify and describe emerging organizational structures.

15-7 Identify factors that can adversely affect organizational structure.

4LTR PRESS ONLINE

Have students access their 4LTR Press Online account to…

- Create StudyBits and post to their Study Board
- Review key terms and create flash-cards
- Create practice quizzes from their StudyBits
- Complete assessment content: matching, drag and drop, and fill-in-the-blank problems
- View Chapter Highlight Boxes: these include chapter videos and key exhibits/figures

VIDEO

*PROFILE ON MODERN SHED

Run time: 7:31 minutes
Like his stylish sheds, Ryan Smith's company is built to be adaptive, scalable, and suited to the needs of the environment. Modem Shed counts only twelve to fourteen full-time employees; however, at times the company's output rivals that of a large builder, due to close collaboration with a network of thirty-five independent contractors. According to Smith, partnering with outside specialists is the most efficient, effective, and flexible way to run a startup company. Small, flexible, responsive—these are the qualities that have enabled Modem Shed to thrive even during an economic recession.

Ask your students:

1. How did Ryan Smith determine whether his company needed a mechanistic structure with a tall vertical hierarchy or an organic one involving free-flowing partnerships?

2. What are the advantages and disadvantages of Modem Shed's organizational structure?

3. Give an example of how Modem Shed's structure enables fast response to rapidly changing market opportunities.

CHAPTER PREP 15

DISCUSSION QUESTIONS

1. How would you describe the organization you work for (or your college) on each of the basic design dimensions? For example, is it a very formal organization or an informal organization?

2. Do the size, technology, and mission of your organization directly affect you? How?

3. Who are your organization's competitors? What changes do you see in information technology where you work?

EXPERIENTIAL EXERCISE

DESIGN AND BUILD A CASTLE

Purpose: To give students an opportunity to design an organization and produce a product.

Group Size: Three teams of six to eight members each.

Time: Students are given forty-five minutes to complete the project.

Activity: Three product-development teams are working within the research and development division of the General Turret and Moat Corporation. Each of the three teams designs a castle for the company to produce and sell. Given limited resources, the company cannot put more than one design on the market. Therefore, the company will have to decide which of the three designs it will use and discard the others.

Exercise Schedule:

1. (5 minutes) Each group is designated #1, #2, or #3. Members read **only** one memorandum, the appropriate one for their group. One observer (or two for larger groups) is selected for each group. Observers read their materials. Memoranda are in the Instructor Manual.

2. (10 minutes) Groups design their organization in order to complete the goal.

3. (15–20 minutes) Each group designs its own castle and draws it on newsprint.

4. (5–10 minutes) "Typical consumers" (may be observers or others) tour building locations and

hear sales pitches. Judges caucus to determine the winner.

5. (10–15 minutes) Groups meet again and write up the central goal statement of the group. Also, they write the organization chart on newsprint with the goal written beneath. These are posted around the room.

6. (5–15 minutes) Instructor leads a class discussion on how the different memos affected organization design. Which design seemed most effective for this task?

Discussion Questions:

1. What do you think made one castle win over the others?

2. How much difference did the sales pitch make?

3. Is one group's organizing structure better than another's? Are others more useful in different "Castle Companies" or different situations?

4. Was communication influenced by any particular structure?

5. What other dynamics of your group seemed to be important and influenced your final product?

ASSIGNMENTS

- Have students write a memo classifying and describing the structural configuration of their university based on the five choices in Table 15.1. If they need more information for their classification and description, have them determine and cite additional sources they can use.

WHAT'S NEW TO ORGB5

- New box feature, "McDonald's Changes Its Structure to Respond Better to Customers"

- New box feature, "Hot Trend: Retailers Respond to Declining Sales with Downsizing"

- New box feature, "Fast Fact: Top Air Carriers Align Structural Elements for Success"

- New box feature, "Seven Designs for Organizations of the Future"

TERMS

organizational design 239
organizational structure 239
differentiation 239
integration 242
formalization 243
centralization 243
specialization 243
standardization 243
complexity 243
hierarchy of authority 243
simple structure 245
machine bureaucracy 245
professional bureaucracy 245
divisionalized form 246
adhocracy 246
contextual variables 246
technological interdependence 248
environment 249
task environment 249
environmental uncertainty 250
mechanistic structure 250
organic structure 250
organizational life cycle 252

WHAT'S INSIDE:

the key role of organizational culture; functions of organizational culture; the leader's role in shaping and reinforcing culture; organizational socialization; assessing organizational culture; changing organizational culture.

CHAPTER OUTLINE

LEARNING OUTCOMES

16-1 Identify the three levels of organizational culture and evaluate the roles they play in an organization.

16-2 Evaluate the four functions of organizational culture within an organization.

16-3 Explain the relationship between organizational culture and performance.

16-4 Describe five ways leaders reinforce organizational culture.

16-5 Describe the three stages of organizational socialization and the ways culture is communicated in each step.

16-6 Discuss how managers assess their organization's culture.

16-7 Explain actions managers can take to change organizational culture.

16-8 Identify the challenges organizations face developing positive, cohesive cultures.

4LTR PRESS ONLINE

Have students access their 4LTR Press Online account to...

- Create StudyBits and post to their Study Board
- Review key terms and create flash-cards
- Create practice quizzes from their StudyBits
- Complete assessment content: matching, drag and drop, and fill-in-the-blank problems
- View Chapter Highlight Boxes: these include chapter videos and key exhibits/figures

VIDEO

*PROFILE ON CAMP BOW WOW

Run time: 5:19 minutes
According to Heidi Ganahl, Camp Bow Wow's top dog, corporate culture has many elements: it can mean logos and branded material a presence on the Internet, or even the relationships developed with customers and employees. But a key element of Camp Bow Wow's culture that doesn't exist in other franchises is the staffs deep emotional connection with animals. The connection is immediately apparent at Camp Bow Wow's corporate headquarters, where offices are bustling with employees and pets alike. "It's all about the pets," Ganahl says. "If we keep that focus and that commitment. I think our culture will be alive and Well for a long time."

Ask your students:

1. What aspects of Camp Bow Wow's corporate culture are visible and conscious? What aspects are invisible and unconscious?

2. Why did Camp Bow Wow have to change its culture when it became a national franchise?

3. What impact does Heidi Ganahl's story have on employees at Camp Bow Wow?

CHAPTER PREP 16

DISCUSSION QUESTIONS

1. Name a company with a visible organizational culture. What do you think are the company's values? Has the culture contributed to the organization's performance? Explain.

2. Name a leader you think manages organizational culture well. How does the leader do this? Use Schein's description of how leaders reinforce culture to analyze the leader's behavior.

3. Suppose you want to change your organization's culture. What sort of resistance would you expect from employees? How would you deal with this resistance?

EXPERIENTIAL EXERCISE

CONTRASTING ORGANIZATIONAL CULTURES

To complete this exercise, groups of four or five students should be formed. Each group should select one of the following pairs of organizations:

American Airlines and Northwest Airlines
Anheuser-Busch and Coors
Hewlett-Packard and Xerox
Albertsons and Winn-Dixie
Dayton-Hudson (Target) and J. C. Penney Company

Use your university library's resources to gather information about the companies' cultures. Contrast the cultures of the two organizations using the following dimensions:

- Strength of the culture.
- Fit of the culture with the industry's environment.
- Adaptiveness of the culture.

Which of the two is the better performer? On what did you base your conclusion? How does the performance of each relate to its organizational culture?

SOURCE: Adapted ·with the permission of The Free Press, a Division of Simon & Schuster, Inc., from Corporate Culture and Performance by John P. Kotter and James L. Heskett. Copyright © 1992 by Kotter Associates, Inc., and James L. Heskett.

ASSIGNMENTS

- Have students select an organization that they might like to work for and learn as much as they can about that company's culture using library resources, online sources, contacts within the company, and as many creative means as they can. Assign students to prepare a brief presentation summarizing the culture for the class.

- Have students research two culturally different organizations of their choice and then prepare a brief description of both companies. Explain why the culture, though different, works for each company and the benefits to each organization.

WHAT'S NEW TO ORGB5

- Updated section 16-1a, Artifacts
- Updated section 16-1c, Assumptions
- Updated section 16-3a, The Strong-Culture Perspective
- New box feature, "IDEO's Creative Culture of Helping"
- Updated section 16-4e, How Leaders Hire and Fire Individuals
- Updated section 16-5, Organizational Socialization
- New box feature, "Hot Trend: GE Changes Its Culture by Crowdsourcing Its Employees"
- Updated section 16-8a, Merger Acquisition
- New box feature, "Southwest Airlines' Culture of Sustainability"

TERMS

organizational (corporate) culture 259

artifacts 259

espoused values 262

enacted values 262

assumptions 262

strong culture 263

adaptive culture 264

organizational socialization 266

anticipatory socialization 266

encounter 267

change and acquisition 268

triangulation 269

WHAT'S INSIDE:

careers as joint responsibilities; career choices and types of jobs; the career stage model; career paths; mentoring; dual-career households; work-home conflicts; career anchors.

CHAPTER OUTLINE

Occupational and Organizational Choice Decisions
Preparing for the World of Work
Occupational Choice
Organizational Choice and Entry

Foundations for a Successful Career
Becoming Your Own Career Coach
Emotional Intelligence and Career Success

The Career Stage Model

The Establishment Stage
Psychological Contracts

The Advancement Stage
Career Paths and Career Ladders
Finding a Mentor
Dual-Career Partnerships
Work–Home Conflicts

The Maintenance Stage
Sustaining Performance
Becoming a Mentor

The Withdrawal Stage
Planning for Change
Retirement

Career Anchors

WHAT'S NEW TO ORGB5

- Updated section 17-1c and 17-2b,
- New box feature, "Genentech Gets Employees' Goats—Literally"
- New box feature, "Hot Trend: Unleashing the Power of Women at Kimberly-Clark"
- Updated section 17-5b, Finding a Mentor
- New box feature, "Fast Fact: Intel Offers Bonding Leave for New Moms and Dads"
- Updated section 17-5d, Work-Home Conflicts
- New box feature, "Merrill Edge's Face Retirement Mobile App"
- Updated "By the Numbers" feature
- Updated section 17-7b, Retirement

LEARNING OUTCOMES

17-1 Explain occupational and organizational choice decisions.

17-2 Identify foundations for a successful career.

17-3 Explain the career stage model.

17-4 Explain the major tasks facing individuals in the establishment stage of the career stage model.

17-5 Identify the issues confronting individuals in the advancement stage of the career stage model.

17-6 Describe how individuals can navigate the challenges of the maintenance stage of the career stage model.

17-7 Explain how individuals withdraw from the workforce.

17-8 Explain how career anchors help form a career identity.

4LTR PRESS ONLINE

Have students access their 4LTR Press Online account to…

- Create StudyBits and post to their Study Board
- Review key terms and create flashcards
- Create practice quizzes from their StudyBits
- Complete assessment content: matching, drag and drop, and fill-in-the-blank problems
- View Chapter Highlight Boxes: these include chapter videos and key exhibits/figures

VIDEO

*PROFILE ON LIVING SOCIAL ESCAPES

Run time: 5:53 minutes
Although there is no single formula for success, Maia Josebachvili and Bram Levy say that hard work, intelligence, and luck are essential for any career. The luck part came when an outside company, LivingSocial, took interest in buying Urban Escapes following the firm's appearance in *Inc.* magazine. Executives arranged to meet Josebachvili at a local pub, and a few months later the acquisition was complete. Now with an abundant supply of capital and resources, Josebachvili and Levy are seeing their careers change in new and exciting ways. "What I'm most happy with," Josebachvili says, "is that I'm now part of a company that is growing faster than we were, but I still get to do exactly what I love to do."

Ask your students:

1. At what stage of the career stage model are Maia Josebachvili and Bram Levy? Explain.

2. Describe how Maia Josebachvili chose her occupation as a business owner and trip planner, and determine if her choice fits her personality type.

3. What challenges is Maia Josebachvili likely to face as she manages her career through her thirties?

DISCUSSION QUESTION

1. What do you think will be the most stressful career stage? What type of stressors led you to make this choice?

CHAPTER PREP 17

EXPERIENTIAL EXERCISE

DUAL CAREERS

Purpose: (1) to help students be more aware of how underlying biases regarding gender roles can influence their decisions affecting the careers of others and (2) to help students be more conscious of their own and others' differing values and perceptions regarding family roles and of issues related to career decisions involving dual-career couples. The handouts for students are in the Instructor Manual.

Suggestions on Delivery:

- Tell students that you have a short exercise that will help them to identify and examine important issues related to personal career decisions. Place students in two or more groups composed of four to six persons each.
- Tell the students to first *Individually* read the case that you are about to hand out, and then quickly respond to the questions at the end. Also, tell them that after they have finished their individual responses, they should then begin to share one-by-one within the group their individual responses (e.g., accept or reject the promotion offer and why they decided to accept or reject).

Activities:

1. Distribute the case exercise—half of the groups receiving the Chris as *male* form and half receiving the Chris as female form.

2. After group sharing and discussion have been completed by most groups (typically lasting fifteen to twenty minutes), tell the students that you would now like to begin to examine, in a total class discussion format, the issues, concerns, and problems that this exercise helped to identify. Ask the students to now go beyond this particular case and to identify what general career issues came up in their sharing of why they responded the way they did to the case, List these issue topics as they are identified, and discuss their importance—but *don't* talk about this particular case yet. This general discussion typically promotes a useful examination of the importance of such topics as:

- Dual-career couple challenges
- Self-sacrifice versus actualization
- Child care for working parents
- Career opportunities in academia versus business
- Influence of earning power on career decisions
- An organization's career advancement expectations/policy
- Temporary spouse separation for conflicting career opportunities
- Allegiance to company versus spouse and family
- Family financial support/security

- Following career dreams versus pragmatism
- Traditional roles of husband and wife in providing family financial support and child care

3. After you have exhausted this class discussion, ask for a show of hands of those who believe that Chris should accept the promotion offer, and then a show of hands of those who believe that Chris should reject the promotion.

4. Ask one of the students to explain why he or she believes that Chris should accept the offer. As the student begins to explain and refers to Chris as a male or female, depending upon the form received, what typically occurs is:

   a. others in the class with a different Chris gender will spontaneously begin to correct the student

   b. the explaining student's group members and others will vociferously support the student's correctness of Chris's gender

   c. as students look again at their forms, brief mass confusion will take place, and

   d. the students will collectively come to realize that they've been had and, in good humor, accuse the instructor of underhanded trickery.

5. At this point, admit to the deception, and inform the students that identical cases were passed out but that in half of the forms Chris was identified as male and his spouse, Kim, as female, and in the other half the gender is switched.

Discussion Questions:

1. Ask the students if it matters whether Chris is male or female.

2. Should Chris's gender influence your decision to accept or reject?

ASSIGNMENTS

- Have students contact the human resources manager of a local business and ask if or she would take a few minutes to discuss some issues about resumes with you. Structure the discussion around the following questions:

   a. How often do you encounter "padded" résumés? What is the most common "padding" and how do you react to it?

   b. Do you verify the information on resumes? How do you do this? How long does it take for you to be sure that an applicant has been honest about his/her qualifications?

   c. What would you do if you found that a productive, loyal employee had lied on a résumé when he or she applied for a job? Is "résumé fraud" an offense that warrants firing?

Tell students to summarize the findings from their interview in a memo to you.

TERMS

LEARNING OUTCOMES

18-1 Identify the major external and internal forces for change in organizations.

18-2 Describe how different types of change vary in scope.

18-3 Discuss methods organizations can use to manage resistance to change.

18-4 Explain Lewin's organizational change model.

18-5 Explain how companies determine the need to conduct an organization development intervention.

18-6 Discuss the major group-focused techniques for organization development intervention.

18-7 Discuss the major individual-focused techniques for organization development intervention.

4LTR PRESS ONLINE

Have students access their 4LTR Press Online account to…

- Create StudyBits and post to their Study Board
- Review key terms and create flashcards
- Create practice quizzes from their StudyBits
- Complete assessment content: matching, drag and drop, and fill-in-the-blank problems
- View Chapter Highlight Boxes: these include chapter videos and key exhibits/figures

VIDEO

*PROFILE ON HOLDEN OUTERWEAR

Run time: 7:06 minutes
When it comes to trends, Holden has always been a leader, never a follower. Soon after the company launched, it was heralded in the press as the new and improved outerwear. Holden's snow pants and jackets possess unique features like leather covered snaps, leather shoulders, and urban-style stitching. Unlike brands that make garments using faux materials, Holden works with true cotton denim twill. which is cut for style and then laminated with waterproofing. By far Holden's greatest innovation has been the creation of a new eco-friendly fabric, In 2005, Mikey LeBlanc and his business partner hatched an idea to make a natural-fiber waterproof breathable fabric, which didn't exist anywhere in the market. In addition to being technically durable, the designers' new eco-material was hailed as an environmental breakthrough.

Ask your students:

1. Describe the type of change that Holden's leaders are managing.

2. What resistance is Holden encountering, especially as the company seeks to design and manufacture highly innovative outerwear garments?

3. Using Kurt Lewin's change model, give a force field analysis for Holden's challenges in delivering innovative products. Suggest how the company might overcome resistance and foster permanent change.

CHAPTER PREP 18

DISCUSSION QUESTIONS

1. What do you think are the major external forces for change in today's organizations?

2. Do you think organizations can prevent resistance to change? If so, how?

3. What organization development techniques are the easiest to implement? What techniques are the most difficult to implement? Why?

EXPERIENTIAL EXERCISE

TEAM BUILDING FOR TEAM EFFECTIVENESS

This exercise will allow you and your team to engage in an organization development activity for team building. The two parts of the exercise are diagnosis and intervention.

Part 1. Diagnosis

Working as a team, complete the following four steps:

1. Describe how you have worked together this semester as a team.

2. What has your team done especially well? What has enabled this?

3. What problems or conflicts have you had as a team? (Be specific.) What was the cause of the problems your team experienced? Have the conflicts been over ideas, methods, or people?

4. Would you assess the overall effectiveness of your team as excellent, good, fair, poor, or a disaster? Explain your effectiveness rating.

Part 2. Intervention

A diagnosis provides the basis for intervention and action in organization development. Team building is a way to improve the relationships and effectiveness of teams at work. It is concerned with the results of work activities and the relationships among the members of the team. Complete the following three steps as a team.

Step 1. Answer the following questions with regard to the relationships within the team:

    a. How could conflicts have been handled better?

    b. How could specific relationships have been improved?

    c. How could the interpersonal atmosphere of the team have been improved?

Step 2. Answer the following questions with regard to the results of the team's work:

    a. How could the team have been more effective?

    b. Are there any team process changes that would have improved the team's effectiveness?

    c. Are there any team structure changes that would have improved the team's effectiveness?

Step 3. Answer the following questions with regard to the work environment in your place of employment:

    a. What have you learned about team building that you can apply there?

    b. What have you learned about team building that would not be applicable there?

ASSIGNMENTS

- Find an article that describes an Organization that has gone through change and managed it well. Develop a Hot Trend or other box feature of your own about the example you find using the format in this book. Prepare a brief oral presentation of your feature for your class.

- Think of a change you would like to make in your life, Using Figure 18.1 as a guide, prepare your own force field analysis for that change. How will you overcome the forces for the status quo? How will you make sure to "refreeze" following the change? Summarize your analysis in an action plan.

WHAT'S NEW TO ORGB5

- New box feature, "Hot Trend: Warby Parker—A Brand Made on the Internet"
- Updated section 18-1a, External Forces
- New box feature, "Fast Fact: Panera Goes High Tech"
- Updated section 18-2, The Scope of Change
- New box feature, "Apple's Data Centers in Europe"
- New box feature, "New Belgium Brewery Becomes Employee-Owned"
- Updated section 18-6d, Team Building
- Updated section 18-7a, Skills Training
- Updated section 18-7b, Leadership Training and Development
- Updated section 18-7e, Job Redesign

ORGB
ONLINE
REVIEW FLASHCARDS
ANYTIME, ANYWHERE!

Create Flashcards from Your StudyBits

Review Key Term Flashcards Already Loaded on the StudyBoard

4LTR
PRESS

Access ORGB ONLINE at www.cengagebrain.com

TEACH³

HIST⁴

BCOM⁸

SPEAK³

ORGB⁵

GLOBAL³

IPC³

COMM⁴

GOVT⁸

MKTG¹⁰

MIS⁶

WORLD RELG³

CFIN⁵

BUSN⁹

SELL⁵

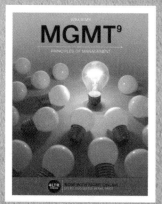
MGMT⁹

4LTR PRESS

LEARNING **YOUR** WAY

www.cengage.com/4ltrpress